Fiat Punto

Service and Repair Manual

A K Legg LAE MIMI and Spencer Drayton

Models covered

(3251 - 272 - 2AG3)

Fiat Punto Hatchback, including Selecta and special/limited editions
Petrol engines: 1.1 litre (1108 cc) and 1.2 litre (1242 cc, 8-valve and 16-valve)
Diesel & turbo-diesel engines: 1.7 litre (1698 cc)

Does NOT cover 1.4 litre (1372 cc) or 1.6 litre (1581 cc) petrol engines, or Cabriolet

ABCDE
FG

A book in the **Haynes Service and Repair Manual Series**

ISBN **1 85960 561 3**

British Library Cataloguing in Publication Data
A catalogue record for this book is available from the British Library.

Printed in the USA

Haynes Publishing
Sparkford, Yeovil, Somerset BA22 7JJ, England

Haynes North America, Inc
861 Lawrence Drive, Newbury Park, California 91320, USA

Editions Haynes
4, Rue de l'Abreuvoir
92415 COURBEVOIE CEDEX, France

Haynes Publishing Nordiska AB
Box 1504, 751 45 UPPSALA, Sverige

Contents

LIVING WITH YOUR FIAT PUNTO

Contents

The Fiat Punto range was introduced in March 1994 with 1108 cc, 1242 cc and 1372 cc petrol engines and a 1698 cc diesel engine. At first, models were only available in 5-door Hatchback form, however 3-door versions followed in May 1994 and Cabriolet and Automatic versions in June 1994. At the same time a turbo diesel model was launched. Power-assisted steering and ABS were offered as options in October 1994, and the 6-speed 55SX and normally-aspirated diesel followed in June 1995. In June 1997 a minor facelift was undertaken which included improvements to the suspension and steering and various cosmetic changes. This facelift also saw the introduction of the 1242 cc DOHC 16-valve engine available in top of the range models.

All engines covered in this Manual are fitted with single- or double-overhead-camshaft engines, and all models have fully independent front and rear suspension. The distinguished lines of the bodywork together with the high level rear lighting have made the Fiat Punto a very popular small car.

Provided that regular servicing is carried out in accordance with the manufacturer's recommendations, the Fiat Punto should prove reliable and economical. The engine compartment is well-designed, and most of the items needing frequent attention are easily accessible.

Fiat Punto 55 SX 5-door

Fiat Punto 55 S 3-door

The Fiat Punto Team

Haynes manuals are produced by dedicated and enthusiastic people working in close co-operation. The team responsible for the creation of this book included:

Authors	**A.K. Legg** LAE MIMI **Spencer Drayton**
Sub-editor	**Ian Barnes**
Page Make-up	**Steve Churchill**
Workshop manager	**Paul Buckland**
Photo Scans	**Steve Tanswell** **John Martin**
Cover illustration & Line Art	**Roger Healing**
Wiring diagrams	**Matthew Marke**

We hope the book will help you to get the maximum enjoyment from your car. By carrying out routine maintenance as described you will ensure your car's reliability and preserve its resale value.

Your Fiat Punto Manual

The aim of this manual is to help you get the best value from your vehicle. It can do so in several ways. It can help you decide what work must be done (even should you choose to get it done by a garage), provide information on routine maintenance and servicing, and give a logical course of action and diagnosis when random faults occur. However, it is hoped that you will use the manual by tackling the work yourself. On simpler jobs, it may even be quicker than booking the car into a garage and going there twice, to leave and collect it. Perhaps most important, a lot of money can be saved by avoiding the costs a garage must charge to cover its labour and overheads.

The manual has drawings and descriptions to show the function of the various components, so that their layout can be understood. Then the tasks are described and photographed in a clear step-by-step sequence.

References to the 'left' or 'right' are in the sense of a person in the driver's seat, facing forward.

Acknowledgements

Thanks are due to Draper Tools Limited, who provided some of the workshop tools, and to all those people at Sparkford who helped in the production of this manual.

Working on your car can be dangerous. This page shows just some of the potential risks and hazards, with the aim of creating a safety-conscious attitude.

General hazards

Scalding

• Don't remove the radiator or expansion tank cap while the engine is hot.
• Engine oil, automatic transmission fluid or power steering fluid may also be dangerously hot if the engine has recently been running.

Burning

• Beware of burns from the exhaust system and from any part of the engine. Brake discs and drums can also be extremely hot immediately after use.

Crushing

• When working under or near a raised vehicle, always supplement the jack with axle stands, or use drive-on ramps. ***Never venture under a car which is only supported by a jack.***

• Take care if loosening or tightening high-torque nuts when the vehicle is on stands. Initial loosening and final tightening should be done with the wheels on the ground.

Fire

• Fuel is highly flammable; fuel vapour is explosive.
• Don't let fuel spill onto a hot engine.
• Do not smoke or allow naked lights (including pilot lights) anywhere near a vehicle being worked on. Also beware of creating sparks (electrically or by use of tools).
• Fuel vapour is heavier than air, so don't work on the fuel system with the vehicle over an inspection pit.
• Another cause of fire is an electrical overload or short-circuit. Take care when repairing or modifying the vehicle wiring.
• Keep a fire extinguisher handy, of a type suitable for use on fuel and electrical fires.

Electric shock

• Ignition HT voltage can be dangerous, especially to people with heart problems or a pacemaker. Don't work on or near the ignition system with the engine running or the ignition switched on.

• Mains voltage is also dangerous. Make sure that any mains-operated equipment is correctly earthed. Mains power points should be protected by a residual current device (RCD) circuit breaker.

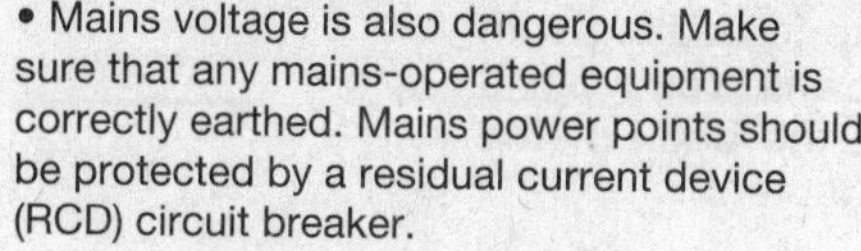

Fume or gas intoxication

• Exhaust fumes are poisonous; they often contain carbon monoxide, which is rapidly fatal if inhaled. Never run the engine in a confined space such as a garage with the doors shut.

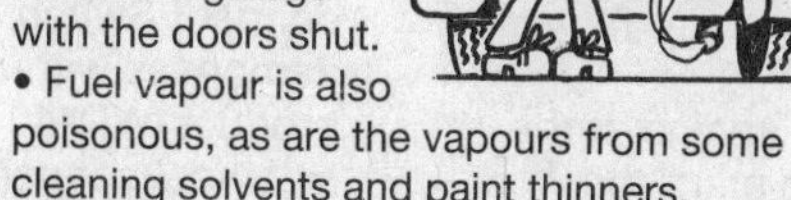

• Fuel vapour is also poisonous, as are the vapours from some cleaning solvents and paint thinners.

Poisonous or irritant substances

• Avoid skin contact with battery acid and with any fuel, fluid or lubricant, especially antifreeze, brake hydraulic fluid and Diesel fuel. Don't syphon them by mouth. If such a substance is swallowed or gets into the eyes, seek medical advice.
• Prolonged contact with used engine oil can cause skin cancer. Wear gloves or use a barrier cream if necessary. Change out of oil-soaked clothes and do not keep oily rags in your pocket.
• Air conditioning refrigerant forms a poisonous gas if exposed to a naked flame (including a cigarette). It can also cause skin burns on contact.

Asbestos

• Asbestos dust can cause cancer if inhaled or swallowed. Asbestos may be found in gaskets and in brake and clutch linings. When dealing with such components it is safest to assume that they contain asbestos.

Special hazards

Hydrofluoric acid

• This extremely corrosive acid is formed when certain types of synthetic rubber, found in some O-rings, oil seals, fuel hoses etc, are exposed to temperatures above $400^{\circ}C$. The rubber changes into a charred or sticky substance containing the acid. *Once formed, the acid remains dangerous for years. If it gets onto the skin, it may be necessary to amputate the limb concerned.*
• When dealing with a vehicle which has suffered a fire, or with components salvaged from such a vehicle, wear protective gloves and discard them after use.

The battery

• Batteries contain sulphuric acid, which attacks clothing, eyes and skin. Take care when topping-up or carrying the battery.
• The hydrogen gas given off by the battery is highly explosive. Never cause a spark or allow a naked light nearby. Be careful when connecting and disconnecting battery chargers or jump leads.

Air bags

• Air bags can cause injury if they go off accidentally. Take care when removing the steering wheel and/or facia. Special storage instructions may apply.

Diesel injection equipment

• Diesel injection pumps supply fuel at very high pressure. Take care when working on the fuel injectors and fuel pipes.

Warning: Never expose the hands, face or any other part of the body to injector spray; the fuel can penetrate the skin with potentially fatal results.

Remember...

DO

• Do use eye protection when using power tools, and when working under the vehicle.

• Do wear gloves or use barrier cream to protect your hands when necessary.

• Do get someone to check periodically that all is well when working alone on the vehicle.

• Do keep loose clothing and long hair well out of the way of moving mechanical parts.

• Do remove rings, wristwatch etc, before working on the vehicle – especially the electrical system.

• Do ensure that any lifting or jacking equipment has a safe working load rating adequate for the job.

DON'T

• Don't attempt to lift a heavy component which may be beyond your capability – get assistance.

• Don't rush to finish a job, or take unverified short cuts.

• Don't use ill-fitting tools which may slip and cause injury.

• Don't leave tools or parts lying around where someone can trip over them. Mop up oil and fuel spills at once.

• Don't allow children or pets to play in or near a vehicle being worked on.

The following pages are intended to help in dealing with common roadside emergencies and breakdowns. You will find more detailed fault finding information at the back of the manual, and repair information in the main chapters.

If your car won't start and the starter motor doesn't turn

- ☐ If it's a model with automatic transmission, make sure the selector is in P or N.
- ☐ Open the bonnet and make sure that the battery terminals are clean and tight.
- ☐ Switch on the headlights and try to start the engine. If the headlights go very dim when you're trying to start, the battery is probably flat. Get out of trouble by jump starting (see next page) using a friend's car.

If your car won't start even though the starter motor turns as normal

- ☐ Is there fuel in the tank?
- ☐ Is there moisture on electrical components under the bonnet? Switch off the ignition, then wipe off any obvious dampness with a dry cloth. Spray a water-repellent aerosol product (WD-40 or equivalent) on ignition and fuel system electrical connectors like those shown in the photos. Pay special attention to the ignition coil wiring connector and HT leads. (Note that Diesel engines don't normally suffer from damp.)

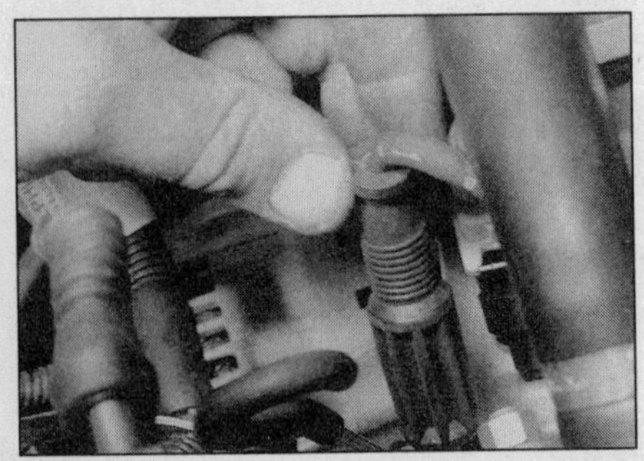

A Check that the spark plug HT leads are securely connected by pushing them onto the plugs (petrol engine models).

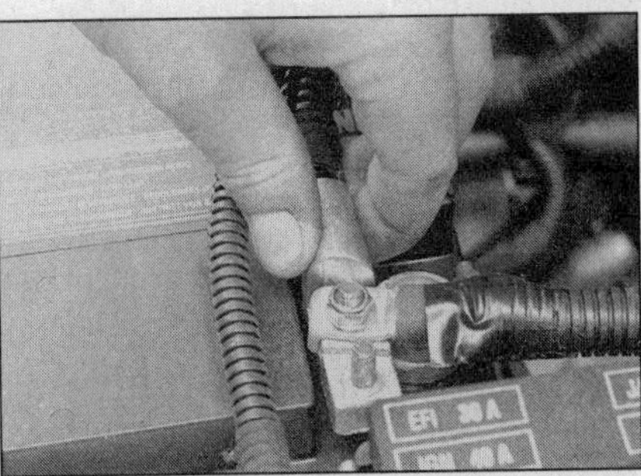

B Check that the wiring to the engine compartments is securely connected.

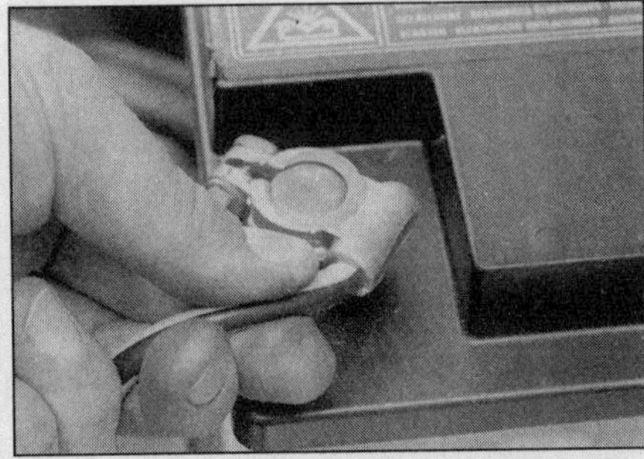

C Check the security and condition of the battery terminals.

Check that electrical connections are secure (with the ignition switched off) and spray them with a water dispersant spray like WD40 if you suspect a problem due to damp

Jump starting will get you out of trouble, but you must correct whatever made the battery go flat in the first place. There are three possibilities:

***1** The battery has been drained by repeated attempts to start, or by leaving the lights on.*

***2** The charging system is not working properly (alternator drivebelt slack or broken, alternator wiring fault or alternator itself faulty).*

***3** The battery itself is at fault (electrolyte low, or battery worn out).*

Jump starting

When jump-starting a car using a booster battery, observe the following precautions:

- ✔ Before connecting the booster battery, make sure that the ignition is switched off.
- ✔ Ensure that all electrical equipment (lights, heater, wipers, etc) is switched off.
- ✔ Take note of any special precautions printed on the battery case.
- ✔ Make sure that the booster battery is the same voltage as the discharged one in the vehicle.
- ✔ If the battery is being jump-started from the battery in another vehicle, the two vehicles MUST NOT TOUCH each other.
- ✔ Make sure that the transmission is in neutral (or PARK, in the case of automatic transmission).

1 Connect one end of the red jump lead to the positive (+) terminal of the flat battery

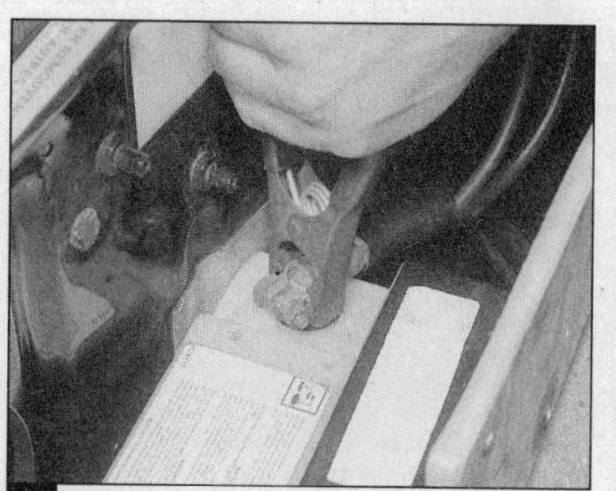

2 Connect the other end of the red lead to the positive (+) terminal of the booster battery.

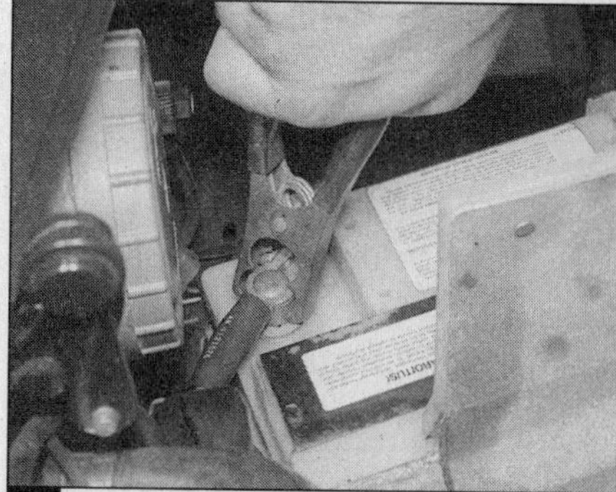

3 Connect one end of the black jump lead to the negative (-) terminal of the booster battery

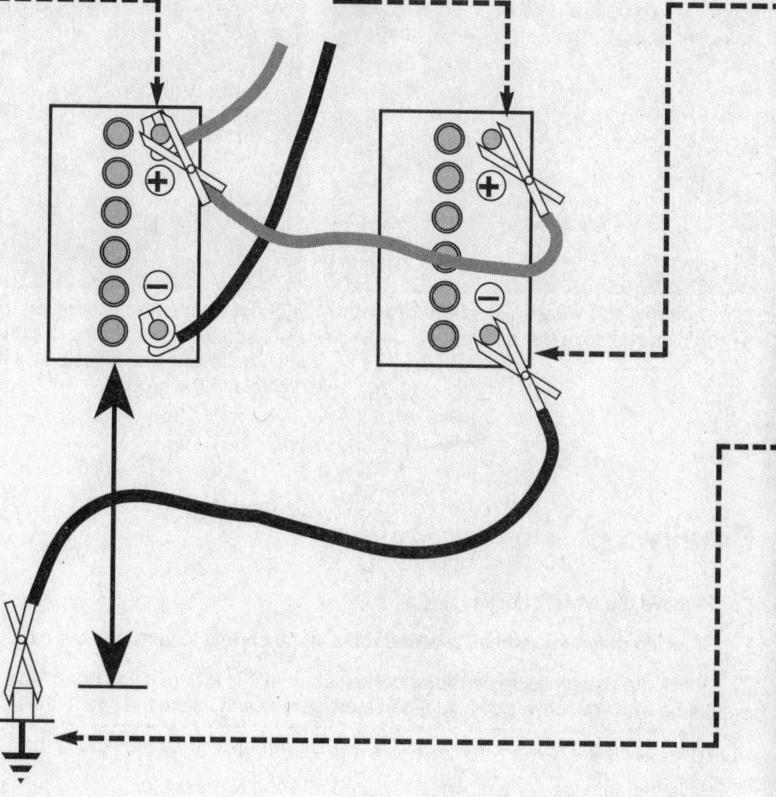

4 Connect the other end of the black jump lead to a bolt or bracket on the engine block, well away from the battery, on the vehicle to be started.

5 Make sure that the jump leads will not come into contact with the fan, drive-belts or other moving parts of the engine.

6 Start the engine using the booster battery and run it at idle speed. Switch on the lights, rear window demister and heater blower motor, then disconnect the jump leads in the reverse order of connection. Turn off the lights etc.

Wheel changing

Some of the details shown here will vary according to model. For instance, the location of the spare wheel and jack is not the same on all cars. However, the basic principles apply to all vehicles.

Warning: Do not change a wheel in a situation where you risk being hit by another vehicle. On busy roads, try to stop in a lay-by or a gateway. Be wary of passing traffic while changing the wheel - it is easy to become distracted by the job in hand.

Preparation

- ☐ When a puncture occurs, stop as soon as it is safe to do so.
- ☐ Park on firm level ground, if possible, and well out of the way of other traffic.
- ☐ Use hazard warning lights if necessary.
- ☐ If you have one, use a warning triangle to alert other drivers of your presence.
- ☐ Apply the handbrake and engage first or reverse gear (or P on models with automatic transmission).
- ☐ Chock the wheel diagonally opposite the one being removed – a couple of large stones will do for this.
- ☐ If the ground is soft, use a flat piece of wood to spread the load under the jack.

Changing the wheel

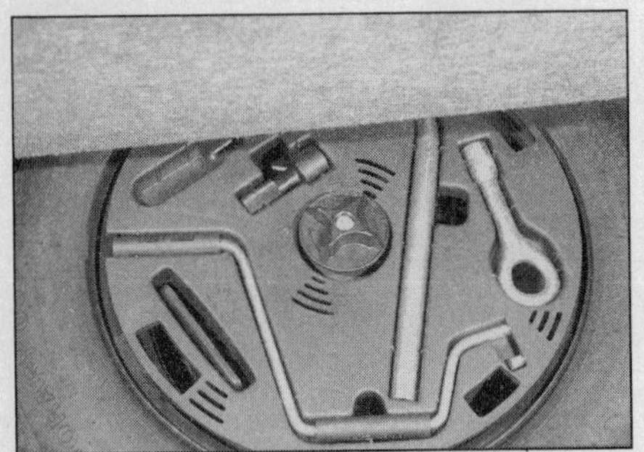

1 The spare wheel and tools (including the jack) are stored in the luggage compartment beneath the floor covering. Unscrew the central plastic nut to remove the tool holder.

2 Slacken each wheel bolt by a half turn

3 Locate the jack under the triangular mark on the sill next to the wheel to be changed, on firm ground

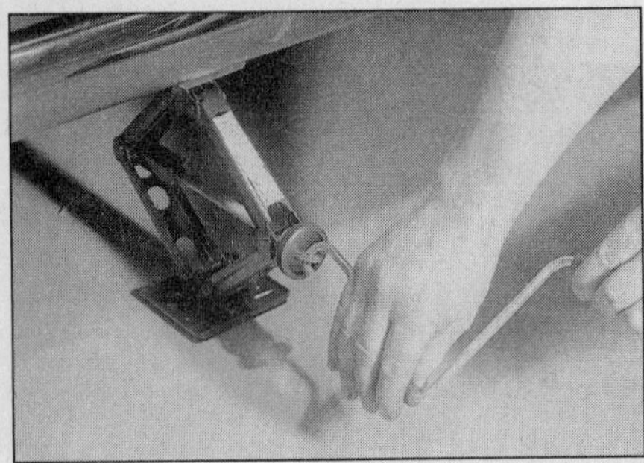

4 Turn the jack handle clockwise until the wheel is raised clear of the ground

5 Unscrew the wheel bolts, withdraw the trim and remove the wheel

6 Fit the spare wheel on the pins, and screw in the bolts. Lightly tighten the bolts with the wheelbrace then lower the vehicle to the ground

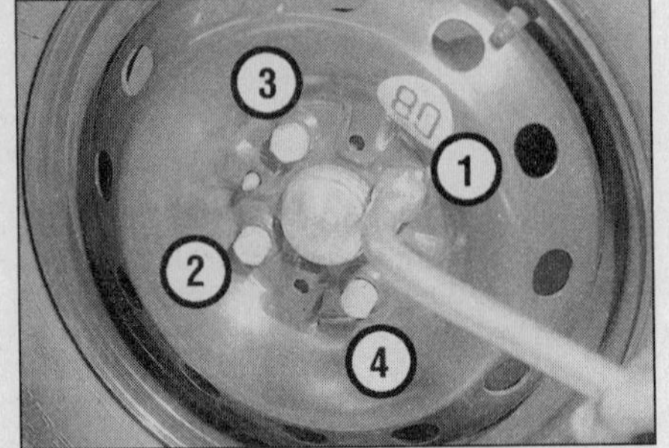

7 Securely tighten the wheel bolts in the sequence shown. Note that the wheel bolts should be slackened and retightened to the specified torque at the earliest possible opportunity.

Finally...

- ☐ Remove the wheel chocks.
- ☐ Stow the punctured wheel, jack and tools in the correct locations in the car.
- ☐ Check the tyre pressure on the wheel just fitted. If it is low, or if you don't have a pressure gauge with you, drive slowly to the nearest garage and inflate the tyre to the right pressure.
- ☐ When using the space-saver spare wheel, do not exceed 50 mph (80 kph).
- ☐ Have the damaged tyre or wheel repaired as soon as possible.

Identifying leaks

Puddles on the garage floor or drive, or obvious wetness under the bonnet or underneath the car, suggest a leak that needs investigating. It can sometimes be difficult to decide where the leak is coming from, especially if the engine bay is very dirty already. Leaking oil or fluid can also be blown rearwards by the passage of air under the car, giving a false impression of where the problem lies.

Warning: Most automotive oils and fluids are poisonous. Wash them off skin, and change out of contaminated clothing, without delay.

The smell of a fluid leaking from the car may provide a clue to what's leaking. Some fluids are distinctively coloured. It may help to clean the car carefully and to park it over some clean paper overnight as an aid to locating the source of the leak. Remember that some leaks may only occur while the engine is running.

Sump oil

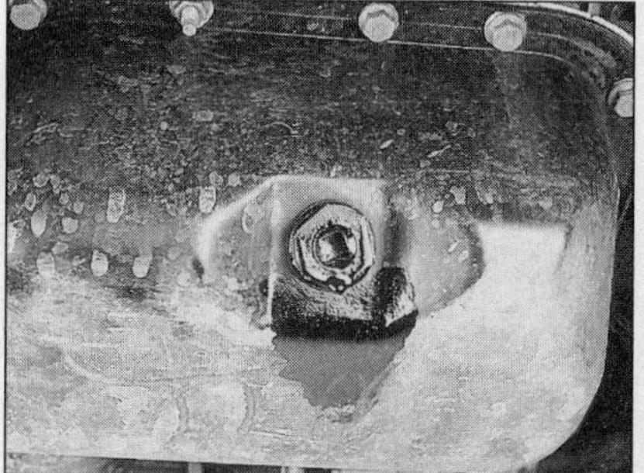

Engine oil may leak from the drain plug...

Oil from filter

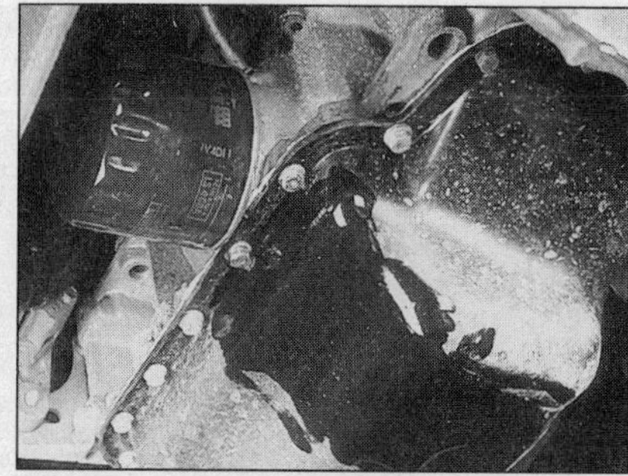

...or from the base of the oil filter.

Gearbox oil

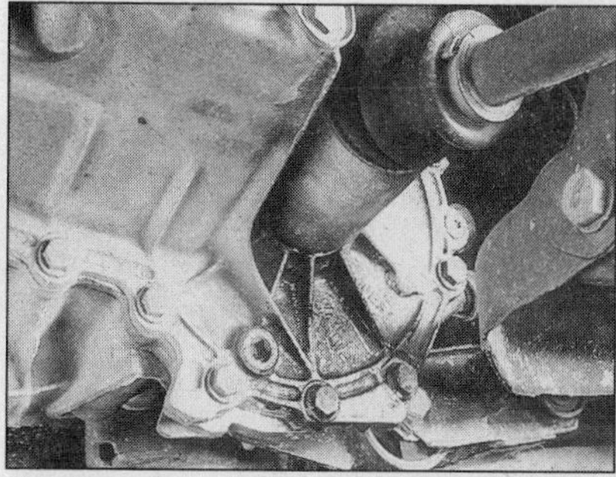

Gearbox oil can leak from the seals at the inboard ends of the driveshafts.

Antifreeze

Leaking antifreeze often leaves a crystalline deposit like this.

Brake fluid

A leak occurring at a wheel is almost certainly brake fluid.

Power steering fluid

Power steering fluid may leak from the pipe connectors on the steering rack.

Towing

When all else fails, you may find yourself having to get a tow home – or of course you may be helping somebody else. Long-distance recovery should only be done by a garage or breakdown service. For shorter distances, DIY towing using another car is easy enough, but observe the following points:

☐ Use a proper tow-rope – they are not expensive. The vehicle being towed must display an ON TOW sign in its rear window.

☐ Always turn the ignition key to the ON position when the vehicle is being towed, so that the steering lock is released, and that the direction indicator and brake lights will work.

☐ Only attach the tow-rope to the towing eyes provided.

☐ Before being towed, release the handbrake and select neutral on the transmission.

☐ Note that greater-than-usual pedal pressure will be required to operate the brakes, since the vacuum servo unit is only operational with the engine running.

☐ On models with power steering, greater-than-usual steering effort will also be required.

☐ The driver of the car being towed must keep the tow-rope taut at all times to avoid snatching.

☐ Make sure that both drivers know the route before setting off.

☐ Only drive at moderate speeds and keep the distance towed to a minimum. Drive smoothly and allow plenty of time for slowing down at junctions.

☐ On models with automatic transmission, special precautions apply(see Chapter 7B, Section 1). If in doubt, do not tow, or transmission damage may result.

☐ The front towing eye is supplied as part of the tool kit stored in the luggage compartment. To fit the eye prise out the plastic cover from the front or rear bumper using a screwdriver, then screw the eye onto the threaded pin as tightly as possible.

Warning: To prevent damage to the catalytic converter, a vehicle must not be push-started, or started by towing, when the engine is at operating temperature. Use jump leads (see Jump starting).

Introduction

There are some very simple checks which need only take a few minutes to carry out, but which could save you a lot of inconvenience and expense.

These *Weekly checks* require no great skill or special tools, and the small amount of time they take to perform could prove to be very well spent, for example;

☐ Keeping an eye on tyre condition and pressures, will not only help to stop them wearing out prematurely, but could also save your life.

☐ Many breakdowns are caused by electrical problems. Battery-related faults are particularly common, and a quick check on a regular basis will often prevent the majority of these.

☐ If your car develops a brake fluid leak, the first time you might know about it is when your brakes don't work properly. Checking the level regularly will give advance warning of this kind of problem.

☐ If the oil or coolant levels run low, the cost of repairing any engine damage will be far greater than fixing the leak, for example.

Underbonnet check points

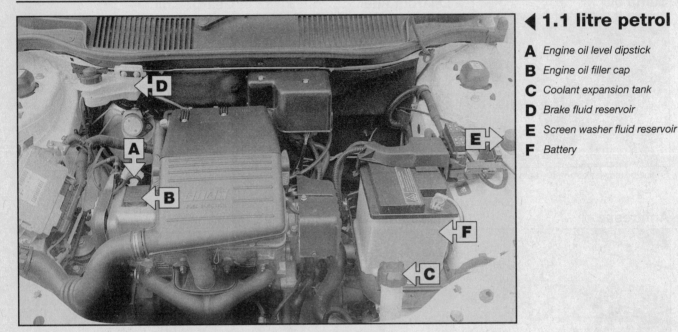

◀ **1.1 litre petrol**

A *Engine oil level dipstick*
B *Engine oil filler cap*
C *Coolant expansion tank*
D *Brake fluid reservoir*
E *Screen washer fluid reservoir*
F *Battery*

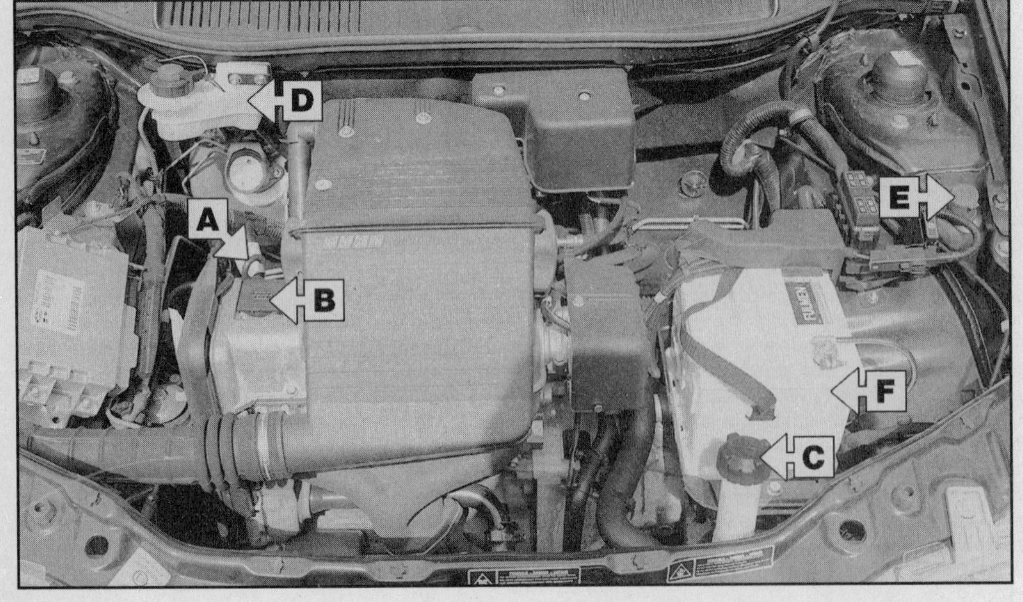

◀ **1.2 litre (8-valve) petrol**

A *Engine oil level dipstick*
B *Engine oil filler cap*
C *Coolant expansion tank*
D *Brake fluid reservoir*
E *Screen washer fluid reservoir*
F *Battery*

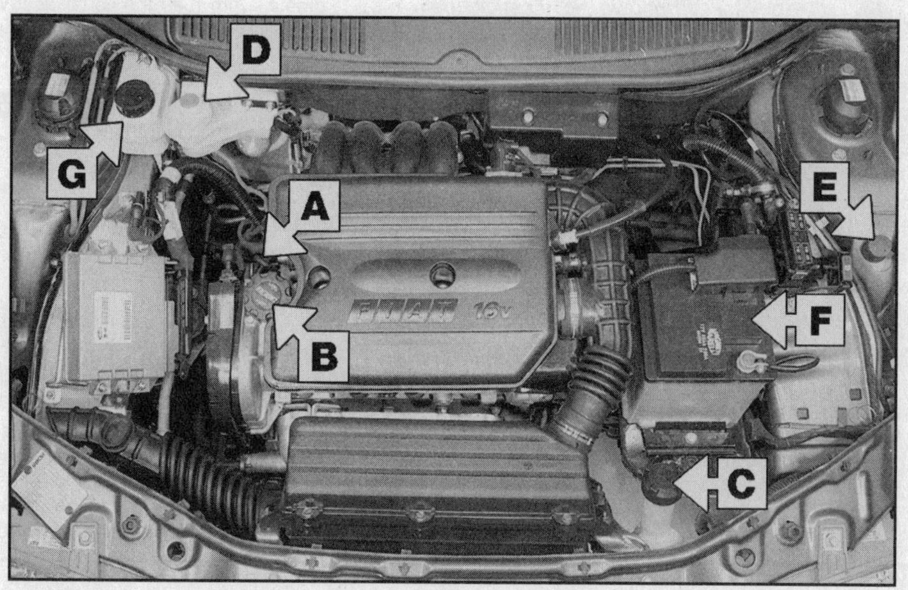

◀ **1.2 litre (16-valve) petrol**

A *Engine oil level dipstick*
B *Engine oil filler cap*
C *Coolant expansion tank*
D *Brake fluid reservoir*
E *Screen washer fluid reservoir*
F *Battery*
G *Power steering fluid reservoir*

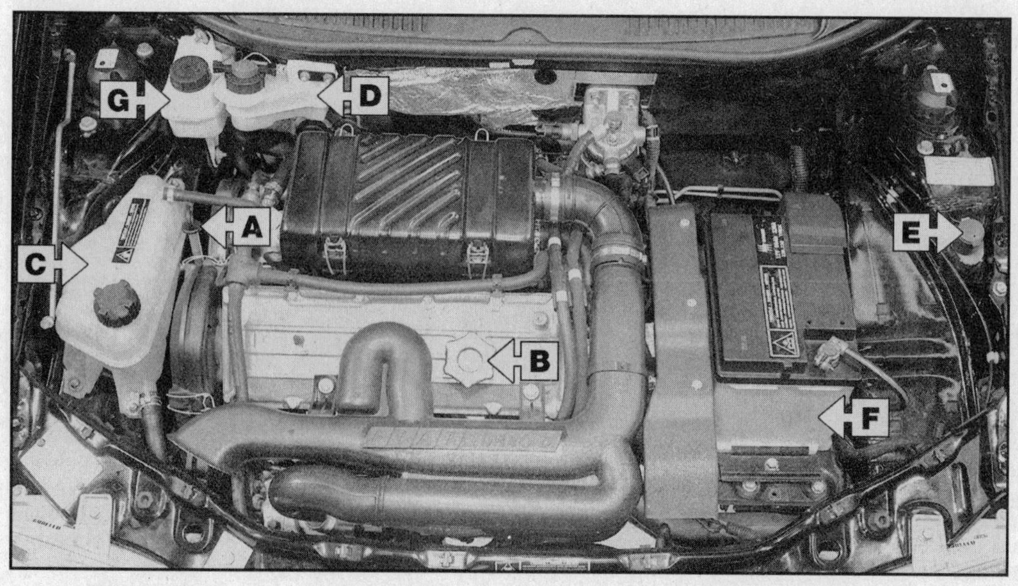

◀ **1.7 litre Turbo diesel**

A *Engine oil level dipstick*
B *Engine oil filler cap*
C *Coolant expansion tank*
D *Brake fluid reservoir*
E *Screen washer fluid reservoir*
F *Battery*
G *Power steering fluid reservoir*

Engine oil level

Before you start

✔ Make sure that your car is on level ground.
✔ Check the oil level before the car is driven, or at least 5 minutes after the engine has been switched off.

If the oil is checked immediately after driving the vehicle, some of the oil will remain in the upper engine components, resulting in an inaccurate reading on the dipstick!

The correct oil

Modern engines place great demands on their oil. It is very important that the correct oil for your car is used (See Lubricants and fluids).

Car Care

● If you have to add oil frequently, you should check whether you have any oil leaks. Place some clean paper under the car overnight, and check for stains in the morning. If there are no leaks, the engine may be burning oil.

● Always maintain the level between the upper and lower dipstick marks (see photo 2). If the level is too low severe engine damage may occur. Oil seal failure may result if the engine is overfilled by adding too much oil.

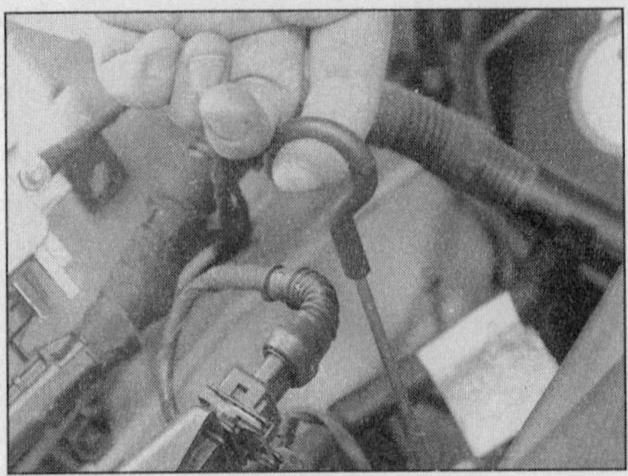

1 The dipstick is brightly coloured for easy identification (see Underbonnet check points). Withdraw the dipstick (petrol engine shown).

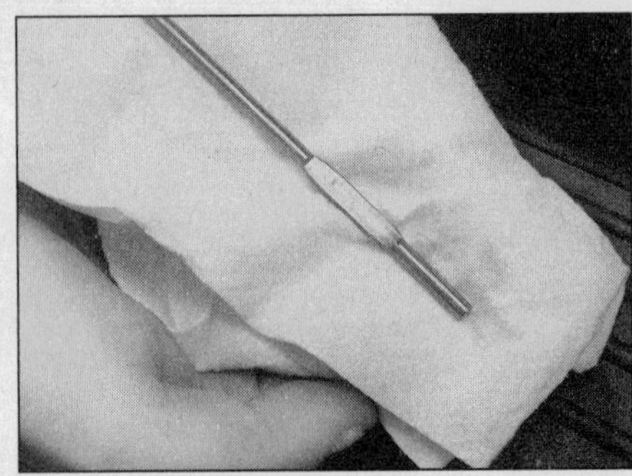

2 Using a clean rag or paper towel remove all oil from the dipstick. Insert the clean dipstick into the tube as far as it will go, then withdraw it again. The level should be between the upper and lower marks.

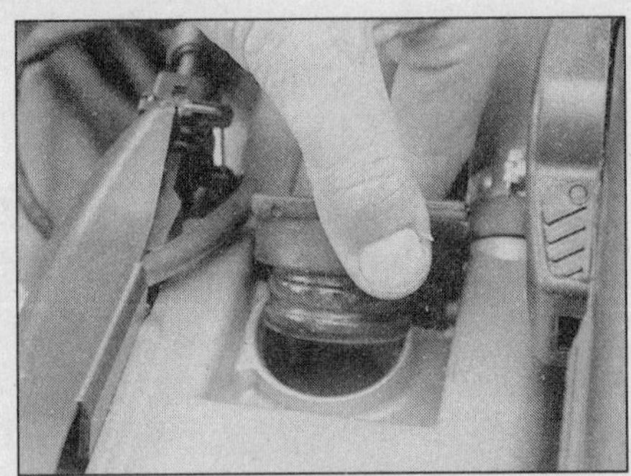

3 If more oil is needed, remove the oil filler cap from the top of the engine (petrol engine shown).

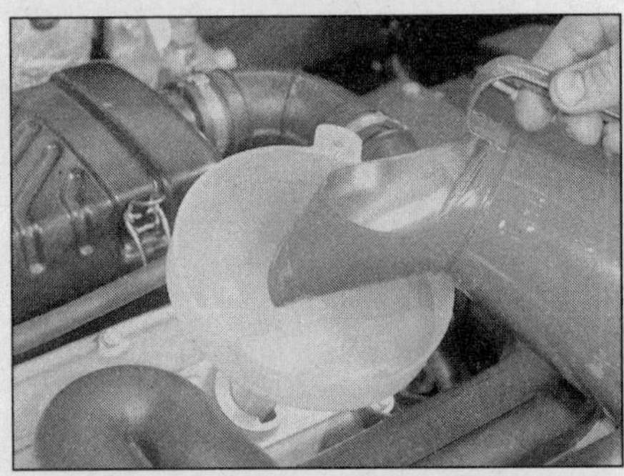

4 Oil is added through the filler cap aperture (diesel engine shown). Add the oil a little at a time, checking the level on the dipstick often. Using a funnel will help to reduce spillage. Don't overfill (see *Car Care*).

Coolant level

Warning: DO NOT attempt to remove the expansion tank pressure cap when the engine is hot, as there is a very great risk of scalding. Do not leave open containers of coolant about, as it is poisonous.

Car Care

● With a sealed-type cooling system, adding coolant should not be necessary on a regular basis. If frequent topping-up is required, it is likely there is a leak. Check the radiator, all hoses and joint faces for signs of staining or wetness, and rectify as necessary.

● It is important that antifreeze is used in the cooling system all year round, not just during the winter months. Don't top-up with water alone, as the antifreeze will become too diluted.

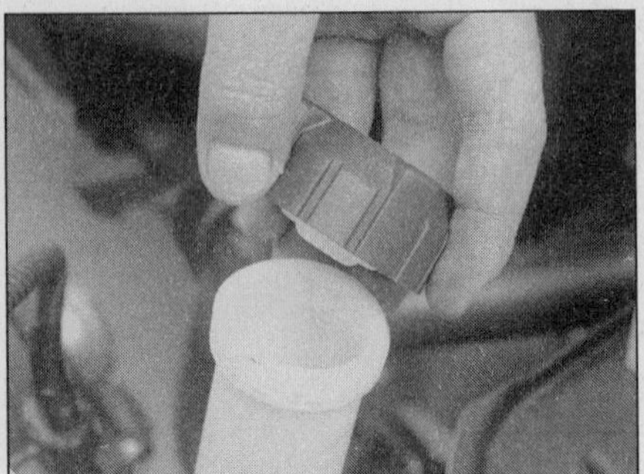

1 Check that the coolant level is between the MIN and MAX marks. If topping up is necessary, **wait until the engine is cold**. Slowly unscrew the expansion tank cap to release any pressure present in the cooling system, and remove it (petrol engine shown).

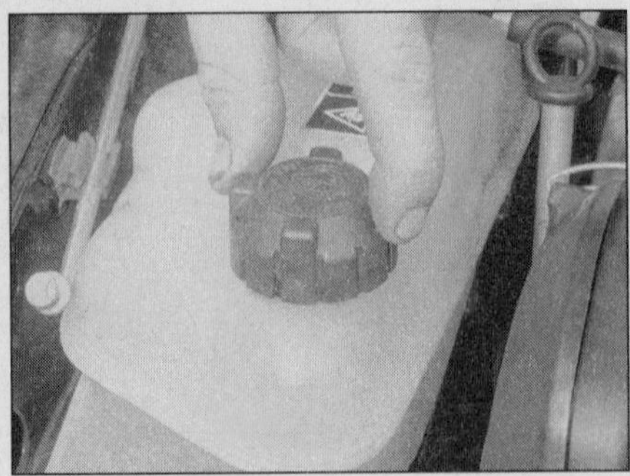

2 On diesel engine models, the coolant expansion tank is a different shape, but the same procedure applies as for petrol engine models (see photo 1). The MIN and MAX marks appear on the side of the tank nearest the engine.

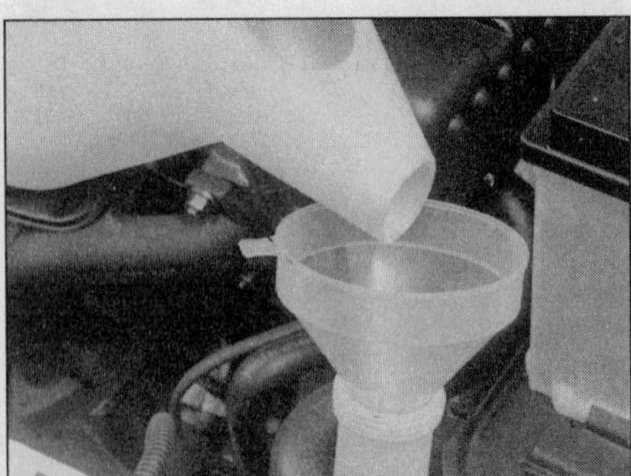

3 Add a mixture of water and antifreeze to the expansion tank until the coolant level is up to the MAX mark (petrol engine shown). The MIN and MAX marks appear on the tank below the filler neck.

Brake fluid level

Warning:

● Brake fluid can harm your eyes and damage painted surfaces, so use extreme caution when handling and pouring it.

● Do not use fluid that has been standing open for some time, as it absorbs moisture from the air, which can cause a dangerous loss of braking effectiveness.

• Make sure that your car is on level ground.
• The fluid level in the reservoir will drop slightly as the brake pads wear down, but the fluid level must never be allowed to drop below the "MIN" mark.

Safety First!

● If the reservoir requires repeated topping-up this is an indication of a fluid leak somewhere in the system, which should be investigated immediately.

● If a leak is suspected, the car should not be driven until the braking system has been checked. Never take any risks where brakes are concerned.

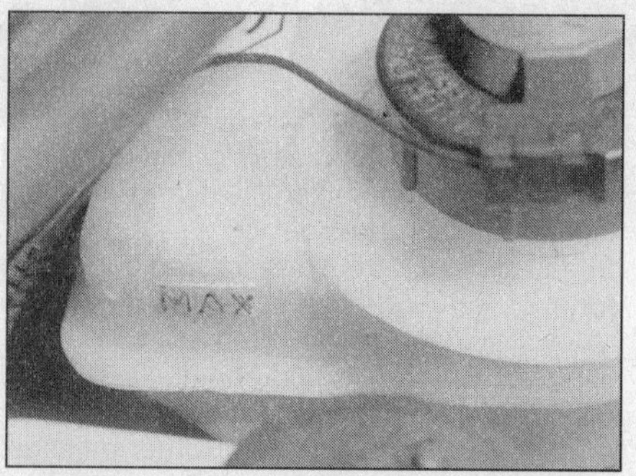

1 The MIN and MAX marks are indicated on the side of the reservoir. The fluid level must be kept between the marks at all times.

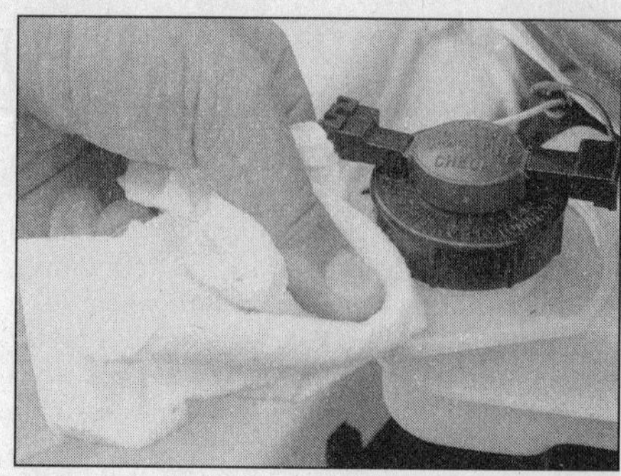

2 If topping-up is necessary, first wipe clean the area around the filler cap to prevent dirt entering the hydraulic system.

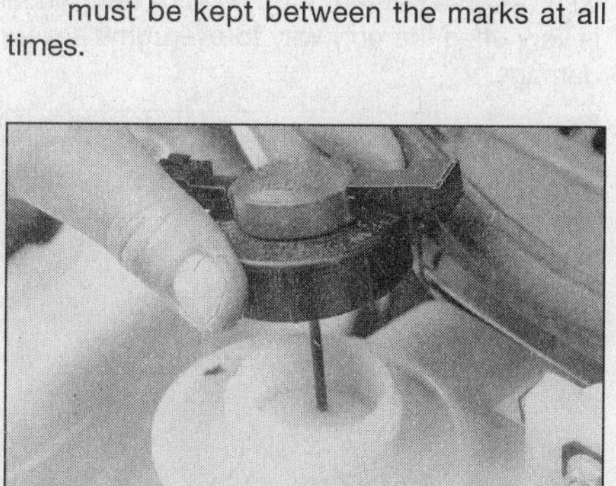

3 Unscrew the reservoir cap and carefully lift it out of position, taking care not to damage the level switch float. Inspect the reservoir; if the fluid is dirty the hydraulic system should be drained and refilled (see Chapter 1A or 1B).

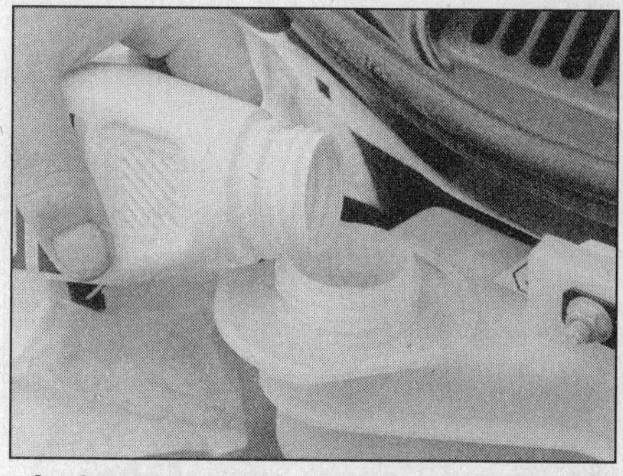

4 Carefully add fluid, taking care not to spill it onto the surrounding components. Use only the specified fluid; mixing different types can cause damage to the system. After topping-up to the correct level, securely refit the cap and wipe off any spilt fluid.

Power steering fluid level

Before you start:

✔ Park the vehicle on level ground.
✔ Set the steering wheel straight-ahead.
✔ The engine should be turned off.

For the check to be accurate, the steering must not be turned once the engine has been stopped.

Safety First!

● The need for frequent topping-up indicates a leak, which should be investigated immediately.

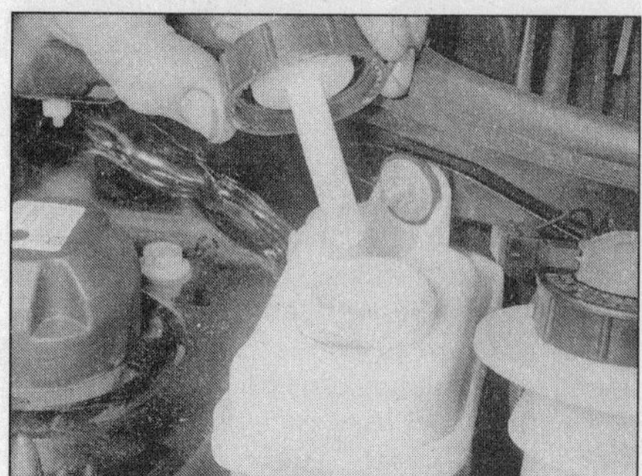

1 The reservoir is located on the right-hand side of the bulkhead in the engine compartment. Wipe clean the area around the reservoir filler cap then unscrew it from the reservoir.

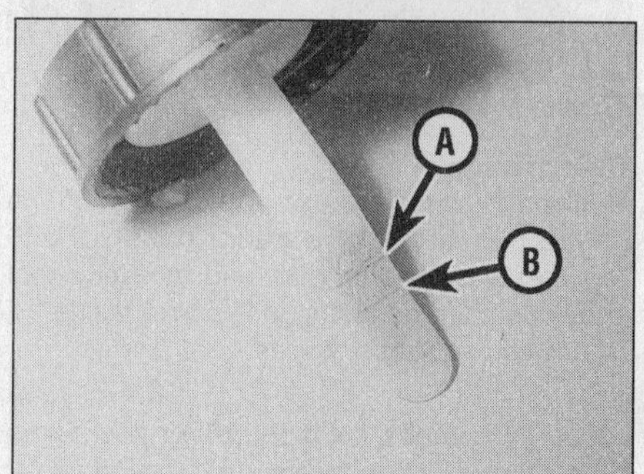

2 Dip the fluid with the reservoir cap/dipstick (do not screw the cap into position). When the engine is cold, the fluid level should be up to the MIN mark (B); when hot, it should be on the MAX mark (A).

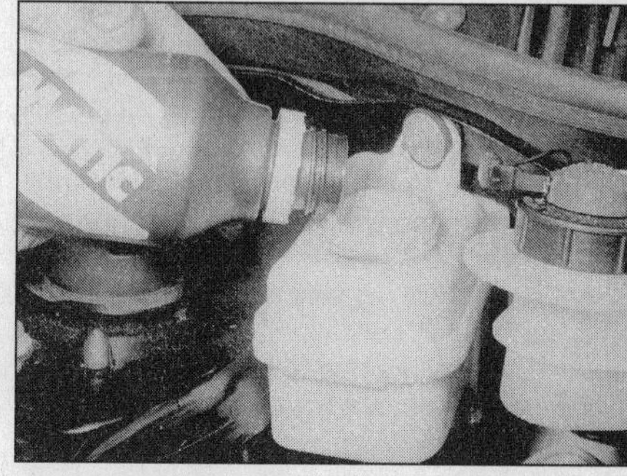

3 When topping-up, use the specified type of fluid and do not overfill the reservoir. When the level is correct, securely refit the cap.

Tyre condition and pressure

It is very important that tyres are in good condition, and at the correct pressure - having a tyre failure at any speed is highly dangerous. Tyre wear is influenced by driving style - harsh braking and acceleration, or fast cornering, will all produce more rapid tyre wear. As a general rule, the front tyres wear out faster than the rears. Interchanging the tyres from front to rear ("rotating" the tyres) may result in more even wear. However, if this is completely effective, you may have the expense of replacing all four tyres at once!

Remove any nails or stones embedded in the tread before they penetrate the tyre to cause deflation. If removal of a nail does reveal that the tyre has been punctured, refit the nail so that its point of penetration is marked. Then immediately change the wheel, and have the tyre repaired by a tyre dealer.

Regularly check the tyres for damage in the form of cuts or bulges, especially in the sidewalls. Periodically remove the wheels, and clean any dirt or mud from the inside and outside surfaces. Examine the wheel rims for signs of rusting, corrosion or other damage. Light alloy wheels are easily damaged by "kerbing" whilst parking; steel wheels may also become dented or buckled. A new wheel is very often the only way to overcome severe damage.

New tyres should be balanced when they are fitted, but it may become necessary to re-balance them as they wear, or if the balance weights fitted to the wheel rim should fall off. Unbalanced tyres will wear more quickly, as will the steering and suspension components. Wheel imbalance is normally signified by vibration, particularly at a certain speed (typically around 50 mph). If this vibration is felt only through the steering, then it is likely that just the front wheels need balancing. If, however, the vibration is felt through the whole car, the rear wheels could be out of balance. Wheel balancing should be carried out by a tyre dealer or garage.

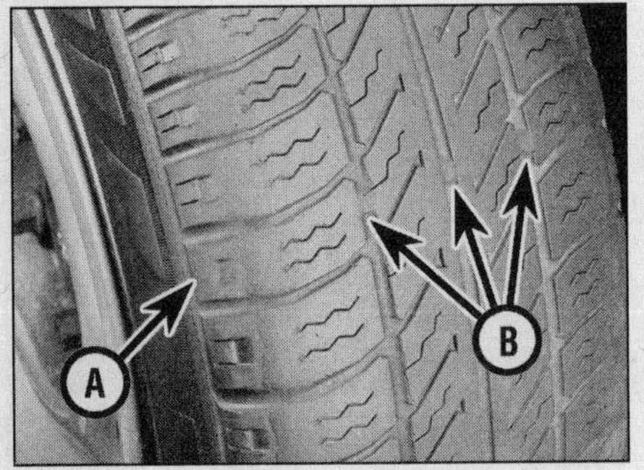

1 ***Tread Depth - visual check***
The original tyres have tread wear safety bands (B), which will appear when the tread depth reaches approximately 1.6 mm. The band positions are indicated by a triangular mark on the tyre sidewall (A).

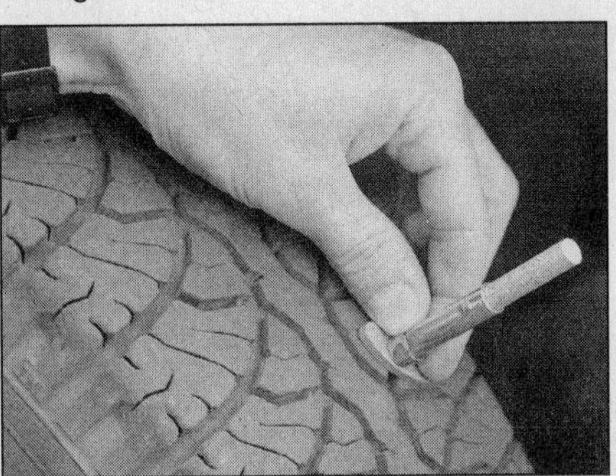

2 ***Tread Depth - manual check***
Alternatively, tread wear can be monitored with a simple, inexpensive device known as a tread depth indicator gauge.

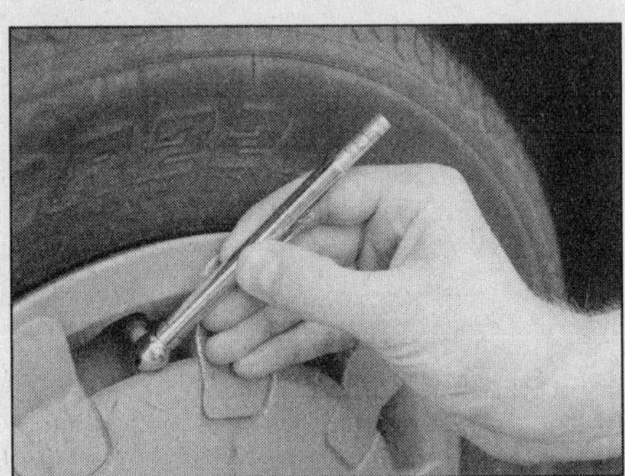

3 ***Tyre Pressure Check***
Check the tyre pressures regularly with the tyres cold. Do not adjust the tyre pressures immediately after the vehicle has been used, or an inaccurate setting will result. Tyre pressures are shown on page 0•18.

Tyre tread wear patterns

Shoulder Wear

Underinflation (wear on both sides)
Under-inflation will cause overheating of the tyre, because the tyre will flex too much, and the tread will not sit correctly on the road surface. This will cause a loss of grip and excessive wear, not to mention the danger of sudden tyre failure due to heat build-up.
Check and adjust pressures
Incorrect wheel camber (wear on one side)
Repair or renew suspension parts
Hard cornering
Reduce speed!

Centre Wear

Overinflation
Over-inflation will cause rapid wear of the centre part of the tyre tread, coupled with reduced grip, harsher ride, and the danger of shock damage occurring in the tyre casing.
Check and adjust pressures

If you sometimes have to inflate your car's tyres to the higher pressures specified for maximum load or sustained high speed, don't forget to reduce the pressures to normal afterwards.

Uneven Wear

Front tyres may wear unevenly as a result of wheel misalignment. Most tyre dealers and garages can check and adjust the wheel alignment (or "tracking") for a modest charge.
Incorrect camber or castor
Repair or renew suspension parts
Malfunctioning suspension
Repair or renew suspension parts
Unbalanced wheel
Balance tyres
Incorrect toe setting
Adjust front wheel alignment
Note: *The feathered edge of the tread which typifies toe wear is best checked by feel.*

Automatic transmission fluid level

Before you start:

✔ Park the vehicle on level ground, and apply the handbrake firmly. Let the engine idle, and select P or N.

Safety First!

● The need for frequent topping-up indicates a leak, which should be investigated immediately.

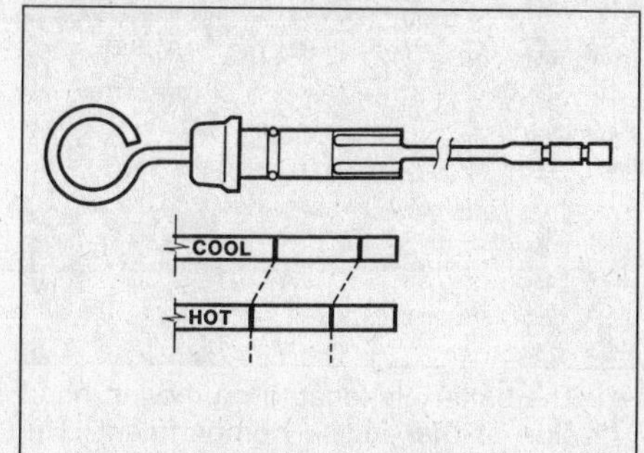

1 Open the bonnet. Withdraw the transmission dipstick, and wipe it with a clean non-fluffy rag. Re-insert the dipstick fully, withdraw it again and read the fluid level. It should be between the two level marks. There are two sets of marks. Use the COOL marks if the transmission is cold (20° to 40°C) or the HOT marks if it is hot (60° to 80°C).

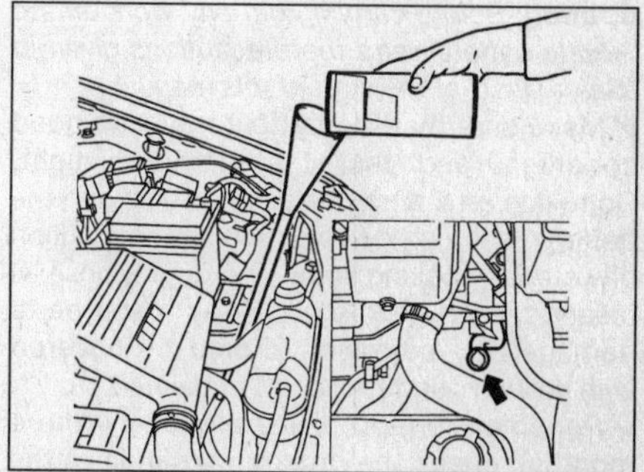

2 If topping up is necessary, add the specified fluid via the dipstick tube, using a funnel with a fine mesh filter. Take great care not to introduce dirt into the transmission.

Screen washer fluid level

Screenwash additives not only keep the winscreen clean during foul weather, they also prevent the washer system freezing in cold weather - which is when you are likely to need it most. Don't top up using plain water as the screenwash will become too diluted, and will freeze during cold weather. ***On no account use coolant antifreeze in the washer system - this could discolour or damage paintwork.***

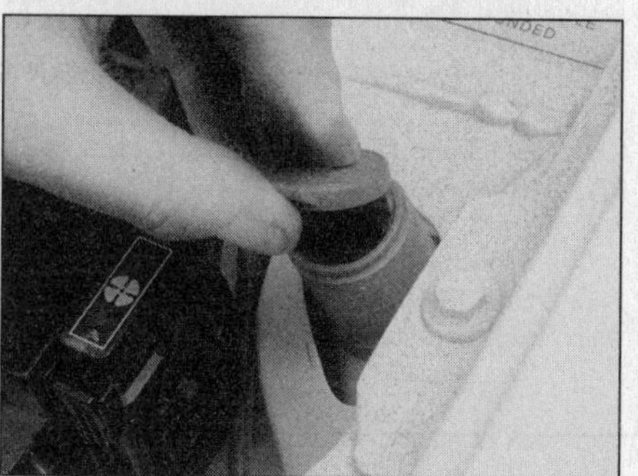

1 The screen washer fluid reservoir is located on the left-hand side of the engine compartment, next to the battery. Prise off the cap and pull out the telescopic filler.

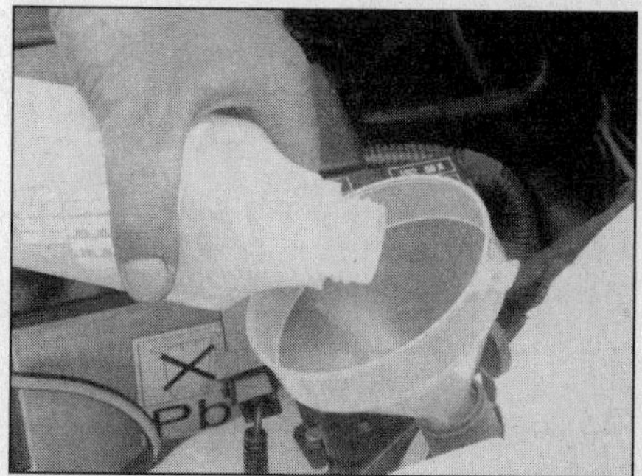

2 When topping-up the reservoir, add a screenwash additive in the quantities recommended on the bottle. Use of a funnel will prevent spillage.

Wiper blades

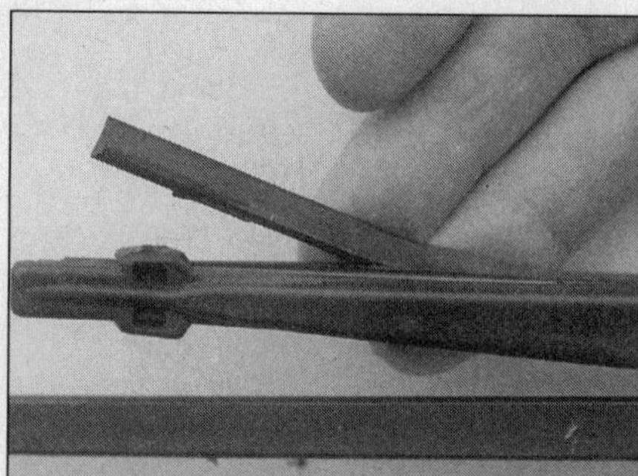

1 Check the condition of the wiper blades; if they are cracked or show any signs of deterioration, or if the glass swept area is smeared, renew them. Wiper blades should be renewed annually. Don't forget to check the tailgate wiper as well.

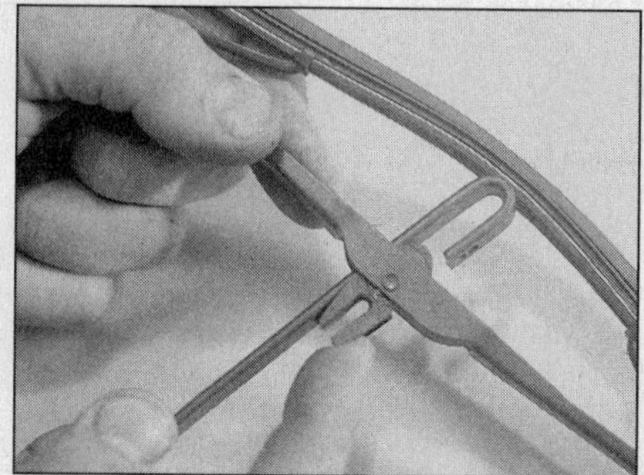

2 To remove a wiper blade, pull the arm fully away from the screen until it locks. Swivel the blade through 90°, press the locking tab with your fingers and slide the blade out of the arm's hooked end.

Battery

***Caution:** Before carrying out any work on the vehicle battery, read the precautions given in "Safety first" at the start of this manual.*

✔ Make sure that the battery tray is in good condition, and that the clamp is tight. Corrosion on the tray, retaining clamp and the battery itself can be removed with a solution of water and baking soda. Thoroughly rinse all cleaned areas with water. Any metal parts damaged by corrosion should be covered with a zinc-based primer, then painted.

✔ Periodically (approximately every three months), check the charge condition of the battery as described in Chapter 5A.

✔ If the battery is flat, and you need to jump start your vehicle, see ***Roadside Repairs.***

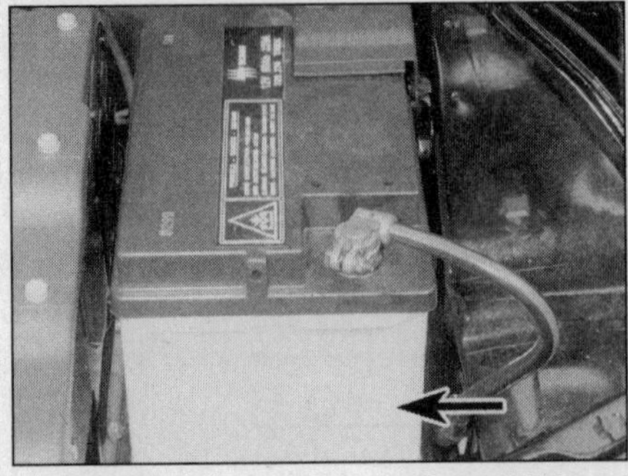

1 The battery is located on the left-hand side of the engine compartment. The exterior of the battery should be inspected periodically for damage such as a cracked case or cover.

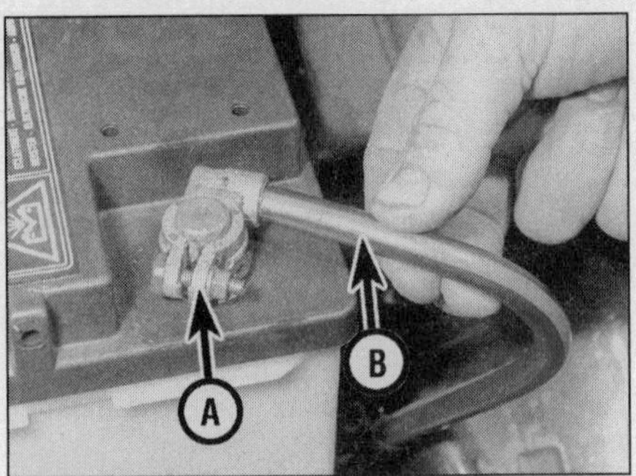

2 Check the tightness of battery clamps (A) to ensure good electrical connections. You should not be able to move them. Also check each cable (B) for cracks and frayed conductors.

Battery corrosion can be kept to a minimum by applying a layer of petroleum jelly to the clamps and terminals after they are reconnected.

3 If corrosion (white, fluffy deposits) is evident, remove the cables from the battery terminals, clean them with a small wire brush, then refit them. Automotive stores sell a tool for cleaning the battery post . . .

4 . . . as well as the battery cable clamps

Electrical systems

✔ Check all external lights and the horn. Refer to the appropriate Sections of Chapter 12 for details if any of the circuits are found to be inoperative.

✔ Visually check all accessible wiring connectors, harnesses and retaining clips for security, and for signs of chafing or damage.

If you need to check your brake lights and indicators unaided, back up to a wall or garage door and operate the lights. The reflected light should show if they are working properly.

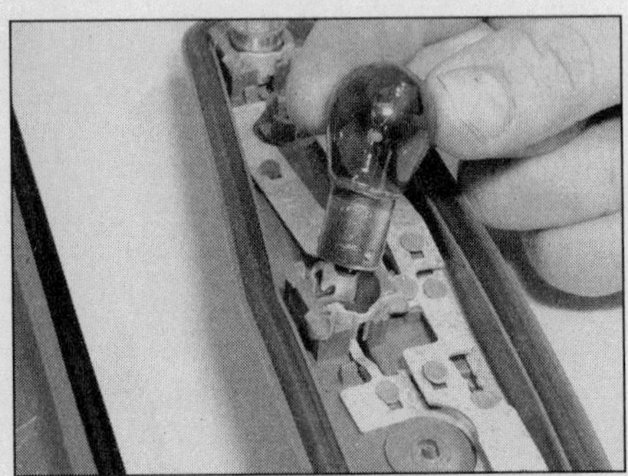

1 If a single indicator light, stop-light or headlight has failed, it is likely that a bulb has blown and will need to be replaced. Refer to Chapter 12 for details. If both stop-lights have failed, it is possible that the switch has failed (see Chapter 9).

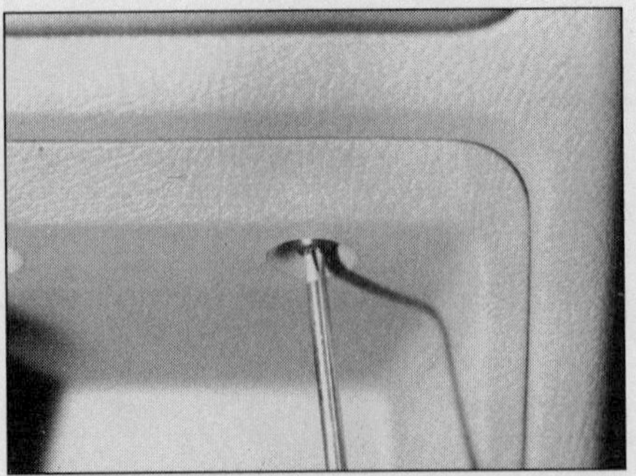

2 If more than one indicator light or tail light has failed it is likely that either a fuse has blown or that there is a fault in the circuit (see Chapter 12). The fuses are located behind the oddments tray on the facia. First unscrew the two screws and swivel the tray down.

3 To replace a blown fuse, simply pull it out using the special plastic tool and fit a new fuse of the correct rating (see Chapter 12). If the fuse blows again, it is important that you find out why - a complete checking procedure is given in Chapter 12.

Lubricants and fluids

Engine	
Petrol	Multigrade engine oil, viscosity SAE15W/40, to API SG/CD or better
Diesel	Multigrade engine oil, viscosity SAE15W/40, to API SG/CD or better
Cooling system	Ethylene glycol-based antifreeze and soft water
Manual gearbox	Hypoid gear oil, viscosity SAE80W to API GL4
Automatic transmission	Dexron type II automatic transmission fluid (ATF)
Braking system	Hydraulic fluid to SAE J1703F or DOT 4
Power steering	Dexron type II automatic transmission fluid (ATF)

Choosing your engine oil

Engines need oil, not only to lubricate moving parts and minimise wear, but also to maximise power output and to improve fuel economy.

HOW ENGINE OIL WORKS

• *Beating friction*

Without oil, the moving surfaces inside your engine will rub together, heat up and melt, quickly causing the engine to seize. Engine oil creates a film which separates these moving parts, preventing wear and heat build-up.

• *Cooling hot-spots*

Temperatures inside the engine can exceed 1000° C. The engine oil circulates and acts as a coolant, transferring heat from the hot-spots to the sump.

• *Cleaning the engine internally*

Good quality engine oils clean the inside of your engine, collecting and dispersing combustion deposits and controlling them until they are trapped by the oil filter or flushed out at oil change.

OIL CARE - FOLLOW THE CODE

To handle and dispose of used engine oil safely, always:

- ***Avoid skin contact with used engine oil. Repeated or prolonged contact can be harmful.***
- ***Dispose of used oil and empty packs in a responsible manner in an authorised disposal site. Call 0800 663366 to find the one nearest to you. Never tip oil down drains or onto the ground.***

Tyre pressures (cold)

	Front	Rear
Petrol models (average load):		
155/70R13, 165/60R14, 165/65R13, 165/65R14, 175/60R14	2.0 (29)	1.9 (28)
165/65R14 78Q (M+S)	2.5 (36)	2.2 (32)
185/55/R14	2.4 (35)	2.0 (29)
135/80B13, 135/80B14 (space-saver spare tyre)	2.8 (41)	2.8 (41)
Petrol models (fully laden):		
155/70R13, 165/60R14, 165/65R14, 175/60R14	2.2 (32)	2.2 (32)
165/65R14 78Q (M+S)	2.5 (36)	2.2 (32)
185/55/R14	2.4 (35)	2.2 (32)
135/80B13, 135/80B14 (space-saver spare tyre)	2.8 (41)	2.8 (41)
Diesel models (average load):		
165/70R13, 165/65R14, 175/60R14	2.4 (35)	2.0 (29)
135/80B13, 135/80B14 (space-saver spare tyre)	2.8 (41)	2.8 (41)
Diesel models (fully laden):		
165/70R13, 165/65R14, 175/60R14	2.4 (35)	2.2 (32)
135/80B13, 135/80B14 (space-saver spare tyre)	2.8 (41)	2.8 (41)

Advanced driving

Many people see the words 'advanced driving' and believe that it won't interest them or that it is a style of driving beyond their own abilities. Nothing could be further from the truth. Advanced driving is straightforward safe, sensible driving - the sort of driving we should all do every time we get behind the wheel.

An average of 10 people are killed every day on UK roads and 870 more are injured, some seriously. Lives are ruined daily, usually because somebody did something stupid. Something like 95% of all accidents are due to human error, mostly driver failure. Sometimes we make genuine mistakes - everyone does. Sometimes we have lapses of concentration. Sometimes we deliberately take risks.

For many people, the process of 'learning to drive' doesn't go much further than learning how to pass the driving test because of a common belief that good drivers are made by 'experience'.

Learning to drive by 'experience' teaches three driving skills:

- ☐ Quick reactions. (Whoops, that was close!)
- ☐ Good handling skills. (Horn, swerve, brake, horn).
- ☐ Reliance on vehicle technology. (Great stuff this ABS, stop in no distance even in the wet...)

Drivers whose skills are 'experience based' generally have a lot of near misses and the odd accident. The results can be seen every day in our courts and our hospital casualty departments.

Advanced drivers have learnt to control the risks by controlling the position and speed of their vehicle. They avoid accidents and near misses, even if the drivers around them make mistakes.

The key skills of advanced driving are **concentration,** effective all-round **observation, anticipation** and **planning.** When **good vehicle handling** is added to these skills, all driving situations can be approached and negotiated in a safe, methodical way, leaving nothing to chance.

Concentration means applying your mind to safe driving, completely excluding anything that's not relevant. Driving is usually the most dangerous activity that most of us undertake in our daily routines. It deserves our full attention.

Observation means not just looking, but seeing and seeking out the information found in the driving environment.

Anticipation means asking yourself what is happening, what you can reasonably expect to happen and what could happen unexpectedly. (One of the commonest words used in compiling accident reports is 'suddenly'.)

Planning is the link between seeing something and taking the appropriate action. For many drivers, planning is the missing link.

If you want to become a safer and more skilful driver and you want to enjoy your driving more, contact the Institute of Advanced Motorists at www.iam.org.uk, phone 0208 996 9600, or write to IAM House, 510 Chiswick High Road, London W4 5RG for an information pack.

Chapter 1 Part A: Routine maintenance & servicing - petrol models

Contents

Degrees of difficulty

Easy, suitable for novice with little experience 

Fairly easy, suitable for beginner with some experience 

Fairly difficult, suitable for competent DIY mechanic 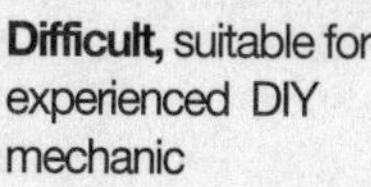

Difficult, suitable for experienced DIY mechanic 

Very difficult, suitable for expert DIY or professional

Lubricants and fluids Refer to end of *Weekly checks* on page 0•17

Capacities

Engine oil (including filter)

1108 cc engine	3.47 litres
1242 cc (8-valve) engine	3.74 litres
1242 cc (16-valve) engine	2.80 litres
Cooling system	4.6 litres
Manual transmission	
5-speed	1.65 litres
6-speed	1.87 litres
Automatic transmission	1.98 litres
Power-assisted steering	0.65 litres
Fuel tank	47 litres
Washer reservoir	
Without headlight washers	2.5 litres
With headlight washers	7.0 litres

Engine

Auxiliary drivebelt tension	5.0 mm deflection midway between pulleys	
Valve clearances - engine cold:	**Inlet**	**Exhaust**
1108 cc and 1242 cc (single-point petrol injection)	0.40 ± 0.05 mm	0.50 ± 0.05 mm
1242 cc (multi-point petrol injection	0.40 ± 0.05 mm	0.45 ± 0.05 mm

Cooling system

Antifreeze mixture (50% antifreeze) ..... Protection down to -35°C

Note: *Refer to antifreeze manufacturer for latest recommendations.*

Fuel system

Engine idle speed	900 ± 50 rpm
CO%	0.35 maximum

Ignition system

Ignition timing	Refer to Chapter 5B	
Spark plugs:	**Type**	**Electrode gap**
All engines	Bosch FR 7 D+	0.9 mm

Brakes

Brake pad lining minimum thickness	1.5 mm
Brake shoe friction material minimum thickness	2.0 mm

Torque wrench settings

	Nm	lbf ft
Automatic transmission fluid drain plug	25	18
Automatic transmission fluid sump bolts	4	3
Manual transmission oil drain plug:		
Stage 1	12	9
Stage 2	Angle-tighten a further 180°	
Manual transmission oil filler plug	40	30
Roadwheel bolts	86	63
Spark plugs	27	20
Sump drain plug	10	7

The maintenance intervals in this manual are provided with the assumption that you, not the dealer, will be carrying out the work. These are the minimum maintenance intervals recommended by us for vehicles driven daily. If you wish to keep your vehicle in peak condition at all times, you may wish to perform some of these procedures more often. We encourage frequent maintenance, because it enhances the efficiency, performance and resale value of your vehicle.

When the vehicle is new, it should be serviced by a factory-authorised dealer service department, in order to preserve the factory warranty.

Every 250 miles (400 km) or weekly

- ☐ Refer to *Weekly checks*

Every 5000 miles (7500 km) or 6 months - whichever comes first

- ☐ Renew the engine oil and filter (Section 3)

Note: *Frequent oil and filter changes are good for the engine. We recommend changing the oil at the mileage specified here, or at least twice a year if the mileage covered is a less.*

Every 10 000 miles (15 000 km) or 12 months - whichever comes first

In addition to the items listed above, carry out the following:

- ☐ Check the operation of the brake warning lamp (Section 4)
- ☐ Check the front brake pads for wear (Section 5)
- ☐ Check the underbody and sealant for damage (Section 6)
- ☐ Hose and fluid leak check (Section 7)
- ☐ Check the condition of the exhaust system and its mountings (Section 8)
- ☐ Check the condition of the driveshaft gaiters (Section 9)
- ☐ Renew pollen filter (Section 10)
- ☐ Check exhaust gas content and idle speed (Section 11)
- ☐ Check the steering and suspension components for condition and security (Section 12)

Every 20 000 miles (30 000 km) or 2 years - whichever comes first

In addition to the items listed above, carry out the following:

- ☐ Check and if necessary adjust the tension of the auxiliary drivebelt(s) (Section 13)
- ☐ Check the freeplay and height of the clutch pedal (Section 14)
- ☐ Check and if necessary adjust the valve clearances (Section 15)
- ☐ Check and if necessary tighten inlet and exhaust manifold mountings (Section 16)
- ☐ Renew the fuel filter (Section 17)
- ☐ Renew the air filter element (Section 18)
- ☐ Renew the spark plugs (Section 19)
- ☐ Check the condition of the HT cables (Section 20)
- ☐ Check the engine management system (Section 21)
- ☐ Lubricate all hinges and locks (Section 22)
- ☐ Check the headlight beam adjustment (Section 23)
- ☐ Carry out a road test (Section 24)

Every 30 000 miles (45 000 km) or 3 years - whichever comes first

In addition to the items listed above, carry out the following:

- ☐ Check the operation of the Lambda sensor (Section 25)
- ☐ Check and if necessary top-up the manual transmission oil level (Section 26)
- ☐ Check the operation of the evaporative loss system (Section 27)
- ☐ Automatic transmission inner filter and fluid renewal (Section 28)

Every 40 000 miles (60 000 km) or 4 years - whichever comes first

In addition to the items listed above, carry out the following:

- ☐ Check the rear brake shoes for wear (Section 29)
- ☐ Renew the timing belt (Section 30)*

***Note:** *Although the normal interval for timing belt renewal is 70 000 miles (105 000 km), it is strongly recommended that the belt is renewed at 40 000 miles (60 000 km) on vehicles which are subjected to intensive use, ie. mainly short journeys or a lot of stop-start driving. The actual belt renewal interval is therefore very much up to the individual owner, but bear in mind that severe engine damage will result if the belt breaks.*

Every 60 000 miles (90 000 km) or 6 years - whichever comes first

In addition to the items listed above, carry out the following:

- ☐ Check the condition and operation of the crankcase emission control system (Section 31)

Every 80 000 miles (120 000 km)

- ☐ Renew the manual transmission oil (Section 32)

Every 2 years (regardless of mileage)

- ☐ Renew the engine coolant (Section 33)
- ☐ Renew the brake fluid (Section 34)

Underbonnet view - 1242 cc engine model

1 Engine oil filler cap
2 Engine oil dipstick
3 Brake vacuum servo unit
4 Brake fluid reservoir
5 Air cleaner cover
6 Coolant expansion tank
7 Windscreen washer fluid reservoir
8 Front suspension strut upper mounting
9 Ignition coil cover
10 Engine wiring connector cover
11 Battery
12 ECU

Underbonnet view - 1108 cc (8-valve) engine model

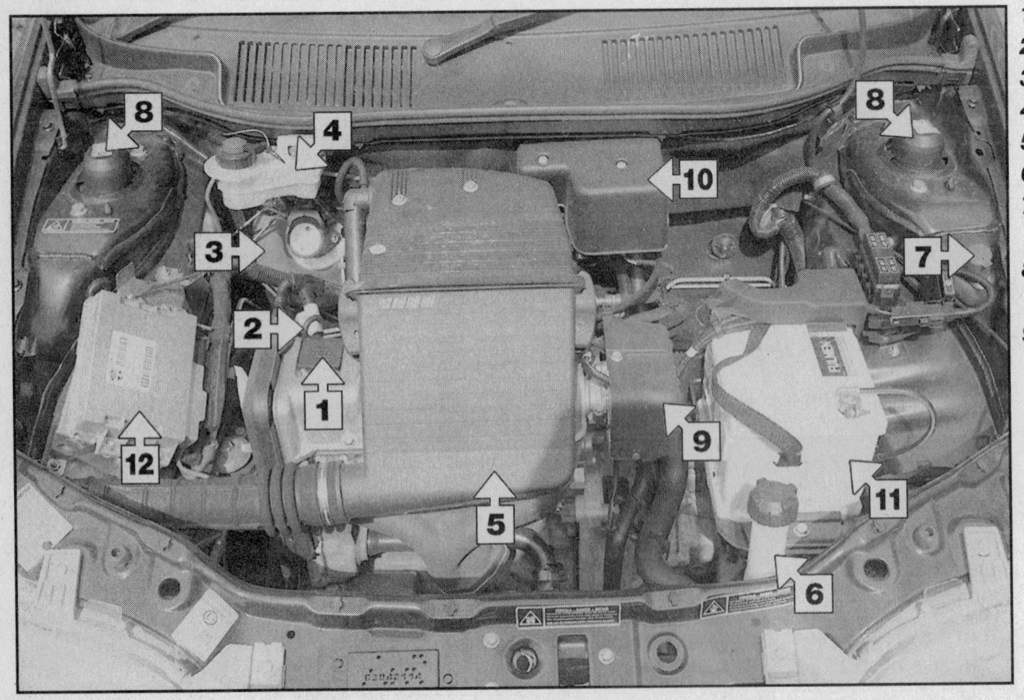

1 Engine oil filler cap
2 Engine oil dipstick
3 Brake vacuum servo unit
4 Brake fluid reservoir
5 Air cleaner cover
6 Coolant expansion tank
7 Windscreen washer fluid reservoir
8 Front suspension strut upper mounting
9 Ignition coil cover
10 Engine wiring connector cover
11 Battery
12 ECU

Underbonnet view - 1242 cc (16-valve) engine model

1 *Engine oil filler cap*
2 *Engine oil dipstick*
3 *Brake fluid reservoir*
4 *Power steering fluid reservoir*
5 *Engine wiring connector cover*
6 *Windscreen washer fluid reservoir*
7 *Battery*
8 *Coolant expansion tank*
9 *Air cleaner cover*
10 *Resonator*
11 *ECU*

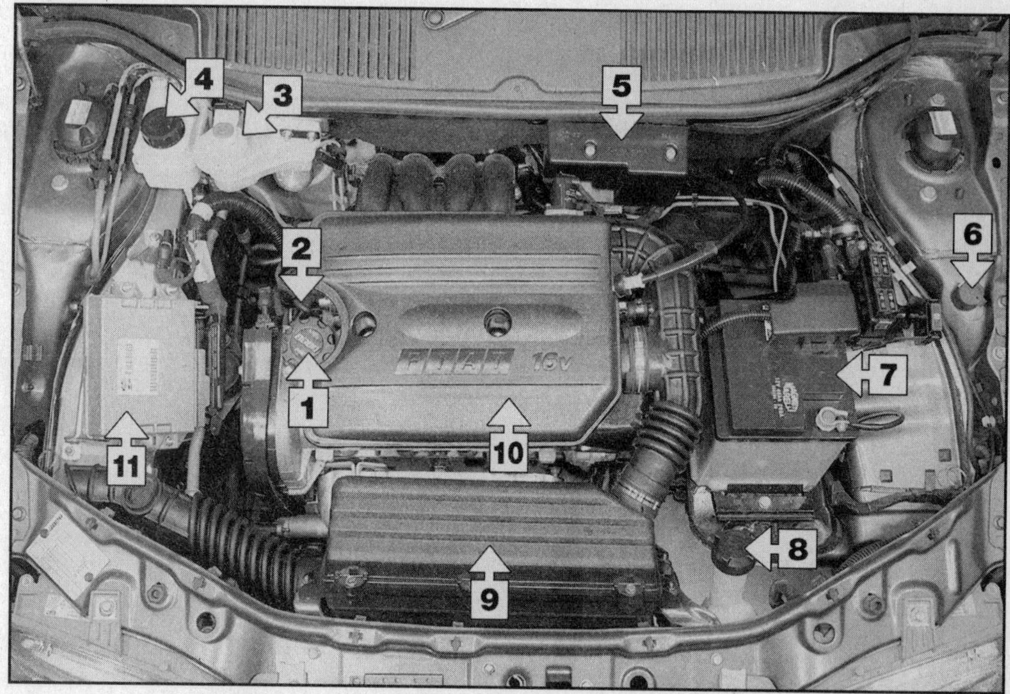

Front underbody view (diesel model shown, petrol model similar)

1 *Oil filter*
2 *Sump drain plug*
3 *Transmission drain plug*
4 *Electric cooling fan unit*
5 *Left-hand driveshaft*
6 *Intermediate shaft*
7 *Right-hand driveshaft*
8 *Front suspension lower arms*
9 *Front anti-roll bar*
10 *Exhaust downpipe*
11 *Front brake calipers*
12 *Rear engine mounting*
13 *Radiator bottom hose*

Rear underbody view (diesel model shown, petrol model similar)

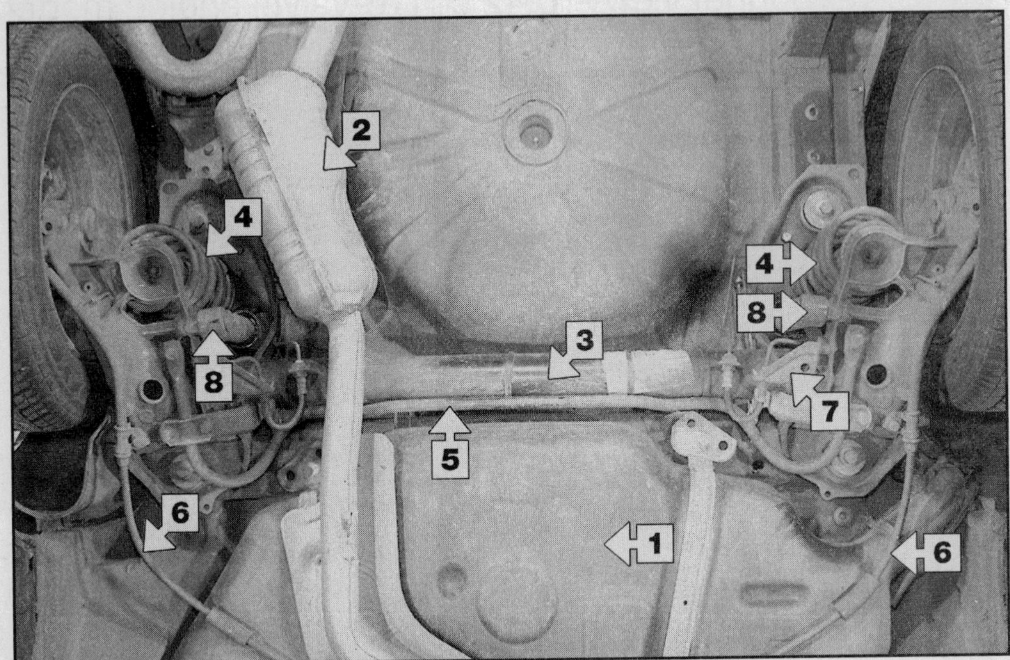

1 *Fuel tank*
2 *Exhaust tailpipe and silencer*
3 *Rear axle*
4 *Coil springs*
5 *Rear anti-roll bar*
6 *Handbrake cables*
7 *Rear brake pressure regulating valve*
8 *Rear shock absorber lower mountings*

Maintenance procedures

1 Introduction

This Chapter is designed to help the home mechanic maintain his/her vehicle for safety, economy, long life and peak performance.

The Chapter contains a master maintenance schedule, and Sections dealing specifically with each task in the schedule. Visual checks, adjustments, component renewal and other helpful items are included. Refer to the accompanying illustrations of the engine compartment and the underside of the vehicle for the locations of the various components.

Servicing your vehicle in accordance with the mileage/time maintenance schedule and the following Sections will provide a planned maintenance programme, which should result in a long and reliable service life. This is a comprehensive plan, so maintaining some items but not others at the specified service intervals, will not produce the same results.

As you service your vehicle, you will discover that many of the procedures can, and should, be grouped together, because of the particular procedure being performed, or because of the proximity of two otherwise-unrelated components to one another. For example, if the vehicle is raised for any reason, the exhaust can be inspected at the same time as the suspension and steering components.

The first step in this maintenance programme is to prepare yourself before the actual work begins. Read through all the Sections relevant to the work to be carried out, then make a list and gather all the parts and tools required. If a problem is encountered, seek advice from a parts specialist, or a dealer service department.

2 Regular maintenance

1 If, from the time the vehicle is new, the routine maintenance schedule is followed closely, and frequent checks are made of fluid levels and high-wear items, as suggested throughout this manual, the engine will be kept in relatively good running condition, and the need for additional work will be minimised.

2 It is possible that there will be times when the engine is running poorly due to the lack of regular maintenance. This is even more likely if a used vehicle, which has not received regular and frequent maintenance checks, is purchased. In such cases, additional work may need to be carried out, outside of the regular maintenance intervals.

3 If engine wear is suspected, a compression test (refer to the relevant Part of Chapter 2) will provide valuable information regarding the overall performance of the main internal components. Such a test can be used as a basis to decide on the extent of the work to be carried out. If, for example, a compression test indicates serious internal engine wear, conventional maintenance as described in this Chapter will not greatly improve the performance of the engine, and may prove a waste of time and money, unless extensive overhaul work is carried out first.

4 The following series of operations are those usually required to improve the performance of a generally poor-running engine:

Primary operations

a) Clean, inspect and test the battery (See Weekly checks).
b) Check all the engine-related fluids (See Weekly checks).
c) Check the condition and tension of the auxiliary drivebelt(s) (Section 13).
d) Renew the spark plugs (Section 19).
e) Inspect the ignition HT leads (Section 20).
f) Check the condition of the air filter, and renew if necessary (Section 18).
g) Check the fuel filter (Section 17).
h) Check the condition of all hoses, and check for fluid leaks (Section 7).
i) Check the exhaust gas emissions (Section 11).

5 If the above operations do not prove fully effective, carry out the following secondary operations:

Secondary operations

All items listed under *Primary operations*, plus the following:

a) Check the charging system (Chapter 5A, Section 4).
b) Check the ignition system (Chapter 5B).
c) Check the fuel system (see relevant Part of Chapter 4).
d) Renew the ignition HT leads (Section 20)

Every 5000 miles (7500 km) or 6 months

3 Engine oil and filter renewal

1 Frequent oil and filter changes are the most important preventative maintenance which can be undertaken by the DIY owner. As engine oil ages, it becomes diluted and contaminated, which leads to premature engine wear.

2 Before starting this procedure, gather all the necessary tools and materials. Also make sure that you have plenty of clean rags and newspapers handy, to mop up any spills. Ideally, the engine oil should be warm, as it will drain better, and more built-up sludge will be removed with it. Take care, however, not to touch the exhaust or any other hot parts of the engine when working under the vehicle. To avoid any possibility of scalding, and to protect yourself from possible skin irritants and other harmful contaminants in used engine oils, it is advisable to wear gloves when carrying out this work. Access to the underside of the vehicle will be greatly improved if it can be raised on a lift, driven onto ramps, or jacked up and supported on axle stands (see *Jacking and vehicle support*). Whichever method is chosen, make sure that the vehicle remains level, or if it is at an angle, that the drain plug is at the lowest point.

3 Slacken the drain plug about half a turn using an Allen key. Position the draining container under the drain plug, then remove the plug completely **(see Haynes Hint)**.

4 Allow some time for the old oil to drain, noting that it may be necessary to reposition the container as the oil flow slows to a trickle.

5 After all the oil has drained, wipe off the drain plug with a clean rag, then clean the area around the drain plug opening and refit the plug. Tighten the plug securely.

HAYNES HiNT

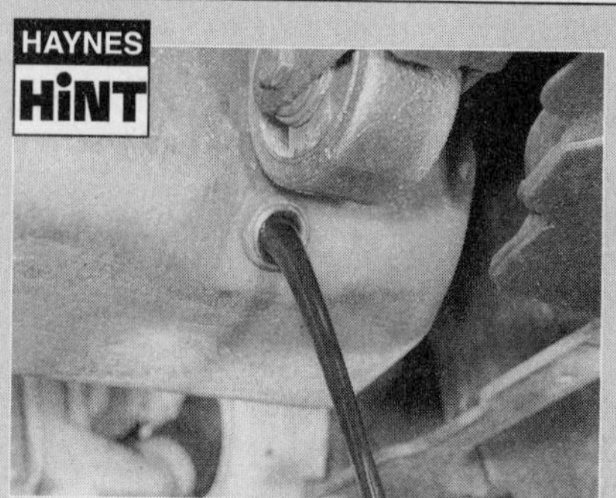

Keep the drain plug pressed into the sump while unscrewing it by hand the last couple of turns. As the plug releases, move it away sharply so that the stream of oil issuing from the sump runs into the container, not up your sleeve.

6 If the filter is also to be renewed, move the container into position under the oil filter, which is located on the front right-hand side of the engine **(see illustration)**.

7 Using an oil filter removal tool if necessary, slacken the filter initially, then unscrew it by hand the rest of the way. Empty the oil in the old filter into the container.

8 Use a clean rag to remove all oil, dirt and sludge from the filter sealing area on the engine. Check the old filter to make sure that the rubber sealing ring has not stuck to the engine. If it has, carefully remove it.

9 Apply a light coating of clean engine oil to the sealing ring on the new filter, then screw it into position on the engine. Tighten the filter firmly by hand only - **do not** use any tools.

10 Remove the old oil and all tools from under the vehicle then lower the vehicle to the ground (if applicable).

3.6 Oil filter location (viewed from above)

11 Remove the dipstick, then pull out the oil filler cap from the cylinder head cover. Fill the engine, using the correct grade and type of oil (see *Weekly checks*). An oil can spout or funnel may help to reduce spillage. Pour in half the specified quantity of oil first, then wait a few minutes for the oil to fall to the sump. Continue adding oil a small quantity at a time until the level is up to the MAX mark on the dipstick. Refit the filler cap.

12 Start the engine and run it for a few minutes; check for leaks around the oil filter seal and the sump drain plug. Note that there may be a delay of a few seconds before the oil pressure warning light goes out when the engine is first started, as the oil circulates through the engine oil galleries and the new oil filter before the pressure builds up.

13 Switch off the engine, and wait a few minutes for the oil to settle in the sump once more. With the new oil circulated and the filter completely full, recheck the level on the dipstick, and add more oil as necessary.

14 Dispose of the used engine oil safely, with reference to *General repair procedures* in the reference Sections of this manual.

Every 10 000 miles (15 000 km) or 12 months

4 Brake warning lamp operation check

1 With the ignition key inserted and turned to the MAR position, open the bonnet and depress the button on the top of the brake fluid reservoir cap **(see illustration)**.

2 As the button is depressed, the brake warning lamp on the instrument panel should illuminate.

3 If the lamp fails to illuminate, check the operation of the level switch using a continuity tester, then refer to Chapter 12, Section 5, and check the instrument panel bulb.

5 Front brake pad check

1 Firmly apply the handbrake, then jack up the front of the car and support it securely on axle stands (see *Jacking and vehicle support*). Remove the front roadwheels.

2 Using a steel rule, measure the thickness of the friction material of the brake pads on both front brakes. This must not be less than 1.5 mm. Check the thickness of the pad friction material through the hole on the front of the caliper **(see illustration)**.

3 For a comprehensive check, the brake pads

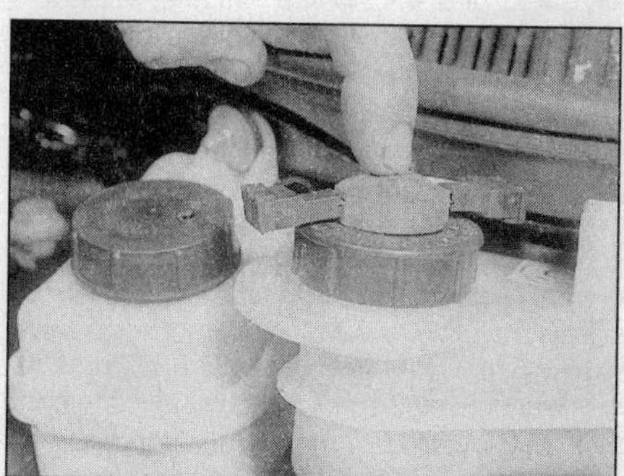

4.1 Depress the button on the top of the brake fluid reservoir cap

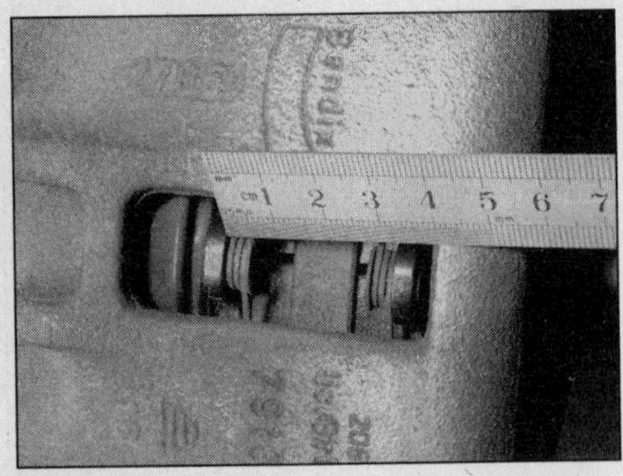

5.2 Check the thickness of the pad friction material through the hole on the front of the caliper

should be removed and cleaned. The operation of the caliper can then also be checked, and the condition of the brake disc itself can be fully examined on both sides. Refer to Chapter 9 for further information.

4 If any pad's friction material is worn to the specified thickness or less, *all four pads must be renewed as a set.* Refer to Chapter 9.

5 On completion refit the roadwheels and lower the car to the ground

6 Underbody sealant check

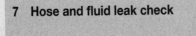

1 Jack up the front and rear of the car and support it securely on axle stands (see *Jacking and vehicle support*). Alternatively position the car over an inspection pit.

2 Check the underbody, wheel housings and side sills for rust and/or damage to the underbody sealant. If evident, repair as necessary.

7 Hose and fluid leak check

1 Visually inspect the engine joint faces, gaskets and seals for any signs of water or oil leaks. Pay particular attention to the areas around the camshaft cover, cylinder head, oil filter and sump joint faces. Bear in mind that, over a period of time, some very slight seepage from these areas is to be expected - what you are really looking for is any indication of a serious leak **(see Haynes Hint)**. Should a leak be found, renew the offending gasket or oil seal by referring to the appropriate Chapters in this manual.

A leak in the cooling system will usually show up as white or rust-coloured deposits on the area adjoining the leak

2 Also check the security and condition of all the engine-related pipes and hoses. Ensure that all cable-ties or securing clips are in place and in good condition. Clips which are broken or missing can lead to chafing of the hoses, pipes or wiring, which could cause more serious problems in the future.

3 Carefully check the radiator hoses and heater hoses along their entire length. Renew any hose which is cracked, swollen or deteriorated. Cracks will show up better if the hose is squeezed. Pay close attention to the hose clips that secure the hoses to the cooling system components. Hose clips can pinch and puncture hoses, resulting in cooling system leaks.

4 Inspect all the cooling system components (hoses, joint faces etc.) for leaks. A leak in the cooling system will usually show up as white- or rust-coloured deposits on the area adjoining the leak. Where any problems of this nature are found on system components, renew the component or gasket with reference to Chapter 3.

5 Where applicable, inspect the automatic transmission fluid cooler hoses for leaks or deterioration.

6 With the vehicle raised, inspect the fuel tank and filler neck for punctures, cracks and other damage. The connection between the filler neck and tank is especially critical. Sometimes a rubber filler neck or connecting hose will leak due to loose retaining clamps or deteriorated rubber.

7 Carefully check all rubber hoses and metal fuel lines leading away from the fuel tank. Check for loose connections, deteriorated hoses, crimped lines, and other damage. Pay particular attention to the vent pipes and hoses, which often loop up around the filler neck and can become blocked or crimped. Follow the lines to the front of the vehicle, carefully inspecting them all the way. Renew damaged sections as necessary.

8 From within the engine compartment, check the security of all fuel hose attachments and pipe unions, and inspect the fuel hoses and vacuum hoses for kinks, chafing and deterioration.

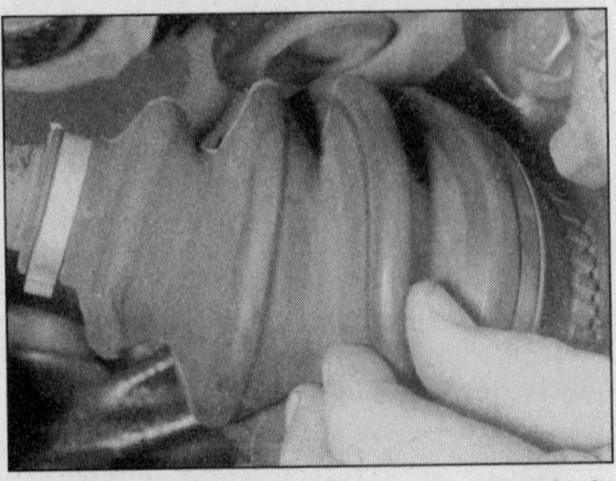

9.1 Checking the condition of a driveshaft gaiter

9 Where applicable, check the condition of the power steering fluid hoses and pipes.

8 Exhaust system check

1 With the engine cold (at least an hour after the vehicle has been driven), check the complete exhaust system from the engine to the end of the tailpipe. The exhaust system is most easily checked with the vehicle raised on a hoist, or suitably supported on axle stands (see *Jacking and vehicle support*), so that the exhaust components are readily visible and accessible.

2 Check the exhaust pipes and connections for evidence of leaks, severe corrosion and damage. Make sure that all brackets and mountings are in good condition, and that all relevant nuts and bolts are tight. Leakage at any of the joints or in other parts of the system will usually show up as a black sooty stain in the vicinity of the leak.

3 Rattles and other noises can often be traced to the exhaust system, especially the brackets and mountings. Try to move the pipes and silencers. If the components are able to come into contact with the body or suspension parts, secure the system with new mountings. Otherwise separate the joints (if possible) and twist the pipes as necessary to provide additional clearance.

9 Driveshaft gaiter check

1 With the vehicle raised and securely supported on stands (see *Jacking and vehicle support*), turn the steering onto full lock, then slowly rotate the roadwheel. Inspect the condition of the outer constant velocity (CV) joint rubber gaiters, squeezing the gaiters to open out the folds. Check for signs of cracking, splits or deterioration of the rubber, which may allow the grease to escape, and lead to water and grit entry into the joint. Also check the security and condition of the retaining clips. Repeat these checks on the inner CV joints **(see illustration)**. If any damage or deterioration is found, the gaiters should be renewed (see Chapter 8, Section 3).

2 At the same time, check the general condition of the CV joints themselves by first holding the driveshaft and attempting to rotate the wheel. Repeat this check by holding the inner joint and attempting to rotate the driveshaft. Any appreciable movement indicates wear in the joints, wear in the driveshaft splines, or a loose driveshaft retaining nut.

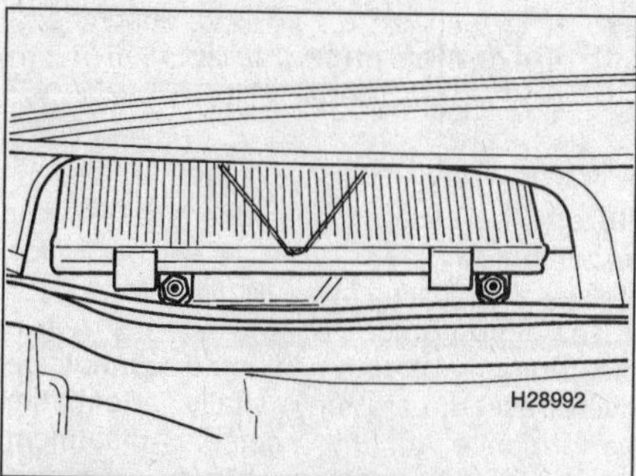

10.5 Location of pollen filter

10 Pollen filter renewal

1 The pollen filter (where fitted) is located under the engine bulkhead cover panel.
2 Refer to Chapter 12 and remove both windscreen wiper arms.
3 Unclip the rubber seal from the relevant end of the top of the engine compartment bulkhead.
4 Unscrew the retaining fastener screws and pull out the fasteners securing the bulkhead cover panel in position. Release the cover panel from the base of the windscreen and remove it from the vehicle.
5 Pivot the pollen filter cover upwards and away then release the retaining clips and withdraw the filter from its housing **(see illustration)**.
6 Wipe clean the filter housing then fit the new filter. Clip the filter securely in position and refit the cover.
7 Refit the trim cover, securing it in position with the fasteners, and seat the rubber seal on the bulkhead.

11 Idle speed and CO content check and adjustment

1 The idle speed is controlled by the ECU via a stepper motor located on the side of the throttle body and is not adjustable.
2 The exhaust gas oxygen content is constantly monitored by the ECU via the Lambda sensor, which is mounted in the exhaust downpipe. The ECU then uses this information to modify the injection timing and duration to maintain the optimum air/fuel ratio.
3 Experienced home mechanics with a considerable amount of skill and equipment (including a good-quality tachometer and a good-quality, carefully calibrated exhaust gas analyser) may be able to check the exhaust CO level and the idle speed. However, if these are found to be in need of adjustment, the car **must** be taken to a suitably-equipped Fiat dealer for testing using the special test equipment which is plugged into the diagnostic connector.

12 Steering and suspension check

Front suspension and steering check

1 Raise the front of the vehicle, and securely support it on axle stands (see *Jacking and vehicle support*).
2 Inspect the balljoint dust covers and the steering rack-and-pinion gaiters for splits, chafing or deterioration. Any wear of these will cause loss of lubricant, together with dirt and water entry, resulting in rapid deterioration of the balljoints or steering gear.
3 On vehicles with power steering, check the fluid hoses for chafing or deterioration, and the pipe and hose unions for fluid leaks. Also check for signs of fluid leakage under pressure from the steering gear rubber gaiters, which would indicate failed fluid seals within the steering gear.
4 Grasp the roadwheel at the 12 o'clock and 6 o'clock positions, and try to rock it **(see illustration)**. Very slight free play may be felt, but if the movement is appreciable, further investigation is necessary to determine the source. Continue rocking the wheel while an assistant depresses the footbrake. If the movement is now eliminated or significantly reduced, it is likely that the hub bearings are at fault. If the free play is still evident with the footbrake depressed, then there is wear in the suspension joints or mountings.
5 Now grasp the wheel at the 9 o'clock and 3 o'clock positions, and try to rock it as before. Any movement felt now may again be caused by wear in the hub bearings or the steering track-rod balljoints. If the inner or outer balljoint is worn, the visual movement will be obvious.

12.4 Rocking a roadwheel to check for wear in the steering/suspension components

6 Using a large screwdriver or flat bar, check for wear in the suspension mounting bushes by levering between the relevant suspension component and its attachment point. Some movement is to be expected as the mountings are made of rubber, but excessive wear should be obvious. Also check the condition of any visible rubber bushes, looking for splits, cracks or contamination of the rubber.
7 With the car standing on its wheels, have an assistant turn the steering wheel back and forth about an eighth of a turn each way. There should be very little, if any, lost movement between the steering wheel and roadwheels. If this is not the case, closely observe the joints and mountings previously described, but in addition, check the steering column universal joints for wear, and the rack-and-pinion steering gear itself.

Suspension strut/ shock absorber check

8 Check for any signs of fluid leakage around the suspension strut/shock absorber body, or from the rubber gaiter around the piston rod. Should any fluid be noticed, the suspension strut/shock absorber is defective internally, and should be renewed. **Note:** *Suspension struts/shock absorbers should always be renewed in pairs on the same axle.*
9 The efficiency of the suspension strut/shock absorber may be checked by bouncing the vehicle at each corner. Generally speaking, the body will return to its normal position and stop after being depressed. If it rises and returns on a rebound, the suspension strut/shock absorber is probably suspect. Examine also the suspension strut/shock absorber upper and lower mountings for any signs of wear.

Every 20 000 miles (30 000 km) or 2 years

13 Auxiliary drivebelt(s) check and renewal

Note: *Fiat specify the use of a special tool to correctly set the drivebelt tension. If access to this equipment cannot be obtained, an approximate setting can be achieved using the method described below. If the method described is used, the tension should be checked using the special tool at the earliest possible opportunity.*
1 Depending on equipment fitted, one, two or three auxiliary drivebelts may be fitted. The alternator, power steering pump and air conditioning compressor, as applicable, are each driven by an individual drivebelt.

Checking

2 Disconnect the battery negative terminal (refer to *Disconnecting the battery* in the Reference Section of this manual).
3 Firmly apply the handbrake, then jack up

the front of the car and support it securely on axle stands (see *Jacking and vehicle support*).

4 Remove the right-hand front wheel.

5 Remove the inner cover from under the right-hand wheelarch for access to the right-hand side of the engine.

6 Using a socket on the crankshaft sprocket bolt, rotate the crankshaft so that the full length of the auxiliary drivebelt(s) can be examined. Look for cracks, splitting and fraying on the surface of the belt; check also for signs of glazing (shiny patches) and separation of the belt plies. If damage or wear is visible, the relevant belt should be renewed.

7 If the condition of the belt is satisfactory, check the drivebelt tension as described below.

Renewal

Alternator drivebelt

Note: *On certain models with power steering but without air conditioning, it will be necessary to remove the power steering pump drivebelt first, as described below.*

8 Where fitted, undo the bolts and remove the belt guard from the alternator.

9 Loosen the pivot and adjustment bolts then swivel the alternator towards the engine and slip off the drivebelt.

10 Unbolt and remove the crankshaft sensor from the front of the engine (refer to Chapter 4A, Section 5, if necessary).

11 Remove the drivebelt from the engine.

12 When renewing a drivebelt, ensure that the correct type is used. Fit the belt around the two pulleys then swivel the alternator outwards to take up any slack in the belt. Adjust the tension correctly as described below.

Power steering pump drivebelt

13 Slacken the bolts securing the power steering pump to the mounting bracket.

14 Slacken the adjusting bolt locknut and turn the adjusting bolt until all the tension is removed from the drivebelt.

15 Undo the bolts and remove the pulley guard from the power steering pump then slip the drivebelt off the pulleys.

16 Ensuring that the correct type of drivebelt is used, fit the belt around the pulleys and turn the adjusting bolt to just take up the slack in the belt. Adjust the tension correctly as described below.

Air conditioning compressor drivebelt

17 Remove the alternator and power steering pump drivebelts as described previously.

18 Slacken the bolts securing the compressor to the mounting bracket.

19 Slacken the adjusting bolt locknut and turn the adjusting bolt until all the tension is removed from the drivebelt, then slip the belt off the pulleys.

20 Ensuring that the correct type of drivebelt is used, fit the belt around the pulleys and turn the adjusting bolt to just take up the slack in the belt. Adjust the tension correctly as described below.

15.7 Checking a valve clearance with a feeler blade

Tensioning

21 Correct tensioning of the belt will ensure that it has a long life. A belt which is too slack will slip and perhaps squeal. Beware, however, of overtightening, as this can cause wear in the alternator, power steering pump or air conditioning compressor bearings. **Note:** *Fiat recommend use of their special tensioning tool however the following procedure will set the tension correctly.*

22 The belt(s) should be tensioned so that, under firm thumb pressure, there is approximately 5.0 mm of free movement at the mid-point between the pulleys. To adjust the alternator drivebelt, slightly tighten the adjustment bolt then swivel the alternator outwards until the belt tension is correct. Fully tighten the adjustment bolt followed by the pivot bolt then refit the rpm sensor.

23 On models with power steering and/or air conditioning, fit the relevant drivebelt over the pulleys then turn the adjusting bolt until the tension is correct. Secure the adjusting bolt by tightening the locknut, then tighten the remaining mounting bolts. Refit any remaining drivebelts and all the components removed.

24 Refit the inner cover and wheel, lower the vehicle to the ground, then reconnect the battery negative terminal.

14 Clutch adjustment check

Refer to Chapter 6, Section 2.

15.11 Using a modified C-spanner and a screwdriver to remove a shim

15 Valve clearance check and adjustment

Note: *The following procedure is not applicable to 1242 cc, 16-valve engines which utilise self-adjusting hydraulic tappets.*

1 The importance of having the valve clearances correctly adjusted cannot be overstressed, as they vitally affect the performance of the engine. Adjustment should only be necessary when the valve gear has become noisy, after engine overhaul, or when trying to trace the cause of power loss. The clearances are checked as follows. The engine must be cold for the check to be accurate.

2 Apply the handbrake then jack up the right-hand front of the vehicle and support on an axle stand (*see Jacking and vehicle support).* Engage 4th gear. The engine can now be rotated by turning the right-hand front roadwheel.

3 Remove all spark plugs as described in Section 19.

4 Remove the camshaft cover as described in Chapter 2A.

5 Each valve clearance must be checked when the high point of the cam lobe is pointing directly upward away from the cam follower.

6 Check the clearances in the firing order 1-3-4-2, No 1 cylinder being at the timing belt end of the engine. This will minimise the amount of crankshaft rotation required.

7 Insert the appropriate feeler blade between the heel of the cam and the cam follower shim of the first valve **(see illustration)**. If necessary alter the thickness of the feeler blade until it is a stiff, sliding fit. Record the thickness, which will, of course, represent the valve clearance for this particular valve.

8 Turn the engine, check the second valve clearance and record it.

9 Repeat the operations on all the remaining valves, recording their respective clearances.

10 Remember that the clearance for inlet and exhaust valves differs - see *Specifications*. Counting from the timing cover end of the engine, the valve sequence is:

Inlet	2-4-5-7
Exhaust	1-3-6-8

11 Where clearances are incorrect, the particular shim will have to be changed. To remove the shim, turn the crankshaft until the high point of the cam is pointing directly upward. The cam follower will now have to be depressed so that the shim can be extracted. Special tools are available from your Fiat dealer to do the job, otherwise you will have to make up a forked lever to locate on the rim of the cam follower. This must allow room for the shim to be prised out by means of the cut-outs provided in the cam follower rim **(see illustration).**

12 Once the shim is extracted, establish its thickness and change it for a thicker or thinner one to bring the previously recorded clearance within specification. For example, if the measured valve clearance was 1.27 mm too great, a shim *thicker* by this amount will be required. Conversely, if the clearance was 1.27 mm too small, a shim *thinner* by this amount will be required.

13 Shims have their thickness (mm) engraved on them; although the engraved side should be fitted so as not to be visible, wear still occurs and often obliterates the number. In this case, measuring their thickness with a metric micrometer is the only method to establish their thickness **(see illustration)**.

14 In practice, if several shims have to be changed, they can often be interchanged, so avoiding the necessity of having to buy more new shims than is necessary.

15 If more than two or three valve clearances are found to be incorrect, it will be more convenient to remove the camshaft for easier removal of the shims.

16 Where no clearance can be measured, even with the thinnest available shim in position, the valve will have to be removed and the end of its stem ground off squarely. This will reduce its overall length by the minimum amount to provide a clearance. This job should be entrusted to your dealer as it is important to keep the end of the valve stem square.

17 On completion, refit the camshaft cover and gasket, air cleaner and duct, and spark plugs.

18 Lower the vehicle to the ground.

16 Manifold mounting check

Refer to Chapters 4A, 4B and 4D and check the tightness of the nuts and bolts securing the inlet and exhaust manifolds.

17 Fuel filter renewal

Warning: Before carrying out the following operation, refer to the precautions given in Safety first! at the beginning of this manual, and follow them implicitly. Petrol is a highly-dangerous and volatile liquid, and the precautions necessary when handling it cannot be overstressed.

15.13 Shim thickness is marked on the lower face (here 4.20 mm)

Note: *1242 cc (8-valve) engine models from 1998 onwards are equipped with a modified fuel system incorporating a fuel filter integral with the fuel pump. On these engines fuel filter renewal is not required.*

1 The fuel filter is situated underneath the rear of the vehicle, on the right-hand side of the fuel tank **(see illustration)**. To gain access to the filter, chock the front wheels, then jack up the rear of the vehicle and support it on axle stands (see *Jacking and vehicle support*).

2 Unscrew the bolt securing the filter to its support bracket.

3 Noting the fitted position of the filter body, release the retaining clips and disconnect the fuel hoses from the filter. The correct position is indicated by an arrow marked on the filter body

4 Remove the filter from the vehicle. Dispose safely of the old filter; it will be highly flammable, and may explode if thrown on a fire.

5 Locate the new filter into position, ensuring that the arrow on the filter body is pointing in the direction of the fuel flow, as noted when removing the old filter. The flow direction can otherwise be determined by tracing the fuel hoses back along their length.

6 Connect the fuel hoses to the filter and tighten the clips, then locate it in the support bracket and tighten the mounting bolt.

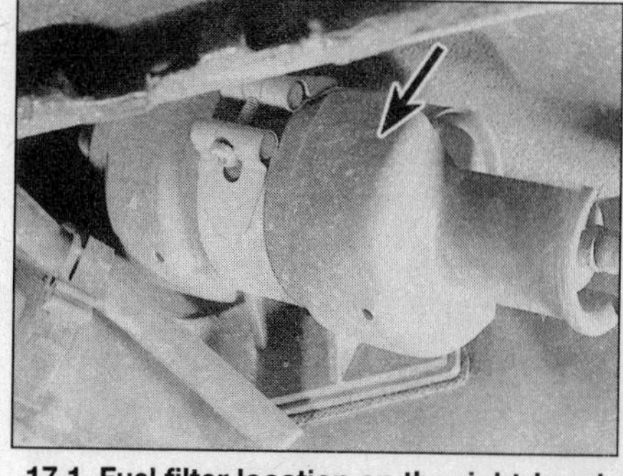

17.1 Fuel filter location on the right-hand side of the fuel tank

7 Start the engine, check the filter hose connections for leaks, then lower the vehicle to the ground.

18 Air filter renewal

1108 cc and 1242 cc (8-valve) engines

1 Prise open the spring clips and withdraw the air cleaner cover a little way from the main body **(see illustration)**. Leave the cover attached to the hot air tube and inlet duct.

2 Lift out the filter element **(see illustration)**.

3 Remove any debris that may have collected inside the air cleaner and wipe the inner surfaces clean.

4 Fit a new air filter element in position, ensuring that the edges are securely seated.

5 Refit the air cleaner top cover and snap the retaining clips into position.

1242 cc (16-valve) engines

6 Undo the three bolts securing the front of the air cleaner cover to the main body. Lift the cover up at the front, disconnect the rear retainers and move it clear of the main body **(see illustration)**. Leave the cover attached to the hot air tube and inlet duct.

7 Lift out the filter element **(see illustration)**.

8 Remove any debris that may have collected inside the air cleaner and wipe the inner surfaces clean.

18.1 Prise open the spring clips . . .

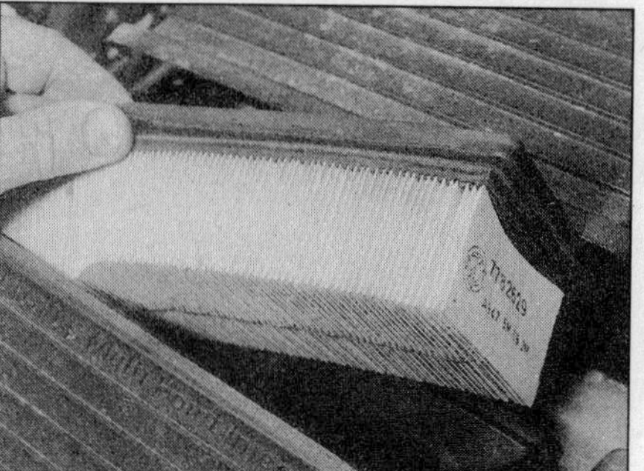

18.2 . . . and remove the filter element (8-valve engines)

18.6 Undo the three bolts (arrowed) and disconnect the air cleaner cover rear retainers (16-valve engines)

18.7 Lift up the cover and remove the filter element (16-valve engines)

9 Fit a new air filter element in position, ensuring that the edges are securely seated.

10 Refit the air cleaner cover, engage the rear retainers and secure with the three bolts.

19 Spark plug renewal

1 The correct functioning of the spark plugs is vital for the correct running and efficiency of the engine. It is essential that the plugs fitted are appropriate for the engine (a suitable type is specified at the beginning of this Chapter). If this type is used and the engine is in good condition, the spark plugs should not need attention between scheduled replacement intervals. Spark plug cleaning is rarely necessary, and should not be attempted unless specialised equipment is available, as damage can easily be caused to the firing ends.

2 To remove the plugs first remove the air cleaner assembly (8-valve engines) or the air cleaner, resonator and inlet air duct (16-valve engines) with reference to Chapter 4A or 4B. If the marks on the original-equipment spark plug (HT) leads cannot be seen, mark the leads 1 to 4, to correspond to the cylinder the lead serves (No 1 cylinder is at the timing belt end of the engine). Pull the leads from the plugs by gripping the end fitting, not the lead, otherwise the lead connection may be fractured **(see illustrations)**.

3 It is advisable to remove the dirt from the spark plug recesses using a clean brush, vacuum cleaner or compressed air before removing the plugs, to prevent dirt dropping into the cylinders.

4 Unscrew the plugs using a spark plug spanner, suitable box spanner or a deep socket and extension bar **(see illustration)**. Keep the socket aligned with the spark plug - if it is forcibly moved to one side, the ceramic insulator may be broken off. As each plug is removed, examine it as follows.

5 Examination of the spark plugs will give a good indication of the condition of the engine. If the insulator nose of the spark plug is clean and white, with no deposits, this is indicative of a weak mixture or too hot a plug (a hot plug transfers heat away from the electrode slowly, a cold plug transfers heat away quickly).

6 If the tip and insulator nose are covered with hard black-looking deposits, this indicates that the mixture is too rich. If the plug is black and oily, then it is likely that the engine is fairly worn, as well as the mixture being too rich.

7 If the insulator nose is covered with light tan to greyish-brown deposits, then the mixture is correct and it is likely that the engine is in good condition.

8 The spark plug electrode gap is of considerable importance as, if it is too large or too small, the size of the spark and its efficiency will be seriously impaired. The gap should be set to the value given in the *Specifications* at the beginning of this Chapter.

9 To set the gap, measure it with a feeler blade and then bend open, or closed, the outer plug electrode until the correct gap is achieved. The centre electrode should never be bent, as this may crack the insulator and cause plug failure, if nothing worse. If using feeler blades, the gap is correct when the appropriate-size blade is a firm sliding fit **(see illustration)**.

10 Special spark plug electrode gap adjusting tools are available from most motor accessory shops, or from some spark plug manufacturers.

11 Before fitting the spark plugs, check that the threaded connector sleeves are tight, and that the plug exterior surfaces and threads are clean **(see Haynes Hint)**.

12 Remove the rubber hose (if used), and tighten the plug to the specified torque using the spark plug socket and a torque wrench. Refit the remaining spark plugs in the same manner.

13 Connect the HT leads in their correct order, and refit any components removed for access.

19.2a Disconnecting the HT leads from the spark plugs on 8-valve engines . . .

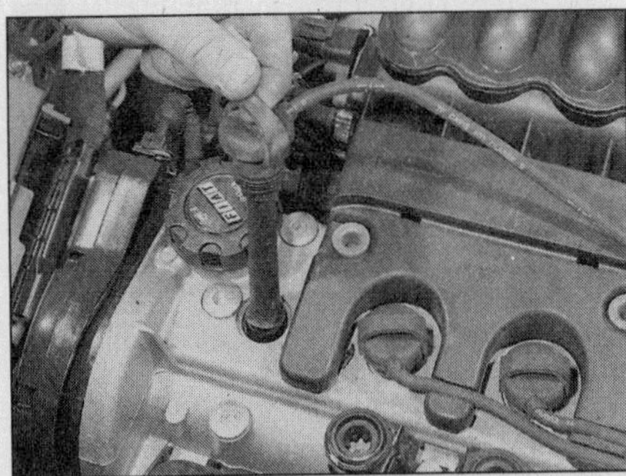

19.2b . . . and on 16-valve engines

19.4 Removing the spark plugs

19.9 Adjusting a spark plug electrode gap

HAYNES HiNT

It is very often difficult to insert spark plugs into their holes without cross-threading them. To avoid this possibility, fit a short length of 5/16 inch internal diameter rubber hose over the end of the spark plug. The flexible hose acts as a universal joint to help align the plug with the plug hole. Should the plug beginto cross-thread, the hose will slip on the spark plug, preventing thread damage to the cylinder head

20 Ignition system check

Warning: Voltages produced by an electronic ignition system are considerably higher than those produced by conventional ignition systems. Extreme care must be taken when working on the system with the ignition switched on. Persons with surgically-implanted cardiac pacemaker devices should keep well clear of the ignition circuits, components and test equipment.

1 The ignition system components should be checked for damage or deterioration as follows.

General component check

2 The spark plug (HT) leads should be checked whenever new spark plugs are fitted.

3 Pull the leads from the plugs by gripping the end fitting, not the lead, otherwise the lead connection may be fractured.

HAYNES HiNT ***Ensure that the leads are numbered before removing them, to avoid confusion when refitting***

4 Check inside the end fitting for signs of corrosion, which will look like a white crusty powder. Push the end fitting back onto the spark plug, ensuring that it is a tight fit on the plug. If not, remove the lead again and use pliers to carefully crimp the metal connector inside the end fitting until it fits securely on the end of the spark plug.

5 Using a clean rag, wipe the entire length of the lead to remove any built-up dirt and grease. Once the lead is clean, check for burns, cracks and other damage. Do not bend the lead excessively, nor pull the lead lengthways - the conductor inside might break.

6 Disconnect the other end of the lead from the ignition coil. Again, pull only on the end fitting. Check for corrosion and a tight fit in the same manner as the spark plug end. Refit the lead securely on completion.

7 Check the remaining leads one at a time, in the same way.

8 If new spark plug (HT) leads are required, purchase a set for your specific car and engine.

9 Even with the ignition system in first-class condition, some engines may still occasionally experience poor starting attributable to damp ignition components. To disperse moisture, a water-dispersant aerosol should be liberally applied.

Ignition timing - check and adjustment

10 Check the ignition timing as described in Chapter 5B.

21 Engine management system check

1 This check is part of the manufacturer's maintenance schedule, and involves testing the engine management system using special dedicated test equipment. Such testing will allow the test equipment to read any fault codes stored in the electronic control unit memory.

2 Unless a fault is suspected, this test is not essential, although it should be noted that it is recommended by the manufacturers.

3 If access to suitable test equipment is not possible, make a thorough check of all ignition, fuel and emission control system components, hoses, and wiring, for security and obvious signs of damage. Further details of the fuel system, emission control system and ignition system can be found in the relevant parts of Chapters 4 and 5.

22 Hinge and lock lubrication

1 Lubricate the hinges of the bonnet, doors and tailgate with a light general-purpose oil. Similarly, lubricate all latches, locks and lock strikers. At the same time, check the security and operation of all the locks, adjusting them if necessary (see Chapter 11).

2 Lightly lubricate the bonnet release mechanism and cable with a suitable grease.

23 Headlight beam adjustment

1 Accurate adjustment of the headlight beam is only possible using optical beam-setting equipment, and this work should therefore be carried out by a Fiat dealer or service station with the necessary facilities. In an emergency, however, the following procedure will provide an acceptable light pattern.

2 Position the car on a level surface with tyres correctly inflated, approximately 10 metres in front of, and at right-angles to, a wall or garage door.

3 Draw a horizontal line on the wall or door at headlamp centre height. Draw a vertical line corresponding to the centre line of the car, then measure off a point either side of this, on the horizontal line, corresponding with the headlamp centres.

4 Switch on the main beam and check that the areas of maximum illumination coincide with the headlamp centre marks on the wall. If not, turn the adjustment screw located on the upper inside edge of the headlight unit to adjust the beam laterally, and the adjustment screw located on the upper outside edge of the headlight unit to adjust the beam vertically. On models with electric headlight adjustment, make sure that it is set at its basic setting before making the adjustment.

24 Road test

Instruments and electrical equipment

1 Check the operation of all instruments and electrical equipment.

2 Make sure that all instruments read correctly, and switch on all electrical equipment in turn, to check that it functions properly.

Steering and suspension

3 Check for any abnormalities in the steering, suspension, handling or road feel.

4 Drive the vehicle, and check that there are no unusual vibrations or noises.

5 Check that the steering feels positive, with no excessive sloppiness, or roughness, and check for any suspension noises when cornering and driving over bumps.

Drivetrain

6 Check the performance of the engine, clutch (where applicable), transmission and driveshafts.

7 Listen for any unusual noises from the engine, clutch and gearbox/transmission.

8 Make sure that the engine runs smoothly when idling, and that there is no hesitation when accelerating.

9 Check that, where applicable, the clutch action is smooth and progressive, that the drive is taken up smoothly, and that the pedal travel is not excessive. Also listen for any noises when the clutch pedal is depressed.

10 On manual gearbox models, check that all gears can be engaged smoothly without noise, and that the gear lever action is not abnormally vague or notchy.

11 On automatic transmission models, check that all the gear positions can be selected with the vehicle at rest. If any problems are found, they should be referred to a Fiat dealer.

12 Listen for a metallic clicking sound from the front of the vehicle, as the vehicle is driven slowly in a circle with the steering on full-lock. Carry out this check in both directions. If a clicking noise is heard, this indicates wear in a driveshaft joint, in which case renew the joint if necessary.

Check the braking system

13 Make sure that the vehicle does not pull to one side when braking, and that the wheels do not lock prematurely when braking hard.

14 Check that there is no vibration through the steering when braking.

15 Check that the handbrake operates correctly without excessive movement of the lever, and that it holds the vehicle stationary on a slope.

16 Test the operation of the brake servo unit as follows. With the engine off, depress the footbrake four or five times to exhaust the vacuum. Hold the brake pedal depressed, then start the engine. As the engine starts, there should be a noticeable give in the brake pedal as vacuum builds up. Allow the engine to run for at least two minutes, and then switch it off. If the brake pedal is depressed now, it should be possible to detect a hiss from the servo as the pedal is depressed. After about four or five applications, no further hissing should be heard, and the pedal should feel considerably harder.

Every 30 000 miles (45 000 km) or 3 years

25 Lambda/oxygen sensor check

If the CO level at the exhaust tailpipe is too high or low, the vehicle should be taken to a Fiat dealer so that the complete fuel-injection and ignition systems, including the Lambda/oxygen sensor, can be thoroughly checked using the special diagnostic equipment. Once these have been checked and are known to be free from faults, the fault must be in the catalytic converter, which must be renewed as described in Chapter 4D, Section 6.

26 Manual transmission oil level check

1 Park the vehicle on a level surface, if possible over an inspection pit or on a ramp as the filler/level plug is best reached from under the engine compartment. The oil level must be checked before the car is driven, or at least 5 minutes after the engine has been switched off. If the oil is checked immediately after driving the car, some of the oil will remain distributed around the transmission components, resulting in an inaccurate level reading.

2 Wipe clean the area around the filler/level plug, which is situated on the front of the transmission **(see illustration)**. Using an Allen key, unscrew the plug and clean it.

3 The oil level should reach the lower edge of the filler/level hole. A certain amount of oil will have gathered behind the filler/level plug, and will trickle out when it is removed; this does **not** necessarily indicate that the level is correct. To ensure that a true level is established, wait until the initial trickle has stopped, then add oil as necessary until a trickle of new oil can be seen emerging. The level will be correct when the flow ceases; use only good-quality oil of the specified type. Make sure that the vehicle is completely level when checking the level and do not overfill.

4 When the level is correct refit and tighten the plug and wipe away any spilt oil.

27 Evaporative loss system check

Refer to Chapter 4D Section 2 and check that all wiring and hoses are correctly connected to the evaporative loss system components.

28 Automatic transmission filter and fluid change

1 Take the vehicle on a short run, to warm the transmission up to operating temperature. Park the car on level ground, then switch off the ignition.

2 Firmly apply the handbrake, then jack up the front of the car and support it securely on axle stands (see *Jacking and vehicle support*). Note that, when refilling and checking the fluid level, the car must be lowered to the ground, and level, to ensure accuracy.

3 Remove the dipstick, then position a suitable container under the transmission. Unscrew the sump drain plug and allow the fluid to drain for at least 10 minutes. Refit and tighten the drain plug when the fluid has completely drained.

Warning: The transmission fluid may be very hot and precautions must be taken to avoid scalding.

4 Clean around the transmission sump mating flange. Unbolt and remove the sump and remove the gasket.

5 Remove the two bolts and withdraw the transmission fluid filter **(see illustration)**.

6 Fit the new filter, and secure it with the two bolts.

7 Refit the sump using a new gasket, then lower the vehicle to the ground.

8 Fill the transmission with the specified quantity of fluid via the dipstick tube, using a funnel with a fine mesh filter.

9 Run the engine to normal operating temperature, then check the fluid level as described in *Weekly checks*.

10 Dispose of the old fluid safely.

26.2 Transmission filler/level plug location

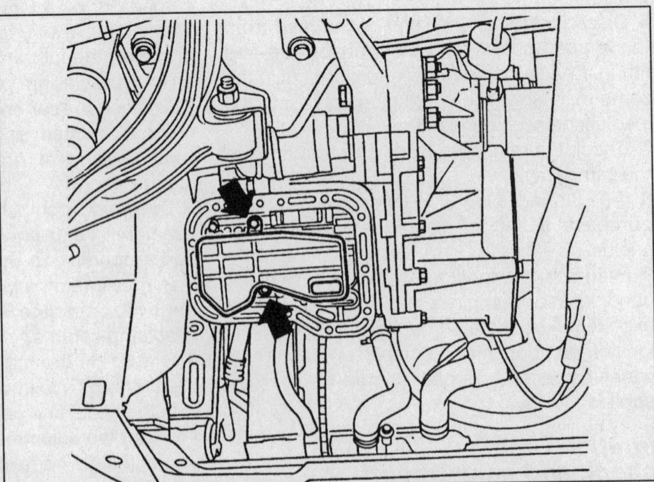

28.5 Automatic transmission fluid filter retaining bolts

Every 40 000 miles (60 000 km) or 4 years

29 Rear brake shoe check

1 Chock the front wheels then jack up the rear of the car and support it on axle stands (see *Jacking and Vehicle Support*). Remove the rear roadwheels.
2 Using the inspection hole at the edge of the brake drum, check that the linings are not worn below the minimum thickness given in the *Specifications* **(see illustration)**. If necessary use a torch.
3 If the friction material on any shoe is worn down to the specified minimum thickness or less, all four shoes must be renewed as a set.
4 At the same time check for signs of brake fluid leakage.
5 For a comprehensive check, the brake drum should be removed and cleaned. This will allow the wheel cylinders to be checked, and the condition of the brake drum itself to be fully examined (see Chapter 9).
6 Refit the rubber plugs then lower the car to the ground.

30 Timing belt renewal

Refer to Chapter 2A or 2B.
Note: *Although the normal interval for timing belt renewal is 70 000 miles (105 000 km), it is strongly recommended that the interval is reduced on vehicles which are subjected to intensive use, ie, mainly short journeys or a lot of stop-start driving. The actual belt renewal interval is therefore very much up to the individual owner. That being said, it is highly recommended to err on the side of safety, and renew the belt at 40 000 miles (60 000 km), bearing in mind the drastic consequences resulting from belt failure.*

29.2 Check the thickness of the shoe friction material through the hole on the edge of the drum (arrowed)

Every 60 000 miles (90 000 km) or 6 years

31 Emission control system check

Refer to Chapter 4D. A full check of the emissions control systems must be made by a Fiat dealer.

Every 80 000 miles (120 000 km)

32 Manual transmission oil renewal

1 Park the vehicle on a level surface, if possible over an inspection pit or on a ramp as the filler/level and drain plugs are accessed from under the engine compartment. If necessary jack up the vehicle and support on axle stands (see *Jacking and vehicle support*).
2 Wipe clean the area around the filler/level and drain plugs, which are on the front and bottom of the transmission **(see illustration)**.
3 Using an Allen key, unscrew the filler/level plug and clean it.
4 Position a suitable container beneath the transmission, then use the Allen key to unscrew the drain plug. Allow the oil to completely drain.
5 Wipe clean the drain plug then refit and tighten it.
6 Fill the transmission with the correct grade and quantity of oil, referring to Section 26 when checking the level. Refit and tighten the filler/level plug.
7 Where applicable lower the vehicle to the ground.

32.2 Transmission drain plug location (viewed from under the vehicle)

1A

Every 2 years (regardless of mileage)

33 Coolant renewal

Cooling system draining

Warning: Wait until the engine is cold before starting this procedure. Do not allow antifreeze to come in contact with your skin, or with the painted surfaces of the vehicle. Rinse off spills immediately with plenty of water. Never leave antifreeze lying around in an open container, or in a puddle in the driveway or on the garage floor. Children and pets are attracted by its sweet smell, but antifreeze can be fatal if ingested.

1 With the engine completely cold, cover the expansion tank cap with a wad of rag, and slowly turn the cap anti-clockwise to relieve the pressure in the cooling system (a hissing sound will normally be heard). Wait until any pressure remaining in the system is released, then continue to turn the cap until it can be removed.
2 Position a suitable container beneath the radiator bottom hose connection, then release the retaining clip and ease the hose from the radiator stub **(see illustration)**. If the hose

33.2 Disconnecting the radiator bottom hose to drain the coolant

joint has not been disturbed for some time, it will be necessary to gently manipulate the hose to break the joint. Do not use excessive force, or the radiator stub could be damaged. Allow the coolant to drain into the container.

3 Certain models are fitted with cooling system bleed plugs, which should be opened to aid the draining process and help prevent airlocks. These are located on the top right hand edge of the radiator, on the heater inlet hose and additionally, on 16-valve engines, on the heater outlet hose **(see illustrations)**. If the coolant has been drained for a reason other than renewal, then provided it is clean and less than two years old, it can be re-used, though this is not recommended.

4 Once all the coolant has drained, reconnect the hose to the radiator and secure it in position with the retaining clip.

Cooling system flushing

5 If coolant renewal has been neglected, or if the antifreeze mixture has become diluted, then in time, the cooling system may gradually lose efficiency, as the coolant passages become restricted due to rust, scale deposits, and other sediment. The cooling system efficiency can be restored by flushing the system clean.

6 The radiator should be flushed independently of the engine, to avoid contamination.

Radiator flushing

7 To flush the radiator disconnect the top and bottom hoses and any other relevant hoses from the radiator, with reference to Chapter 3.

8 Insert a garden hose into the radiator top inlet. Direct a flow of clean water through the radiator, and continue flushing until clean water emerges from the radiator bottom outlet.

9 If after a reasonable period, the water still does not run clear, the radiator can be flushed with a good proprietary cooling system cleaning agent. It is important that their manufacturer's instructions are followed carefully. If the contamination is particularly bad, insert the hose in the radiator bottom outlet, and reverse-flush the radiator.

Engine flushing

10 To flush the engine, remove the thermostat as described in Chapter 3 then temporarily refit the thermostat cover.

11 With the top and bottom hoses disconnected from the radiator, insert a garden hose into the radiator top hose. Direct a clean flow of water through the engine, and continue flushing until clean water emerges from the radiator bottom hose.

12 On completion of flushing, refit the thermostat and reconnect the hoses with reference to Chapter 3.

Cooling system filling

13 Before attempting to fill the cooling system, make sure that all hoses and clips are in good condition, and that the clips are tight. Note that an antifreeze mixture must be used all year round, to prevent corrosion of the engine components (see below).

14 Remove the expansion tank filler cap, and fill the system by slowly pouring the coolant into the expansion tank to prevent airlocks from forming. Ensure that all bleed plugs/screws are open.

15 If the coolant is being renewed, begin by pouring in a couple of litres of water, followed by the correct quantity of antifreeze, then top-up with more water.

16 Once the level in the expansion tank starts to rise, squeeze the radiator top and bottom hoses to help expel any trapped air in the system. Once all the air is expelled, top-up the coolant level to the MAX mark and refit the expansion tank cap. Close all bleed plugs. Continue the filling procedure as follows according to engine type.

1108 cc and 1242 cc (8-valve) engines

17 Start the engine and run it until it reaches normal operating temperature, then stop the engine and allow it to cool.

18 Check for leaks, particularly around disturbed components. Check the coolant level in the expansion tank, and top-up if necessary. Note that the system must be cold before an accurate level is indicated in the expansion tank. If the expansion tank cap is removed while the engine is still warm, cover the cap with a thick cloth, and unscrew the cap slowly to gradually relieve the system pressure (a hissing sound will normally be heard). Wait until any pressure remaining in the system is released, then continue to turn the cap until it can be removed.

1242 cc (16-valve) engines

19 Remove the expansion tank filler cap, start the engine and run it at idling speed for two to three minutes. Allow the engine to continue running until the electric cooling fan operates, but during this time, briefly increase the engine speed to 2000 to 3000 rpm every 30 seconds. Maintain the coolant level in the expansion tank to the MAX mark during this procedure, adding more coolant as necessary.

20 On models without air conditioning, with the engine still idling, carefully unscrew the bleed plug on the top of the radiator. Increase the engine speed until fluid emerges from the bleed plug, then close the plug and return the engine to idle.

Warning: Take suitable precautions against scalding when opening the bleed plug as the coolant will be very hot.

21 On all models, allow the engine to continue running at idle for a further five minutes. After this time, switch the engine off, allow it to cool completely and when cool

33.3a Location of cooling system bleed plugs (arrowed)

33.3b Bleed screw located on the top right hand edge of the radiator

check, and if necessary top-up, the level in the expansion tank. Refit the cap on completion.

Antifreeze mixture

22 The antifreeze should always be renewed at the specified intervals. This is necessary not only to maintain the antifreeze properties, but also to prevent corrosion which would otherwise occur as the corrosion inhibitors become progressively less effective.

23 Always use an ethylene-glycol based antifreeze which is suitable for use in mixed-metal cooling systems. The quantity of antifreeze and levels of protection are indicated in the *Specifications*.

24 Before adding antifreeze, the cooling system should be completely drained, preferably flushed, and all hoses checked for condition and security.

25 After filling with antifreeze, a label should be attached to the expansion tank, stating the type and concentration of antifreeze used, and the date installed. Any subsequent topping-up should be made with the same type and concentration of antifreeze.

26 Do not use engine antifreeze in the windscreen/tailgate washer system, as it will cause damage to the vehicle paintwork. A screenwash additive should be added to the washer system in the quantities stated on the bottle.

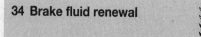

34 Brake fluid renewal

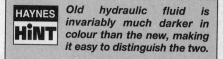

Warning: Brake hydraulic fluid can harm your eyes and damage painted surfaces, so use extreme caution when handling and pouring it. Do not use fluid that has been standing open for some time, as it absorbs moisture from the air. Excess moisture can cause a dangerous loss of braking effectiveness.

1 The procedure is similar to that for the bleeding of the hydraulic system as described in Chapter 9, except that the brake fluid reservoir should be emptied by siphoning, using a clean poultry baster or similar before starting, and allowance should be made for the old fluid to be expelled when bleeding a section of the circuit.

2 Working as described in Chapter 9, open the first bleed screw in the sequence, and pump the brake pedal gently until nearly all the old fluid has been emptied from the master cylinder reservoir.

Old hydraulic fluid is invariably much darker in colour than the new, making it easy to distinguish the two.

3 Top-up to the MAX level with new fluid, and continue pumping until only the new fluid remains in the reservoir, and new fluid can be seen emerging from the bleed screw. Tighten the screw, and top the reservoir level up to the MAX level line.

4 Work through all the remaining bleed screws in the sequence until new fluid can be seen at all of them. Be careful to keep the master cylinder reservoir topped-up to above the MIN level at all times, or air may enter the system and greatly increase the length of the task.

5 When the operation is complete, check that all bleed screws are securely tightened, and that their dust caps are refitted. Wash off all traces of spilt fluid, and recheck the master cylinder reservoir fluid level.

6 Check the operation of the brakes before taking the car on the road.

Chapter 1 Part B:
Routine maintenance & servicing - diesel models

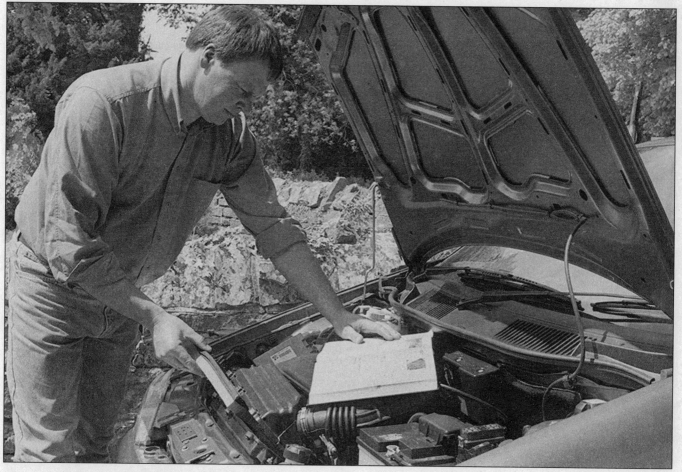

Contents

Degrees of difficulty

Easy, suitable for novice with little experience 	**Fairly easy,** suitable for beginner with some experience 	**Fairly difficult,** suitable for competent DIY mechanic	**Difficult,** suitable for experienced DIY mechanic 	**Very difficult,** suitable for expert DIY or professional

Lubricants and fluids

Refer to end of *Weekly checks* on page 0•17

Capacities

Engine oil (including filter)	
Non-turbo diesel engine	4.95 litres
Turbo diesel engine	4.84 litres
Cooling system	7.2 litres
Manual transmission	
Non-turbo diesel engine	2.37 litres
Turbo diesel engine	1.98 litres
Power-assisted steering	0.65 litres
Fuel tank	47 litres
Washer reservoir	
Without headlight washers	2.5 litres
With headlight washers	7.0 litres

Engine

Engine idle speed:	
Non-turbo diesel engine	810 ± 40 rpm
Turbo diesel engine	900 ± 20 rpm
Auxiliary drivebelt tension	5.0 mm deflection midway between pulleys
Valve clearances - engine cold:	
Inlet	0.30 mm ± 0.05 mm
Exhaust	0.35 mm ± 0.05 mm

Cooling system

Antifreeze mixture:	
50% antifreeze	Protection down to –35°C

Note: *Refer to antifreeze manufacturer for latest recommendations.*

Brakes

Brake pad lining minimum thickness	1.5 mm
Brake shoe friction material minimum thickness	2.0 mm

Tyre pressures

See end of *Weekly checks* on page 0•18

Torque wrench settings

	Nm	lbf ft
Fuel filter bracket to body	18	13
Fuel filter to bracket	24	18
Manual transmission oil drain plug:		
Non-turbo diesel engine:		
Stage 1	12	9
Stage 2	Angle-tighten a further 180°	
Turbo diesel engine	46	34
Manual transmission oil filler plug	46	34
Roadwheel bolts	86	63

The maintenance intervals in this manual are provided with the assumption that you, not the dealer, will be carrying out the work. These are the minimum maintenance intervals recommended by us for vehicles driven daily. If you wish to keep your vehicle in peak condition at all times, you may wish to perform some of these procedures more often. We encourage frequent maintenance, because it enhances the efficiency, performance and resale value of your vehicle.

When the vehicle is new, it should be serviced by a factory-authorised dealer service department, in order to preserve the factory warranty.

Every 250 miles (400 km) or weekly

- ☐ Refer to *Weekly checks*

Every 5000 miles (7500 km) or 6 months - whichever comes first

- ☐ Renew the engine oil and filter (Section 3)
- ☐ Drain any water from the fuel filter (Section 4)

Every 10 000 miles (15 000 km) or 12 months - whichever comes first

In addition to the items listed above, carry out the following:

- ☐ Check the operation of the brake warning lamp (Section 5)
- ☐ Check the front brake pads for wear (Section 6)
- ☐ Check the underbody and sealant for damage (Section 7)
- ☐ Hose and fluid leak check (Section 8)
- ☐ Check the condition of the exhaust system and its mountings (Section 9)
- ☐ Check the condition of the driveshaft gaiters (Section 10)
- ☐ Check and adjust the idle speed (Section 11)
- ☐ Renew the fuel filter (Section 12)
- ☐ Renew the air filter element (Section 13)
- ☐ Renew the pollen filter (Section 14)
- ☐ Check the steering and suspension components for condition and security (Section 15)

Every 20 000 miles (30 000 km) or 2 years - whichever comes first

In addition to the items listed above, carry out the following:

- ☐ Check and if necessary adjust the tension of the auxiliary drivebelt(s) (Section 16)
- ☐ Check the freeplay and height of the clutch pedal (Section 17)
- ☐ Check and if necessary adjust the valve clearances (Section 18)
- ☐ Lubricate all hinges and locks (Section 19)
- ☐ Check the headlight beam adjustment (Section 20)
- ☐ Carry out a road test (Section 21)

Every 30 000 miles (45 000 km) or 3 years - whichever comes first

In addition to the items listed above, carry out the following:

- ☐ Check and if necessary top-up the manual transmission oil level (Section 22)

Every 40 000 miles (60 000 km) or 4 years - whichever comes first

In addition to the items listed above, carry out the following:

- ☐ Check the rear brake shoes for wear (Section 23)
- ☐ Renew the timing belt (Section 24)*

***Note:** Although the normal interval for timing belt renewal is 70 000 miles (105 000 km), it is strongly recommended that the belt is renewed at 40 000 miles (60 000 km) on vehicles which are subjected to intensive use, ie. mainly short journeys or a lot of stop-start driving. The actual belt renewal interval is therefore very much up to the individual owner, but bear in mind that severe engine damage will result if the belt breaks.*

Every 60 000 miles (90 000 km) or 6 years - whichever comes first

In addition to the items listed above, carry out the following:

- ☐ Check the condition and operation of the emission control system components (Section 25)

Every 80 000 miles (120 000 km)

- ☐ Renew the manual transmission oil (Section 26)

Every 2 years (regardless of mileage)

- ☐ Renew the engine coolant (Section 27)
- ☐ Renew the brake fluid (Section 28)

Underbonnet view - turbo diesel model

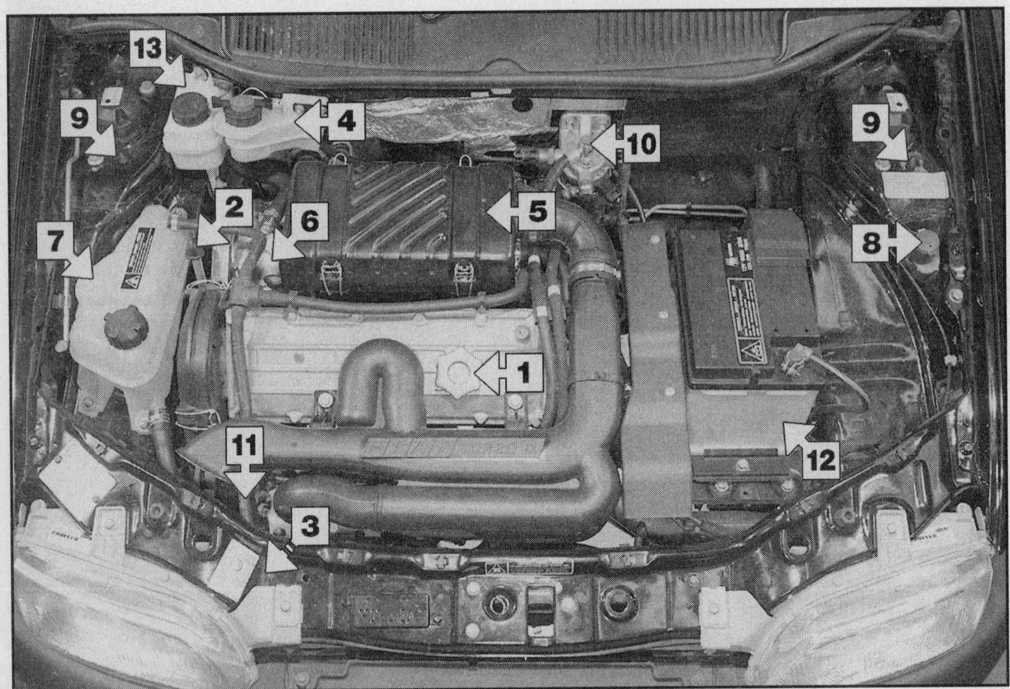

1 *Engine oil filler cap*
2 *Engine oil dipstick*
3 *Oil filter*
4 *Brake/clutch fluid reservoir*
5 *Air cleaner cover*
6 *Power steering pump*
7 *Coolant expansion tank*
8 *Windscreen washer fluid reservoir*
9 *Front suspension strut upper mounting*
10 *Fuel filter/heater housing*
11 *Fuel injection pump*
12 *Battery*
13 *Power steering fluid reservoir*

Front underbody view - turbo diesel model

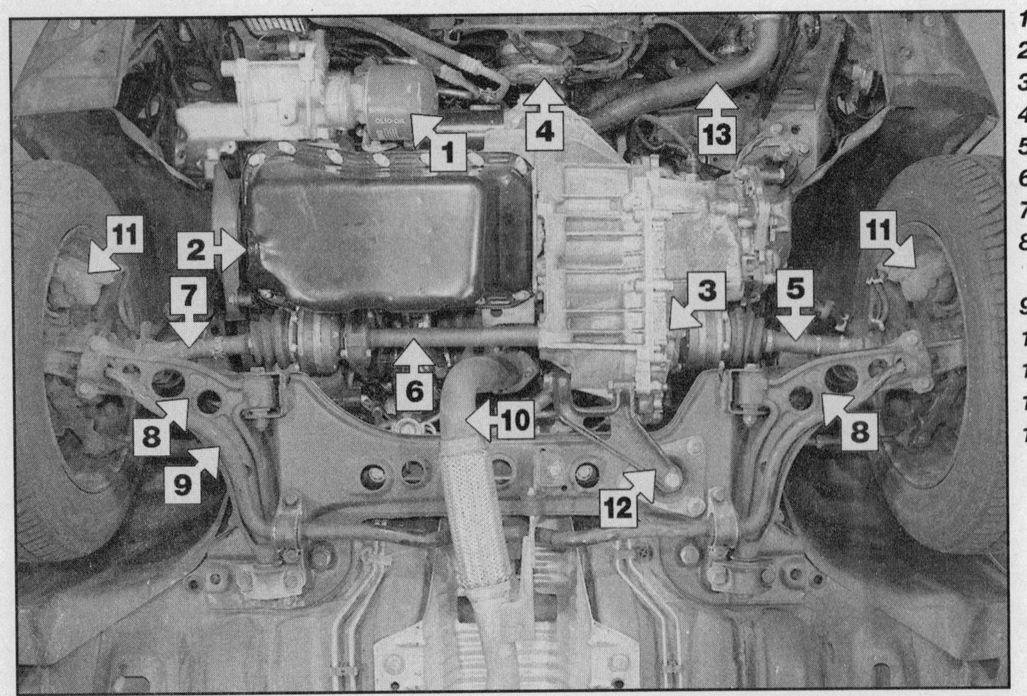

1 *Oil filter*
2 *Sump drain plug*
3 *Transmission drain plug*
4 *Electric cooling fan unit*
5 *Left-hand driveshaft*
6 *Intermediate shaft*
7 *Right-hand driveshaft*
8 *Front suspension lower arms*
9 *Front anti-roll bar*
10 *Exhaust downpipe*
11 *Front brake calipers*
12 *Rear engine mounting*
13 *Radiator bottom hose*

Rear underbody view - turbo diesel model

1 Fuel tank
2 Exhaust tailpipe and silencer
3 Rear axle
4 Coil springs
5 Rear anti-roll bar
6 Handbrake cables
7 Rear brake pressure regulating valve
8 Rear shock absorber lower mountings

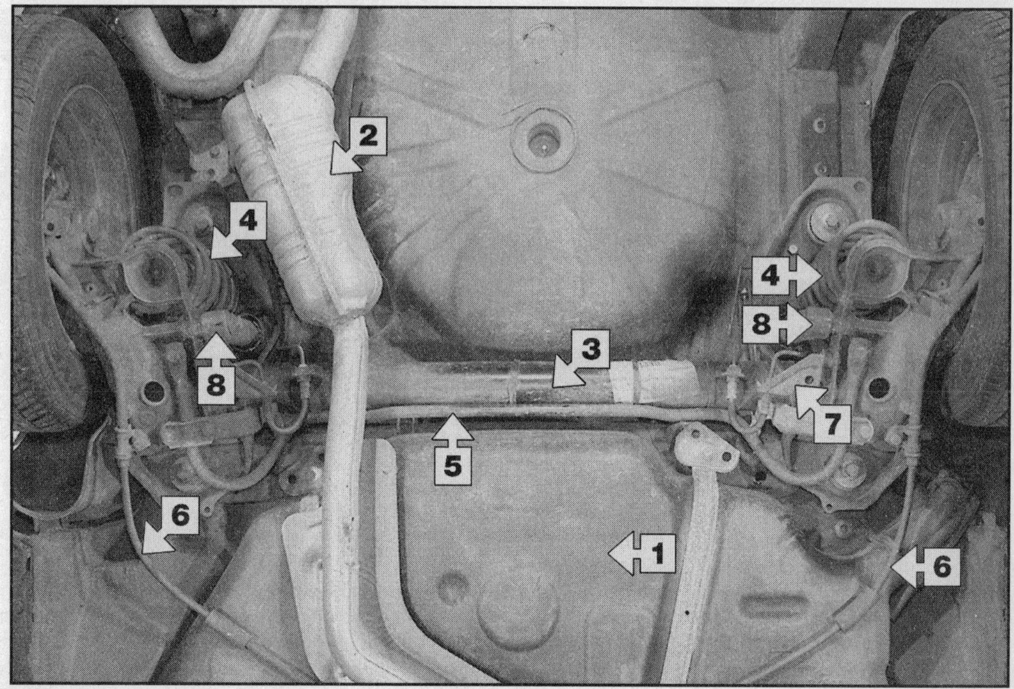

Maintenance procedures

1 Introduction

This Chapter is designed to help the home mechanic maintain his/her vehicle for safety, economy, long life and peak performance.

The Chapter contains a master maintenance schedule, and Sections dealing specifically with each task in the schedule. Visual checks, adjustments, component renewal and other helpful items are included. Refer to the accompanying illustrations of the engine compartment and the underside of the vehicle for the locations of the various components.

Servicing your vehicle in accordance with the mileage/time maintenance schedule and the following Sections will provide a planned maintenance programme, which should result in a long and reliable service life. This is a comprehensive plan, so maintaining some items but not others at the specified service intervals, will not produce the same results.

As you service your vehicle, you will discover that many of the procedures can, and should, be grouped together, because of the particular procedure being performed, or because of the proximity of two otherwise-unrelated components to one another. For example, if the vehicle is raised for any reason, the exhaust can be inspected at the same time as the suspension and steering components.

The first step in this maintenance programme is to prepare yourself before the actual work begins. Read through all the Sections relevant to the work to be carried out, then make a list and gather all the parts and tools required. If a problem is encountered, seek advice from a parts specialist, or a dealer service department.

2 Regular maintenance

1 If, from the time the vehicle is new, the routine maintenance schedule is followed closely, and frequent checks are made of fluid levels and high-wear items, as suggested throughout this manual, the engine will be kept in relatively good running condition, and the need for additional work will be minimised.

2 It is possible that there will be times when the engine is running poorly due to the lack of regular maintenance. This is even more likely if a used vehicle, which has not received regular and frequent maintenance checks, is purchased. In such cases, additional work may need to be carried out, outside of the regular maintenance intervals.

3 If engine wear is suspected, a compression test (refer to Chapter 2C) will provide valuable information regarding the overall performance of the main internal components. Such a test can be used as a basis to decide on the extent of the work to be carried out. If, for example, a compression test indicates serious internal engine wear, conventional maintenance as described in this Chapter will not greatly improve the performance of the engine, and may prove a waste of time and money, unless extensive overhaul work is carried out first.

4 The following series of operations are those usually required to improve the performance of a generally poor-running engine:

Primary operations

a) Clean, inspect and test the battery (See Weekly checks).
b) Check all the engine-related fluids (See Weekly checks).
c) Drain the water from the fuel filter (Section 4).
d) Check the condition and tension of the auxiliary drivebelt(s) (Section 16).
e) Check the condition of the air filter, and renew if necessary (Section 13).
f) Check the condition of all hoses, and check for fluid leaks (Section 8).
g) Check the engine idle speed setting (Section 11).
h) Check the exhaust gas emissions (Section 25).

5 If the above operations do not prove fully effective, carry out the following secondary operations:

Secondary operations

All items listed under *Primary operations*, plus the following:

a) Check the charging system (Chapter 5A, Section 4).
b) Renew the fuel filter (Section 12) and check the fuel system (see Chapter 4C).

Every 5000 miles (7500 km) or 6 months

3 Engine oil and filter renewal

1 Frequent oil and filter changes are the most important preventative maintenance procedures which can be undertaken by the DIY owner. As engine oil ages, it becomes diluted and contaminated, which leads to premature engine wear.

2 Before starting this procedure, gather all the necessary tools and materials. Also make sure that you have plenty of clean rags and newspapers handy, to mop up any spills. Ideally, the engine oil should be warm, as it will drain better, and more built-up sludge will be removed with it. Take care, however, not to touch the exhaust or any other hot parts of the engine when working under the vehicle. To avoid any possibility of scalding, and to protect yourself from possible skin irritants and other harmful contaminants in used engine oils, it is advisable to wear gloves when carrying out this work. Access to the underside of the vehicle will be greatly improved if it can be raised on a lift, driven onto ramps, or jacked up and supported on axle stands (see *Jacking and vehicle support*). Whichever method is chosen, make sure that the vehicle remains level, or if it is at an angle, that the drain plug is at the lowest point.

3 Slacken the drain plug about half a turn using a 12 mm Allen key **(see illustration)**. Position the draining container under the drain plug, then remove the plug completely **(see Haynes Hint)**.

4 Allow some time for the old oil to drain, noting that it may be necessary to reposition the container as the oil flow slows to a trickle.

5 After all the oil has drained, wipe off the drain plug with a clean rag, then clean the area around the drain plug opening and refit the plug. Tighten the plug securely.

6 If the filter is also to be renewed, move the container into position under the oil filter, which is located on the front right-hand side of the engine.

7 Using an oil filter removal tool if necessary, slacken the filter initially, then unscrew it by hand the rest of the way **(see illustrations)**.

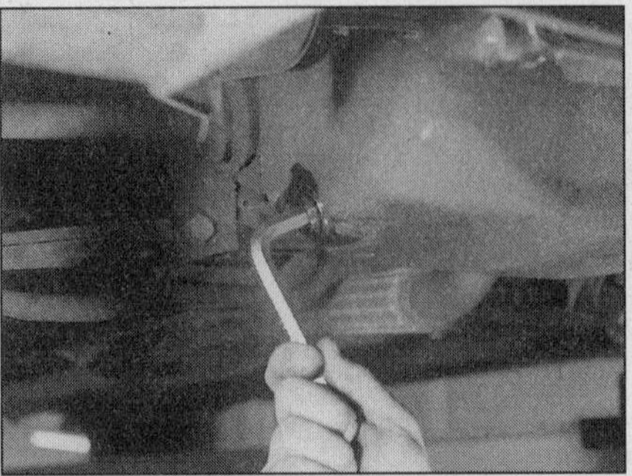

3.3 Using a 12 mm Allen key to loosen the engine oil drain plug

Empty the oil in the old filter into the container.

8 Use a clean rag to remove all oil, dirt and sludge from the filter sealing area on the engine. Check the old filter to make sure that the rubber sealing ring has not stuck to the engine. If it has, carefully remove it.

9 Apply a light coating of clean engine oil to the sealing ring on the new filter, then screw it into position on the engine. Tighten the filter firmly by hand only - **do not** use any tools **(see illustration)**.

10 Remove the old oil and all tools from under the vehicle then lower the vehicle to the ground (if applicable).

11 Remove the dipstick, then unscrew the oil filler cap from the cylinder head cover. Fill the engine, using the correct grade and type of oil (see *Weekly checks*). An oil can spout or funnel may help to reduce spillage. Pour in half the specified quantity of oil first, then wait a few minutes for the oil to fall to the sump. Continue adding oil a small quantity at a time until the level is up to the MAX mark on the dipstick. Refit the filler cap.

12 Start the engine and run it for a few minutes; check for leaks around the oil filter seal and the sump drain plug. Note that there may be a delay of a few seconds before the oil pressure warning light goes out when the engine is first started, as the oil circulates through the engine oil galleries and the new oil filter before the pressure builds up.

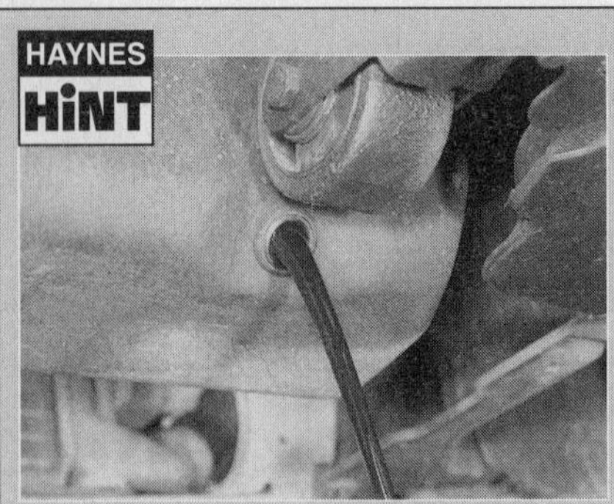

Keep the drain plug pressed into the sump while unscrewing it by hand the last couple of turns. As the plug releases, move it away sharply so that the stream of oil issuing from the sump runs into the container, not up your sleeve.

13 Switch off the engine, and wait a few minutes for the oil to settle in the sump once more. With the new oil circulated and the filter completely full, recheck the level on the dipstick, and add more oil as necessary.

14 Dispose of the used engine oil safely, with reference to *General repair procedures* in the reference Sections of this manual.

4 Fuel filter water draining

1 A water drain screw is provided at the base of the fuel filter.

2 Position a suitable container under the fuel filter. Loosen the bleed screw on the top of the filter, and open the drain screw at the base of the filter by turning it anti-clockwise. Allow fuel and water to drain until fuel, free from water, emerges from the drain screw outlet. Close the drain and bleed screws and tighten them securely.

3 Dispose of the drained fuel safely.

4 Start the engine. If difficulty is experienced, bleed the fuel system (see Chapter 4C).

3.7a Using an oil filter removal chain strap

3.7b Removing the oil filter

3.9 New oil filter tightened by hand

Every 10 000 miles (15 000 km) or 12 months

5 Brake warning lamp operation check

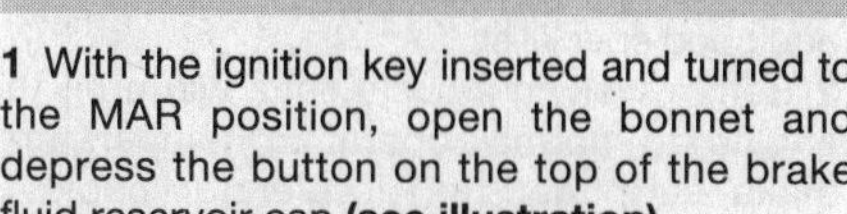

1 With the ignition key inserted and turned to the MAR position, open the bonnet and depress the button on the top of the brake fluid reservoir cap **(see illustration)**.

2 As the button is pressed, the brake warning lamp on the instrument panel should light.

3 If the lamp fails to illuminate, check the operation of the level switch using a continuity tester, then refer to Chapter 12, Section 5, and check the instrument panel bulb.

5.1 Depress the button on the top of the brake fluid reservoir cap

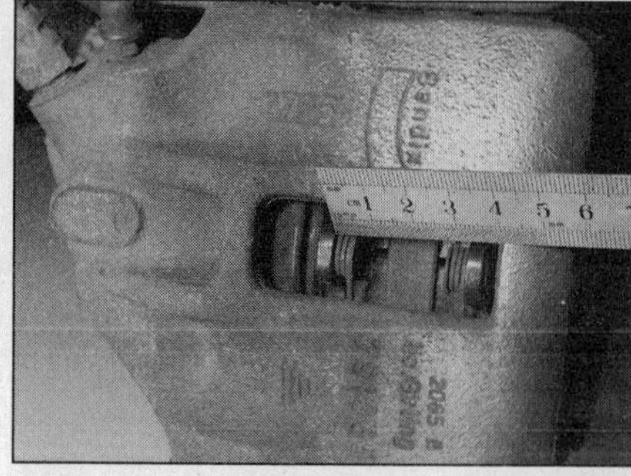

6.2 Check the thickness of the pad friction material through the hole on the front of the caliper

6 Front brake pad check

1 Firmly apply the handbrake, then jack up the front of the car and support it securely on axle stands (see *Jacking and vehicle support*). Remove the front roadwheels.

2 Using a steel rule, measure the thickness of the friction material of the brake pads on both front brakes. This must not be less than 1.5 mm. Check the thickness of the pad friction material through the hole on the front of the caliper **(see illustration)**.

3 For a comprehensive check, the brake pads should be removed and cleaned. The operation of the caliper can then also be checked, and the condition of the brake disc itself can be fully examined on both sides. Refer to Chapter 9 for further information.

4 If any pad's friction material is worn to the specified thickness or less, *all four pads must be renewed as a set.* Refer to Chapter 9.

5 On completion refit the roadwheels and lower the car to the ground.

7 Underbody sealant check

1 Jack up the front and rear of the car and support on axle stands (see *Jacking and vehicle support*). Alternatively position the car over an inspection pit.

2 Check the complete underbody, wheel housings and side sills for corrosion and/or damage to the underbody sealant. If evident, repair as necessary.

8 Hose and fluid leak check

1 Visually inspect the engine joint faces, gaskets and seals for any signs of water or oil leaks. Pay particular attention to the areas around the camshaft cover, cylinder head, oil filter and sump joint faces. Bear in mind that, over a period of time, some very slight seepage from these areas is to be expected - what you are really looking for is any indication of a serious leak **(see Haynes Hint)**. Should a leak be found, renew the offending gasket or oil seal by referring to the appropriate Chapters in this manual.

2 Also check the security and condition of all the engine-related pipes and hoses. Ensure that all cable-ties or securing clips are in place and in good condition. Clips which are broken or missing can lead to chafing of the hoses, pipes or wiring, which could cause more serious problems in the future.

3 Carefully check the radiator hoses and heater hoses along their entire length. Renew any hose which is cracked, swollen or deteriorated. Cracks will show up better if the hose is squeezed. Pay close attention to the hose clips that secure the hoses to the cooling system components. Hose clips can pinch and puncture hoses, resulting in leaks.

4 Inspect all the cooling system components (hoses, joint faces etc.) for leaks. A leak in the cooling system will usually show up as white or rust-coloured deposits on the area adjoining the leak. Where any problems of this nature are found on system components, renew the component or gasket with reference to Chapter 3.

5 With the vehicle raised, inspect the fuel tank and filler neck for punctures, cracks and other damage. The connection between the filler neck and tank is especially critical. Sometimes a rubber filler neck or connecting hose will leak due to loose retaining clamps or deteriorated rubber.

6 Carefully check all rubber hoses and metal fuel lines leading away from the fuel tank. Check for loose connections, deteriorated hoses, crimped lines, and other damage. Pay particular attention to the vent pipes and hoses, which often loop up around the filler neck and can become blocked or crimped. Follow the lines to the front of the vehicle, carefully inspecting them all the way. Renew damaged sections as necessary.

7 With the vehicle raised, check along the length of the underside for leaks from the metal brake lines, caused by damage or corrosion.

8 At each front brake caliper, check the area around the brake pipe unions and the bleed nipples for hydraulic fluid leakage.

9 Remove the front roadwheels and check for fluid leakage from the area around the caliper piston seal. Check that the lip of the piston dust seal is correctly located in its groove. If it has been displaced, the brake caliper should be removed and overhauled as described in Chapter 9, to check for internal dirt ingress or corrosion.

10 Check the area surrounding the master cylinder and vacuum servo unit for signs of corrosion, insecurity or hydraulic fluid leakage. Examine the vacuum hose leading to the servo unit for signs of damage or chafing.

11 From within the engine compartment, check the security of all fuel hose attachments and pipe unions, and inspect the fuel hoses and vacuum hoses for kinks, chafing and deterioration.

12 Where applicable, check the condition of the power steering fluid hoses and pipes.

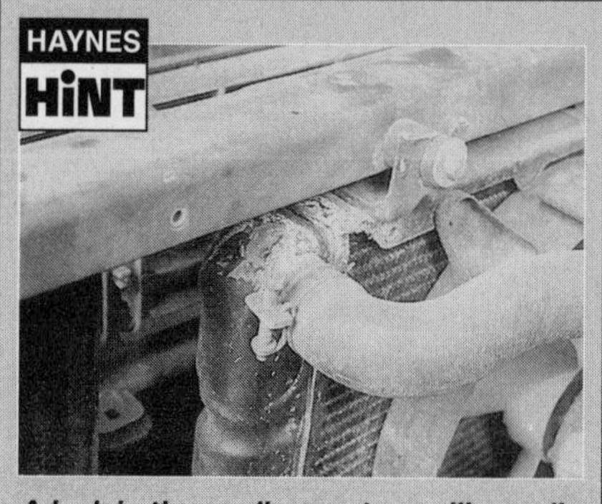

A leak in the cooling system will usually show up as white or rust coloured deposits on the area adjoining the leak.

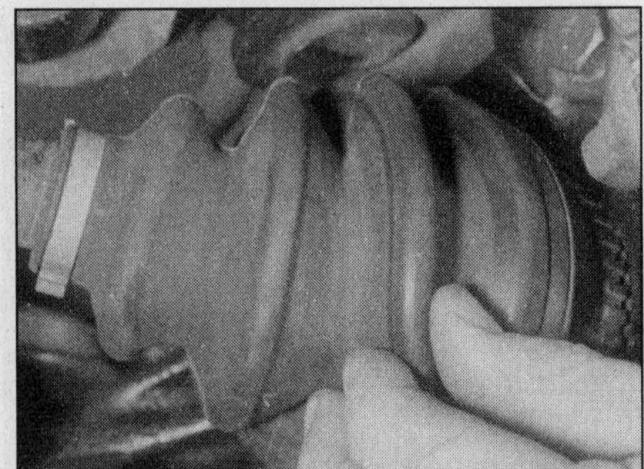

10.1 Checking the condition of a driveshaft gaiter

9 Exhaust system check

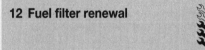

1 With the engine cold (at least an hour after the vehicle has been driven), check the complete exhaust system from the engine to the end of the tailpipe. The exhaust system is most easily checked with the vehicle raised on a hoist, or suitably supported on axle stands (see *Jacking and vehicle support*), so that the exhaust components are readily visible and accessible.

2 Check the exhaust pipes and connections for evidence of leaks, severe corrosion and damage. Make sure that all brackets and mountings are in good condition, and that all relevant nuts and bolts are tight. Leakage at any of the joints or in other parts of the system will usually show up as a black sooty stain in the vicinity of the leak.

3 Rattles and other noises can often be traced to the exhaust system, especially the brackets and mountings. Try to move the pipes and silencers. If the components are able to come into contact with the body or suspension parts, secure the system with new mountings. Otherwise separate the joints (if possible) and twist the pipes as necessary to provide additional clearance.

10 Driveshaft gaiter check

1 With the vehicle raised and securely supported on stands (see *Jacking and vehicle support*), turn the steering onto full lock, then slowly rotate the roadwheel. Inspect the condition of the outer constant velocity (CV) joint rubber gaiters, squeezing the gaiters to open out the folds. Check for signs of cracking, splits or deterioration of the rubber, which may allow the grease to escape, and lead to water and grit entry into the joint. Also check the security and condition of the retaining clips. Repeat these checks on the inner CV joints **(see illustration)**. If any damage or deterioration is found, the gaiters should be renewed (see Chapter 8, Section 3).

2 At the same time, check the general condition of the CV joints themselves by first holding the driveshaft and attempting to rotate the wheel. Repeat this check by holding the inner joint and attempting to rotate the driveshaft. Any appreciable movement indicates wear in the joints, wear in the driveshaft splines, or a loose driveshaft retaining nut.

11 Idle speed check and adjustment

1 The usual type of tachometer (rev counter), which works from ignition system pulses, cannot be used on diesel engines. A diagnostic socket is provided for the use of Fiat test equipment, but this will not normally be available to the home mechanic. If it is not felt that adjusting the idle speed by ear is satisfactory, it will be necessary to purchase or hire an appropriate tachometer, or else leave the task to a Fiat dealer or other suitably equipped specialist.

2 Before making adjustments, warm up the engine to normal operating temperature. Make sure that the accelerator cable is correctly adjusted (see Chapter 4C).

3 The adjustment must be made with all electrical components (including the cooling fan) switched off. If the fan comes on during the adjustment, wait until it switches off automatically before proceeding.

4 The idle adjustment screw is located on the top of the fuel injection pump **(see illustration)**. To adjust the idle speed loosen the locknut and turn the screw as required then tighten the locknut.

5 On completion switch off the engine.

12 Fuel filter renewal

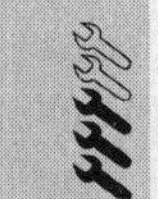

1 The fuel filter is located on the bulkhead in the engine compartment. An electrically-operated heater is located between the filter and the housing.

2 Position a suitable container under the fuel filter. Loosen the bleed screw on the top of the filter, then disconnect the wiring from the water sensor and loosen the water drain screw on the bottom of the filter. Allow the fuel to drain completely **(see illustration)**.

3 Tighten the drain and bleed screws, then use an oil filter strap to loosen the fuel filter **(see illustration)**.

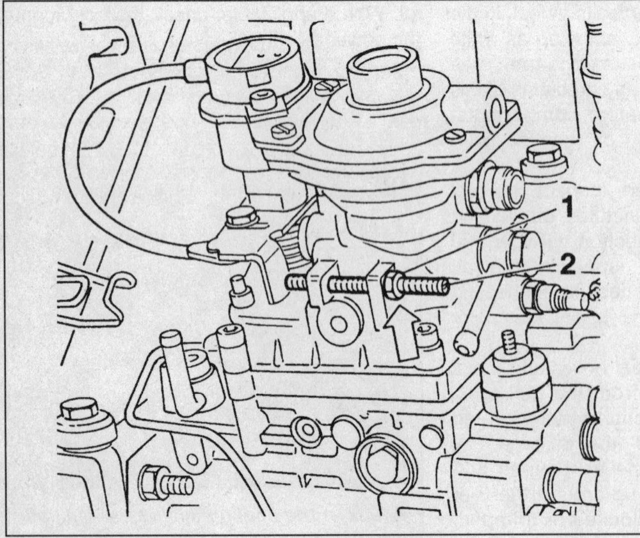

11.4 Idle speed adjustment

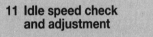

1 Locknut *2 Adjustment screw*

12.2 Loosening the bleed screw on the top of the fuel filter

4 Completely unscrew the filter and pour the remaining contents into the container. Ensure that the rubber sealing ring comes away with the filter and unscrew the drain screw from the bottom of the filter **(see illustrations)**.
5 Wipe clean the contact surfaces then smear a little fuel on the sealing rubber of the new filter.
6 Screw on the new filter fully using the hands only.
7 Prime the fuel system and start the engine with reference to Chapter 4C. Check for any signs of fuel leakage around the new filter.

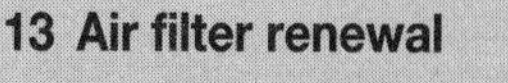

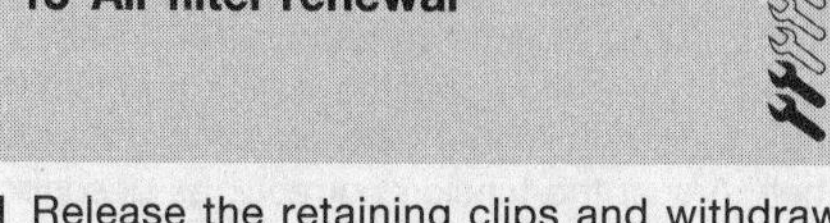

13 Air filter renewal

1 Release the retaining clips and withdraw the air cleaner cover a little way from the main body. Leave the cover attached to the inlet duct.
2 Lift out the filter element **(see illustration)**.
3 Remove any debris that may have collected inside the air cleaner and wipe the inner surfaces clean.
4 Fit a new air filter element in position, ensuring that the edges are securely seated.
5 Refit the air cleaner top cover and snap the retaining clips into position.

14 Pollen filter renewal

1 The pollen filter (where fitted) is located under the engine bulkhead cover panel.
2 Refer to Chapter 12 and remove both windscreen wiper arms.
3 Unclip the rubber seal from the relevant end of the top of the engine compartment bulkhead.
4 Unscrew the retaining fastener screws and pull out the fasteners securing the bulkhead cover panel in position. Release the cover panel from the base of the windscreen and remove it from the vehicle.
5 Pivot the pollen filter cover upwards and away then release the retaining clips and withdraw the filter from its housing **(see illustration)**.

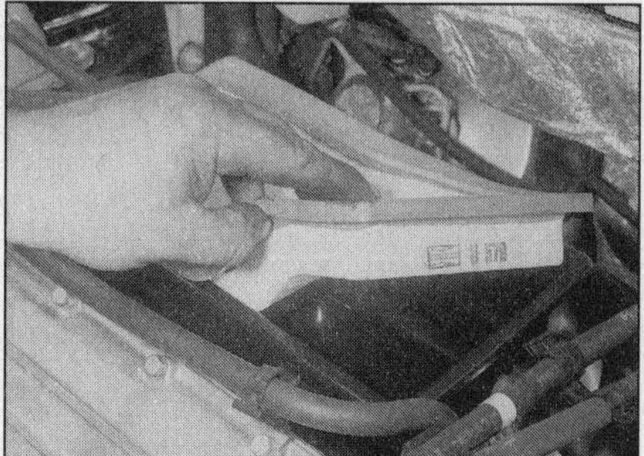

13.2 Removing the air filter element

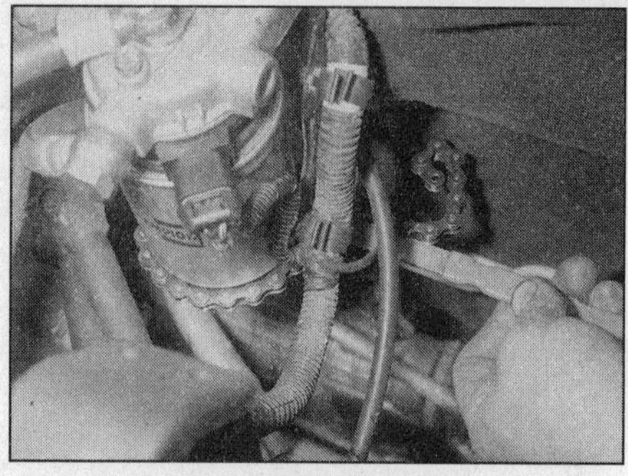

12.3 Using an oil filter strap to loosen the fuel filter

6 Wipe clean the filter housing then fit the new filter. Clip the filter securely in position and refit the cover.
7 Refit the trim cover, securing it in position with the fasteners, and seat the rubber seal on the bulkhead.

15 Steering and suspension check

Front suspension and steering check

1 Raise the front of the vehicle, and securely support it on axle stands (see *Jacking and vehicle support*).
2 Visually inspect the balljoint dust covers and the steering rack-and-pinion gaiters for splits, chafing or deterioration. Any wear of these components will cause loss of lubricant, together with dirt and water entry, resulting in rapid deterioration of the balljoints or steering gear.
3 On vehicles with power steering, check the fluid hoses for chafing or deterioration, and the pipe and hose unions for fluid leaks. Also check for signs of fluid leakage under pressure from the steering gear rubber gaiters, which would indicate failed fluid seals within the steering gear.
4 Grasp the roadwheel at the 12 o'clock and 6 o'clock positions, and try to rock it **(see illustration)**. Very slight free play may be felt, but if the movement is appreciable, further investigation is necessary to determine the source. Continue rocking the wheel while an assistant depresses the footbrake. If the movement is now eliminated or significantly reduced, it is likely that the hub bearings are at fault. If the free play is still evident with the footbrake depressed, then there is wear in the suspension joints or mountings.
5 Now grasp the wheel at the 9 o'clock and 3 o'clock positions, and try to rock it as before. Any movement felt now may again be caused by wear in the hub bearings or the steering track-rod balljoints. If the inner or outer balljoint is worn, the visual movement will be obvious.
6 Using a large screwdriver or flat bar, check for wear in the suspension mounting bushes by levering between the relevant suspension component and its attachment point. Some movement is to be expected as the mountings are made of rubber, but excessive wear should be obvious. Also check the condition of any visible rubber bushes, looking for splits, cracks or contamination of the rubber.

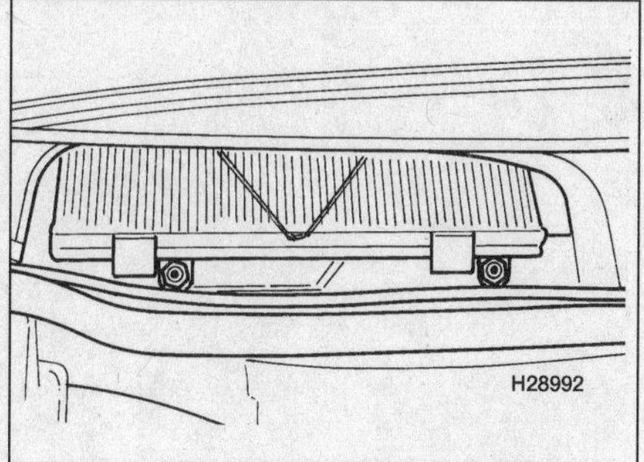

14.5 Location of pollen filter

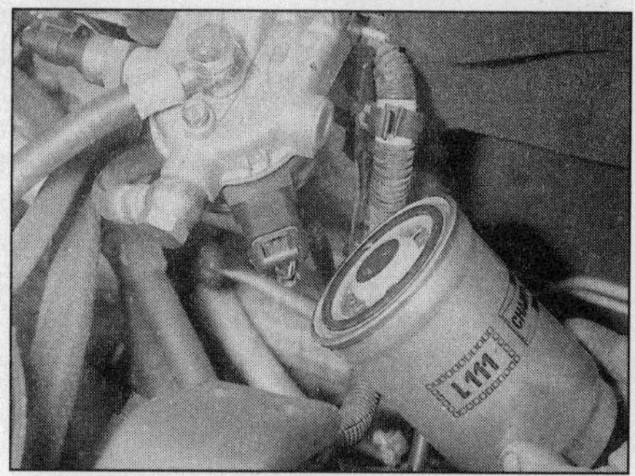

12.4a Removing the fuel filter

12.4b Showing the drain screw components on the bottom of the fuel filter

15.4 Rocking a roadwheel to check for wear in the steering/suspension components

7 With the car standing on its wheels, have an assistant turn the steering wheel back and forth about an eighth of a turn each way. There should be very little, if any, lost movement between the steering wheel and roadwheels. If this is not the case, closely observe the joints and mountings previously described, but in addition, check the steering column universal joints for wear, and the rack-and-pinion steering gear itself.

Suspension strut/ shock absorber check

8 Check for any signs of fluid leakage around the suspension strut/shock absorber body, or from the rubber gaiter around the piston rod. Should any fluid be noticed, the suspension strut/shock absorber is defective internally, and should be renewed. **Note:** *Suspension struts/shock absorbers should always be renewed in pairs on the same axle.*

9 The efficiency of the suspension strut/shock absorber may be checked by bouncing the vehicle at each corner. Generally speaking, the body will return to its normal position and stop after being depressed. If it rises and returns on a rebound, the suspension strut/shock absorber is probably suspect. Examine also the suspension strut/shock absorber upper and lower mountings for any signs of wear.

Every 20 000 miles (30 000 km) or 2 years

16 Auxiliary drivebelt(s) check and renewal

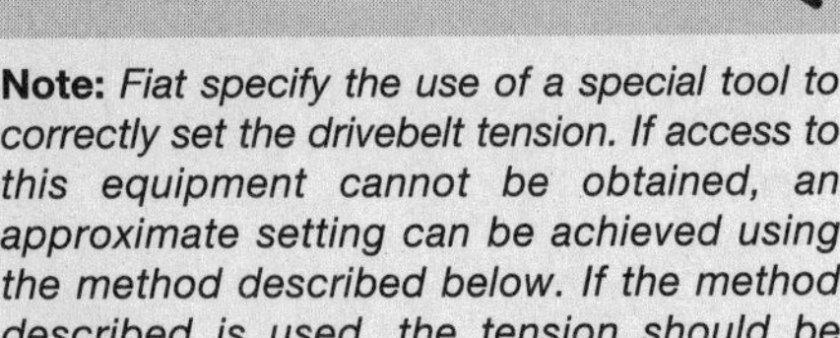

Note: *Fiat specify the use of a special tool to correctly set the drivebelt tension. If access to this equipment cannot be obtained, an approximate setting can be achieved using the method described below. If the method described is used, the tension should be checked using the special tool at the earliest possible opportunity.*

1 Depending on equipment fitted, one, two or three auxiliary drivebelts may be fitted. The alternator, power steering pump and air conditioning compressor, as applicable, are each driven by an individual drivebelt.

Checking

2 Disconnect the battery negative terminal (refer to *Disconnecting the battery* in the Reference Section of this manual).

3 Firmly apply the handbrake, then jack up the front of the car and support it securely on axle stands (see *Jacking and vehicle support*).

4 Remove the right-hand wheel.

5 Remove the inner cover(s) from under the right-hand wheelarch for access to the right-hand side of the engine.

6 Using a socket on the crankshaft sprocket bolt, rotate the crankshaft so that the full length of the auxiliary drivebelt(s) can be examined. Look for cracks, splitting and fraying on the surface of the belt; check also for signs of glazing (shiny patches) and separation of the belt plies. If damage or wear is visible, the belt should be renewed.

7 If the condition of the belt is satisfactory, check the drivebelt tension as described below.

Renewal

Alternator drivebelt

8 On models with air conditioning, remove the compressor drivebelt as described below.

9 Unclip and remove the upper timing belt cover, then unbolt and remove the lower timing belt cover.

10 Loosen the pivot bolt and adjustment lockbolt then unscrew the adjustment bolt to move the alternator towards the engine so that the drivebelt may be slipped off the alternator, crankshaft, and, on models with air conditioning, the idler pulley **(see illustrations)**.

11 When renewing a drivebelt, ensure that the correct type is used. Fit the belt around the pulleys then tighten the adjustment bolt to take up any slack in the belt. Adjust the tension correctly as described below.

Power steering pump drivebelt

12 Remove the alternator drivebelt as described previously.

13 Slacken the bolts securing the power steering pump to the mounting bracket.

14 Slacken the adjusting bolt locknut and turn the adjusting bolt until all the tension is removed from the drivebelt.

15 Undo the bolts and remove the pulley guard from the power steering pump then slip the drivebelt off the pulleys.

16 Ensuring that the correct type of drivebelt is used, fit the belt around the pulleys and turn the adjusting bolt to just take up the slack in the belt. Adjust the tension correctly as described below.

Air conditioning compressor drivebelt

17 Slacken the bolts securing the adjustment pulley bracket to the engine.

18 Slacken the adjusting bolt locknut and turn the adjusting bolt until all the tension is removed from the drivebelt, then slip the belt off the pulleys.

19 Ensuring that the correct type of drivebelt is used, fit the belt around the pulleys and turn the adjusting bolt to just take up the slack in the belt. Adjust the tension correctly as described below.

Tensioning

20 Correct tensioning of the belt will ensure that it has a long life. A belt which is too slack will slip and perhaps squeal. Beware, however, of overtightening, as this can cause wear in the alternator, power steering pump or air conditioning compressor bearings. **Note:** *Fiat recommend use of their special tensioning tool however the following procedure will set the tension correctly.*

21 The belt(s) should be tensioned so that, under firm thumb pressure, there is approximately 5.0 mm of free movement at the mid-point between the pulleys. To adjust, tighten or loosen the relevant adjustment bolt until the tension is correct. Fully tighten the pivot and adjustment lockbolts. Repeat this procedure for any remaining drivebelts removed for access.

22 Refit the lower timing belt cover and tighten the mounting bolts.

23 Refit the upper timing belt cover and secure with the clips.

24 Refit the inner cover and wheel, lower the vehicle to the ground, then reconnect the battery negative terminal.

16.10a Loosening the alternator drivebelt adjustment bolt

16.10b Removing the drivebelt from the alternator pulley

17 Clutch adjustment check

Refer to Chapter 6, Section 2.

18.7 Using feeler blades to check the valve clearances

18.11 Valve clearance adjustment shim

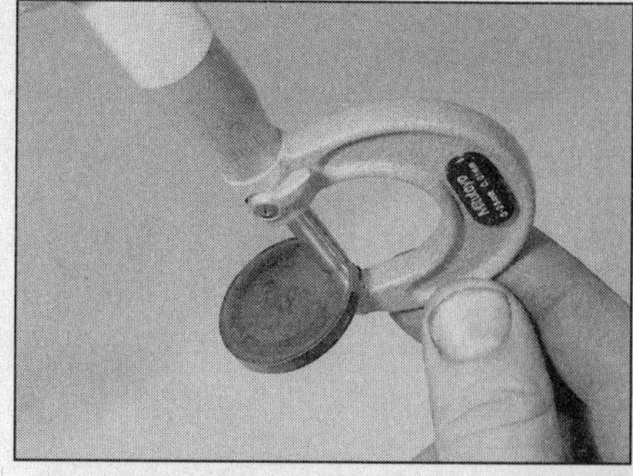

18.13 Measuring the thickness of a shim using a micrometer

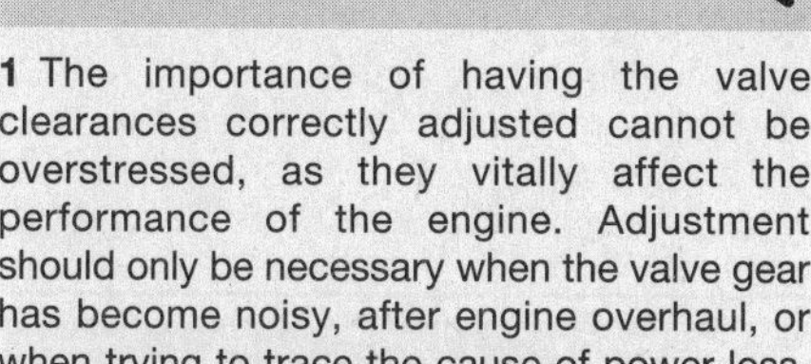

18 Valve clearance check and adjustment

1 The importance of having the valve clearances correctly adjusted cannot be overstressed, as they vitally affect the performance of the engine. Adjustment should only be necessary when the valve gear has become noisy, after engine overhaul, or when trying to trace the cause of power loss. The clearances are checked as follows. The engine must be cold for the check to be accurate.

2 Apply the handbrake then jack up the right-hand front of the vehicle and support on an axle stand (*see Jacking and vehicle support*). Engage 4th gear. The engine can now be rotated by turning the right-hand front roadwheel.

3 Remove all four glow plugs as described in Chapter 5C.

4 Remove the air cleaner cover and air duct then remove the camshaft cover as described in Chapter 2C.

5 Each valve clearance must be checked when the high point of the cam is pointing directly upward away from the cam follower.

6 Check the clearances in the firing order 1-3-4-2, No 1 cylinder being at the timing belt end of the engine. This will minimise the amount of crankshaft rotation required.

7 Insert the appropriate feeler blade between the heel of the cam and the cam follower shim of the first valve **(see illustration)**. If necessary alter the thickness of the feeler blade until it is a stiff, sliding fit. Record the thickness, which will, of course, represent the valve clearance for this particular valve.

8 Turn the engine, check the second valve clearance and record it.

9 Repeat the operations on all the remaining valves, recording their respective clearances.

10 Remember that the clearance for inlet and exhaust valves differs - see *Specifications*. Counting from the timing cover end of the engine, the valve sequence is:

Inlet	*2-4-5-7*
Exhaust	*1-3-6-8*

11 Where clearances are incorrect the particular shim will have to be changed. To remove the shim, turn the crankshaft until the high point of the cam is pointing directly upward. The cam follower will now have to be depressed so that the shim can be extracted. Special tools are available from your Fiat dealer to do the job, otherwise you will have to make up a forked lever to locate on the rim of the cam follower. This must allow room for the shim to be prised out by means of the cut-outs provided in the cam follower rim **(see illustration)**.

12 Once the shim is extracted, establish its thickness and change it for a thicker or thinner one to bring the previously recorded clearance within specification. For example, if the measured valve clearance was 1.27 mm too great, a shim *thicker* by this amount will be required. Conversely, if the clearance was 1.27 mm too small, a shim *thinner* by this amount will be required.

13 Shims have their thickness (mm) engraved on them; although the engraved side should be fitted so as not to be visible, wear still occurs and often obliterates the number. In this case, measuring their thickness with a metric micrometer is the only method to establish their thickness **(see illustration)**.

14 In practice, if several shims have to be changed, they can often be interchanged, so avoiding the necessity of having to buy more new shims than is necessary.

15 If more than two or three valve clearances are found to be incorrect, it will be more convenient to remove the camshaft for easier removal of the shims.

16 Where no clearance can be measured, even with the thinnest available shim in position, the valve will have to be removed and the end of its stem ground off squarely. This will reduce its overall length by the minimum amount to provide a clearance. This job should be entrusted to your dealer as it is important to keep the end of the valve stem square.

17 On completion, refit the camshaft cover and gasket, air cleaner and duct, and glowplugs.

18 Lower the vehicle to the ground.

19 Hinge and lock lubrication

1 Lubricate the hinges of the bonnet, doors and tailgate with a light general-purpose oil. Similarly, lubricate all latches, locks and lock strikers. At the same time, check the security and operation of all the locks, adjusting them if necessary (see Chapter 11).

2 Lightly lubricate the bonnet release mechanism and cable with a suitable grease.

20 Headlight beam adjustment

1 Accurate adjustment of the headlight beam is only possible using optical beam-setting equipment, and this work should therefore be carried out by a Fiat dealer or service station with the necessary facilities. In an emergency, however, the following procedure will provide an acceptable light pattern.

2 Position the car on a level surface with tyres correctly inflated, approximately 10 metres in front of, and at right-angles to, a wall or garage door.

3 Draw a horizontal line on the wall or door at headlamp centre height. Draw a vertical line corresponding to the centre line of the car, then measure off a point either side of this, on the horizontal line, corresponding with the headlamp centres.

4 Switch on the main beam and check that the areas of maximum illumination coincide with the headlamp centre marks on the wall. If not, turn the adjustment screw located on the upper inside edge of the headlight unit to adjust the beam laterally, and the adjustment screw located on the upper outside edge of the headlight unit to adjust the beam vertically. On models with electric headlight adjustment, make sure that it is set at its basic setting before making the adjustment.

21 Road test

Instruments and electrical equipment

1 Check the operation of all instruments and electrical equipment.

2 Make sure that all instruments read correctly, and switch on all electrical equipment in turn, to check that it functions properly.

Steering and suspension

3 Check for any abnormalities in the steering, suspension, handling or road feel.

4 Drive the vehicle, and check that there are no unusual vibrations or noises.

5 Check that the steering feels positive, with no excessive sloppiness, or roughness, and check for any suspension noises when cornering and driving over bumps.

Drivetrain

6 Check the performance of the engine, clutch, transmission and driveshafts.

7 Listen for any unusual noises from the engine, clutch and transmission.

8 Make sure that the engine runs smoothly when idling, and that there is no hesitation when accelerating.

9 Check that the clutch action is smooth and progressive, that the drive is taken up smoothly, and that the pedal travel is not excessive. Also listen for any noises when the clutch pedal is depressed.

10 Check that all gears can be engaged smoothly without noise, and that the gear lever action is not abnormally vague or notchy.

11 Listen for a metallic clicking sound from the front of the vehicle, as the vehicle is driven slowly in a circle with the steering on full-lock. Carry out this check in both directions. If a clicking noise is heard, this indicates wear in a driveshaft joint, in which case renew the joint if necessary.

Check the braking system

12 Make sure that the vehicle does not pull to one side when braking, and that the wheels do not lock prematurely when braking hard.

13 Check that there is no vibration through the steering when braking.

14 Check that the handbrake operates correctly without excessive movement of the lever, and that it holds the vehicle stationary on a slope.

15 Test the operation of the brake servo unit as follows. With the engine off, depress the footbrake four or five times to exhaust the vacuum. Hold the brake pedal depressed, then start the engine. As the engine starts, there should be a noticeable give in the brake pedal as vacuum builds up. Allow the engine to run for at least two minutes, and then switch it off. If the brake pedal is depressed now, it should be possible to detect a hiss from the servo as the pedal is depressed. After about four or five applications, no further hissing should be heard, and the pedal should feel considerably harder. **Note:** *The vacuum for the servo unit is provided by the vacuum pump mounted on the left-hand end of the cylinder head.*

Every 30 000 miles (45 000 km) or 3 years

22 Manual transmission oil level check

1 Park the vehicle on a level surface, if possible over an inspection pit or on a ramp as the filler/level plug is best reached from under the engine compartment. The oil level must be checked before the car is driven, or at least 5 minutes after the engine has been switched off. If the oil is checked immediately after driving the car, some of the oil will remain distributed around the transmission components, resulting in an inaccurate level reading.

2 Wipe clean the area around the filler/level plug, which is situated on the front of the transmission **(see illustration)**. Using an Allen key, unscrew the plug and clean it.

3 The oil level should reach the lower edge of the filler/level hole. A certain amount of oil will have gathered behind the filler/level plug, and will trickle out when it is removed; this does **not** necessarily indicate that the level is correct. To ensure that a true level is established, wait until the initial trickle has stopped, then add oil as necessary until a trickle of new oil can be seen emerging. The level will be correct when the flow ceases; use only good-quality oil of the specified type. Make sure that the vehicle is completely level when checking the level and do not overfill.

4 When the level is correct refit and tighten the plug and wipe away any spilt oil.

22.2 Transmission filler/level plug location

Every 40 000 miles (60 000 km) or 4 years

23 Rear brake shoe check

1 Chock the front wheels then jack up the rear of the car and support it on axle stands (see *Jacking and Vehicle Support*). Remove the rear roadwheels.

2 Using the inspection hole at the edge of the brake drum, check that the linings are not worn below the minimum thickness given in the Specifications **(see illustration)**. If necessary use a torch.

3 If the friction material on any shoe is worn down to the specified minimum thickness or less, all four shoes must be renewed as a set.

4 At the same time check for signs of brake fluid leakage.

5 For a comprehensive check, the brake drum should be removed and cleaned. This will allow the wheel cylinders to be checked, and the condition of the brake drum itself to be fully examined (see Chapter 9).

6 Refit the rubber plugs then lower the car to the ground.

24 Timing belt renewal

Refer to Chapter 2C.

Note: *Although the normal interval for timing belt renewal is 70 000 miles (105 000 km), it is strong recommended that the interval is reduced on vehicles which are subjected to intensive use, ie, mainly short journeys or a lot of stop-start driving. The actual belt renewal interval is therefore very much up to the individual owner. That being said, it is highly recommended to err on the side of safety, and renew the belt at this earlier interval, bearing in mind the drastic consequences resulting from belt failure.*

23.2 Check the thickness of the shoe friction material through the hole on the edge of the drum (arrowed)

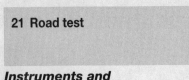

Every 60 000 miles (90 000 km) or 6 years

25 Emissions control systems check

Refer to Chapter 4D. A full check of the emissions control systems must be made by a Fiat dealer.

Every 80 000 miles (120 000 km)

26 Manual transmission oil renewal

1 Park the vehicle on a level surface, if possible over an inspection pit or on a ramp as the filler/level and drain plugs are accessed from under the engine compartment. If necessary jack up the vehicle and support on axle stands (see *Jacking and vehicle support*).

2 Wipe clean the area around the filler/level and drain plugs, which are situated on the front and bottom of the transmission **(see illustration)**.

3 Using an Allen key, unscrew the filler/level plug and clean it.

4 Position a suitable container beneath the transmission, then use the Allen key to unscrew the drain plug. Allow the oil to completely drain.

5 Wipe clean the drain plug then refit and tighten it.

6 Fill the transmission with the correct grade and quantity of oil, referring to Section 22 when checking the level. Refit and tighten the filler/level plug.

7 Where applicable lower the vehicle to the ground.

26.2 Transmission drain plug location (viewed from under the vehicle)

Every 2 years (regardless of mileage)

27 Coolant renewal

Cooling system draining

Warning: Wait until the engine is cold before starting this procedure. Do not allow anti-freeze to come in contact with your skin, or with the painted surfaces of the vehicle. Rinse off spills immediately with plenty of water. Never leave antifreeze lying around in an open container, or in a puddle in the driveway or on the garage floor. Children and pets are attracted by its sweet smell, but antifreeze can be fatal if ingested.

1 With the engine completely cold, cover the expansion tank cap with a wad of rag, and slowly turn the cap anti-clockwise to relieve the pressure in the cooling system (a hissing sound will normally be heard). Wait until any pressure remaining in the system is released, then continue to turn the cap until it can be removed.

2 Position a suitable container beneath the radiator bottom hose connection, then release the retaining clip and ease the hose from the radiator stub **(see illustration)**. If the hose joint has not been disturbed for some time, it will be necessary to gently manipulate the hose to break the joint. Do not use excessive force, or the radiator stub could be damaged. Allow the coolant to drain into the container.

3 Certain models are fitted with cooling system bleed plugs, which should be opened to aid the draining process and help prevent airlocks. These are located on the heater inlet hose and on the top right hand edge of the radiator **(see illustrations)**. If the coolant has been drained for a reason other than renewal, then provided it is clean and less than two years old, it can be re-used, though this is not recommended.

4 Once all the coolant has drained, reconnect the hose to the radiator and secure it in position with the retaining clip.

Cooling system flushing

5 If coolant renewal has been neglected, or if the antifreeze mixture has become diluted, then in time, the cooling system may gradually lose efficiency, as the coolant passages become restricted due to rust, scale deposits, and other sediment. The cooling system efficiency can be restored by flushing the system clean.

6 The radiator should be flushed independently of the engine, to avoid unnecessary contamination.

27.2 Disconnecting the radiator bottom hose to drain the coolant

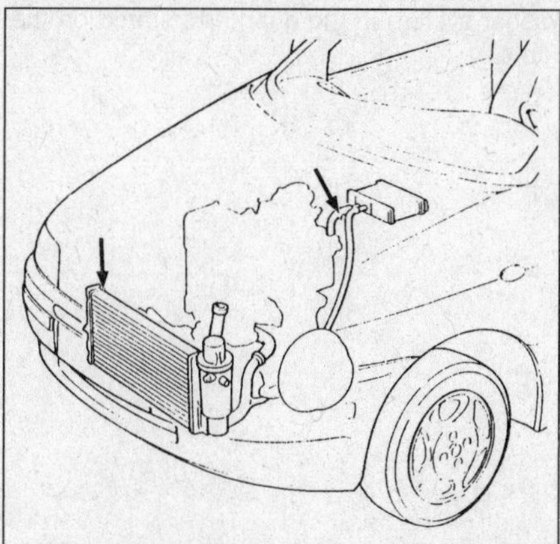

27.3a Location of cooling system bleed plugs (arrowed)

27.3b Bleed screw located on the top right hand edge of the radiator

Radiator flushing

7 To flush the radiator disconnect the top and bottom hoses and any other relevant hoses from the radiator, with reference to Chapter 3.

8 Insert a garden hose into the radiator top inlet. Direct a flow of clean water through the radiator, and continue flushing until clean water emerges from the radiator bottom outlet.

9 If after a reasonable period, the water still does not run clear, the radiator can be flushed with a good proprietary cooling system cleaning agent. It is important that their manufacturer's instructions are followed carefully. If the contamination is particularly bad, insert the hose in the radiator bottom outlet, and reverse-flush the radiator.

Engine flushing

10 To flush the engine, remove the thermostat as described in Chapter 3.

11 With the bottom hose disconnected, direct a clean flow of water through the engine, and continue flushing until clean water emerges from the radiator bottom hose.

12 On completion of flushing, refit the thermostat and reconnect the hose with reference to Chapter 3.

Cooling system filling

13 Before attempting to fill the cooling system, make sure that all hoses and clips are in good condition, and that the clips are tight. Note that an antifreeze mixture must be used all year round, to prevent corrosion of the engine components (see following sub-Section).

14 Remove the expansion tank filler cap, and fill the system by slowly pouring the coolant into the expansion tank to prevent airlocks from forming. Ensure that all bleed plugs/screws are open.

15 If the coolant is being renewed, begin by pouring in a couple of litres of water, followed by the correct quantity of antifreeze, then top-up with more water.

16 Once the level in the expansion tank starts to rise, squeeze the radiator top and bottom hoses to help expel any trapped air in the system. Once all the air is expelled, top-up the coolant level to the MAX mark and refit the expansion tank cap. Close all bleed plugs.

17 Start the engine and run it until it reaches normal operating temperature, then stop the engine and allow it to cool.

18 Check for leaks, particularly around disturbed components. Check the coolant level in the expansion tank, and top-up if necessary. Note that the system must be cold before an accurate level is indicated in the expansion tank. If the expansion tank cap is removed while the engine is still warm, cover the cap with a thick cloth, and unscrew the cap slowly to gradually relieve the system pressure (a hissing sound will normally be heard). Wait until any pressure remaining in the system is released, then continue to turn the cap until it can be removed.

Antifreeze mixture

19 The antifreeze should always be renewed at the specified intervals. This is necessary not only to maintain the antifreeze properties, but also to prevent corrosion which would otherwise occur as the corrosion inhibitors become progressively less effective.

20 Always use an ethylene-glycol based antifreeze which is suitable for use in mixed-metal cooling systems. The quantity of antifreeze and levels of protection are indicated in the *Specifications*.

21 Before adding antifreeze, the cooling system should be completely drained, preferably flushed, and all hoses checked for condition and security.

22 After filling with antifreeze, a label should be attached to the expansion tank, stating the type and concentration of antifreeze used, and the date installed. Any subsequent topping-up should be made with the same type and concentration of antifreeze.

23 Do not use engine antifreeze in the windscreen/tailgate washer system, as it will cause damage to the vehicle paintwork. A screenwash additive should be added to the washer system in the quantities stated on the bottle.

28 Brake fluid renewal

Warning: Brake hydraulic fluid can harm your eyes and damage painted surfaces, so use extreme caution when handling and pouring it. Do not use fluid that has been standing open for some time, as it absorbs moisture from the air. Excess moisture can cause a dangerous loss of braking effectiveness.

1 The procedure is similar to that for the bleeding of the hydraulic system as described in Chapter 9, except that the brake fluid reservoir should be emptied by siphoning, using a clean poultry baster or similar before starting, and allowance should be made for the old fluid to be expelled when bleeding a section of the circuit.

2 Working as described in Chapter 9, open the first bleed screw in the sequence, and pump the brake pedal gently until nearly all the old fluid has been emptied from the master cylinder reservoir.

Old hydraulic fluid is invariably much darker in colour than the new, making it easy to distinguish the two.

3 Top-up to the MAX level with new fluid, and continue pumping until only the new fluid remains in the reservoir, and new fluid can be seen emerging from the bleed screw. Tighten the screw, and top the reservoir level up to the MAX level line.

4 Work through all the remaining bleed screws in the sequence until new fluid can be seen at all of them. Be careful to keep the master cylinder reservoir topped-up to above the MIN level at all times, or air may enter the system and greatly increase the length of the task.

5 When the operation is complete, check that all bleed screws are securely tightened, and that their dust caps are refitted. Wash off all traces of spilt fluid, and recheck the master cylinder reservoir fluid level.

6 Check the operation of the brakes before taking the car on the road.

Chapter 2 Part A: SOHC (8-valve) petrol engine in-car repair procedures

Contents

Degrees of difficulty

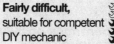

Easy, suitable for novice with little experience 	**Fairly easy,** suitable for beginner with some experience 	**Fairly difficult,** suitable for competent DIY mechanic 	**Difficult,** suitable for experienced DIY mechanic	**Very difficult,** suitable for expert DIY or professional

2A

Specifications

General

Engine code:*	
1108 cc engine (55 models):	
Up to May 1997	176.A6.000
May 1997 onwards	176.B2.000
1242 cc engine (60 models):	
Up to May 1997	176.B1.000
May 1997 onward	176.B4.000
1242 cc engine (75 models)	176.A8.000

***Note:** *See Vehicle Identification for the location of code marking on the engine.*

Bore:	
1108 cc engine	70.0 mm
1242 cc engine	70.8 mm
Stroke:	
1108 cc engine	72.0 mm
1242 cc engine	78.86 mm
Compression ratio:	
1108 cc engine	9.6:1
1242 cc engine with single-point injection	9.6:1
1242 cc engine with multi-point injection	9.8:1
Firing order	1-3-4-2
No 1 cylinder location	Timing belt end of engine
Timing belt tension	See text

Lubrication system

Oil pump type	By-rotor driven from front of crankshaft
Outer rotor-to-housing clearance	0.080 to 0.186 mm
Axial clearance	0.025 to 0.056 mm

Torque wrench settings	Nm	lbf ft
Camshaft cover	8	6
Camshaft sprocket	70	52
Cylinder head:		
Stage 1	30	22
Stage 2	Angle-tighten a further 90°	
Stage 3	Angle-tighten a further 90°	
Crankshaft sprocket centre bolt	100	74
Engine mounting bolt:		
M10 x 1.25	59	44
M8	25	18
Engine mounting nut (M10 x 1.25)	60	44
Flywheel/driveplate	44	32
Sump	10	7
Timing belt tensioner	28	21

1 General information

Using this Chapter

Chapter 2 is divided into four Parts; A, B, C and D. Repair operations that can be carried out with the engine in the vehicle are described in Part A, SOHC (8-valve) petrol engines, Part B, DOHC (16-valve) petrol engines and Part C, diesel engines. Part D covers the removal of the engine/transmission as a unit, and describes the engine dismantling and overhaul procedures.

In Parts A, B and C, the assumption is made that the engine is installed in the vehicle, with all ancillaries connected. If the engine has been removed for overhaul, the preliminary dismantling information which precedes each operation may be ignored.

Engine description

Throughout this Chapter, engines are identified by their capacities. A listing of all engines covered, together with their code letters, is given in the Specifications.

The engines covered in this Part of Chapter 2 are water-cooled, single overhead camshaft, in-line four-cylinder units, with cast iron cylinder blocks and aluminium-alloy cylinder heads. All are mounted transversely at the front of the vehicle, with the transmission bolted to the left-hand side of the engine.

The cylinder head carries the camshaft which is driven by a toothed timing belt and runs in three bearings. It also houses the inlet and exhaust valves, which are closed by single coil springs, and which run in guides pressed into the cylinder head. The camshaft actuates the valves directly via cam followers mounted in the cylinder head. Adjustment of the valve clearances is by means of shims located on top of the followers. The cylinder head contains integral oilways which supply and lubricate the tappets.

The crankshaft is supported by five main bearings, and endfloat is controlled by a thrust bearing fitted to the upper section of the centre main bearing.

Engine coolant is circulated by a pump, driven by the timing belt. For details of the cooling system, refer to Chapter 3.

Lubricant is circulated under pressure by a pump, driven from the front of the crankshaft. Oil is drawn from the sump through a strainer, and then forced through an externally-mounted, replaceable screw-on filter. From there, it is distributed to the cylinder head, where it lubricates the camshaft journals and tappets, and also to the crankcase, where it lubricates the main bearings, connecting rod big and small-ends, gudgeon pins and cylinder bores. On 1242 cc engines, oil jets are fitted to the base of each cylinder bore - these spray oil onto the underside of the pistons, to improve cooling.

Repair operations possible with the engine in the car

The following work can be carried out with the engine in the car:

a) Compression pressure - testing
b) Auxiliary drivebelt - removal and refitting (refer to Chapter 1A)
c) Valve clearances - checking and adjustment (refer to Chapter 1A)
d) Camshaft cover - removal and refitting
e) Timing belt and covers - removal and refitting
f) Timing belt tensioner and sprockets - removal and refitting
*g) Cylinder head - removal and refitting**
*h) Camshaft and cam followers - removal and refitting**
i) Camshaft oil seal - renewal
j) Crankshaft oil seals - renewal
k) Flywheel/driveplate - removal, inspection and refitting
l) Engine mountings - inspection and renewal
m) Sump - removal and refitting
n) Oil pump and pick-up tube assembly - removal, inspection and refitting

**Cylinder head dismantling procedures are detailed in Chapter 2D, with details of camshaft and cam follower removal.*

Note: *It is possible to remove the pistons and connecting rods (after removing the cylinder head and sump) without removing the engine. However, this is not recommended. Work of this nature is more easily and thoroughly completed with the engine on the bench, as described in Chapter 2D.*

2 Location of TDC on No 1 cylinder

General information

1 The camshaft is driven by the crankshaft, by means of sprockets and a timing belt. Both sprockets rotate in phase with each other and this provides the correct valve timing as the engine rotates. When the timing belt is removed during servicing or repair, it is possible for the camshaft and crankshaft to rotate independently of each other and the correct valve timing is then lost.

2 The design of the engines covered in this Chapter are such that potentially damaging piston-to-valve contact may occur if the camshaft is rotated when any of the pistons are stationary at, or near, the top of their stroke.

3 For this reason it is important that the correct phasing between the camshaft and crankshaft is preserved whilst the timing belt is off the engine. This is achieved by setting the engine in a reference position (known as Top Dead Centre or TDC) before the timing belt is removed and then preventing the camshaft and crankshaft from rotating until the belt is refitted. Similarly, if the engine has been dismantled for overhaul, the engine can be set to TDC during reassembly to ensure that the correct shaft phasing is restored.

4 TDC is the highest point in the cylinder that each piston reaches as the crankshaft turns. Each piston reaches TDC at the end of the compression stroke and again at the end of the exhaust stroke. However, for the purpose of timing the engine, TDC refers to the position of No 1 piston at the end of its compression stroke. On all engines in this manual, No 1 piston (and cylinder) is at the timing belt end of the engine.

5 The camshaft sprocket is equipped with a marking which, when aligned with a reference marking on the cylinder head, indicates that the camshaft is correctly positioned for cylinder No 1 at TDC on its compression stroke.

2.11 Unscrewing the crankshaft pulley bolts

2.13a Camshaft sprocket and cylinder head TDC timing marks (arrowed) aligned - shown with timing belt removed

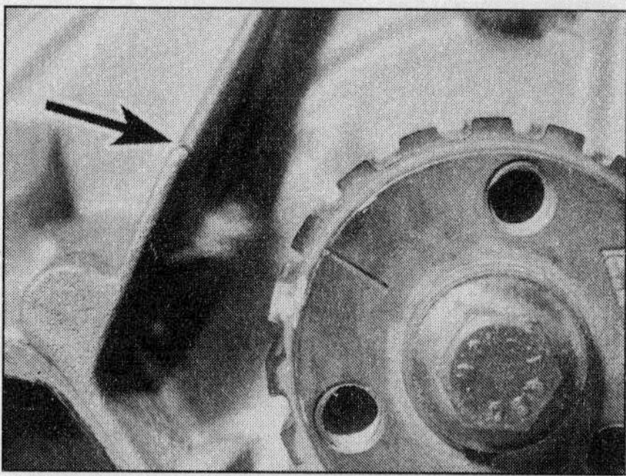
2.13b Crankshaft sprocket and oil pump cover TDC timing marks (arrowed) aligned

6 The crankshaft sprocket is also equipped with a timing mark - when this is aligned with a reference marking on the oil pump cover, the engine is set with cylinders No 1 and 4 at TDC. Note that it is the camshaft positioning that determines whether a cylinder is on its compression or exhaust stroke.

Location of TDC on cylinder No 1

7 Remove the air cleaner and ducting as described in Chapter 4A or 4B. Remove the spark plug from No 1 cylinder as described in Chapter 1A.
8 Firmly apply the handbrake, then jack up the front of the car and support it securely on axle stands (see *Jacking and vehicle support*).
9 Remove the auxiliary drivebelt(s) as described in Chapter 1A.
10 Unbolt and remove the timing belt cover. Note the bolt located at the bottom of the cover; this can be easily overlooked.
11 Undo the three bolts and remove the crankshaft pulley from the sprocket **(see illustration)**.
12 Turn the engine in its normal direction of rotation (using a socket or spanner on the crankshaft sprocket centre bolt) until pressure can be felt at No 1 cylinder spark plug hole.

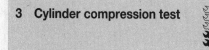

Remove all four spark plugs; this will make the engine easier to turn; refer to Chapter 1A for details.

13 Continue turning the engine until the camshaft sprocket TDC timing mark is aligned with the mark on the cylinder head and the crankshaft sprocket timing mark is aligned with the mark on the oil pump cover **(see illustrations)**.
14 The engine is now set at TDC for No 1 cylinder on compression.

3 Cylinder compression test

1 When engine performance is down, or if misfiring occurs which cannot be attributed to the ignition or fuel systems, a compression test can provide diagnostic clues as to the engine's condition. If the test is performed regularly, it can give warning of trouble before any other symptoms become apparent.
2 The engine must be fully warmed-up to normal operating temperature, the battery must be fully charged, and all the spark plugs must be removed (Chapter 1A). The aid of an assistant will also be required.
3 Disable the ignition system by disconnecting the LT wiring plug to the ignition coils.
4 Fit a compression tester to the No 1 cylinder spark plug hole - the type of tester which screws into the plug thread is to be preferred.
5 Have the assistant hold the throttle wide open, and crank the engine on the starter motor; after one or two revolutions, the compression pressure should build up to a maximum figure, and then stabilise. Record the highest reading obtained.
6 Repeat the test on the remaining cylinders, recording the pressure in each.
7 All cylinders should produce very similar pressures; any excessive difference indicates the existence of a fault. Note that the compression should build up quickly in a healthy engine; low compression on the first stroke, followed by gradually increasing pressure on successive strokes, indicates worn piston rings. A low compression reading on the first stroke, which does not build up during successive strokes, indicates leaking valves or a blown head gasket (a cracked head could also be the cause).
8 If the pressure in any cylinder is very low, carry out the following test to isolate the cause. Introduce a teaspoonful of clean oil into that cylinder through its spark plug hole and repeat the test.
9 If the addition of oil temporarily improves the compression pressure, this indicates that bore or piston wear is responsible for the pressure loss. No improvement suggests that leaking or burnt valves, or a blown head gasket, may be to blame.
10 A low reading from two adjacent cylinders is almost certainly due to the head gasket having blown between them; the presence of coolant in the engine oil will confirm this.
11 If one cylinder is about 20 percent lower than the others and the engine has a slightly rough idle, a worn camshaft lobe could be the cause.
12 On completion of the test, refit the spark plugs and reconnect the ignition LT wiring plug.

4 Timing belt and covers - removal and refitting

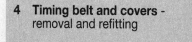

Note: *Fiat specify the use of a special timing belt tension measuring tool to correctly set the timing belt tension. If access to this equipment cannot be obtained, an approximate setting can be achieved using the method described below. If the method described is used, the tension must be checked using the special tool at the earliest possible opportunity. Do not drive the vehicle over large distances, or use high engine speeds, until the belt tension is known to be correct. Refer to a Fiat dealer for advice.*

General information

1 The function of the timing belt is to drive the camshaft and coolant pump. Should the belt slip or break in service, the valve timing will be disturbed and piston-to-valve contact will occur, resulting in serious engine damage.
2 The timing belt should be renewed at the specified intervals (see Chapter 1A), or earlier if it is contaminated with oil, or if it is at all noisy in operation (a scraping noise due to uneven wear).
3 If the timing belt is being removed, it is a wise precaution to check the condition of the coolant pump at the same time (check for signs of coolant leakage). This may avoid the need to remove the timing belt again at a later stage, should the coolant pump fail.

Removal

4 Firmly apply the handbrake, then jack up the front of the car and support it securely on axle stands (see *Jacking and vehicle support*). Remove the right-hand front roadwheel.
5 Remove the air cleaner and air ducting as described in Chapter 4A or 4B.
6 Remove the auxiliary drivebelt(s) and the spark plugs as described in Chapter 1A.

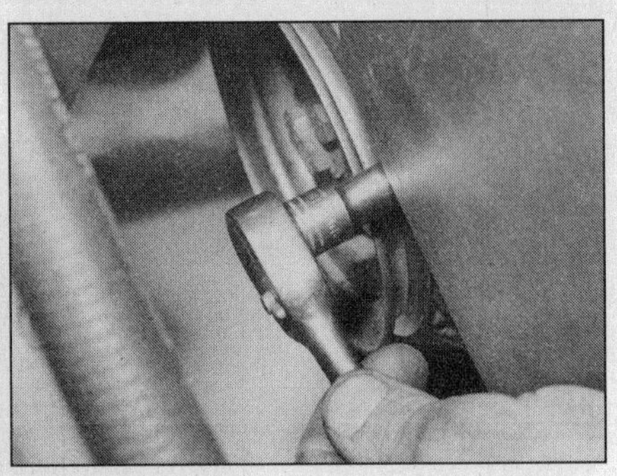
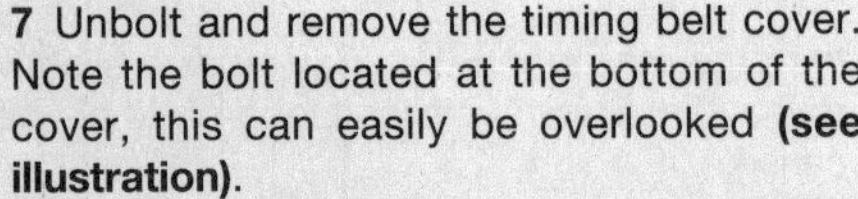

4.7 Removing the timing belt cover bottom bolt

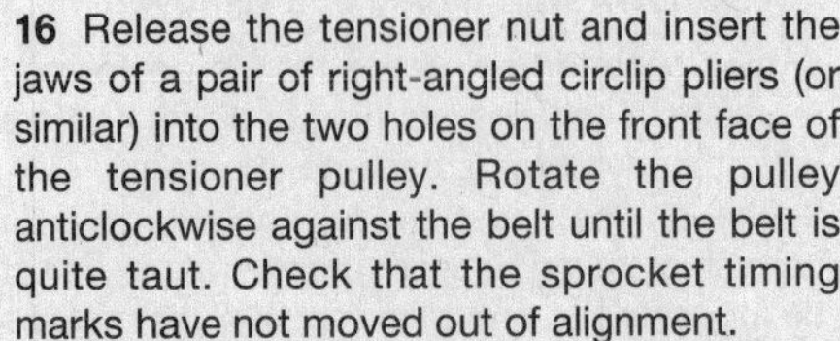

4.8 Removing the crankshaft pulley

4.10 Releasing the timing belt tensioner nut

7 Unbolt and remove the timing belt cover. Note the bolt located at the bottom of the cover, this can easily be overlooked **(see illustration)**.

8 Undo the three bolts and remove the crankshaft pulley from the sprocket **(see illustration)**.

9 Set the engine at TDC on No 1 cylinder as described in Section 2.

10 Release the nut on the timing belt tensioner, move the tensioner pulley away from the belt and retighten the nut to hold the pulley in the retracted position **(see illustration)**.

11 If the timing belt is to be re-used, use white paint or chalk to mark the direction of rotation on the belt (if markings do not already exist), then slip the belt off the sprockets. Note that the crankshaft and camshaft must not be rotated whilst the belt is removed.

12 Check the timing belt carefully for any signs of uneven wear, splitting, or oil contamination. Pay particular attention to the roots of the teeth. Renew it if there is the slightest doubt about its condition. If the engine is undergoing an overhaul, renew the belt as a matter of course, regardless of its apparent condition. The cost of a new belt is nothing compared with the cost of repairs, should the belt break in service. If signs of oil contamination are found, trace the source of the oil leak and rectify it. Wash down the engine timing belt area and all related components, to remove all traces of oil.

Refitting

13 Before refitting, thoroughly clean the timing belt sprockets. Check that the tensioner pulley rotates freely, without any sign of roughness. If necessary, renew the tensioner pulley as described in Section 5.

14 When refitting the new belt, make sure that the sprocket timing marks are still in alignment and fit the belt so that the arrows on the belt point in the direction of engine rotation, and the lines of the belt coincide with the sprocket marks.

15 Engage the timing belt with the crankshaft sprocket first, then place it around the coolant pump sprocket and the camshaft sprocket **(see illustration)**. Finally slip the belt around the tensioner pulley.

16 Release the tensioner nut and insert the jaws of a pair of right-angled circlip pliers (or similar) into the two holes on the front face of the tensioner pulley. Rotate the pulley anticlockwise against the belt until the belt is quite taut. Check that the sprocket timing marks have not moved out of alignment.

17 Maintain the effort applied to the tensioner pulley, then tighten the retaining nut.

18 Turn the crankshaft through two complete turns in the normal direction of rotation and check that when the centre of the longest run of the belt is gripped between finger and thumb it can just be twisted through 90°.

19 If the belt appears too be too slack or too tight, slacken the tensioner nut and repeat steps 16 to 18 until the correct tension is achieved.

Caution: The above procedure serves only as a rough guide to setting the belt tension. The tension must be checked accurately by a Fiat dealer using specialised checking equipment, at the earliest opportunity.

20 Refit the timing belt cover, the crankshaft pulley, auxiliary drivebelt(s), spark plugs and the air cleaner/ducting. Adjust the tension of the auxiliary drivebelt(s) as described in Chapter 1A.

21 Refit the front wheel and lower the car to the ground.

5 Timing belt tensioner and sprockets - removal, inspection and refitting

Timing belt tensioner

Removal

1 Firmly apply the handbrake, then jack up the front of the car and support it securely on axle stands (see *Jacking and vehicle support*). Remove the right-hand front roadwheel.

2 Remove the air cleaner and air ducting as described in Chapter 4A or 4B.

3 Remove the auxiliary drivebelt(s) as described in Chapter 1A.

4 Undo the three bolts and remove the crankshaft pulley from the sprocket.

5 Unbolt and remove the timing belt cover. Note the bolt located at the bottom of the cover, this can easily be overlooked.

4.15 Fitting the timing belt

6 Set the engine at TDC on No 1 cylinder as described in Section 2.

7 Loosen the nut on the timing belt tensioner and move the tensioner pulley away from the belt **(see illustration)**. Keep the belt engaged with the sprockets using a cable-tie or string.

8 Completely unscrew the nut and slide the tensioner off the mounting stud.

Inspection

9 Wipe the tensioner clean but do not use solvents that may contaminate the bearings. Spin the tensioner pulley on its hub by hand. Stiff movement or excessive freeplay is an indication of severe wear; the tensioner is not a serviceable component, and should be renewed.

Refitting

10 Slide the tensioner pulley over the mounting stud and fit the securing nut.

5.7 Timing belt tensioner retaining nut (arrowed) - shown with timing belt removed

TOOL TiP

To make a camshaft sprocket holding tool, obtain two lengths of steel strip about 6 mm thick by 30 mm wide or similar, one 600 mm long, the other 200 mm long (all dimensions approximate). Bolt the two strips together to form a forked end, leaving the bolt slack so that the shorter strip can pivot freely. At the end of each 'prong' of the fork, secure a bolt with a nut and a locknut, to act as the fulcrums; these will engage with the cut-outs in the sprocket, and should protrude by about 30 mm

11 Check and adjust the tension of the timing belt with reference to Section 4.

12 Refit the timing belt cover and tighten the bolts.

13 Refit the crankshaft pulley.

14 Refit and tension the auxiliary drivebelt(s) as described in Chapter 1.

15 Refit the air cleaner and air ducting as described in Chapter 4A or 4B.

16 Refit the roadwheel and lower the vehicle to the ground.

Camshaft sprocket

Removal

17 Remove the timing belt as described in Section 4.

18 The camshaft sprocket must now be held stationary while the retaining bolt is loosened. To do this, make up a tool as follows and engage it with the holes in the sprocket **(see Tool Tip)**.

19 Alternatively pass a rod through one of the holes in the camshaft sprocket to prevent it rotating. Position a pad of rag or a piece of wood under the rod to avoid damaging the cylinder head.

5.20a Unscrew the camshaft sprocket securing bolt and washer . . .

5.20b . . . and slide the sprocket from the end of the camshaft. Integral location key (arrowed)

20 Unscrew the bolt and slide the sprocket from the end of the camshaft. Note the integral location key on the inner face of the sprocket **(see illustrations)**.

Inspection

21 With the sprocket removed, examine the camshaft oil seal for signs of leaking. If necessary, refer to Section 7 and renew it.

22 Check the sprocket teeth for damage.

23 Wipe clean the sprocket and camshaft mating surfaces.

Refitting

24 Locate the sprocket on the end of the camshaft, then refit the bolt and washer and tighten to the specified torque while holding the camshaft stationary using the method described previously.

25 Refit the timing belt as described in Section 4.

Crankshaft sprocket

Removal

26 Remove the timing belt as described in Section 4.

27 Working beneath the engine, unbolt and remove the flywheel lower cover, then hold the flywheel stationary preferably using a tool which engages the flywheel starter ring gear (see Section 10). Alternatively have an assistant engage a wide-bladed screwdriver with the starter ring gear.

28 Unscrew the crankshaft sprocket retaining bolt and slide the sprocket off the end of the crankshaft. The sprocket may have an integral location key on its inner face **(see illustration)**, or a separate key which locates in a groove in the crankshaft nose may be fitted.

Inspection

29 With the sprocket removed, examine the crankshaft oil seal for signs of leaking. If necessary, refer to Section 8 and renew it.

30 Check the sprocket teeth for damage.

31 Wipe clean the sprocket and crankshaft mating surfaces.

Refitting

32 Slide the sprocket onto the crankshaft making sure it engages the integral key or separate key, then refit the bolt and washer and tighten the bolt to the specified torque while holding the crankshaft stationary using the method described in paragraph 27 **(see illustration)**.

33 Refit the timing belt as described in Section 4.

2A

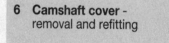

6 Camshaft cover - removal and refitting

Removal

1 Remove the air cleaner assembly and inlet duct as described in Chapter 4A or 4B.

2 Progressively unscrew the mounting bolts from the top of the camshaft cover and lift off the cover - note the location of any supports on the bolts **(see illustration)**. If it sticks, do

5.28 Crankshaft sprocket located by integral key

5.32 Tighten the crankshaft sprocket bolt to the specified torque

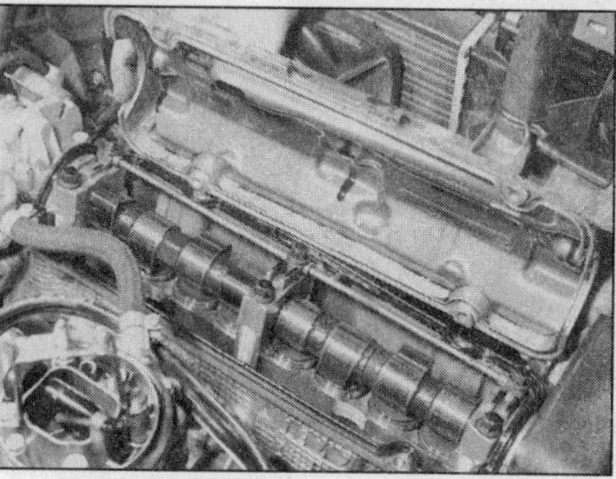

6.2 Removing the camshaft cover

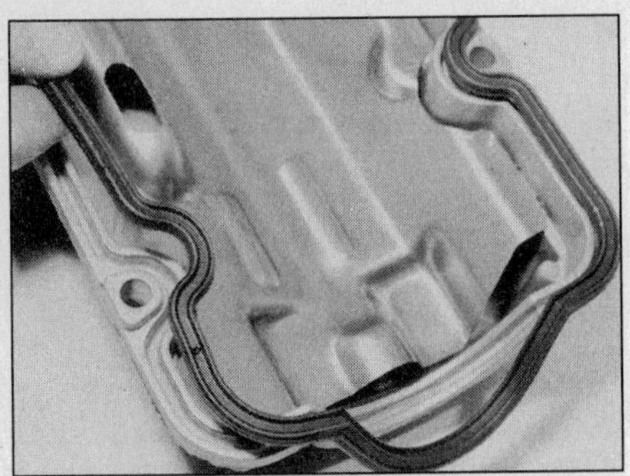

6.3 Camshaft cover gasket

not attempt to lever it off - instead free it by working around the cover and tapping it lightly with a soft-faced mallet.

3 Recover the camshaft cover gasket **(see illustration)**. Inspect the gasket carefully, and renew it if damage or deterioration is evident.

4 Clean the mating surfaces of the cylinder head and camshaft cover thoroughly, removing all traces of oil and old gasket - take care to avoid damaging the surfaces as you do this.

Refitting

5 Locate a new gasket on the cylinder head and make sure it is correctly seated.

6 Lower the cover onto the gasket making sure the gasket is not displaced.

7 Insert the mounting bolts and tighten them progressively to the specified torque.

8 Refit the air cleaner assembly and inlet duct with reference to Chapter 4A or 4B.

7 Camshaft oil seal - renewal

1 Remove the timing belt and camshaft sprocket as described in Sections 4 and 5.

2 Using a suitable hooked instrument, remove the oil seal from the cylinder head taking care not to damage the surface of the camshaft.

3 Clean the seating in the cylinder head and the end of the camshaft. To prevent damage to the new oil seal as it is being fitted, wrap some adhesive tape around the end of the camshaft and lightly oil it.

9.8 Removing the timing belt inner covers

4 Dip the new oil seal in oil then locate it over the camshaft making sure that the sealing lips are facing inwards.

5 Using a suitable tubular drift, drive the oil seal squarely into the cylinder head. Remove the adhesive tape.

6 Refit the camshaft sprocket and timing belt with reference to Sections 5 and 4.

8 Crankshaft oil seals - renewal

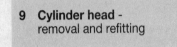

Front (right-hand side) oil seal

1 The front oil seal is located in the oil pump on the front of the crankshaft. Remove the timing belt as described in Section 4 and the crankshaft sprocket as described in Section 5.

2 Using a hooked instrument, remove the oil seal from the oil pump casing taking care not to damage the surface of the crankshaft.

3 Clean the seating in the housing and the surface of the crankshaft. To prevent damage to the new oil seal as it is being fitted, wrap some adhesive tape around the end of the crankshaft and lightly oil it.

4 Dip the new oil seal in oil then offer it up to the oil pump casing making sure that the sealing lips are facing inwards.

5 Using a suitable tubular drift, drive the oil seal squarely into the casing. Remove the adhesive tape.

6 Refit the crankshaft sprocket and timing belt with reference to Sections 5 and 4.

Rear (left-hand side) oil seal

Note: *The following paragraphs describe renewal of the rear oil seal leaving the housing in position. Refer to Chapter 2D for details of removing the housing.*

7 Remove the flywheel/driveplate as described in Section 10.

8 Using a suitable hooked instrument, remove the oil seal from the rear oil seal housing taking care not to damage the surface of the crankshaft.

9 Clean the seating in the housing and the surface of the crankshaft. Check the crankshaft for burrs which may damage the sealing lip of the new seal, and if necessary use a fine file to remove them.

9.12 Removing the cylinder head

10 Dip the new seal in clean engine oil and carefully locate it over the crankshaft rear flange making sure that it is the correct way round.

11 Progressively tap the oil seal into the housing keeping it square to prevent distortion. A block of wood is useful for this purpose.

12 Refit the flywheel/driveplate with reference to Section 10.

9 Cylinder head - removal and refitting

Removal

1 Disconnect the battery negative terminal (refer to *Disconnecting the battery* in the Reference Section of this manual).

2 Drain the cooling system as described in Chapter 1A, then remove the air cleaner and ducting as described in Chapter 4A or 4B.

3 Disconnect the accelerator cable and controls from the throttle housing.

4 Disconnect the fuel hoses.

5 Disconnect the coolant and vacuum hoses from the cylinder head and inlet manifold.

6 Disconnect all electrical leads noting their location.

7 Remove the ignition coils with reference to Chapter 5B.

8 Remove the timing belt as described in Section 4, then unbolt and remove the timing belt inner covers **(see illustration)**.

9 Unbolt and remove the inlet manifold, complete with throttle housing. On MPI models unbolt the fuel rail.

10 Unbolt the exhaust manifold from the cylinder head, and tie it to the front of the engine compartment. If preferred remove the manifold completely by unbolting the downpipe. Also disconnect the downpipe bracket.

11 Unscrew the cylinder head bolts half a turn at a time in the reverse order to that shown in illustration 9.24b. When the bolts are free, remove them with their washers.

12 Lift the cylinder head from the block **(see illustration)**. If it is stuck tight insert pieces of wood into the exhaust or inlet ports, and use them as levers to rock the head off the block. On no account drive levers into the gasket joint, nor attempt to tap the head sideways, as it is located on positioning dowels.

13 Remove and discard the cylinder head gasket and the manifold gaskets.

14 The cylinder head can be dismantled after removing the camshaft and cam followers as described in Chapter 2D.

15 If the valves have been ground-in, the valve clearances will require adjusting, as described in Chapter 1A. This should be done before the cylinder head is refitted to the engine.

Preparation for refitting

16 The mating faces of the cylinder head and cylinder block must be perfectly clean before refitting the head. Use a hard plastic or wooden scraper to remove all traces of gasket and carbon; also clean the piston crowns. Take particular care when cleaning the piston crowns as the soft aluminium alloy is easily damaged. Make sure that the carbon is not allowed to enter the oil and water passages - this is particularly important for the lubrication system, as carbon could block the oil supply to the engine's components. Using adhesive tape and paper, seal the water, oil and bolt holes in the cylinder block. To prevent carbon entering the gap between the pistons and bores, smear a little grease in the gap. After cleaning each piston, use a small brush to remove all traces of grease and carbon from the gap, then wipe away the remainder with a clean rag. Clean all the pistons in the same way.

17 Check the mating surfaces of the cylinder block and the cylinder head for nicks, deep scratches and other damage. If slight, they may be removed carefully with a file, but if excessive, machining may be the only alternative to renewal. If warpage of the cylinder head gasket surface is suspected, use a straight-edge to check it for distortion. Refer to Part D of this Chapter if necessary.

18 Check the condition of the cylinder head bolts, and particularly their threads, whenever they are removed. Wash the bolts in a suitable solvent, and wipe them dry. Check each bolt for any sign of visible wear or damage, renewing them if necessary.

Refitting

19 Before refitting the assembled cylinder head, make sure that the head and block mating surfaces are perfectly clean, and that the bolt holes in the cylinder block have been mopped out to clear any oil.

20 Check that the camshaft and crankshaft sprocket timing marks are still aligned with their respective cylinder head and oil pump cover marks as described in Section 2.

21 The new gasket should not be removed from its nylon cover until required for use. Fit the gasket dry, and make sure that the mating surfaces on the head and block are perfectly clean.

9.22a Place the cylinder head gasket on the cylinder block . . .

9.22b . . . so that the ALTO marking can be read from above

22 Place the gasket on the cylinder block so that the word ALTO can be read from above **(see illustrations)**.

23 Lower the cylinder head onto the block so that it locates on the positioning dowel.

24 The cylinder head bolt threads must be clean. Dip the bolts in engine oil, and allow them to drain for thirty minutes. Screw the bolts in finger-tight then working progressively and in the sequence shown, tighten all the cylinder head bolts to the Stage 1 torque setting given in the Specifications, using a torque wrench and a suitable socket. With all the bolts tightened to their Stage 1 setting, working again in the specified sequence, first angle-tighten the bolts through the specified Stage 2 angle, then again through the Stage 3 angle, using a socket and extension bar. It is recommended that an angle-measuring gauge is used during this stage of tightening, to ensure accuracy **(see illustrations)**.

25 Refit the inlet manifold and throttle body using a new gasket (refer to Chapter 4A or 4B).

26 Refit the exhaust manifold using a new gasket. Tighten all nuts. Reconnect the exhaust downpipe bracket.

27 Refit the timing belt inner covers and tighten the bolts.

28 Refit the timing belt, and tension it as described in Section 4. Refit the timing belt outer cover.

29 Refit the ignition coils and camshaft cover.

30 Reconnect all hoses, electrical leads and controls referring the relevant Chapters of this manual.

31 Fit the air cleaner and ducting.

32 Reconnect the battery then fill and bleed the cooling system as described in Chapter 1A.

10 Flywheel/driveplate - removal, inspection and refitting

Removal

1 Remove the transmission as described in Chapter 7A or 7B. On manual transmission models also remove the clutch (Chapter 6).

2 Mark the position of the flywheel/driveplate with respect to the crankshaft using a dab of paint. Note that on some models although there is only one location dowel on the flywheel/driveplate there are two holes in the end of the crankshaft and it is therefore possible to locate the flywheel 180° out. The flywheel/driveplate must now be held stationary while the bolts are loosened. A home-made locking tool may be fabricated from a piece of scrap metal and used to lock the ring gear. Bolt the tool to one of the transmission bellhousing mounting holes.

3 Unscrew then remove the mounting bolts then lift off the flywheel/driveplate. Recover the spacer plate on manual transmission models. Discard the flywheel/driveplate bolts; new ones must be used on refitting.

Inspection

Manual transmission models

4 If the flywheel's clutch mating surface is deeply scored, cracked or otherwise damaged, the flywheel must be renewed.

9.24a Oil the cylinder head bolts as described before refitting

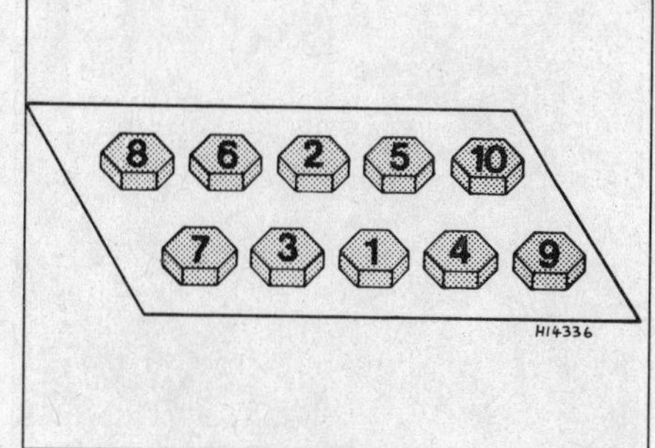

9.24b Cylinder head bolt tightening sequence

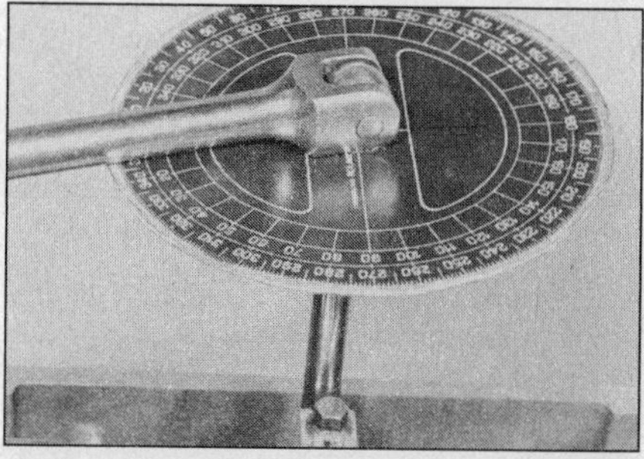

9.24c Using an angle gauge to tighten the cylinder head bolts to their second and third stage torque settings

10.10 Tighten the flywheel bolt to the specified torque

However, it may be possible to have it surface-ground; seek the advice of a Fiat dealer or engine reconditioning specialist.

5 If the ring gear is badly worn or has missing teeth, the flywheel must be renewed.

Automatic transmission models

6 Check the driveplate for signs of damage and renew it if necessary. If the ring gear is badly worn or has missing teeth, the driveplate must be renewed.

Refitting

7 Clean the mating surfaces of the flywheel/driveplate and crankshaft. Remove any remaining locking compound from the threads of the crankshaft holes, using the correct-size tap, if available.

If a suitable tap is not available, cut two slots down the threads of one of the old bolts with a hacksaw, and use the bolt to remove the locking compound from the threads.

8 If the new retaining bolts are not supplied with their threads already pre-coated, apply a suitable thread-locking compound to the threads of each bolt.

9 Offer up the flywheel/driveplate to the crankshaft, using the alignment marks made during removal, and fit the new retaining bolts (together with the spacer plate on manual transmission models).

10 Lock the flywheel/driveplate using the method employed on dismantling, and tighten the retaining bolts to the specified torque **(see illustration)**.

11 Refit the clutch on manual transmission models as described in Chapter 6.

12 Refit the transmission as described in Chapter 7A or 7B.

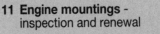

11 Engine mountings - inspection and renewal

Inspection

1 Firmly apply the handbrake, then jack up the front of the car and support it securely on axle stands (see *Jacking and vehicle support*).

2 Check the mounting rubbers to see if they are cracked, hardened or separated from the metal at any point; renew the mounting if any such damage or deterioration is evident.

3 Check that all the mounting's fasteners are securely tightened; use a torque wrench to check if possible.

4 Using a large screwdriver or a crowbar, check for wear in the mounting by carefully levering against it to check for free play. Where this is not possible enlist the aid of an assistant to move the engine/transmission back and forth, or from side to side, while you watch the mounting. While some free play is to be expected even from new components, excessive wear should be obvious. If excessive free play is found, check first that the fasteners are correctly secured, then renew any worn components as described below.

Renewal

Right-hand mounting

5 Firmly apply the handbrake, then jack up the front of the car and support it securely on axle stands (see *Jacking and vehicle support*).

6 Place a trolley jack beneath the right-hand side of the engine, with a block of wood on the jack head. Raise the jack until it is supporting the weight of the engine.

7 Unscrew the nut securing the engine bracket to the mounting.

8 Lower the engine slightly then unbolt the mounting from the body.

9 Locate the new mounting on the body, insert the bolts and tighten to the specified torque.

10 Raise the engine and locate the bracket on the mounting. Refit the nut and tighten to the specified torque.

11 Remove the trolley jack and lower the vehicle to the ground.

Left-hand mounting

12 Firmly apply the handbrake, then jack up the front of the car and support it securely on axle stands (see *Jacking and vehicle support*).

13 Place a trolley jack beneath the transmission, with a block of wood on the jack head. Raise the jack until it is supporting the weight of the engine/transmission.

14 Unscrew the bolts securing the left-hand mounting to the body.

15 Unscrew the nut securing the mounting to the transmission bracket and recover the washers.

16 Lower the transmission sufficiently to remove the mounting from the transmission bracket.

17 Locate the new mounting in the transmission bracket and refit the nut and washers. Tighten the nut to the specified torque.

18 Raise the engine and refit the mounting-to-body bolts. Tighten the bolts to the specified torque.

19 Remove the trolley jack and lower the vehicle to the ground.

Rear mounting

20 Firmly apply the handbrake, then jack up the front of the car and support it securely on axle stands (see *Jacking and vehicle support*).

21 Working beneath the vehicle, unscrew the bolts securing the rear engine mounting to the underbody.

22 Temporarily support the weight of the engine/transmission using a trolley jack.

23 Unbolt the rear mounting assembly from the transmission and withdraw from under the vehicle.

24 Unscrew the bolt and separate the bracket from the mounting.

25 Fitting the new mounting is a reversal of the removal procedure.

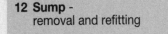

12 Sump - removal and refitting

Removal

1 Firmly apply the handbrake, then jack up the front of the car and support it securely on axle stands (see *Jacking and vehicle support*). Drain the engine oil as described in Chapter 1A.

2 Unbolt and remove the cover plate from the lower part of the flywheel housing **(see illustration)**.

3 Refer to Chapter 4D and unbolt the exhaust front pipe from the manifold. Undo the support bracket fastenings and lower the front pipe clear of the sump.

4 Unscrew the sump securing screws and nuts and pull the sump downwards to remove it **(see illustration)**. The joint sealant will

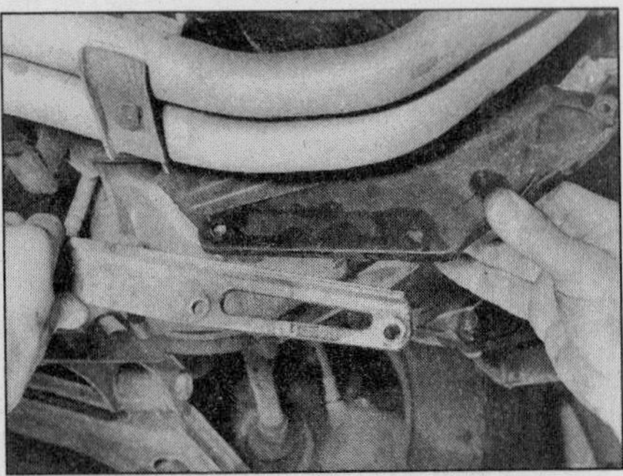

12.2 Removing the flywheel housing cover plate

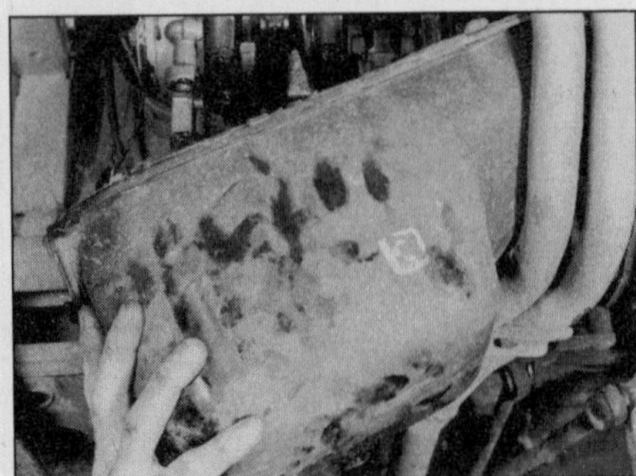

12.4 Removing the sump

require cutting with a sharp knife to release the sump. Clean away all old gasket material.

Refitting

5 When refitting, a bead of RTV silicone instant gasket 3 mm in diameter should be applied to the sump flange. Fit the sump, screw in the fixing screws and tighten to the specified torque. Note the flange end fixing nuts **(see illustrations)**.

6 Wait one hour for the gasket compound to harden before filling with engine oil.

7 Refit the flywheel housing cover plate and exhaust system front pipe.

8 Lower the vehicle to the ground and fill the engine with oil (see Chapter 1A). Check the oil level after running the engine for a few minutes.

12.5a Tightening a sump fixing screw

12.5b Sump fixing screw and flange end fixing nut

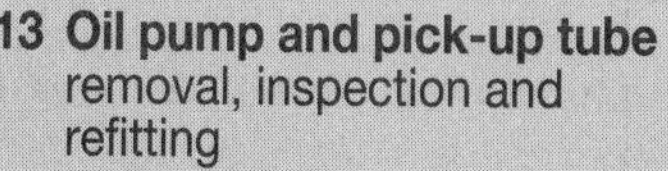

13 Oil pump and pick-up tube - removal, inspection and refitting

Removal

1 Drain the engine oil and remove the sump as described in Section 12.

2 Unscrew and remove the oil filter cartridge (see Chapter 1A).

3 Remove the timing belt as described in Section 4.

4 Lock the crankshaft against rotation either by placing a block of wood between a crankshaft web and the inside of the crankcase, or by jamming the flywheel starter ring gear with a suitable tool.

5 Unscrew and remove the crankshaft sprocket bolt and take off the sprocket. If it is tight, use two screwdrivers to lever it off, or use a two or three-legged puller.

6 Unbolt and remove the oil pick-up/filter screen assembly. Note the sealing washer.

7 Extract the oil pump fixing bolts and withdraw the pump. Remove the gasket.

Inspection

8 The oil pump incorporates a pressure relief valve, which can be removed for examination by depressing the spring plunger and pulling out the keeper plate **(see illustrations)**.

9 If pump wear is suspected, check the gears in the following way. Extract the fixing screws and remove the rear cover plate. The screws are very tight, and will probably require the use of an impact screwdriver **(see illustration)**.

10 Check the clearance between the outer gear and the pump housing using feeler blades. Check the gear endfloat by placing a straightedge across the pump body, and checking the gap between the straight-edge and gear face **(see illustrations)**. If the clearances are outside the specified tolerance, renew the oil pump complete.

11 If the pump is unworn, refit the rear cover plate and tighten the screws fully.

12 Apply air pressure from a tyre pump to the oil pump oil ducts, to clear any sludge or other material. Prime the pump by pouring clean engine oil into its inlet duct, at the same time turning the oil pump inner gear with the fingers.

13 Lever out the oil seal and drive a new one squarely into the oil pump casing **(see illustrations)**. Lubricate the oil seal lips.

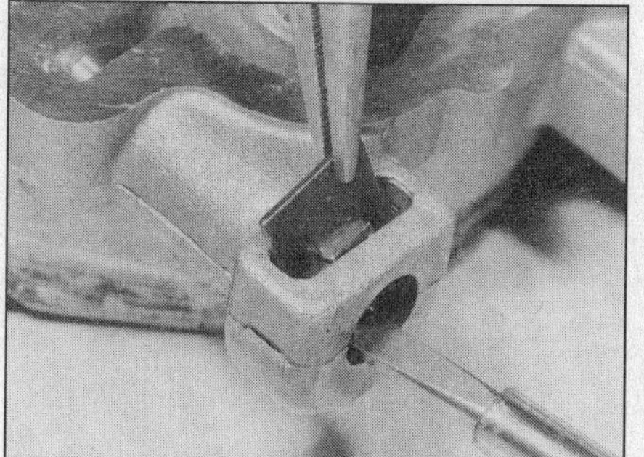

13.8a Removing the oil pump pressure relief valve

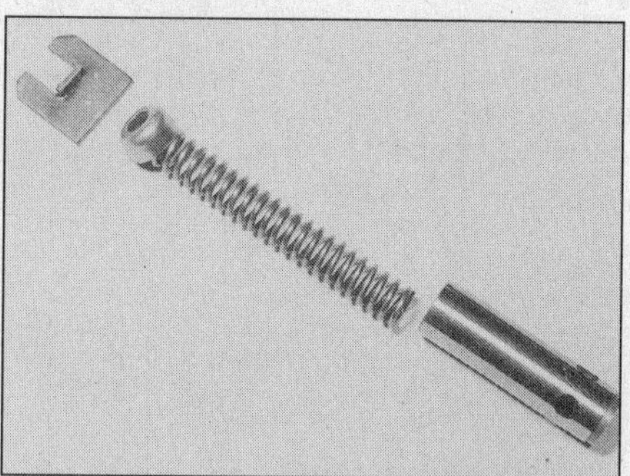

13.8b Components of the oil pump pressure relief valve

13.9 Using an impact screwdriver to remove the oil pump rear cover plate screws

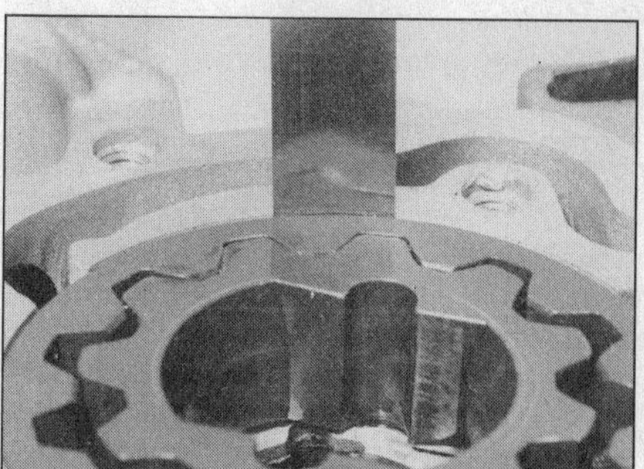

13.10a Measuring oil pump outer gear-to-pump housing clearance

13.10b Measuring oil pump gear endfloat

13.13a Removing the oil pump oil seal

13.13b Using a socket to fit a new oil seal to the oil pump

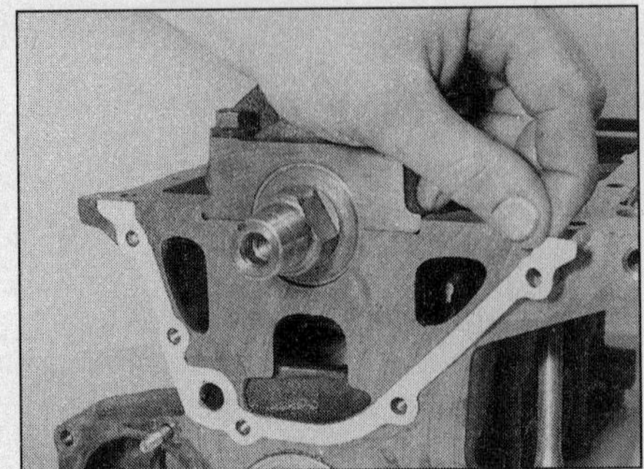
13.14a Using a new gasket . . .

13.14b . . . refit the oil pump

Refitting

14 Bolt the pump into position using a new joint gasket **(see illustrations)**. Note that one bolt is longer than the others.

15 Bolt on the oil pick-up assembly using a new sealing washer.

16 Lock the crankshaft as described in paragraph 4, then fit the crankshaft sprocket and tighten the bolt to the specified torque.

17 Fit the sump as described in Section 12. Screw on a new oil filter cartridge.

18 Fit and tension the timing belt as described in Section 4.

19 Fill the engine with oil (see Chapter 1A).

20 Run the engine for a few minutes, then check and top-up the oil level (see *Weekly checks*).

Chapter 2 Part B: DOHC (16-valve) petrol engine in-car repair procedures

Contents

Degrees of difficulty

Easy, suitable for novice with little experience 	**Fairly easy,** suitable for beginner with some experience 	**Fairly difficult,** suitable for competent DIY mechanic	**Difficult,** suitable for experienced DIY mechanic	**Very difficult,** suitable for expert DIY or professional

Specifications

General

Engine code*	176.B9.000

***Note:** See Vehicle Identification for the location of code marking on the engine.*

Bore	70.8 mm
Stroke	78.86 mm
Capacity	1242 cc
Compression ratio	10.2:1
Firing order	1-3-4-2
No 1 cylinder location	Timing belt end of engine
Timing belt tension	See text

Camshaft

Drive	Toothed belt
No of bearings	3
Camshaft bearing journal diameters:	
No 1 bearing	35.000 to 35.015 mm
No 2 bearing	48.000 to 48.015 mm
No 3 bearing	49.000 to 49.015 mm
Camshaft bearing journal running clearance	0.030 to 0.070 mm
Camshaft endfloat	0.15 to 0.34 mm

Cylinder head extension

Camshaft bearing diameters:	
No 1 bearing	35.045 to 35.070 mm
No 2 bearing	48.045 to 48.070 mm
No 3 bearing	49.045 to 49.070 mm
Cam follower (tappet) type	Hydraulic
Cam follower (tappet) diameter	28.353 to 28.370 mm
Cam follower (tappet) bore diameter in cylinder head extension	28.400 to 28.421 mm
Cam follower (tappet) running clearance	0.046 to 0.051 mm

Lubrication system

Oil pump type	By-rotor driven from front of crankshaft	
Outer rotor-to-housing clearance	0.100 to 0.210 mm	
Axial clearance	0.025 to 0.070 mm	

Torque wrench settings

	Nm	lbf ft
Camshaft driven gears	120	89
Camshaft sprocket	120	89
Crankshaft sprocket centre bolt:		
Stage 1	20	15
Stage 2	Angle-tighten a further 90°	
Cylinder head:		
Stage 1	30	22
Stage 2	Angle-tighten a further 90°	
Stage 3	Angle-tighten a further 90°	
Cylinder head extension to cylinder head	15	11
Engine mounting bolt:		
M10 x 1.25	59	44
M8	25	18
Engine mounting nut (M10 x 1.25)	60	44
Flywheel	44	32
Timing belt tensioner	25	18
Sump	10	7

1 General information

Using this Chapter

Chapter 2 is divided into four Parts; A, B, C and D. Repair operations that can be carried out with the engine in the vehicle are described in Part A, SOHC (8-valve) petrol engines, Part B, DOHC (16-valve) petrol engines and Part C, diesel engines. Part D covers the removal of the engine/transmission as a unit, and describes the engine dismantling and overhaul procedures.

In Parts A, B and C, the assumption is made that the engine is installed in the vehicle, with all ancillaries connected. If the engine has been removed for overhaul, the preliminary dismantling information which precedes each operation may be ignored.

Engine description

Throughout this Chapter, engines are identified by their capacities. A listing of all engines covered, together with their code letters, is given in the Specifications.

The engine covered in this Part of Chapter 2 is a water-cooled, double overhead camshaft, in-line four-cylinder unit, with cast iron cylinder block and aluminium-alloy cylinder head. The unit is mounted transversely at the front of the vehicle, with the transmission bolted to the left-hand side of the engine.

The cylinder head houses the eight inlet and eight exhaust valves, which are closed by single coil springs, and which run in guides pressed into the cylinder head. The two camshafts are housed in a cylinder head extension which is bolted to the top of the cylinder head. The exhaust camshaft is driven by a toothed timing belt and in turn drives the inlet camshaft via a pair of gears located at the left-hand end of the cylinder head extension. The camshafts actuate the valves directly via self-adjusting hydraulic cam followers mounted in the cylinder head extension.

The crankshaft is supported by five main bearings, and endfloat is controlled by a thrust bearing fitted to the upper section of the centre main bearing.

Engine coolant is circulated by a pump, driven by the timing belt. For details of the cooling system, refer to Chapter 3.

Lubricant is circulated under pressure by a pump, driven from the front of the crankshaft. Oil is drawn from the sump through a strainer, and then forced through an externally-mounted, replaceable screw-on filter. From there, it is distributed to the cylinder head and cylinder head extension, where it lubricates the camshaft journals and cam followers, and also to the crankcase, where it lubricates the main bearings, connecting rod big and small-ends, gudgeon pins and cylinder bores. Oil jets are fitted to the base of each cylinder bore - these spray oil onto the underside of the pistons, to improve cooling.

Repair operations possible with the engine in the car

The following work can be carried out with the engine in the car:

a) Auxiliary drivebelt - removal and refitting (refer to Chapter 1A)
b) Oil pump and pick-up tube assembly - removal, inspection and refitting
c) Timing belt and covers - removal and refitting
d) Timing belt tensioner and sprockets - removal and refitting
*e) Cylinder head - removal and refitting**
f) Cylinder head extension - removal and refitting
g) Camshaft and cam followers - removal and refitting
h) Camshaft oil seal - renewal
i) Crankshaft oil seals - renewal
j) Flywheel - removal, inspection and refitting
k) Engine mountings - inspection and renewal
l) Sump - removal and refitting

**Cylinder head dismantling procedures are detailed in Chapter 2D.*

Note 1: *It is possible to remove the pistons and connecting rods (after removing the cylinder head and sump) without removing the engine. However, this is not recommended. Work of this nature is more easily and thoroughly completed with the engine on the bench, as described in Chapter 2D.*

Note 2: *Many of the procedures in this Chapter entail the use of numerous special tools. Where possible, suitable alternatives are described with details of their fabrication. Before starting any operations on the engine, read through the entire procedure first to familiarise yourself with the work involved, tools to be obtained and new parts that may be necessary.*

2 Engine assembly/ valve timing holes - general information and usage

Note: *Do not attempt to rotate the engine whilst the camshafts are locked in position. If the engine is to be left in this state for a long period of time, it is a good idea to place suitable warning notices inside the vehicle, and in the engine compartment. This will reduce the possibility of the engine being accidentally cranked on the starter motor, which is likely to cause damage with the locking tools in place.*

1 To accurately set the valve timing for all operations requiring removal and refitting of the timing belt, timing holes are drilled in the camshafts and cylinder head extension. The holes are used in conjunction with camshaft locking tools and crankshaft positioning rods to lock the camshafts when all the pistons are positioned at the mid-point of their stroke. This

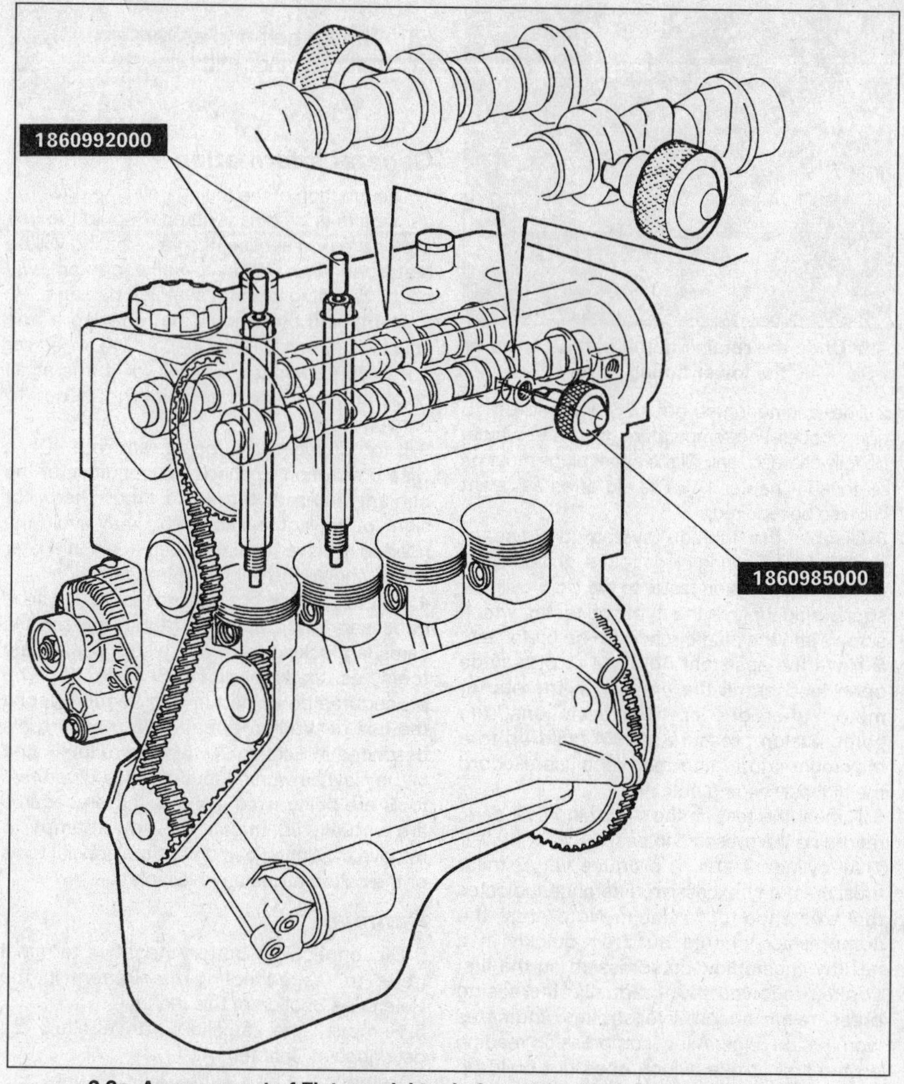

2.2a Arrangement of Fiat special tools for setting the piston position and locking the camshafts

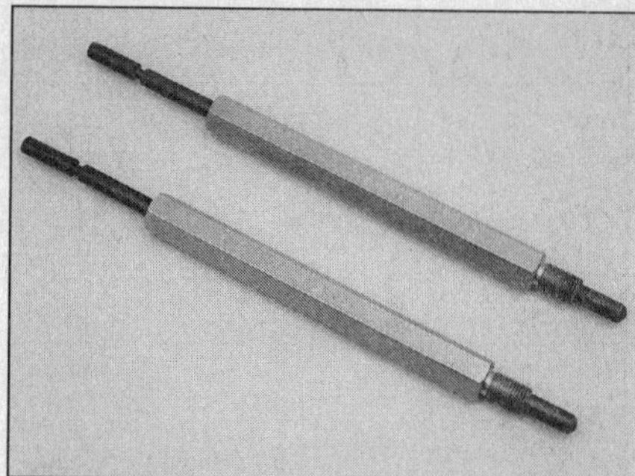

2.2b Fiat special tool for setting piston position . . .

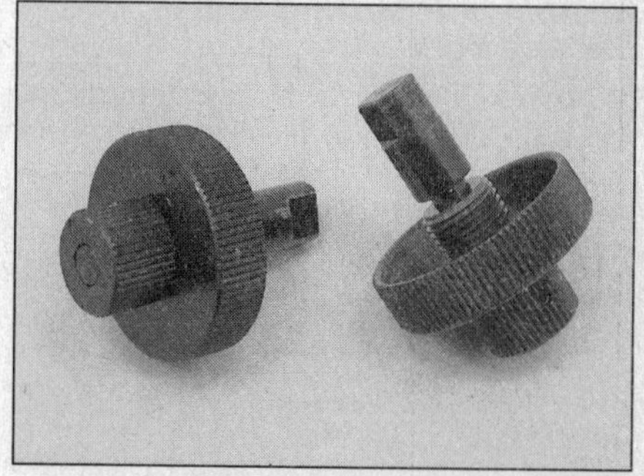

2.2c . . . and locking the camshafts

arrangement prevents the possibility of the valves contacting the pistons when refitting the cylinder head or timing belt, and also ensures that the correct valve timing can be obtained. The design of the engine is such that there are no conventional timing marks on the crankshaft or camshaft sprockets to indicate the normal TDC position. Therefore, for any work on the timing belt, camshafts or cylinder head, the locking and positioning tools must be used.

2 The special Fiat tools for setting the camshafts and pistons consist of two rods which slide in sleeves that are screwed into No 1 and No 2 cylinder spark plug holes. The rods are pushed down to contact the pistons, and the crankshaft is then turned until both rods protrude from their sleeves by the same amount. With the crankshaft correctly set, two camshaft locking pins are used, one for the inlet camshaft and one for the exhaust camshaft. The pins are screwed into holes on each side of the cylinder head extension so that they engage with slots machined in the camshafts. The arrangement of the Fiat special tools are shown **(see illustrations)**. The tool numbers are as follows:

Camshaft locking tools	*Tool No 1860985000*
Piston positioning tool	*Tool No 1860992000*

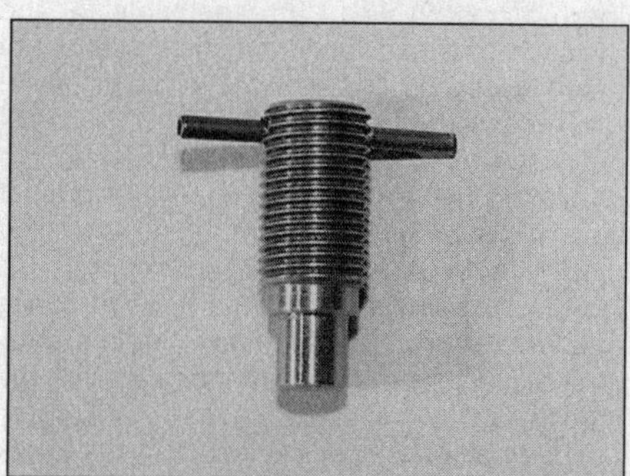

2.6a To make an alternative camshaft locking tool . . .

3 Although the special Fiat tools are relatively inexpensive and should be readily available from Fiat dealers, it is possible to fabricate suitable alternatives, with the help of a local machine shop, as described below. Once the tools have been made up, their usage is described in the relevant Sections of this Chapter where the tools are required.

Camshaft locking tool fabrication

4 Remove the air cleaner, inlet air duct and resonator as described in Chapter 4B.

5 Unscrew the sealing plug from the front face of the cylinder head extension.

6 Using the sealing plug as a pattern, obtain a length of threaded dowel rod or two suitable bolts to screw into the sealing plug hole. With the help of a machine shop or engineering works, make up the camshaft locking tools by having the dowel rod or bolts machined to the dimensions shown **(see illustrations)**. Note that two will be needed, one for each camshaft.

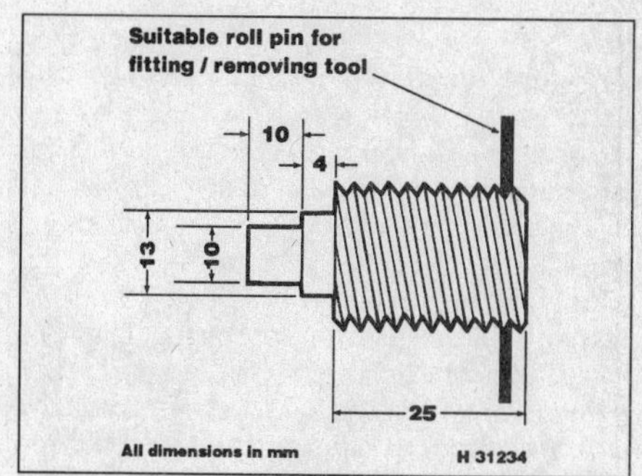

2.6b . . . have suitable dowel rods or bolts machined to the dimensions shown

4.8 Undo the three bolts and remove the crankshaft pulley from the sprocket

Crankshaft setting tool fabrication

7 To make the crankshaft setting tools, four old spark plugs will be required, together with four lengths of dowel rod. The length of each dowel rod is not critical, but it must be long enough to protrude about 100 mm above the top of the cylinder head extension when resting on top of a piston located half way down its bore. What is critical, however, is that all four dowel rods must be **exactly** the same length.

8 Break off the ceramic upper section of each plug and remove the centre electrode and earth tip. The easiest way to do this is to mount each spark plug in a vice (after removing the ceramic upper plug section) and drill a hole down through the centre of the plug. The diameter of the drill bit should be the same as the diameter of the dowel rod to be used. When finished you should have four spark plug bodies and four equal length dowel rods which will slide through the centre of the spark plugs.

3 Cylinder compression test

1 When engine performance is down, or if misfiring occurs which cannot be attributed to the ignition or fuel systems, a compression test can provide diagnostic clues as to the engine's condition. If the test is performed regularly, it can give warning of trouble before any other symptoms become apparent.

4.10 Undo the upper timing cover upper retaining bolt, and the rear retaining bolt

4.9 Undo the retaining bolt in the centre of the lower timing cover

2 The engine must be fully warmed-up to normal operating temperature, the battery must be fully charged, and all the spark plugs must be removed (Chapter 1A). The aid of an assistant will also be required.

3 Disable the ignition system by disconnecting the LT wiring plugs to the ignition coils.

4 Fit a compression tester to the No 1 cylinder spark plug hole - the type of tester which screws into the plug thread is to be preferred.

5 Have the assistant hold the throttle wide open, and crank the engine on the starter motor; after one or two revolutions, the compression pressure should build up to a maximum figure, and then stabilise. Record the highest reading obtained.

6 Repeat the test on the remaining cylinders, recording the pressure in each.

7 All cylinders should produce very similar pressures; any excessive difference indicates the existence of a fault. Note that the compression should build up quickly in a healthy engine; low compression on the first stroke, followed by gradually increasing pressure on successive strokes, indicates worn piston rings. A low compression reading on the first stroke, which does not build up during successive strokes, indicates leaking valves or a blown head gasket (a cracked head could also be the cause).

8 If the pressure in any cylinder is very low, carry out the following test to isolate the cause. Introduce a teaspoonful of clean oil into that cylinder through its spark plug hole and repeat the test.

9 If the addition of oil temporarily improves the compression pressure, this indicates that bore or piston wear is responsible for the pressure loss. No improvement suggests that leaking or burnt valves, or a blown head gasket, may be to blame.

10 A low reading from two adjacent cylinders is almost certainly due to the head gasket having blown between them; the presence of coolant in the engine oil will confirm this.

11 If one cylinder is about 20 percent lower than the others and the engine has a slightly rough idle, a worn camshaft lobe could be the cause.

12 On completion of the test, refit the spark plugs and reconnect the ignition LT wiring plug.

4 Timing belt and covers - removal and refitting

General information

1 The function of the timing belt is to drive the camshafts and coolant pump. Should the belt slip or break in service, the valve timing will be disturbed and piston-to-valve contact will occur, resulting in serious engine damage.

2 The timing belt should be renewed at the specified intervals (see Chapter 1A), or earlier if it is contaminated with oil, or if it is at all noisy in operation (a scraping noise due to uneven wear).

3 If the timing belt is being removed, it is a wise precaution to check the condition of the coolant pump at the same time (check for signs of coolant leakage). This may avoid the need to remove the timing belt again at a later stage, should the coolant pump fail.

4 Before carrying out this procedure, it will be necessary to obtain or fabricate suitable camshaft locking tools and piston positioning tools as described in Section 2. The procedures contained in this Section depict the use of the home-made alternative tools described in Section 2, which were fabricated in the Haynes workshop. If the manufacturers tools are being used instead, the procedures are virtually identical. Do not attempt to remove the timing belt unless the special tools or their alternatives are available.

Removal

5 Disconnect the battery negative terminal (refer to *Disconnecting the battery* in the Reference Section of this manual).

6 Remove the auxiliary drivebelt(s) as described in Chapter 1A.

7 Remove the air cleaner, inlet air duct and resonator as described in Chapter 4B.

8 Undo the three bolts and remove the crankshaft pulley from the sprocket **(see illustration)**.

9 Undo the retaining bolt in the centre of the lower timing cover **(see illustration)**.

10 Undo the upper timing cover upper retaining bolt, and the rear retaining bolt located above the alternator **(see illustration)**.

11 Release the crankshaft TDC sensor wiring from the clip on the upper timing cover, then withdraw the cover slightly and slide the wiring plug and socket from the timing cover slot **(see illustrations)**.

12 Release the TDC sensor wiring from the periphery of the upper and lower timing covers and remove both covers **(see illustrations)**.

13 Free the accelerator inner cable from the throttle cam, remove the outer cable spring clip, then pull the outer cable out from its mounting bracket rubber grommet.

14 From the side of the throttle body, disconnect the wiring connectors from the

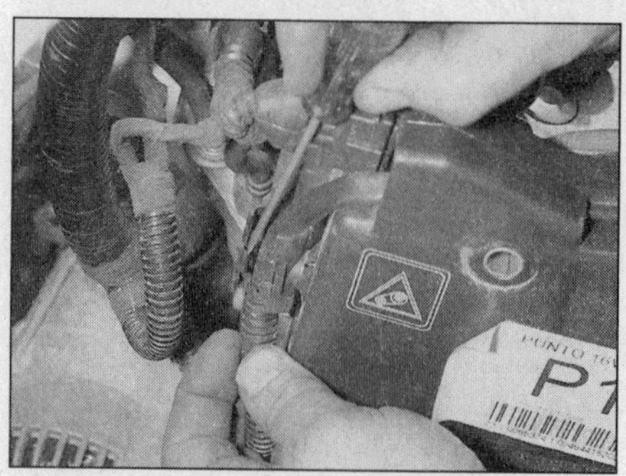

4.11a Release the crankshaft TDC sensor wiring from the clip on the upper timing cover . . .

throttle potentiometer and the idle control stepper motor. Disconnect the coolant temperature sensor wiring connector located in the inlet manifold below the throttle body, and disconnect the brake servo vacuum hose.

15 Disconnect the wiring connectors for the fuel injector harness and the intake air temperature/pressure sensor, then disconnect the fuel pressure regulator vacuum hose and the EVAP purge valve hose.

16 Undo the two bolts securing the plastic inlet manifold upper section to the lower section. Release the spark plug HT lead from the location groove in the manifold upper section, then lift the upper section, complete with throttle body, off the engine. Recover the O-rings from the manifold ports.

17 Unscrew the two bolts securing the fuel

4.21a Screw the spark plug bodies of the home-made piston positioning tools into each spark plug hole . . .

4.21b . . . place a suitable washer or similar into the recess to keep the dowel rod vertical . . .

4.11b . . . then slide the wiring plug and socket from the timing cover slot

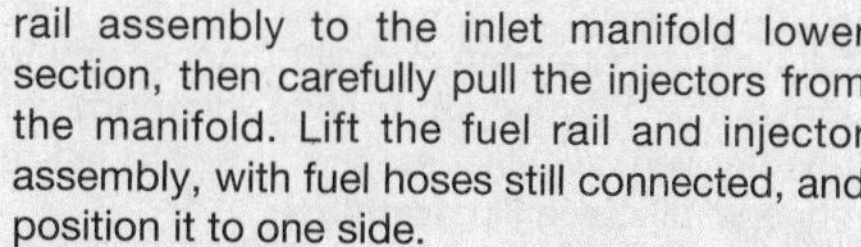

rail assembly to the inlet manifold lower section, then carefully pull the injectors from the manifold. Lift the fuel rail and injector assembly, with fuel hoses still connected, and position it to one side.

18 Undo the bolts securing the engine management ECU mounting brackets to the body and move the ECU to one side without disconnecting the wiring connector.

19 Remove the spark plugs as described in Chapter 1A.

20 Unscrew the two sealing plugs from the front and rear of the cylinder head extension to enable the camshaft locking tools to be inserted.

21 Screw the spark plug bodies of the home-made piston positioning tools into each spark plug hole and insert the dowel rods into each body. To keep the dowel rods vertical, locate a suitable washer or similar over the rod and into the recess at the top of the spark plug hole. In the photos shown here, an old valve stem oil seal housing was used but anything similar will suffice **(see illustrations)**.

22 Using a socket on the crankshaft sprocket centre bolt, turn the crankshaft in the normal direction of rotation until all four dowel rods are protruding from the top of the cylinder head extension by the same amount. As the engine is turned, two of the rods will move up and two will move down until the position is reached where they are all at the same height. The best way to check this is to place a straight edge along the top of the rods and turn the crankshaft very slowly until the straight edge contacts all four rods **(see illustration)**.

23 When all four rods are at the same height, all the pistons will be at the mid-point of their stroke. Using a screwdriver or similar inserted into the front timing hole in the cylinder head extension, check that the timing slot in the exhaust camshaft is approximately aligned with the timing hole. If the camshaft slot cannot be felt, turn the crankshaft through one complete revolution and realign the dowel rods using the straight edge. Check again for the camshaft slot. Note that although the pistons can be at the mid-point of their stroke twice for each cycle of the engine, the camshaft slots will only be positioned correctly once per cycle.

24 With the pistons correctly set, it should now be possible to screw in the camshaft

4.21c . . . then insert the dowel rods

4.12a Remove the upper . . .

4.12b . . . and lower timing covers

4.22 Place a straight edge along the top of the rods and turn the crankshaft until the straight edge contacts all four rods

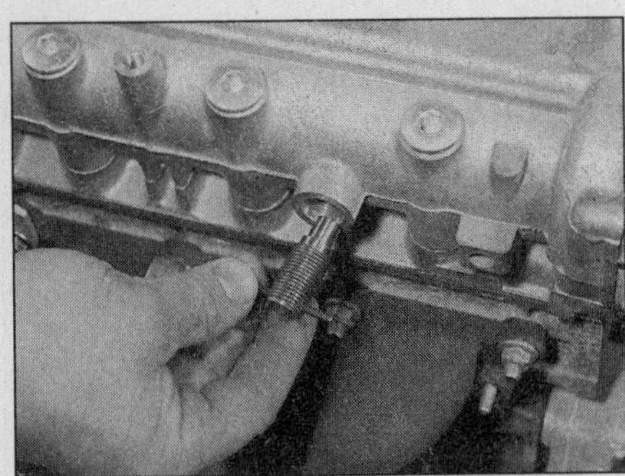
4.24a Screw in the camshaft locking tools into the timing holes in the cylinder head extension

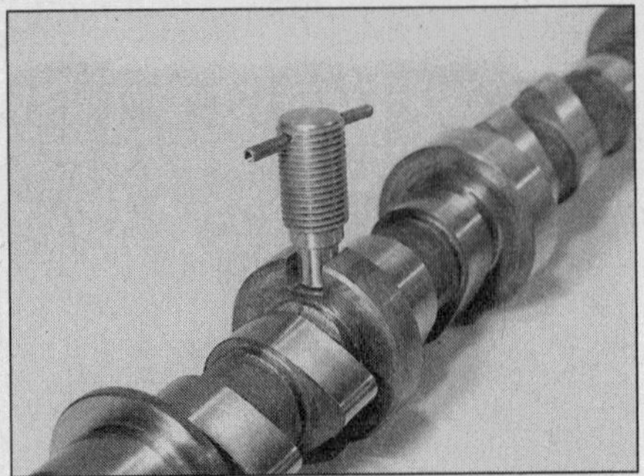
4.24b The tools engage in the camshaft slots when fitted (shown removed for clarity)

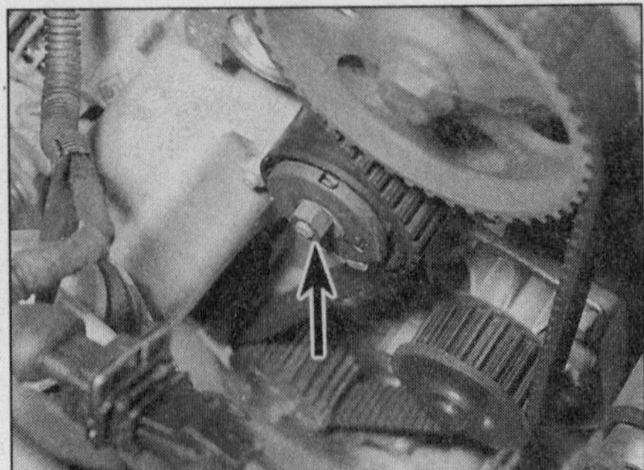
4.25 Release the nut on the timing belt tensioner (arrowed)

locking tools into the timing holes in the cylinder head extension. To provide the necessary degree of timing accuracy, the machined end of the locking tools are a very close fit in the slots machined in the camshafts. To allow the tools to be screwed fully into engagement, it may be necessary to move the crankshaft in one direction or another *very slightly* until the tools are felt to engage fully **(see illustrations)**.

25 Release the nut on the timing belt tensioner to release the tension on the belt **(see illustration)**.

26 If the timing belt is to be re-used, use white paint or chalk to mark the direction of rotation on the belt (if markings do not already exist), then slip the belt off the sprockets **(see illustration)**. Note that the crankshaft must not be rotated whilst the belt is removed.

27 Check the timing belt carefully for any signs of uneven wear, splitting, or oil contamination. Pay particular attention to the roots of the teeth. Renew it if there is the slightest doubt about its condition. If the engine is undergoing an overhaul, renew the belt as a matter of course, regardless of its apparent condition. The cost of a new belt is nothing compared with the cost of repairs, should the belt break in service. If signs of oil contamination are found, trace the source of the oil leak and rectify it. Wash down the engine timing belt area and all related components, to remove all traces of oil.

4.26 Slip the timing belt off the sprockets

TOOL TiP

To make a camshaft sprocket holding tool, obtain two lengths of steel strip about 6 mm thick by 30 mm wide or similar, one 600 mm long, the other 200 mm long (all dimensions approximate). Bolt the two strips together to form a forked end, leaving the bolt slack so that the shorter strip can pivot freely. At the end of each 'prong' of the fork, secure a bolt with a nut and a locknut, to act as the fulcrums; these will engage with the cut-outs in the sprocket, and should protrude by about 30 mm

Refitting

28 Before refitting, thoroughly clean the timing belt sprockets. Check that the tensioner pulley rotates freely, without any sign of roughness. If necessary, renew the tensioner pulley as described in Section 5.

29 The camshaft sprocket retaining bolt must now be slackened to allow the sprocket to move as the timing belt is refitted and tensioned. To hold the sprocket stationary while the retaining bolt is loosened, make up a tool as follows and engage it with the holes in the sprocket **(see Tool Tip)**. With the sprocket held, slacken the retaining bolt.

30 Check that the pistons are still correctly positioned at the mid-point of their stroke and that the camshafts are locked with the locking tools.

31 Ensuring that the direction markings on the timing belt point in the normal direction of engine rotation, engage the timing belt with the crankshaft sprocket first, then place it around the coolant pump sprocket and the camshaft sprocket **(see illustration)**. Finally slip the belt around the tensioner pulley.

32 Insert the jaws of a pair of right-angled circlip pliers (or similar) into the two holes on the front face of the tensioner pulley **(see illustration)**. Rotate the pulley to tension the belt until the belt is quite taut. Maintain the effort applied to the tensioner pulley, then tighten the pulley retaining nut.

33 Tighten the camshaft sprocket retaining bolt to the specified torque while holding the camshaft stationary using the method described previously **(see illustration)**.

34 Remove the piston positioning tools and camshaft locking tools and turn the crankshaft through two complete turns in the normal direction of rotation.

4.31 Fit the new belt around the sprockets observing the direction markings

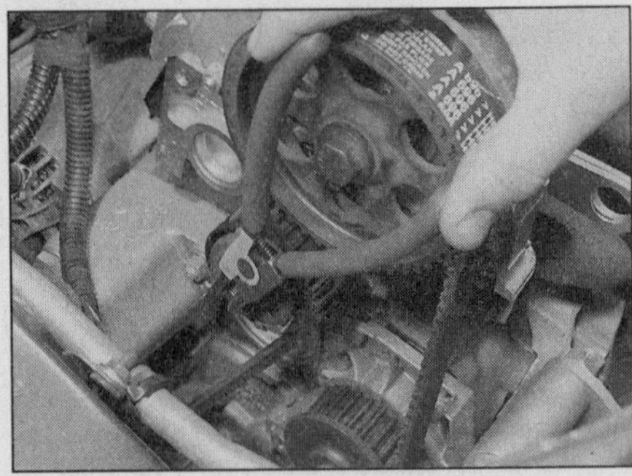
4.32 Using right-angled circlip pliers, turn the tensioner pulley to fully tension the belt

35 Slacken the tensioner pulley retaining nut and reposition the tensioner to align the mobile indicator with the fixed reference mark on the pulley face **(see illustration)**. Hold the pulley in this position and tighten the retaining nut to the specified torque.

36 Turn the crankshaft through a further two complete turns in the normal direction of rotation. Check that the timing is correct by refitting the piston positioning tools and camshaft locking tools as described previously.

37 When all is correct, remove the setting and locking tools and refit the sealing plugs to the cylinder head extension, using new O-rings if necessary. Tighten the plugs securely.

38 Refit the spark plugs as described in Chapter 1A.

39 Refit the ECU and secure with the mounting bolts.

40 Renew the injector O-ring seals, smear them with a little Vaseline then locate the injectors and fuel rail onto the inlet manifold lower section. Secure the fuel rail with the two retaining bolts.

41 Refit the inlet manifold upper section using new sealing O-rings if necessary and secure with the two bolts.

42 Reconnect the wiring connectors for the fuel injector harness and the intake air temperature/pressure sensor, then connect the fuel pressure regulator vacuum hose and the EVAP purge valve hose.

43 Reconnect the wiring connectors for the throttle potentiometer, idle control stepper motor and coolant temperature sensor. Reconnect the brake servo vacuum hose.

44 Refit and adjust the accelerator cable as described in Chapter 4B.

45 Refit the upper and lower timing belt covers together with the TDC sensor wiring.

46 Refit the crankshaft pulley and tighten the three retaining bolts securely.

47 Refit the air cleaner, inlet air duct and resonator as described in Chapter 4B.

48 Refit the auxiliary drivebelt(s) as described in Chapter 1A, then reconnect the battery negative terminal.

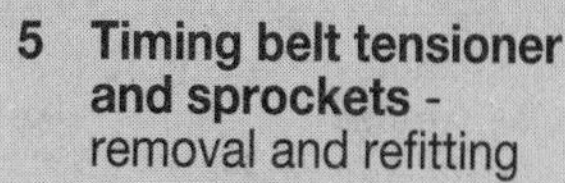

5 Timing belt tensioner and sprockets - removal and refitting

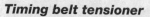

Timing belt tensioner

Removal

1 Remove the timing belt as described in Section 4.

2 Completely unscrew the tensioner nut and slide the tensioner off the mounting stud.

Inspection

3 Wipe the tensioner clean but do not use solvents that may contaminate the bearings. Spin the tensioner pulley on its hub by hand. Stiff movement or excessive freeplay is an indication of severe wear; the tensioner is not a serviceable component, and should be renewed.

4.33 Holding the camshaft sprocket with the tool described previously while tightening the sprocket bolt

Refitting

4 Slide the tensioner pulley over the mounting stud and fit the securing nut.

5 Refit the timing belt as described in Section 4.

Camshaft sprocket

Removal

6 Remove the timing belt as described in Section 4.

7 Unscrew the bolt and slide the sprocket from the end of the camshaft.

Inspection

8 With the sprocket removed, examine the camshaft oil seal for signs of leaking. If necessary, refer to Section 6 and renew it.

9 Check the sprocket teeth for damage.

10 Wipe clean the sprocket and camshaft mating surfaces.

Refitting

11 Locate the sprocket on the end of the camshaft, then refit the retaining bolt finger tight only at this stage.

12 Refit the timing belt as described in Section 4.

Crankshaft sprocket

Removal

13 Remove the timing belt as described in Section 4.

14 Working beneath the engine, unbolt and remove the flywheel lower cover, then hold the flywheel stationary preferably using a tool which engages the flywheel starter ring gear.

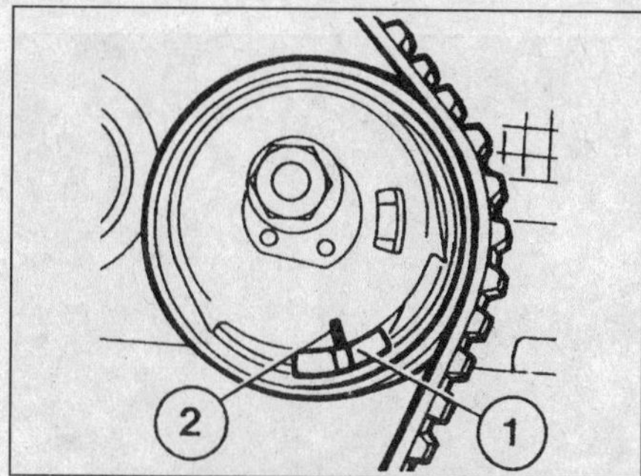

4.35 Position the tensioner so that the mobile indicator (1) is aligned with the fixed reference mark (2)

Alternatively have an assistant engage a wide-bladed screwdriver with the starter ring gear.

15 Unscrew the crankshaft sprocket retaining bolt and slide the sprocket off the end of the crankshaft. The sprocket may have an integral location key on its inner face, or a separate key which locates in a groove in the crankshaft nose may be fitted.

Inspection

16 With the sprocket removed, examine the crankshaft oil seal for signs of leaking. If necessary, refer to Section 7 and renew it.

17 Check the sprocket teeth for damage.

18 Wipe clean the sprocket and crankshaft mating surfaces.

Refitting

19 Slide the sprocket onto the crankshaft making sure it engages the integral key or separate key, then refit the bolt and washer and tighten the bolt to the specified torque while holding the crankshaft stationary using the method described in paragraph 14.

20 Refit the timing belt as described in Section 4.

6 Camshaft oil seal - renewal

1 Remove the timing belt and camshaft sprocket as described in Sections 4 and 5.

2 Punch or drill a small hole in the oil seal. Screw a self-tapping screw into the hole, and pull on the screws with pliers to extract the seal.

3 Clean the seal housing, and polish off any burrs or raised edges, which may have caused the seal to fail in the first place.

4 Lubricate the lips of the new seal with clean engine oil, and drive it into position until it seats on its locating shoulder. Use a suitable tubular drift, such as a socket, which bears only on the hard outer edge of the seal. Take care not to damage the seal lips during fitting. Note that the seal lips should face inwards.

5 Refit the camshaft sprocket and timing belt as described in Sections 5 and 4.

7 Crankshaft oil seals - renewal

Front (right-hand side) oil seal

1 The front oil seal is located in the oil pump on the front of the crankshaft. Remove the timing belt as described in Section 4 and the crankshaft sprocket as described in Section 5.

2 Using a hooked instrument, remove the oil seal from the oil pump casing taking care not to damage the surface of the crankshaft.

3 Clean the seating in the housing and the surface of the crankshaft. To prevent damage to the new oil seal as it is being fitted, wrap some adhesive tape around the end of the crankshaft and lightly oil it.

8.3a Disconnect the LT wiring plugs from the two ignition coils . . .

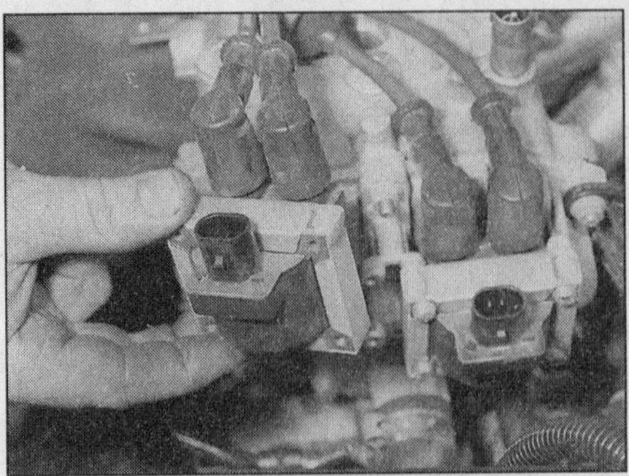

8.3b . . . then unscrew the mounting bolts and remove the ignition coils

8.5 Unscrew the protective caps covering the cylinder head extension retaining bolts

4 Dip the new oil seal in oil then offer it up to the oil pump casing making sure that the sealing lips are facing inwards.

5 Using a suitable tubular drift, drive the oil seal squarely into the casing. Remove the adhesive tape.

6 Refit the crankshaft sprocket and timing belt with reference to Sections 5 and 4.

Rear (left-hand side) oil seal

Note: *The following paragraphs describe renewal of the rear oil seal leaving the housing in position. Refer to Chapter 2D for details of removing the housing.*

7 Remove the flywheel as described in Section 11.

8 Using a suitable hooked instrument, remove the oil seal from the rear oil seal housing taking care not to damage the surface of the crankshaft.

9 Clean the seating in the housing and the surface of the crankshaft. Check the crankshaft for burrs which may damage the sealing lip of the new seal, and if necessary use a fine file to remove them.

10 Dip the new seal in clean engine oil and carefully locate it over the crankshaft rear flange making sure that it is the correct way round.

11 Progressively tap the oil seal into the housing keeping it square to prevent distortion. A block of wood is useful for this purpose.

12 Refit the flywheel with reference to Section 11.

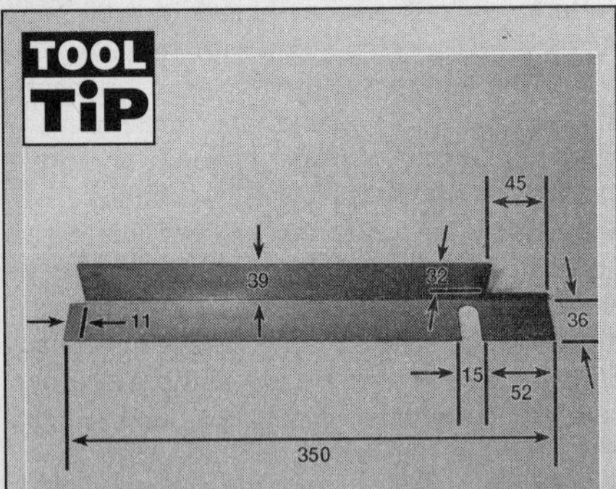

To make a cam follower retaining tool, obtain two lengths of thin metal angle and cut both to the dimensions (in mm) shown

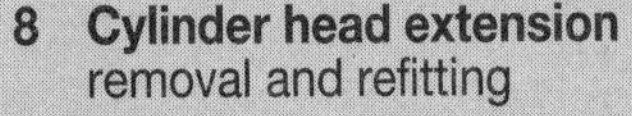

8 Cylinder head extension - removal and refitting

Removal

1 Remove the timing belt as described in Section 4.

2 Identify the two HT leads for position then disconnect them from the coil HT terminals.

3 Disconnect the LT wiring plugs from the two ignition coils, then unscrew the mounting bolts and remove the ignition coils from the end of the cylinder head extension **(see illustrations)**.

4 Undo the bolt and remove the resonator support bracket from the top of the cylinder head extension.

5 Unscrew the protective caps covering the cylinder head extension retaining bolts **(see illustration)**.

6 To retain the cam followers in place as the cylinder head extension is removed, Fiat special tool No 1860988000 will be required. This tool consists of two strips of suitably slotted thin metal angle which slip between the cylinder head extension and cylinder head mating faces as the extension is lifted off. The tool holds the cam followers in place in the extension allowing the assembly to be withdrawn without fouling the inlet and exhaust valves. The tools are relatively inexpensive and readily available from Fiat dealers. Suitable alternatives can be fabricated, if desired, using thin metal angle strip cut to the dimensions shown **(see Tool tip)**.

7 Progressively slacken and remove the bolts securing the cylinder head extension to the cylinder head.

8 Lift the cylinder head extension up very slightly, keeping it square to the cylinder head. Slip the tools in place to hold the cam followers, then lift the extension off the cylinder head **(see illustrations)**. Recover the gasket between the two assemblies.

9 Dismantling and inspection procedures for the cylinder head extension and camshafts are given in Section 9.

Refitting

10 Ensure that the mating faces of the cylinder head and extension are thoroughly cleaned, with all traces of old gasket removed, then locate a new gasket on the cylinder head **(see illustration)**.

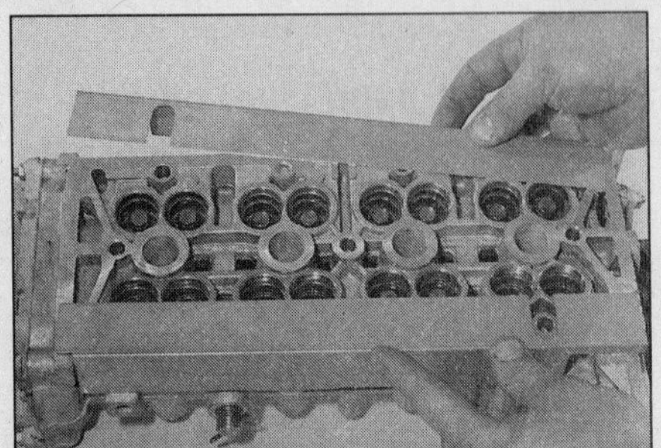

8.8a Lift the cylinder head extension slightly and insert the tools (shown with cylinder head removed for clarity) . . .

8.8b . . . then remove the cylinder head extension

8.10 Locate a new gasket on the cylinder head

8.12 Refit the cylinder head extension retaining bolts and tighten them to the specified torque

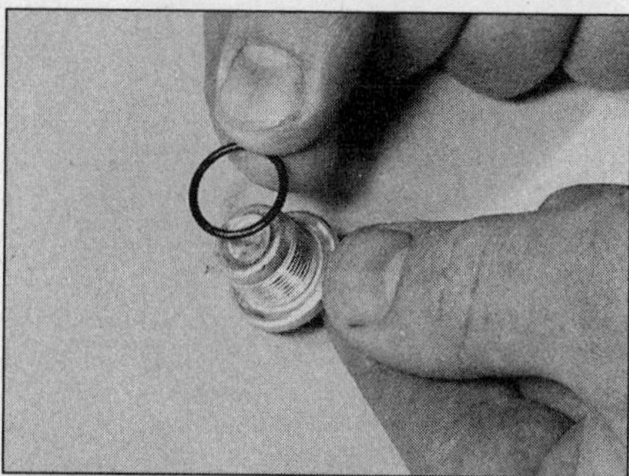
8.13 Renew the O-ring seals on the protective caps covering the cylinder head extension retaining bolts

11 Locate the cam follower retaining tools in position then lower the extension assembly onto the cylinder head. When all the cam followers have engaged their respective valves, remove the tools.

12 Refit the retaining bolts and tighten them progressively to pull the extension down onto the cylinder head. Do this slowly and carefully as the valve springs will be compressed during this operation and it is essential to keep the extension square and level as the bolts are tightened. Once all the bolts are initially tightened, progressively tighten them further to the specified torque **(see illustration)**.

13 If necessary renew the O-ring seals on the protective caps covering the cylinder head extension retaining bolts **(see illustration)**. Refit the caps and tighten them securely.

14 Refit the resonator support bracket to the top of the cylinder head extension.

15 Refit the ignition coils and reconnect the wiring.

16 Refit the timing belt as described in Section 4.

9 Camshafts and cam followers - removal, inspection and refitting

Removal

1 Remove the cylinder head extension as described in Section 8.

2 Place the assembly upside down on a bench and lift off the cam follower retaining tools.

3 Remove the cam followers from their locations in the cylinder head extension and place them in an oil tight compartmented box labelled 1 to 8 (inlet) and 1 to 8 (exhaust) **(see illustration)**. Alternatively, place them into individual storage jars or containers suitably marked. Fill the box or the jars with clean engine oil until each cam follower is just submerged.

4 Undo the camshaft sprocket retaining bolt while holding the sprocket with a suitable tool as described in Section 4.

5 Remove the camshaft sprocket, then undo the bolt and nut and remove the cover plate over the inlet camshaft **(see illustrations)**.

6 At the other end of the cylinder head extension, undo the nuts and remove the end cover **(see illustration)**. Recover the gasket.

7 Undo the two bolts securing the camshaft drive gears to the inlet and exhaust camshafts **(see illustration)**. The camshaft locking tools used in the timing belt removal procedure (which should still be in place) are sufficient to prevent the camshafts rotating while the gear retaining bolts are undone. Remove the bolts and withdraw the camshaft gears.

8 Remove the camshaft locking tools.

9 Carefully remove the inlet camshaft from the cylinder head extension **(see illustration)**. Suitably mark the camshaft IN to avoid confusion when refitting.

10 Punch or drill a small hole in the exhaust camshaft oil seal. Screw a self-tapping screw into the hole, and pull on the screw with pliers to extract the seal **(see illustration)**.

11 Carefully remove the exhaust camshaft from the cylinder head extension **(see illustration)**. Suitably mark the camshaft EX to avoid confusion when refitting.

9.3 Remove the cam followers from their locations in the cylinder head extension

9.5a Remove the camshaft sprocket . . .

9.5b . . . then undo the bolt and nut and remove the cover plate over the inlet camshaft

9.6 Undo the nuts and remove the end cover

9.7 Undo the two bolts securing the camshaft drive gears to the inlet and exhaust camshafts

9.9 Carefully remove the inlet camshaft from the cylinder head extension

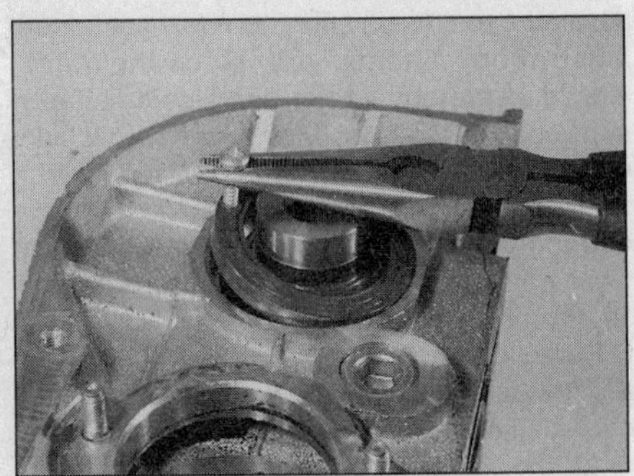
9.10 Extract the exhaust camshaft oil seal . . .

9.11 . . . then remove the exhaust camshaft from the cylinder head extension

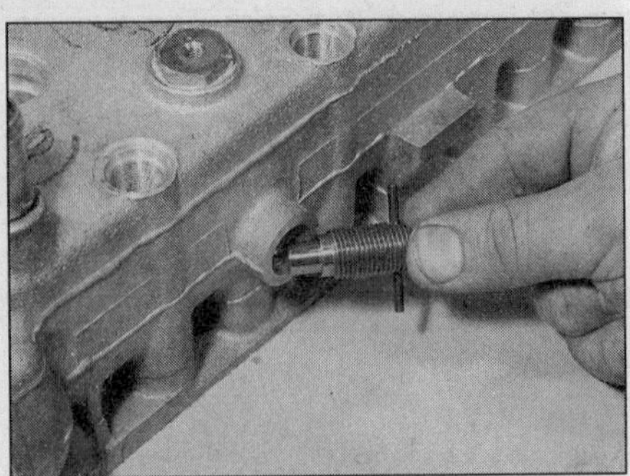
9.15 Refit the camshaft locking tools

Inspection

12 Examine the camshaft bearing surfaces and cam lobes for signs of wear ridges and scoring. Renew the camshaft if any of these conditions are apparent. Examine the condition of the bearing surfaces, both on the camshaft journals and in the cylinder head extension. If the head extension bearing surfaces are worn excessively, the extension will need to be renewed. If suitable measuring equipment is available, camshaft bearing journal wear can be checked by direct measurement.

13 Examine the cam follower bearing surfaces which contact the camshaft lobes for wear ridges and scoring. Renew any follower on which these conditions are apparent. If a follower bearing surface is badly scored, also examine the corresponding lobe on the camshaft for wear, as it is likely that both will be worn. Renew worn components as necessary.

Refitting

14 Liberally lubricate the camshaft journals and cylinder head extension bearings, then locate both camshafts in position. Note that the exhaust camshaft is nearest to the front facing side of the engine.

15 With the camshafts in position, rotate them as necessary until the camshaft locking tools can be re-inserted **(see illustration)**.

16 Lubricate the lips of a new exhaust camshaft oil seal with clean engine oil, and drive it into position until it seats on its locating shoulder **(see illustration)**. Use a suitable tubular drift, such as a socket, which bears only on the hard outer edge of the seal. Take care not to damage the seal lips during fitting. Note that the seal lips should face inwards.

17 Refit the inlet camshaft drive gear and retaining bolt then tighten the bolt to the specified torque **(see illustration)**.

18 Refit the exhaust camshaft drive gear to the exhaust camshaft. As the gear is being fitted, it will be necessary to align the anti-backlash inner gear teeth using a screwdriver to enable the teeth of both the gears to mesh **(see illustration)**.

19 At this stage it is advisable to check the camshaft endfloat using a dial gauge mounted on the cylinder head extension, with its probe in contact with the camshaft being checked. Move the camshaft one way, zero the gauge, then move the camshaft as far as it will go the other way. Record the reading on the dial gauge and compare the figure with that given in the Specifications. Repeat on the other camshaft. If either of the readings exceeds the tolerance given, a new cylinder head extension will be required.

20 Locate a new gasket on the cylinder head extension end cover, then wrap round the protruding tangs on the gasket to retain it in position **(see illustrations)**.

21 Locate the end cover on the cylinder head extension and secure with the retaining nuts securely tightened.

22 Locate a new O-ring on the inlet camshaft cover plate, then apply RTV gasket sealant to the cover plate contact face **(see illustrations)**. Fit the cover plate and secure with the nut and bolt.

23 Refit the camshaft sprocket and secure with the retaining bolt tightened finger tight only at this stage.

24 Liberally lubricate the cam followers and place them in position in their respective cylinder head extension bores **(see illustration)**.

9.16 Fit a new exhaust camshaft oil seal

9.17 Tighten the inlet camshaft drive gear retaining bolt to the specified torque

9.18 Refit the exhaust camshaft drive gear while aligning the anti-backlash inner gear teeth

9.20a Locate a new gasket on the cylinder head extension end cover . . .

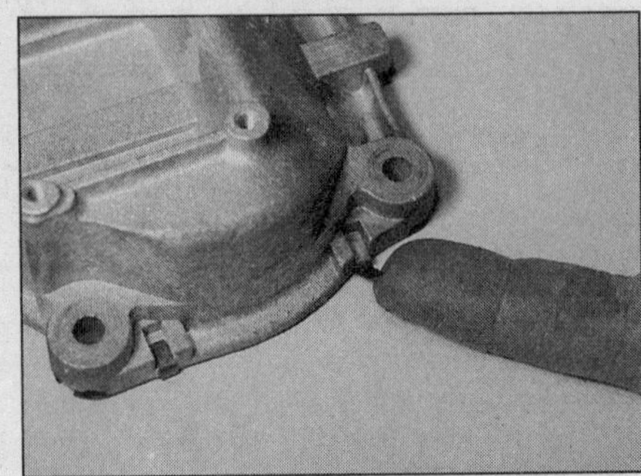
9.20b . . . then wrap round the protruding tangs to retain the gasket

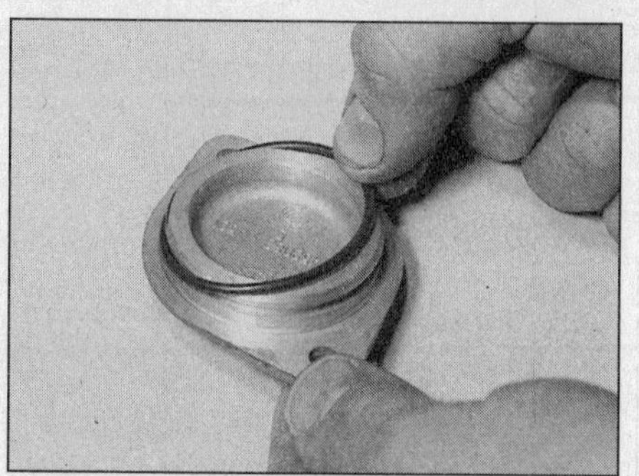

9.22a Locate a new O-ring on the inlet camshaft cover plate . . .

25 Locate the cam follower retaining tools in position and refit the cylinder head extension as described in Section 8.

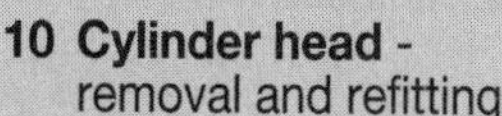

10 Cylinder head - removal and refitting

Removal

Note: *The cylinder head bolts are of special splined design and a Fiat tool should be obtained to unscrew them. A Torx key will not fit however in practise it was found that a close-fitting Allen key could be used as an alternative.*

1 Drain the cooling system as described in Chapter 1A.

2 Remove the cylinder head extension as described in Section 8.

3 Disconnect the radiator hose from the thermostat housing on the left-hand end of the cylinder head.

4 Disconnect the heater hose from the outlet at the rear of the cylinder head.

5 Disconnect the coolant temperature sensor and temperature gauge sensor wiring plugs from the left-hand end of the cylinder head.

6 Undo the engine oil dipstick tube bracket retaining bolt and the two bolts securing the wiring harness support clips to the inlet manifold lower section.

7 Undo the retaining nuts and separate the exhaust system front pipe from the exhaust manifold flange.

8 Check that nothing remains attached to the cylinder head likely to impede removal. It is assumed that the head will be removed complete with exhaust manifold and inlet manifold lower section.

9 Unscrew the cylinder head bolts half a turn at a time in the reverse order to that shown in **illustration 10.20a**. When the bolts are free, remove them from their locations..

10 Lift the cylinder head from the block. If it is stuck tight rock the head to break the joint by means of the manifolds. On no account drive levers into the gasket joint, nor attempt to tap the head sideways, as it is located on positioning dowels.

11 Remove and discard the cylinder head gasket.

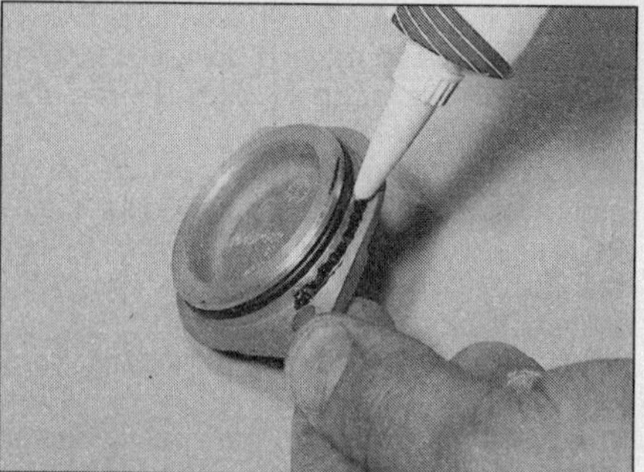

9.22b . . . then apply RTV gasket sealant to the cover plate contact face

12 Refer to Chapter 2D for cylinder head dismantling and inspection procedures.

Preparation for refitting

13 The mating faces of the cylinder head and cylinder block must be perfectly clean before refitting the head. Use a hard plastic or wooden scraper to remove all traces of gasket and carbon; also clean the piston crowns. Take particular care when cleaning the piston crowns as the soft aluminium alloy is easily damaged. Make sure that the carbon is not allowed to enter the oil and water passages - this is particularly important for the lubrication system, as carbon could block the oil supply to the engine's components. Using adhesive tape and paper, seal the water, oil and bolt holes in the cylinder block. To prevent carbon entering the gap between the pistons and bores, smear a little grease in the gap. After cleaning each piston, use a small brush to remove all traces of grease and carbon from the gap, then wipe away the remainder with a clean rag. Clean all the pistons in the same way.

14 Check the mating surfaces of the cylinder block and the cylinder head for nicks, deep scratches and other damage. If slight, they may be removed carefully with a file, but if excessive, machining may be the only alternative to renewal. If warpage of the cylinder head gasket surface is suspected, use a straight-edge to check it for distortion. Refer to Part D of this Chapter if necessary.

15 Check the condition of the cylinder head bolts, and particularly their threads, whenever they are removed. Wash the bolts in a suitable solvent, and wipe them dry. Check each bolt for any sign of visible wear or damage, renewing them if necessary.

9.24 Lubricate the cam followers and place them in position in their respective bores

Refitting

16 Before refitting the assembled cylinder head, make sure that the head and block mating surfaces are perfectly clean, and that the bolt holes in the cylinder block have been mopped out to clear any oil.

17 The new gasket should not be removed from its nylon cover until required for use. Fit the gasket dry, and make sure that the mating surfaces on the head and block are perfectly clean.

18 Place the gasket on the cylinder block so that the word ALTO can be read from above.

19 Lower the cylinder head onto the block so that it locates on the positioning dowel.

20 The cylinder head bolt threads must be clean and lightly lubricated. Screw the bolts in finger-tight then working progressively and in the sequence shown, tighten all the cylinder head bolts to the Stage 1 torque setting given in the Specifications, using a torque wrench and a suitable socket. With all the bolts tightened to their Stage 1 setting, working again in the specified sequence, first angle-tighten the bolts through the specified Stage 2 angle, then again through the Stage 3 angle, using a socket and extension bar. It is recommended that an angle-measuring gauge is used during this stage of tightening, to ensure accuracy **(see illustrations)**.

21 Reconnect the exhaust system front pipe to the manifold using a new flange gasket.

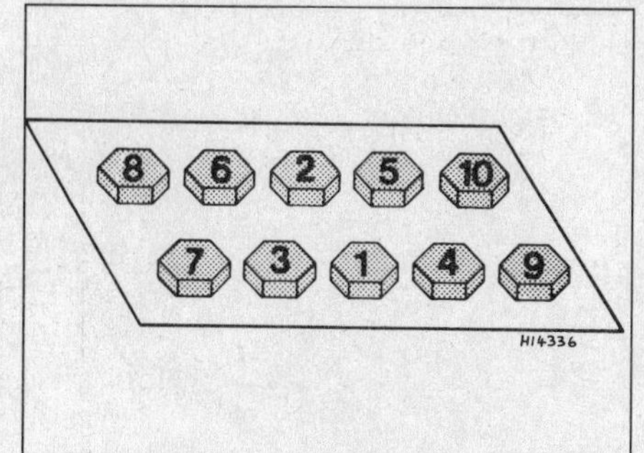

10.20a Cylinder head bolt tightening sequence

10.20b Tighten the cylinder head bolts to the Stage 1 torque setting . . .

10.20c . . . then through the Stage 2 and Stage 3 angle

22 Refit the engine oil dipstick tube bracket retaining bolt and the two bolts securing the wiring harness support clips to the inlet manifold lower section.
23 Connect the coolant temperature sensor and temperature gauge sensor wiring plugs.
24 Connect the radiator hose to the thermostat housing and the heater hose to the cylinder head outlet.
25 Refit the cylinder head extension as described in Section 8.
26 On completion, refill the cooling system as described in Chapter 1A.

11 Flywheel - removal, inspection and refitting

Refer to Chapter 2A, Section 10.

12 Engine mountings - inspection and renewal

Refer to Chapter 2A, Section 11.

13 Sump - removal and refitting

Refer to Chapter 2A, Section 12.

14 Oil pump and pick-up tube - removal, inspection and refitting

Refer to Chapter 2A, Section 13.

Chapter 2 Part C:
Diesel engine in-car repair procedures

Contents

Degrees of difficulty

Easy, suitable for novice with little experience 
Fairly easy, suitable for beginner with some experience 
Fairly difficult, suitable for competent DIY mechanic 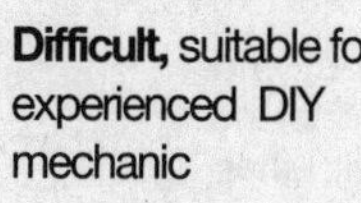
Difficult, suitable for experienced DIY mechanic
Very difficult, suitable for expert DIY or professional

Specifications

General

Engine code:*	
1698 cc non-turbo engine	176.B3.000
1698 cc turbo engine:	
Up to 1997	176.A3.000 or 176.A5.000
1997 onward	176.A3.000 or 176.B7.000

***Note:** See Vehicle Identification for the location of the code marking on the engine.*

Bore	82.6 mm
Stroke	79.2 mm
Compression ratio:	
Non-turbo engine	20.5:1
Turbo engine	19:1
Firing order	1-3-4-2
No 1 cylinder location	Timing belt end of engine
Timing belt tension	See text

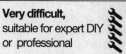

Lubrication system

Oil pump type	By-rotor driven from front of crankshaft
Outer rotor-to-housing clearance	0.080 to 0.186 mm
Axial clearance	0.025 to 0.056 mm

Torque wrench settings

	Nm	lbf ft
Camshaft cover	10	7
Camshaft sprocket	118	87
Crankshaft sprocket centre bolt	190	140
Cylinder head:		
Stage 1	50	37
Stage 2	100	74
Stage 3	Angle-tighten a further 90°	
Stage 4	Angle-tighten a further 90°	
Cylinder head front bolts	30	22
Flywheel	142	105
Fuel injection pump sprocket	49	36
Inlet and exhaust manifolds	25	18
Sump	10	7
Timing belt tensioner and idler	44	32

1 General information

Using this Chapter

Chapter 2 is divided into four Parts; A, B, C and D. Repair operations that can be carried out with the engine in the vehicle are described in Part A, SOHC (8-valve) petrol engines, Part B, DOHC (16-valve) petrol engines and Part C, diesel engines. Part D covers the removal of the engine/transmission as a unit, and describes the engine dismantling and overhaul procedures.

In Parts A, B and C, the assumption is made that the engine is installed in the vehicle, with all ancillaries connected. If the engine has been removed for overhaul, the preliminary dismantling information which precedes each operation may be ignored.

Engine description

Both normally aspirated (non-turbo) and turbocharged diesel engines are fitted to the Punto range. The engines together with their codes are given in the *Specifications* at the start of this Chapter.

The engines are water-cooled, single-overhead camshaft, in-line four cylinder units with cast-iron cylinder blocks and aluminium-alloy cylinder heads. The engine is mounted transversely at the front of the vehicle, with the transmission bolted to the left-hand side of the engine.

The cylinder head carries the camshaft which is driven by a toothed timing belt. It also houses the inlet and exhaust valves which are closed by single coil valve springs and run in valve guides pressed into the cylinder head. The valves are operated by cam followers fitted over each valve, and the clearances are adjusted by shims positioned between the followers and the camshaft lobes. The camshaft is supported by four bearings - the end bearings are machined in the cylinder head and the remaining bearings have caps bolted to the cylinder head. The cylinder head contains integral oilways which supply and lubricate the camshaft and followers and it also incorporates renewable swirl chambers.

The crankshaft is supported by five main bearings, and endfloat is controlled by a thrust bearing fitted on the rear main bearing.

All diesel engines are fitted with a brake servo vacuum pump driven from the left-hand end of the camshaft.

Engine coolant is circulated by a pump, driven by the auxiliary drivebelt. For details of the cooling system refer to Chapter 3.

Lubricant is circulated under pressure by a pump, driven from the front of the crankshaft. Oil is drawn from the sump through a strainer, and then forced through an externally-mounted, replaceable screw-on filter. From there, it is distributed to the cylinder head, where it lubricates the camshaft journals and followers, and also to the crankcase, where it lubricates the main bearings, connecting rod big- and small-ends, gudgeon pins and cylinder bores. Oil jets are fitted to the base of each cylinder bore - these spray oil onto the underside of the pistons, to improve cooling. An oil cooler is also fitted to reduce the temperature of oil before it re-enters the engine.

Repair operations possible with the engine in the car

The following work can be carried out with the engine in the car:

a) Compression pressure - testing
b) Auxiliary drivebelt - removal and refitting (refer to Chapter 1B)
c) Valve clearances - checking and adjustment (refer to Chapter 1B)
d) Camshaft cover - removal and refitting
e) Timing belt and covers - removal and refitting
f) Timing belt tensioner and sprockets - removal and refitting
*g) Cylinder head - removal and refitting**
*h) Camshaft and cam followers - removal and refitting**
i) Camshaft oil seal - renewal
j) Crankshaft oil seals - renewal
k) Flywheel - removal, inspection and refitting
l) Engine mountings - inspection and renewal
m) Sump - removal and refitting
n) Oil pump and pick-up tube assembly - removal, inspection and refitting

**Cylinder head dismantling procedures are detailed in Chapter 2D, with details of camshaft and cam follower removal.*

Note: *It is possible to remove the pistons and connecting rods (after removing the cylinder head and sump) without removing the engine. However, this is not recommended. Work of this nature is more easily and thoroughly completed with the engine on the bench as described in Chapter 2D.*

2 Location of TDC on No 1 cylinder

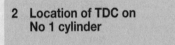

General information

1 The camshaft and fuel injection pump are driven by the crankshaft, by means of sprockets and a timing belt. All three sprockets rotate in phase with each other and this provides the correct valve and injection pump timing as the engine rotates. When the timing belt is removed during servicing or repair, it is possible for the camshaft, injection pump and crankshaft to rotate independently of each other and the correct timing is then lost.

2 It is therefore important that the correct phasing between the camshaft, injection pump and crankshaft is preserved whilst the timing belt is off the engine. This is achieved by setting the engine in a reference position (known as Top Dead Centre or TDC) before the timing belt is removed and then preventing the camshaft, pump and crankshaft from rotating until the belt is refitted. Similarly, if the engine has been dismantled for overhaul, the engine can be set to TDC during reassembly to ensure that the correct phasing is restored.

3 TDC is the highest point in the cylinder that each piston reaches as the crankshaft turns. Each piston reaches TDC at the end of the compression stroke and again at the end of the exhaust stroke. However, for the purpose of timing the engine, TDC refers to the position of No 1 piston at the end of its compression stroke. On all engines in this manual, No 1 piston (and cylinder) is at the timing belt end of the engine.

4 The camshaft and fuel injection pump sprockets are each equipped with a marking which, when aligned with a reference marking on the timing belt inner cover, indicates that the camshaft and pump are correctly positioned for cylinder No 1 at TDC on its compression stroke.

5 The crankshaft sprocket is also equipped with a timing mark - when this is aligned with a reference marking on the oil pump cover, the engine is set with cylinders No 1 and 4 at TDC. Note that it is the camshaft positioning that determines whether a cylinder is on its compression or exhaust stroke.

Location of TDC on cylinder No 1

6 Remove the air inlet ducting as described in Chapter 4C, Section 2.

7 Remove the heater glow plugs with reference to Chapter 5C. Due to the high compression ratio of diesel engines this is necessary to allow the engine to be turned by hand.

8 Unscrew the mounting bolts and move the coolant expansion tank to one side for access to the timing covers. Release the hose from the clips on the camshaft cover.

9 Release the toggle clips and remove the upper timing cover **(see illustration)**.

2.9 Removing the upper timing cover

10 Firmly apply the handbrake, then jack up the front of the car and support it securely on axle stands (see *Jacking and vehicle support*). Remove the right-hand front roadwheel.

11 Working under the wheelarch, remove the splash guard, then unbolt and remove the outer cover over the crankshaft pulley **(see illustration)**.

12 Remove the auxiliary drivebelt(s) as described in Chapter 1B.

13 Unbolt and remove the lower timing cover from the cylinder block **(see illustration)**. Note that one of the bolts is located at the front of the engine.

14 Unscrew the four socket-headed bolts and remove the pulley from the front of the crankshaft **(see illustrations)**. Recover the spacer plate.

15 Turn the engine in its normal direction of rotation (using a socket or spanner on the crankshaft sprocket centre bolt) until pressure can be felt at No 1 cylinder glowplug hole.

16 Continue turning the engine until the TDC timing marks on the camshaft and fuel injection pump sprockets are aligned with the corresponding marks on the timing belt inner cover, and the crankshaft sprocket timing mark is aligned with the mark on the oil pump cover **(see illustration)**.

17 The engine is now set at TDC for No 1 cylinder on compression.

2.11 Removing the outer cover over the crankshaft pulley

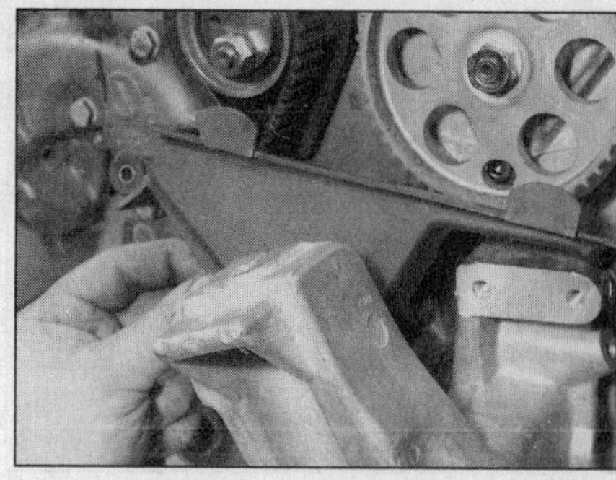

2.13 Removing the lower timing cover

2.14a Unscrew and remove the socket-headed bolts and spacer . . .

2.14b . . . and remove the pulley from the front of the crankshaft

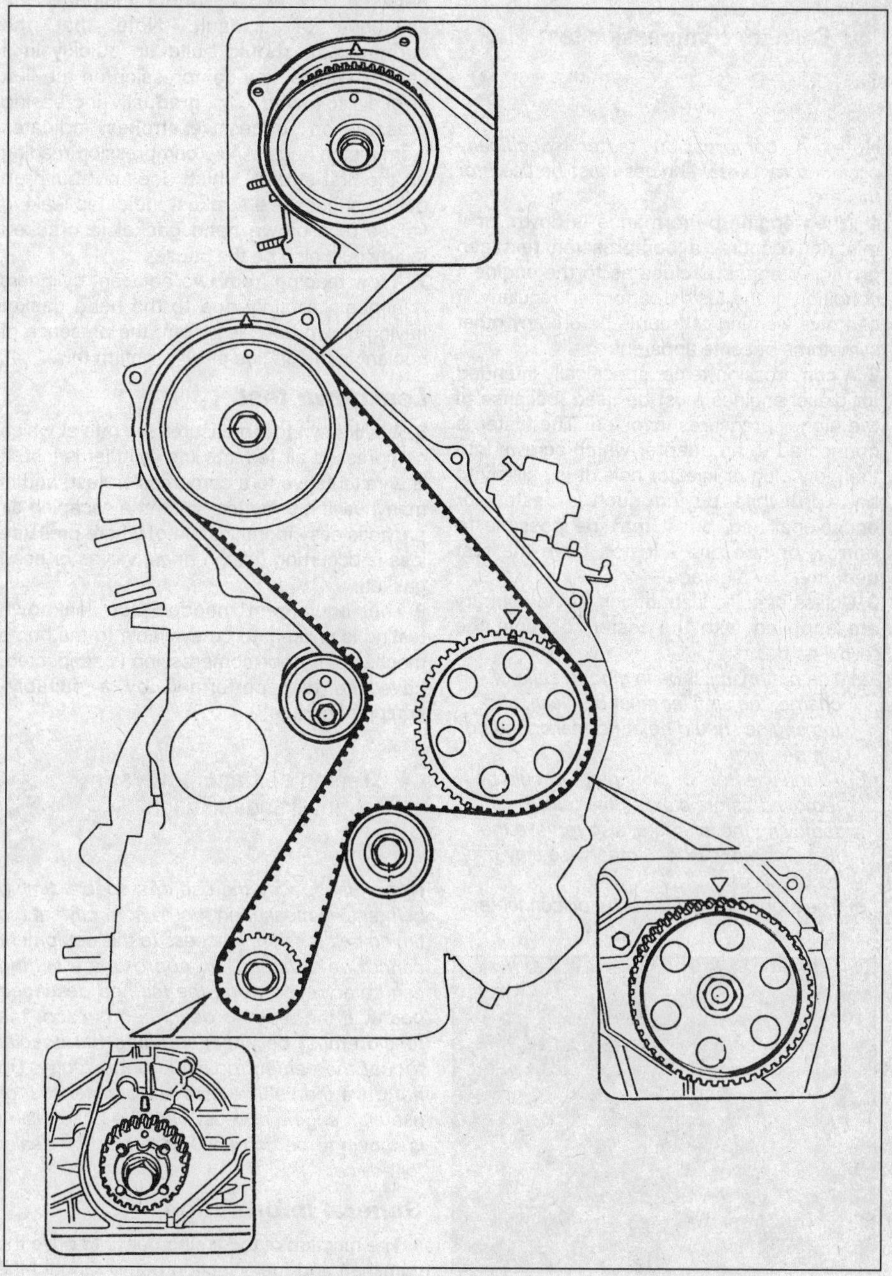

2.16 Sprocket timing mark positioning with No 1 cylinder at TDC

2C

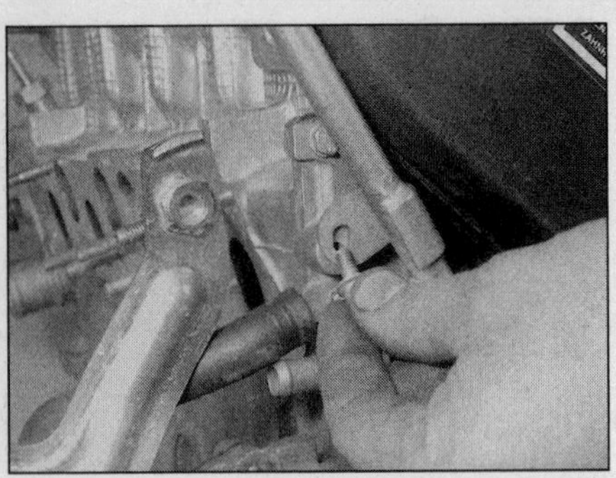

4.4a Unbolt the engine oil dipstick tube . . .

3 Cylinder compression test

Note: *A compression tester specifically designed for diesel engines must be used for this test.*

1 When engine performance is down, or if misfiring occurs, a compression test can provide diagnostic clues as to the engine's condition. If the test is performed regularly, it can give warning of trouble before any other symptoms become apparent.

2 A compression tester specifically intended for diesel engines must be used, because of the higher pressures involved. The tester is connected to an adapter which screws into the glow plug or injector hole. It is unlikely to be worthwhile buying such a tester for occasional use, but it may be possible to borrow or hire one - if not, have the test performed by a garage.

3 Unless specific instructions to the contrary are supplied with the tester, observe the following points:

a) *The battery must be in a good state of charge, the air filter must be clean, and the engine should be at normal operating temperature.*

b) *All the injectors or glow plugs should be removed before starting the test. If removing the injectors, also remove the flame shield washers, otherwise they may be blown out.*

c) *The stop solenoid must be disconnected, to prevent the engine from running or fuel from being discharged.*

4.4b . . . and remove it from the rubber grommet in the oil pump housing

4 There is no need to hold the accelerator pedal down during the test, because the diesel engine air inlet is not throttled.

5 The cause of poor compression is less easy to establish on a diesel engine than on a petrol one. The effect of introducing oil into the cylinders (wet testing) is not conclusive, because there is a risk that the oil will sit in the recess on the piston crown, instead of passing to the rings. However the following can be used as a rough guide to diagnosis.

6 All cylinders should produce very similar pressures; a difference of more than 5 bars between any two cylinders indicates the existence of a fault. Note that the compression should build up quickly in a healthy engine; low compression on the first stroke, followed by gradually-increasing pressure on successive strokes, indicates worn piston rings. A low compression reading on the first stroke, which does not build up during successive strokes, indicates leaking valves or a blown head gasket (a cracked head could also be the cause).

7 A low reading from two adjacent cylinders is almost certainly due to the head gasket having blown between them; the presence of coolant in the engine oil will confirm this.

Leakdown test

8 A leakdown test measures the rate at which compressed air fed into the cylinder is lost. It is an alternative to a compression test, and in many ways it is better, since the escaping air provides easy identification of where pressure loss is occurring (piston rings, valves or head gasket).

9 The equipment needed for leakdown testing is unlikely to be available to the home mechanic. If poor compression is suspected, have the test performed by a suitably-equipped garage.

4 Timing belt and covers - removal and refitting

Note: *Fiat specify the use of a special timing belt tension measuring tool to correctly set the timing belt tension. If access to this equipment cannot be obtained, an approximate setting can be achieved using the method described below. If the method described is used, the tension must be checked using the special tool at the earliest possible opportunity. Do not drive the vehicle over large distances, or use high engine speeds, until the belt tension is known to be correct. Refer to a Fiat dealer for advice.*

General information

1 The function of the timing belt is to drive the camshaft and fuel injection pump. Should the belt slip or break in service, the valve timing will be disturbed and piston-to-valve contact will occur, resulting in serious engine damage.

2 The timing belt should be renewed at the specified intervals (see Chapter 1B), or earlier if it is contaminated with oil, or if it is at all noisy in operation (a scraping noise due to uneven wear).

Removal

3 Set the engine at TDC on No 1 cylinder as described in Section 2.

4 Unbolt and remove the engine oil dipstick tube and remove it from the rubber grommet in the oil pump housing **(see illustrations)**.

5 Before removing the timing belt check its tension by turning the belt through 90° with finger and thumb midway between the injection pump and camshaft sprockets. This will give you an idea of the tension to apply when refitting, assuming the tension is already correct. Also note the position of the tensioner pulley as a reference mark.

6 Release the nut on the timing belt tensioner, move the tensioner pulley away from the belt and retighten the nut to hold the pulley in the retracted position.

7 If the timing belt is to be re-used, use white paint or chalk to mark the direction of rotation on the belt (if markings do not already exist), then slip the belt off the camshaft, crankshaft and injection pump sprockets, and the idler and tensioner pulleys.

Caution: If the belt appears to be in good condition and can be re-used, it is essential that it is refitted the same way round, otherwise accelerated wear will result, leading to premature failure.

8 Check the timing belt carefully for any signs of uneven wear, splitting, or oil contamination. Pay particular attention to the roots of the teeth. Renew it if there is the slightest doubt about its condition. If the engine is undergoing an overhaul, renew the belt as a matter of course, regardless of its apparent condition. The cost of a new belt is nothing compared with the cost of repairs, should the belt break in service. If signs of oil contamination are found, trace the source of the oil leak and rectify it. Wash down the engine timing belt area and all related components, to remove all traces of oil.

Refitting

9 Before refitting, thoroughly clean the timing belt sprockets. Check that the tensioner and idler pulleys rotate freely, without any sign of roughness. If necessary, renew them as described in Section 5.

10 Ensure that the crankshaft, camshaft and injection pump sprockets are still at their TDC positions as described in Section 2.

11 Engage the timing belt with the crankshaft sprocket, then locate it around the idler pulley and onto the injection pump sprocket making sure that it is kept taught. Continue to locate it around the camshaft sprocket and finally around the tensioner pulley **(see illustration)**. Ensure the belt teeth seat correctly on the sprockets.

4.11 Locating the timing belt around the tensioner pulley

4.12a Using two bolts and a screwdriver to tension the timing belt

4.12b Tightening the tensioner nut

Caution: Where applicable observe the direction of rotation markings on the belt.

12 Tension the timing belt by turning the eccentrically-mounted tensioner clockwise; two holes are provided in the side of the tensioner hub for this purpose - a pair of sturdy right-angled circlip pliers can be used to do this or alternatively two bolts and a long screwdriver may be used. Fiat use a special tensioner tool located in the holes - this consists of a calibrated rod and weight. The weight is positioned 60 mm along the rod to provide the correct tension to the belt, then the tensioner nut is tightened. Tighten the tensioner nut to the specified torque **(see illustrations)**.

13 If the tensioner tool is not available, test the tension by grasping the timing belt between the finger and thumb midway between the camshaft and injection pump pulleys, and twisting it through 90° (see paragraph 5).

5.2a Remove the nut . . .

Caution: The above procedure serves only as a rough guide to setting the belt tension. The tension must be checked accurately by a Fiat dealer using the special tensioner tool, at the earliest opportunity.

14 Turn the engine two complete turns clockwise, check that all the timing marks are still aligned then recheck the timing belt tension. If necessary carry out the tensioning procedure again.

15 Refit the components disturbed for access, using the reverse of the removal procedure and bearing in mind the following points:

a) Tighten all nuts and bolts to the specified torque, where given.

b) Refit the auxiliary drivebelt(s) as described in Chapter 1B.

5 Timing belt tensioner and sprockets - removal, inspection and refitting

Timing belt tensioner

Removal

1 Follow the procedure for removing the timing belt in Section 4, however it is not necessary to completely remove the belt from the timing sprockets provided it is kept fully engaged with them.

2 Unscrew the nut and slide the tensioner off the mounting stud **(see illustrations)**.

Inspection

3 Wipe the tensioner clean but do not use solvents that may contaminate the bearings. Spin the tensioner pulley on its hub by hand. Stiff movement or excessive freeplay is an indication of severe wear; the tensioner is not a serviceable component, and should be renewed.

Refitting

4 Slide the tensioner pulley over the mounting stud and screw on the nut.

5 Refer to Section 4 and refit the timing belt.

Timing belt idler pulley

Removal

6 Remove the timing belt as described in Section 4.

7 Unscrew the mounting bolt and remove the idler pulley from the front of the cylinder block **(see illustration)**.

Inspection

8 Wipe the idler clean but do not use solvents that may contaminate the bearings. Spin the idler pulley on its hub by hand. Stiff movement or excessive freeplay is an indication of severe wear; the idler is not a serviceable component, and should be renewed.

Refitting

9 Refit the idler to the front of the block and tighten the bolt to the specified torque **(see illustration)**.

10 Refer to Section 4 and refit the timing belt.

5.2b . . . followed by the timing belt tensioner pulley

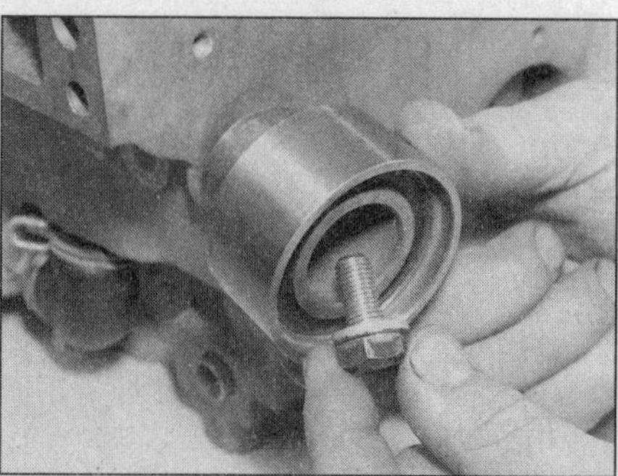

5.7 Removing the idler pulley

5.9 Tightening the idler pulley mounting bolt

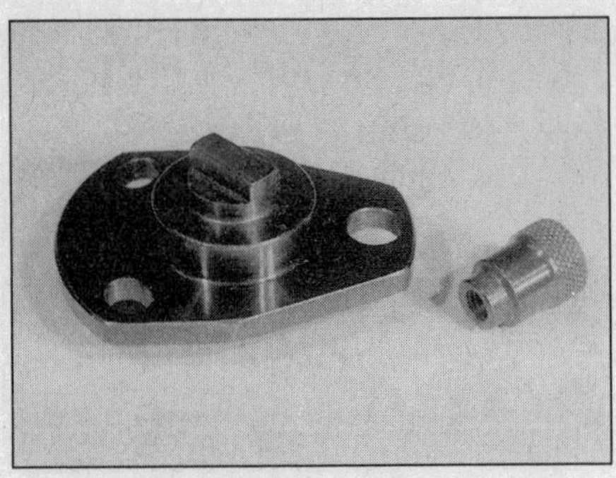

5.11 Special Fiat tool necessary to accurately position the camshaft before fitting the sprocket

Camshaft sprocket

Removal

11 Remove the timing belt as described in Section 4. A special Fiat tool **(see illustration)** is necessary to position the camshaft before refitting the sprocket, however if the original camshaft is being re-used, use of the special tool can be avoided by accurately marking the camshaft position before removing the sprocket.

Caution: On later 1996 models the camshaft sprocket can be moved in either direction on the camshaft location dowel.

12 The camshaft sprocket must now be held stationary whilst the retaining bolt is loosened. This is no problem on later models where the sprocket incorporates holes, however some early models have a sprocket without holes - on this type Fiat technicians use a special tool which clamps on the sprocket teeth. If this tool is not available, it may be possible to make up a similar tool. On later models a sprocket holding tool can easily be made **(see Tool Tip)**.

To make a camshaft sprocket holding tool, obtain two lengths of steel strip about 6 mm thick by 30 mm wide or similar, one 600 mm long, the other 200 mm long (all dimensions approximate). Bolt the two strips together to form a forked end, leaving the bolt slack so that the shorter strip can pivot freely. At the end of each 'prong' of the fork, secure a bolt with a nut and a locknut, to act as the fulcrums; these will engage with the cut-outs in the sprocket, and should protrude by about 30 mm

13 On 1996-on models mark the position of the camshaft in relation to the cylinder head. This is best achieved by removing the vacuum pump from the flywheel end of the head and marking the head in relation to the drive slot in the end of the camshaft. Note the location of the hose and bracket when removing the vacuum pump **(see illustration)**.

14 Unscrew and remove the bolt and washer and withdraw the sprocket from the end of the camshaft **(see illustrations)**. Note the location peg on the camshaft.

Inspection

15 With the sprocket removed, examine the camshaft oil seal for signs of leaking. If necessary, refer to Section 7 and renew it.

16 Check the sprocket teeth for damage.

17 Wipe clean the sprocket and camshaft mating surfaces.

Refitting

18 Locate the sprocket on the end of the camshaft. On 1996-on models check that the camshaft is positioned accurately to the previously made marks and also make sure that the TDC mark on the sprocket is aligned with the mark on the inner timing cover. If available use the special Fiat tool to locate the camshaft correctly. Refit the bolt and washer and tighten to the specified torque while holding the camshaft sprocket stationary using the method described previously. Recheck all alignment marks.

19 Refit the timing belt as described in Section 4.

Crankshaft sprocket

Caution: The crankshaft sprocket retaining bolt has a left-hand thread.

Removal

20 Remove the timing belt as described in Section 4.

21 Working beneath the engine unbolt and remove the flywheel lower cover, then hold the flywheel stationary preferably using a tool which engages the flywheel starter ring gear (see Section 10). Alternatively have an assistant engage a wide-bladed screwdriver with the starter ring gear

22 Unscrew and remove the crankshaft sprocket retaining bolt (left-hand thread), washer and spacer and slide the sprocket off the end of the crankshaft **(see illustrations)**. It is quite tight and it will be necessary to use a

5.13 Note the location of the hose and bracket when removing the vacuum pump

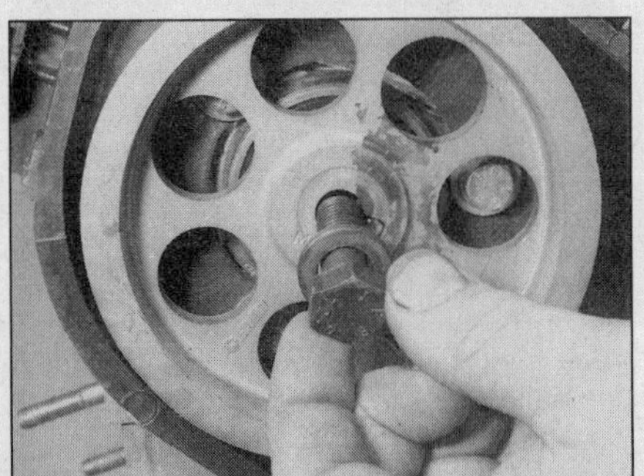

5.14a Unscrew and remove the bolt and washer . . .

5.14b . . . and remove the sprocket from the end of the camshaft

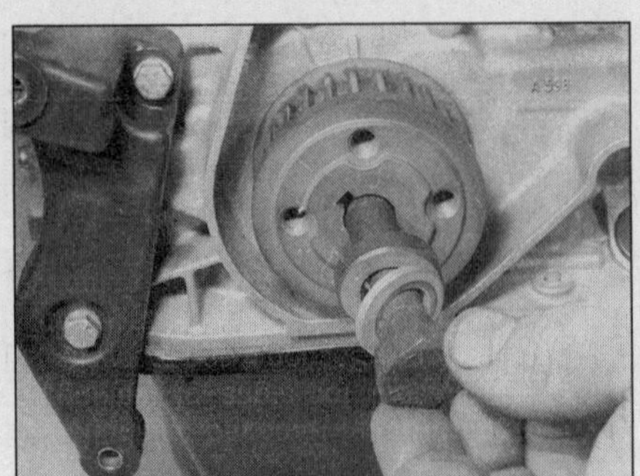

5.22a Unscrew and remove the bolt, washer and spacer . . .

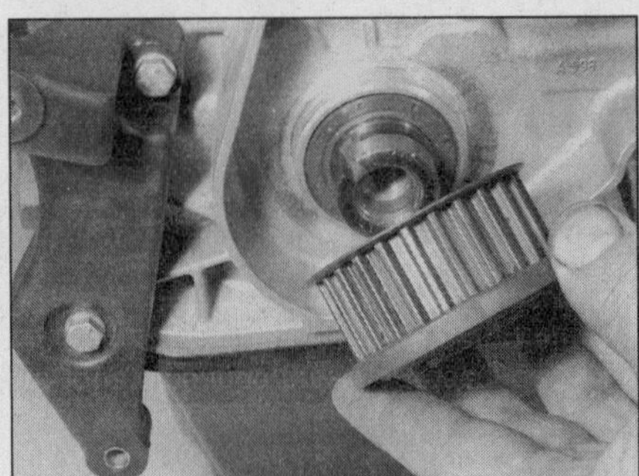

5.22b . . . and remove the crankshaft sprocket

5.30 Unscrewing the retaining nut for the injection pump sprocket

5.31a Use a puller to release the sprocket from the injection pump shaft

5.31b Remove the injection pump sprocket . . .

5.31c . . . followed by the Woodruff key

5.35 Tightening the injection pump sprocket bolt

rocking motion to remove it. Note that the sprocket is located by an integral key.

Inspection

23 With the sprocket removed, examine the crankshaft oil seal for signs of leaking. If necessary, refer to Section 8 and renew it.

24 Check the sprocket teeth for damage. Also check the key and if necessary renew it.

25 Wipe clean the sprocket and crankshaft mating surfaces.

Refitting

26 Slide the sprocket onto the crankshaft and engage the key with the slot in the crankshaft.

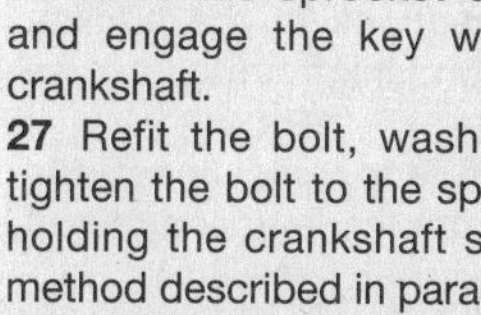

27 Refit the bolt, washer and spacer and tighten the bolt to the specified torque while holding the crankshaft stationary using the method described in paragraph 21.

28 Refit the timing belt as described in Section 4.

Injection pump sprocket

Removal

29 Remove the timing belt as described in Section 4.

30 Using a suitable tool hold the injection pump sprocket stationary, then unscrew the nut securing the sprocket to the injection pump shaft **(see illustration)**.

31 Using a suitable puller remove the sprocket from the end of the injection pump shaft and recover the Woodruff key from the groove **(see illustrations)**.

Inspection

32 With the sprocket removed, check the sprocket teeth for damage. Also check the key and if necessary renew it.

33 Wipe clean the sprocket and injection pump shaft.

Refitting

34 Locate the key in the groove making sure that it is fully inserted and parallel with the shaft surface.

35 Refit the sprocket onto the injection pump shaft then refit the bolt and washer and tighten the bolt to the specified torque while holding the sprocket stationary **(see illustration)**.

36 Refit the timing belt as described in Section 4.

6 Camshaft cover - removal and refitting

Removal

1 Remove the air ducting from the camshaft cover as described in Chapter 4C, Section 2.

2 Unclip the coolant hoses from the camshaft cover and tie them out of the way.

2C

3 Note the position of the support brackets then progressively unscrew the mounting bolts from the top of the camshaft cover and lift off the cover **(see illustrations)**. If it sticks, do not attempt to lever it off - instead free it by working around the cover and tapping it lightly with a soft-faced mallet.

4 Recover the camshaft cover gasket. Inspect the gasket carefully, and renew it if damage or deterioration is evident **(see illustration)**.

5 Clean the mating surfaces of the cylinder head and camshaft cover thoroughly, removing all traces of oil and old gasket - take care to avoid damaging the surfaces as you do this.

6.3a Support bracket positions on the camshaft cover

6.3b Removing the camshaft cover . . .

6.4 . . . and gasket

Refitting

6 Locate a new gasket on the cylinder head and make sure it is correctly seated.

7 Lower the cover onto the gasket making sure the gasket is not displaced.

8 Insert the mounting bolts and tighten them securely in a progressive sequence. Position the support brackets as noted during removal.

9 Clip the coolant hoses in position then refit the air ducting.

7 Camshaft oil seal - renewal

1 Remove the timing belt and camshaft sprocket as described in Sections 4 and 5.

2 Using a suitable hooked instrument, remove the oil seal from the cylinder head taking care not to damage the surface of the camshaft. Alternatively drill a small hole in the oil seal and insert a self-tapping screw - the seal can then be removed by pulling on the screw with a pair of pliers.

3 Clean the seating in the cylinder head and the end of the camshaft. To prevent damage to the new oil seal as it is being fitted, wrap some adhesive tape around the end of the camshaft and lightly oil it.

4 Dip the new oil seal in oil then locate it over the camshaft making sure that the sealing lips are facing inwards.

5 Using a suitable tubular drift, drive the oil seal squarely into the cylinder head. Remove the adhesive tape.

6 Refit the camshaft sprocket and timing belt with reference to Sections 5 and 4.

8 Crankshaft oil seals - renewal

Front (right-hand side) oil seal

1 The front oil seal is located in the oil pump casing on the front of the crankshaft. Remove the timing belt as described in Section 4 and the crankshaft sprocket as described in Section 5.

2 Using a suitable hooked instrument, remove the oil seal from the oil pump casing taking care not to damage the surface of the crankshaft. Alternatively drill a small hole in the oil seal and insert a self-tapping screw - the seal can then be removed by pulling on the screw with a pair of pliers.

3 Clean the seating in the oil pump and the surface of the crankshaft. To prevent damage to the new oil seal as it is being fitted, wrap some adhesive tape around the end of the crankshaft and lightly oil it.

4 Dip the new oil seal in oil then offer it up to the oil pump casing making sure that the sealing lips are facing inwards.

8.8a Rear oil seal and housing

5 Using a suitable tubular drift, drive the oil seal squarely into the casing. Remove the adhesive tape.

6 Refit the crankshaft sprocket and timing belt with reference to Sections 5 and 4.

Rear (left-hand side) oil seal

Note: *The following paragraphs describe renewal of the rear oil seal leaving the housing in position. The alternative method is to remove the housing and renew the oil seal on the bench, however there is then the possibility of damaging the sump gasket. Refer to Chapter 2D for details of removing the rear oil seal housing.*

7 Remove the flywheel as described in Section 10.

8 Using a suitable hooked instrument, remove the oil seal from the rear oil seal housing taking care not to damage the surface of the crankshaft. Alternatively drill a small hole in the oil seal and insert a self-tapping screw - the seal can then be removed by pulling on the screw with a pair of pliers **(see illustrations)**.

9 Clean the seating in the housing and the surface of the crankshaft. Check the crankshaft for burrs which may damage the oil seal lip of the new seal, and if necessary use a fine file to remove them.

10 Dip the new seal in clean engine oil and carefully locate it over the crankshaft rear flange making sure that it the correct way round.

11 Progressively tap the oil seal into the housing keeping it square to prevent distortion. A block of wood is useful for this purpose.

12 Refit the flywheel with reference to Section 10.

8.8b Using a self-tapping screw and pliers to remove the rear oil seal

9 Cylinder head - removal and refitting

Removal

Note: *The cylinder head bolts are of special splined design and a Fiat tool should be obtained to unscrew them. A Torx key will not fit however in practise it was found that a close-fitting Allen key could be used as an alternative.*

1 Disconnect the battery negative terminal (refer to *Disconnecting the battery* in the Reference Section of this manual).

2 Remove the battery as described in Chapter 5A.

3 Refer to Chapter 1B and carry out the following:

a) Drain the engine oil.

b) Drain the cooling system.

4 Remove the timing belt as described in Section 4.

5 Unbolt and remove the relay guard and bracket from the left-hand side of the engine.

6 Unbolt and remove the battery mounting tray and disconnect the wiring and lines from the modulator valve and relays.

7 Remove the air cleaner assembly and air duct with reference to Chapter 4C.

8 Loosen the clip and disconnect the vacuum hose from the vacuum pump on the left-hand end of the cylinder head.

9 Loosen the clips and disconnect the radiator top hose from the cylinder head outlet. Also disconnect the heater inlet hose from the thermostat housing.

10 Loosen the clips and disconnect the expansion tank and heater outlet hoses.

11 Identify all wiring connectors then disconnect them from the cylinder head.

12 Unscrew the expansion tank mounting screws, then disconnect the expansion tank hoses at their connections to the engine. Remove the expansion tank from the engine compartment.

13 Release the clip and disconnect the crankcase breather from the left-hand rear of the cylinder head.

14 Unbolt the power steering pump upper cover bracket then unscrew the pivot and adjustment bolts while leaving the fluid hoses still attached. Release the drivebelt (if still in place) then tie the pump to the bulkhead.

15 Loosen the clips and disconnect the short coolant hose from the cylinder head outlet to the coolant pump **(see illustration)**.

16 At the rear of the engine, unbolt and disconnect the oil delivery pipe from the turbocharger (where applicable) and crankcase **(see illustrations)**.

17 Disconnect the return hose from the thermostat housing to the coolant pump **(see illustration)**.

18 Unbolt the metal coolant return pipe and pull it out from the coolant pump inlet elbow **(see illustrations)**.

9.15 Short coolant hose from the cylinder head outlet to the coolant pump

9.16a Disconnecting the oil delivery pipe from the turbocharger

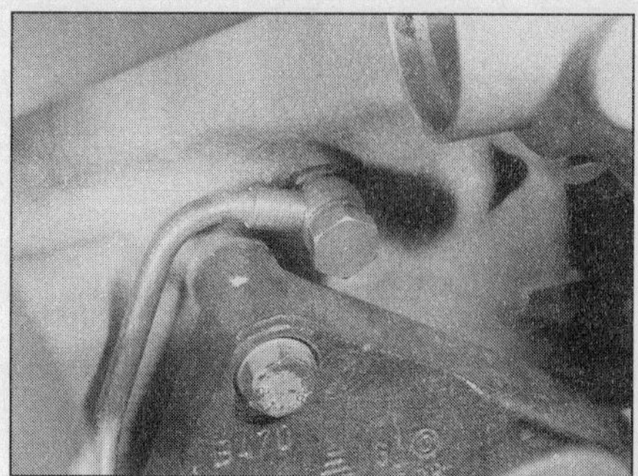

9.16b Oil delivery pipe location on the crankcase

19 Where applicable, unscrew the bolts retaining the bracket to the turbocharger and the crankcase **(see illustration)**.

20 Unscrew the nut and slide the timing belt tensioner off its stud.

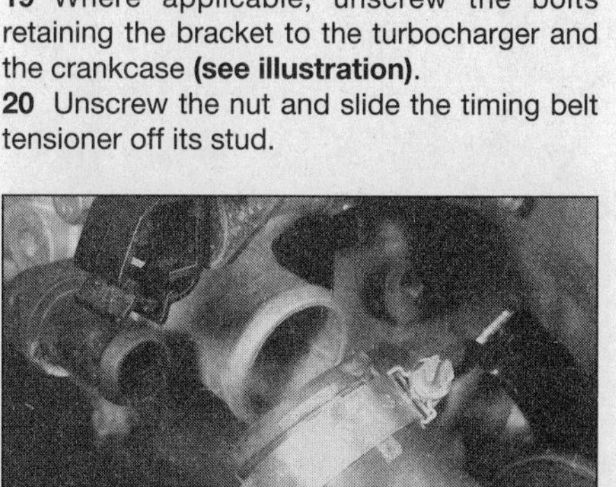

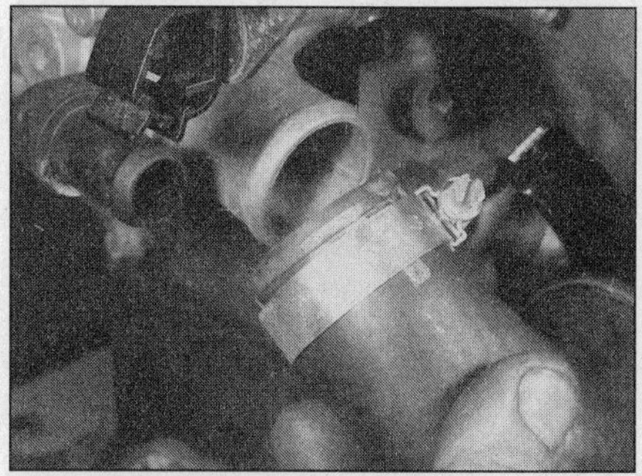

9.17 Disconnecting the return hose from the thermostat housing

21 Release the fuel supply and return hoses from the supports on the cylinder head.

22 Unscrew the union bolt and disconnect the fuel supply hose from the filter on the bulkhead.

23 Loosen the clip and disconnect the fuel return hose from the injection pump.

24 Unscrew the union nuts while holding insert flats, and disconnect the fuel supply lines from the injectors and injection pump **(see illustration)**. Cover the apertures to prevent dust entry.

25 Disconnect the glow plug supply wiring from the terminal on No 4 glow plug heater on the front left-hand side of the engine.

26 Disconnect the wiring from the maximum coolant temperature connector on the front of the engine.

27 Disconnect the fuel return line from No 1 injector.

28 Unscrew the nuts securing the exhaust front pipe to the exhaust manifold. Where necessary, use a screwdriver to bend back the lock tabs. Lower the front pipe and recover the gasket.

29 Where applicable, remove the clip and disconnect the oil return hose from the turbocharger to the sump.

30 Remove the camshaft sprocket as described in Section 5.

31 Unscrew the bolts securing the timing belt inner cover to the cylinder head and injection pump bracket, then remove the inner cover **(see illustrations)**.

32 Unbolt and remove the camshaft cover and recover the gasket. Note the location of the support brackets.

33 Unscrew and remove the bolts and washers located on the front of the cylinder head, alongside the injectors **(see illustration)**.

2C

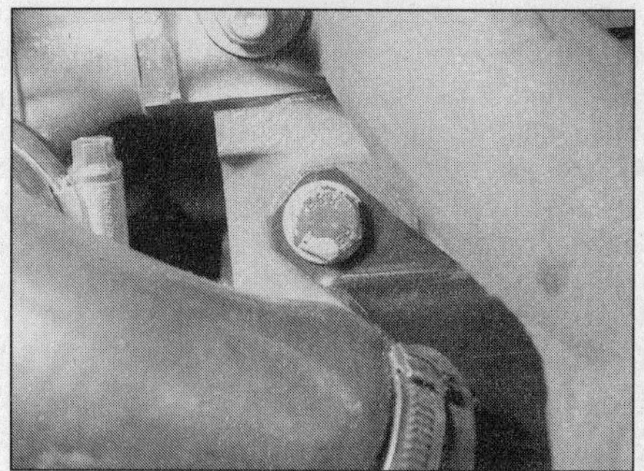

9.18a Metal coolant return pipe mounting bolt

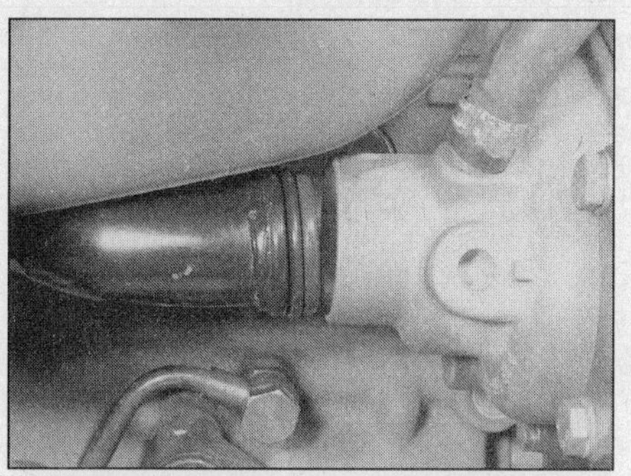

9.18b Removing the metal coolant return pipe from the coolant pump

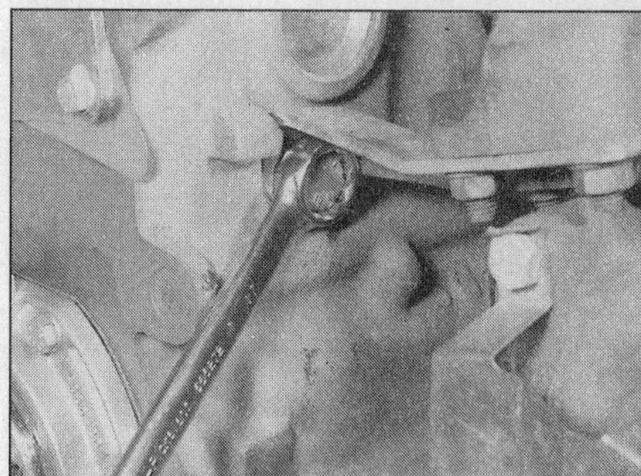

9.19 Unbolt the bracket retaining the turbocharger and manifold to the crankcase

9.24 Unscrewing the union nuts from the injection pump

9.31a Bolts securing the inner timing cover to the cylinder head

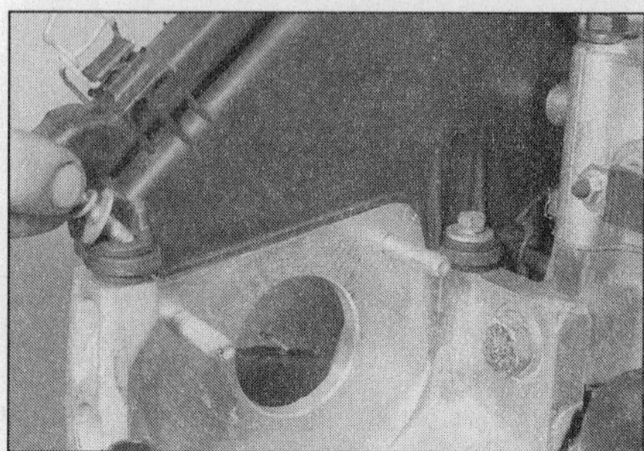

9.31b Removing the bolts securing the inner timing cover to the injection pump/oil filter bracket

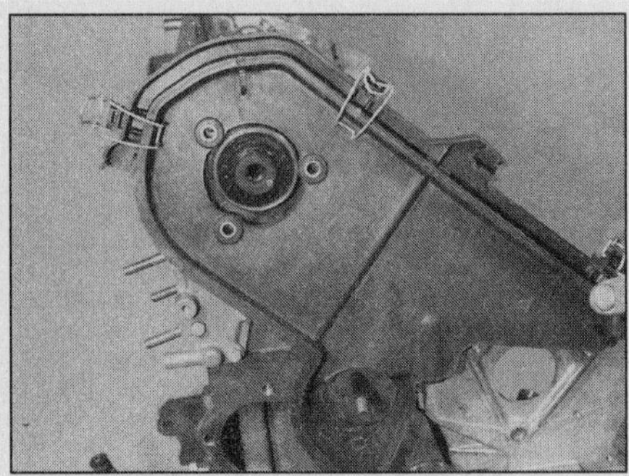

9.31c Removing the inner timing cover

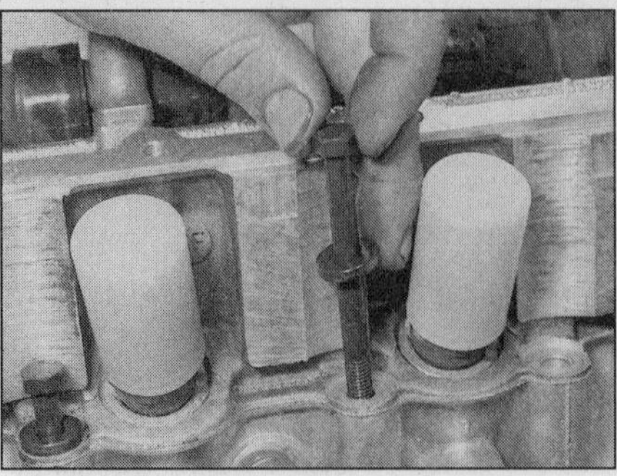

9.33 Removing one of the bolts at the front of the cylinder head

9.34a Unscrewing the cylinder head bolts

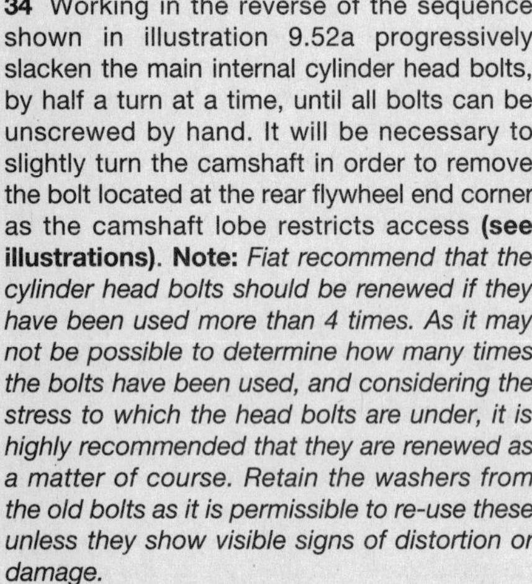

34 Working in the reverse of the sequence shown in illustration 9.52a progressively slacken the main internal cylinder head bolts, by half a turn at a time, until all bolts can be unscrewed by hand. It will be necessary to slightly turn the camshaft in order to remove the bolt located at the rear flywheel end corner as the camshaft lobe restricts access **(see illustrations)**. **Note:** *Fiat recommend that the cylinder head bolts should be renewed if they have been used more than 4 times. As it may not be possible to determine how many times the bolts have been used, and considering the stress to which the head bolts are under, it is highly recommended that they are renewed as a matter of course. Retain the washers from the old bolts as it is permissible to re-use these unless they show visible signs of distortion or damage.*

35 Check that nothing remains connected to the cylinder head, then lift the head away from the cylinder block **(see illustration)**; seek assistance if possible, as it is a heavy assembly, especially as it is being removed complete with the manifolds and turbocharger. If preferred remove the manifolds first.

36 With the cylinder head on a work surface, unscrew the nuts securing the inlet and exhaust manifolds and withdraw them from the studs together with the turbocharger, where applicable.

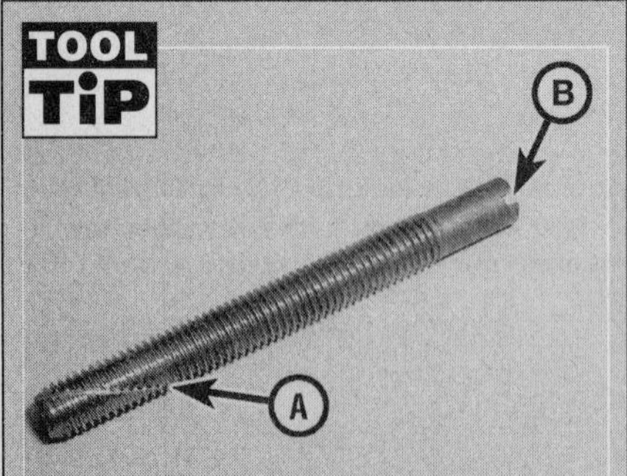

If a tap is not available, make a home-made substitute by cutting a slot (A) down the threads of one of the old cylinder head bolts. After use, the bolt head can be cut off, and the shank can then be used as an alignment dowel to assist cylinder head refitting. Cut a screwdriver slot (B) in the top of the bolt, to allow it to be unscrewed

9.34b Turn the camshaft slightly to remove the rear flywheel end corner bolt

9.35 Lifting the cylinder head off of the block - note the protectors fitted to the injectors

37 Recover the gasket from the studs.

38 If the cylinder head is to be dismantled for overhaul refer to Chapter 2D.

Preparation for refitting

39 The mating surfaces of the cylinder head and cylinder block/crankcase must be perfectly clean before refitting the head. Use a hard plastic or wood scraper to remove all traces of gasket and carbon; also clean the piston crowns. Take particular care during the cleaning operations, as aluminium alloy is easily damaged. Also, make sure that the carbon is not allowed to enter the oil and water passages - this is particularly important for the lubrication system, as carbon could block the oil supply to the engine's components. Using adhesive tape and paper, seal the water, oil and bolt holes in the cylinder block/crankcase.

9.42 Checking the piston protrusion with a dial gauge

40 Check the mating surfaces of the cylinder block and cylinder head for nicks, deep scratches and other damage. If slight, they may be removed carefully with abrasive paper.

41 Clean out the cylinder head bolt drillings using a suitable tap. If a tap is not available, make a home-made substitute **(see Tool Tip)**.

42 Before refitting the cylinder head the correct new gasket must be selected, although unless new pistons have been fitted the new cylinder head gasket will be the same thickness as the old one. The following procedure will verify the correct thickness required. Using a dial gauge positioned on the cylinder block, check the protrusion of each piston by turning the crankshaft until the relevant piston is at TDC **(see illustration)**. Make a note of the protrusion for each cylinder then add them up and divide by 4 to give a mean average protrusion. Using the following table select the correct gasket - the notches are located on the front right-hand end of the gasket.

Average piston protrusion	Gasket thickness	Number of notches
– 0.03 to – 0.1 mm	1.65 mm	-
0.1 to 0.3 mm	1.80 mm	1
0.3 to 0.43 mm	1.95 mm	2

Caution: The cylinder head gasket is made of special material which hardens while the engine is running. Keep the gasket sealed in its plastic bag until just before fitting.

9.46a The locating dowel in the cylinder block

9.46b Locating the cylinder head gasket on the block

9.46c The word ALTO must be uppermost

43 It is possible for the piston crowns to strike and damage the valve heads, if the camshaft is rotated with the timing belt removed and the crankshaft set to TDC. For this reason, the crankshaft must be set to a position other than TDC on No 1 cylinder before the cylinder head is refitted. Use a socket on the crankshaft pulley centre bolt to turn the crankshaft in its normal direction of rotation, until all four pistons are positioned halfway down their bores, with No 1 piston on its upstroke - approximately 90° before TDC.

Refitting

44 If the manifolds are being refitted before refitting the cylinder head proceed as follows, otherwise fit the manifolds later when the head is refitted. Ensure that the inlet and exhaust manifold mating surfaces are completely clean, then locate the new gasket on the studs.

45 Locate the inlet and exhaust manifolds together with the turbocharger, where applicable, on the studs. Refit the nuts and washers and tighten to the specified torque.

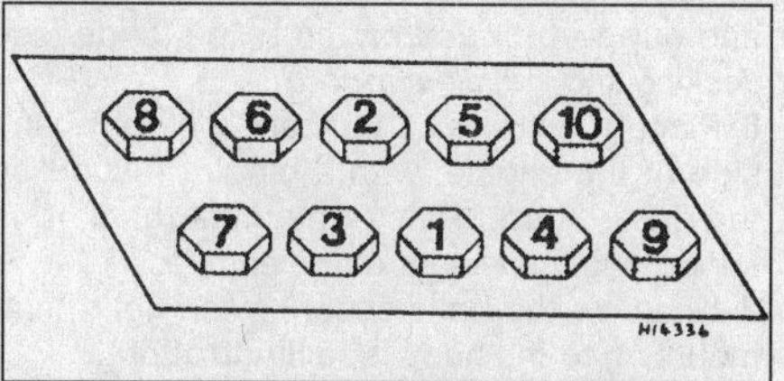

9.52a Cylinder head bolt tightening sequence

46 Lay the new head gasket on the cylinder block engaging it with the locating dowel. The word ALTO must be uppermost **(see illustrations)**.

47 As a means of locating the cylinder head accurately, cut the heads from two of the old cylinder head bolts. Cut a slot, big enough for a screwdriver blade, in the end of each bolt. These can be used as alignment dowels to assist in cylinder head refitting, however if the head is being refitted without the manifolds it is not necessary to take this action.

48 With the help of an assistant, place the cylinder head assembly centrally on the cylinder block ensuring that the locating dowels engage with the holes in the cylinder head. Check that the head gasket is correctly seated before allowing the full weight of the cylinder head to rest on it.

49 Where necessary, unscrew the home-made alignment dowels, using a flat bladed screwdriver.

50 The cylinder head bolt threads must be clean. Dip the bolts in engine oil, and allow them to drain for thirty minutes.

51 Carefully enter each bolt with washer into its relevant hole (*do not drop them in)* and screw in, by hand only, until finger-tight.

52 Working progressively and in the sequence shown, first tighten the cylinder head bolts to their Stage 1 torque setting, using a torque wrench and suitable socket **(see illustrations)**. Go round again, in the sequence shown, and tighten the bolts to the Stage 2 torque setting.

53 Once all the bolts have been tightened to their Stage 2 setting, working again in the given sequence, angle-tighten the bolts through the specified Stage 3 angle, using a socket and extension bar **(see illustration)**. It is recommended that an angle-measuring gauge is used during this stage of the tightening, to ensure accuracy. If a gauge is not available, use white paint to make alignment marks between the bolt head and cylinder head prior to tightening; the marks can then be used to check the bolt has been rotated through the correct angle during tightening. Repeat for the Stage 4 setting.

54 Refit the cylinder head front retaining bolts and tighten to the specified torque.

55 Refit the camshaft cover together with a new gasket and tighten the bolts progressively to the specified torque.

56 The remaining procedure is a reversal of the removal procedure noting the following points.

a) Tighten all nut and bolts to the specified torque where given.

*b) When refitting the metal coolant pipe to the coolant pump, use a new O-ring **(see illustration)**.*

c) Refit the timing belt with reference to Section 4.

d) Use a new exhaust front pipe gasket.

e) Refit the auxiliary drivebelt(s) as described in Chapter 1B.

f) Refer to Chapter 4C when refitting the air cleaner and air duct.

g) Refill the cooling system and fill the engine with new oil with reference to Chapter 1B.

57 Refer to Chapter 2D when starting the engine for the first time.

2C

9.52b Tighten the cylinder head bolts to the Stage 1 and Stage 2 settings using a torque wrench

9.53 Angle-tightening the cylinder head bolts to the Stage 3 and Stage 4 settings

9.56 Use a new O-ring on the coolant pipe before refitting it to the pump

10.2 Locking the flywheel using a home-made tool

10.3a Unscrew the flywheel bolts . . .

10.3b . . . and remove the spacer plate

10 Flywheel - removal, inspection and refitting

Removal

1 Remove the transmission and clutch as described in Chapter 7A and 6.

2 Lock the flywheel in position using a home-made locking tool, fabricated from a piece of scrap metal. Bolt it to one of the transmission bellhousing mounting holes **(see illustration)**. Mark the position of the flywheel with respect to the crankshaft using a dab of paint. Note that although there is only one location dowel on the flywheel, there are two holes in the end of the crankshaft and it is therefore possible to locate the flywheel 180° out resulting in the timing mark being in the incorrect position.

3 Unscrew and remove the flywheel mounting bolts then lift off the flywheel. Recover the spacer plate **(see illustrations)**. Discard the flywheel retaining bolts; new ones must be used on refitting.

Inspection

4 If the flywheel's clutch mating surface is deeply scored, cracked or otherwise damaged, the flywheel must be renewed. However, it may be possible to have it surface-ground; seek the advice of a Fiat dealer or engine reconditioning specialist.

5 If the ring gear is badly worn or has missing teeth, the flywheel must be renewed.

Refitting

6 Clean the mating surfaces of the flywheel and crankshaft. Remove any remaining locking compound from the threads of the crankshaft holes, using the correct-size tap, if available.

If a suitable tap is not available, cut two slots down the threads of one of the old flywheel bolts with a hacksaw, and use the bolt to remove the locking compound form the threads.

7 If the new flywheel retaining bolts are not supplied with their threads already pre-coated, apply a suitable thread-locking compound to the threads of each bolt.

10.8a Location dowel on the flywheel

10.8b Inserting the flywheel bolts

8 Offer up the flywheel to the crankshaft, using the alignment marks made during removal, and fit the new retaining bolts together with the spacer plate **(see illustrations)**.

9 Lock the flywheel using the method employed on dismantling, and tighten the retaining bolts to the specified torque.

10 Refit the clutch as described in Chapter 6. Remove the locking tool and refit the transmission as described in Chapter 7A.

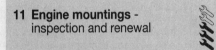

11 Engine mountings - inspection and renewal

Inspection

1 Firmly apply the handbrake, then jack up the front of the car and support it securely on axle stands (see *Jacking and vehicle support*).

2 Check the mounting rubbers to see if they are cracked, hardened or separated from the metal at any point; renew the mounting if any such damage or deterioration is evident.

3 Check that all the mounting's fasteners are securely tightened.

4 Using a large screwdriver or a crowbar, check for wear in the mounting by carefully levering against it to check for free play. Where this is not possible enlist the aid of an assistant to move the engine/transmission back and forth, or from side to side, while you watch the mounting. While some free play is to be expected even from new components, excessive wear should be obvious. If excessive free play is found, check first that the fasteners are correctly secured, then renew any worn components as described below.

Renewal

Right-hand mounting

5 If not already done, firmly apply the handbrake, then jack up the front of the car and support it securely on axle stands (see *Jacking and vehicle support*).

6 Place a trolley jack beneath the right-hand side of the engine, with a block of wood on the jack head. Raise the jack until it is supporting the weight of the engine.

7 Unscrew the bolts securing the right-hand mounting to the body **(see illustration)**.

8 Unscrew the special long nut securing the mounting to the engine and recover the washers.

11.7 Right-hand engine mounting viewed from below

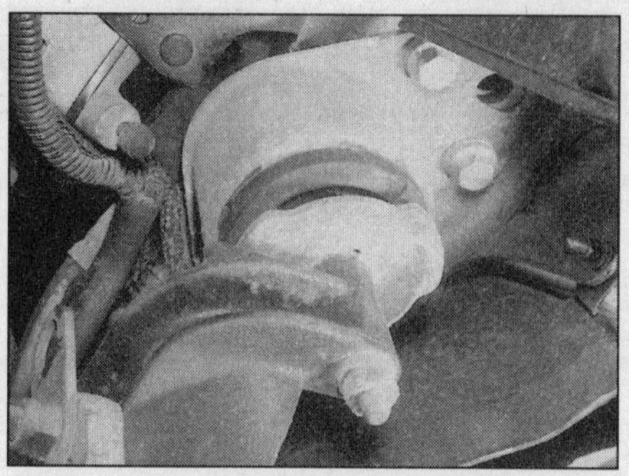
11.15 Left-hand engine mounting viewed from below

11.22 Rear engine mounting viewed from below

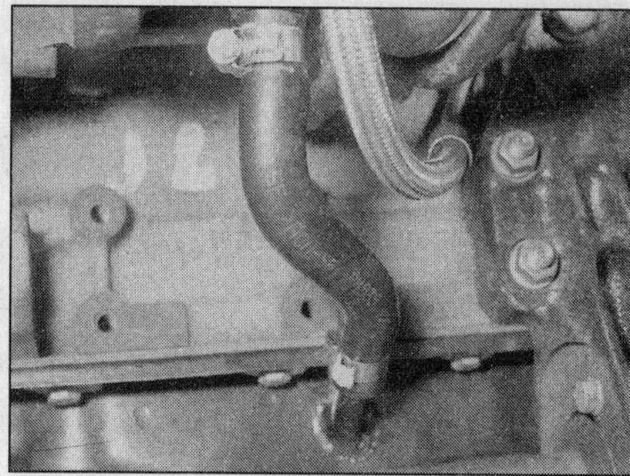
12.4 Turbocharger-to-sump oil drain hose

9 Lower the engine sufficiently to remove the mounting from the engine bracket.
10 Locate the new mounting in the engine bracket, refit the nut and washers and tighten securely.
11 Raise the engine and refit and tighten the mounting-to-body bolts.
12 Remove the trolley jack and lower the vehicle to the ground.

Left-hand mounting

13 If not already done, firmly apply the handbrake, then jack up the front of the car and support it securely on axle stands (see *Jacking and vehicle support*).
14 Place a trolley jack beneath the transmission, with a block of wood on the jack head. Raise the jack until it is supporting the weight of the engine/transmission.
15 Unscrew the bolts securing the left-hand mounting to the body **(see illustration)**.
16 Unscrew the nut securing the mounting to the transmission bracket and recover the washers.
17 Lower the transmission sufficiently to remove the mounting from the transmission bracket.
18 Locate the new mounting in the transmission bracket, refit the nut and washers and tighten securely.
19 Raise the engine and refit and tighten the mounting-to-body bolts.
20 Remove the trolley jack and lower the vehicle to the ground.

Rear mounting

21 If not already done, firmly apply the handbrake, then jack up the front of the car and support it securely on axle stands (see *Jacking and vehicle support*).
22 Working beneath the vehicle, unscrew the bolts securing the rear engine mounting to the underbody **(see illustration)**.
23 Temporarily support the weight of the engine/transmission using a trolley jack.
24 Unbolt the rear mounting assembly from the transmission and withdraw from under the vehicle.
25 Unscrew the bolt and separate the bracket from the mounting.
26 Fitting the new mounting is a reversal of the removal procedure.

12 Sump - removal and refitting

Removal

1 Disconnect the battery negative terminal (refer to *Disconnecting the battery* in the Reference Section of this manual).
2 Firmly apply the handbrake, then jack up the front of the car and support it securely on axle stands (see *Jacking and vehicle support*).
3 Drain the engine oil as described in Chapter 1B. Where applicable, remove the screws and lower the engine undertray away from the vehicle.
4 On turbo models disconnect the turbocharger oil drain hose from the sump **(see illustration)**.
5 Working around the outside of the sump, progressively loosen and withdraw the sump retaining bolts.
6 Break the joint by striking the sump with the palm of your hand, then lower the sump and withdraw it from underneath the vehicle. Recover and discard the sump gasket.
7 While the sump is removed, take the opportunity to check the oil pump pick-up/strainer for signs of clogging. If necessary, clean or renew the strainer.

Refitting

8 Thoroughly clean the sump inside and out ensuring that all traces of gasket are removed from the mating surfaces of both the sump and the cylinder block/crankcase.
9 Ensure that the mating surfaces are clean and dry, then apply a little grease to the surface of the sump. This will retain the gasket in position while refitting the sump.
10 Lay the new sump gasket in position on the sump mating surface, then offer up the sump and refit the retaining bolts. Tighten the bolts evenly and progressively to the specified torque.
11 On turbo models reconnect the turbocharger oil drain hose.
12 Lower the vehicle to the ground then refer to Chapter 1B and refill the engine with the specified grade and quantity of oil.
13 Reconnect the battery negative terminal.

13 Oil pump and pick-up tube - removal, inspection and refitting

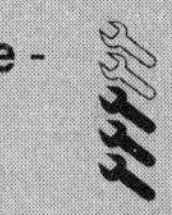

2C

Removal

1 The oil pump is mounted on the timing belt end of the cylinder block and is driven by flats on the crankshaft nose. Incorporated in the oil pump body is the crankshaft oil seal.
2 Remove the timing belt as described in Section 4, and the crankshaft sprocket as described in Section 5.
3 Remove the sump as described in Section 12.
4 Unscrew the bolts securing the pick-up tube to the bottom of the oil pump. Also unscrew the bolt securing the tube to the No 2 main bearing cap. Withdraw the tube from the oil pump and crankcase. Recover the gasket **(see illustrations)**.

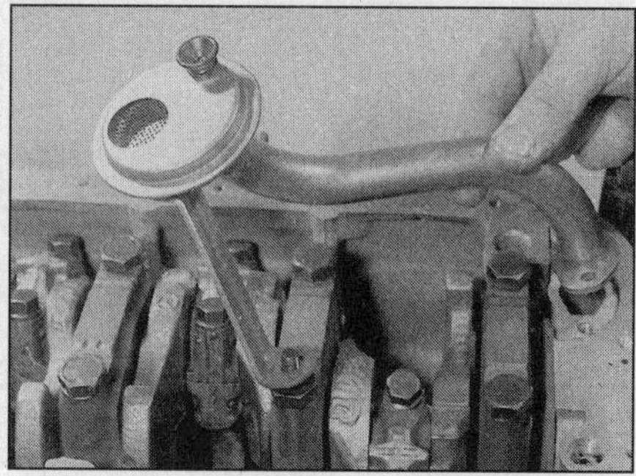
13.4a Removing the oil pump pick-up tube . . .

13.4b . . . and gasket

13.5 Note the location of the bracket on the oil pump

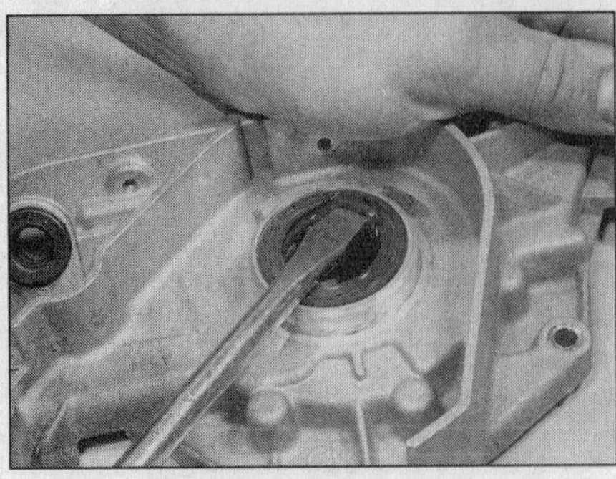
13.6 Prising the oil seal from the oil pump housing

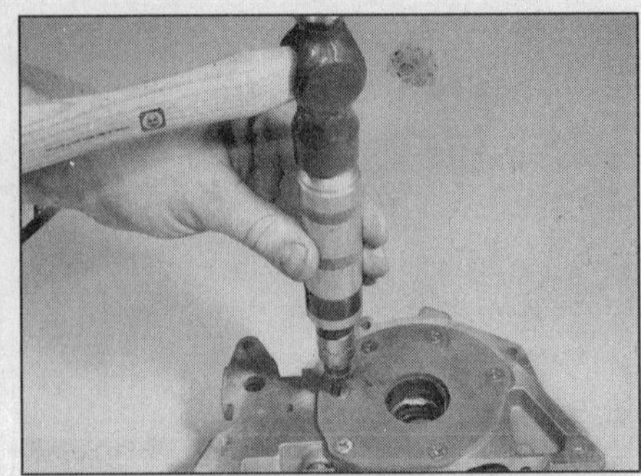
13.7 Using an impact driver to loosen the oil pump cover screws

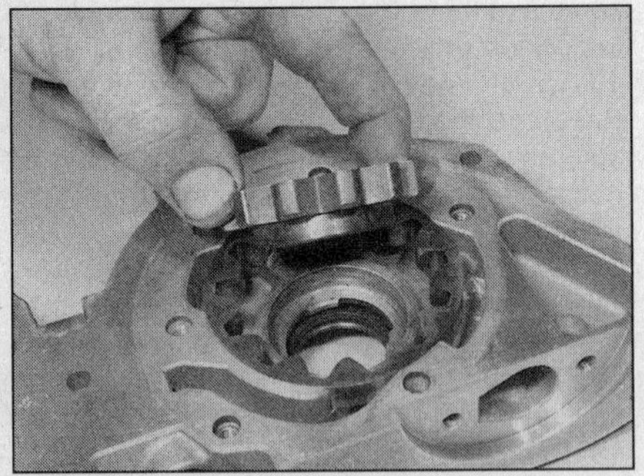
13.8a Removing the inner rotor . . .

13.8b . . . and outer rotor

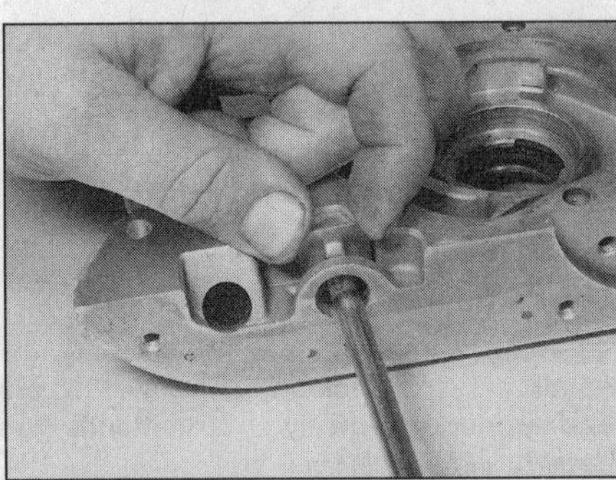
13.9a Depress the relief valve collar and remove the retaining plate . . .

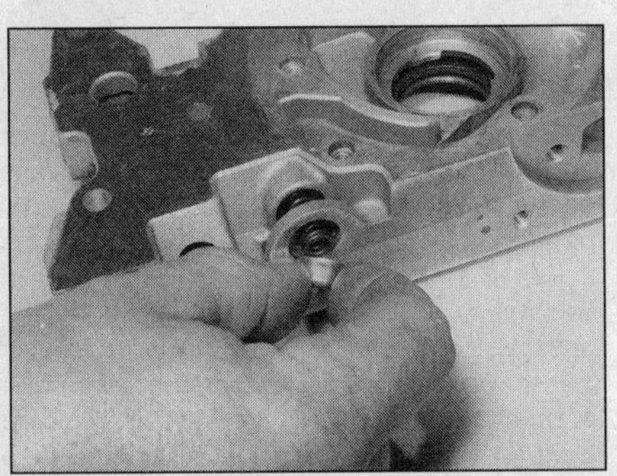
13.9b . . . then remove the seat . . .

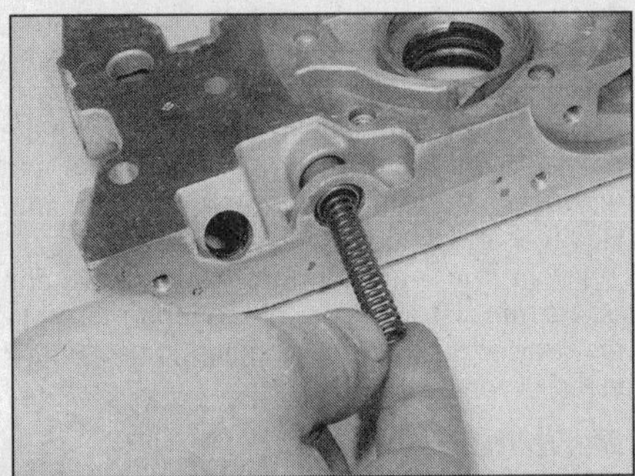
13.9c . . . spring . . .

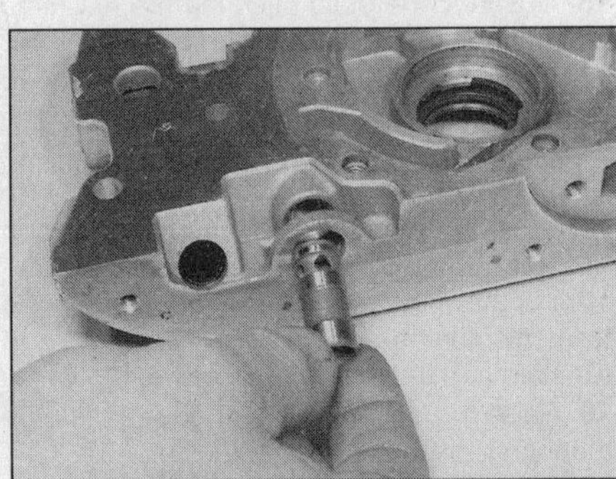
13.9d . . . and valve

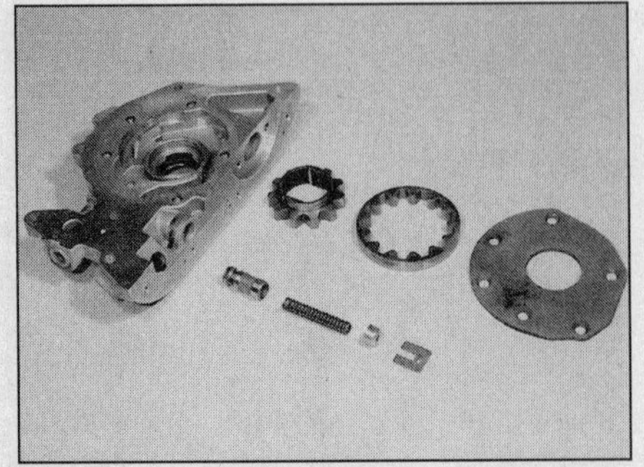
13.9e Oil pump housing and components

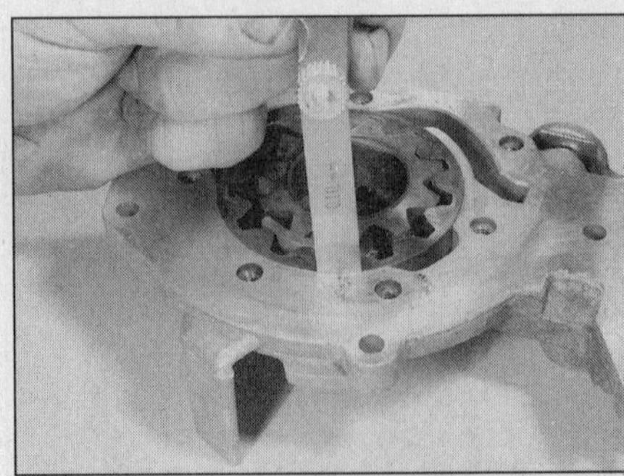
13.10a Checking the outer rotor-to-casing clearance

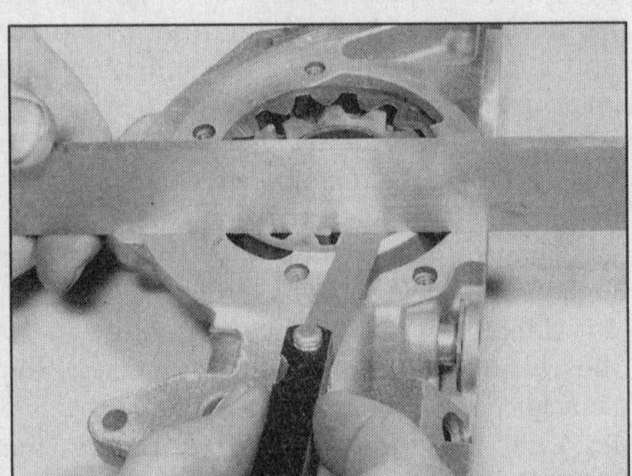
13.10b Checking the rotor endplay

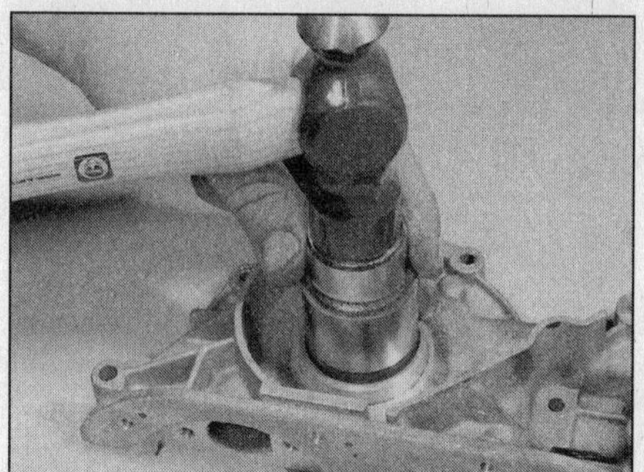
13.14 Fitting the new oil seal to the oil pump casing

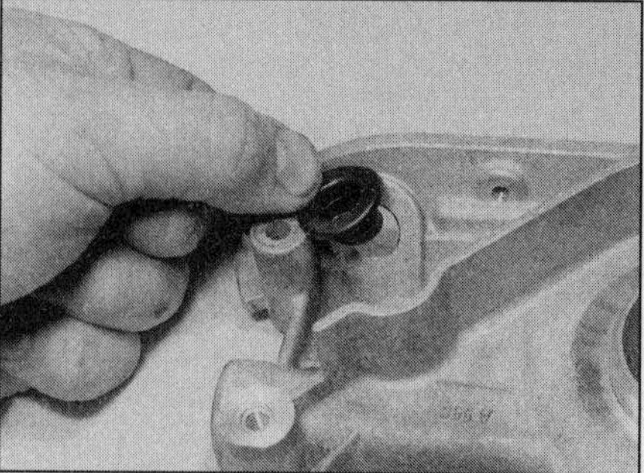
13.15 Engine oil dipstick rubber grommet in the oil pump casing

13.16 Positioning the oil pump gasket on the cylinder block

5 Unscrew the bolts securing the oil pump to the front of the cylinder block and withdraw it over the nose of the crankshaft. Note the location of the bracket **(see illustration)**. Recover the gasket.

Inspection

6 Prise the oil seal from the front of the oil pump using a screwdriver **(see illustration)**.
7 Unscrew the crosshead screws and lift off the cover. The screws are tight and are best loosened using an impact driver **(see illustration)**.
8 Lift out the two rotors keeping them identified for position in relation to each other **(see illustrations)**.
9 Depress the relief valve collar, then extract the retaining plate and withdraw the seat, spring and valve **(see illustrations)**.
10 Clean the pump thoroughly, and inspect the rotors for signs of damage or wear. Using a feeler blade, check the wear between the outer rotor and oil pump casing. Using the feeler blade and a straight-edge, check the endplay of the rotors. If the rotors are worn in excess of the specified amount given in Specifications, the oil pump should be renewed as a complete unit **(see illustrations)**.
11 Check the condition of the relief valve and seating - if worn excessively the pump must be renewed.
12 If the components are in good condition, reassemble the pump using a reversal of the dismantling procedure. Before fitting the cover the rotors should be oiled and the cavity between them filled with clean engine oil. Make sure the cover screws are fully tightened.
13 Thoroughly clean the mating surfaces of the oil pump and cylinder block.
14 Dip the new oil seal in engine oil then locate it on the front of the oil pump with the sealing lips facing inwards. Use a suitable tubular drift (or socket) to drive the seal into the oil pump casing **(see illustration)**.
15 Examine the dipstick tube rubber grommet in the oil pump and renew it if necessary **(see illustration)**.

Refitting

16 Smear a little engine oil on both sides of the new gasket then locate it on the cylinder block **(see illustration)**.
17 To prevent damage to the new oil seal as it is passed over the nose of the crankshaft, wrap some adhesive tape around it and lightly oil it.
18 Carefully locate the oil pump over the crankshaft taking care not to damage the oil seal then insert the bolts loosely. Remove the adhesive tape **(see illustration)**.
19 Using a straight-edge, position the oil pump so that the sump mating surface is level with the surface of the crankcase **(see illustration)**. With the pump correctly positioned, securely tighten the bolts in an even and progressive sequence.
20 Refit the oil pick-up tube together with a new gasket, and securely tighten the mounting bolts.
21 Refit the sump with reference to Section 12.
22 Refit the crankshaft sprocket with reference to Section 5 and the timing belt with reference to Section 4.
23 When starting the engine, let it idle until the oil pressure warning light goes out.

14 Oil cooler - removal and refitting

Removal

1 The oil cooler is located on the right-hand side of the engine compartment. First remove the front bumper as described in Chapter 11.
2 Unbolt the support bar for the radiator and oil cooler.
3 Support the oil cooler then unscrew the upper mounting bolt. Lower the cooler to the extent of the hoses.
4 Position a container beneath the cooler then unscrew the inlet and outlet union nuts and disconnect the hoses from the oil filter. Note the fitted positions of the hoses for correct refitting. Allow the oil to drain into the container.
5 Fully unscrew the union nuts and disconnect the hoses from the oil cooler.

Refitting

6 Refitting is a reversal of removal, but top-up the engine oil level as necessary. Run the engine and check for leaks.

13.18 Locating the oil pump over the end of the crankshaft

13.19 Checking that the oil pump and sump mating surfaces are correctly aligned with a straight-edge

Chapter 2 Part D:
Engine removal and overhaul procedures

Contents

Degrees of difficulty

Easy, suitable for novice with little experience 	**Fairly easy,** suitable for beginner with some experience 	**Fairly difficult,** suitable for competent DIY mechanic	**Difficult,** suitable for experienced DIY mechanic	**Very difficult,** suitable for expert DIY or professional 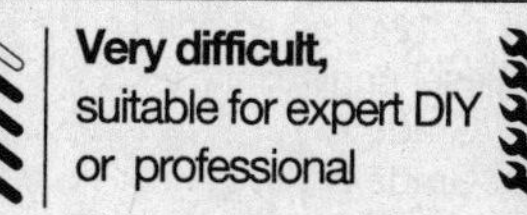

Specifications

Engine codes

See Chapter 2A, 2B or 2C.

Cylinder head

Camshaft bearing diameters:*	
Petrol engines:	
No 1 bearing	24.045 to 24.070 mm
No 2 bearing	23.545 to 23.570 mm
No 3 bearing	24.025 to 24.070 mm
Diesel engine:	
No 1 bearing (in right-hand side mount)	29.990 to 30.015 mm
No 2 bearing	25.545 to 25.570 mm
No 3 bearing	24.045 to 24.070 mm
No 4 bearing (in left-hand side mount)	23.990 to 24.015 mm
Valve seat angle	45° ± 5'
Cam follower (tappet) running clearance in head*	0.005 to 0.050 mm
Difference between swirl chamber and cylinder head surface (diesel engine only)	-0.765 to 0.055 mm

** Refer to Chapter 2B for camshaft and cam follower specifications on 1242 cc (16-valve) petrol engines.*

Valves

Valve stem diameter (inlet and exhaust):	
Petrol engines:	
1108 cc and 1242 cc (8-valve) engines	6.982 to 7.000 mm
1242 cc (16-valve) engine	5.974 to 5.992 mm
Diesel engine	7.974 to 7.992 mm
Valve face angle	45° 30' ± 5'
Valve stem-to-guide clearance:	
Petrol engines:	
1108 cc and 1242 cc (8-valve) engines	0.022 to 0.058 mm
1242 cc (16-valve) engine	0.030 to 0.066 mm
Diesel engine	0.030 to 0.066 mm
Cam follower (tappet) shim sizes	3.20 to 4.70 mm in increments of 0.05 mm

Camshaft

Camshaft bearing journal diameters:*	**Petrol engines**	**Diesel engine**
No 1 bearing	24.000 to 24.015 mm	29.945 to 29.960 mm
No 2 bearing	23.500 to 23.515 mm	25.500 to 25.515 mm
No 3 bearing	24.000 to 24.015 mm	24.000 to 24.015 mm
No 4 bearing	N/A	23.945 to 23.960 mm
Camshaft bearing running clearance*	0.030 to 0.070 mm	
Camshaft endfloat*	0.070 to 0.250 mm	

** Refer to Chapter 2B for camshaft specifications on 1242 cc (16-valve) engines.*

Cylinder block

Bore diameter:	
Petrol engines:	
1108 cc engine	70.000 to 70.030 mm
1242 cc engine	70.800 to 70.830 mm
Diesel engine	82.600 to 82.650 mm
Undersizes	Increments of 0.010 mm

Pistons and piston rings

Piston diameter:	
Petrol engines:	
Grade A:	
1108 cc engine	69.960 to 69.970 mm
1242 cc engine	70.760 to 70.770 mm
Grade B:	
1108 cc engine	69.970 to 69.980 mm
1242 cc engine	70.770 to 70.780 mm
Grade C:	
1108 cc engine	69.980 to 69.990 mm
1242 cc engine	70.780 to 70.790 mm
Diesel engine:	
Grade A	82.530 to 82.540 mm
Grade B	-
Grade C	82.550 to 82.560 mm
Grade E	82.570 to 82.580 mm
Piston projection above top of bore:	
Diesel engine	0.637 to 1.162 mm
Piston to bore clearance:	
Petrol engines	0.030 to 0.050 mm
Diesel engine	0.060 to 0.080 mm
Maximum difference in weight between pistons	± 5g
Gudgeon pin diameter	17.970 to 17.974 mm
Gudgeon pin-to-piston clearance:	
Petrol engines	0.008 to 0.016 mm
Diesel engine	0.003 to 0.009 mm
Piston ring-to-groove clearance:	
Petrol engines:	
Top compression ring:	
1108 cc engine	0.040 to 0.075 mm
1242 cc (8-valve) engine	0.040 to 0.080 mm
1242 cc (16-valve) engine	0 to 0.06 mm
2nd compression ring:	
1108 cc and 1242 cc (8-valve) engines	0.020 to 0.055 mm
1242 cc (16-valve) engine	0 to 0.055 mm
Oil scraper ring:	
1108 cc and 1242 cc (8-valve) engines	0.020 to 0.055 mm
1242 cc (16-valve) engine	0 to 0.055 mm
Diesel engine:	
Top compression ring	0.080 to 0.130 mm
2nd compression ring	0.020 to 0.052 mm
Oil scraper ring	0.030 to 0.065 mm
Piston ring end gap:	
Petrol engines:	
Top compression ring:	
1108 cc engine	0.25 to 0.45 mm
1242 cc engine	0.20 to 0.40 mm
2nd compression ring	0.25 to 0.45 mm
Oil scraper ring	0.20 to 0.45 mm
Diesel engine:	
Top compression ring	0.020 to 0.350 mm
2nd compression ring	0.300 to 0.500 mm
Oil scraper ring	0.250 to 0.500 mm

Connecting rods

Gudgeon pin-to-small end clearance:	
Petrol engines	Interference fit
Diesel engine	0.014 to 0.020 mm

Crankshaft

Main bearing journal diameters:	
Petrol engines:	
1108 cc engine:	
Grade 1	43.994 to 44.000 mm
Grade 2	43.988 to 43.994 mm
Grade 3	43.982 to 43.988 mm
1242 cc engine:	
Grade 1	47.994 to 48.000 mm
Grade 2	47.988 to 47.994 mm
Grade 3	47.982 to 47.988 mm
Diesel engine:	
Grade 1	52.995 to 53.004 mm
Grade 2	52.986 to 52.995 mm
Crankpin journal diameters:	
Petrol engines:	
1108 cc engine:	
Grade A	38.001 to 38.008 mm
Grade B	37.995 to 38.001 mm
Grade C	37.988 to 37.995 mm
1242 cc (8-valve) engine:	
Grade A	42.001 to 42.008 mm
Grade B	41.995 to 42.001 mm
Grade C	41.988 to 41.995 mm
1242 cc (16-valve) engine:	
Grade A	41.990 to 42.008 mm
Diesel engine:	
Grade A	50.796 to 50.805 mm
Grade B	50.787 to 50.796 mm
Main bearing running clearance:	
Petrol engines:	
1108 cc and 1242 cc (8-valve) engines	0.025 to 0.049 mm
1242 cc (16-valve) engine	0.025 to 0.040 mm
Diesel engine	0.027 to 0.066 mm
Big-end bearing running clearance:	
Petrol engines:	
1108 cc and 1242 cc (8-valve) engines	0.024 to 0.062 mm
1242 cc (16-valve) engine	0.024 to 0.060 mm
Diesel engine	0.026 to 0.063 mm
Crankshaft endfloat:	
Petrol engines	0.055 to 0.265 mm
Diesel engine	0.049 to 0.231 mm

Torque wrench settings	Nm	lbf ft
Petrol engines		
Big-end bolt	41	30
Camshaft bearing caps (1108 cc and 1242 cc (8-valve) engines:		
M8 x 1.25	20	15
M8	10	7
Main bearing cap:		
Stage 1	40	30
Stage 2	Angle-tighten a further 90°	
Diesel engines		
Big-end bolt:		
Stage 1	25	18
Stage 2	Angle-tighten a further 50°	
Camshaft bearing caps	19	14
Camshaft side mounts	19	14
Main bearing cap	113	83
Swirl chamber to head	118	87

1 General information

Included in this Part of Chapter 2 are details of removing the engine/transmission from the car and general overhaul procedures for the cylinder head, cylinder block/crankcase and all other engine internal components.

The information given ranges from advice concerning preparation for an overhaul and the purchase of replacement parts, to detailed step-by-step procedures covering removal, inspection, renovation and refitting of engine internal components.

After Section 5, all instructions are based on the assumption that the engine has been removed from the car. For information concerning in-car engine repair, as well as the removal and refitting of those external components necessary for full overhaul, refer to Part A, B or C of this Chapter (as applicable) and to Section 5. Ignore any preliminary dismantling operations described in Part A, B or C that are no longer relevant once the engine has been removed from the car.

2 Engine overhaul - general information

1 It is not always easy to determine when, or if, an engine should be completely overhauled, as a number of factors must be considered.

2 High mileage is not necessarily an indication that an overhaul is needed, while low mileage does not preclude the need for an overhaul. Frequency of servicing is probably the most important consideration. An engine which has had regular and frequent oil and filter changes, as well as other required maintenance, should give many thousands of miles of reliable service. Conversely, a neglected engine may require an overhaul very early in its life.

3 Excessive oil consumption is an indication that piston rings, valve seals and/or valve guides are in need of attention. Make sure that oil leaks are not responsible before deciding that the rings and/or guides are worn. Perform a compression test, as described in Parts A or B (petrol engines) or C (diesel engines) of this Chapter, to determine the likely cause of the problem.

4 Check the oil pressure with a gauge fitted in place of the oil pressure switch. If it is extremely low, the main and big-end bearings, and/or the oil pump, are probably worn out.

5 Loss of power, rough running, knocking or metallic engine noises, excessive valve gear noise, and high fuel consumption may also point to the need for an overhaul, especially if they are all present at the same time. If a complete service does not remedy the situation, major mechanical work is the only solution.

6 An engine overhaul involves restoring all internal parts to the specification of a new engine. During an overhaul, the cylinders are rebored (where applicable), the pistons and the piston rings are renewed. New main and big-end bearings are generally fitted; if necessary, the crankshaft may be reground, to restore the journals.

7 The valves are also serviced as well, since they are usually in less-than-perfect condition at this point. While the engine is being overhauled, other components, such as the starter and alternator, can be overhauled as well. The end result should be an as-new engine that will give many trouble-free miles. **Note:** *Critical cooling system components such as the hoses, thermostat and coolant pump should be renewed when an engine is overhauled. The radiator should be checked carefully, to ensure that it is not clogged or leaking. Also, it is a good idea to renew the oil pump whenever the engine is overhauled.*

8 Before beginning the engine overhaul, read through the entire procedure, to familiarise yourself with the scope and requirements of the job. Overhauling an engine is not difficult if you follow carefully all of the instructions, have the necessary tools and equipment, and pay close attention to all specifications. It can, however, be time-consuming. Plan on the car being off the road for a minimum of two weeks, especially if parts must be taken to an engineering works for repair or reconditioning.

9 Check on the availability of parts and make sure that any necessary special tools and equipment are obtained in advance. Most work can be done with typical hand tools, although a number of precision measuring tools are required for inspecting parts to determine if they must be renewed. Often the engineering works will handle the inspection of parts and offer advice concerning reconditioning and renewal. **Note:** *Always wait until the engine has been completely dismantled, and until all components (especially the cylinder block/crankcase and the crankshaft) have been inspected, before deciding what service and repair operations must be performed by an engineering works. The condition of these components will be the major factor to consider when determining whether to overhaul the original engine, or to buy a reconditioned unit. Do not, therefore, purchase parts or have overhaul work done on other components until they have been thoroughly inspected.* As a general rule, time is the primary cost of an overhaul, so it does not pay to fit worn or sub-standard parts.

10 As a final note, to ensure maximum life and minimum trouble from a reconditioned engine, everything must be assembled with care, in a spotlessly-clean environment.

3 Engine and transmission removal - methods and precautions

1 If you have decided that the engine must be removed for overhaul or major repair work, several preliminary steps should be taken.

2 Locating a suitable place to work is extremely important. Adequate work space, along with storage space for the car, will be needed. If a workshop or garage is not available, at the very least, a flat, level, clean work surface is required.

3 Cleaning the engine compartment and engine/transmission before beginning the removal procedure will help keep tools clean and organised.

4 An engine hoist or A-frame will also be necessary. Make sure the equipment is rated in excess of the combined weight of the engine and transmission. Safety is of primary importance, considering the potential hazards involved in lifting the engine/transmission out of the car.

5 If this is the first time you have removed an engine, an assistant should ideally be available. Advice and aid from someone more experienced would also be helpful. There are many instances when one person cannot simultaneously perform all of the operations required when lifting the engine out of the vehicle.

6 Plan the operation ahead of time. Before starting work, arrange for the hire of or obtain all of the tools and equipment you will need. Some of the equipment necessary to perform engine/transmission removal and installation safely and with relative ease (in addition to an engine hoist) is as follows: a heavy duty trolley jack, complete sets of spanners and sockets as described in the reference section of this manual, wooden blocks, and plenty of rags and cleaning solvent for mopping up spilled oil, coolant and fuel. If the hoist must be hired, make sure that you arrange for it in advance, and perform all of the operations possible without it beforehand. This will save you money and time.

7 Plan for the car to be out of use for quite a while. An engineering works will be required to perform some of the work which the do-it-yourselfer cannot accomplish without special equipment. These places often have a busy schedule, so it would be a good idea to consult them before removing the engine, in order to accurately estimate the amount of time required to rebuild or repair components that may need work.

8 Always be extremely careful when removing and refitting the engine/transmission. Serious injury can result from careless actions. Plan ahead and take your time, and a job of this nature, although major, can be accomplished successfully.

4 Engine and transmission - removal, separation, connection and refitting

Note: *The engine is lowered from the engine compartment as a complete unit with the transmission; the two are then separated for overhaul.*

Removal

1 Remove the bonnet and disconnect the washer tubing as described in Chapter 11 **(see illustrations)**.

2 Apply the handbrake, then jack up the front of the vehicle and support on axle stands (see *Jacking and vehicle support*). Remove both front wheels. In order to remove the engine/transmission assembly in an upright position from under the vehicle, there must be a minimum clearance of 660 mm between the floor and the front crossmember. Additional height is necessary if the assembly is to be lowered onto a trolley.

3 Where fitted, unbolt and remove the engine compartment lower cover.

4 Remove the auxiliary drivebelt(s) with reference to Chapter 1A or 1B.

5 Drain the engine oil, transmission oil/fluid and coolant with reference to Chapter 1A or 1B.

6 Remove the battery (see Chapter 5A).

7 On manual transmission models with a cable clutch, disconnect the clutch cable from the transmission (refer to Chapter 6). On manual transmission models with a hydraulic clutch unbolt the clutch slave cylinder from the top of the transmission then fit a cable-tie around it to prevent the piston coming out **(see illustration)**. Position the cylinder to one side.

8 Unscrew the nut and disconnect the earth lead from the transmission **(see illustration)**.

Petrol engines

9 Unbolt and remove the battery tray.

10 Disconnect the wiring from the reversing light switch.

11 On manual transmission models disconnect the reverse inhibition cable from the transmission then disconnect the gear selector rod from the lever on the transmission.

12 Remove the air cleaner and ducting as described in Chapter 4A or 4B.

13 On automatic transmission models disconnect the kickdown cable and gear selector cable as described in Chapter 7B. Also disconnect the wiring for the electro-magnetic clutch.

14 Unbolt and remove the cover from the bulkhead then disconnect the oxygen sensor wiring.

15 Disconnect the remaining wiring at the bulkhead and release the fuse holders at the mounting.

16 Disconnect the vacuum pipe from the inlet manifold, and also disconnect the wiring connector located next to it.

4.1a Unscrewing the bonnet hinge bolts

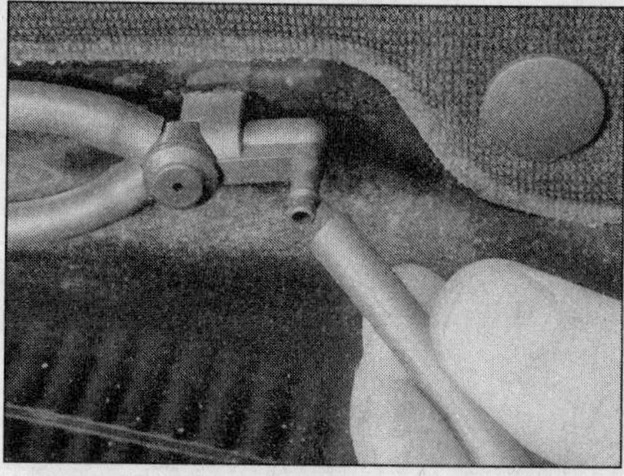

4.1b Disconnecting the washer tubing

17 Unscrew the nuts and separate the engine wiring harness lead from the battery positive cable terminal.

18 Disconnect the accelerator cable from the engine as described in Chapter 4A or 4B.

19 Loosen the clip and disconnect the radiator top hose from the elbow on the left-hand end of the cylinder head. Similarly disconnect the bottom hose. On 16-valve models, remove the radiator electric cooling fan as described in Chapter 3.

20 Identify the hoses connected to the throttle housing, then disconnect them.

21 Identify the coolant heater hoses on the bulkhead for position, then loosen the clips and disconnect the hoses.

22 Loosen the clip and disconnect the brake servo vacuum hose from the inlet manifold. Where applicable, disconnect the remaining emission control system vacuum hoses from the inlet manifold after identifying their locations to aid refitting.

23 Disconnect the fuel supply and return hoses from the throttle housing.

24 Release the connector from the ignition/fuel ECU located on the right-hand side of the engine compartment.

25 Unscrew the nut and detach the earth cable from its location near the ECU.

26 Disconnect the diagnostic connector located near the ECU.

27 On models fitted with power steering, refer to Chapter 10 and unbolt the power steering pump from the front of the engine without disconnecting the hydraulic fluid lines then tie it to one side so that it will not obstruct the removal of the engine. On models with air conditioning, similarly unbolt the air conditioning compressor and position it clear of the engine. Do not disconnect the air conditioning refrigerant pipes/hoses.

28 On manual transmission models pull out the retaining plate and disconnect the gear selector cable from the lever on the transmission.

29 Unscrew the nuts retaining the track rod ends on the swivel hubs and use a balljoint separator tool to disconnect them.

30 Release the flexible brake fluid hoses and ABS system sensor wiring from the front suspension struts.

31 On manual transmission models, unscrew the nuts from the outer ends of each driveshaft. To prevent the hubs from turning either have an assistant depress the brake pedal, or temporarily insert two wheel bolts and use a lever to hold the hub.

32 On automatic transmission models use a suitable drift to drive out the roll pins securing the inner ends of the driveshafts to the transmission output stubs. Turn the driveshafts as necessary to access the roll pins .

33 Unscrew the two bolts securing the right-hand swivel hub assembly to the front suspension strut, then move the hub assembly outwards. On manual transmission models release the outer end of the driveshaft from the hub assembly - on automatic transmission models slide the inner end of the driveshaft **off** the final drive output stub. Take care not to strain the flexible brake hose while doing this. Move the driveshaft to one side then temporarily refit the hub assembly to the strut. On manual transmission models, make

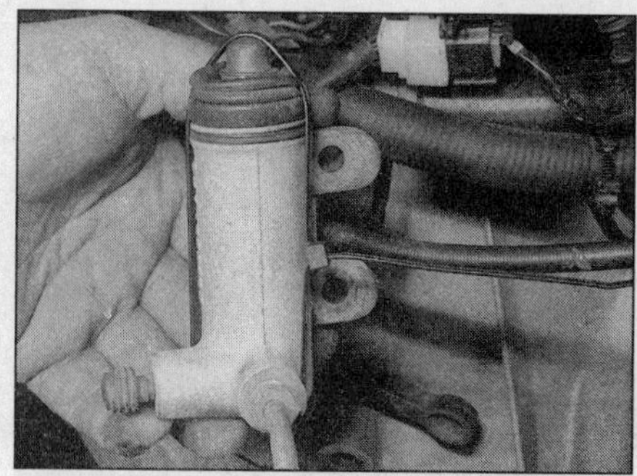

4.7 Fit a cable tie around the clutch slave cylinder to prevent the piston coming out

4.8 Disconnecting the earth lead from the transmission

4.36a Relay guard mounting nuts

4.36b Battery tray and mounting bolts

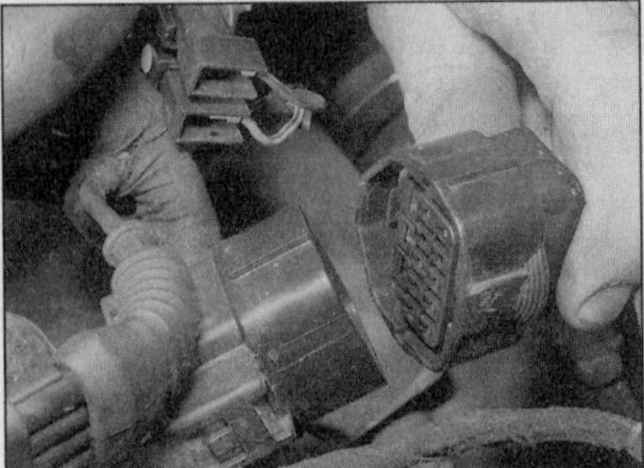
4.36c Disconnect the engine wiring harness located above the transmission . . .

4.36d . . . the inner wiring plug . . .

4.36e . . . and the outer wiring plug

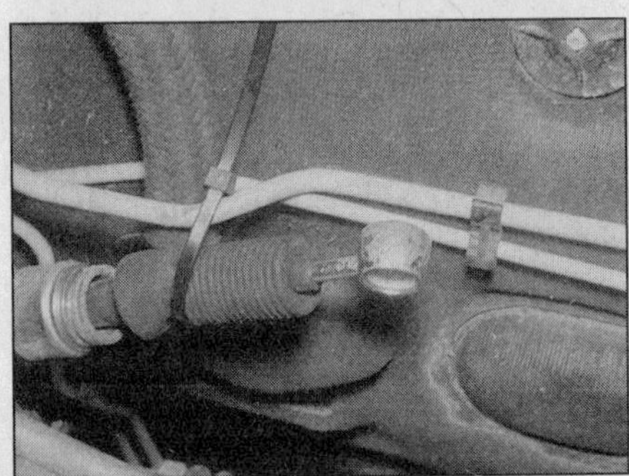
4.37 Tie the gear selector cable to the bulkhead

sure that the driveshaft is positioned to clear the lower suspension arm when the engine is removed.

34 Disconnect the left-hand driveshaft using the same procedure.

4.41 Engine wiring harness connections to the battery positive cable

35 Remove the exhaust front downpipe with reference to Chapter 4D.

Diesel engines

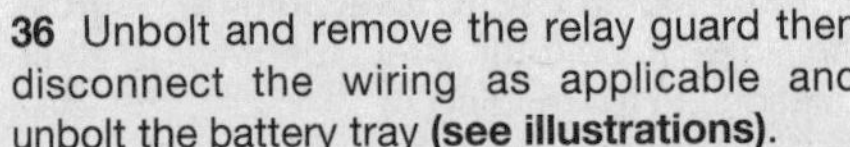

36 Unbolt and remove the relay guard then disconnect the wiring as applicable and unbolt the battery tray **(see illustrations)**.

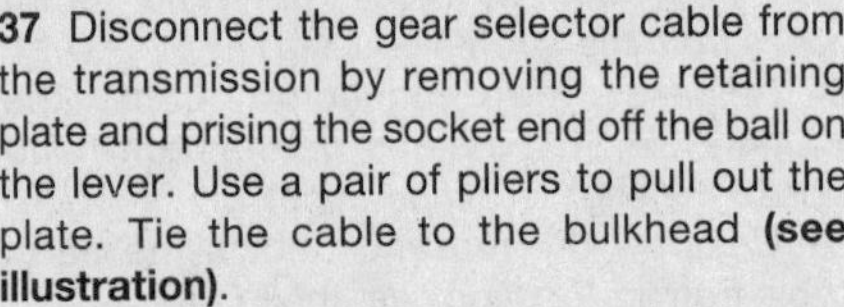

37 Disconnect the gear selector cable from the transmission by removing the retaining plate and prising the socket end off the ball on the lever. Use a pair of pliers to pull out the plate. Tie the cable to the bulkhead **(see illustration)**.

38 Unscrew the nut and disconnect the gear selector rod from the lever on the top of the transmission.

39 Remove the air cleaner and air inlet duct by unscrewing the two bolts securing the duct to the valve cover and loosening the clip securing the duct to the air cleaner. Refer to Chapter 4C if necessary.

40 Disconnect the vacuum pipe from the vacuum pump on the left-hand side of the cylinder head and disconnect the wiring plug located over the transmission.

41 Unscrew the nuts and disconnect the engine wiring harness from the battery positive cable **(see illustration)**.

42 At the fuel filter unscrew the union bolt and disconnect the fuel delivery hose for the injection pump. Use polythene and an elastic band to cover the end of the hose **(see illustrations)**.

43 At the fuel injection pump unscrew the clip and disconnect the fuel return hose **(see illustration)**.

44 Disconnect the radiator top hose from the thermostat housing on the left-hand side of the cylinder head, and also disconnect the heater hose at the engine **(see illustrations)**.

45 Disconnect the heater return hose and expansion tank hose from the elbow on the

4.42a Unscrew the union bolt and disconnect the fuel delivery hose from the fuel filter

4.42b Cover the end of the hose to prevent dust entry

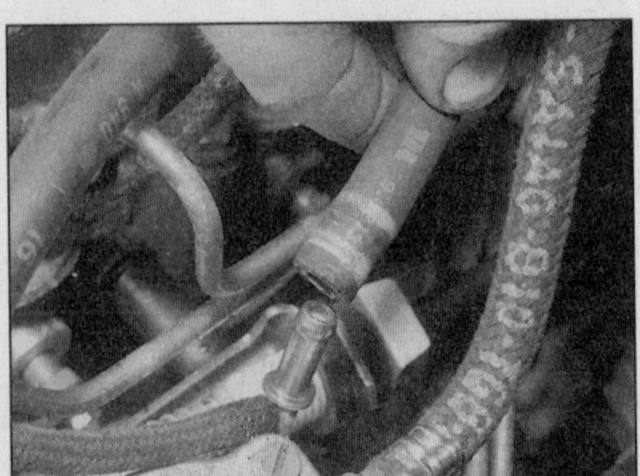
4.43 Disconnecting the fuel return hose from the fuel injection pump

4.44a Disconnecting the radiator top hose from the thermostat housing

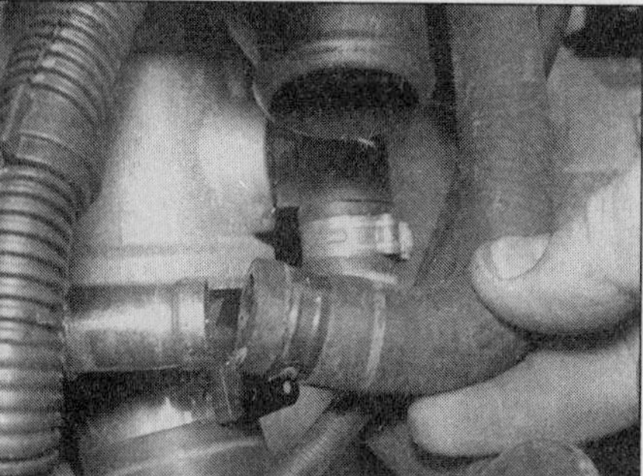
4.44b Disconnecting the heater hose at the engine

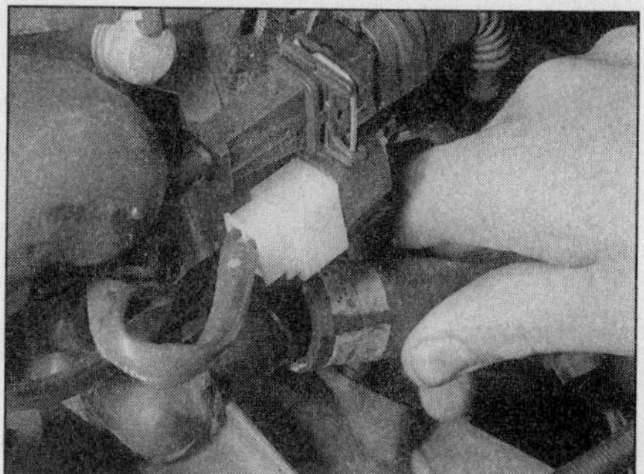
4.45a Disconnecting the heater return hose . . .

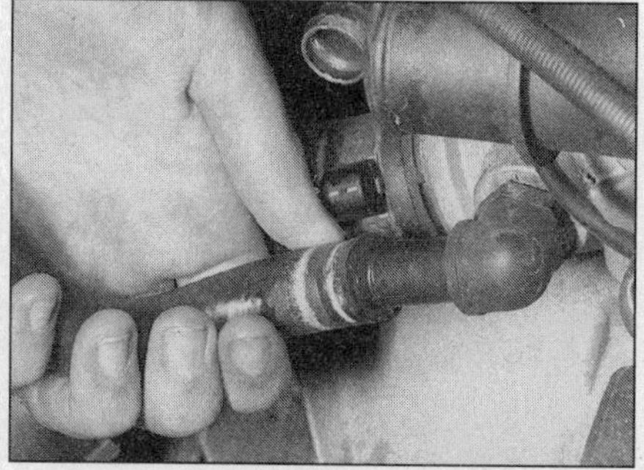
4.45b . . . and expansion tank hose

4.49a Remove the front bracket bolt . . .

4.49b . . . the belt adjustment bolt . . .

left-hand side of the cylinder head, from the top of the radiator and from the expansion tank **(see illustrations)**.

46 Disconnect the radiator bottom hose from the elbow on the cylinder head.

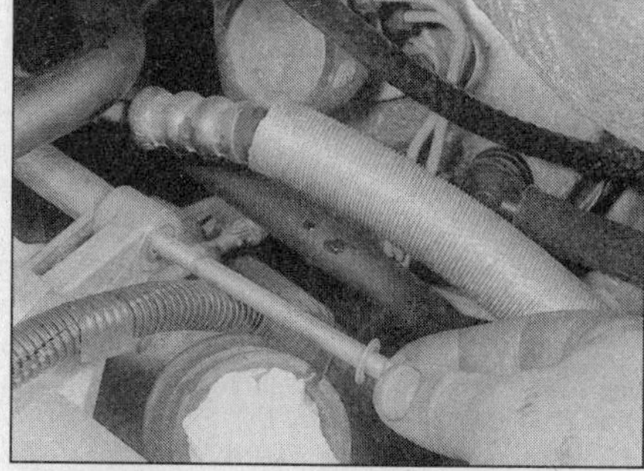
4.49c . . . the rear through-bolt . . .

47 On models with a speedometer cable, disconnect the cable from the transmission.

48 On models with an electronic speedometer, if necessary disconnect the wiring connector on the support bracket. The cable may be left attached if the transmission is not being detached from the engine.

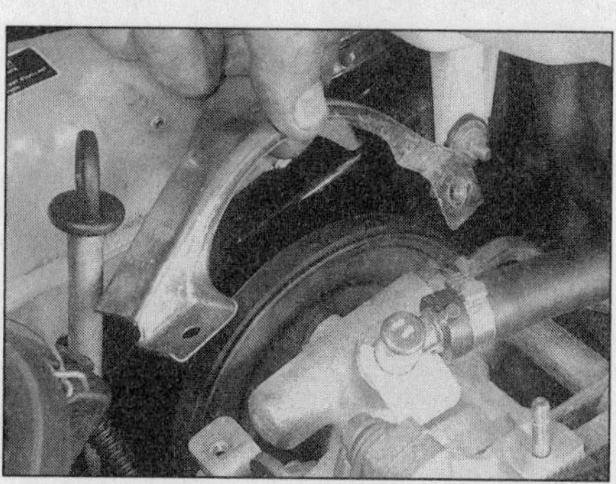
4.49d . . . the cover . . .

49 On models fitted with power steering, unbolt the power steering pump from the rear right-hand side of the engine without disconnecting the hydraulic fluid lines then tie it to one side on the bulkhead so that it will not obstruct the removal of the engine. To do this first remove the front bracket bolt, remove the belt adjustment bolt, remove the rear through-bolt, lift away the cover and remove the adjustment lockbolt **(see illustrations)**. On models with air conditioning, similarly unbolt the air conditioning compressor and position it clear of the engine. Do not disconnect the air conditioning refrigerant pipes/hoses.

50 Disconnect the coolant purge hoses from the top of the radiator and expansion tank **(see illustrations)**.

51 Disconnect the accelerator cable from the injection pump (see Chapter 4C).

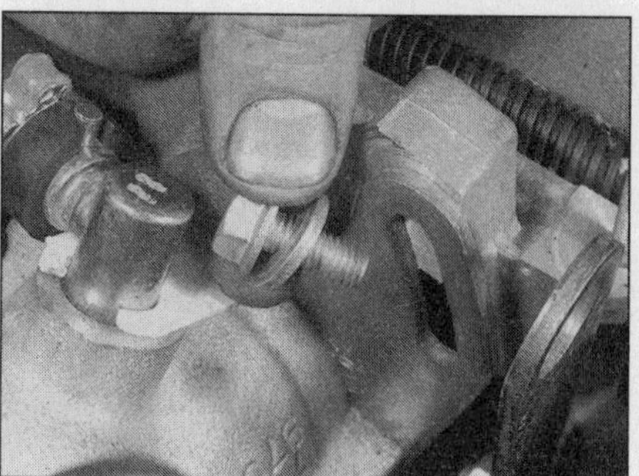
4.49e . . . and the adjustment lockbolt . . .

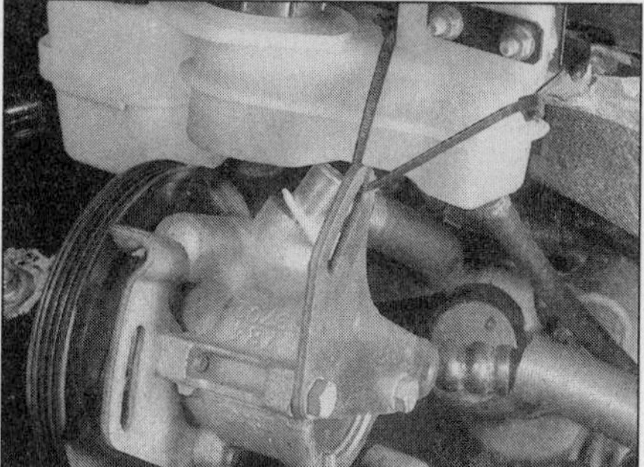
4.49f . . . and tie the power steering pump to the bulkhead

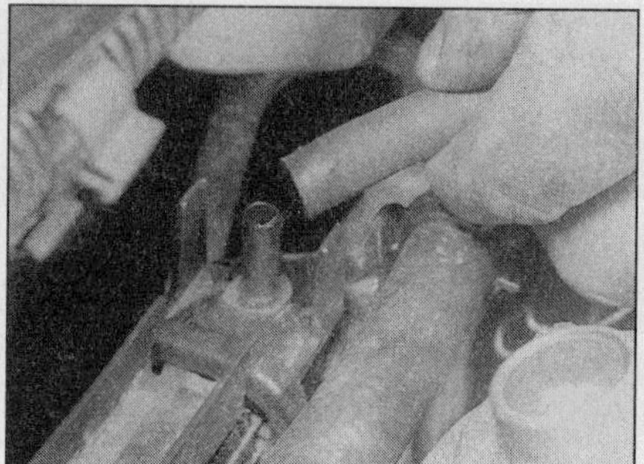
4.50a Disconnecting the coolant purge hoses from the radiator . . .

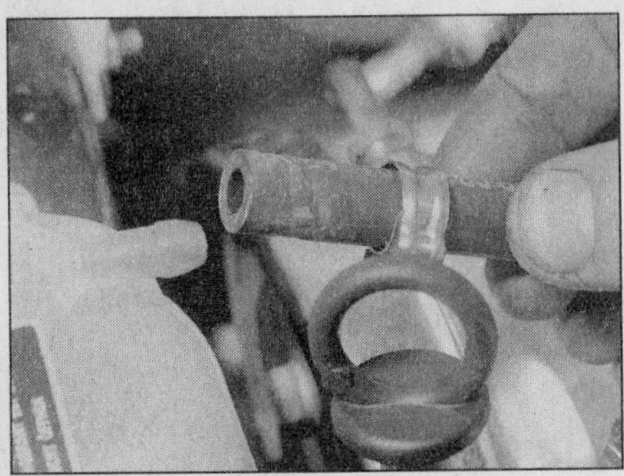

4.50b . . . and expansion tank

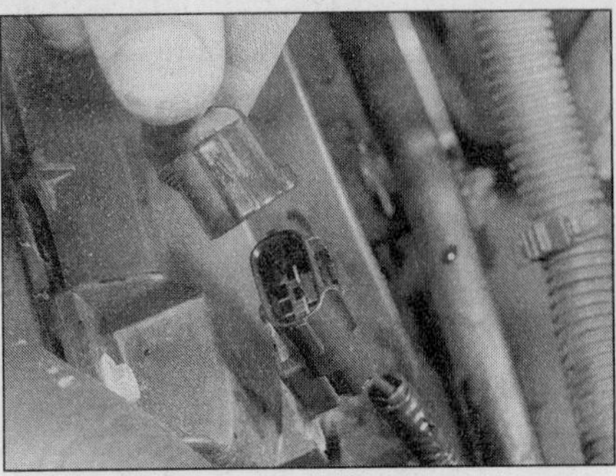

4.52 Disconnecting the radiator coolant temperature sensor wiring plug

4.53a Wheel arch liner retaining screws

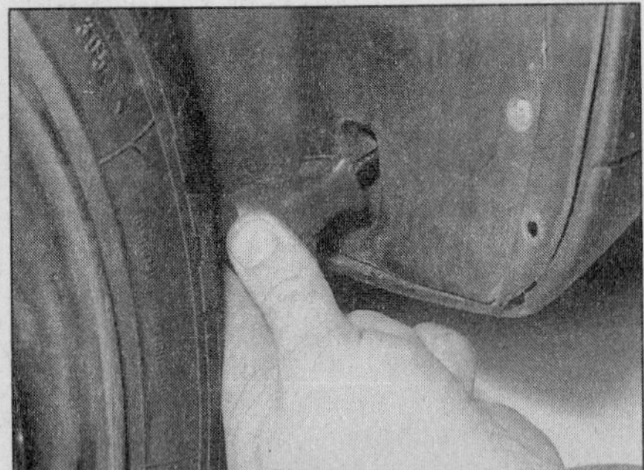

4.53b One of the wheel arch liner retaining screws is hidden in a recess

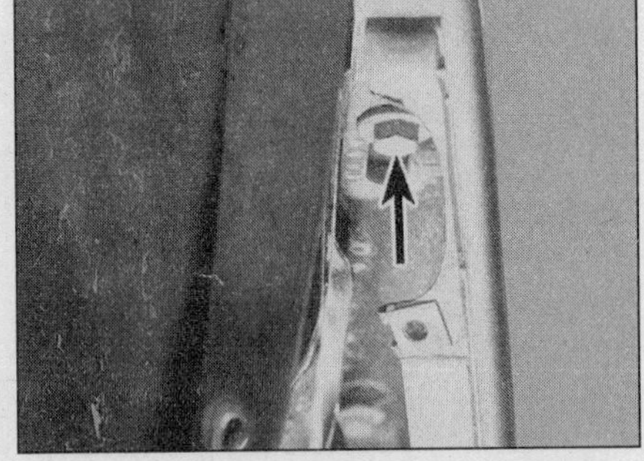

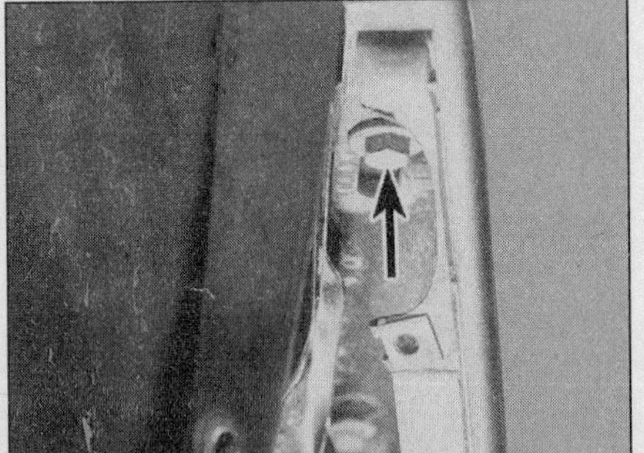

4.53c Bolt securing the front bumper to the valance

4.54 One of the front bumper lower retaining screws

52 On the radiator cooling fan housing, disconnect the wiring plug for the coolant temperature sensor **(see illustration)**.

53 Unscrew the four front screws on each side retaining the wheel arch liners in order to access the front bumper mounting bolts - one of the screws is hidden in a recess. Pull back the liners and use an extension and socket to unscrew the bolts securing the front bumper to the valance **(see illustrations)**.

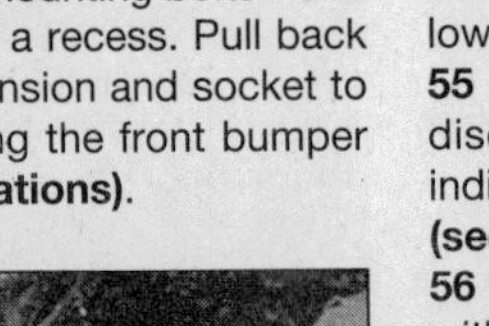

54 Unscrew and remove the front bumper lower retaining screws **(see illustration)**.

55 From inside the engine compartment, disconnect the wiring from the rear of the indicator lights and release the retaining clips **(see illustration)**.

56 Unscrew the upper retaining screws and withdraw the front bumper from the body **(see illustrations)**.

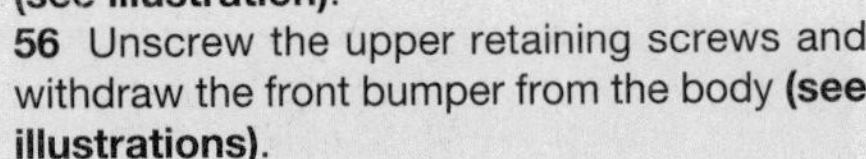

57 Unscrew the bolts securing the radiator lower mounting bracket to the body then prise the bracket from the rubbers on the bottom of the radiator **(see illustrations)**.

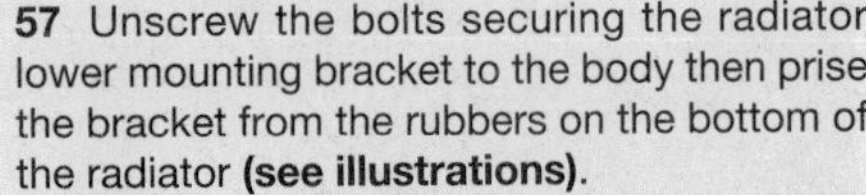

58 Unscrew the upper mounting bolt securing the engine oil cooler then lower the cooler and support on an axle stand **(see illustration)**. Take care not to damage the hoses.

59 Support the radiator then unscrew the radiator upper mounting bolts, and remove the radiator from the vehicle **(see illustrations)**.

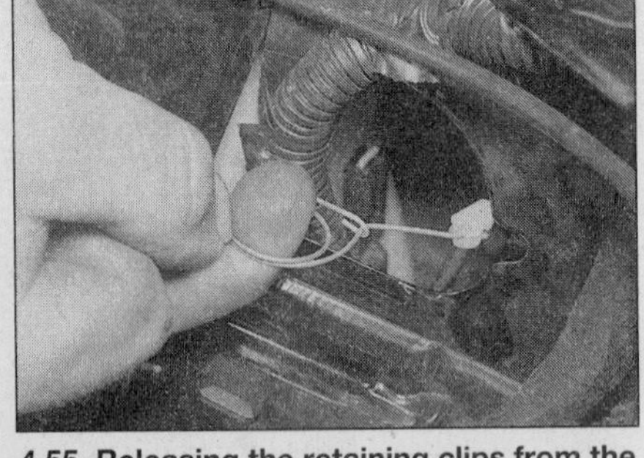

4.55 Releasing the retaining clips from the rear of the indicator lights

4.56a Side bumper retaining screw

4.56b Centre bumper retaining screw

4.57a Radiator lower mounting bracket bolt

4.57b Removing the bracket from the rubbers on the bottom of the radiator

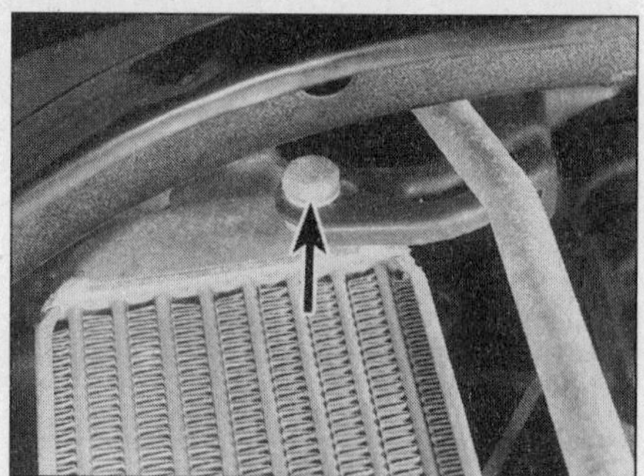
4.58 Engine oil cooler upper mounting bolt

4.59a Left-hand side radiator mounting bolt removal

4.59b Right-hand side radiator mounting bolt

60 At the oil filter, unscrew the union nuts and disconnect the oil cooler lines/hoses then remove the oil cooler from the vehicle **(see illustration)**. Be prepared for some oil leakage. Note the fitted position of the hoses before disconnecting them so that they can be refitted correctly.

61 Disconnect the reversing light wiring from the switch on the front of the transmission **(see illustration)**.

62 Using an Allen key, unscrew the bolts securing the inner ends of the driveshafts to the flanges on the transmission. The right-hand driveshaft is disconnected from the intermediate shaft flange on the rear of the engine. Recover the plates beneath the heads of the driveshaft bolts **(see illustrations)**.

63 Unscrew the bolts securing the front swivel hub assemblies to the struts. Also release the flexible brake hoses from the struts.

64 Move the swivel hub assemblies outwards and support the inner ends of the driveshafts on axle stands (see *Jacking and vehicle support*). Take care not to strain the flexible brake hoses.

65 Remove the exhaust front pipe with reference to Chapter 4D. If difficulty is experienced in separating the front pipe from the intermediate pipe, it may prove easier to remove the complete exhaust system.

All models

66 Attach a suitable hoist to the engine and transmission lifting eyes **(see illustration)**. The left-hand eye is located on the transmission and the right-hand one on the right-hand side of the engine. Take the weight of the engine/transmission.

67 Working beneath the vehicle, unscrew the bolts securing the rear engine mounting to the underbody and transmission, and withdraw the mounting.

68 In the engine compartment, unscrew the bolts securing the right-hand engine mounting to the body and engine. For additional working room completely remove the mounting.

69 Unscrew the bolts securing the left-hand engine/transmission mounting to the body. For additional working room completely remove the mounting.

70 With the help of an assistant lower the engine/transmission from the engine compartment taking care not to damage the surrounding components **(see illustration)**. Ideally lower the unit onto a low trolley so that it may be withdrawn from under the vehicle. Disconnect the hoist from the assembly.

4.59c Removing the radiator from the vehicle

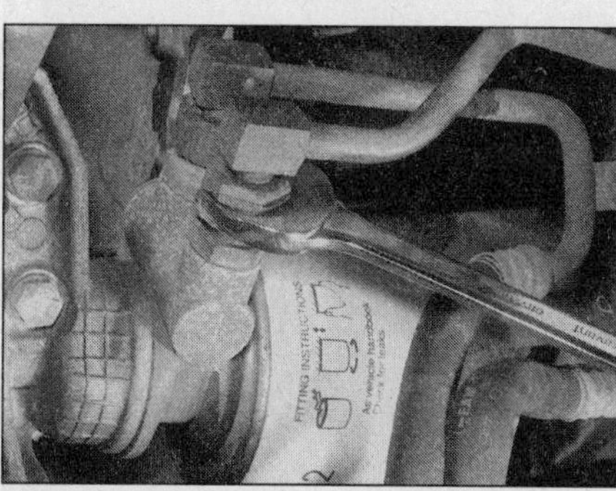

4.60 Loosening the union nuts securing the oil cooler lines to the oil filter housing

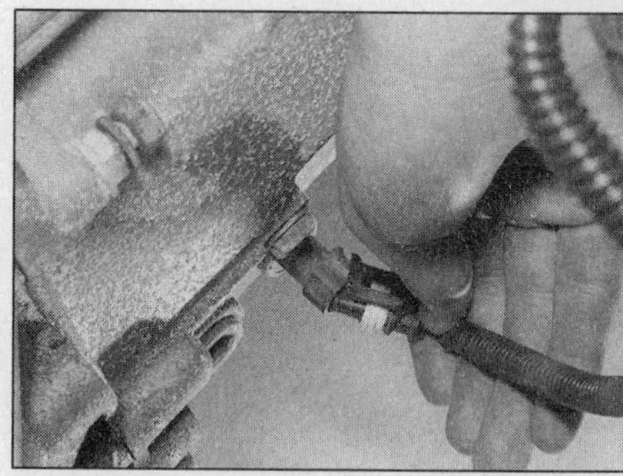
4.61 Disconnecting the reversing light wiring

4.62a Use an Allen key to unscrew the inner driveshaft bolts

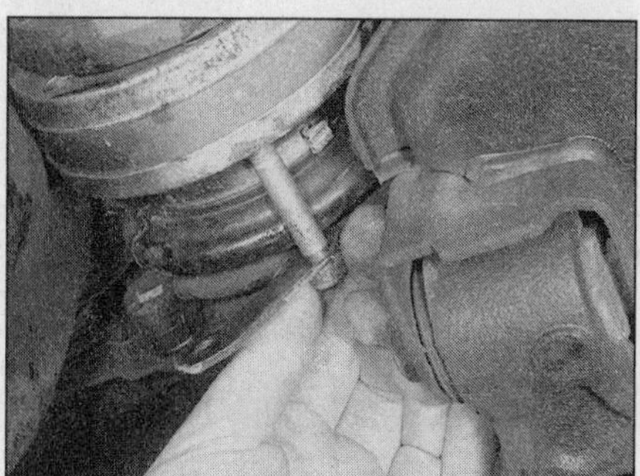
4.62b Removing the driveshaft bolts and plates

4.66 Attaching a hoist to the engine and transmission assembly

4.70 Lowering the engine/transmission assembly to the floor

4.77 Removing the transmission lower cover

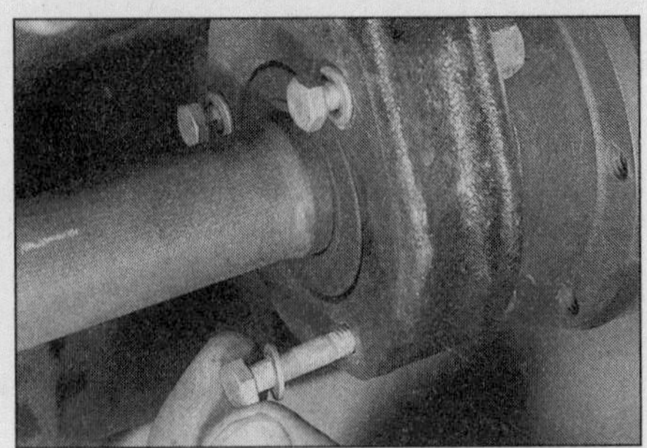
4.78 Removing the bolts securing the intermediate shaft to the bracket on the rear of the cylinder block

4.79a Withdraw the intermediate shaft . . .

4.79b . . . and recover the dust boot

Separation

71 Rest the engine and transmission assembly on a firm, flat surface, and use wooden blocks as wedges to keep the unit steady.

72 Note the routing and location of the wiring harness on the engine/transmission assembly, then methodically disconnect it.

73 Remove the starter motor (Chapter 5A).

Petrol engines

74 Note the location of the earth leads on the transmission support bracket on the rear of the cylinder block, then unscrew the securing bolts and move the leads to one side.

75 Unscrew the bolts on the transmission and remove the support bracket.

76 Unscrew the remaining bolts and remove the transmission lower cover.

Diesel engines

77 Unscrew the bolts and remove the transmission lower cover **(see illustration).**

78 Unscrew the bolts securing the intermediate shaft to the bracket on the rear of the cylinder block **(see illustration).**

79 Withdraw the intermediate shaft through the bracket and recover the dust boot from the inner end **(see illustrations).**

80 Unscrew the mounting bolts and remove the rpm sensor from the transmission **(see illustrations).**

Manual transmission models

81 Support the transmission with blocks of wood.

82 Unscrew the transmission-to-engine bolts. Also unscrew the nut securing the transmission to the rear of the cylinder block **(see illustrations).**

83 Lift the transmission complete with driveshafts directly from the rear of the engine, taking care to keep it level so that the transmission input shaft does not hang on the clutch **(see illustration).**

Automatic transmission models

84 Support the transmission with blocks of wood.

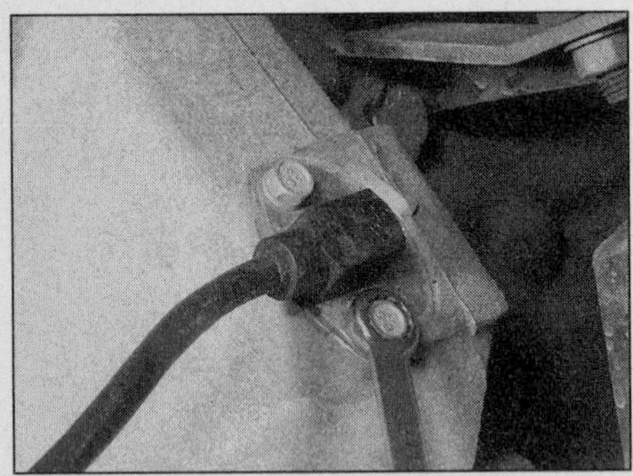
4.80a Unscrew the bolts . . .

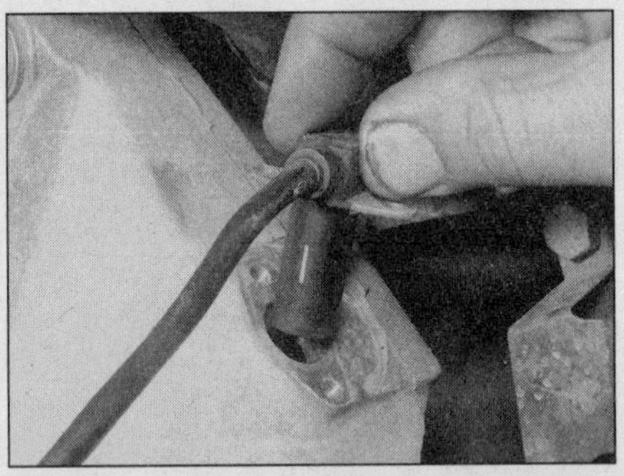
4.80b . . . and remove the rpm sensor from the transmission

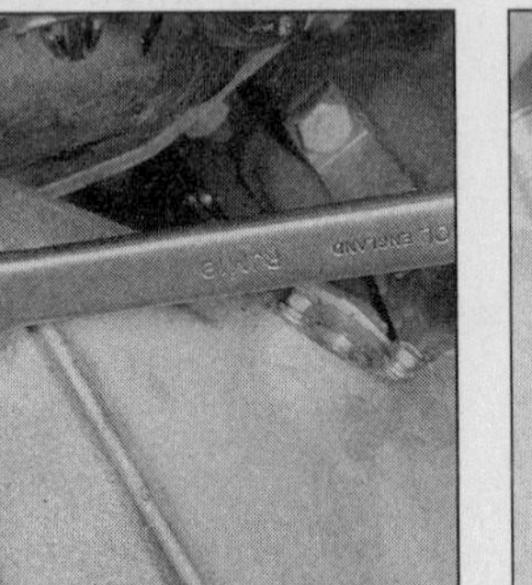
4.82a Unscrewing the transmission-to-engine bolts

4.82b Nut securing the transmission to the rear of the cylinder block

4.83 Separating the engine from the transmission (petrol engine)

85 Remove the brush holder assembly from the automatic transmission as described in Chapter 7B, Section 4. The brushes bear on the slip rings at the rear of the electro-magnetic clutch housing and they may be damaged when the transmission is removed.

86 Unscrew and remove the transmission-to-engine bolts then carefully draw the transmission away from the engine, resting it securely on wooden blocks. Collect the locating dowels if they are loose enough to be extracted.

87 If the oil pump driveshaft remains engaged with the crankshaft, remove it and insert into the transmission to protect it from damage.

Connection

88 If the engine and transmission have not been separated, go to paragraph 104.

Manual transmission models

89 Smear a little high-melting-point grease on the splines of the transmission input shaft. Do not use an excessive amount as there is the risk of contaminating the clutch friction plate.

90 Carefully offer up the transmission to the engine cylinder block, guiding the input shaft through the clutch friction plate.

91 Refit the transmission-to-engine bolts and the single nut, hand tightening them to secure the transmission in position. **Note:** *Do not tighten them to force the engine and transmission together.* Ensure that the bellhousing and cylinder block mating faces will butt together evenly without obstruction, before finally tightening the bolts and nut securely.

Automatic transmission models

92 Check that the oil pump driveshaft is correctly engaged with the oil pump in the transmission.

93 Carefully offer up the transmission to the rear of the engine and insert the oil pump driveshaft in the centre of the electro-magnetic clutch housing. Locate the transmission on the locating dowels then insert the bolts and tighten them securely.

94 Refit the brush holder assembly to the automatic transmission with reference to Chapter 7B, Section 4.

Petrol engines

95 Refit the transmission lower cover and tighten the bolts.

96 Locate the support bracket on the lower cover, then insert the bolts hand-tight. Also insert the bolts securing the bracket to the rear of the cylinder block. With all the bolts inserted, tighten them securely.

97 Refit the earth leads and tighten the bolts.

Diesel engines

98 Refit the rpm sensor and tighten the bolts.

99 Insert the intermediate shaft through the bracket then locate the dust boot on it and insert the inner end in the transmission.

100 Refit and tighten the bolts securing the intermediate shaft to the bracket on the rear of the cylinder block.

101 Refit the transmission lower cover and tighten the bolts.

All models

102 Refit the starter motor (see Chapter 5A).

103 Refit the wiring harness to the components on the engine/transmission assembly making sure it is routed correctly.

Refitting

104 Locate the engine/transmission assembly beneath the engine compartment and attach the hoist to the lifting eyes.

105 Carefully lift the assembly up into the engine compartment taking care not to damage the surrounding components.

106 Reconnect the left-hand engine/transmission mounting to the body and tighten the bolts.

107 Reconnect the right-hand engine mounting to the body and tighten the bolts.

108 Working beneath the vehicle, refit the rear engine mounting and tighten the bolts.

109 Disconnect the hoist from the engine and transmission lifting eyes and remove the hoist from under the vehicle.

110 The remainder of the refitting procedure is the direct reverse of the removal procedure, noting the following points:

a) Ensure that all sections of the wiring harness follow their original routing; use new cable-ties to secure the harness in position, keeping it away from sources of heat and abrasion.
b) On vehicles with manual transmission check and if necessary adjust the gearchange cable and rod with reference to Chapter 7A.
c) On vehicles with automatic transmission use new roll pins to secure the driveshafts to the transmission output stubs. Also check and if necessary adjust the kickdown and selector cables with reference to Chapter 7B.
d) Ensure that all hoses are correctly routed and are secured with the correct hose clips, where applicable. If the hose clips cannot be used again; proprietary worm drive clips should be fitted in their place.
e) Refill the cooling system as described in Chapter 1A or 1B.
f) Refill the engine with appropriate grades and quantities of oil (Chapter 1A or 1B).
g) Refit and adjust the auxiliary drivebelt(s) with reference to Chapter 1A or 1B.
h) Check and if necessary adjust the accelerator cable with reference to Chapter 4A, 4B or 4C.
i) When the engine is started for the first time, check for air, coolant, lubricant and fuel leaks from manifolds, hoses etc. If the engine has been overhauled, read the notes in Section 13 before attempting to start it.

5 Engine overhaul - dismantling sequence

1 It is much easier to dismantle and work on the engine if it is mounted on a portable engine stand. These stands can often be hired from a tool hire shop. Before the engine is mounted on a stand, the flywheel should be removed, so that the stand bolts can be tightened into the end of the cylinder block/crankcase.

2 If a stand is not available, it is possible to dismantle the engine with it blocked up on a sturdy workbench, or on the floor. Be very careful not to tip or drop the engine when working without a stand.

3 If you intend to obtain a reconditioned engine, all ancillaries must be removed first, to be transferred to the replacement engine (just as they will if you are doing a complete engine overhaul yourself). These components include the following:

Petrol engines

a) Power steering pump if removed with the engine (Chapter 10).
b) Alternator (including mounting brackets) and starter motor (Chapter 5A).
c) The ignition system and HT components including all sensors, HT leads and spark plugs (Chapters 1A and 5B).
d) The fuel injection system components (Chapters 4A and 4B).
e) All electrical switches, actuators and sensors, and the engine wiring harness (Chapters 4A, 4B, 5B).
f) Inlet and exhaust manifolds (Chapters 4A, 4B and 4D).
g) Engine oil dipstick and tube.
h) Engine mountings (Chapter 2A).
i) Flywheel/driveplate (Chapter 2A).
j) Clutch components (Chapter 6) - manual transmission.
k) Electro-magnetic clutch components (Chapter 7B) - automatic transmission.
l) Cooling system components (Chapter 3).

Diesel engines

a) Power steering pump if removed with the engine (Chapter 10).
b) Alternator (including mounting brackets) and starter motor (Chapter 5A).
c) The glow plug/pre-heating system components (Chapter 5C).
d) All fuel system components, including the fuel injection pump, all sensors and actuators (Chapter 4C).
e) The vacuum pump.
f) All electrical switches, actuators and sensors, and the engine wiring harness (Chapter 4C and 5C).
g) Inlet and exhaust manifolds and, where applicable, the turbocharger (Chapter 4C and 4D).
h) The engine oil level dipstick and its tube.
i) Engine mountings (Chapter 2C).

6.5a Prising out the feed stub of the camshaft lubricating pipe

6.5b Unscrewing the camshaft bearing/banjo union bolt

6.5c Removing the camshaft lubricating pipe

j) Flywheel (Chapter 2C).
k) Clutch components (Chapter 6).
l) Cooling system components (Chapter 3).

Note: *When removing the external components from the engine, pay close attention to details that may be helpful or important during refitting. Note the fitted position of gaskets, seals, spacers, pins, washers, bolts, and other small components.*

4 If you are obtaining a short engine (the engine cylinder block/crankcase, crankshaft, pistons and connecting rods, all fully assembled), then the cylinder head, sump, oil pump, timing belt (together with its tensioner and covers), coolant pump, thermostat housing, coolant outlet elbows, oil filter housing and where applicable oil cooler will also have to be removed.

5 If you are planning a full overhaul, the engine can be dismantled in the order given below:

a) Flywheel/driveplate.
b) Timing belt, sprockets, and tensioner.
c) Inlet and exhaust manifolds.
d) Cylinder head.
e) Sump.
f) Oil pump.
g) Pistons and crankshaft.

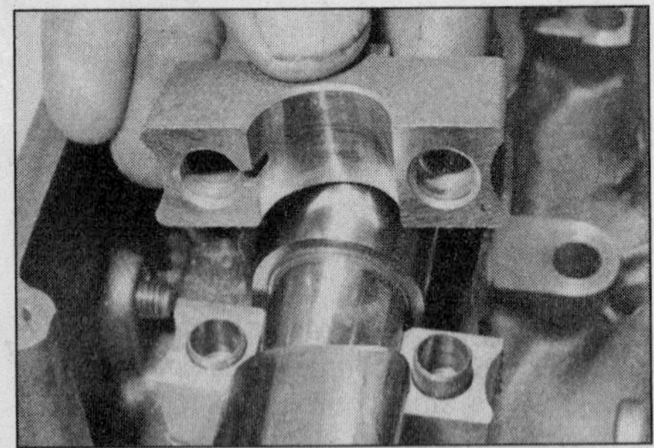

6.5d When removing the camshaft bearing caps, note the position of the long and short locating dowels

6 Cylinder head - dismantling, cleaning, inspection and reassembly

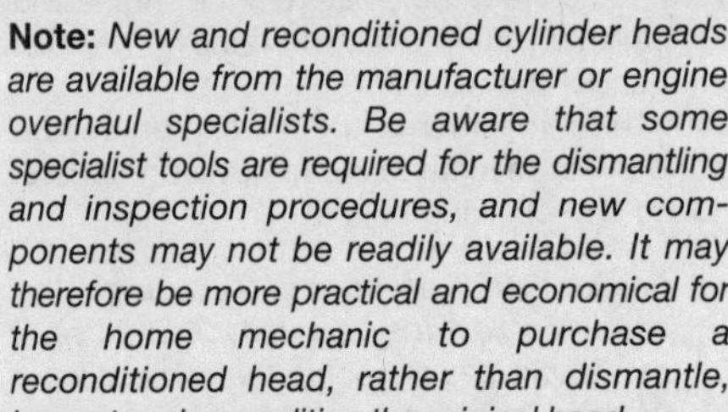

Note: *New and reconditioned cylinder heads are available from the manufacturer or engine overhaul specialists. Be aware that some specialist tools are required for the dismantling and inspection procedures, and new components may not be readily available. It may therefore be more practical and economical for the home mechanic to purchase a reconditioned head, rather than dismantle, inspect and recondition the original head.*

Dismantling

Note: *On 8-valve petrol engines and diesel engines, the camshaft and cam followers are located in the cylinder head assembly and the relevant dismantling and reassembly procedures are contained in this Section. On 16-valve petrol engines, the camshafts and cam followers are located in a separate housing (cylinder head extension) which is bolted to the top of the cylinder head. All procedures relating to the camshafts and cam followers on 16-valve engines are therefore contained in Chapter 2B. Proceed to paragraph 15 for cylinder head dismantling procedures on 16-valve engines, and ignore any references to camshafts, cam followers and oil seals in the paragraphs that follow.*

1 Remove the cylinder head as described in Part A, B or C of this Chapter (as applicable).

2 If not already done, remove the inlet and exhaust manifolds with reference to the relevant Part of Chapter 4. Also remove the spark plugs, glow plugs and injectors as applicable.

3 Remove the camshaft sprocket with reference to Chapter 2A or 2C.

Petrol engines

4 Mark the positions of the camshaft bearing caps, numbering them from the timing end.

5 Unbolt and remove the lubrication pipe (prise the oil feed stub out with a screwdriver). Unscrew the remaining bolts and take off the bearing caps **(see illustrations)**.

6 Lift the camshaft carefully from the cylinder head, checking that the valve clearance shims and cam followers are not withdrawn by the adhesion of the oil **(see illustration)**.

7 Remove the shims and cam followers, but keep them in their originally fitted order.

Diesel engines

8 Unbolt the thermostat housing and gasket, and vacuum pump from the left-hand end of the cylinder head. Also if necessary unbolt the coolant cover and gasket from the right-hand end of the head. Note the location of brackets **(see illustrations)**.

9 Using a soft metal drift, carefully tap out the left-hand side mount and recover the gasket **(see illustrations)**.

10 At the timing belt end of the cylinder head,

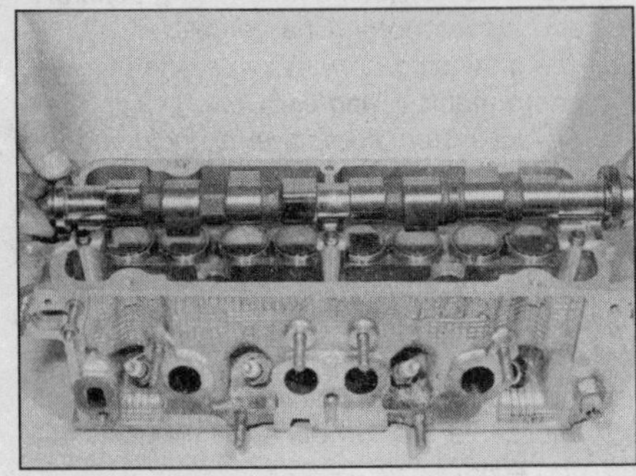

6.6 Removing the camshaft

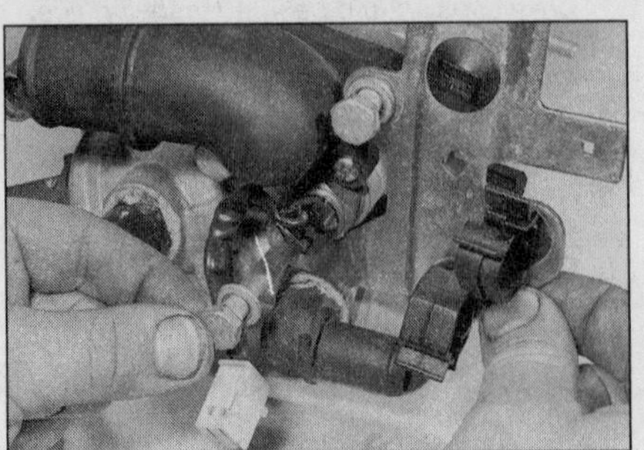

6.8a Unscrew and remove the bolts from the thermostat housing, noting the location of the bracket

6.8b Removing the thermostat housing . . .

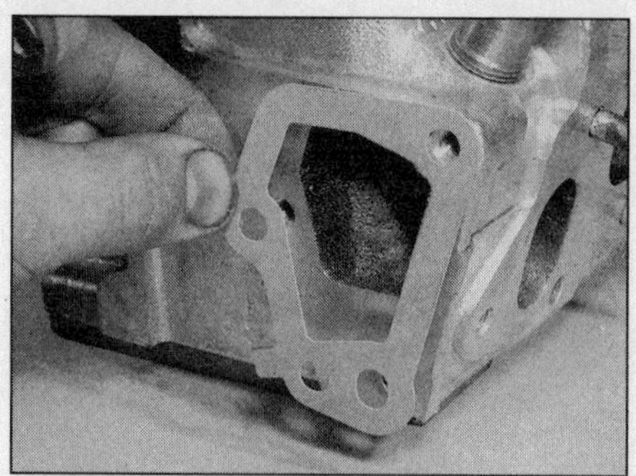

6.8c . . . and gasket

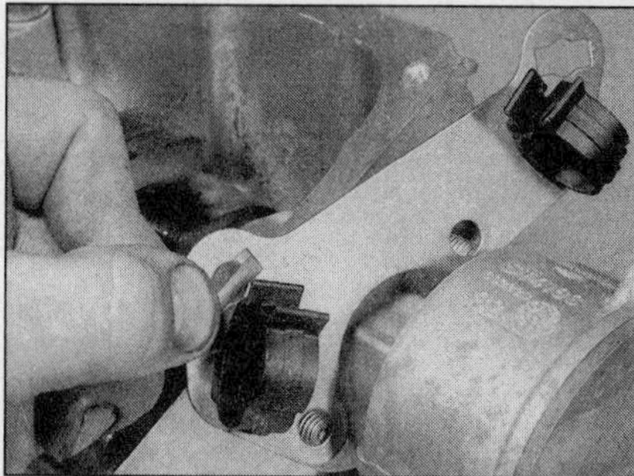

6.8d Unscrew the vacuum pump mounting nuts noting the location of the bracket

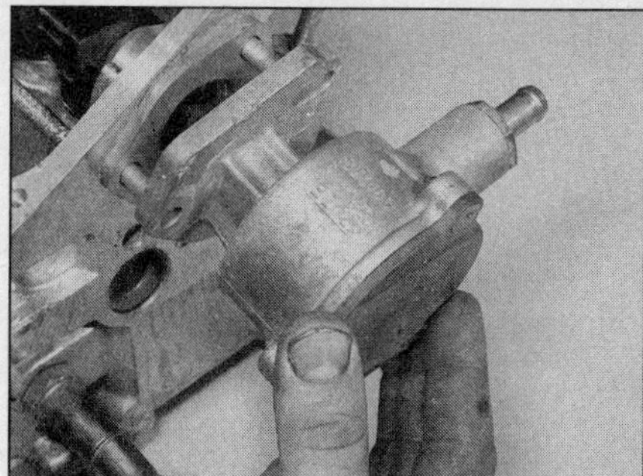

6.8e Removing the vacuum pump

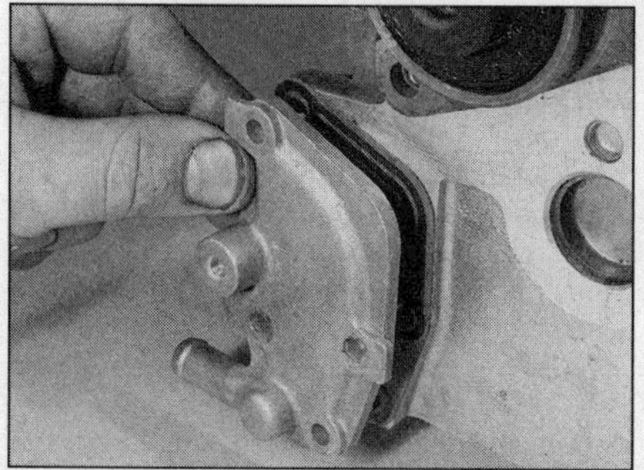

6.8f Removing the coolant cover

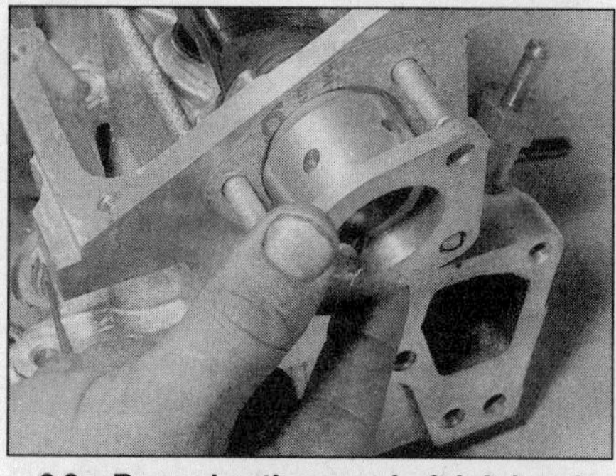

6.9a Removing the camshaft left-hand side mount . . .

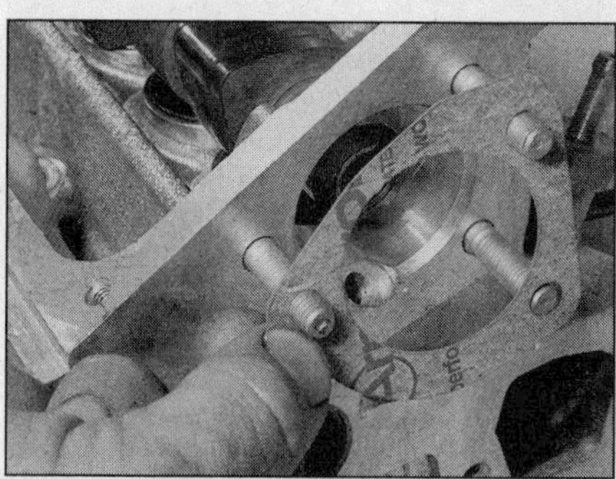

6.9b . . . and gasket

unscrew the bolts securing the right-hand side mount to the head. Carefully tap out the right-hand side mount and recover the gasket **(see illustrations)**.

11 Mark the positions of the camshaft bearing caps, numbering from the timing belt end.

12 Progressively unscrew the bearing cap nuts then take off the bearing caps. Note the location dowels on the mounting studs **(see illustrations)**.

13 Lift the camshaft towards the timing end, then remove it from the cylinder head **(see illustration)**. Make sure the valve clearance shims and cam followers are not withdrawn by the adhesion of the oil.

6.10a Removing the camshaft right-hand side mount . . .

6.10b . . . and gasket

6.12a Unscrew the nuts . . .

6.12b . . . and remove the bearing caps

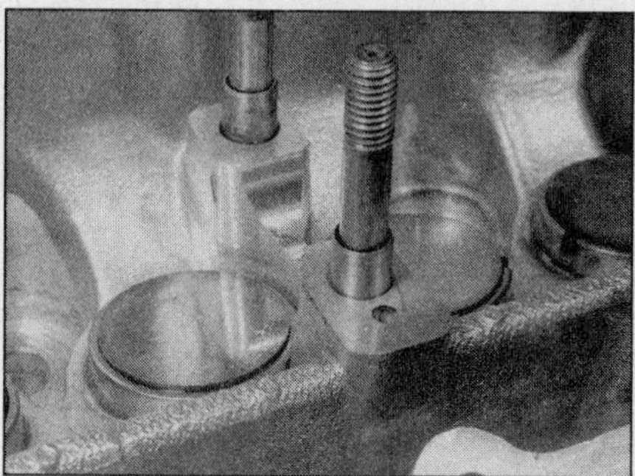

6.12c The camshaft mounting studs incorporate location dowels

6.13 Removing the camshaft from the cylinder head

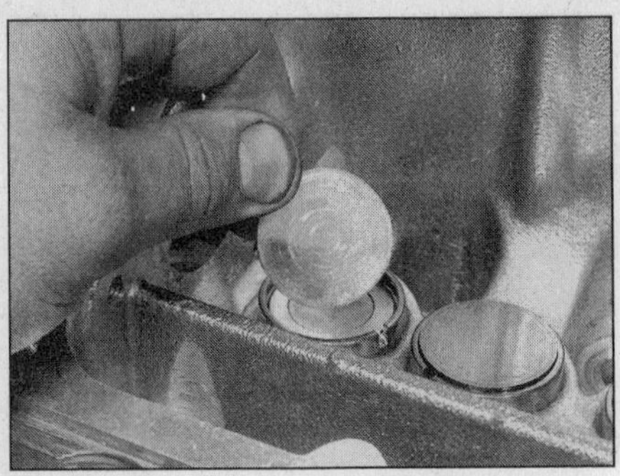
6.14a Removing the shims . . .

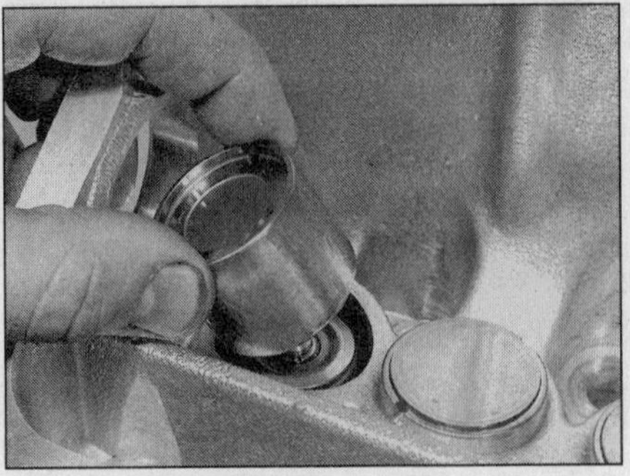
6.14b . . . and cam followers

6.16a Removing the upper spring seat . . .

14 Remove the shims and cam followers, but keep them in their originally fitted order **(see illustrations)**.

All engines

15 Stand the cylinder head on its end. Using a valve spring compressor, compress each valve spring in turn, extracting the split collets when the upper valve spring seat has been pushed far enough down the valve stem to free them. If the spring seat sticks, lightly tap the upper jaw of the spring compressor with a hammer to free it.

16 Release the valve spring compressor and remove the upper spring seat, valve spring and lower spring seat **(see illustrations)**.

17 Withdraw the valve from the head gasket side of the cylinder head, then use a pair of pliers to extract the valve stem oil seal from the top of the guide **(see illustrations)**. If the valve sticks in the guide, carefully deburr the end face with fine abrasive paper. Repeat this process for the remaining valves.

18 On diesel engines, if the swirl chambers are badly coked or burned and are in need of renewal, they may be removed by unscrewing the retaining collars and carefully tapping them out from the combustion chamber side. Recover the washers and keep them identified for position **(see illustration)**.

19 It is essential that each valve is stored together with its collets, retainer, spring, and spring seat. The valves should also be kept in their correct sequence, unless they are so badly worn that they are to be renewed. If they are going to be kept and used again, place each valve assembly in a labelled polythene bag or similar small container **(see illustration)**. Note that No 1 valve is at the timing belt end of the engine.

Cleaning

20 Using a suitable degreasing agent, remove all traces of oil deposits from the cylinder head, paying particular attention to the journal bearings, cam follower bores, valve guides and oilways, as applicable. Scrape off any traces of old gasket from the mating surfaces, taking care not to score or gouge them. If using emery paper, do not use a grade of less than 100. Turn the head over and using a blunt blade, scrape any carbon deposits from the combustion chambers and ports.

Caution: Do not erode the sealing surface of the valve seat.

21 Finally, wash the entire head casting with a suitable solvent to remove the remaining debris.

22 Clean the valve heads and stems using a fine wire brush. If the valve is heavily coked,

6.16b . . . spring . . .

6.16c . . . and lower spring seat

6.17a Removing the valve stem oil seals

6.17b Valve and cam follower components

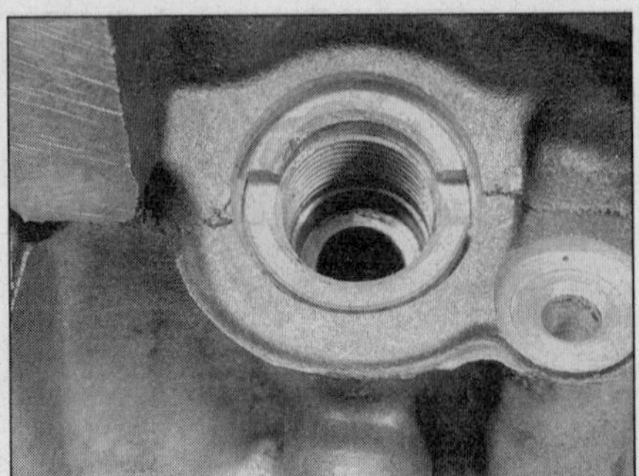
6.18 Swirl chamber retaining collar (diesel engine)

6.19 Keep groups of components together in labelled bags or boxes

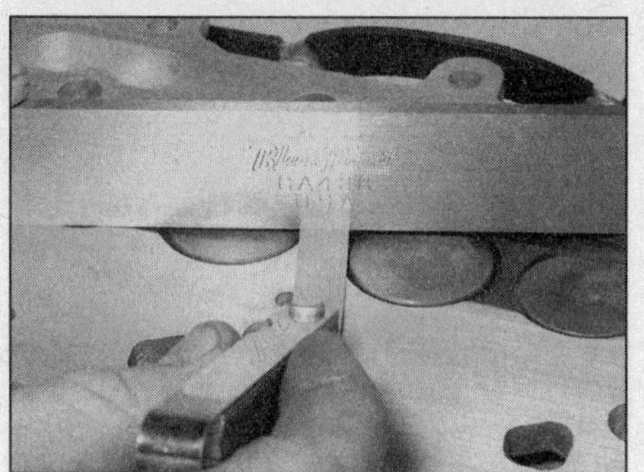

6.25 Checking the cylinder head for distortion

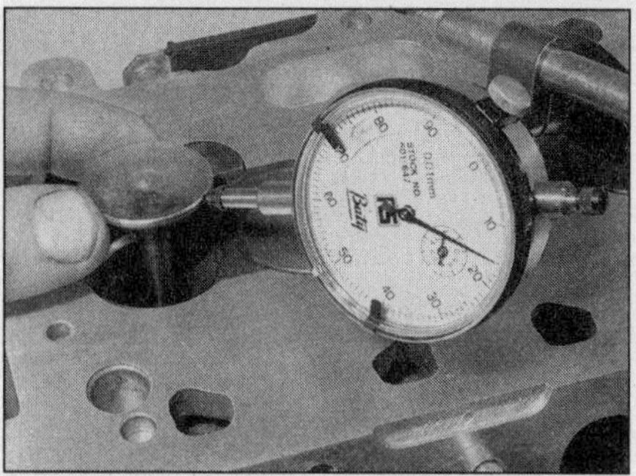

6.27 Checking the valve guides and valves for wear

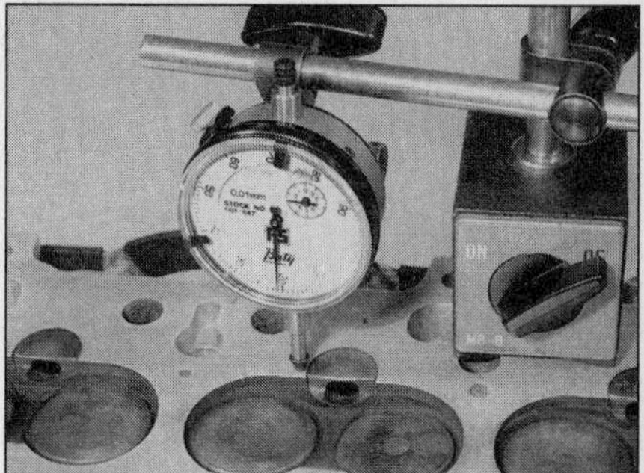

6.29a Diesel swirl chamber protrusion can be checked using a dial gauge . . .

scrape off the majority of the deposits with a blunt blade first, then use the wire brush.

Caution: Do not erode the sealing surface of the valve face.

23 Thoroughly clean the remainder of the components using solvent and allow them to dry completely. On 8-valve petrol and diesel engines, discard the oil seals, as new items must be fitted when the cylinder head is reassembled.

Inspection

Cylinder head

24 Inspect the head very carefully for cracks, evidence of coolant leakage, and other damage. If cracks are found, a new cylinder head should be obtained.

25 Use a straight-edge and feeler blade to check that the cylinder head gasket surface is not distorted **(see illustration)**. If it is, it may be possible to have it machined, provided that the cylinder head thickness is not excessively reduced. As no specifications as to permissible distortion limits or cylinder head thickness tolerances are given by the manufacturer, seek the advice of an engine overhaul specialist if distortion is apparent.

26 Examine the valve seats in each of the combustion chambers. If they are severely pitted, cracked, or burned, they will need to be renewed or re-cut by an engine overhaul specialist. If they are only slightly pitted, this can be removed by grinding-in the valve heads and seats with fine valve-grinding compound, as described below.

27 Check the valve guides for wear by inserting the relevant valve, and checking for side-to-side motion of the valve **(see illustration)**. A very small amount of movement is acceptable. If the movement seems excessive, remove the valve. Measure the valve stem diameter at several points, and renew the valve if it is worn. If the valve stem is not worn, the wear must be in the valve guide, and the guide must be renewed. The renewal of valve guides should be carried out by an engine overhaul specialist, who will have the necessary tools required.

28 If renewing the valve guides, the valve seats should be re-cut or re-ground only *after* the new guides have been fitted.

29 On diesel engines, inspect the swirl chambers for burning or damage such as cracking. Small cracks in the chambers are acceptable; renewal of the chambers will only be required if chamber tracts are badly burned and disfigured, or if they are no longer a tight fit in the cylinder head. If there is any doubt as to the swirl chamber condition, seek the advice of a Fiat dealer or a suitable repairer who specialises in diesel engines. Swirl chamber renewal should be entrusted to a specialist. Using a dial test indicator, check that the difference between the swirl chamber and the cylinder head surface is within the limits given in the Specifications. Alternatively feeler blades and a straight-edge may be used **(see illustrations)**. Zero the dial test indicator on the gasket surface of the cylinder head, then measure the protrusion of the swirl chamber. If the protrusion is not within the specified limits, the advice of a Fiat dealer or suitable repairer who specialises in diesel engines should be sought.

Camshaft

30 Inspect the camshaft for wear on the surfaces of the lobes and journals. Normally their surfaces should be smooth and have a dull shine; look for scoring and pitting. Accelerated wear will occur once the hardened exterior of the camshaft has been damaged.

31 Examine the bearing cap and journal surfaces for signs of wear.

32 To measure the camshaft endfloat, temporarily refit the camshaft then push the camshaft to one end of the cylinder head as far as it will travel. Attach a dial test indicator to the cylinder head and zero it, then push the camshaft as far as it will go to the other end of the cylinder head and record the gauge reading. Verify the reading by pushing the camshaft back to its original position and checking that the gauge indicates zero again **(see illustration)**.

33 The camshaft bearing running clearance may be checked using Plastigauge as described later in this Chapter.

34 Where the camshaft and bearings are worn excessively consider renewing the complete cylinder head together with camshaft and cam followers. A reconditioned head may be available from engine repairers. Wear of cam followers may be checked using a micrometer **(see illustration)**.

6.29b . . . or feeler blades

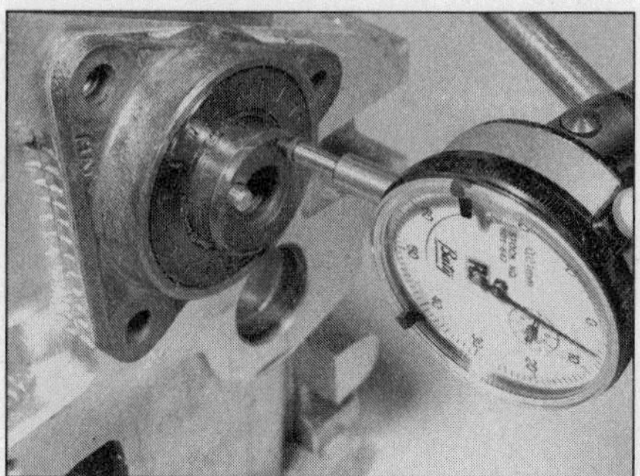

6.32 Checking the camshaft endfloat with a dial gauge

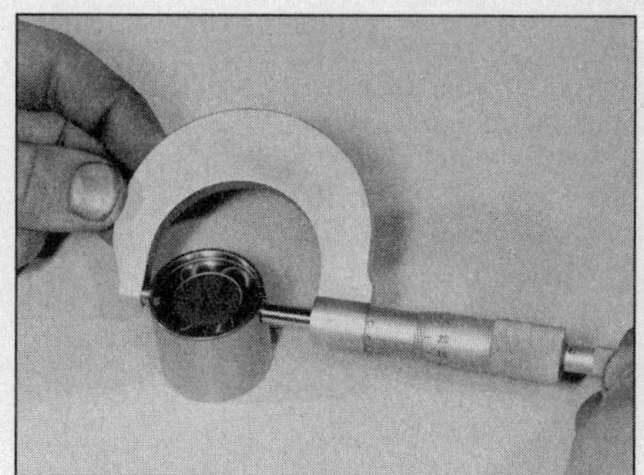

6.34 Checking the wear of the cam followers

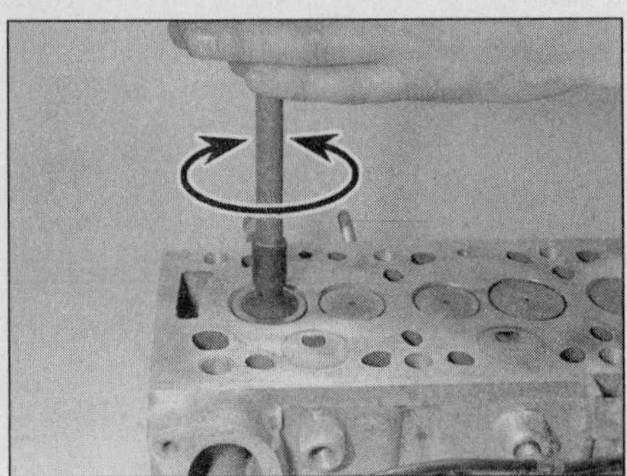

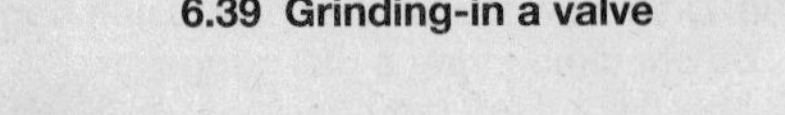

6.39 Grinding-in a valve

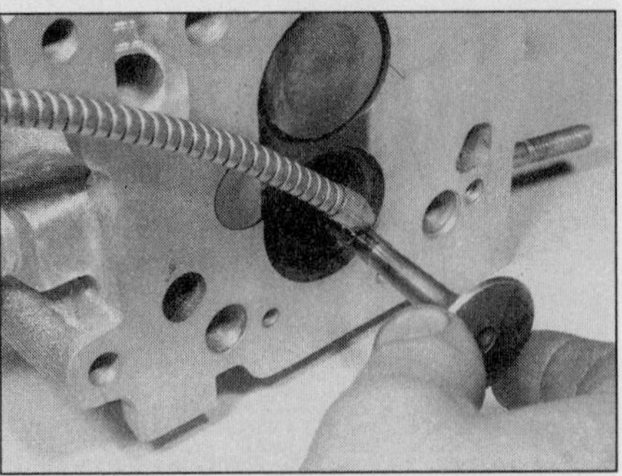

6.45 Lubricate the valves before locating them

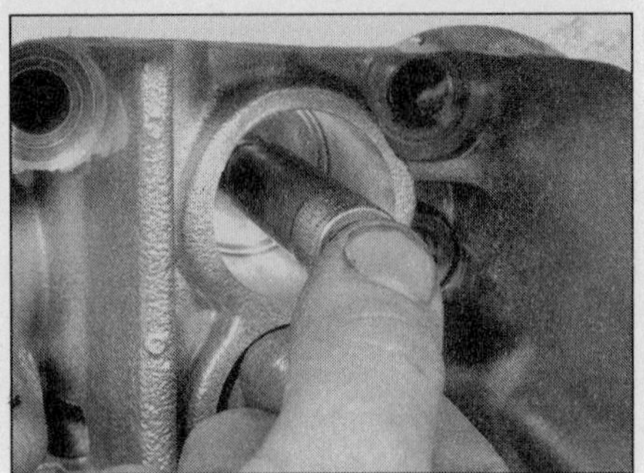

6.46 Using a socket to press the valve stem seals onto the guides

Valves and associated components

35 Examine the head of each valve for pitting, burning, cracks, and general wear. Check the valve stem for scoring and wear ridges. Rotate the valve, and check for any obvious indication that it is bent. Look for pits or excessive wear on the tip of each valve stem. Renew any valve that shows any such signs of wear or damage.

36 If the valve appears satisfactory at this stage, measure the valve stem diameter at several points using a micrometer. Any significant difference in the readings obtained indicates wear of the valve stem. Should any of these conditions be apparent, the valve(s) must be renewed.

37 If the valves are in satisfactory condition, they should be ground (lapped) into their respective seats, to ensure a smooth, gas-tight seal. If the seat is only lightly pitted, or if it has been re-cut, fine grinding compound *only* should be used to produce the required finish. Coarse valve-grinding compound should *not* be used, unless a seat is badly burned or deeply pitted. If this is the case, the cylinder head and valves should be inspected by an expert, to decide whether seat re-cutting, or even the renewal of the valve or seat insert (where possible) is required.

38 Valve grinding is carried out as follows. Place the cylinder head upside-down on blocks on a bench.

39 Smear a trace of (the appropriate grade of) valve-grinding compound on the seat face, and press a suction grinding tool onto the valve head. With a semi-rotary action, grind the valve head to its seat, lifting the valve occasionally to redistribute the grinding compound **(see illustration)**. A light spring placed under the valve head will greatly ease this operation.

40 If coarse grinding compound is being used, work only until a dull, matt even surface is produced on both the valve seat and the valve, then wipe off the used compound, and repeat the process with fine compound. When a smooth unbroken ring of light grey matt finish is produced on both the valve and seat, the grinding operation is complete. *Do not* grind-in the valves any further than absolutely necessary, or the seat will be prematurely sunk into the cylinder head.

41 When all the valves have been ground-in, carefully wash off *all* traces of grinding compound using paraffin or a suitable solvent, before reassembling the cylinder head.

42 Examine the valve springs for signs of damage and discoloration. If possible compare the length of the springs with new ones and renew them if necessary.

43 Stand each spring on a flat surface, and check it for squareness. If any of the springs are damaged, distorted or have lost their tension, obtain a complete new set of springs. It is normal to renew the valve springs as a matter of course if a major overhaul is being carried out.

44 Renew the valve stem oil seals regardless of their apparent condition.

Reassembly

45 Lubricate the stems of the valves, and insert the valves into their original locations **(see illustration)**. If new valves are being fitted, insert them into the locations to which they have been ground.

46 Refit the spring seat then, working on the first valve, dip the new valve stem seal in fresh engine oil. Carefully locate it over the valve and onto the guide. Take care not to damage the seal as it is passed over the valve stem. Use a suitable socket or metal tube to press the seal firmly onto the guide **(see illustration)**.

47 Locate the valve spring on top of its seat, then refit the spring retainer.

48 Compress the valve spring, and locate the split collets in the recess in the valve stem. Release the compressor, then repeat the procedure on the remaining valves **(see illustration)**.

Use a dab of grease to hold the collets in position on the valve stem while the spring compressor is released.

49 With all the valves installed, place the cylinder head on blocks on the bench and, using a hammer and interposed block of wood, tap the end of each valve stem to settle the components.

50 On diesel engines, refit the swirl chambers together with their washers and tighten the retaining collars to the specified torque.

51 Oil the cam followers and locate them in their correct positions in the cylinder head. Locate the shims in the cam followers making sure they are in their original positions.

52 Oil the journals then locate the camshaft in the cylinder head with the cam lobes of No 1 cylinder facing upwards (ie No 1 cylinder at TDC).

53 Refit the bearing caps in their correct positions and progressively tighten the nuts/bolts to the specified torque **(see illustration)**. On petrol engines locate the lubrication pipe on the head and press in the oil feed stub before refitting the bolts.

54 On diesel engines fit a new oil seal to the right-hand side mount, then refit both side mounts together with new gaskets. Tighten the right-hand mount bolts. Also refit the coolant cover and thermostat housing together with new gaskets **(see illustrations)**.

6.48 Compressing the valve spring and fitting the split collets

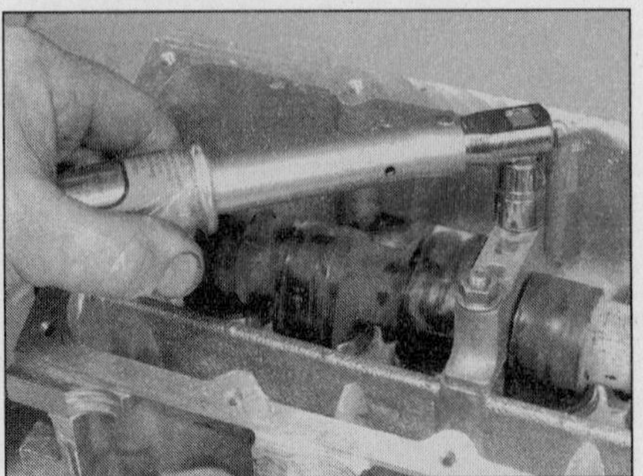

6.53 Tightening the camshaft bearing cap nuts (diesel engines)

55 On diesel engines, fit new O-ring seals to the vacuum pump then refit it to the left-hand end of the cylinder head and tighten the nuts **(see illustrations)**.

56 Refit the camshaft sprocket with reference to Chapter 2A or 2C.

57 Refit the spark plugs, glow plugs and injectors as applicable.

58 If required, refit the inlet and exhaust manifolds at this point. The valve clearances can also be checked now. The cylinder head is now ready for refitting as described in Part A, B or C of this Chapter (as applicable).

6.54a Fitting a new oil seal to the right-hand side mount

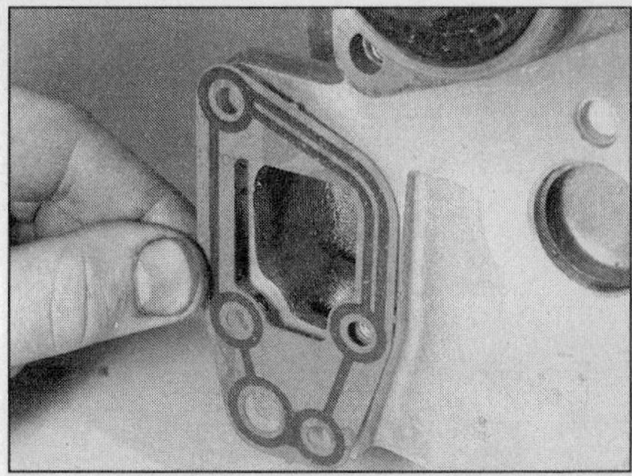

6.54b Coolant cover gasket

6.55a Fitting a new large O-ring on the vacuum pump

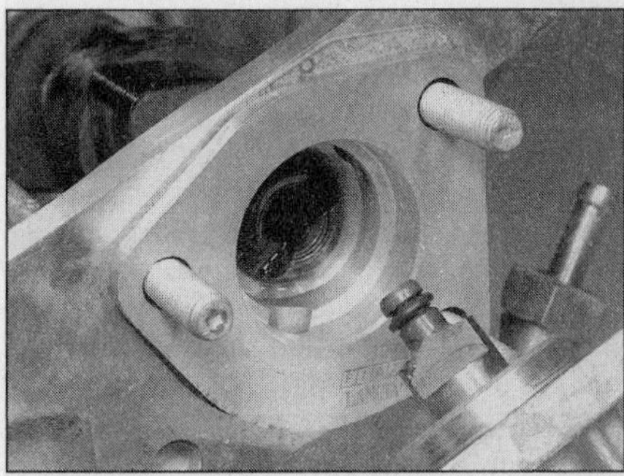

6.55b Fitting the vacuum pump - note the small O-ring on the end of the shaft

7 Pistons and connecting rods - removal, inspection, and big-end running clearance check

Removal

1 Remove the sump and gasket with reference to Chapter 2A, 2B or 2C.

2 Unbolt and remove the oil pump pick-up/filter screen assembly. On 16-valve engines, unbolt and remove the anti-vibration plate from the main bearing caps.

3 The big-end bearing shells can be renewed without having to remove the cylinder head, if the caps are unbolted and the piston/connecting rod pushed gently up the bore slightly (the crankpin being at its lowest point). If these shells are worn, however, the main bearing shells will almost certainly be worn as well. In this case, the crankshaft should be removed for inspection.

4 To remove the pistons and connecting rods, remove the cylinder head first with reference to Chapter 2A, 2B or 2C.

5 Check to see if the big-end caps and connecting rods are numbered. If no numbers are visible, use a hammer and centre-punch, paint or similar, to mark each connecting rod and big-end cap with its respective cylinder number on the flat machined surface provided.

6 Turn the crankshaft as necessary to bring the first crankpin to its lowest point, then unscrew the bolts and remove the big-end cap and shell bearing **(see illustrations)**.

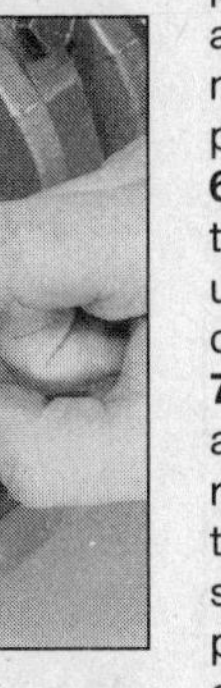

7 Push the piston/rod assembly up the bore and out of the cylinder block. There is one reservation; if a wear ridge has developed at the top of the bores, remove this by careful scraping before trying to remove the piston/rod assemblies. The ridge will otherwise prevent removal, or will break the piston rings during the attempt.

8 Remove the remaining pistons/rods in a similar way. If the bearing shells are to be used again, tape them to their respective caps or rods **(see illustrations)**.

Inspection

9 Before the inspection process can begin, the piston/connecting rod assemblies must be cleaned, and the original piston rings removed from the pistons.

10 Carefully expand the old rings over the top of the pistons. The use of two or three old feeler blades will be helpful in preventing the rings dropping into empty grooves. Be careful not to scratch the piston with the ends of the ring. The rings are brittle, and will snap if they are spread too far. They are also very sharp - protect your hands and fingers. Always remove the rings from the top of the piston. Keep each set of rings with its piston if the old rings are to be re-used.

7.6a Unscrew the bolts . . .

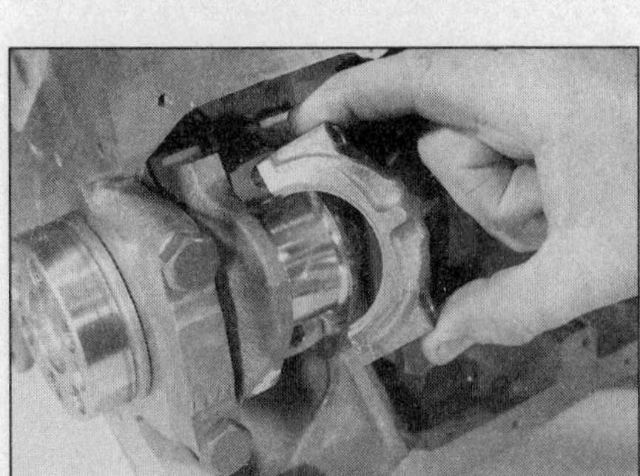

7.6b . . . and remove the big-end cap and shell bearing

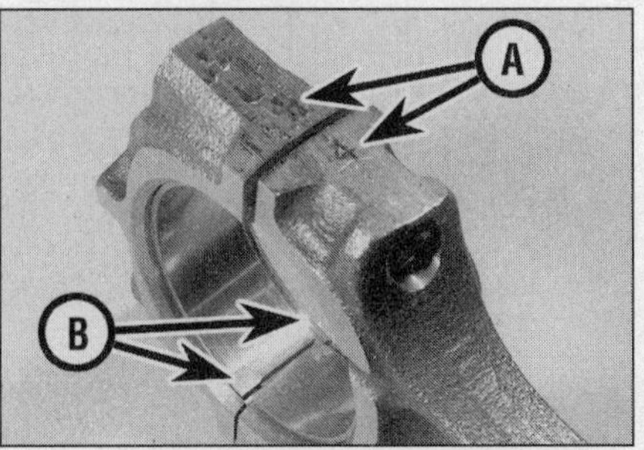

7.8a Connecting rod and cap (diesel engine) showing cylinder numbering (A) and shell location tags (B)

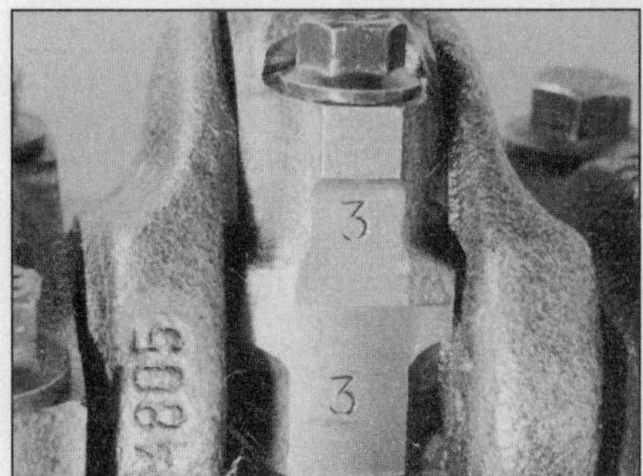

7.8b Connecting rod and cap numbers (petrol engine)

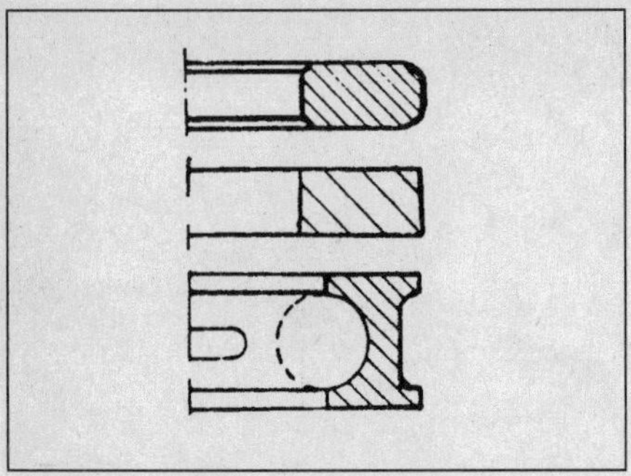
7.13 Positioning of piston rings (petrol engine)

11 Scrape away all traces of carbon from the top of the piston. A hand-held wire brush (or a piece of fine emery cloth) can be used, once the majority of the deposits have been scraped away.

12 Remove the carbon from the ring grooves in the piston, using an old ring. Break the ring in half to do this (be careful not to cut your fingers - piston rings are sharp). Be careful to remove only the carbon deposits - do not remove any metal, and do not nick or scratch the sides of the ring grooves.

13 Once the deposits have been removed, clean the piston/connecting rod assembly with paraffin or a suitable solvent, and dry thoroughly. Make sure that the oil return holes in the ring grooves are clear. Fit the rings to their respective grooves making sure they are positioned the correct way round where applicable **(see illustration)**.

14 If the pistons and cylinder bores are not damaged or worn excessively, and if the cylinder block does not need to be rebored, the original pistons can be refitted. Normal piston wear shows up as even vertical wear on the piston thrust surfaces, and slight looseness of the top ring in its groove. New piston rings should always be used when the engine is reassembled.

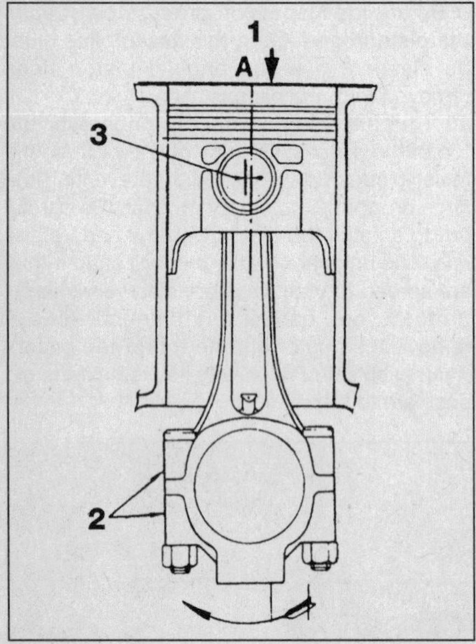

7.26a Piston to connecting rod assembly (petrol engine)

1 *Piston grade (A) and directional arrow on piston crown (towards timing belt end)*
2 *Connecting rod/cap matching numbers*
3 *Gudgeon pin offset in piston (0.9 to 1.1 mm)*
Arrow indicates direction of crankshaft rotation

7.22 Prising out the gudgeon pin retaining circlips

15 Carefully inspect each piston for cracks around the skirt, around the gudgeon pin holes, and at the piston ring lands (between the ring grooves).

16 Look for scoring and scuffing on the piston skirt, holes in the piston crown, and burned areas at the edge of the crown. If the skirt is scored or scuffed, the engine may have been suffering from overheating, and/or abnormal combustion which caused excessively high operating temperatures. The cooling and lubrication systems should be checked thoroughly. Scorch marks on the sides of the pistons show that blow-by has occurred. A hole in the piston crown, or burned areas at the edge of the piston crown, indicates that abnormal combustion has been occurring. If any of the above problems exist, the causes must be investigated and corrected, or the damage will occur again. The causes may include incorrect ignition/injection pump timing, or a faulty injector (as applicable).

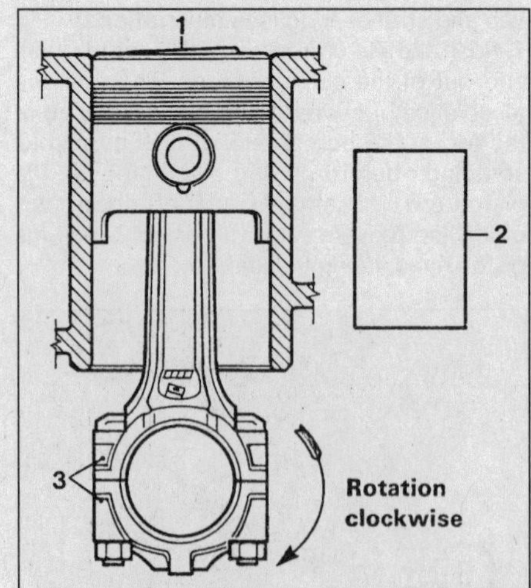

7.26b Piston to connecting rod assembly (diesel engine)

1 *Piston crown*
2 *Injection pump location*
3 *Connecting rod/cap matching numbers*

17 Corrosion of the piston, in the form of pitting, indicates that coolant has been leaking into the combustion chamber and/or the crankcase. Again, the cause must be corrected, or the problem may persist in the rebuilt engine.

18 Examine each connecting rod carefully for signs of damage, such as cracks around the big-end and small-end bearings. Check that the rod is not bent or distorted. Damage is highly unlikely, unless the engine has been seized or badly overheated. Detailed checking of the connecting rod assembly can only be carried out by an engine repair specialist with the necessary equipment.

19 Although not essential, it is highly recommended that the big-end cap bolts are renewed as a complete set prior to refitting.

20 On petrol engines piston and/or connecting rod renewal should be entrusted to an engine repair specialist, who will have the necessary tooling to remove and install the interference fit gudgeon pins.

21 On diesel engines, the gudgeon pins are of the floating type, secured in position by two circlips. On these engines, the pistons and connecting rods can be separated as follows.

22 Using a small flat-bladed screwdriver, prise out the circlips, and push out the gudgeon pin **(see illustration)**. Identify the piston and rod to ensure correct reassembly. Discard the circlips - new ones *must* be used on refitting.

23 Examine the gudgeon pin and connecting rod small-end bearing bush for signs of wear or damage. Bush renewal should be entrusted to an engine overhaul specialist.

24 The connecting rods themselves should not be in need of renewal, unless seizure or some other major mechanical failure has occurred. Check the alignment of the connecting rods visually, and if the rods are not straight, take them to an engine overhaul specialist for a more detailed check.

25 Examine all components, and obtain any new parts as necessary. If new pistons are purchased, they will be supplied complete with gudgeon pins and circlips.

26 On reassembly position the piston on the connecting rod as shown **(see illustrations)**.

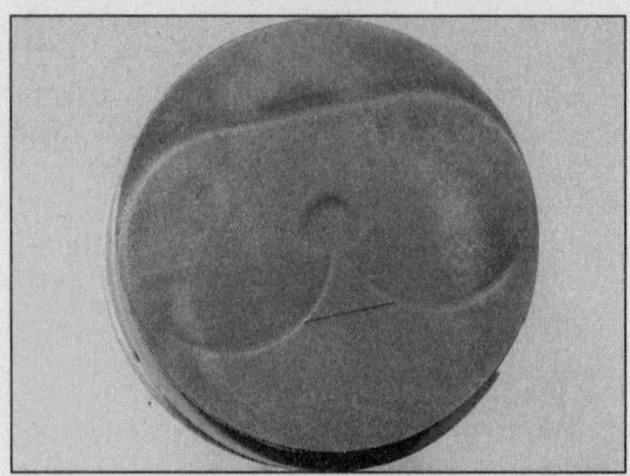
7.26c Piston crown on diesel engines

Apply a smear of clean engine oil to the gudgeon pin. Slide it into the piston and through the connecting rod small-end. Check that the piston pivots freely on the rod, then secure the gudgeon pin in position with two new circlips. Ensure that each circlip is correctly located in its groove in the piston.

Refitting and big-end bearing running clearance check

27 Prior to refitting the piston/connecting rod assemblies, it is recommended that the big-end bearing running clearance is checked as follows.

Big-end bearing running clearance check

28 Clean the backs of the bearing shells, and the bearing locations in both the connecting rod and bearing cap.

29 Press the bearing shells into their locations, ensuring that the tab on each shell engages in the notch in the connecting rod and cap. Take care not to touch any shell's bearing surface with your fingers. If the original bearing shells are being used for the check, ensure that they are refitted in their original locations. The clearance can be checked in either of two ways.

30 One method is to refit the big-end bearing cap to the connecting rod, ensuring that they are fitted the correct way around, with the bearing shells in place. With the cap retaining bolts correctly tightened, use an internal micrometer or vernier caliper to measure the internal diameter of each assembled pair of bearing shells. If the diameter of each corresponding crankshaft journal is measured and then subtracted from the bearing internal diameter, the result will be the big-end bearing running clearance.

31 The second, and more accurate method is to use a product called Plastigauge. Ensure that the bearing shells are correctly fitted then place a strand of Plastigauge on each (cleaned) crankpin journal.

32 Refit the (clean) piston/connecting rod assemblies to the crankshaft, and refit the big-end bearing caps, using the marks made or noted on removal to ensure that they are fitted the correct way around.

33 Tighten the bearing cap bolts taking care not to disturb the Plastigauge or rotate the connecting rod during the tightening sequence.

34 Dismantle the assemblies without rotating the connecting rods. Use the scale printed on the Plastigauge envelope to obtain the big-end bearing running clearance.

35 If the clearance is significantly different from that expected, the bearing shells may be the wrong size (or excessively worn, if the original shells are being re-used). Make sure that no dirt or oil was trapped between the bearing shells and the caps or block when the clearance was measured. If the Plastigauge was wider at one end than at the other, the crankshaft journal may be tapered.

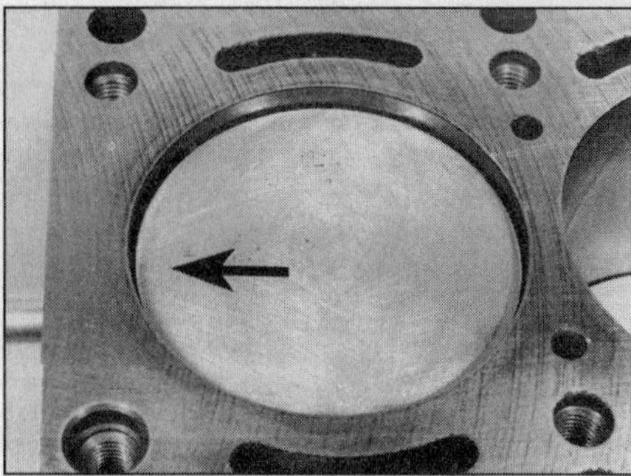

7.40a The arrow on the piston crown must point towards the timing belt end of the engine (petrol engine)

36 On completion, carefully scrape away all traces of the Plastigauge material from the crankshaft and bearing shells. Use your fingernail, or some other object which is unlikely to score the bearing surfaces.

Final piston/connecting rod refitting

37 Ensure that the bearing shells are correctly fitted. If new shells are being fitted, ensure that all traces of the protective grease are cleaned off using paraffin. Wipe dry the shells and connecting rods with a lint-free cloth.

38 Lubricate the cylinder bores, the pistons, and piston rings, then lay out each piston/connecting rod assembly in its respective position.

39 Start with assembly No 1. Position the piston ring gaps 120° apart, then clamp them in position with a piston ring compressor.

40 Insert the piston/connecting rod assembly into the top of cylinder making sure it is the correct way round. On petrol engines, ensure that the arrow on the piston crown is pointing towards the timing belt end of the engine and on diesel engines, ensure that the cloverleaf-shaped cut-out on the piston crown is towards the front (oil filter side) of the cylinder block. Using a block of wood or hammer handle against the piston crown, tap the assembly into the cylinder until the piston crown is flush with the top of the cylinder **(see illustrations)**.

41 Ensure that the bearing shell is still correctly installed. Liberally lubricate the crankpin and both bearing shells. Taking care not to mark the cylinder bores, pull the piston/connecting rod assembly down the bore and onto the crankpin.

7.43a Torque-tightening the big-end bearing cap bolts (diesel engine)

7.40b Inserting the piston/connecting rod assembly into the cylinder bore using a hammer handle (diesel engine)

42 Refit the big-end bearing cap, tightening its retaining bolts finger-tight at first. Note that the faces with the identification marks must match (which means that the bearing shell locating tabs abut each other).

43 Tighten the bearing cap retaining bolts evenly and progressively to the specified torque setting. On diesel engines tighten the bolts to the Stage 1 torque then angle-tighten them to the specified Stage 2 angle using an angle-measuring gauge. **(see illustrations)**

44 Once the bearing cap retaining bolts have been correctly tightened, rotate the crankshaft. Check that it turns freely; some stiffness is to be expected if new components have been fitted, but there should be no signs of binding or tight spots.

45 Refit the remaining three piston/connecting rod assemblies in the same way.

46 Refit the cylinder head, anti-vibration plate (16-valve engines), oil pump pick-up/filter screen assembly and sump with reference to Chapter 2A, 2B or 2C.

8 Crankshaft - removal and inspection

Removal

1 Remove the sump, oil pump and pick-up tube, and flywheel/driveplate with reference to the relevant Sections of Chapter 2 Parts A, B or C. On 16-valve engines, unbolt and remove the anti-vibration plate from the main bearing caps.

7.43b Angle-tightening the big-end bearing cap bolts (diesel engine)

8.4 Using a dial gauge to check the crankshaft endfloat

8.6 Main bearing markings (petrol engine)

2 Remove the pistons and connecting rods, as described in Section 7. However, if no work is to be done on the pistons and connecting rods there is no need to remove the cylinder head, or to push the pistons out of the cylinder bores. The pistons should just be pushed far enough up the bores that they are positioned clear of the crankshaft journals.

3 Unbolt the crankshaft rear oil seal housing from the cylinder block and recover the gasket where fitted.

4 Before removing the crankshaft, check the endfloat using a dial gauge. Push the crankshaft fully one way, and then zero the gauge. Push the crankshaft fully the other way, and check the endfloat **(see illustration)**. The result can be compared with the specified amount, and will give an indication as to whether new thrustwashers are required.

5 If a dial gauge is not available, feeler blades can be used. First push the crankshaft fully towards the flywheel end of the engine, then use feeler blades to measure the gap - on petrol engines measure between the centre main bearing thrustwasher and the crankshaft web, and on diesel engines measure between the rear main bearing and the crankshaft web.

6 Note the markings on the main bearing caps which vary according to type. On 8-valve petrol engines there is one line on the cap nearest the timing belt end, two on the second cap, C on the centre cap, then three and four lines on the remaining caps **(see illustration)**. On 16-valve petrol engines, the caps are marked one to five with a series of lines (one line for the cap nearest the timing belt end, two for the next cap and so on). On diesel engines the caps are marked one to five in the same way but with notches instead of lines. Note also that on some diesel engines the cap nearest the timing belt end is not marked and the notches therefore start with No 2 cap.

7 Loosen and remove the main bearing cap retaining bolts, and lift off each bearing cap. Recover the lower bearing shells, and tape them to their respective caps for safe-keeping. On some diesel engines note that the centre main bearing cap bolts are longer than the other bolts.

8 Lift the crankshaft from the crankcase and remove the upper bearing shells from the crankcase. If the shells are to be used again, keep them identified for position. Also remove the thrustwashers from their position either side of the centre main bearing (petrol engines) or rear main bearing (diesel engines) **(see illustrations)**.

Inspection

9 Wash the crankshaft in a suitable solvent and allow it to dry. Flush the oil holes thoroughly, to ensure that they are not blocked - use a pipe cleaner or a needle brush if necessary. Remove any sharp edges from the edge of the holes which may damage the new bearings when they are installed.

10 Inspect the main bearing and crankpin journals carefully; if uneven wear, cracking, scoring or pitting are evident then the crankshaft should be reground by an engineering workshop, and refitted to the engine with undersize bearings.

11 Use a micrometer to measure the diameter of each main bearing journal. Taking a number of measurements on the surface of each journal will reveal if it is worn unevenly. Differences in diameter measured at 90° intervals indicate that the journal is out of round. Differences in diameter measured along the length of the journal, indicate that the journal is tapered. Again, if wear is detected, the crankshaft can be reground by an engineering workshop and refitted with undersize bearings.

12 Check the oil seal journals at either end of the crankshaft. If they appear excessively scored or damaged, they may cause the new seals to leak when the engine is reassembled. It may be possible to repair the journal; seek the advice of an engineering workshop.

13 Measure the crankshaft runout by setting up a DTI gauge on the centre main bearing journal and rotating the shaft in V - blocks. The maximum deflection of the gauge will indicate the runout. Take precautions to protect the bearing journals and oil seal mating surfaces from damage during this procedure. A maximum runout figure is not quoted by the manufacturer, but use the figure of 0.05 mm as a rough guide. If the runout exceeds this figure, crankshaft renewal should be considered - consult your Fiat dealer or an engine rebuilding specialist for advice.

14 Refer to Section 10 for details of main and big-end bearing inspection.

9 Cylinder block/crankcase - cleaning and inspection

Cleaning

1 Remove all external components, brackets and electrical switches/sensors from the block including the rear engine plate, injection pump/oil filter bracket and gasket, intermediate shaft bracket, oil vapour breather casing, and coolant pump. Also unbolt and remove the oil return tube from the crankcase **(see illustrations)**. For complete cleaning, the core plugs should ideally be removed. Drill a small hole in the plugs, then insert a self-tapping screw into the hole. Pull out the plugs by

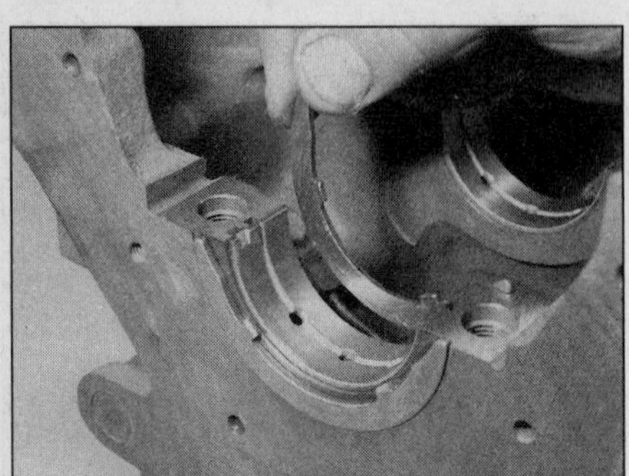

8.8a Removing the thrustwashers . . .

8.8b . . . and upper bearing shells (diesel engine)

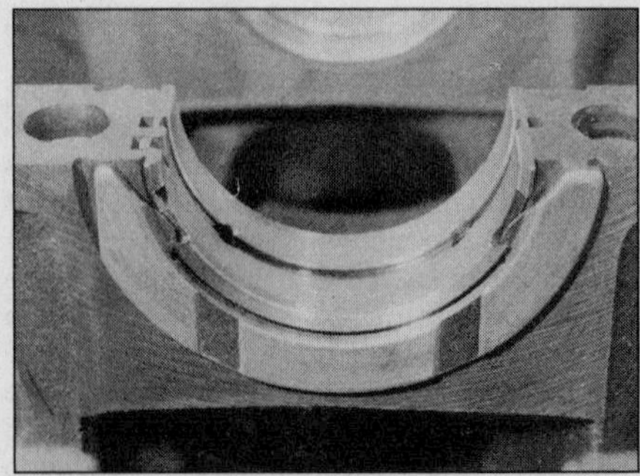

8.8c Thrustwashers located on the centre main bearing (petrol engine)

9.1a Removing the oil return tube from the crankcase

9.1b Removing the injection pump/oil filter bracket

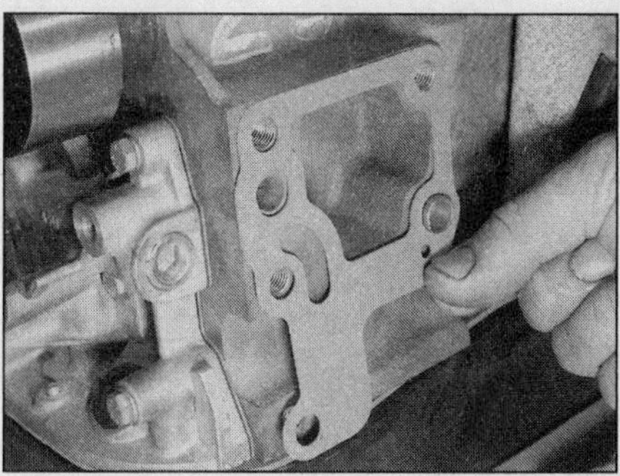
9.1c Removing the injection pump/oil filter bracket gasket from the cylinder block

pulling on the screw with a pair of grips, or by using a slide hammer.

2 Where applicable, undo the retaining bolts and remove the piston oil jet spray tubes from inside the cylinder block.

3 Scrape all traces of gasket from the cylinder block/crankcase, taking care not to damage the gasket/sealing surfaces.

4 Remove all oil gallery plugs (where fitted). The plugs are usually very tight - they may have to be drilled out, and the holes re-tapped. Use new plugs when the engine is reassembled.

5 If the block is very dirty have it steam-cleaned, otherwise use paraffin to clean it.

6 Clean all oil holes and oil galleries again and dry thoroughly, then apply a light film of oil to all mating surfaces, to prevent rusting. Smear the cylinder bores with a light coating of oil.

7 All threaded holes must be clean, to ensure accurate torque readings during reassembly. To clean the threads, run the correct-size tap into each of the holes to remove rust, corrosion, thread sealant or sludge, and to restore damaged threads **(see illustration)**. If possible, use compressed air to clear the holes of debris produced by this operation.

8 Apply suitable sealant to the new oil gallery plugs, and insert them into the holes in the block. Tighten them securely.

9 Where applicable, refit the piston oil jet spray tubes to the cylinder block, and securely tighten the retaining bolts. Bend over the tabs to lock the bolts **(see illustration)**.

10 Fit the new core plugs with sealant applied to their perimeters before using a suitable metal tube to drive them into position.

11 Refit the oil return tube to the crankcase and tighten the mounting bolts.

12 Refit the injection pump/oil filter bracket together with a new gasket and tighten the bolts.

13 Refit the rear engine plate and tighten the bolts. Also refit any other removed brackets etc.

Inspection

14 Visually check the cylinder block for cracks and corrosion. Look for stripped threads in the threaded holes. If there has been any history of internal water leakage, it may be worthwhile having an engine overhaul

9.1d Removing the intermediate shaft bracket

9.1e Removing the oil vapour breather casing

specialist check it with special equipment.

15 Check each cylinder bore for scuffing and scoring. Check for signs of a wear ridge at the top of the cylinder, indicating that the bore is excessively worn.

16 If the necessary measuring equipment is available, measure the bore diameters at the top (just under the wear ridge), centre, and bottom, parallel to the crankshaft axis.

17 Next, measure the bore diameters at the same three locations, at right-angles to the crankshaft axis. If there is any doubt about the condition of the cylinder bores seek the advice of a Fiat dealer or suitable engine reconditioning specialist.

18 If the engine is not going to be reassembled right away, cover it with a large plastic bag to keep it clean and prevent rusting. If the engine is ready for reassembly, refit all the components and brackets removed.

10 Main and big-end bearings - inspection and selection

2D

Inspection

1 Even though the main and big-end bearings should be renewed during the engine overhaul, the old bearings should be retained for close examination, as they may reveal valuable information about the condition of the engine **(see illustration overleaf)**. The bearing shells are available in different thicknesses to match the diameter of the journal.

2 Bearing failure can occur due to lack of lubrication, the presence of dirt or other foreign particles, overloading the engine, or corrosion. Regardless of the cause of bearing

9.7 To clean the cylinder block threads, run a correct-size tap into the holes

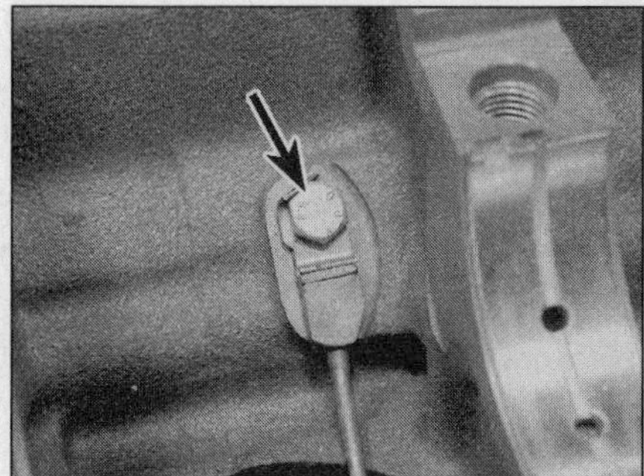
9.9 Piston oil jet spray tube showing locking tab

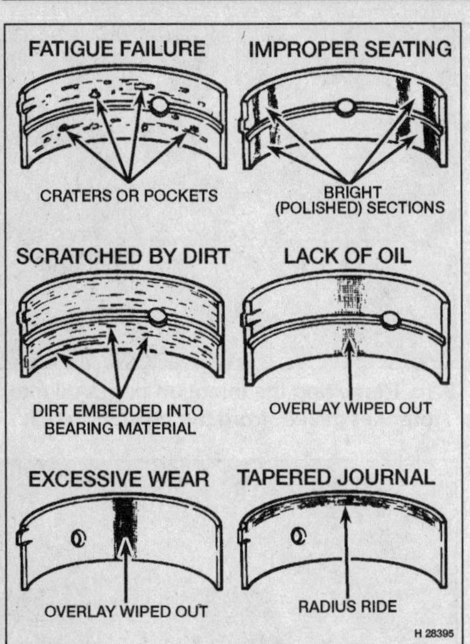

10.1 Typical bearing failures

failure, the cause must be corrected (where applicable) before the engine is reassembled, to prevent it from happening again.

3 When examining the bearing shells, remove them from the cylinder block/crankcase, the main bearing caps, the connecting rods and the connecting rod big-end bearing caps. Lay them out on a clean surface in the same general position as their location in the engine. This will enable you to match any bearing problems with the corresponding crankshaft journal. *Do not* touch any shell's bearing surface with your fingers while checking it.

4 Dirt and other foreign matter gets into the engine in a variety of ways. It may be left in the engine during assembly, or it may pass through filters or the crankcase ventilation system. It may get into the oil, and from there into the bearings. Metal chips from machining operations and normal engine wear are often present. Abrasives are sometimes left in engine components after reconditioning, especially when parts are not thoroughly cleaned using the proper cleaning methods. Whatever the source, these foreign objects often end up embedded in the soft bearing material, and are easily recognised. Large particles will not embed in the bearing, and will score or gouge the bearing and journal. The best prevention for this cause of bearing failure is to clean all parts thoroughly, and keep everything spotlessly-clean during engine assembly. Frequent and regular engine oil and filter changes are also recommended.

5 Lack of lubrication (or lubrication breakdown) has a number of interrelated causes. Excessive heat (which thins the oil), overloading (which squeezes the oil from the bearing face) and oil leakage (from excessive bearing clearances, worn oil pump or high engine speeds) all contribute to lubrication breakdown. Blocked oil passages, which can be the result of misaligned oil holes in a bearing shell, will also oil-starve a bearing, and destroy it. When lack of lubrication is the cause of bearing failure, the bearing material is wiped or extruded from the steel backing of the bearing. Temperatures may increase to the point where the steel backing turns blue from overheating.

6 Driving habits can have a definite effect on bearing life. Full-throttle, low-speed operation (labouring the engine) puts very high loads on bearings, tending to squeeze out the oil film. These loads cause the bearings to flex, which produces fine cracks in the bearing face (fatigue failure). Eventually, the bearing material will loosen in pieces, and tear away from the steel backing.

7 Short-distance driving leads to corrosion of bearings, because insufficient engine heat is produced to drive off the condensed water and corrosive gases. These products collect in the engine oil, forming acid and sludge. As the oil is carried to the engine bearings, the acid attacks and corrodes the bearing material.

8 Incorrect bearing installation during engine assembly will lead to bearing failure as well. Tight-fitting bearings leave insufficient bearing running clearance, and will result in oil starvation. Dirt or foreign particles trapped behind a bearing shell result in high spots on the bearing, which lead to failure.

9 *Do not* touch any shell's bearing surface with your fingers during reassembly; there is a risk of scratching the delicate surface, or of depositing particles of dirt on it.

10 As mentioned at the beginning of this Section, the bearing shells should be renewed as a matter of course during engine overhaul; to do otherwise is false economy.

Selection

11 Main and big-end bearings are available in standard sizes and a range of undersizes to suit reground crankshafts - refer to the Specifications for details. The engine reconditioner will select the correct bearing shells for a machined crankshaft.

12 The running clearances can be checked when the crankshaft is refitted with its new bearings.

11 Engine overhaul - reassembly sequence

1 Before reassembly begins, ensure that all new parts have been obtained, and that all necessary tools are available. Read through the entire procedure to familiarise yourself with the work involved, and to ensure that all items necessary for reassembly of the engine are at hand. In addition to all normal tools and materials, thread-locking compound will be needed. A tube of sealant will also be required for the joint faces that are fitted without gaskets.

2 In order to save time and avoid problems, engine reassembly can be carried out in the following order:

a) Crankshaft (Section 12).
b) Piston/connecting rod assemblies (Section 7).
c) Oil pump (see Part A, B or C - as applicable).
d) Sump (see Part A, B or C - as applicable).
e) Flywheel/driveplate (see Part A, B or C - as applicable).
f) Cylinder head (see Part A, B or C - as applicable).
g) Coolant pump (see Chapter 3)
h) Timing belt tensioner and sprockets, and timing belt (See Part A, B or C - as applicable).
i) Engine external components.

3 At this stage, all engine components should be absolutely clean and dry, with all faults repaired. The components should be laid out on a completely clean work surface.

12 Crankshaft - refitting and main bearing running clearance check

Crankshaft - initial refitting

1 Crankshaft refitting is the first stage of engine reassembly following overhaul. At this point, it is assumed that the crankshaft, cylinder block/crankcase and bearings have been cleaned, inspected and reconditioned or renewed.

2 Place the cylinder block on a clean, level work surface, with the crankcase facing upwards. Where necessary, unbolt the bearing caps and lay them out in order to ensure correct reassembly. If they are still in place, remove the bearing shells from the caps and the crankcase and wipe out the inner surfaces with a clean rag - they must be kept spotlessly clean.

3 Clean the rear surface of the new bearing shells with a rag and fit them on the bearing saddles. Ensure that the orientation lugs on the shells engage with the recesses in the saddles and that the oil holes are correctly aligned. Do not hammer or otherwise force the bearing shells into place. It is critically important that the surfaces of the bearings are kept free from damage and contamination.

4 Give the newly fitted bearing shells and the crankshaft journals a final clean with a rag. Check that the oil holes in the crankshaft are free from dirt, as any left here will become embedded in the new bearings when the engine is first started.

5 Carefully lay the crankshaft in the crankcase, taking care not to dislodge the bearing shells **(see illustration)**.

Main bearing running clearance check

6 When the crankshaft and bearings are refitted, a clearance must exist between them

12.5 Lowering the crankshaft into the crankcase

12.7 Lay the Plastigauge on the main bearing journals

12.8 Locating a lower half main bearing shell in its cap

12.9 Fit the main bearing caps . . .

12.10a . . . insert the bolts . . .

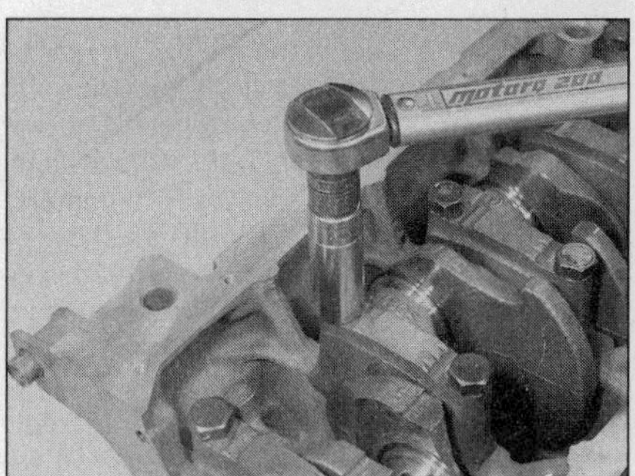

12.10b . . . and torque-tighten them

to allow lubricant to circulate. This clearance is impossible to check using feeler blades, however Plastigauge can be used. This consists of a thin strip of soft plastic that is crushed between the bearing shells and journals when the bearing caps are tightened up. Its width then indicates the size of the clearance gap.

7 Cut off five pieces of Plastigauge, just shorter than the length of the crankshaft journal. Lay a piece on each journal, in line with its axis **(see illustration)**.

8 Wipe off the rear surfaces of the new lower half main bearing shells and fit them to the main bearing caps, again ensuring that the locating lugs engage correctly **(see illustration)**.

9 Fit the caps in their correct locations on the bearing saddles, using the manufacturers markings as a guide **(see illustration)**. Ensure that they are correctly orientated - the caps should be fitted such that the recesses for the bearing shell locating lugs are on the same side as those in the bearing saddle.

10 Insert and tighten the bolts until they are all correctly torqued **(see illustrations)**. Do not allow the crankshaft to rotate at all whilst the Plastigauge is in place. Progressively unbolt the bearing caps and remove them, taking care not to dislodge the Plastigauge.

11 The width of the crushed Plastigauge can now be measured, using the scale provided **(see illustration)**. Use the correct scale, as both imperial and metric are printed. This measurement indicates the running clearance - compare it with that listed in the Specifications. If the clearance is outside the tolerance, it may be due to dirt or debris trapped under the bearing surface; try cleaning them again and repeat the clearance check. If the results are still unacceptable, re-check the journal diameters and the bearing sizes. Note that if the Plastigauge is thicker at one end, the journals may be tapered and as such, will require regrinding.

12 When you are satisfied that the clearances are correct, carefully remove the remains of the Plastigauge from the journals and bearings faces. Use a soft, plastic or wooden scraper as anything metallic is likely to damage the surfaces.

Crankshaft - final refitting

13 Lift the crankshaft out of the crankcase. Wipe off the surfaces of the bearings in the crankcase and the bearing caps. Fit the thrust bearings using grease to hold them in position. Ensure they are seated correctly in the machined recesses, with the oil grooves facing outwards

14 Liberally coat the bearing shells in the crankcase with clean engine oil **(see illustration)**.

15 Lower the crankshaft into position in the crankcase.

16 Lubricate the lower bearing shells in the main bearing caps with clean engine oil. Make sure that the locating lugs on the shells are still engaged with the corresponding recesses in the caps.

17 Fit the main bearing caps in the correct order and orientation. Insert the bearing cap bolts and hand tighten them only.

18 Working from the centre bearing cap outwards, tighten the retaining bolts to their specified torque. On petrol engines, tighten all the bolts to the first stage, then angle-tighten them to the Stage 2 angle **(see illustration)**.

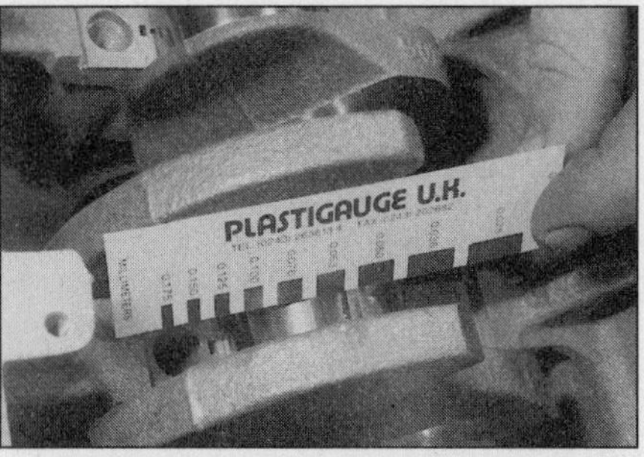

12.11 Use the special scale card to determine the main bearing running clearance

12.14 Lubricate the main bearing shells before final assembly

12.18 Angle-tightening the main bearing cap bolts (petrol engine)

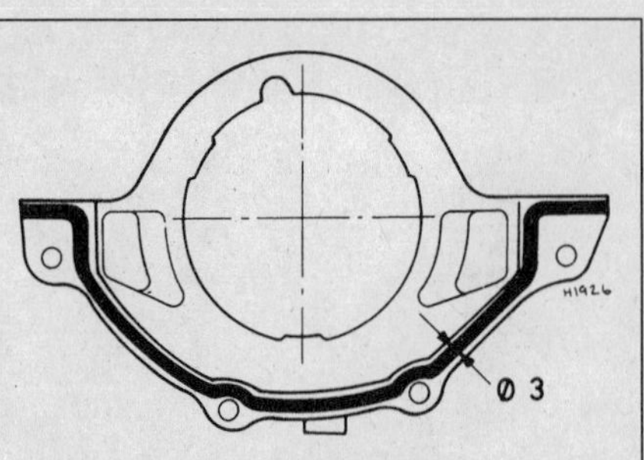

12.19a Application area for silicone instant gasket on crankshaft rear oil seal housing (petrol engine)

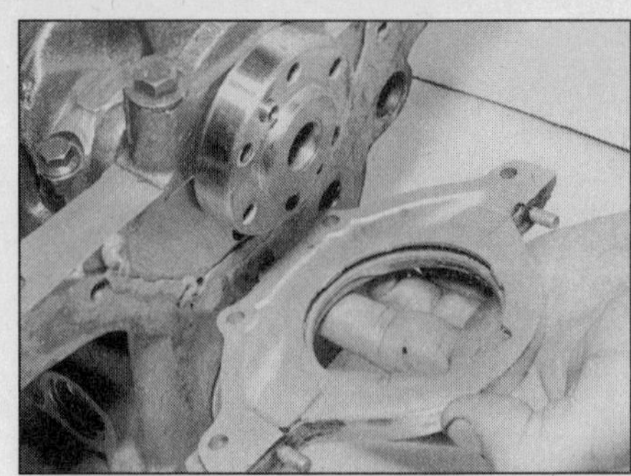

12.19b Refitting the crankshaft rear oil seal housing (petrol engine)

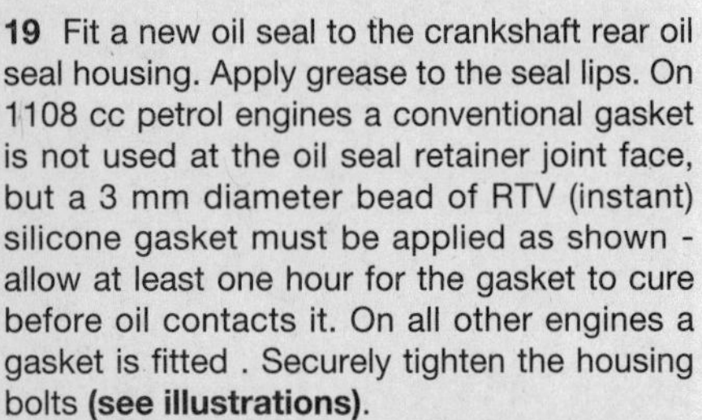

19 Fit a new oil seal to the crankshaft rear oil seal housing. Apply grease to the seal lips. On 1108 cc petrol engines a conventional gasket is not used at the oil seal retainer joint face, but a 3 mm diameter bead of RTV (instant) silicone gasket must be applied as shown - allow at least one hour for the gasket to cure before oil contacts it. On all other engines a gasket is fitted . Securely tighten the housing bolts **(see illustrations)**.

20 Check that the crankshaft rotates freely by turning it by hand. If resistance is felt, re-check the running clearances, as described above.

21 Carry out a check of the crankshaft endfloat as described at the beginning of Section 8. If the thrust surfaces of the crankshaft have been checked and new thrust washers have been fitted, then the endfloat should be within specification.

22 Refit the pistons and connecting rods as described in Section 7.

23 Refit the flywheel/driveplate, anti-vibration plate (16-valve engines), oil pump and pick-up tube, and sump with reference to the relevant Sections of Parts A, B or C of this Chapter.

13 Engine - initial start-up after overhaul and reassembly

1 With the engine refitted in the vehicle, double-check the engine oil and coolant levels. Make a final check that everything has been reconnected, and that there are no tools or rags left in the engine compartment.

Petrol engine models

2 Remove the spark plugs, then disable the ignition system by disconnecting the LT wiring plug to the ignition coils.

3 Turn the engine on the starter until the oil pressure warning light goes out. Refit the spark plugs, and reconnect the LT wiring.

Diesel engine models

4 Disconnect the wiring from the stop solenoid on the injection pump, then turn the engine on the starter motor until the oil pressure warning light goes out. Reconnect the wire to the stop solenoid.

5 Fully depress the accelerator pedal, turn the ignition key to its first position and wait for the preheating warning light to go out.

All models

6 Start the engine, noting that this may take a little longer than usual, due to the fuel system components having been disturbed.

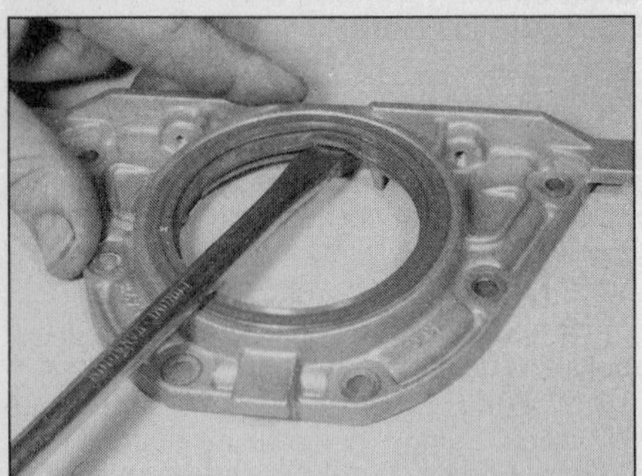

12.19c On diesel engines use a screwdriver to prise out the rear oil seal

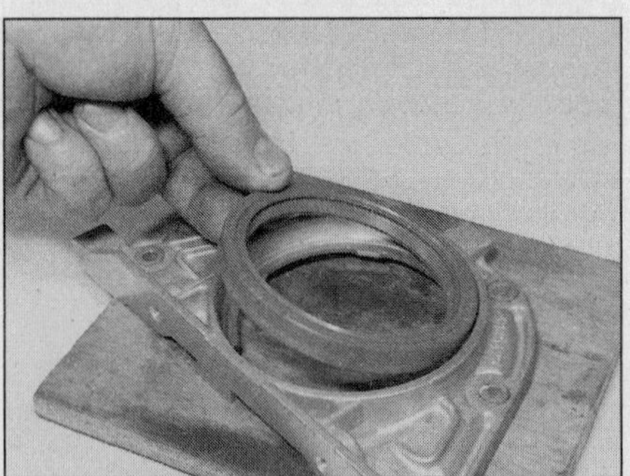

12.19d Locate the new oil seal in the housing (diesel engine) . . .

12.19e . . . and use a block of wood to drive it in

12.19f On Diesel engines fit the gasket to the cylinder block . . .

12.19g . . . then locate the rear oil seal housing . . .

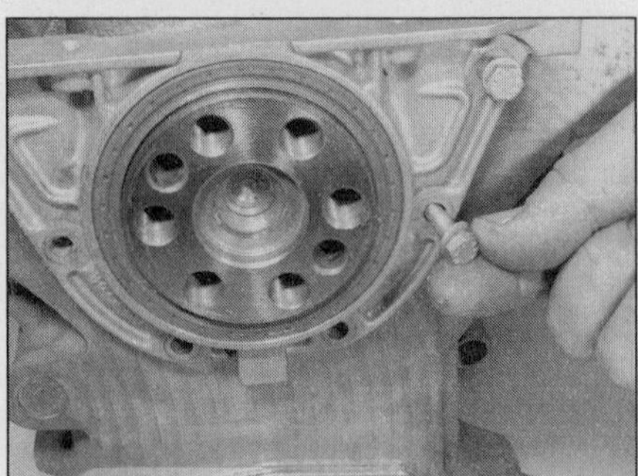

12.19h . . . and insert the bolts

7 While the engine is idling, check for fuel, water and oil leaks. Don't be alarmed if there are some odd smells and smoke from parts getting hot and burning off oil deposits.

8 Assuming all is well, keep the engine idling until hot water is felt circulating through the top hose, then switch off the engine.

9 Recheck the oil and coolant levels as described in Chapter 1A or 1B, and top-up as necessary.

10 There is no need to re-tighten the cylinder head bolts once the engine has first run after reassembly.

11 If new pistons, rings or crankshaft bearings have been fitted, the engine must be treated as new, and run-in for the first 500 miles (800 km). *Do not* operate the engine at full-throttle, or allow it to labour at low engine speeds in any gear. It is recommended that the oil and filter be changed at the end of this period.

Chapter 3
Cooling, heating and ventilation systems

Contents

Degrees of difficulty

Easy, suitable for novice with little experience 	**Fairly easy,** suitable for beginner with some experience 	**Fairly difficult,** suitable for competent DIY mechanic 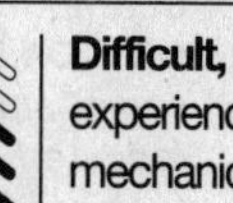	**Difficult,** suitable for experienced DIY mechanic	**Very difficult,** suitable for expert DIY or professional 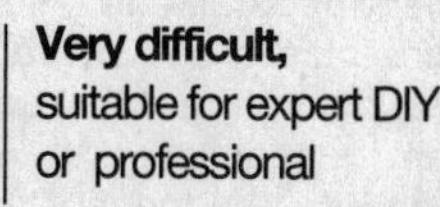

Specifications

General

Expansion tank relief valve opening pressure	0.98 bar
Coolant pump impeller-to-casing clearance:	
Diesel engine models	0.53 to 1.37 mm
Petrol engine models	0.4 to 0.9 mm

Thermostat

Diesel engine models:	
Opening temperature:	
Starts to open	78 to 82°C
Fully open	88°C
Maximum valve travel (approximate)	7.5 mm
Petrol engine models:	
Opening temperature:	
1108 cc and 1242 cc (8-valve) engines:	
Starts to open	85 to 89°C
Fully open	100°C
1242 cc (16-valve) engines:	
Starts to open	81 to 85°C
Fully open	103°C
Maximum valve lift (approximate)	7.5 mm

Electric cooling fan

Petrol engine models with single speed fan:	
Cut-in temperature	90 to 94°C
Cut-out temperature	85 to 89°C
Diesel engine models with twin speed fan:	
Cut-in temperature:	
Primary fan	86 to 90° C
Secondary fan	90 to 94°C
Cut-out temperature:	
Primary fan	81 to 85°C
Secondary fan	85 to 89°C

Torque wrench settings

Torque wrench settings	Nm	lbf ft
Coolant pump pulley securing bolts (diesel engine models)	23	17
Coolant pump securing bolts:		
Diesel engine models	23	17
Petrol engine models	8	6
Coolant pump securing nuts (petrol engine models)	10	7

3

1 General information and precautions

General information

The engine cooling/cabin heating system is of pressurised type, comprising a coolant pump driven by the camshaft timing belt (petrol engine models) or auxiliary drivebelt (diesel engine models), a crossflow radiator, a coolant expansion tank, an electric cooling fan, a thermostat, heater matrix, and all associated hoses and switches.

The system functions as follows: the coolant pump circulates cold water around the cylinder block and head passages, and through the inlet manifold, heater matrix and throttle body to the thermostat housing.

When the engine is cold, the thermostat remains closed and prevents coolant from circulating through the radiator. When the coolant reaches a predetermined temperature, the thermostat opens, and the coolant passes through the top hose to the radiator. As the coolant circulates through the radiator, it is cooled by the in-rush of air when the car is in forward motion. The airflow is supplemented by the action of the electric cooling fan, when necessary. As the temperature of the coolant in the radiator drops, it flows to the bottom of the radiator by convection, and passes out through the bottom hose to the coolant pump - the cycle is then repeated.

When the engine is at normal operating temperature, the coolant expands, and some of it is displaced into the expansion tank. Coolant collects in the tank, and is returned to the radiator when the system cools. On petrol engine models, the expansion tank is integrated into the side of the radiator. On diesel engine models, and certain petrol engine models with air conditioning, the tank is a separate unit, mounted on the right hand side of the engine compartment.

On turbo diesel engine models, the coolant is also passed through a supplementary engine oil cooler, to assist in controlling the engine lubricant temperature.

The electric cooling fan mounted in front of the radiator is controlled by a thermostatic switch. At a predetermined coolant temperature, the switch/sensor actuates the fan to provide additional airflow through the radiator. The switch cuts the electrical supply to the fan when the coolant temperature has dropped below a preset threshold (see Specifications).

Precautions

Warning: Do not attempt to remove the expansion tank pressure cap, or to disturb any part of the cooling system, while the engine is hot, as there is a high risk of scalding. If the expansion tank pressure cap must be removed before the engine and radiator have fully cooled (even though this is not recommended), the pressure in the cooling system must first be relieved. Cover the cap with a thick layer of cloth, to avoid scalding, and slowly unscrew the pressure cap until a hissing sound is heard. When the hissing stops, indicating that the pressure has reduced, slowly unscrew the pressure cap until it can be removed; if more hissing sounds are heard, wait until they have stopped before unscrewing the cap completely. At all times, keep your face well away from the pressure cap opening, and protect your hands.

Warning: Do not allow antifreeze to come into contact with your skin, or with the painted surfaces of the vehicle. Rinse off spills immediately, with plenty of water. Never leave antifreeze lying around in an open container, or in a puddle in the driveway or on the garage floor. Children and pets are attracted by its sweet smell, but antifreeze can be fatal if ingested.

Warning: If the engine is hot, the electric cooling fan may start rotating even if the engine and ignition are switched off. Be careful to keep your hands, hair, and any loose clothing well clear when working in the engine compartment.

2 Cooling system hoses - disconnection and renewal

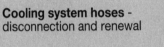

1 The number, routing and pattern of hoses will vary according to model, but the same basic procedure applies. Before commencing work, make sure that the new hoses are to hand, along with new hose clips if needed. It is good practice to renew the hose clips at the same time as the hoses.

2 Drain the cooling system, as described in Chapter 1A or 1B, saving the coolant if it is fit for re-use. Apply a little penetrating oil onto the hose clips if they are corroded.

3 Release the hose clips from the hose concerned. Three types of clip are used; worm-drive, spring and 'sardine-can'. The worm-drive clip is released by turning its screw anti-clockwise. The spring clip is released by squeezing its tags together with pliers, at the same time working the clip away from the hose stub. The sardine-can clips are not re-usable, and are best cut off with snips or side cutters.

4 Unclip any wires, cables or other hoses which may be attached to the hose being removed. Make notes for reference when reassembling if necessary.

5 Release the hose from its stubs with a twisting motion. Be careful not to damage the stubs on delicate components such as the radiator, or thermostat housings. If the hose is stuck fast, the best course is often to cut it off using a sharp knife, but again be careful not to damage the stubs.

6 Before fitting the new hose, smear the stubs with washing-up liquid or a suitable rubber lubricant to aid fitting. Do not use oil or grease, which may attack the rubber.

7 Fit the hose clips over the ends of the hose, then fit the hose over its stubs. Work the hose into position. When satisfied, locate and tighten the hose clips.

8 Refill the cooling system as described in Chapter 1A or 1B. Run the engine, and check that there are no leaks.

9 Recheck the tightness of the hose clips on any new hoses after a few hundred miles.

10 Top-up the coolant level if necessary.

3 Radiator - removal, inspection and refitting

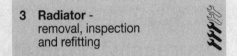

Removal

Note: *If leakage is the reason for removing the radiator, bear in mind that minor leaks can often be cured using proprietary radiator sealing compound, with the radiator in situ.*

1 Disconnect the battery negative terminal (refer to *Disconnecting the battery* in the Reference Section of this manual). On diesel engine models, unbolt the relay bracket from the side of the battery tray.

2 Drain the cooling system as described in Chapter 1A or 1B.

3 On 1242 cc (16-valve) petrol engine models, remove the air cleaner and inlet ducts as described in Chapter 4B.

4 Slacken the clips and disconnect the top and bottom coolant hoses from the radiator. In addition on diesel engine models, and petrol engine models with a remotely-sited expansion tank, disconnect the expansion tank coolant hose from the right hand side of the radiator **(see illustrations)**.

5 Unscrew the fixings and lift the plastic trim panel from above the front bumper. Unscrew the bolt(s) securing the radiator to the upper body panel **(see illustration)**. Note that the radiator and cooling fan assembly share the same upper mounting bolt.

6 Unbolt the cooling fan(s) and shroud assembly from the rear of the radiator, as described in Section 5.

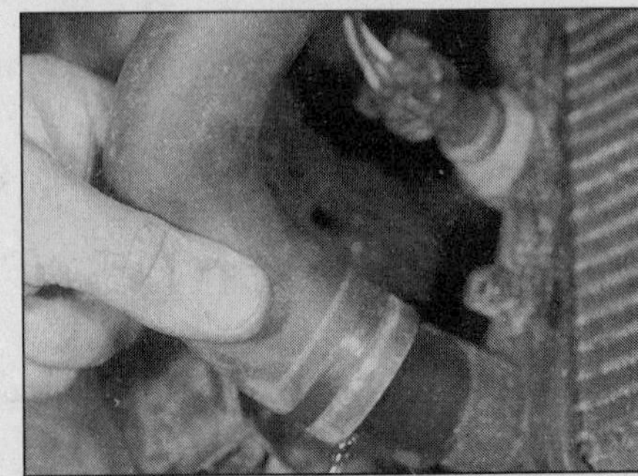

3.4a Slacken the clip and disconnect the radiator bottom hose

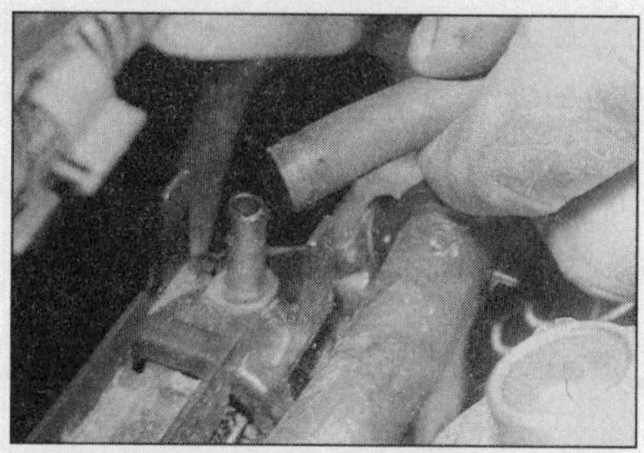
3.4b On diesel engine models, disconnect the expansion tank coolant hose from the radiator

3.5 Unscrew the bolts securing the radiator to the upper body panel

3.8 Disengage the lower mountings studs from the engine compartment lower crossmember

4.6a Removing the thermostat housing (petrol engine)

4.6b Thermostat housing location - ignition distributor removed for clarity (petrol engine)

7 Withdraw the mounting brackets (where applicable), and recover the upper mounting rubbers.

8 Carefully tilt the radiator back towards the engine, then disengage the lower mountings studs from the crossmember and lift the radiator from the engine compartment **(see illustration)**. Recover the lower mounting rubbers if they are loose.

Inspection

9 If the radiator has been removed due to suspected blockage, it may be flushed out as described in Chapter 1A or 1B. Clean dirt and debris from the radiator fins, using an air line (in which case, wear eye protection) or a soft brush. Be careful, as the fins are sharp, and can also be easily damaged.

10 If necessary, a radiator specialist can perform a flow test on the radiator, to establish whether an internal blockage exists.

11 A leaking radiator must be referred to a specialist for permanent repair. Do not attempt to weld or solder a leaking radiator, as damage to the plastic components may result. **Note:** *In an emergency, minor leaks from the radiator can often be cured by using a suitable radiator sealing compound, in accordance with its manufacturer's instructions, with the radiator in situ.*

12 If the radiator is to be sent for repair or is to be renewed, remove all hoses (and where applicable, the cooling fan switch).

13 Inspect the radiator mounting rubbers, and renew them if necessary.

Refitting

14 Refitting is a reversal of removal, bearing in mind the following points:

a) Ensure that the radiator lower lugs engage correctly with the lower mounting rubbers.

b) On completion, refill the cooling system as described in Chapter 1A or 1B.

4 Thermostat - removal, testing and refitting

General

1 The thermostat housing is bolted to the left hand end of the cylinder head. The thermostat itself cannot be separated from the housing and can only be renewed as part of a complete assembly.

Removal

2 Drain the cooling system as described in Chapter 1A or 1B.

3 On diesel engine models, unbolt the wiring harness/fuel hose support bracket from the housing. On 1242 cc (16-valve) petrol engine models, remove the air cleaner and inlet ducts as described in Chapter 4B.

4 Slacken the clip(s) and detach the coolant hose(s) from the thermostat housing. Make a careful note of their orientation to aid refitting.

5 Where applicable, disconnect the wiring plug from the cooling fan switch and coolant temperature sensor, which are threaded into the thermostat cover.

6 Unscrew the securing bolts, and remove the thermostat housing from the cylinder head **(see illustrations)**. If it sticks, tap it gently first on one side and then the other to free it - do not lever between the mating faces. Recover the remains of the old gasket.

4.6c Removing the thermostat housing (diesel engine)

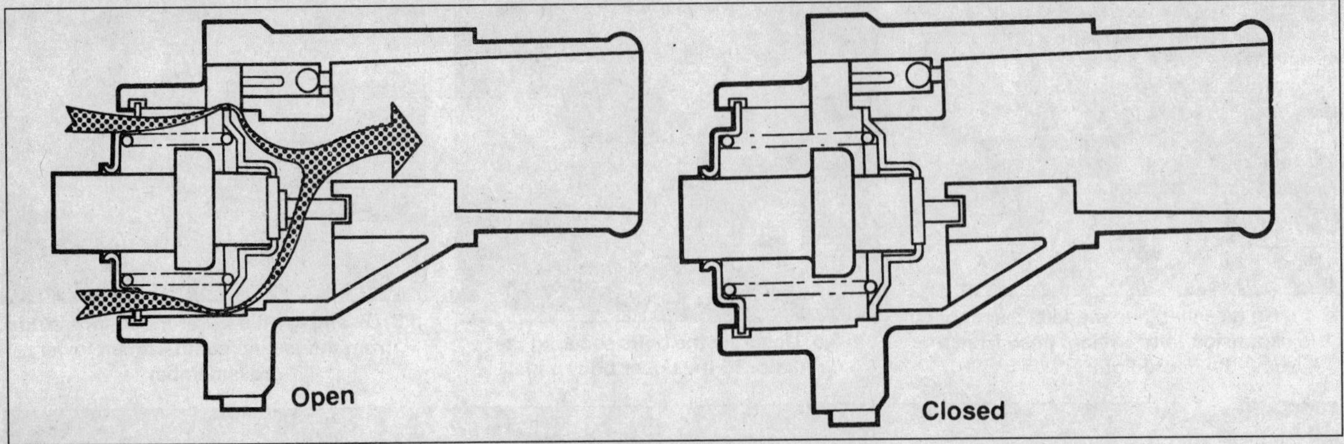

4.7a Thermostat operation (petrol engine)

Testing

7 A rough test of the thermostat may be made by suspending it with a piece of string in a container full of water. Heat the water to bring it to the boil and observe the movement of the valve shaft through the inlet port **(see illustrations)**.

8 The thermostat valve must be fully open, by the time the water boils. If not, renew the complete thermostat/housing assembly.

9 If a thermometer is available, the precise opening temperature of the thermostat may be determined; compare with the figures given in the Specifications. The opening temperature is also marked on the thermostat housing.

10 Note that a thermostat which fails to close completely as the water cools must also be renewed.

Refitting

11 Ensure that the cylinder head and thermostat housing mating surfaces are completely clean and free from all traces of the old gasket material.

12 Lay a new gasket in position on the cylinder head, then fit the thermostat housing and insert retaining bolts, tightening them securely.

Caution: Do not over-tighten the retaining bolts, as the alloy casting could easily be damaged

13 Where applicable, transfer the cooling fan switch and coolant temperature sensor to the new housing.

14 Refit the coolant hose(s) to the ports on the thermostat housing and tighten the clips securely.

15 Where applicable, refit the harness/hose support bracket to the thermostat housing and tighten the bolts securely. Also refit the air cleaner and inlet ducts as described in Chapter 4B

15 Refill the cooling system as described in Chapter 1A or 1B.

5 Electric cooling fan(s) - testing, removal and refitting

Testing

1 Detailed fault diagnosis should be carried out by a Fiat dealer using dedicated test equipment, but basic diagnosis can be carried out as follows.

2 If the fan does not appear to work, run the engine until normal operating temperature is reached, then allow it to idle. The fan should cut in within a few minutes (before the temperature gauge needle enters the red section). If not, switch off the engine and disconnect the cooling fan motor wiring connector.

3 The motor can be tested by disconnecting it from the wiring loom, and connecting a 12-volt supply directly to it. The motor should operate - if not, the motor, or the motor wiring, is faulty.

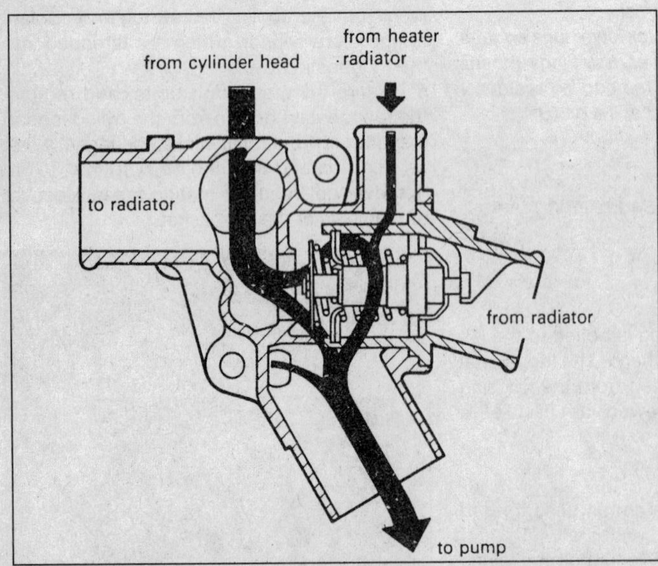

4.7b Thermostat operation in the fully closed position (diesel engine)

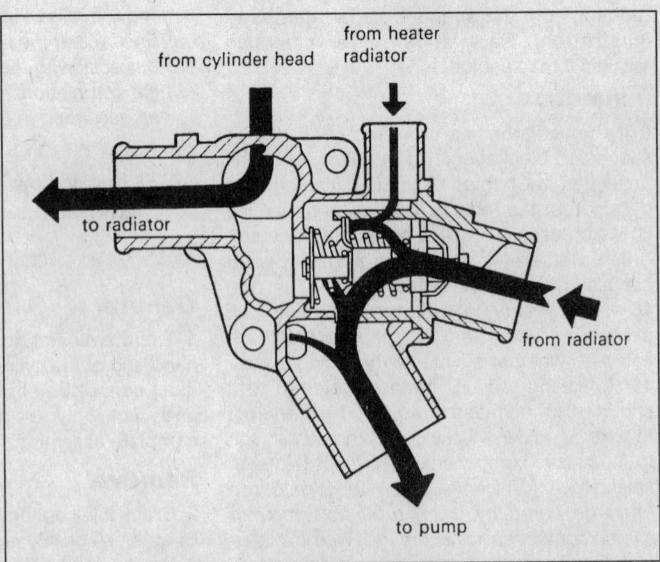

4.7c Thermostat operation in the fully open position (diesel engine)

4 If the motor operates when tested as described, the fault must lie in the engine wiring harness or the temperature sensor. The temperature sensor/switch can be tested as described in Section 6. Any further fault diagnosis should be referred to a suitably-equipped Fiat dealer - **do not** attempt to test the electronic control unit.

Removal

5 Disconnect the battery negative terminal (refer to *Disconnecting the battery* in the Reference Section of this manual).
6 On diesel engine models, unbolt the relay bracket from the side of the battery tray to improve access. On 1242 cc (16-valve) petrol engine models, remove the air cleaner and inlet ducts as described in Chapter 4B.
7 Disconnect the motor wiring connector(s).
8 Unbolt the shroud from the rear of the radiator, then lift out the cooling fan assembly.

Refitting

9 Refitting is a reversal of removal.

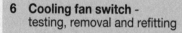

6 Cooling fan switch - testing, removal and refitting

Testing

1 The switch is threaded into the lower left hand corner of the radiator.
2 The switch can be tested by removing it, and checking that the switching action occurs at the correct temperature (heat the sensor in a container of water, and monitor the temperature with a thermometer).
3 There should be no continuity between the switch terminals, until the specified cooling fan cut-in temperature is reached, when continuity (and zero resistance) should exist between the terminals.

Removal

4 Disconnect the battery negative terminal (refer to *Disconnecting the battery* in the Reference Section of this manual).
5 Allow the engine to cool completely, then drain the cooling system as described in Chapter 1A or 1B.
6 Disconnect the wiring plug from the sensor.

7.4a Unscrew the securing bolts . . .

7 Carefully unscrew the sensor and, where applicable, recover the sealing ring.

Refitting

8 If the sensor was originally fitted using sealing compound, clean the sensor threads thoroughly, and coat them with fresh sealing compound.
9 If the sensor was originally fitted using a sealing ring, use a new sealing ring on refitting.
10 Refitting is a reversal of removal, but refill the cooling system as described in Chapter 1A or 1B.
11 On completion, start the engine and run it until it reaches normal operating temperature. Continue to run the engine until the cooling fan cuts in and out correctly.

7 Coolant pump - removal, inspection and refitting

Removal

Petrol engine models

1 Disconnect the battery negative terminal (refer to *Disconnecting the battery* in the Reference Section of this manual).
2 Drain the cooling system and remove the auxiliary drivebelt(s) as described in Chapter 1A.
3 Remove the timing belt as described in Chapter 2A or 2B.
4 Unscrew the securing bolts/nuts, and withdraw the coolant pump **(see illustrations)**.

7.4b . . . and withdraw the coolant pump (petrol engine)

If the pump is stuck, tap it gently using a soft-faced mallet - **do not** lever between the pump and cylinder block mating faces.

Diesel engine models

5 Disconnect the battery negative terminal (refer to *Disconnecting the battery* in the Reference Section of this manual).
6 Drain the cooling system as described in Chapter 1B.
7 Remove the auxiliary drivebelt(s) as described in Chapter 1B.
8 On models fitted with power steering, refer to Chapter 10 and remove the power steering pump from its mountings; this can be achieved without disconnecting the power steering fluid hoses from the pump. Tie the pump away from the work area, taking care to avoid kinking the fluid hoses.
9 Unscrew the securing bolts, and remove the coolant pump pulley. It will be necessary to counterhold the pulley in order to unscrew the bolts, and this is most easily achieved by wrapping an old drivebelt tightly around the pulley to act in a similar manner to a strap wrench. Alternatively, a stout screwdriver can be braced between two of the pulley bolts while the third is slackened **(see illustrations)**.
10 Disconnect the bypass hoses from the coolant pump outlet stubs.
11 Unscrew the securing bolts, and withdraw the coolant pump assembly. Note that the pump must be detached from the transfer pipe than runs behind the cylinder block to the thermostat housing **(see illustration)**. The pipe is a push fit in the port on the rear of the coolant pump

7.9a Unscrew the coolant pump pulley bolts . . .

7.9b . . . and lift off the pulley (diesel engine)

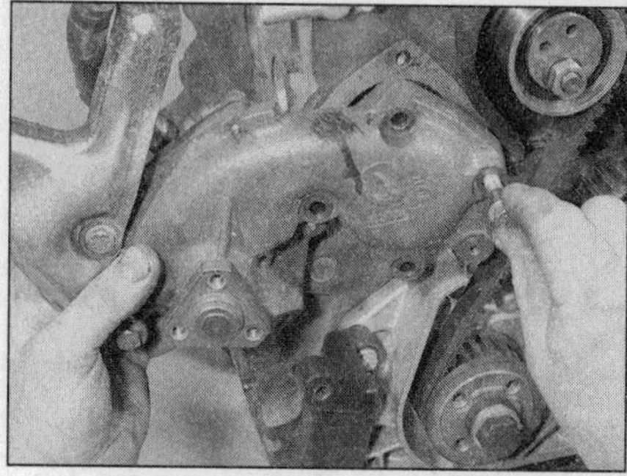

7.11 Removing the coolant pump assembly (diesel engine)

12 If the pump is stuck, tap it gently using a soft-faced mallet - **do not** lever between the pump and cylinder block mating faces.

Inspection

13 Check the pump body and impeller for signs of excessive corrosion. Turn the impeller, and check for stiffness due to corrosion, or roughness due to excessive end play.

14 Check the clearance between the pump impeller and the casing using a feeler blade **(see illustration)**. If the clearance is different to that given in the *Specifications*, the pump must be renewed. No spare components are available; the pump can only be renewed as a complete assembly.

15 On diesel engine models, remove the O-ring at the end of the transfer pipe, which runs behind the cylinder block and fits into the rear of the coolant pump. A new O-ring should be fitted as a matter of course.

Refitting

Petrol engine models

16 Commence refitting by thoroughly cleaning all traces of sealant from the mating faces of the pump and cylinder block/pump housing.

17 Apply a continuous bead of sealant (liquid gasket) to the cylinder block mating face of the pump, taking care not to apply excessive sealant, which may enter the pump itself **(see illustration)**.

18 Place the pump in position in its housing, then refit and tighten the bolts/nuts to the specified torque.

19 Refit the timing belt as described in Chapter 2A or 2B.

20 Refit the auxiliary drivebelt(s) and refill the cooling system as described in Chapter 1A.

21 Reconnect the battery negative terminal.

Diesel engine models

22 Commence refitting by thoroughly cleaning all traces of old gasket from the mating faces of the pump housing and cylinder block.

23 Place a new gasket in position on the cylinder block, locate the pump in position, then refit and tighten the bolts **(see

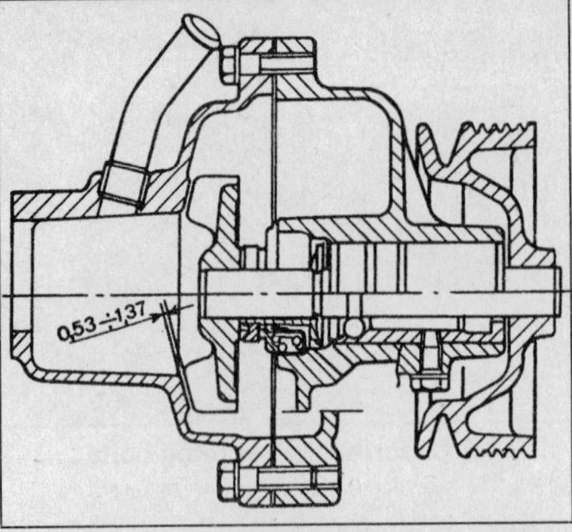

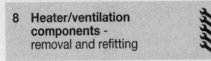

7.14 Checking the clearance between the pump impeller and the casing using a feeler blade (diesel engine)

illustration)**. Ensure that the end of the coolant transfer pipe seats firmly in the port at the rear of the coolant pump, without displacing the O-ring seal.

24 Refit the pump pulley, then refit the securing bolts and tighten to the specified torque. Counterhold the pulley using the same method employed during removal.

25 Where applicable, refit the power steering pump with reference to Chapter 10.

26 Refit and tension the auxiliary drivebelt(s) as described in Chapter 1B.

27 Refill the cooling system as described in Chapter 1B.

28 Reconnect the battery negative terminal.

8 Heater/ventilation components - removal and refitting

Complete heater assembly

Warning: On models fitted with air conditioning, do not attempt to remove the cooling unit, which is located between the heater blower motor casing and the main heater assembly. Removal of the cooling unit entails disconnection of refrigerant lines - refer to Section 10 for precautions to be observed.

If in any doubt as to the procedure to follow on models with air conditioning, consult a Fiat dealer for advice.

Note: *This is an involved procedure, and it is recommended that the following Section is read thoroughly before commencing work. Plenty of time should be allowed to complete the operation. During dismantling, make notes on the routing of all wiring and cables, and the locations of all fixings, to aid reassembly.*

Removal

1 Disconnect the battery negative terminal (refer to *Disconnecting the battery* in the Reference Section of this manual).

2 Set the heater control to HOT, then drain the cooling system as described in Chapter 1A or 1B.

3 Working in the engine bay, slacken the clips and detach the heater unit coolant hoses from the ports at the bulkhead **(see illustration)**. Recover the rubber grommets.

4 Refer to Chapter 11 and remove the entire facia assembly from the vehicle bulkhead. Rest the assembly on the front seats.

5 At this stage, access to the air inlet/distribution/blending control cables is possible. These can be easily disconnected from their respective control levers and renewed if required.

6 Working from the engine bay, remove the protective plastic caps to expose the heater assembly mounting studs and remove the nuts.

7 Label the electrical connections to the heater assembly, to aid correct refitting later and then unplug them at the connectors

8 Slacken and remove the nuts and lift the heater assembly off its mounting studs.

Refitting

9 To refit the assembly, reverse the steps described for removal, bearing in mind the following points:

a) Make sure that all wiring and cables are routed as noted during dismantling.
b) Make sure that all air ducts are securely reconnected.
c) Refit the facia components with reference to Chapter 11.
d) On completion, refill the cooling system as described in Chapter 1A or 1B.

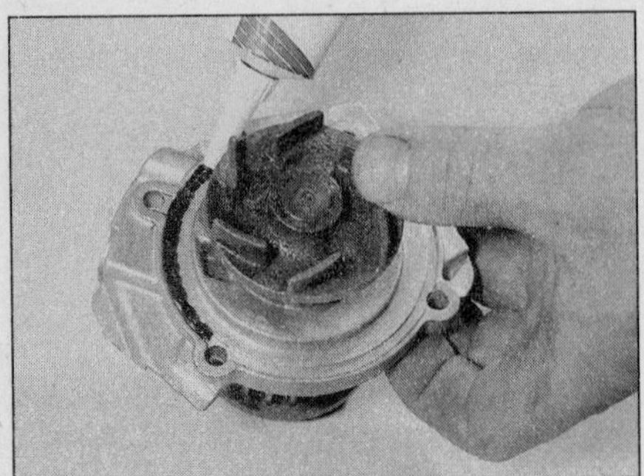

7.17 On petrol engine models, apply a continuous bead of sealant (liquid gasket) to the pump mating face

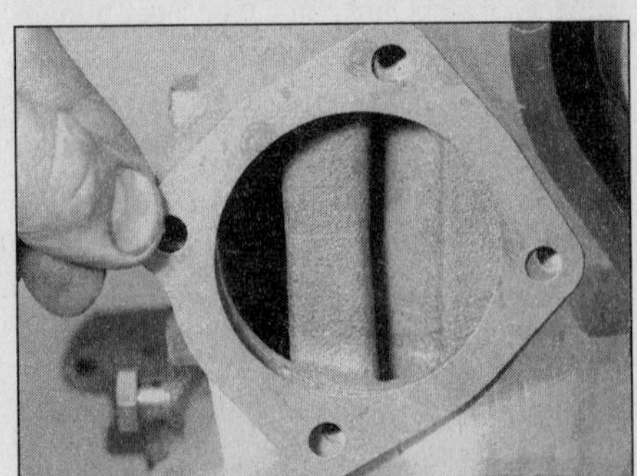

7.23 On diesel engine models, place a new gasket in position on the cylinder block

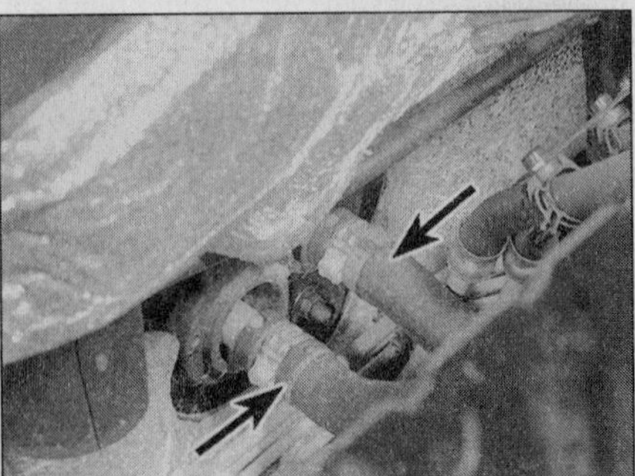

8.3 Slacken the clips (arrowed) and detach the heater unit coolant hoses from the ports at the bulkhead

Heater matrix

Removal

10 Remove the complete heater assembly as described previously in this Section.

11 Slacken and remove the securing screws, then withdraw the heater matrix from the heater assembly casing.

Refitting

12 Refitting is a reversal of removal; refit the heater assembly as described previously in this Section.

Heater blower motor

Removal

13 Disconnect the battery negative terminal (refer to *Disconnecting the battery* in the Reference Section of this manual).

14 Unplug the wiring from the blower motor at the connector.

15 Working in the passenger front footwell, under the glovebox, remove the securing screws and lower the blower motor and rotor assembly from its casing **(see illustration)**.

Refitting

16 Refitting is a reversal of removal.

Heater blower motor resistor

Removal

17 The resistor is located at the bottom of the heater casing, behind the blower motor.

18 Disconnect the battery negative terminal (refer to *Disconnecting the battery* in the Reference Section of this manual).

19 For improved access, remove the blower motor as described in the previous sub-Section.

20 Disconnect the wiring plug from the resistor.

21 Working under the glovebox, remove the two securing screws, and withdraw the resistor from the blower unit case **(see illustrations)**.

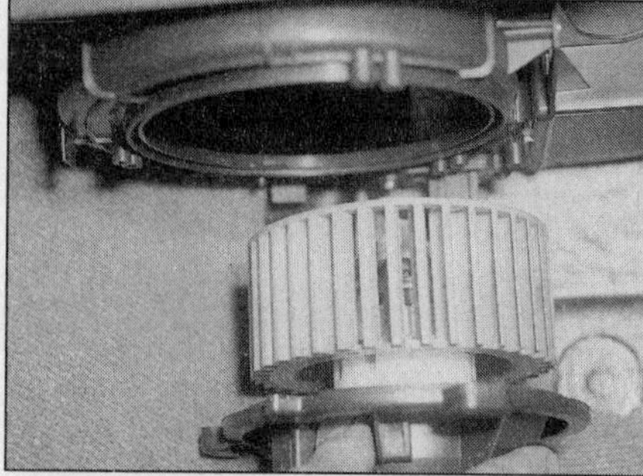

8.15 Remove the securing screws and lower the blower motor and rotor assembly from its casing

Refitting

22 Refitting is a reversal of removal.

Heater control panel

Removal

23 Pull the ventilation fan speed control knob from the panel.

24 Unscrew and remove the three screws securing the panel cover. Two screws are under the lower edge of the panel, whilst the remaining screw is located in the ventilation fan speed control knob recess. Remove the panel.

25 Unscrew and remove the four screws securing the control panel to the facia. The screws are located in each corner of the panel.

26 Remove the facia as described in Chapter 11.

27 Make a careful note of the cable and electrical connections. Unscrew the cable clamps and unclip the inner cables from the controls. Unplug the ventilation fan speed control.

28 Unclip and remove the control panel from the heater distributor box assembly.

Refitting

29 Refitting is a reversal of removal.

9 Air conditioning system - general information and precautions

General information

An air conditioning system is available on certain models. It enables the temperature of incoming air to be lowered, and also dehumidifies the air, which allows rapid demisting and increased comfort.

The cooling side of the system works in the same way as a domestic refrigerator. Refrigerant gas is drawn into a belt-driven compressor where the increase in pressure causes the refrigerant gas to turn to liquid. It then passes through a condenser mounted on the front of the radiator, where it is cooled. The liquid then passes through an expansion valve to an evaporator, where it changes from liquid under high pressure to gas under low pressure. This change is accompanied by a drop in temperature, which cools the evaporator and hence the air passing over it. The refrigerant returns to the compressor, and the cycle begins again.

The air blown through the evaporator passes to the air distribution unit where it is mixed, if required, with hot air blown through the heater matrix to achieve the desired temperature in the passenger compartment.

The heating side of the system works in the same way as on models without air conditioning (see Section 8).

The system is electronically-controlled. Any problems with the system should be referred to a Fiat dealer.

Precautions

With an air conditioning system, it is necessary to observe special precautions whenever dealing with any part of the system, or its associated components. If for any reason the system must be disconnected, it is

3

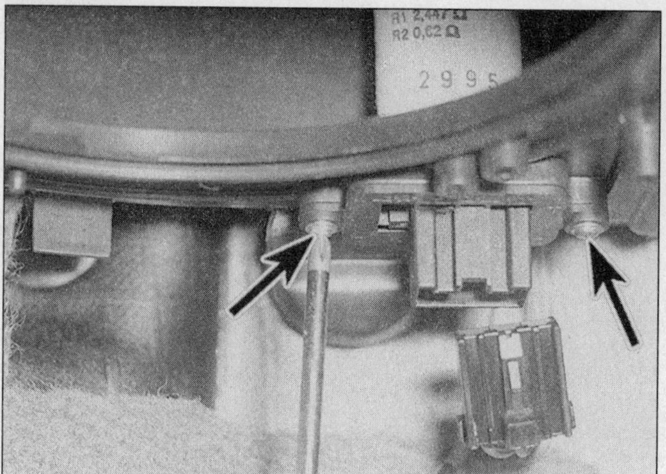

8.21a Remove the two securing screws (arrowed) . . .

8.21b . . . and withdraw the resistor from the blower unit case

essential that you entrust this task to your Fiat dealer or a refrigeration engineer.

Warning: The refrigeration circuit contains a liquid refrigerant and it is dangerous to disconnect any part of the system without specialist knowledge and equipment.

The refrigerant is potentially dangerous, and should only be handled by qualified persons. If it is splashed onto the skin, it can cause severe frostbite. It is not itself poisonous, but in the presence of a naked flame (including a cigarette), it forms a poisonous gas. Uncontrolled discharging of the refrigerant is dangerous and potentially damaging to the environment.

10 Air conditioning components - removal and refitting

Note: *Do not operate the air conditioning system if it is known to be short of refrigerant, as this may damage the compressor.*

1 The only operation which can be carried out easily without discharging the refrigerant is renewal of the auxiliary (compressor) drivebelt - this procedure is described in Chapter 1A or 1B. All other operations must be referred to a Fiat dealer or an air conditioning specialist.

2 If necessary for access to other components, the compressor can be unbolted and moved aside, *without disconnecting its flexible hoses*, after removing the drivebelt.

Warning: Do not attempt to open the refrigerant circuit. Refer to the precautions given in Section 9.

Chapter 4 Part A:
Fuel system - single-point petrol injection models

Contents

Degrees of difficulty

Easy, suitable for novice with little experience 	**Fairly easy,** suitable for beginner with some experience 	**Fairly difficult,** suitable for competent DIY mechanic 	**Difficult,** suitable for experienced DIY mechanic 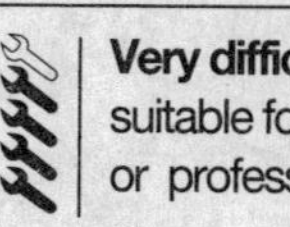	**Very difficult,** suitable for expert DIY or professional

4A

Specifications

System type . . . . Weber-Marelli integrated single-point fuel injection/ignition system

Fuel system data

Fuel pump type	Electric, immersed in fuel tank
Fuel pump delivery rate	110 litres/hour minimum
Regulated fuel pressure	1.0 ± 0.2 bar
Crankshaft TDC sensor resistance at 20°C	650 to 720 ohms
Injector duration (at idle)	1.5 ms

Recommended fuel

Minimum octane rating	95 RON unleaded

Torque wrench settings

Torque wrench settings	Nm	lbf ft
Coolant temperature sensor	3	2
Fuel filter collar nut	5	4
Fuel tank	28	21
Idle control stepper motor	4	3
Inlet manifold	27	20
Inlet union to filter	31	23
Outlet union to filter	15	11
Throttle body to manifold	7	5
Throttle potentiometer	3	2

1 General information and precautions

General information

The IAW Weber-Marelli single point injection (SPI) system is a self-contained engine management system, which controls both the fuel injection and ignition **(see illustration)**. This Chapter deals with the fuel injection system components only - refer to Chapter 5B for details of the ignition system components.

The fuel injection system comprises a fuel tank, an electric fuel pump, a fuel filter, fuel supply and return lines, a throttle body with an integral electronic fuel injector, and an Electronic Control Unit (ECU) together with its associated sensors, actuators and wiring.

The fuel pump delivers a constant supply of fuel through a cartridge filter to the throttle body, and the fuel pressure regulator (integral with the throttle body) maintains a constant fuel pressure at the fuel injector and returns excess fuel to the tank via the return line. This constant flow system also helps to reduce fuel temperature and prevents vaporisation.

The fuel injector is opened and closed by an Electronic Control Unit (ECU), which calculates the injection timing and duration according to engine speed, throttle position and rate of opening, inlet air temperature, coolant temperature and exhaust gas oxygen content information, received from sensors mounted on the engine.

Inlet air is drawn into the engine through the air cleaner, which contains a renewable paper filter element. The inlet air temperature is regulated by a vacuum operated valve mounted in the air ducting, which blends air at ambient temperature with hot air, drawn from over the exhaust manifold.

Idle speed is controlled by a stepper motor located on the side of the throttle body. Cold starting enrichment is controlled by the ECU using the coolant temperature and inlet air temperature parameters to increase the injector opening duration.

The exhaust gas oxygen content is constantly monitored by the ECU via the Lambda (oxygen) sensor, which is mounted in the exhaust downpipe. The ECU then uses this information to modify the injection timing and duration to maintain the optimum air/fuel ratio. An exhaust catalyst is fitted to all SPI models. The ECU also controls the operation of the activated charcoal filter evaporative loss system - refer to Chapter 4D for further details.

It should be noted that fault diagnosis of the IAW Weber-Marelli system is only possible with dedicated electronic test equipment. Problems with the system should therefore be referred to a Fiat dealer for assessment. Once the fault has been identified, the removal/refitting procedures detailed in the following Sections can then be followed.

Precautions

Warning: Many procedures in this Chapter require the removal of fuel lines and connections, which may result in fuel spillage. Before carrying out any operation on the fuel system, refer to the precautions given in Safety first! at the beginning of this manual, and follow them implicitly. Petrol is a highly dangerous and volatile liquid, and the precautions

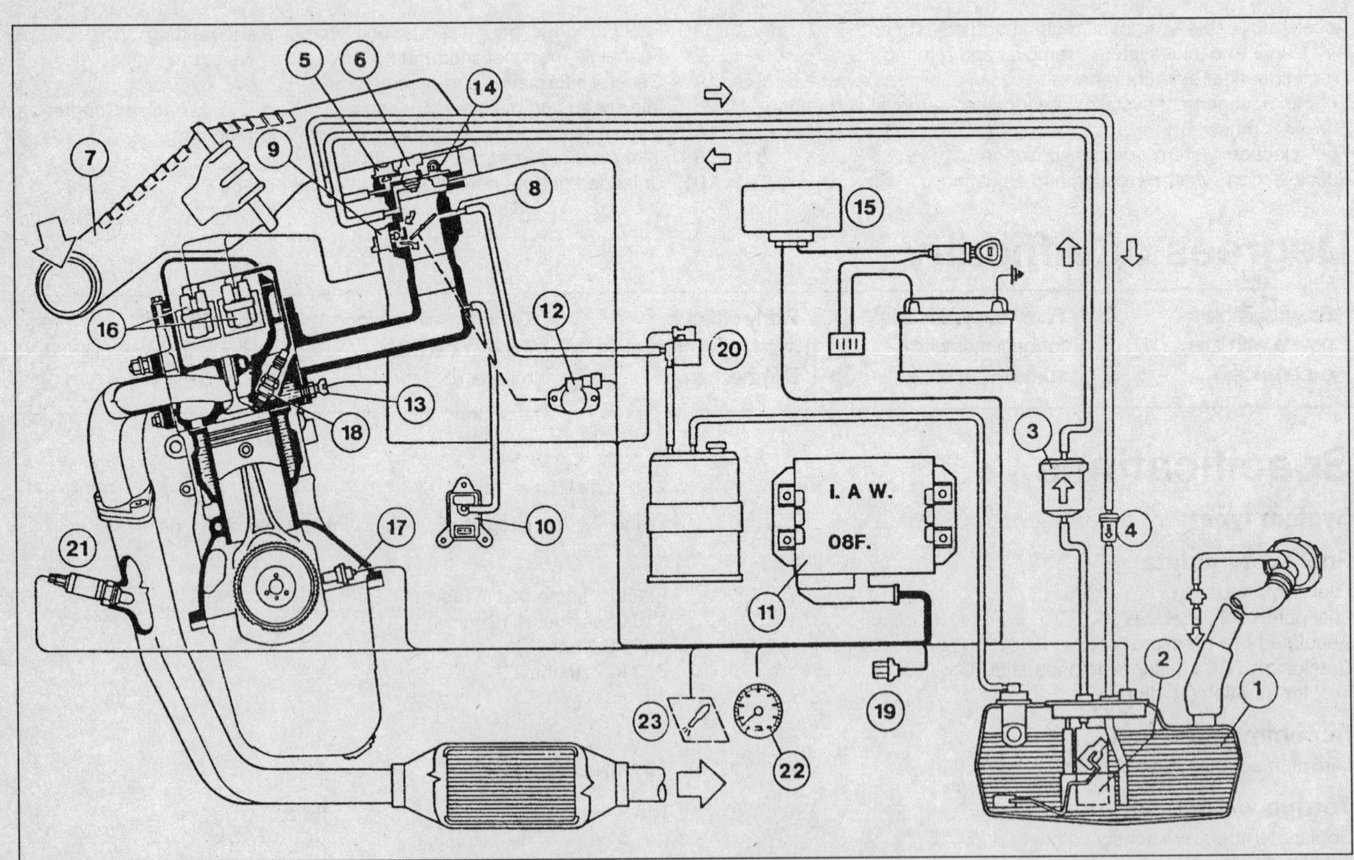

1.1 IAW Weber-Marelli single point injection (SPI) system

1 Fuel tank
2 Fuel pump
3 Fuel filter
4 Anti-reflux valve
5 Fuel pressure regulator
6 Injector
7 Air cleaner
8 Fuel vapour trap
9 Idle stepper motor
10 Absolute pressure sensor
11 Injection/ignition ECU
12 Throttle position sensor
13 Engine coolant temperature sensor
14 Intake air temperature sensor
15 Injection/ignition dual relay
16 Ignition coils
17 Rpm and TDC sensor
18 Spark plugs
19 Diagnostic socket
20 EVAP solenoid
21 Lambda/oxygen sensor
22 Rev counter
23 IAW failure warning light

2.4a Disconnect the large breather hose . . .

2.4b . . . and the small breather hose . . .

necessary when handling it cannot be overstressed. Note that residual pressure will remain in the fuel lines long after the vehicle was last used, When disconnecting any fuel line, first depressurise the fuel system (see Section 8).

2 Air cleaner and inlet system - removal and refitting

Removal

1 Remove the air cleaner element as described in Chapter 1A.

2 Disconnect the outer section from the hot air tube and the inlet air duct and remove it from the engine compartment.

3 If necessary remove the inlet air duct.

4 Disconnect the large and small breather hoses from the inner section of the air cleaner, then unscrew the retaining nuts and lift the section from the throttle body **(see illustrations)**.

5 Recover the sealing ring. Check the ring for condition and renew it if necessary.

6 Wipe clean the inner surfaces of both the inner and outer sections of the air cleaner.

Refitting

7 Refitting is a reversal of removal but renew the element if necessary.

3 Inlet air temperature regulator - removal and refitting

Removal

1 The thermostatically-controlled cold air flap opener is located in the air cleaner outer casing section. To check the unit, disconnect the air inlet duct with the engine cold and use a mirror to check that the flap is positioned to admit only hot air from the shroud on the exhaust manifold. Next, warm up the engine and check that the flap moves to admit only cold air from the inlet duct. If the unit is faulty it must be renewed.

2 Remove the air cleaner element as described in Chapter 1A.

3 Unscrew the retaining screw and remove the regulator from the air cleaner outer section.

Refitting

4 Refitting is a reversal of removal.

4 Accelerator cable - removal, refitting and adjustment

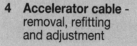

Removal

1 Remove the air cleaner and air inlet ducting as described in Section 2.

2 To release the cable from the throttle body, unscrew the outer cable locknuts, then disengage the inner cable from the throttle cam, and release the outer cable from its mounting bracket.

3 Working under the instrument panel inside the vehicle, unhook the cable from the fork at the top of the pedal arm.

4 Release the bulkhead grommet and withdraw the accelerator cable from inside the engine compartment.

Refitting and adjustment

5 Refitting is a reverse of the removal process, but adjust the cable (by means of the outer cable locknuts) so that there is only a very small amount of free play present at the throttle body end of the inner cable. Have an assistant depress the accelerator pedal, and check that the throttle cam opens fully and returns to the at-rest position, then securely tighten the cable locknuts. On Selecta models, check the kickdown cable adjustment as described in Chapter 7B before adjusting the accelerator cable - in its rest position the accelerator pedal should have approximately 8.0 mm free travel.

5 Engine management system components - removal and refitting

Note: *Refer to the warning given in Section 1 before proceeding.*

Throttle body assembly

Removal

1 Remove the air cleaner and air duct as described in Section 2.

2 Disconnect the wiring connectors from the throttle potentiometer, idle control stepper motor, inlet air temperature sensor and the injector wiring loom connector situated on the front of the throttle body.

3 Depressurise the fuel system with reference to Section 8, then release the retaining clips and disconnect the fuel feed and return hoses from the throttle body assembly. If the original Fiat retaining clips are still fitted, cut the clips and discard them; replace them with standard fuel hose clips on refitting.

4 Slacken the accelerator cable locknuts, then disengage the inner cable from the throttle cam and free the outer cable from its retaining bracket. Position the cable clear of the throttle body.

5 Disconnect the EVAP purge valve hose, and the MAP sensor hose from the rear of the throttle body.

6 Slacken and remove the four bolts securing the throttle body assembly to the inlet manifold, then remove the assembly along with its insulating spacer.

Refitting

7 Refitting is a reversal of the removal procedure, bearing in mind the following points:

a) *Examine the insulating spacer for signs of damage, and renew if necessary.*

b) *Ensure that the throttle body, inlet manifold and insulating spacer mating surfaces are clean and dry, then fit the throttle body and spacer, and securely tighten the retaining bolts.*

2.4c . . . then remove the retaining nuts . . .

2.4d . . . and remove the air cleaner inner section

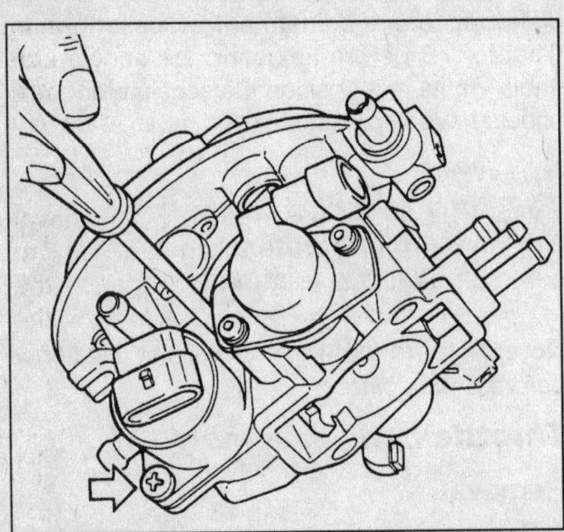

5.16 Removing the idle control stepper motor

c) *Ensure that all hoses are correctly reconnected and, where necessary, that their retaining clips are securely tightened.*
d) *Adjust the accelerator cable as described in Section 4.*

Fuel injector

Note: *If a faulty injector is suspected, before condemning the injector, it is worth trying the effect of one of the proprietary injector cleaning treatments.*

Removal

8 Remove the air cleaner and air duct as described in Section 2.

9 Disconnect the wiring then unscrew the mounting screws and remove the injector from the throttle body.

Refitting

10 Refitting is a reversal of removal.

Fuel pressure regulator

Removal

11 Remove the air cleaner and air duct as described in Section 2.

12 Using a marker pen, make alignment marks between the regulator cover and the throttle body, then undo the four retaining screws. As the screws are loosened, place a rag over the cover to catch any fuel spray which may be released.

13 Lift off the cover, then remove the spring and withdraw the diaphragm, noting its correct fitted orientation. Remove all traces of dirt, and examine the diaphragm for signs of splitting. If damage is found, it will be necessary to renew the complete upper throttle body assembly.

Refitting

14 Refitting is a reversal of removal ensuring that the diaphragm and cover are fitted the correct way round, and that the retaining screws are securely tightened.

Idle control stepper motor

Removal

15 Disconnect the battery negative terminal (refer to *Disconnecting the battery* in the Reference Section of this manual), then remove the air cleaner and air duct as described in Section 2.

16 Using a crosshead screwdriver, unscrew the mounting screws and remove the stepper motor from the throttle body. Recover the gasket **(see illustration)**.

17 Clean the unit and check for damage and wear.

Refitting

18 When refitting the unit use a new gasket and make sure that the plunger is inserted correctly using the following procedure. Insert the unit and refit the mounting screws loosely. Reconnect the wiring then switch on the ignition several times so that the unit centralises itself. Finally fully tighten the mounting screws to the specified torque. **Note:** *The mounting screws are covered with a locking agent and must be renewed every time they are removed.*

19 Leave the battery negative terminal disconnected for about 20 minutes - the injection/ignition ECU will position the idle control stepper motor correctly the first time the engine is started. Reconnect the battery negative terminal.

Throttle potentiometer

Removal

20 Remove the air cleaner and air duct as described in Section 2.

21 Disconnect the wiring from the throttle potentiometer.

22 Using an Allen key unscrew the mounting screws then withdraw the unit from the throttle body **(see illustration)**. **Note:** *The mounting screws are covered with a locking agent and must be renewed every time they are removed.*

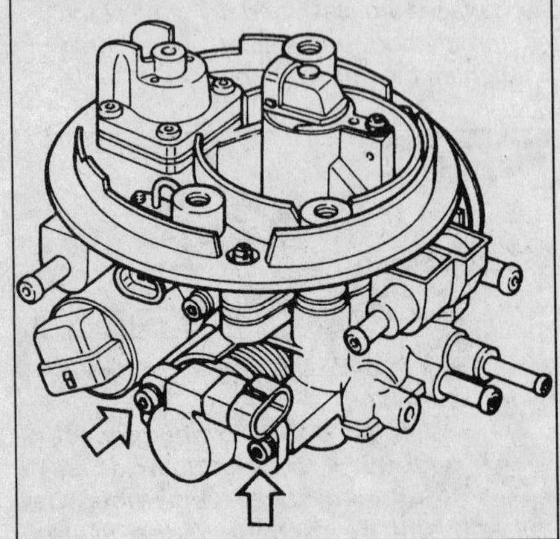

5.22 Throttle potentiometer mounting screws

Refitting

23 When refitting the unit make sure that the pin is correctly engaged, and tighten the mounting screws to the specified torque.

24 If a Fiat test instrument is available, the operation of the throttle potentiometer can be checked at this stage. Before connecting the wiring first turn the ignition key to position MAR and wait a few seconds, then return the key to the STOP position. Reconnect the wiring and connect the test instrument. Turn the ignition key to the MAR position and cancel the error that will appear. The throttle position indicated should be between 0° and 4°. If greater than this, check that the accelerator cable is correctly adjusted however if the correct reading cannot be obtained renew the unit.

Inlet air temperature sensor

Removal

25 Remove the throttle body assembly as described earlier in this Section.

26 Extract the plastic pins and remove the press-fit cover from the top of the throttle body.

27 Invert the cover then unscrew the mounting screws and remove the inlet air temperature sensor from the cover.

Refitting

28 Refitting is a reversal of removal.

Manifold absolute pressure (MAP) sensor

Removal

29 The manifold absolute pressure sensor is located on the left-hand side of the bulkhead.

30 Unscrew the mounting screws and remove the sensor from the bulkhead. Disconnect the wiring and vacuum pipe.

Refitting

31 Refitting is a reversal of removal, but check the condition of the vacuum pipe and renew it if necessary.

Coolant temperature sensor

Removal

32 The coolant temperature sensor is located on the left-hand side of the inlet manifold. Drain the cooling system as described in Chapter 1A before removing it.

33 Disconnect the wiring.

34 Unscrew the sensor and remove it from the inlet manifold. If using a socket take care not to damage the wiring connector on the sensor.

Refitting

35 Refitting is a reversal of removal but tighten the sensor to the specified torque. **Do not** exceed the specified torque otherwise the unit may be damaged.

Crankshaft TDC sensor

Removal

36 The crankshaft TDC sensor is located on the front side of the crankshaft pulley. Firmly apply the handbrake, then jack up the front of the car and support it securely on axle stands (see *Jacking and vehicle support*). Remove the right-hand front roadwheel and the protective plastic cover under the wheelarch.

37 Disconnect the sensor wiring plug on the front of the engine.

38 Detach the sensor from its mounting.

Refitting

39 After refitting the sensor use a feeler blade to check that the gap between sensor and the serrated part of the crankshaft pulley is between 0.5 and 1.5 mm. No adjustment is possible and if the gap is incorrect the sensor and pulley should be checked for possible damage.

Electronic control unit (ECU)

Removal

Note: *The engine management system has a learning capability which allows the ECU to store details of the engine's running characteristics in its memory. This memory will be erased by the disconnection of the battery cables, with the result that the engine may idle roughly, or lack performance for a while, until the engine's characteristics are re-learnt.*

40 The ECU (electronic control unit) is located on the right-hand inner wing **(see illustration)**. The 3-pin socket by the ECU is for connection of diagnostic test equipment.

41 Disconnect the battery negative terminal (refer to *Disconnecting the battery* in the Reference Section of this manual).

42 Disconnect the ECU wiring connector, then undo the retaining nuts and remove the unit from the bracket in the engine compartment.

Refitting

43 Refitting is a reversal of removal making sure that the wiring connector is securely reconnected.

Inertia safety switch

Removal

44 The inertia safety switch is located by the left-hand side passenger seat. First pull back the carpet for access.

45 Disconnect the wiring then unbolt the switch.

Refitting

46 Refitting is a reversal of removal.

Fuel injection system relays

Removal

47 The fuel injection system relay is located under a plastic cover on the bulkhead. The MAP sensor is also located under the same cover.

48 Two separate relays are incorporated in the single housing; the left-hand relay has a 5 amp fuse and the right-hand relay has a 25 amp fuse. The main purpose of the relays is to supply current to the fuel pump, ignition coils, oxygen sensor, injectors and EVAP solenoid. The main relay is controlled by the ignition switch.

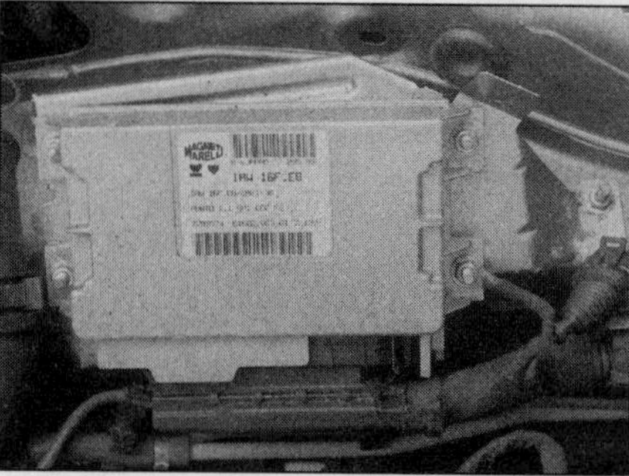

5.40 ECU located on the right-hand inner wing

49 Remove the cover and pull the relay directly from its socket.

Refitting

50 Refitting is a reversal of removal.

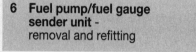

6 Fuel pump/fuel gauge sender unit - removal and refitting

Removal

Note: *Refer to the warning given in Section 1 before proceeding.*

1 Disconnect the battery negative terminal (refer to *Disconnecting the battery* in the Reference Section of this manual).

2 Remove the rear seat as described in Chapter 11. Prise the fuel pump access cover out of the floor panel to gain access to the pump unit.

3 Disconnect the wiring connector.

4 Bearing in mind the warning given in Section 1, disconnect the fuel supply and return lines from the pump unit by pressing the tabs **(see illustration)**. Plug the ends of the lines or cover them with adhesive tape.

5 Using a suitable tool, unscrew the large ring nut and carefully withdraw the fuel pump/fuel tank sender unit assembly from the fuel tank, along with its sealing ring.

6 If necessary, the unit can be dismantled and the pump and sender unit separated. If this is the case, carefully note the correct fitted positions of all components while dismantling the unit, and use these notes on reassembly to ensure that all items are correctly fitted.

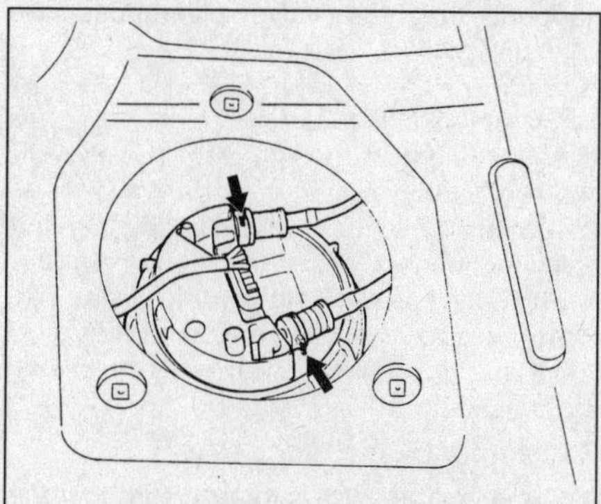

6.4 Press the tabs indicated to disconnect the fuel supply and return lines

Refitting

7 Refitting is a reversal of the removal procedure using a new sealing ring. Prior to refitting the access cover, reconnect the battery, then start the engine and check the feed and return unions for signs of leakage.

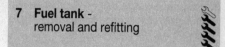

7 Fuel tank - removal and refitting

Note: *Refer to the warning given in Section 1 before proceeding.*

Removal

1 Before removing the fuel tank, all fuel must be drained from the tank. Since a fuel tank drain plug is not provided, it is therefore preferable to carry out the removal operation when the tank is nearly empty. Before proceeding, disconnect the battery negative terminal (refer to *Disconnecting the battery* in the Reference Section of this manual), and syphon or hand-pump the remaining fuel from the tank.

2 Remove the fuel pump/fuel gauge sender unit as described in Section 6.

3 Chock the front wheels, then jack up the rear of the vehicle and support on axle stands (see *Jacking and vehicle support*).

4 Loosen the clip and disconnect the filler pipe from the right-hand side of the fuel tank.

5 Undo the tank flange and strap mounting bolts, then lower the tank out of position until it is possible to access the hose connections on top of the tank.

6 Loosen the clips and disconnect the EVAP purge hose and breather hose from the fuel tank. If necessary, the filler neck can be detached from the body.

7 Check that all hoses and wiring is disconnected, then remove the tank from underneath the vehicle.

Refitting

8 Refitting is a reversal of the removal procedure, ensuring all hoses are correctly routed and securely reconnected.

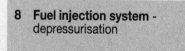

8 Fuel injection system - depressurisation

Note: *Refer to the warning given in Section 1 before proceeding.*

Warning: The following procedure will merely relieve the pressure in the fuel system - remember that fuel will still be present in the system components and take precautions accordingly before disconnecting any of them.

1 The fuel system referred to in this Section is defined as the tank-mounted fuel pump, the fuel filter, the throttle body and pressure regulator components, and the metal pipes and flexible hoses of the fuel lines between these components. All these contain fuel which will be under pressure while the engine is running and/or while the ignition is switched on. The pressure will remain for some time after the ignition has been switched off, and must be relieved before any of these components are disturbed for servicing work.

2 Disconnect the battery negative terminal (refer to *Disconnecting the battery* in the Reference Section of this manual).

3 Place a container beneath the relevant connection/union to be disconnected, and have a large rag ready to soak up any escaping fuel not being caught by the container.

4 Slowly loosen the connection or union nut (as applicable) to avoid a sudden release of pressure, and wrap the rag around the connection to catch any fuel spray which may be expelled. Once the pressure is released, disconnect the fuel line, and insert plugs to minimise fuel loss and prevent the entry of dirt into the fuel system.

9 Inlet manifold - removal and refitting

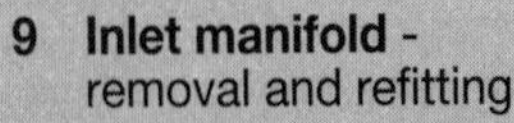

Note: *Refer to the warning given in Section 1 before proceeding.*

Removal

1 Remove the throttle body assembly as described in Section 5.

2 Drain the cooling system as described in Chapter 1A.

3 Disconnect the wiring connector from the coolant temperature sensor (situated on the left-hand side of the manifold).

4 Undo the bolt securing the accelerator cable mounting bracket to the manifold, and position it clear of the manifold.

5 Slacken the retaining clip and disconnect the coolant hose from the rear of the manifold.

6 Disconnect the brake vacuum hose.

7 Undo the seven manifold retaining nuts and bolts, and remove the manifold from the engine. Remove the gasket and discard it; a new one should be used on refitting.

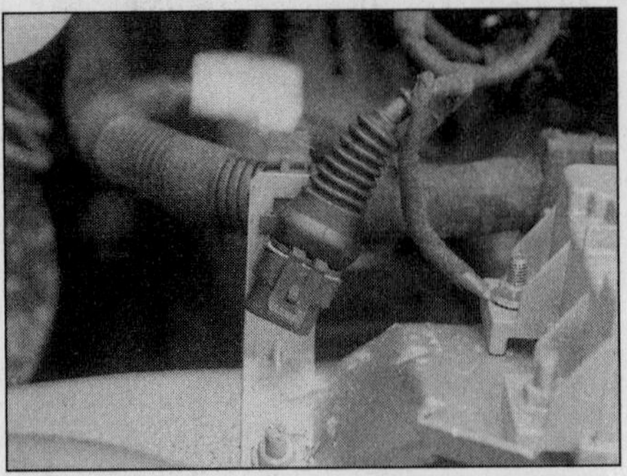

10.2 The diagnostic connector is located behind the ECU

Refitting

8 Refitting is a reverse of the removal procedure, noting the following points:

a) *Ensure that the manifold and cylinder head mating surfaces are clean and dry, and fit a new manifold gasket. Refit the manifold and securely tighten its retaining nuts.*
b) *Ensure that all relevant hoses are reconnected to their original positions and are securely held (where necessary) by the retaining clips.*
c) *Refit the throttle body assembly with reference to Section 5.*
d) *On completion, refill the cooling system as described in Chapter 1A.*

10 Fuel injection system - testing and adjustment

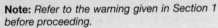

Testing

1 If a fault appears in the fuel injection system, first ensure that all the system wiring connectors are securely connected and free of corrosion. Then ensure that the fault is not due to poor maintenance; ie, check that the air cleaner filter element is clean, the spark plugs are in good condition and correctly gapped, that the valve clearances are correctly adjusted, and that the engine breather hoses are clear and undamaged.

2 If these checks fail to reveal the cause of the problem, the vehicle should be taken to a suitably-equipped Fiat dealer for testing. A wiring block connector is incorporated in the engine management circuit, into which a special electronic diagnostic tester can be plugged; the connector is situated behind the ECU **(see illustration)**. The tester will locate the fault quickly and simply, alleviating the need to test all the system components individually, which is a time-consuming operation that carries a high risk of damaging the ECU.

Adjustments

3 As mentioned above, the idle speed and mixture adjustment are all monitored and controlled by the ECU, and are not adjustable. Experienced home mechanics with a considerable amount of skill and equipment (including a good-quality tachometer and a good-quality, carefully calibrated exhaust gas analyser) may be able to check the exhaust CO level and the idle speed. However, if these are found to be in need of adjustment, the car must be taken to a suitably-equipped Fiat dealer for testing using the special test equipment which is plugged into the diagnostic connector.

11 Unleaded petrol - general information and usage

Note: *The information given in this Chapter is correct at the time of writing. If updated information is thought to be required, check with a Fiat dealer. If travelling abroad, consult one of the motoring organisations (or a similar authority) for advice on the fuel available.*

1 All petrol models are fitted with a catalytic converter and must be run on unleaded fuel only - the fuel recommended by Fiat is given in the Specifications of this Chapter. Under no circumstances should leaded fuel (UK 4-star) be used, as this may damage the converter.

2 Super unleaded petrol (98 octane) can also be used in all models if wished, though there is no advantage in doing so.

Chapter 4 Part B:
Fuel system - multi-point petrol injection models

Contents

Degrees of difficulty

Easy, suitable for novice with little experience 	**Fairly easy,** suitable for beginner with some experience 	**Fairly difficult,** suitable for competent DIY mechanic 	**Difficult,** suitable for experienced DIY mechanic	**Very difficult,** suitable for expert DIY or professional 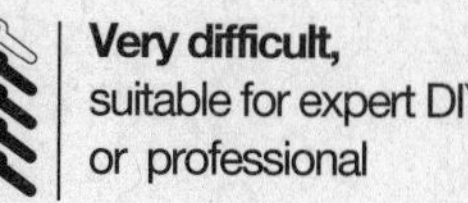

Specifications

System type	Weber-Marelli integrated multi-point fuel injection/ignition system	
Fuel system data		
Fuel pump type	Electric, immersed in fuel tank	
Fuel pump delivery rate:		
1242 cc (8-valve) engine	120 litres/hour minimum	
1242 cc (16-valve) engine	110 litres/hour minimum	
Regulated fuel pressure:		
1242 cc (8-valve) engine:		
Pre-1998 models	2.5 bars	
1998 models onward	3.5 bars	
1242 cc (16-valve) engine	3.0 bars	
Crankshaft TDC sensor resistance at 20°C	650 to 720 ohms	
Injector electrical resistance:		
Pre-1998 models	16.2 ohms	
1998 models onward	13.8 to 15.2 ohms	
Injector duration (at idle)	2.0 ms	
Recommended fuel		
Minimum octane rating	95 RON unleaded	
Torque wrench settings	**Nm**	**lbf ft**
Coolant temperature sensor	3	2
Idle control stepper motor	4	3
Inlet manifold brake servo union	35	26
Inlet manifold upper section-to-lower section (16-valve engines)	9	7
Inlet manifold-to-cylinder head (16-valve engines)	15	11
Inlet manifold-to-cylinder head (8-valve engines)	27	20
Throttle body to manifold	7	5
Throttle potentiometer	3	2

1 General information and precautions

General information

The IAW Weber-Marelli multi-point injection (MPI) system is a self-contained engine management system, which controls both the fuel injection and ignition **(see illustrations)**. This Chapter deals with the fuel injection system components only - refer to Chapter 5B for details of the ignition system components.

The fuel injection system comprises a fuel tank, an electric fuel pump, a fuel filter, fuel supply and return lines, a throttle body, a fuel rail with four electronic injectors, and an Electronic Control Unit (ECU) together with its associated sensors, actuators and wiring.

On pre-1998, 8-valve engines and all 16-valve engines, the fuel pump delivers a constant supply of fuel through a cartridge filter to the fuel rail, and the fuel pressure regulator (located on the fuel rail) maintains a constant fuel pressure at the fuel injectors and returns excess fuel to the tank via the return line. This constant flow system also helps to reduce fuel temperature and prevents vaporisation. On later 8-valve engines, a returnless fuel system is used. With this arrangement, the fuel filter and fuel pressure regulator are an integral part of the fuel pump assembly located in the fuel tank. The regulator maintains a constant fuel pressure in the supply line to the fuel rail and allows excess fuel to recirculate in the fuel tank, by means of a bypass channel, if the regulated fuel pressure is exceeded. As the fuel filter is an integral part of the pump assembly, fuel filter renewal is no longer necessary as part of the maintenance and servicing schedule.

The fuel injectors are opened and closed by an Electronic Control Unit (ECU), which calculates the injection timing and duration according to engine speed, throttle position and rate of opening, inlet air temperature, coolant temperature and exhaust gas oxygen content information, received from sensors mounted on the engine. The injectors are operated simultaneously (ie not sequentially) and inject half of the quantity of fuel required on each turn of the crankshaft.

Inlet air is drawn into the engine through the air cleaner, which contains a renewable paper filter element. On 8-valve engines, the inlet air temperature is regulated by a vacuum operated valve mounted in the air ducting, which blends air at ambient temperature with hot air, drawn from over the exhaust manifold.

Idle speed is controlled by a stepper motor located on the side of the throttle body. Cold starting enrichment is controlled by the ECU using the coolant temperature and inlet air temperature parameters to increase the injector opening duration.

The exhaust gas oxygen content is constantly monitored by the ECU via the Lambda/oxygen sensor, which is mounted in the exhaust downpipe. The ECU then uses this information to modify the injection timing and duration to maintain the optimum air/fuel ratio. An exhaust catalyst is fitted to all models. The ECU also controls the operation of the activated charcoal filter evaporative loss system - refer to Chapter 4D for further details.

It should be noted that fault diagnosis of the IAW Weber-Marelli system is only possible with dedicated electronic test equipment.

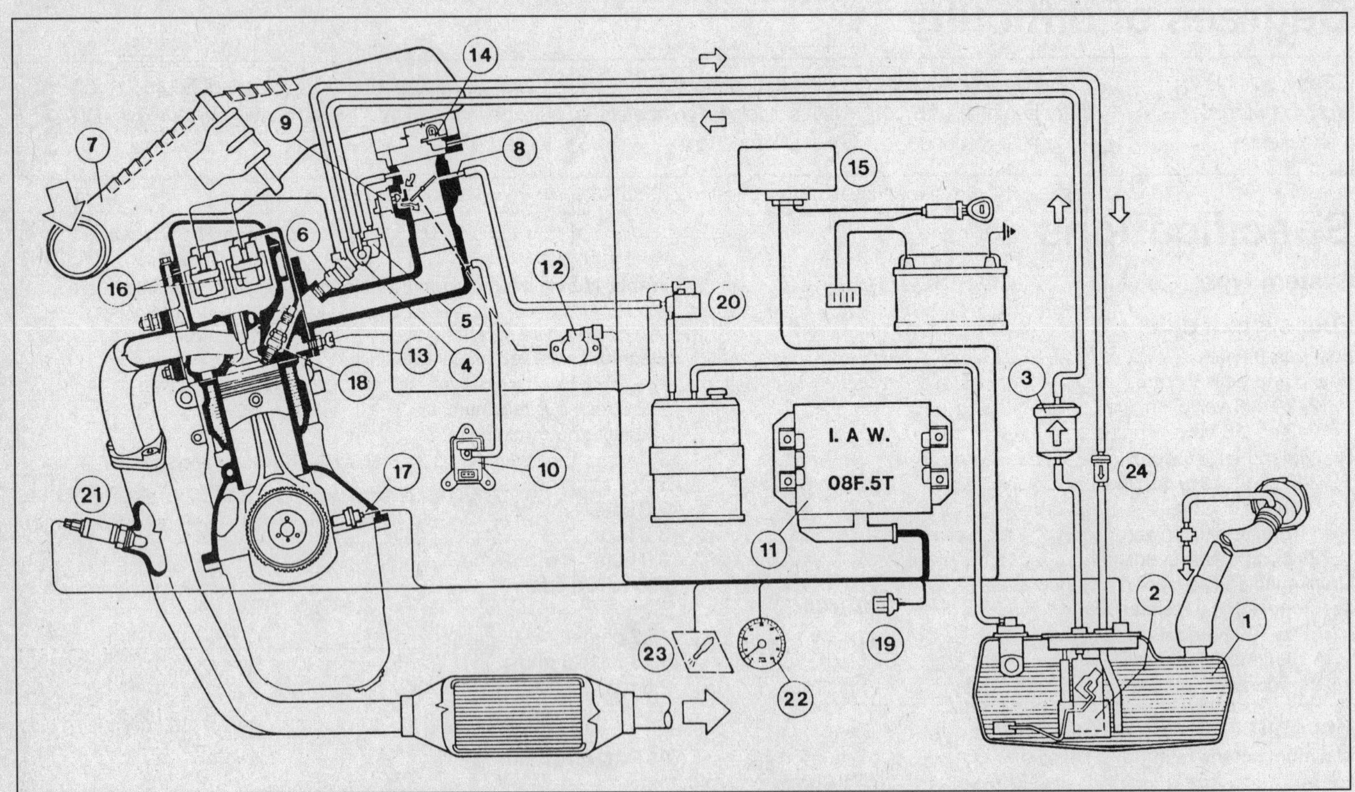

1.1a IAW Weber-Marelli multi-point injection (MPI) system (8-valve engines)

1 Fuel tank
2 Fuel pump
3 Filter (pre-1998 models)
4 Fuel rail
5 Pressure regulator (pre-1998 models)
6 Injectors
7 Air cleaner
8 Fuel vapour trap
9 Idle control stepper motor
10 Manifold absolute pressure sensor
11 ECU
12 Throttle position sensor
13 Coolant temperature sensor
14 Intake air temperature sensor
15 Dual relay
16 Ignition coils
17 Rpm and TDC sensor
18 Spark plugs
19 Diagnostic socket
20 EVAP solenoid
21 Lambda/oxygen sensor
22 Rev counter
23 IAW failure warning light
24 Anti-reflux valve

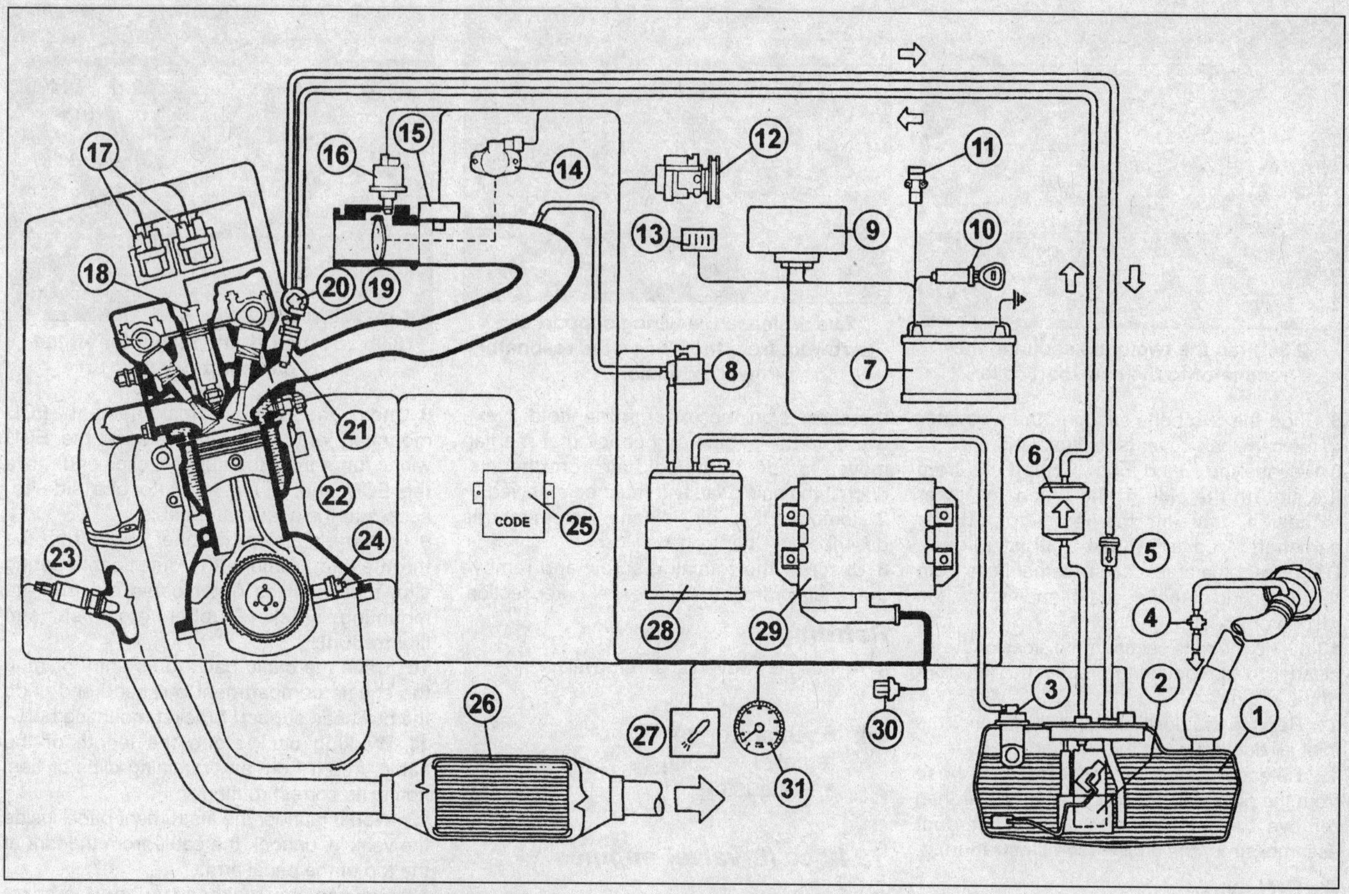

1.1b IAW Weber-Marelli multi-point injection (MPI) system (16-valve engines)

1 Fuel tank
2 Fuel pump
3 Multi-purpose valve
4 Safety valve
5 Anti-reflux valve
6 Filter
7 Battery
8 EVAP solenoid
9 Dual relay
10 Ignition switch
11 Inertia switch
12 Air conditioning compressor
13 Fuse
14 Throttle position sensor
15 Intake air temperature/pressure sensor
16 Idle control stepper motor
17 Ignition coils
18 Spark plugs
19 Fuel rail
20 Pressure regulator
21 Injectors
22 Coolant temperature sensor
23 Lambda/oxygen sensor
24 Rpm and TDC sensor
25 Engine immobiliser control unit
26 Catalytic converter
27 IAW failure warning light
28 EVAP canister
29 ECU
30 Diagnostic socket
31 Rev counter

Problems with the system should therefore be referred to a Fiat dealer for assessment. Once the fault has been identified, the removal/refitting procedures detailed in the following Sections can then be followed.

Precautions

Warning: Many procedures in this Chapter require the removal of fuel lines and connections, which may result in fuel spillage. Before carrying out any operation on the fuel system, refer to the precautions given in Safety first! at the beginning of this manual, and follow them implicitly. Petrol is a highly dangerous and volatile liquid, and the precautions necessary when handling it cannot be overstressed. Note that residual pressure will remain in the fuel lines long after the vehicle was last used, When disconnecting any fuel line, first depressurise the fuel system (see Section 9) .

2 Air cleaner and inlet system - removal and refitting

Removal

1242 cc (8-valve) engines

1 Remove the air cleaner element as described in Chapter 1A.

2 Disconnect the outer section from the hot air tube and the inlet air duct and remove it from the engine compartment.

3 If necessary remove the inlet air duct.

4 Disconnect the large and small breather hoses from the inner section of the air cleaner, then unscrew the retaining nuts and lift the section from the throttle body.

5 Recover the sealing ring. Check the ring for condition and renew it if necessary.

6 Wipe clean the inner surfaces of both the inner and outer sections of the air cleaner.

1242 cc (16-valve) engines

7 Release the hose clip and disconnect the inlet air duct from the resonator **(see illustration)**.

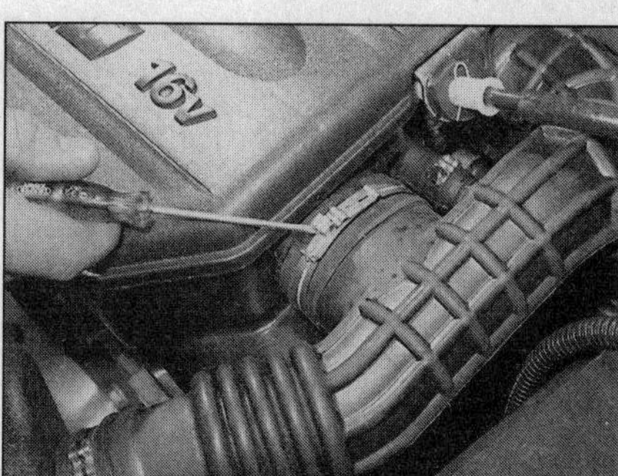

2.7 Release the hose clip and disconnect the inlet air duct from the resonator

2.8 Undo the two bolts securing the resonator to the camshaft cover

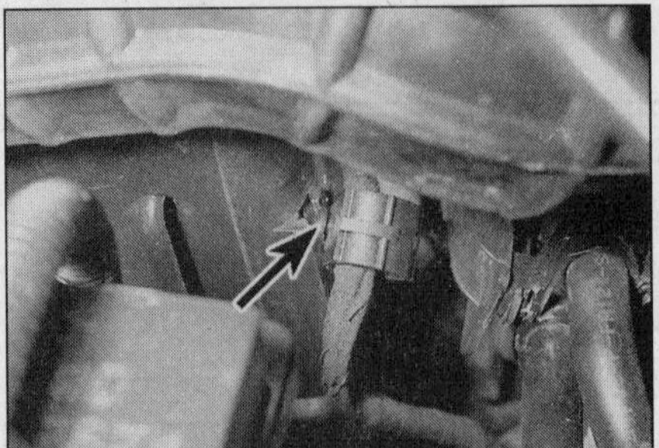

2.9a Release the wiring support clip (arrowed) from the slot on the resonator lower extension . . .

2.9b . . . then lift the resonator off the camshaft cover

8 Undo the two bolts securing the resonator to the camshaft cover **(see illustration)**.

9 Release the wiring loom support clip from the slot on the side of the resonator lower extension, then lift the resonator off the camshaft cover **(see illustrations)**. Disconnect the crankcase breather hose from the underside of the resonator and remove the resonator from the engine.

10 Undo the nuts securing the sides of the air cleaner to the mounting brackets at the front of the engine.

11 Release the hose clip and disconnect the inlet air duct from the throttle body.

12 Release the crankcase ventilation hose from the pipe stub on the camshaft cover then remove the air cleaner and inlet air duct assembly from the engine **(see illustration)**.

Refitting

13 Refitting is a reversal of removal but renew the air cleaner element as described in Chapter 1A, if necessary.

3 Inlet air temperature regulator - removal and refitting

Removal

1 The thermostatically-controlled cold air flap opener, fitted to 8-valve engines, is located in the air cleaner outer casing section. To check the unit, disconnect the air inlet duct with the engine cold and use a mirror to check that the flap is positioned to admit only hot air from

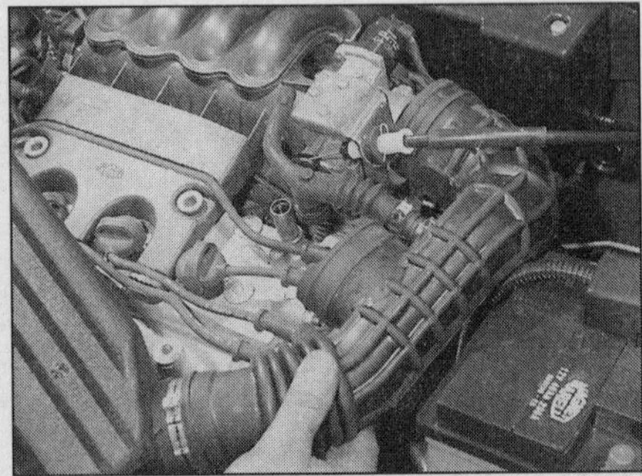

2.12 Removing the air cleaner and inlet air duct assembly

the shroud on the exhaust manifold. Next, warm up the engine and check that the flap moves to admit only cold air from the inlet duct. If the unit is faulty it must be renewed.

2 Remove the air cleaner element as described in Chapter 1A.

3 Unscrew the retaining screw and remove the regulator from the air cleaner outer section.

Refitting

4 Refitting is a reversal of removal.

4 Accelerator cable - removal, refitting and adjustment

1242 cc (8-valve) engines

Removal

1 Remove the air cleaner as described in Section 2.

2 To release the cable from the throttle body, unscrew the outer cable locknuts, then disengage the inner cable from the throttle cam, and release the outer cable from its mounting bracket.

3 Working under the instrument panel inside the vehicle, unhook the cable from the fork at the top of the pedal arm.

4 Release the bulkhead grommet and withdraw the accelerator cable from inside the engine compartment.

Refitting and adjustment

5 Refitting is a reverse of the removal process, but adjust the cable (by means of the outer cable locknuts) so that there is only a very small amount of free play present at the throttle body end of the inner cable. Have an assistant depress the accelerator pedal, and check that the throttle cam opens fully and returns to the at-rest position, then securely tighten the cable locknuts.

1242 cc (16-valve) engines

Removal

6 Disconnect the battery negative terminal (refer to *Disconnecting the battery* in the Reference Section of this manual).

7 Remove the resonator, air cleaner and inlet air duct as described in Section 2.

8 Undo the engine management ECU mounting bracket bolts, release the ECU wiring loom from the support clips and move the ECU and wiring loom to one side for access to the accelerator cable.

9 Free the accelerator inner cable from the throttle cam, remove the outer cable spring clip, then pull the outer cable out from its mounting bracket rubber grommet **(see illustration)**.

10 Trace the cable back to its entry point in the engine compartment bulkhead and undo the bulkhead support bracket mounting bolt.

11 Working back along the length of the cable, free it from any retaining clips or ties, noting its correct routing.

12 Working under the instrument panel inside the vehicle, unhook the cable from the fork at the top of the pedal arm.

13 Release the bulkhead support bracket and withdraw the accelerator cable from inside the engine compartment.

Refitting and adjustment

14 Refitting is a reverse of the removal process, but adjust the cable as follows before refitting the outer cable spring clip.

15 Ensuring that the throttle cam is fully against its stop, gently pull the cable out of its grommet until all free play is removed from the inner cable.

16 With the cable held in this position, fit the spring clip to the first outer cable groove visible in front of the mounting bracket rubber grommet. This should leave a small amount of freeplay in the inner cable which is necessary to ensure correct throttle operation.

4.9 Accelerator outer cable spring clip (arrowed)

17 Have an assistant depress the accelerator pedal and check that the throttle cam opens fully and returns smoothly to its stop. If necessary, reposition the spring clip in the next outer cable groove and recheck the throttle operation.

18 Refit the remainder of the disturbed components.

5 Engine management system components (1242 cc, 8-valve engines) - removal and refitting

Note: *Refer to the warning given in Section 1 before proceeding.*

Throttle body assembly

Removal

1 Remove the air cleaner and inlet air duct as described in Section 2.

2 Disconnect the wiring connectors from the throttle potentiometer, the idle control stepper motor and the inlet air temperature sensor.

3 Slacken the accelerator cable locknuts, then disengage the inner cable from the throttle cam and free the outer cable from its retaining bracket. Position the cable clear of the throttle body.

4 Unclip and disconnect the EVAP purge valve hose, and the MAP sensor hose from the rear of the throttle body then, where applicable, disconnect the fuel pressure regulator vacuum hose from the front of the throttle body.

5 Slacken and remove the four bolts securing the throttle body assembly to the inlet manifold, then remove the assembly along with its insulating spacer.

Refitting

6 Refitting is a reversal of the removal procedure, bearing in mind the following points:

a) *Examine the insulating spacer for signs of damage, and renew if necessary.*
b) *Ensure the throttle body, inlet manifold and insulating spacer mating surfaces are clean and dry, then fit the throttle body and spacer, and securely tighten the retaining bolts.*
c) *Ensure all hoses are correctly reconnected and, where necessary, that their retaining clips are securely tightened.*
d) *Adjust the accelerator cable as described in Section 4.*

Fuel rail and injectors

Removal

7 Disconnect the battery negative terminal (refer to *Disconnecting the battery* in the Reference Section of this manual).

8 Remove the throttle body assembly as described earlier in this Section, however it is only necessary to move the unit to one side for access to the fuel rail and therefore it is unnecessary to disconnect the accelerator cable and hoses etc.

9 Depressurise the fuel system as described in Section 9.

10 Loosen the clips or release the quick-release couplings and disconnect the fuel inlet and, on pre-1998 models, outlet hoses from the fuel rail. Note the fitted positions of the hoses to aid refitting later.

11 Unplug the injector wiring harness connectors, labelling them to aid correct refitting later.

12 Unscrew the bolts securing the fuel rail assembly to the inlet manifold, then carefully pull the injectors from the inlet manifold. Remove the assembly from the engine and remove the injector lower O-ring seals.

13 The injectors can be removed individually from the fuel rail by extracting the relevant metal clip and easing the injector out of the rail. Remove the injector upper O-ring seals **(see illustration)**.

14 On pre-1998 models, if necessary remove the retaining clip and remove the fuel pressure regulator from the fuel rail.

15 Check the electrical resistance of the injector using a multimeter and compare it with the Specifications. **Note:** *If a faulty injector is suspected, before condemning the injector, it is worth trying the effect of one of the proprietary injector-cleaning treatments.*

Refitting

16 Refit the injectors and fuel rail by following the removal procedure, in reverse, noting the following points:

a) *Renew the injector O-ring seals, and smear them with a little Vaseline before assembling. Take care when fitting the injectors to the fuel rail and do not press them in further than required to fit the retaining clip otherwise the O-ring seal may be damaged.*

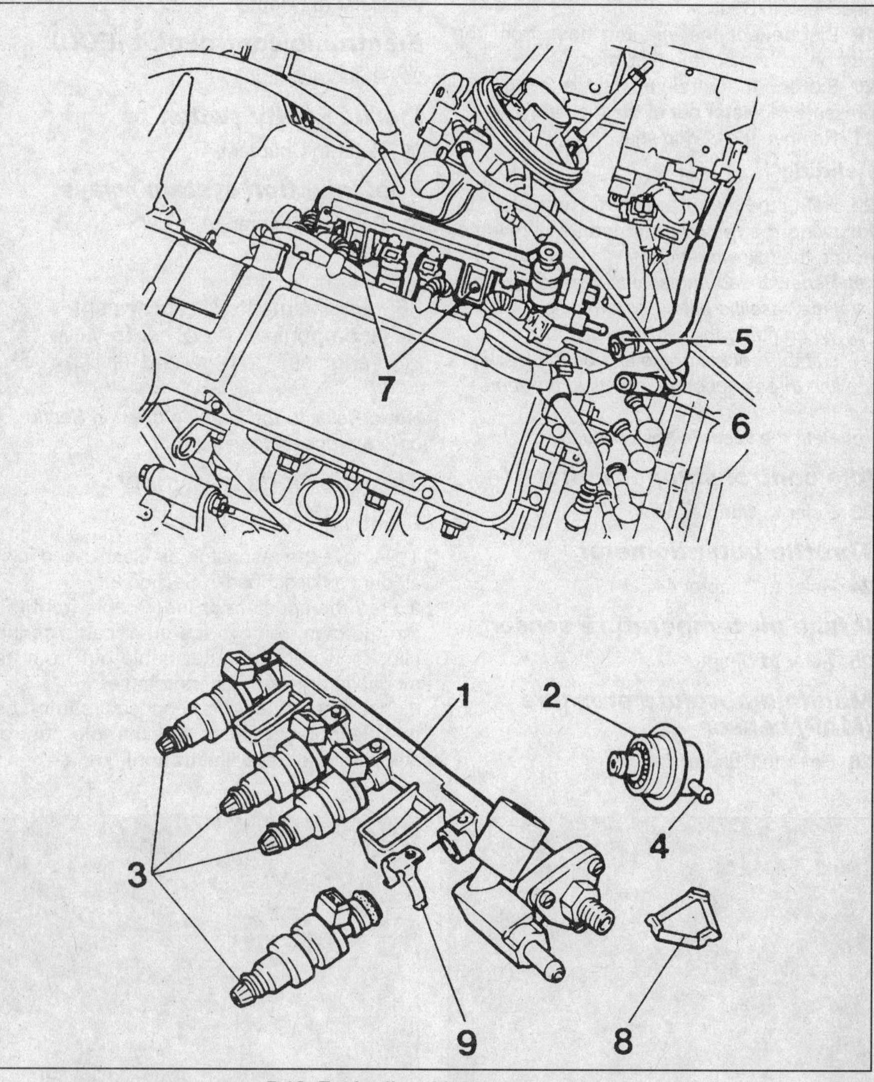

5.13 Fuel rail and injector removal

1 *Fuel rail*
2 *Fuel pressure regulator*
3 *Injectors*
4 *Vacuum stub connection*
5 *Fuel inlet hose*
6 *Fuel return hose*
7 *Mounting bolts*
8 *Injector mounting clip*
9 *Injector mounting clip*

4B

b) *Ensure that the injector retaining clips are securely seated.*
c) *Make sure the fuel supply and return hoses are correctly fitted as noted on removal.*
d) *Check that all vacuum and electrical connections are remade correctly and securely.*
e) *On completion check the fuel rail and injectors for fuel leaks.*

Fuel pressure regulator

Note: *On 1998 models onward, the fuel pressure regulator is an integral part of the fuel pump and cannot be renewed separately. The following procedure applies to pre-1998 models only.*

Removal

17 Remove the air cleaner and inlet air ducts as described in Section 2.

18 Depressurise the fuel system as described in Section 9.

19 Disconnect the vacuum hose from the port on the side of the regulator.

20 Extract the retaining clip and pull the pressure regulator out of the fuel rail.

21 Remove the O-ring seal.

Refitting

22 Refit the fuel pressure regulator by following the removal procedure in reverse, noting the following points:

a) *Renew the O-ring seal and smear it with a little Vaseline before assembling.*
b) *When fitting the retaining clip, use a suitable socket or metal tube to press in the three anchorage points at the same time.*
c) *Refit the vacuum hose securely.*

Idle control stepper motor

23 Refer to Chapter 4A.

Throttle potentiometer

24 Refer to Chapter 4A.

Intake air temperature sensor

25 Refer to Chapter 4A.

Manifold absolute pressure (MAP) sensor

26 Refer to Chapter 4A.

6.3 Disconnect the wiring connectors from the throttle potentiometer and the idle control stepper motor

Coolant temperature sensor

27 Refer to Chapter 4A.

Crankshaft TDC sensor

28 Refer to Chapter 4A.

Electronic control unit (ECU)

29 Refer to Chapter 4A.

Inertia safety switch

30 Refer to Chapter 4A.

Fuel injection system relays

31 Refer to Chapter 4A.

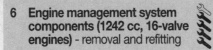

6 Engine management system components (1242 cc, 16-valve engines) - removal and refitting

Note: *Refer to the warning given in Section 1 before proceeding.*

Throttle body assembly

Removal

1 Remove the resonator, air cleaner and inlet air duct as described in Section 2.

2 Free the accelerator inner cable from the throttle cam, remove the outer cable spring clip, then pull the outer cable out from its mounting bracket rubber grommet.

3 Disconnect the wiring connectors from the throttle potentiometer and the idle control stepper motor **(see illustration)**.

4 Slacken and remove the three bolts securing the throttle body assembly to the inlet manifold, then remove the assembly along with its insulating spacer. As the throttle body is withdrawn, disconnect the vacuum hose from the underside of the unit.

Refitting

5 Refitting is a reversal of the removal procedure, bearing in mind the following points:

a) *Examine the insulating spacer for signs of damage, and renew if necessary.*
b) *Ensure the throttle body, inlet manifold and insulating spacer mating surfaces are clean and dry, then fit the throttle body and spacer, and securely tighten the retaining bolts.*
c) *Adjust the accelerator cable as described in Section 4.*

Fuel rail and injectors

Removal

6 Disconnect the battery negative terminal (refer to *Disconnecting the battery* in the Reference Section of this manual).

7 Remove the resonator, air cleaner and inlet air duct as described in Section 2.

8 Free the accelerator inner cable from the throttle cam, remove the outer cable spring clip, then pull the outer cable out from its mounting bracket rubber grommet.

9 From the side of the throttle body, disconnect the wiring connectors from the throttle potentiometer and the idle control stepper motor.

10 Depressurise the fuel system as described in Section 9.

11 Loosen the clips or release the quick-release couplings and disconnect the fuel inlet and outlet hoses from the left-hand end of the fuel rail, below the throttle body. Note the fitted positions of the hoses to aid refitting later. Undo the support bracket retaining bolt and move the fuel hoses to one side.

12 Disconnect the wiring connectors for the fuel injector harness and the intake air temperature/pressure sensor **(see illustrations)**.

13 Disconnect the fuel pressure regulator vacuum hose and the EVAP purge valve hose **(see illustrations)**.

6.12a Disconnect the wiring connectors for the fuel injector harness . . .

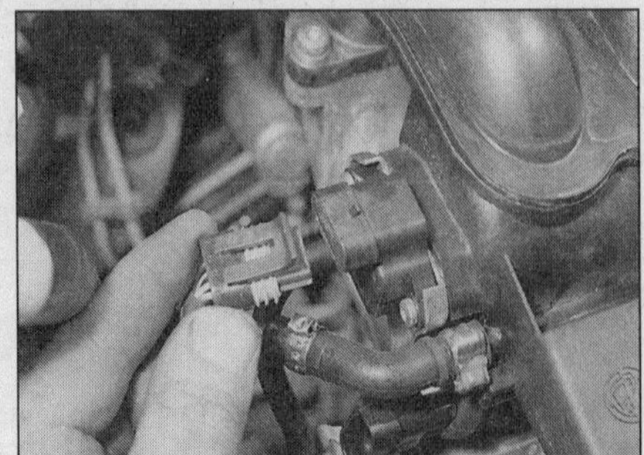

6.12b . . . and intake air temperature/pressure sensor

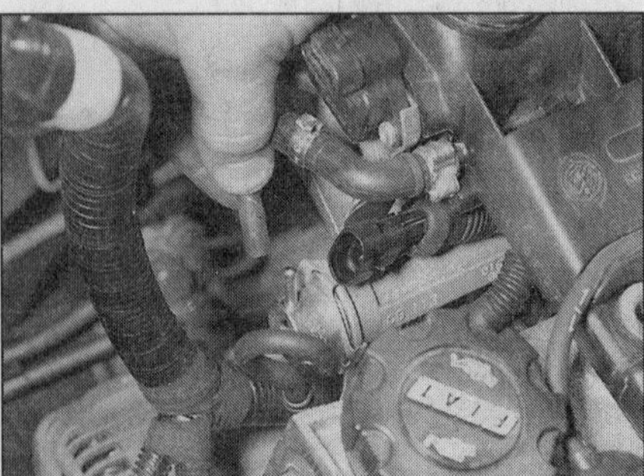

6.13a Disconnect the fuel pressure regulator vacuum hose . . .

6.13b . . . and the EVAP purge valve hose

6.14a Undo the inlet manifold upper section retaining bolts . . .

6.14b . . . and lift off the manifold upper section and throttle body

14 Undo the two bolts securing the plastic inlet manifold upper section to the lower section. Release the spark plug HT lead from the location groove in the manifold upper section, then lift the upper section, complete with throttle body, off the engine **(see illustrations)**. Recover the O-rings from the manifold ports.

15 Unscrew the two bolts securing the fuel rail assembly to the inlet manifold lower section, then carefully pull the injectors from the inlet manifold **(see illustration)**. Remove the assembly from the engine and remove the injector lower O-ring seals.

16 The injectors can be removed individually from the fuel rail by disconnecting the wiring connector, extracting the relevant metal clip and easing the injector out of the rail. Remove the injector upper O-ring seals.

17 Check the electrical resistance of the injector using a multimeter and compare it with the Specifications. **Note:** *If a faulty injector is suspected, before condemning the injector, it is worth trying the effect of one of the proprietary injector-cleaning treatments.*

Refitting

18 Refit the injectors and fuel rail by following the removal procedure, in reverse, noting the following points:

a) Renew the injector O-ring seals, and smear them with a little Vaseline before assembling. Take care when fitting the injectors to the fuel rail and do not press them in further than required to fit the retaining clip otherwise the O-ring seal may be damaged.

b) Ensure that the injector retaining clips are securely seated.

c) Renew the sealing O-rings fitted between the manifold upper and lower sections if in any doubt about their condition.

d) Make sure the fuel supply and return hoses are correctly fitted as noted on removal.

e) Check that all vacuum and electrical connections are remade correctly and securely.

f) On completion check the fuel rail and injectors for fuel leaks.

6.15 Fuel rail securing bolts (arrowed)

Fuel pressure regulator

Removal

19 Remove the resonator, air cleaner and inlet air ducts as described in Section 2.

20 Depressurise the fuel system as described in Section 9.

21 Disconnect the vacuum hose from the port on the side of the regulator.

22 Extract the retaining clip and pull the pressure regulator out of the fuel rail.

23 Remove the O-ring seal.

Refitting

24 Refit the fuel pressure regulator by following the removal procedure in reverse, noting the following points:

a) Renew the O-ring seal and smear it with a little Vaseline before assembling.

b) When fitting the retaining clip, use a suitable socket or metal tube to press in the three anchorage points at the same time.

c) Refit the vacuum hose securely.

Idle control stepper motor

25 The idle control stepper motor is an integral part of the throttle body and cannot be individually renewed.

Throttle potentiometer

26 The throttle potentiometer is an integral part of the throttle body and cannot be individually renewed.

Intake air temperature/pressure sensor

Removal

27 Remove the resonator, air cleaner and inlet air duct as described in Section 2.

28 Disconnect the sensor wiring connector, located on the right-hand side of the inlet manifold upper section.

29 Undo the two screws and remove the sensor from the manifold.

Refitting

30 Refitting is a reversal of the removal procedure.

Coolant temperature sensor

31 Refer to Chapter 4A.

Crankshaft TDC sensor

32 Refer to Chapter 4A.

Electronic control unit (ECU)

Removal

Note: *The engine management system has a learning capability which allows the ECU to store details of the engine's running characteristics in its memory. This memory will be erased by the disconnection of the battery cables, with the result that the engine may idle roughly, or lack performance for a while, until the engine's characteristics are re-learnt.*

33 The ECU (electronic control unit) is located on the right-hand inner wing panel.

34 Disconnect the battery negative terminal (refer to *Disconnecting the battery* in the Reference Section of this manual).

35 Undo the mounting bracket nuts and withdraw the unit from the inner wing **(see illustration)**.

36 Disconnect the ECU wiring connector, then remove the unit from the engine compartment.

6.35 Undo the mounting bracket nuts and withdraw the ECU from the inner wing

Refitting

37 Refitting is a reversal of removal making sure that the wiring connector is securely reconnected.

Inertia safety switch

38 Refer to Chapter 4A.

Fuel injection system relays

Removal

39 The fuel injection system twin relay is located under a plastic cover on the engine compartment bulkhead.

40 The main purpose of the relay is to supply current to the fuel pump, ignition coils, oxygen sensor, injectors and EVAP solenoid. The relay is controlled by the ignition switch. A 15 amp fuse, protecting the fuel pump, oxygen sensor and EVAP solenoid is located adjacent to the relay.

41 Remove the cover and pull the relay directly from its socket.

Refitting

42 Refitting is a reversal of removal.

7 Fuel pump and fuel gauge sender unit - removal and refitting

Removal

Note: *Refer to the warning given in Section 1 before proceeding.*

1 Disconnect the battery negative terminal (refer to *Disconnecting the battery* in the Reference Section of this manual).

2 Depressurise the fuel system as described in Section 9.

3 Remove the rear seat as described in Chapter 11. Prise the fuel pump access cover out of the floor panel to gain access to the pump unit. On later models, undo the three retaining screws to release the cover.

4 Disconnect the wiring connector.

5 Bearing in mind the warning given in Section 1, disconnect the fuel supply and, where applicable, the return lines from the pump unit by pressing the tabs. Plug the ends of the lines or cover them with adhesive tape.

6 Using a suitable tool, unscrew the large ring nut and carefully withdraw the fuel pump/fuel tank sender unit assembly from the fuel tank, along with its sealing ring.

7 If necessary, the unit can be dismantled and the pump and sender unit separated. If this is the case, carefully note the correct fitted positions of all components while dismantling the unit, and use these notes on reassembly to ensure that all items are correctly fitted.

Refitting

8 Refitting is a reversal of the removal procedure using a new sealing ring. Prior to refitting the access cover, reconnect the battery, then start the engine and check the fuel line union(s) for signs of leakage.

8 Fuel tank - removal and refitting

Refer to Chapter 4A.

9 Fuel injection system - depressurisation

Note: *Refer to the warning given in Section 1 before proceeding.*

Warning: The following procedure will merely relieve the pressure in the fuel system - remember that fuel will still be present in the system components and take precautions accordingly before disconnecting any of them.

1 The fuel system referred to in this Section is defined as the tank-mounted fuel pump, the fuel filter, the fuel rail, the fuel injectors, and the metal pipes and flexible hoses of the fuel lines between these components. All these contain fuel which will be under pressure while the engine is running and/or while the ignition is switched on. The pressure will remain for some time after the ignition has been switched off, and must be relieved before any of these components are disturbed for servicing work.

2 Disconnect the battery negative terminal (refer to *Disconnecting the battery* in the Reference Section of this manual).

3 Have a large rag ready to cover the union to be disconnected and, if possible, place a container beneath the relevant connection/union.

4 Slowly loosen the connection or union nut (as applicable) to avoid a sudden release of pressure, and ensure that the rag is wrapped around the connection to catch any fuel spray which may be expelled. Once the pressure is released, disconnect the fuel line, and insert plugs to minimise fuel loss and prevent the entry of dirt into the fuel system. Note that on later models, quick-release fuel couplings are used on many of the fuel line connections. To release these couplings, depress the two clips on the side of the coupling while keeping the fuel line pushed in. With the clips depressed, slowly withdraw the fuel line from the coupling allowing the fuel pressure to release, then withdraw the fuel line fully.

10 Inlet manifold - removal and refitting

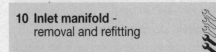

Note: *Refer to the warning given in Section 1 before proceeding.*

1242 cc (8-valve) engines

Removal

1 Remove the throttle body assembly as described in Section 5.

2 Remove the fuel rail and injectors as described in Section 5.

3 Drain the cooling system as described in Chapter 1A.

4 Disconnect the wiring connector from the coolant temperature sensor (situated on the left-hand side of the manifold).

5 Undo the bolt securing the accelerator cable mounting bracket to the manifold, and position it clear of the manifold.

6 Slacken the retaining clip and disconnect the coolant hose from the rear of the manifold.

7 Disconnect the brake vacuum hose.

8 Undo the seven manifold retaining nuts and bolts, and remove the manifold from the engine. Remove the gasket and discard it; a new one should be used on refitting.

Refitting

9 Refitting is a reverse of the removal procedure, noting the following points:

a) *Ensure that the manifold and cylinder head mating surfaces are clean and dry, and fit a new manifold gasket. Refit the manifold and securely tighten its retaining nuts.*
b) *Ensure all relevant hoses are reconnected to their original positions and are securely held (where necessary) by the retaining clips.*
c) *Refit the fuel rail and injectors, and the throttle body assembly with reference to Section 5.*
d) *On completion, refill the cooling system as described in Chapter 1A.*

1242 cc (16-valve) engines

Removal

10 Disconnect the battery negative terminal (refer to *Disconnecting the battery* in the Reference Section of this manual).

11 Remove the resonator, air cleaner and inlet air duct as described in Section 2.

12 Drain the cooling system as described in Chapter 1A.

13 Free the accelerator inner cable from the throttle cam, remove the outer cable spring clip, then pull the outer cable out from its mounting bracket rubber grommet.

14 From the side of the throttle body, disconnect the wiring connectors from the throttle potentiometer and the idle control stepper motor. Disconnect the coolant temperature sensor wiring connector located in the inlet manifold below the throttle body, and disconnect the brake servo vacuum hose.

15 Disconnect the wiring connectors for the fuel injector harness and the intake air temperature/pressure sensor, then disconnect the fuel pressure regulator vacuum hose and the EVAP purge valve hose **(see illustration)**.

16 Undo the two bolts securing the plastic inlet manifold upper section to the lower section. Release the spark plug HT lead from the location groove in the manifold upper section, then lift the upper section, complete with throttle body, off the engine. Recover the O-rings from the manifold ports.

17 Unscrew the two bolts securing the fuel rail assembly to the inlet manifold lower section, then carefully pull the injectors from the manifold. Lift the fuel rail and injector assembly, with fuel hoses still connected, and position it to one side **(see illustration)**.

18 Disconnect the heater hose from the manifold stub.

19 Undo the engine oil dipstick tube bracket retaining bolt and the two bolts securing the wiring harness support clips to the manifold.

20 Undo the ten manifold retaining nuts and remove the manifold from the cylinder head studs. Remove the gasket and discard it; a new one should be used on refitting.

Refitting

21 Refitting is a reverse of the removal procedure, noting the following points:

a) Ensure that the manifold and cylinder head mating surfaces are clean and dry, and fit a new manifold gasket. Refit the manifold and securely tighten its retaining nuts.

b) Renew the sealing O-rings fitted between the manifold upper and lower sections if in any doubt about their condition.

c) Ensure all relevant hoses are reconnected to their original positions and are securely held (where necessary) by the retaining clips.

d) Renew the injector O-ring seals, and smear them with a little Vaseline before assembling.

e) Adjust the accelerator cable as described in Section 4.

f) On completion, refill the cooling system as described in Chapter 1A.

11 Fuel injection system - testing and adjustment

Refer to Chapter 4A.

12 Unleaded petrol - general information and usage

Refer to Chapter 4A.

10.15 Disconnect the wiring connectors and hoses from the fuel rail and manifold

1 *Fuel injector harness wiring connector*
2 *Intake air temperature/pressure sensor wiring connector*
3 *Fuel pressure regulator vacuum hose*
4 *EVAP purge valve hose*

10.17 Lift off the fuel rail and injector assembly, with fuel hoses still connected, and position it to one side

Chapter 4 Part C:
Fuel system - diesel models

Contents

Degrees of difficulty

Easy, suitable for novice with little experience 

Fairly easy, suitable for beginner with some experience 

Fairly difficult, suitable for competent DIY mechanic

Difficult, suitable for experienced DIY mechanic 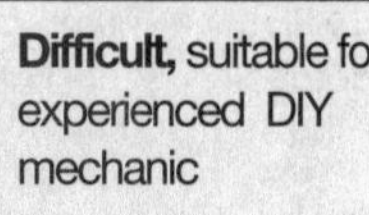

Very difficult, suitable for expert DIY or professional

Specifications

General

System type	Rear-mounted fuel tank, distributor fuel injection pump with integral transfer pump, indirect injection. Turbocharger on TDS, TD and TDSX models
Firing order	1-3-4-2 (No 1 at timing belt end of engine)

Injection pump (Bosch VE)

Direction of rotation	Clockwise, viewed from sprocket end
Static timing:	
Engine position	No 1 piston at TDC
Pump timing measurement	0.93 ± 0.05 mm
Maximum engine speed	5200 to 5300 rpm

Injection pump (Lucas/CAV FT08)

Direction of rotation	Clockwise, viewed from sprocket end
Static timing:	
Engine position	No 1 piston at TDC
Pump timing measurement	0° ± 1° TDC (**Note**: *Value shown on pump - see text*)
Maximum engine speed	5150 ± 50 rpm

Injectors

Type	Pintle
Opening pressure:	
Bosch	150 to 158 bar
Lucas:	
New	124 to 131 bar
After running in	116 to 123 bar

RPM sensor

Sensor-to-flywheel ring gear teeth gap	0.25 to 1.3 mm
Winding resistance	680 ± 100 ohms

Torque wrench settings

	Nm	lbf ft
Fuel injection pump rear bracket	29	21
Fuel injection pump	25	18
Fuel injectors	55	41
Fuel pipe union nuts	30	22
Inlet manifold	24	18
Lower oil filter mounting and injection pump mounting nut	71	52
Turbocharger to exhaust manifold	40	30
Upper oil filter mounting and injection pump mounting nut	98	72

1 General information and precautions

General information

The fuel system consists of a rear-mounted fuel tank, a fuel filter with integral water separator, a fuel injection pump, injectors and associated components. A turbocharger is fitted to TDS, TD and TDSX models.

Fuel is drawn from the fuel tank to the fuel injection pump by a vane-type transfer pump incorporated in the fuel injection pump. Before reaching the pump, the fuel passes through a fuel filter, where foreign matter and water are removed. Excess fuel lubricates the moving components of the pump, and is then returned to the tank. On turbo models with the Bosch fuel injection system, an electrically operated heater is incorporated in the fuel filter housing.

The fuel injection pump is driven at half-crankshaft speed by the timing belt. The high pressure required to inject the fuel into the compressed air in the swirl chambers is achieved by a cam plate acting on a single piston on the Bosch pump, or by two opposed pistons forced together by rollers running in a cam ring on the Lucas (CAV) pump. The fuel passes through a central rotor with a single outlet drilling which aligns with ports leading to the injector pipes.

Fuel metering is controlled by a centrifugal governor, which reacts to accelerator pedal position and engine speed. The governor is linked to a metering valve, which increases or decreases the amount of fuel delivered at each pumping stroke. On turbocharged models, a separate device also increases fuel delivery with increasing boost pressure.

Basic injection timing is determined when the pump is fitted. When the engine is running, it is varied automatically to suit the prevailing engine speed by a mechanism which turns the cam plate or ring.

The four fuel injectors produce a homogeneous spray of fuel into the swirl chambers located in the cylinder head. The injectors are calibrated to open and close at critical pressures to provide efficient and even combustion. Each injector needle is lubricated by fuel, which accumulates in the spring chamber and is channelled to the injection pump return hose by leak-off pipes.

Bosch or Lucas fuel system components may be fitted, depending on the model. Components from the latter manufacturer are marked either CAV, Roto-diesel or Con-diesel, depending on their date and place of manufacture. With the exception of the fuel filter assembly, replacement components must be of the same make as those originally fitted.

Cold starting is assisted by preheater or glow plugs fitted to each swirl chamber. On the Bosch injection pump, an automatic cold injection advance device operated through a thermal switch, advances the injection timing by increasing the fuel pressure. The device operates at coolant temperatures below 55° C **(see illustration)**.

A stop solenoid cuts the fuel supply to the injection pump rotor when the ignition is switched off.

Provided that the specified maintenance is carried out, the fuel injection equipment will give long and trouble-free service. The injection pump itself may well outlast the engine. The main potential cause of damage to the injection pump and injectors is dirt or water in the fuel.

Servicing of the injection pump and injectors is very limited for the home mechanic, and any dismantling or adjustment other than that described in this Chapter must be entrusted to a Fiat dealer or fuel injection specialist.

Precautions

Warning: It is necessary to take certain precautions when working on the fuel system components, particularly the fuel injectors. Before carrying out any operations on the fuel system, refer to the precautions given in Safety first! at the beginning of this manual, and to any additional warning notes at the start of the relevant Sections.

2 Air cleaner and inlet system - removal and refitting

Removal

1 Remove the air cleaner element as described in Chapter 1B **(see illustration)**.

1.9 Cold injection advance device on the injection pump

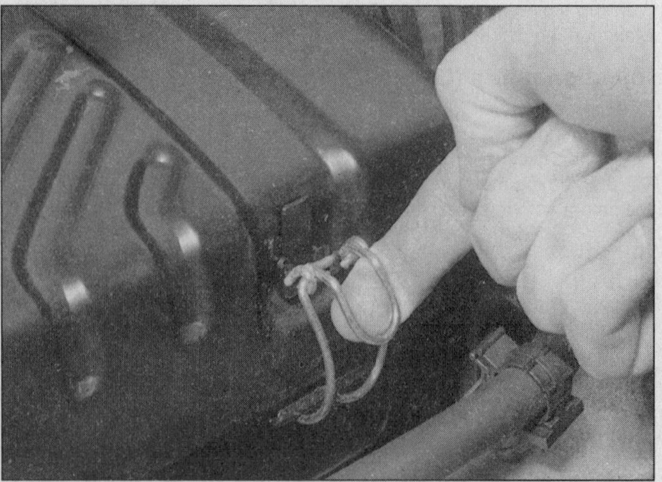

2.1 Releasing the air cleaner cover clips

2.7a Unscrew the bolt . . .

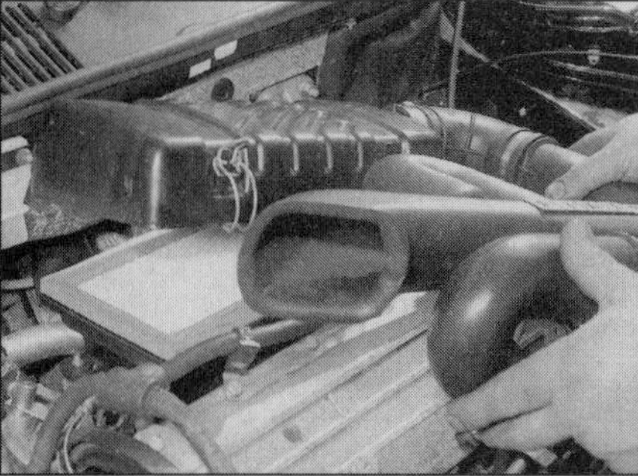

2.7b . . . and remove the inlet air duct assembly

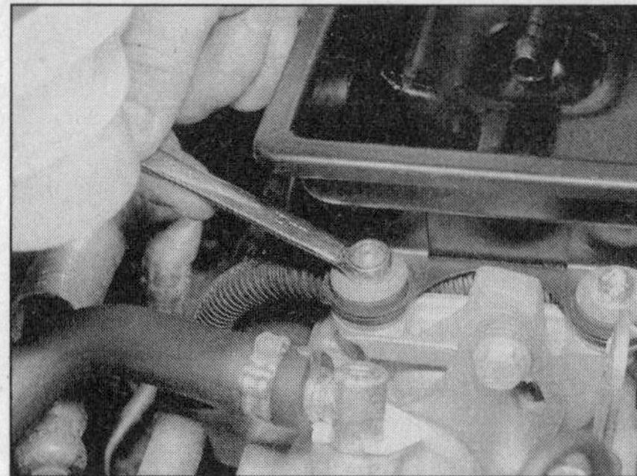

2.9a Unscrew the mounting nuts . . .

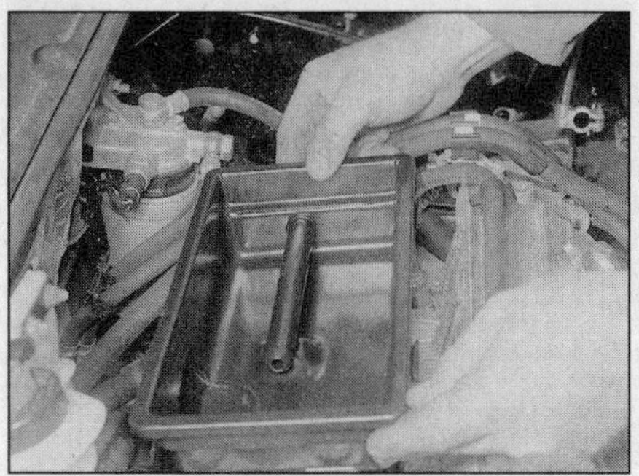

2.9b . . . remove the air cleaner body . . .

2.9c . . . and spacers

Non-turbo models

2 Disconnect the intermediate air duct from the air cleaner cover and the resonance box.

3 Disconnect the inlet duct from the resonance box and unbolt it from the front of the engine compartment.

4 Unscrew the mounting nuts and remove the resonance box. Note the location of the special spacers.

5 If necessary unbolt and remove the support brackets for the resonance box.

Turbo models

6 Disconnect the intermediate air duct from the air cleaner cover and front inlet air duct assembly.

7 Unbolt and remove the inlet air duct assembly **(see illustrations)**.

8 Disconnect the air ducts from between the air cleaner and turbocharger, and between the turbocharger and inlet manifold.

9 Unscrew the mounting nuts and remove the air cleaner body. Note the location of the special spacers **(see illustrations)**.

Refitting

10 Refitting is a reversal of the removal procedure.

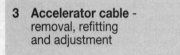

3 Accelerator cable - removal, refitting and adjustment

Removal

1 Remove the air inlet ducting as described in Section 2.

2 Working in the engine compartment, remove the cylindrical spring clip, and release the inner cable from the lever **(see illustration)**.

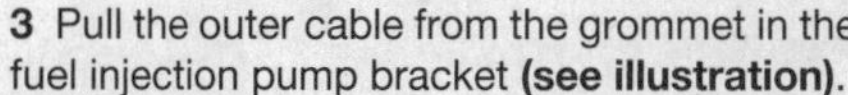

3 Pull the outer cable from the grommet in the fuel injection pump bracket **(see illustration)**.

4 Release the cable from the remaining clips and brackets in the engine compartment, noting its routing.

5 Working under the instrument panel inside the vehicle, unhook the cable from the fork at the top of the pedal arm.

6 Release the bulkhead grommet and withdraw the accelerator cable from inside the engine compartment.

Refitting

7 Refitting is a reversal of removal, but ensure that the cable is routed as noted before removal, and on completion, adjust the cable as follows.

Adjustment

8 Remove the spring clip from the accelerator outer cable **(see illustration)**. Ensuring that the control lever is against its stop, gently pull the cable out of its grommet until all free play is removed from the inner cable.

9 With the cable held in this position, refit the spring clip to the last exposed outer cable groove in front of the rubber grommet and washer. When the clip is refitted and the outer cable is released, there should be only a small amount of free play in the inner cable.

10 Have an assistant depress the accelerator pedal, and check that the control lever opens fully and returns smoothly to its stop.

4C

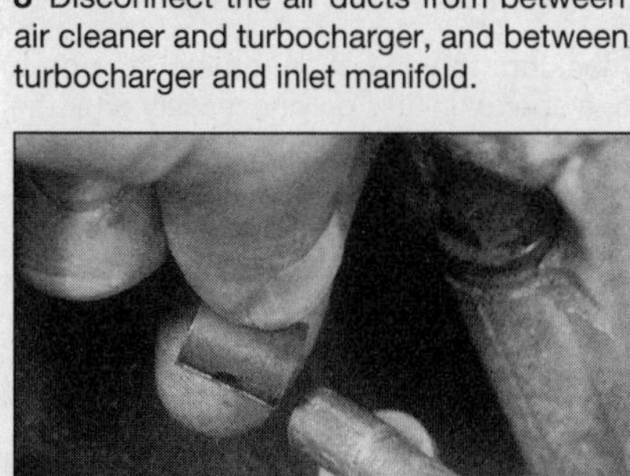

3.2 Remove the spring clip and release the inner cable

3.3 Removing the outer cable

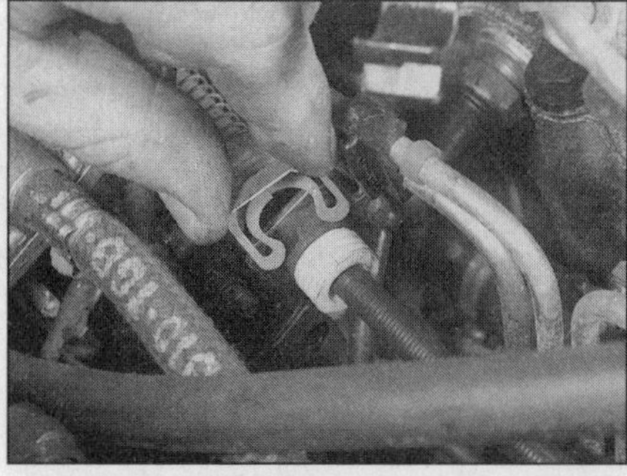

3.8 Removing the spring clip from the accelerator outer cable

5.9 Unscrewing the rear support bracket bolt (Bosch)

5.10a Injection pump lower mounting bolt removal (Bosch)

5.10b Removing the special injection pump mounting bracket (Bosch)

4 Fuel system - priming and bleeding

The injection pump is self-priming and no special procedures are necessary to prime the fuel system. However where the fuel system has been completely drained it is helpful to loosen the injector union nuts while turning the engine on the starter motor in order to purge trapped air.

5 Fuel injection pump - removal and refitting

Removal

1 Disconnect the battery negative terminal (refer to *Disconnecting the battery* in the Reference Section of this manual).
2 Remove the timing belt and injection pump sprocket as described in Chapter 2C.
3 Disconnect the accelerator cable from the fuel injection pump, with reference to Section 3.
4 Loosen the clip, or undo the banjo union, and disconnect the fuel supply hose. Recover the sealing washers from the banjo union, where applicable. Cover the open end of the hose, and refit and cover the banjo bolt to keep dirt out.
5 Disconnect the main fuel return pipe and the injector leak-off return pipe banjo union. Recover the sealing washers from the banjo union. Again, cover the open end of the hose and the banjo bolt to keep dirt out.
6 Disconnect all relevant wiring from the pump.
7 Unscrew the union nuts securing the injector pipes to the fuel injection pump and injectors. Counterhold the unions on the pump, while unscrewing the pipe-to-pump union nuts. Remove the pipes as a set. Cover open unions to keep dirt out, using small plastic bags, or fingers cut from discarded (but clean!) rubber gloves.
8 Mark the fuel injection pump in relation to the mounting bracket, using a scriber or felt tip pen. This will ensure the correct pump timing is retained when refitting.
9 Unscrew the bolt(s) from the rear support bracket **(see illustration)**.
10 Unscrew the mounting nuts/bolt, remove the special bracket, then remove the injection pump from the mounting bracket/housing **(see illustrations)**.

Refitting

11 Locate the injection pump in the mounting bracket and align the marks made on the pump and bracket before removal. If a new pump is being fitted, transfer the mark from the old pump to give an approximate setting. Locate the special bracket and fit the nuts/bolt loosely.
12 Refit the rear support bracket and fit the bolts loosely.
13 Set up the injection timing, as described in Sections 7 and 8 (as applicable).
14 Refit and reconnect the injector fuel pipes.
15 Reconnect all relevant wiring to the pump.
16 Reconnect the fuel supply and return hoses, and tighten the unions, as applicable. Use new sealing washers on the banjo unions.
17 Reconnect and adjust the accelerator cable with reference to Section 3.
18 Refit the injection pump sprocket and timing belt as described in Chapter 2C.
19 Reconnect the battery negative terminal.
20 Start the engine, and check for any leakage at the fuel unions. To enable the engine to start it may be necessary to loosen the injector union nuts while turning the engine on the starter motor in order to purge trapped air.
21 Check and if necessary adjust the idle speed as described in Chapter 1B.

5.10c Removing the injection pump (Bosch)

6 Injection timing - checking methods

1 Checking the injection timing is not a routine operation. It is only necessary after the injection pump has been disturbed.
2 Dynamic timing equipment does exist, but it is unlikely to be available to the home mechanic. The equipment works by converting pressure pulses in an injector pipe into electrical signals. If such equipment is available, use it in accordance with its maker's instructions using the timing mark on the flywheel **(see illustrations)**.
3 Static timing as described in this Chapter gives good results if carried out carefully. A dial test indicator will be needed, with probes and adapters appropriate to the type of injection pump. Read through the procedures before starting work, to find out what is involved.

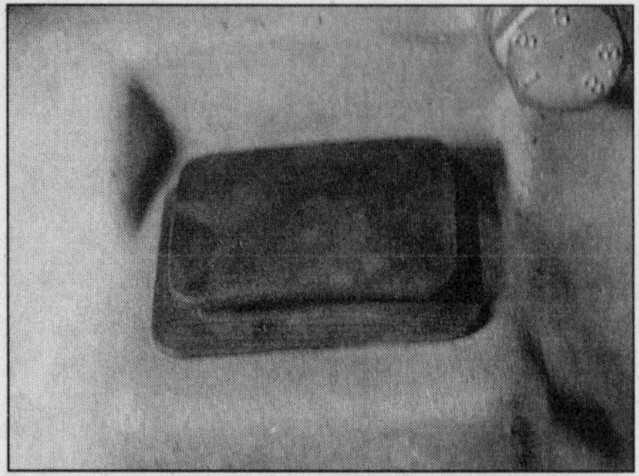

6.2a Remove the rubber bung . . .

6.2b . . . when checking the injection pump timing dynamically. Timing marks shown on flywheel and transmission casing

7 Injection timing (Bosch fuel injection pump) - checking and adjustment

Caution: Some of the injection pump settings and access plugs may be sealed by the manufacturers at the factory, using paint or locking wire and lead seals. Do not disturb the seals if the vehicle is still within the warranty period, otherwise the warranty will be invalidated. Also do not attempt the timing procedure unless accurate instrumentation is available.

Note: *To check the injection pump timing a special timing probe and mounting bracket is required. Without access to this piece of equipment, injection pump timing should be entrusted to a Fiat dealer or other suitably equipped specialist.*

1 If the injection timing is being checked with the pump in position on the engine, rather than as part of the pump refitting procedure, disconnect the battery negative terminal (refer to *Disconnecting the battery* in the Reference Section of this manual), and remove the air inlet ducting from the front of the engine.

2 Unscrew the union nuts and disconnect the injector pipes from the injection pump and injectors. Counterhold the unions on the pump, while unscrewing the pipe-to-pump union nuts. Remove the pipes as a set. Cover open unions to keep dirt out, using small plastic bags, or fingers cut from discarded (but clean!) rubber gloves.

3 Referring to Chapter 2C, set the engine at TDC on cylinder No 1.

4 Unscrew the access screw, situated in the centre of the four injector pipe unions, from the rear of the injection pump **(see illustration)**. As the screw is removed, position a suitable container beneath the pump to catch any escaping fuel. Mop up any spilt fuel with a clean cloth.

5 Screw the adapter into the rear of the pump and mount the dial gauge in the adapter **(see illustration)**. If access to the special Fiat adapter cannot be gained, they can be purchased from most good motor factors. Position the dial gauge so that its plunger is at the mid-point of its travel and securely tighten the adapter locknut.

6 Slowly rotate the crankshaft first back then forwards whilst observing the dial gauge, to determine when the injection pump piston is at the bottom of its travel (BDC). When the piston is correctly positioned, zero the dial gauge.

7 Rotate the crankshaft slowly in the correct direction until the TDC timing marks are aligned on both the crankshaft, camshaft and injection pump sprockets.

8 The reading obtained on the dial gauge should be equal to the specified pump timing measurement given in the Specifications at the start of this Chapter. If adjustment is necessary, slacken the front and rear pump mounting nuts/bolts and slowly rotate the pump body until the point is found where the specified reading is obtained. When the pump is correctly positioned, tighten both its front and rear mounting nuts and bolts securely.

7.4 Unscrew the access screw from the rear of the injection pump (Bosch)

7.5 Dial gauge and adapter (Bosch)

9 Rotate the crankshaft through one and three quarter rotations in the normal direction of rotation. Find the injection pump piston BDC as described in paragraph 6 and zero the dial gauge.

10 Rotate the crankshaft slowly in the correct direction of rotation until the TDC marks are aligned. Recheck the timing measurement.

11 If adjustment is necessary, slacken the pump mounting nuts and bolts and repeat the operations in paragraphs 8 to 10.

12 When the pump timing is correctly set, unscrew the adapter and remove the dial gauge.

13 Refit the screw and sealing washer to the pump and tighten it securely.

14 If the procedure is being carried out as part of the pump refitting sequence, proceed as described in Section 5.

15 If the procedure is being carried out with the pump fitted to the engine, refit the injector pipes tightening their union nuts to the specified torque setting. Reconnect the battery and refit the air inlet ducting.

16 Start the engine, and check for any leakage at the fuel unions. To enable the engine to start it may be necessary to loosen the injector union nuts while turning the engine on the starter motor in order to purge trapped air.

17 Check and if necessary adjust the idle speed as described in Chapter 1B.

8.4 Removing the injection pump timing inspection plug (Lucas)

8 Injection timing (Lucas fuel injection pump) - checking and adjustment

Caution: Some of the injection pump settings and access plugs may be sealed by the manufacturers at the factory, using paint or locking wire and lead seals. Do not disturb the seals if the vehicle is still within the warranty period, otherwise the warranty will be invalidated. Also do not attempt the timing procedure unless accurate instrumentation is available.

Note: *To check the injection pump timing a special timing probe and mounting bracket is required. Without access to this piece of equipment, injection pump timing should be entrusted to a Fiat dealer or other suitably equipped specialist.*

1 If the injection timing is being checked with the pump in position on the engine, rather than as part of the pump refitting procedure, disconnect the battery negative terminal (refer to *Disconnecting the battery* in the Reference Section of this manual), and remove the air inlet ducting from the front of the engine.

2 Unscrew the union nuts and disconnect the injector pipes from the injection pump and injectors. Counterhold the unions on the pump, while unscrewing the pipe-to-pump union nuts. Remove the pipes as a set. Cover open unions to keep dirt out, using small plastic bags, or fingers cut from discarded (but clean!) rubber gloves.

3 Referring to Chapter 2C, set the engine at TDC on cylinder No 1, then turn the crankshaft backwards (anti-clockwise) approximately a quarter of a turn.

4 Unscrew the access plug from the guide on the top of the pump body and recover the sealing washer **(see illustration)**. Insert the special timing probe into the guide, making sure it is correctly seated against the guide sealing washer surface. **Note:** *The timing probe must be seated against the guide sealing washer surface and not the upper lip of the guide for the measurement to be accurate.*

5 Mount the bracket on the pump guide (using adapter tool) and securely mount the dial gauge (dial test indicator) in the bracket

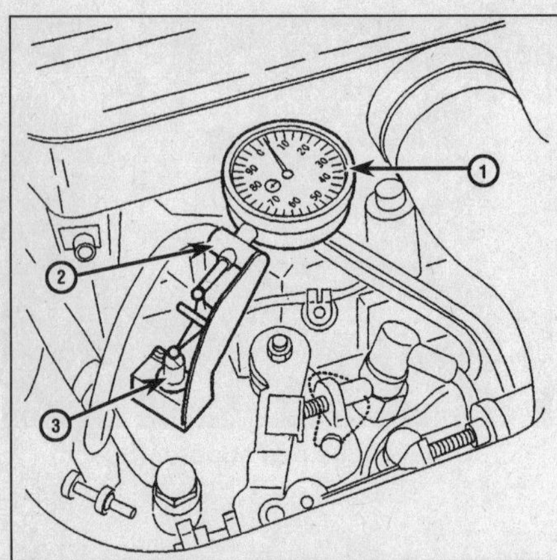

8.5 Dial gauge (1), mounting bracket (2) and setting rod (3) in position on the injection pump (Lucas)

so that its tip is in contact with the bracket linkage **(see illustration)**. Position the dial gauge so that its plunger is at the mid-point of its travel and zero the gauge.

6 Rotate the crankshaft slowly in the correct direction of rotation (clockwise) until the crankshaft is positioned at TDC on No 1 piston with all the sprocket timing marks aligned.

7 Check the reading on the dial gauge which should correspond to the value marked on the pump (there is a tolerance of ± 0.04 mm). The timing value may be marked on a plastic disc attached to the front of the pump, or alternatively on a tag attached to the pump control lever **(see illustrations)**.

8 If adjustment is necessary, slacken the front pump mounting nuts/bolt and the rear mounting bolt, then slowly rotate the pump body until the point is found where the specified reading is obtained on the dial gauge (access to the lower front bolt is gained through the hole in the injection pump sprocket). When the pump is correctly positioned, tighten both its front mounting nuts/bolt and the rear bolt to their specified torque settings.

9 Withdraw the timing probe slightly, so that it is positioned clear of the pump rotor dowel. Rotate the crankshaft through one and three quarter rotations in the normal direction of rotation.

10 Slide the timing probe back into position ensuring that it is correctly seated against the guide sealing washer surface, not the upper lip, then zero the dial gauge.

11 Rotate the crankshaft slowly in the correct direction of rotation to the TDC position and recheck the timing measurement.

12 If adjustment is necessary, slacken the pump mounting nuts and bolt and repeat the operations in paragraphs 8 to 11.

13 When the pump timing is correctly set, remove the dial gauge and mounting bracket and withdraw the timing probe.

14 Refit the screw and sealing washer to the guide and tighten it securely.

8.7a Pump timing value (x) marked on plastic disc (Lucas)

15 If the procedure is being carried out as part of the pump refitting sequence, proceed as described in Section 5.

16 If the procedure is being carried out with the pump fitted to the engine, refit the injector pipes tightening their union nuts to the specified torque setting. Reconnect the battery and refit the air inlet ducting.

17 Start the engine, and check for any leakage at the fuel unions. To enable the engine to start it may be necessary to loosen the injector union nuts while turning the engine on the starter motor in order to purge trapped air.

18 Check and if necessary adjust the idle speed as described in Chapter 1B.

9 Fuel injectors - testing, removal and refitting

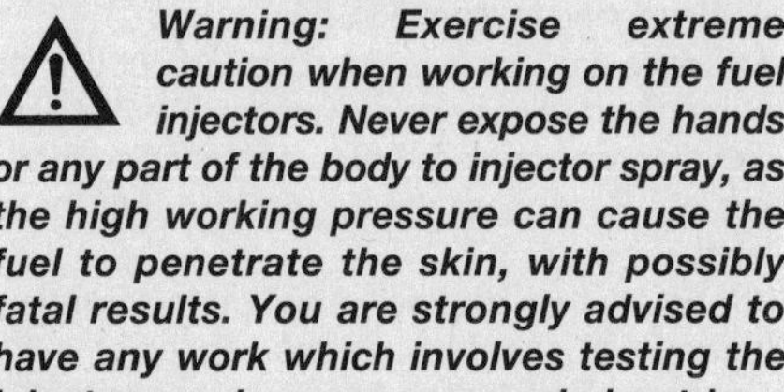

Warning: Exercise extreme caution when working on the fuel injectors. Never expose the hands or any part of the body to injector spray, as the high working pressure can cause the fuel to penetrate the skin, with possibly fatal results. You are strongly advised to have any work which involves testing the injectors under pressure carried out by a dealer or fuel injection specialist.

Testing

1 Injectors do deteriorate with prolonged use, and it is reasonable to expect them to need reconditioning or renewal after 60 000 miles (100 000 km) or so. Accurate testing, overhaul and calibration of the injectors must be left to a specialist. A defective injector which is causing knocking or smoking can be located without dismantling as follows.

8.7b Pump timing values marked on label (1) and tag (2) (Lucas)

2 Run the engine at a fast idle. Slacken each injector union in turn, placing rag around the union to catch spilt fuel, and being careful not to expose the skin to any spray. When the union on the defective injector is slackened, the knocking or smoking will stop.

Removal

3 Remove the air inlet ducting from the front part of the engine.

4 Carefully clean around the injectors and injector pipe union nuts.

5 Pull the leak-off pipes from the injectors **(see illustration)**.

6 Unscrew the union nuts securing the injector pipes to the fuel injection pump. Counterhold the unions on the pump when unscrewing the nuts. Cover open unions to keep dirt out, using small plastic bags, or fingers cut from discarded (but clean!) rubber gloves.

7 Unscrew the union nuts and disconnect the pipes from the injectors. If necessary, the injector pipes may be completely removed. Note carefully the locations of the pipe clamps, for use when refitting. Cover the ends of the injectors, to prevent dirt ingress.

8 Unscrew the injectors using a deep socket or box spanner, and remove them from the cylinder head **(see illustration)**.

9 Recover the fire seal washers from the cylinder head and discard them **(see illustration)**.

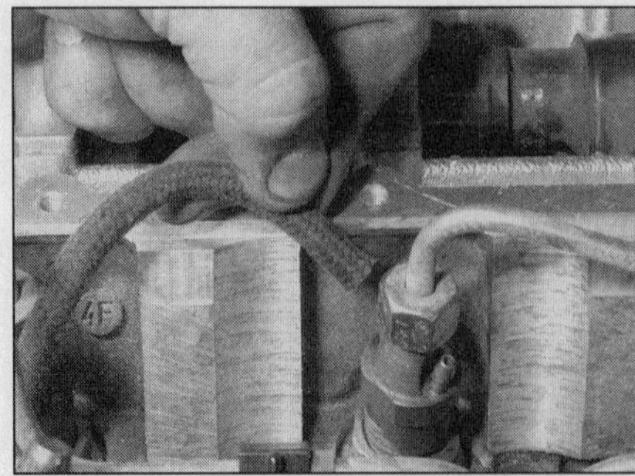

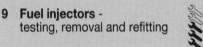

9.5 Disconnecting the injector leak-off pipes

9.8 Removing an injector

9.9 Removing the fire seal washer

9.13 Tightening an injector with a torque wrench

Refitting

10 Obtain new fire seal washers.

11 Take care not to drop the injectors, or allow the needles at their tips to become damaged. The injectors are precision-made to fine limits, and must not be handled roughly. In particular, never mount them in a bench vice.

12 Commence refitting by inserting the fire seal washers (convex face uppermost).

13 Insert the injectors and tighten them to the specified torque **(see illustration)**.

14 Refit the injector pipes and tighten the union nuts. Make sure the pipe clamps are in their previously-noted positions. If the clamps are wrongly positioned or missing, problems may be experienced with pipes breaking or splitting.

15 Reconnect the leak-off pipes.

16 Refit the air ducting.

17 Start the engine, and check for any leakage at the fuel unions. To enable the engine to start it may be necessary to loosen the injector union nuts while turning the engine on the starter motor in order to purge trapped air.

10 Fuel gauge sender unit - removal and refitting

Refer to Chapter 4A, however note that the unit does not incorporate a pump **(see illustrations)**.

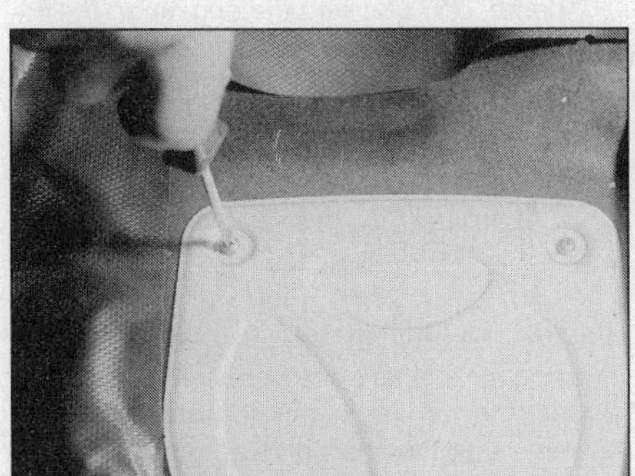
10.1a Remove the cover . . .

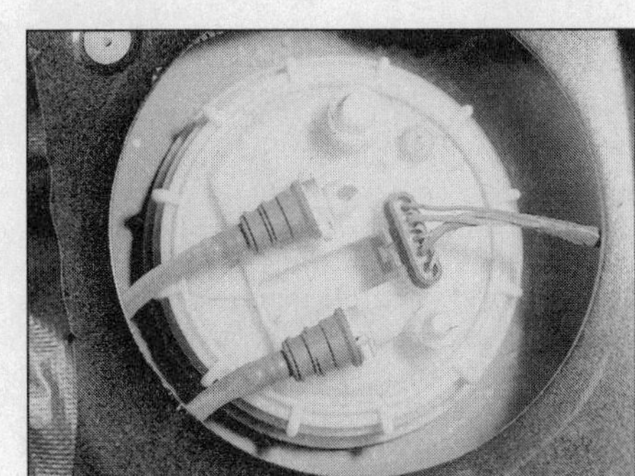
10.1b . . . for access to the fuel gauge sender unit

11 Fuel tank - removal and refitting

Refer to Chapter 4A, however note that in addition a safety valve with an anti-roll device is fitted in the top of the tank with a ventilation pipe to the front of the tank. The fuel gauge sender unit does not incorporate a pump as this unit is located in the injection pump.

12 Inlet manifold - removal and refitting

Note: *The inlet and exhaust manifolds are both located on the rear of the engine and share the same securing bolts and gasket. Although the following procedure describes removal of the inlet manifold separately it may be necessary to remove the exhaust manifold as well in order to renew the gasket.*

Removal

1 Remove the air cleaner and ducting as described in Section 2.

2 Unbolt and remove the relay guard and bracket from the left-hand side of the engine.

3 On turbo models disconnect the air duct from the inlet manifold elbow. If necessary the elbow can be unbolted from the manifold and the sealing ring removed.

4 Unscrew the nuts securing the inlet manifold to the cylinder head noting the position of the support bracket. Note that some of the nuts also secure the exhaust manifold. Withdraw the inlet manifold from the studs **(see illustrations)**.

5 Examine the gasket. If it is damaged it will be necessary to remove the exhaust manifold in order to renew it.

Refitting

6 Refitting is a reversal of removal, but tighten all nuts and bolts to the specified torque.

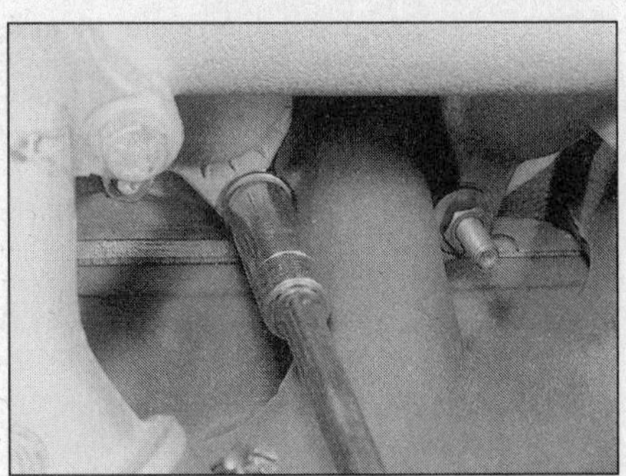
12.4a Unscrew the inlet manifold mounting nuts . . .

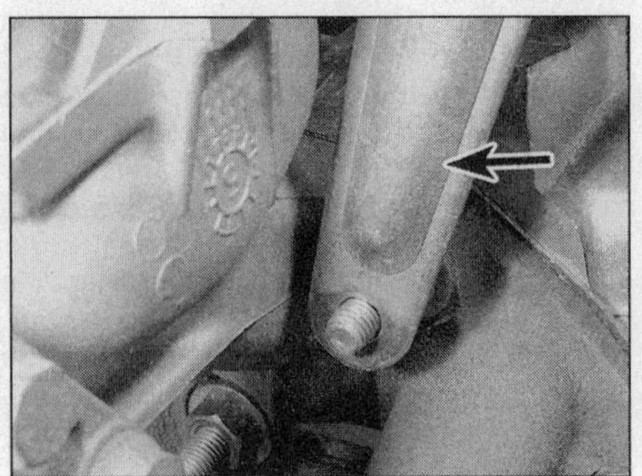
12.4b . . . noting the location of the support bracket

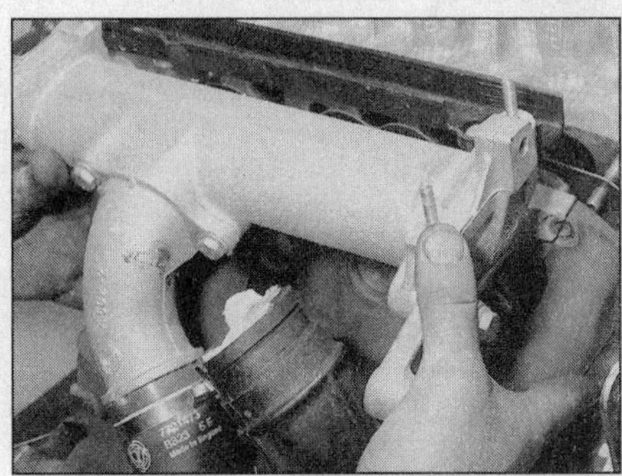
12.4c Removing the inlet manifold

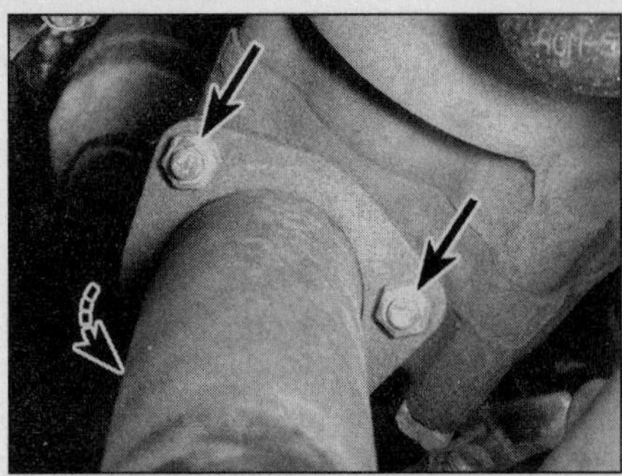

14.6 Nuts securing the exhaust downpipe to the exhaust manifold

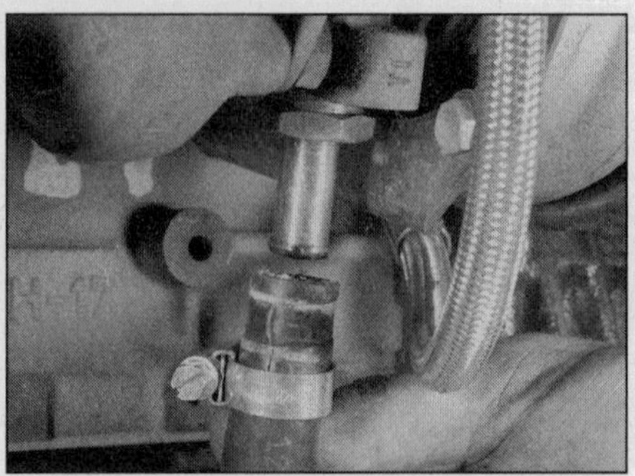

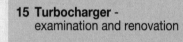

14.8 Disconnecting the oil return pipe from the turbocharger

13 Turbocharger - description and precautions

Description

A turbocharger is fitted to TDS, TD and SX models. It increases engine efficiency by raising the pressure in the inlet manifold above atmospheric pressure. Instead of the air simply being sucked into the cylinders, it is forced in. Additional fuel is supplied by the injection pump in proportion to the increased air inlet.

Energy for the operation of the turbocharger comes from the exhaust gas. The gas flows through a specially-shaped housing (the turbine housing) and in so doing, spins the turbine wheel. The turbine wheel is attached to a shaft, at the end of which is another vaned wheel known as the compressor wheel. The compressor wheel spins in its own housing, and compresses the inlet air on the way to the inlet manifold.

Boost pressure (the pressure in the inlet manifold) is limited by a wastegate, which diverts the exhaust gas away from the turbine wheel in response to a pressure-sensitive actuator. A pressure-operated switch operates a warning light on the instrument panel in the event of excessive boost pressure developing.

The turbo shaft is pressure-lubricated by an oil feed pipe from the main oil gallery. The shaft floats on a cushion of oil. A drain pipe returns the oil to the sump.

Precautions

The turbocharger operates at extremely high speeds and temperatures. Certain precautions must be observed, to avoid premature failure of the turbo, or injury to the operator.

Do not operate the turbo with any of its parts exposed, or with any of its hoses removed. Foreign objects falling onto the rotating vanes could cause excessive damage, and (if ejected) personal injury.

Do not race the engine immediately after start-up, especially if it is cold. Give the oil a few seconds to circulate.

Always allow the engine to return to idle speed before switching it off - do not blip the throttle and switch off, as this will leave the turbo spinning without lubrication.

Allow the engine to idle for several minutes before switching off after a high-speed run.

Observe the recommended intervals for oil and filter changing, and use a reputable oil of the specified quality. Neglect of oil changing, or use of inferior oil, can cause carbon formation on the turbo shaft, leading to subsequent failure.

14 Turbocharger - removal and refitting

Removal

1 Remove the battery as described in Chapter 5A.
2 Unbolt and remove the relay guard and bracket from the left-hand side of the engine.
3 Remove the air cleaner and ducting as described in Section 2.
4 Loosen the clips and remove the air outlet duct between the turbocharger and inlet manifold. Also disconnect the air inlet duct from the turbocharger.
5 Apply the handbrake, then jack up the front of the vehicle and support on axle stands (see *Jacking and vehicle support*).
6 Bend back the locking tabs (if fitted) and unscrew the nuts securing the exhaust downpipe to the exhaust manifold **(see illustration)**. Disconnect the downpipe from the exhaust system (refer to Part 4D) and remove it from under the vehicle. Recover the gasket.
7 Unscrew the union nut and disconnect the oil supply pipe from the turbocharger. Recover the copper ring and tape over the end of the pipe to prevent dust entry.
8 Disconnect the oil return pipe from the turbocharger **(see illustration)**.
9 Unscrew the bolt securing the mounting bracket to the cylinder block.
10 Unscrew the mounting nuts and withdraw the turbocharger from the studs in the exhaust manifold. Recover the gasket. If it is to be refitted, store the turbocharger carefully, and plug its openings to prevent dirt ingress.

Refitting

11 Refitting is a reversal of removal, bearing in mind the following points:

a) If a new turbocharger is being fitted, change the engine oil and filter.

b) Tighten all nuts and bolts to the specified torque.

c) Before starting the engine, prime the turbo lubrication circuit by disconnecting the stop solenoid lead at the injection pump, and cranking the engine on the starter for three ten-second bursts.

15 Turbocharger - examination and renovation

1 With the turbocharger removed, inspect the housing for cracks or other visible damage.
2 Spin the turbine or the compressor wheel, to verify that the shaft is intact and to feel for excessive shake or roughness. Some play is normal, since in use, the shaft is floating on a film of oil. Check that the wheel vanes are undamaged.
3 The wastegate and actuator are integral, and cannot be checked or renewed separately. Consult a Fiat dealer or other specialist if it is thought that testing or renewal is necessary.
4 If the exhaust or induction passages are oil-contaminated, the turbo shaft oil seals have probably failed.
5 No DIY repair of the turbo is possible. A new unit may be available on an exchange basis.

Chapter 4 Part D:
Exhaust and emission control systems

Contents

Degrees of difficulty

Easy, suitable for novice with little experience 	**Fairly easy,** suitable for beginner with some experience 	**Fairly difficult,** suitable for competent DIY mechanic 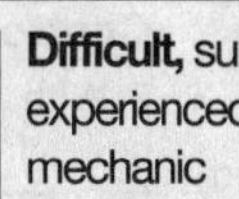	**Difficult,** suitable for experienced DIY mechanic	**Very difficult,** suitable for expert DIY or professional

Specifications

Torque wrench settings	**Nm**	**lbf ft**
Exhaust downpipe to manifold	24	18
Exhaust manifold	24	18
Exhaust system mounting	27	20
Exhaust to catalytic converter:		
M8	24	18
M10x1.25	40	30
Lambda oxygen sensor	53	39

1 General information

Emission control systems

All petrol engine models use unleaded petrol and are controlled by engine management systems that are 'tuned' to give the best compromise between driveability, fuel consumption and exhaust emission production. In addition, a number of systems are fitted that help to minimise other harmful emissions; a crankcase emission-control system (petrol models only) that reduces the release of pollutants from the crankcase, an evaporative loss emission control system (petrol models only) to reduce the release of hydrocarbons from the fuel tank, a catalytic converter (petrol and diesel models) to reduce exhaust gas pollutants, and an Exhaust Gas Recirculation (EGR) system (turbo diesel models only) to reduce exhaust emissions.

Crankcase emission control

To reduce the emission of unburned hydrocarbons from the crankcase into the atmosphere, the engine is sealed and the blow-by gases and oil vapour are drawn from inside the crankcase, through a flame trap, into the inlet tract to be burned by the engine during normal combustion.

Under conditions of high manifold depression (idling, deceleration) the gases will by sucked positively out of the crankcase. Under conditions of low manifold depression (acceleration, full-throttle running) the gases are forced out of the crankcase by the (relatively) higher crankcase pressure; if the engine is worn, the raised crankcase pressure (due to increased blow-by) will cause some of the flow to return under all manifold conditions.

Exhaust emission control - petrol models

To minimise the amount of pollutants which escape into the atmosphere, a catalytic converter is fitted in the exhaust system. The fuel system is of the closed-loop type, in which a Lambda (or oxygen) sensor in the exhaust system provides the engine management system ECU with constant feedback, enabling the ECU to adjust the air/fuel mixture to optimise combustion.

The Lambda sensor has a heating element built-in that is controlled by the ECU through the Lambda sensor relay to quickly bring the sensor's tip to its optimum operating temperature. The sensor's tip is sensitive to oxygen and relays a voltage signal to the ECU that varies according on the amount of oxygen in the exhaust gas. If the inlet air/fuel mixture is too rich, the exhaust gases are low in oxygen so the sensor sends a low-voltage signal, the voltage rising as the mixture weakens and the amount of oxygen rises in the exhaust gases. Peak conversion efficiency of all major pollutants occurs if the inlet air/fuel mixture is maintained at the chemically-correct ratio for the complete combustion of petrol of 14.7 parts (by weight) of air to 1 part of fuel (the stoichiometric ratio). The sensor output voltage alters in a large step at this point, the ECU using the signal change as a reference point and correcting the inlet air/fuel mixture accordingly by altering the fuel injector pulse width.

Exhaust emission control - diesel models

An oxidation catalyst is fitted in the exhaust system of all diesel engine models. This has the effect of removing a large proportion of the gaseous hydrocarbons, carbon monoxide and particulates present in the exhaust gas.

An Exhaust Gas Recirculation (EGR) system is fitted to all turbo diesel engine models. This reduces the level of nitrogen oxides produced during combustion by introducing a proportion of the exhaust gas back into the inlet manifold, under certain engine operating

2.2 Charcoal canister location behind the right-hand headlight

conditions, via a plunger valve. The system is controlled electronically by means of an emissions system control unit.

Evaporative emission control - petrol models

To minimise the escape of unburned hydrocarbons into the atmosphere, an evaporative loss emission control system is fitted to petrol models. The fuel tank filler cap is sealed and a charcoal canister is mounted underneath the right-hand headlamp to collect the petrol vapours released from the fuel contained in the fuel tank. It stores them until they can be drawn from the canister (under the control of the fuel injection/ignition system ECU) via the purge valve into the inlet tract, where they are then burned by the engine during normal combustion.

To ensure that the engine runs correctly when it is cold and/or idling and to protect the catalytic converter from the effects of an over-rich mixture, the purge control valve is not opened by the ECU until the engine has warmed up, and the engine is under load; the valve solenoid is then modulated on and off to allow the stored vapour to pass into the inlet tract.

Exhaust systems

The exhaust system comprises the exhaust manifold, an exhaust downpipe, a catalytic converter, an intermediate pipe with silencer, and a tailpipe with silencer. On turbo diesel models the turbocharger is fitted between the exhaust manifold and the downpipe.

2 Evaporative loss emission control system - information and component renewal

Information

1 The evaporative loss emission control system consists of the control solenoid (or purge valve), the activated charcoal filter canister and a series of connecting vacuum hoses.

2 The control solenoid and charcoal canister are both mounted on the right-hand side of the engine compartment behind the headlight **(see illustration)**.

Component renewal

Control solenoid

3 With the bonnet open, disconnect the hoses from the control solenoid on the top of the charcoal canister.

4 Disconnect the wiring and remove the solenoid.

5 Refitting is a reversal of removal.

Charcoal canister

6 Remove the control solenoid as described previously.

7 Disconnect the fuel tank hose from the canister.

8 Detach the mounting and remove the canister.

9 Refitting is a reversal of removal.

Multifunction valve

10 The multifunction valve is mounted on top of the fuel tank. Removal and refitting is similar to that described for the tank sender gauge/pump (refer to Chapter 4A or 4B).

3 Crankcase emission system - general information

The crankcase emission control system consists of a hose from the camshaft cover to the air cleaner with a branch to the throttle body. The main hose incorporates a flame trap and the inlet to the throttle body incorporates a calibrated hole.

The system requires no attention other than to check at regular intervals that the hoses are free of blockages and undamaged.

4 Lambda oxygen sensor - removal and refitting

Note: *The Lambda oxygen sensor is delicate and will not work if it is dropped or knocked, if its power supply is disrupted, or if any cleaning materials are used on it.*

Removal

1 The sensor is threaded into the exhaust front downpipe. Access if best gained from underneath the vehicle. Apply the handbrake then jack up the front of the vehicle and support on axle stands (see *Jacking and vehicle support*).

2 Disconnect the sensor wiring connector located on the front of the engine.

3 Working beneath the vehicle, unscrew the sensor, taking care to avoid damaging the sensor probe as it is removed. **Note:** *As a flying lead remains connected to the sensor after it has been disconnected, if the correct spanner is not available, a slotted socket will be required to remove the sensor.*

Refitting

4 Apply a little anti-seize grease to the sensor threads - avoid contaminating the probe tip.

5 Refit the sensor to the downpipe, tightening it to the correct torque. Reconnect the wiring.

6 Lower the vehicle to the ground.

5 Exhaust manifold - removal and refitting

Petrol models

Removal

1 On 1242 cc (16-valve) engines, remove the air cleaner and inlet system components as described in Chapter 4B.

2 Firmly apply the handbrake, then jack up the front of the car and support it securely on axle stands (see *Jacking and vehicle support*).

3 Disconnect the oxygen sensor wiring or alternatively remove the sensor completely.

4 Unscrew the nuts and disconnect the exhaust downpipe from the exhaust manifold flange. Recover the gasket.

5 On 1242 cc (16-valve) engines, undo the bolts and remove the manifold heat shield, then remove the bracket at the timing belt end of the manifold **(see illustrations)**.

6 Unscrew the mounting nuts, remove the washers, and recover any additional brackets fitted over the studs, noting their locations. Withdraw the manifold from the studs on the cylinder head.

7 Recover the gaskets from the studs.

5.5a On 16-valve engines, undo the bolts and remove the manifold heat shield . . .

5.5b . . . then remove the bracket

Refitting

8 Refitting is a reversal of the removal procedure but fit new gaskets. Tighten the nuts to the specified torque.

Diesel models

Note: *On diesel models the inlet and exhaust manifolds are located on the rear of the engine and share the same securing nuts and gasket.*

Removal

9 Remove the inlet manifold as described in Part C of this Chapter.

10 Firmly apply the handbrake, then jack up the front of the car and support it securely on axle stands (see *Jacking and vehicle support*).

11 Straighten the tab washers (where fitted), then unscrew and remove the exhaust downpipe retaining nuts. Detach the downpipe from the manifold/turbocharger. Suitably support the downpipe.

12 Undo the manifold-to-cylinder head securing nuts and withdraw the manifold **(see illustration)**.

13 Separate the turbocharger from the manifold with reference to Chapter 4C.

14 Remove the gasket and clean the mating faces of the manifold, cylinder head and downpipe flange **(see illustration)**. The gasket must be renewed when refitting the manifold.

Refitting

15 Refitting is a reversal of the removal procedure but fit a new gasket. Tighten the retaining nuts to the specified torque and where necessary lock them by bending over the locktabs.

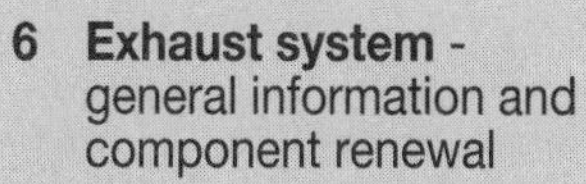

6 Exhaust system - general information and component renewal

General information

1 A three section exhaust system is fitted consisting of a twin-branch front downpipe, a catalytic converter, and a tailpipe with two silencers. The downpipe-to-manifold and downpipe-to-catalytic converter joints are both of flange and gasket type, whereas the remaining joint is of the sleeve type secured with a clamp ring **(see illustration)**.

2 The system is suspended throughout its entire length by rubber mountings.

Removal

3 Each exhaust section can be removed individually or, alternatively, the complete system can be removed as a unit. Where separation of the rear sleeve joint is necessary, it may be more practical to remove the entire system rather than try and separate the joint in position.

4 To remove the system or part of the system, first jack up the front of the vehicle and support on axle stands (*see Jacking and vehicle support*). Alternatively position the vehicle over an inspection pit or on car ramps.

5.12 Removing the exhaust manifold (diesel engine)

Downpipe

5 Support the catalytic converter using an axle stand or blocks of wood. Where applicable on petrol models, refer to Section 4 and remove the oxygen sensor from the exhaust downpipe.

6 Unscrew and remove the bolts securing the downpipe to the catalytic converter, then separate the joint and recover the gasket.

7 Bend back the locktabs (where fitted) then unscrew the nuts securing the downpipe to the exhaust manifold/turbocharger, and lower the downpipe. Recover the gasket.

Catalytic converter

8 Support the tailpipe section of the exhaust using an axle stand or blocks of wood.

9 Unscrew and remove the bolts securing the downpipe to the catalytic converter, then separate the joint and recover the gasket.

10 Unscrew the clamp bolt and separate the converter from the tailpipe section.

11 Release the mounting rubber and remove the converter from under the vehicle.

Tailpipe and silencers

12 Support the catalytic converter using an axle stand or blocks of wood.

13 Unscrew the clamp bolt and separate the catalytic converter from the tailpipe section.

14 Release the tailpipe section from its mounting rubbers and remove from under the vehicle.

Complete system

15 Disconnect the downpipe from the exhaust manifold as described in paragraph 7.

6.1 Exhaust clamp ring securing the tailpipe to the front exhaust system

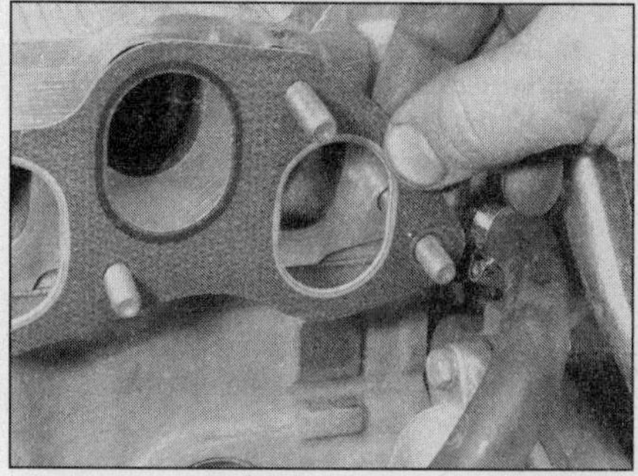

5.14 Removing the exhaust manifold gasket (diesel engine)

16 With the aid of an assistant, free the system from all its mounting rubbers and manoeuvre it out from underneath the vehicle.

Heatshield

17 The heatshield is secured to tne underbody by bolts and is easily removed once the exhaust system has been removed.

Refitting

18 Each section is refitted by a reverse of the removal sequence, noting the following points.

a) Ensure that all traces of corrosion have been removed from the flanges and renew all necessary gaskets.

b) Inspect the rubber mountings for signs of damage or deterioration and renew as necessary.

c) Before refitting the tailpipe joint, smear some exhaust system jointing paste to the joint mating surfaces to ensure an air-tight seal. Tighten the clamp bolt.

d) Prior to fully tightening the rear joint clamp, ensure that all rubber mountings are correctly located and that there is adequate clearance between the exhaust system and vehicle underbody.

7 Catalytic converter - general information and precautions

The catalytic converter is a reliable and simple device which needs no maintenance in itself, but there are some facts of which an owner should be aware if the converter is to function properly for its full service life.

Petrol models

a) DO NOT use leaded petrol in a car equipped with a catalytic converter - the lead will coat the precious metals, reducing their converting efficiency and will eventually destroy the converter.

b) Always keep the ignition and fuel systems well-maintained in accordance with the manufacturer's schedule.

c) If the engine develops a misfire, do not drive the car at all (or at least as little as possible) until the fault is cured.

d) *DO NOT push- or tow-start the car - this will soak the catalytic converter in unburned fuel, causing it to overheat when the engine does start.*

e) *DO NOT switch off the ignition at high engine speeds.*

f) *DO NOT use fuel or engine oil additives - these may contain substances harmful to the catalytic converter.*

g) *DO NOT continue to use the car if the engine burns oil to the extent of leaving a visible trail of blue smoke.*

h) *Remember that the catalytic converter operates at very high temperatures. DO NOT, therefore, park the car in dry undergrowth, over long grass or piles of dead leaves after a long run.*

i) *Remember that the catalytic converter is FRAGILE - do not strike it with tools during servicing work.*

j) *In some cases a sulphurous smell (like that of rotten eggs) may be noticed from the exhaust. This is common to many catalytic converter-equipped cars and once the car has covered a few thousand miles the problem should disappear.*

k) *The catalytic converter, used on a well-maintained and well-driven car, should last for between 50 000 and 100 000 miles - if the converter is no longer effective it must be renewed.*

Diesel models

Refer to the information given in parts f, g, h and i of the petrol models information given above.

Chapter 5 Part A:
Starting and charging systems

Contents

Degrees of difficulty

Easy, suitable for novice with little experience 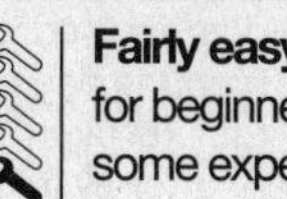

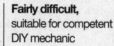

Fairly easy, suitable for beginner with some experience 

Fairly difficult, suitable for competent DIY mechanic

Difficult, suitable for experienced DIY mechanic

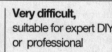

Very difficult, suitable for expert DIY or professional

Specifications

General

System type	12 volt, negative earth

Starter motor

Type:	
Petrol engines	Magneti-Marelli pre-engaged
Diesel engines	Bosch pre-engaged with reduction gear
Output:	
Petrol engines	0.8 kW (1108 cc) or 0.9 kW (1242 cc)
Diesel engines	1.7 kW

Battery

Capacity:	
Petrol engines	32 to 50 amp/hr
Diesel engines	60 amp/hr
Charge condition:	
Poor	12.5 volts
Normal	12.6 volts
Good	12.7 volts

Alternator

Type	Magneti-Marelli
Output	65 to 85 amp

Torque wrench settings	Nm	lbf ft
Alternator	60	44
Battery tray	29	21
Oil pressure switch:		
Petrol engine	32	24
Diesel engine	37	27

5A

1 General information and precautions

General information

The engine electrical system consists mainly of the charging and starting systems. Because of their engine-related functions, these components are covered separately from the body electrical devices such as the lights, instruments, etc (which are covered in Chapter 12). On petrol engine models refer to Part B for information on the ignition system, and on diesel models refer to Part C for information on the preheating system.

The electrical system is of 12-volt negative earth type.

The battery fitted as original equipment is of maintenance-free (sealed for life) type and is charged by the alternator, which is belt-driven from the crankshaft pulley. If a non-original battery is fitted it may be of standard or low maintenance type.

The starter motor is of the pre-engaged type incorporating an integral solenoid. On starting, the solenoid moves the drive pinion into engagement with the flywheel ring gear before the starter motor is energised. Once the engine has started, a one-way clutch prevents the motor armature being driven by the engine until the pinion disengages from the flywheel.

Precautions

Further details of the various systems are given in the relevant Sections of this Chapter. While some repair procedures are given, the usual course of action is to renew the component concerned. The owner whose interest extends beyond mere component renewal should obtain a copy of the *Automobile Electrical & Electronic Systems Manual*, available from the publishers of this manual.

It is necessary to take extra care when working on the electrical system to avoid damage to semi-conductor devices (diodes and transistors), and to avoid the risk of personal injury. In addition to the precautions given in *Safety first!* at the beginning of this manual, observe the following when working on the system:

Always remove rings, watches, etc before working on the electrical system. Even with the battery disconnected, capacitive discharge could occur if a component's live terminal is earthed through a metal object. This could cause a shock or nasty burn.

Do not reverse the battery connections. Components such as the alternator, electronic control units, or any other components having semi-conductor circuitry could be irreparably damaged.

If the engine is being started using jump leads and a slave battery, connect the batteries *positive-to-positive* and *negative-to-negative* (see *Jump starting*). This also applies when connecting a battery charger but in this case both of the battery terminals should first be disconnected.

Never disconnect the battery terminals, the alternator, any electrical wiring or any test instruments when the engine is running.

Do not allow the engine to turn the alternator when the alternator is not connected.

Never test for alternator output by flashing the output lead to earth.

Never use an ohmmeter of the type incorporating a hand-cranked generator for circuit or continuity testing.

Always ensure that the battery negative lead is disconnected when working on the electrical system.

Before using electric-arc welding equipment on the car, disconnect the battery, alternator and components such as the fuel injection/ignition electronic control unit to protect them from the risk of damage.

Several systems fitted to the vehicle require battery power to be available at all times, either to ensure their continued operation (such as the clock) or to maintain control unit memories or security codes which would be wiped if the battery were to be disconnected. To ensure that there are no unforeseen consequences of this action, Refer to *Disconnecting the battery* in the Reference Section of this manual for further information.

2 Battery - testing and charging

Standard and low maintenance battery - testing

1 If the vehicle covers a small annual mileage, it is worthwhile checking the specific gravity of the electrolyte every three months to determine the state of charge of the battery. Use a hydrometer to make the check and compare the results with the following table. Note that the specific gravity readings assume an electrolyte temperature of 15°C (60°F); for every 10°C (18°F) below 15°C (60°F) subtract 0.007. For every 10°C (18°F) above 15°C (60°F) add 0.007.

	Ambient temperature	
	Above 25°C	**Below 25°C**
Charged	*1.210 to 1.230*	*1.270 to 1.290*
70% charged	*1.170 to 1.190*	*1.230 to 1.250*
Discharged	*1.050 to 1.070*	*1.110 to 1.130*

2 If the battery condition is suspect, first check the specific gravity of electrolyte in each cell. A variation of 0.040 or more between any cells indicates loss of electrolyte or deterioration of the internal plates.

3 If the specific gravity variation is 0.040 or more, the battery should be renewed. If the cell variation is satisfactory but the battery is discharged, it should be charged as described later in this Section.

Maintenance-free battery - testing

4 In cases where a sealed for life maintenance-free battery is fitted, topping-up and testing of the electrolyte in each cell is not possible. The condition of the battery can therefore only be tested using a battery condition indicator or a voltmeter.

5 Certain models may be fitted with a maintenance-free battery with a built-in charge condition indicator. The indicator is located in the top of the battery casing, and indicates the condition of the battery from its colour. If the indicator shows green, then the battery is in a good state of charge. If the indicator turns darker, eventually to black, then the battery requires charging, as described later in this Section. If the indicator shows clear/yellow, then the electrolyte level in the battery is too low to allow further use, and the battery should be renewed. **Do not** attempt to charge, load or jump start a battery when the indicator shows clear/yellow.

6 If testing the battery using a voltmeter, connect the voltmeter across the battery and compare the result with those given in the *Specifications* under 'charge condition'. The test is only accurate if the battery has not been subjected to any kind of charge for the previous six hours. If this is not the case, switch on the headlights for 30 seconds, then wait four to five minutes before testing the battery after switching off the headlights. All other electrical circuits must be switched off, so check that the doors and tailgate are fully shut when making the test.

7 If the voltage reading is less than 12.2 volts, then the battery is discharged, whilst a reading of 12.2 to 12.4 volts indicates a partially discharged condition.

8 If the battery is to be charged, remove it from the vehicle (Section 3) and charge it as described later in this Section.

Standard and low maintenance battery - charging

Note: *The following is intended as a guide only. Always refer to the manufacturer's recommendations (often printed on a label attached to the battery) before charging a battery.*

9 Charge the battery at a rate of 3.5 to 4 amps and continue to charge the battery at this rate until no further rise in specific gravity is noted over a four hour period.

10 Alternatively, a trickle charger charging at the rate of 1.5 amps can safely be used overnight.

11 Specially rapid boost charges which are claimed to restore the power of the battery in 1 to 2 hours are not recommended, as they can cause serious damage to the battery plates through overheating.

12 While charging the battery, note that the temperature of the electrolyte should never exceed 37.8°C (100°F).

Maintenance-free battery - charging

Note: *The following is intended as a guide only. Always refer to the manufacturer's recommendations (often printed on a label attached to the battery) before charging a battery.*

13 This battery type takes considerably longer to fully recharge than the standard type, the time taken being dependent on the extent of discharge, but it can take anything up to three days.

14 A constant voltage type charger is required, to be set, when connected, to 13.9 to 14.9 volts with a charger current below 25 amps. Using this method, the battery should be usable within three hours, giving a voltage reading of 12.5 volts, but this is for a partially discharged battery and, as mentioned, full charging can take considerably longer.

15 If the battery is to be charged from a fully discharged state (condition reading less than 12.2 volts), have it recharged by your FIAT dealer or local automotive electrician, as the charge rate is higher and constant supervision during charging is necessary.

3 Battery - removal and refitting

Note: *Refer to Disconnecting the battery in the Reference Section of this manual before proceeding.*

Removal

1 Slacken the clamp bolts and disconnect the clamp from the battery negative (earth) terminal.

2 Remove the insulation cover (where fitted) and disconnect the positive terminal lead(s) in the same way.

3 At the base of the battery, unscrew the bolt from the battery holding clamp plate and remove the clamp plate **(see illustration)**.

4 Remove the battery from the engine compartment.

5 If necessary the mounting tray may be removed by unscrewing the bolts. On diesel models it will be necessary to remove the relay guard bolts as well.

Refitting

6 Refitting is a reversal of removal but make sure that the positive terminal is connected first followed by the negative terminal.

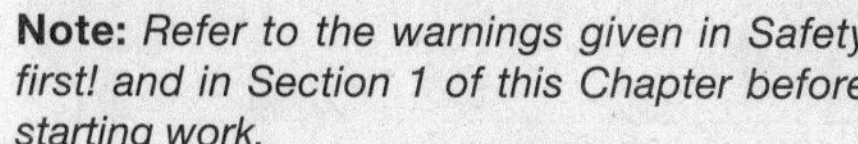

4 Alternator/charging system - testing in vehicle

Note: *Refer to the warnings given in Safety first! and in Section 1 of this Chapter before starting work.*

1 If the ignition warning light fails to illuminate when the ignition is switched on, first check the alternator wiring connections for security. If satisfactory, check that the warning light bulb has not blown, and that the bulbholder is secure in its location in the instrument panel. If the light still fails to illuminate, check the continuity of the warning light feed wire from the alternator to the bulbholder. If all is satisfactory, the alternator is at fault and should be renewed or taken to an auto-electrician for testing and repair.

2 If the ignition warning light illuminates when the engine is running, stop the engine and check that the drivebelt is correctly tensioned (see Chapter 1A or 1B) and that the alternator connections are secure. If all is so far satisfactory, have the alternator checked by an auto-electrician.

3 If the alternator output is suspect even though the warning light functions correctly, the regulated voltage may be checked as follows.

4 Connect a voltmeter across the battery terminals and start the engine.

5 Increase the engine speed until the voltmeter reading remains steady; the reading should be approximately 12 to 13 volts, and no more than 14 volts.

6 Switch on as many electrical accessories (eg, the headlights, heated rear window and heater blower) as possible, and check that the alternator maintains the regulated voltage at around 13 to 14 volts.

7 If the regulated voltage is not as stated, the fault may be due to worn brushes, weak brush springs, a faulty voltage regulator, a faulty diode, a severed phase winding or worn or damaged slip rings. The alternator should be renewed or taken to an auto-electrician for testing and repair.

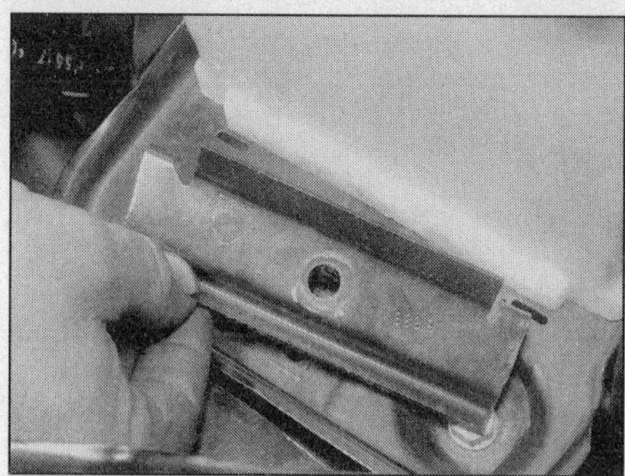

3.3 Removing the battery clamp plate

5 Alternator - removal and refitting

Removal

1 Disconnect the battery negative terminal (refer to *Disconnecting the battery* in the Reference Section of this manual).

2 Firmly apply the handbrake, then jack up the front of the car and support it securely on axle stands (see *Jacking and vehicle support*). Remove the right-hand front roadwheel.

3 Remove the inner cover from under the right-hand wheelarch for access to the right-hand side of the engine.

4 Disconnect the cables from the rear of the alternator **(see illustration)**.

Petrol models

5 Loosen the pivot and adjustment bolts then swivel the alternator towards the engine and slip off the drivebelt. Note that the position of the rpm sensor will prevent complete removal of the drivebelt from the crankshaft pulley.

6 Unscrew and remove the pivot and adjustment bolts then unscrew the upper slot-mounted bolt. Withdraw the alternator from the engine **(see illustrations)**.

Diesel models

7 For additional working room, unclip and remove the upper timing belt cover then unbolt and remove the lower timing belt cover.

5.4 Cable connections on the rear of the alternator

5.6a Alternator adjustment and pivot bolts (petrol engine)

B Adjuster bolt C Pivot bolt

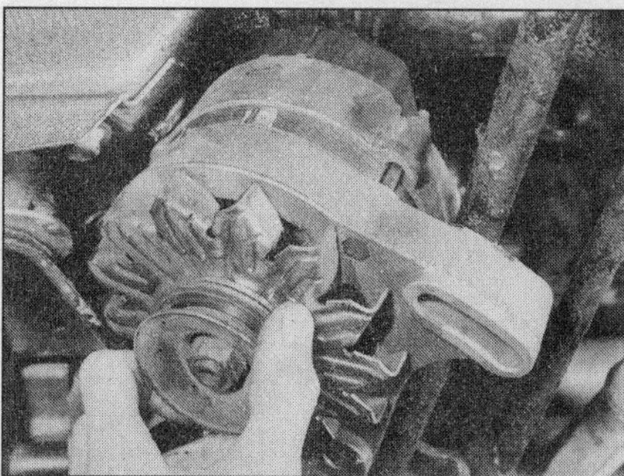

5.6b Removing the alternator (petrol engine)

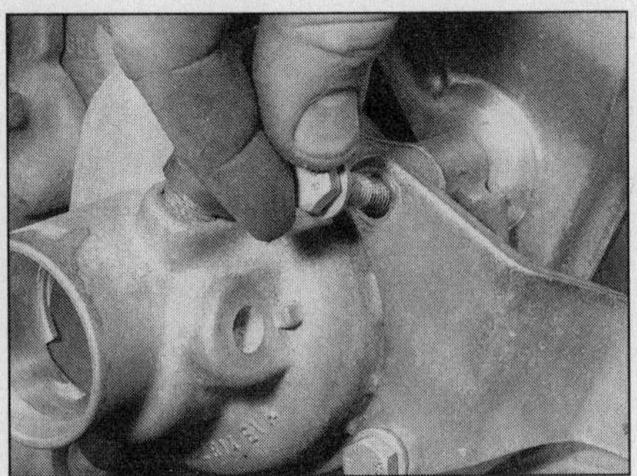

5.9a Unbolting the alternator upper bracket from the rear of the coolant pump

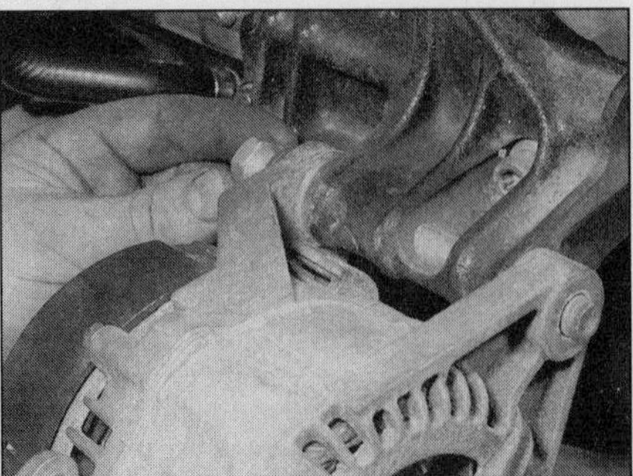

5.9b Removing the pivot bolt and alternator from the engine

8 Loosen the pivot bolt and adjustment locknut then unscrew the adjustment bolt and swivel the alternator towards the engine so that the drivebelt may be slipped off the alternator pulley.

9 Unscrew and remove the pivot and adjustment bolts and withdraw the alternator from the engine compartment. If preferred the upper alternator bracket may be unbolted from the rear of the coolant pump **(see illustrations)**.

Refitting

10 Refitting is a reversal of removal. Refer to Chapter 1A or 1B as applicable for details of tensioning the auxiliary drivebelt. On completion tighten the pivot and adjustment bolts/nut to the specified torque.

6 Alternator - brush holder/regulator module renewal

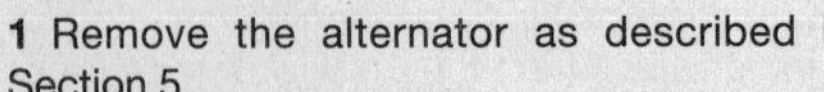

1 Remove the alternator as described in Section 5.

2 Extract the two small bolts and withdraw the brush box. Note the small plastic grille on the Marelli alternator **(see illustrations)**.

3 Using a steel rule check the length of the brushes. If less than 5.0 mm the complete brush holder assembly should be renewed. **Note:** *On Bosch alternators it may be possible to obtain the brushes separately, in which case the brush leads should be unsoldered from the terminals and the new brush leads soldered onto the terminals.*

4 Check the slip rings for excessive wear and clean them with a rag soaked in fuel.

5 Fit the new holder using a reversal of the removal procedure but make sure that each brush moves freely.

7 Starting system - testing

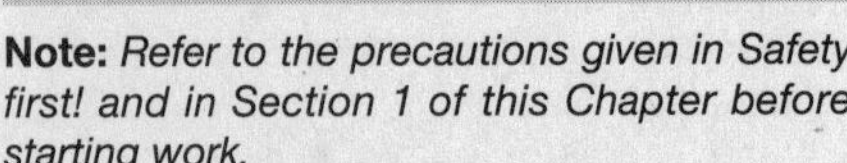

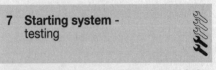

Note: *Refer to the precautions given in Safety first! and in Section 1 of this Chapter before starting work.*

1 If the starter motor fails to operate when the ignition key is turned to the appropriate position, the following possible causes may be to blame.

a) The battery is faulty.
b) The electrical connections between the switch, solenoid, battery and starter motor are somewhere failing to pass the necessary current from the battery through the starter to earth.
c) The solenoid is faulty.
d) The starter motor is mechanically or electrically defective.

2 To check the battery, switch on the headlights. If they dim after a few seconds, this indicates that the battery is discharged - recharge (see Section 2) or renew the battery. If the headlights glow brightly, operate the ignition switch and observe the lights. If they dim, then this indicates that current is reaching the starter motor, therefore the fault must lie in the starter motor. If the lights continue to glow brightly (and no clicking sound can be heard from the starter motor solenoid), this indicates that there is a fault in the circuit or solenoid - see following paragraphs. If the starter motor turns slowly when operated, but the battery is in good condition, then this indicates that either the starter motor is faulty, or there is considerable resistance somewhere in the circuit.

3 If a fault in the circuit is suspected, disconnect the battery leads (including the earth connection to the body), the starter/solenoid wiring and the engine/transmission earth strap. Thoroughly clean the connections, and reconnect the leads and wiring, then use a voltmeter or test lamp to check that full battery voltage is available at the battery positive lead connection to the solenoid, and that the earth is sound. Smear petroleum jelly around the battery terminals to prevent corrosion - corroded connections are amongst the most frequent causes of electrical system faults.

4 If the battery and all connections are in good condition, check the circuit by disconnecting the wire from the solenoid blade terminal. Connect a voltmeter or test lamp between the wire end and a good earth (such as the battery negative terminal), and check that the wire is live when the ignition switch is turned to the start position. If it is, then the circuit is sound - if not, the circuit wiring can be checked as described in Chapter 12, Section 2.

5 The solenoid contacts can be checked by connecting a voltmeter or test lamp across the solenoid. When the ignition switch is turned to the start position, there should be a reading or lighted bulb, as applicable. If there is no reading or lighted bulb, the solenoid is faulty and should be renewed.

6 If the circuit and solenoid are proved sound, the fault must lie in the starter motor. In this event, it may be possible to have the starter motor overhauled by a specialist, but check on the cost of spares before proceeding, as it may prove more economical to obtain a new or exchange motor.

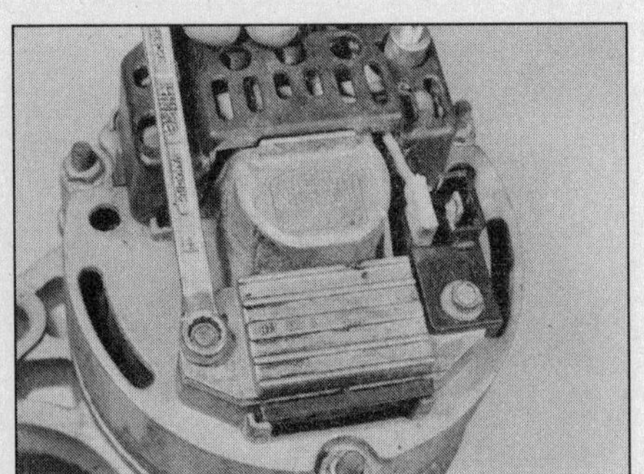

6.2a Remove the retaining bolts . . .

6.2b . . . noting the small plastic grille on the Marelli alternator . . .

6.2c . . . and withdraw the brush box

8.4a Starter motor wiring connections (petrol engine)

8.4b On diesel engines, raise the plastic cover . . .

8.4c . . . and disconnect the solenoid trigger wire

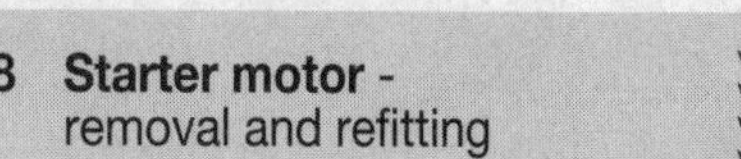

8 Starter motor - removal and refitting

Removal

1 Disconnect the battery negative terminal (refer to *Disconnecting the battery* in the Reference Section of this manual).

2 Apply the handbrake then jack up the front of the vehicle and support on axle stands (see *Jacking and Vehicle Support*).

3 On petrol engines, unscrew and remove the starter motor mounting bolt located at the top of the transmission bellhousing. Access is gained from behind the battery.

4 Working beneath the vehicle, raise the plastic cover then disconnect the wiring from the solenoid located on top of the starter motor **(see illustrations)**.

5 Unscrew the nut and disconnect the positive cable from the solenoid terminal **(see illustration)**.

6 Unscrew the mounting bolts (noting the location of the support bracket on petrol engines), then withdraw the starter motor from the transmission **(see illustrations)**.

Refitting

7 Refit the starter motor by following the removal procedure in reverse.

9 Starter motor - testing and overhaul

If the starter motor is thought to be suspect, it should be removed from the vehicle and taken to an auto-electrician for testing. Most auto-electricians will be able to supply and fit brushes at a reasonable cost. However, check on the cost of repairs before proceeding as it may prove more economical to obtain a new or exchange motor.

8.5 Disconnecting the battery cable from the starter motor

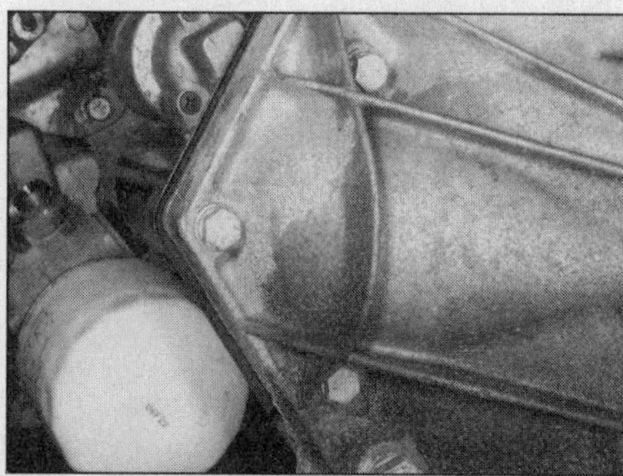

8.6a Starter motor mounting bolt locations (diesel engine)

8.6b Removing the starter motor (diesel engine)

Chapter 5 Part B:
Ignition system - petrol models

Contents

Degrees of difficulty

Easy, suitable for novice with little experience 	**Fairly easy,** suitable for beginner with some experience 	**Fairly difficult,** suitable for competent DIY mechanic	**Difficult,** suitable for experienced DIY mechanic 	**Very difficult,** suitable for expert DIY or professional

Specifications

General

System type . . . . Weber-Marelli static (distributorless), wasted spark ignition system controlled by engine management ECU
Firing order . . . . 1-3-4-2 (No 1 cylinder at timing belt end of engine)
Ignition timing at idle speed (non-adjustable, for reference only):
  8-valve engines:
    Single-point injection engine with manual transmission . . . . 10° ± 3° BTDC
    Single-point injection engine with automatic transmission . . . . 8° ± 3° BTDC
    Multi-point injection engine . . . . 13° ± 3° BTDC
  16-valve engines . . . . 8° ± 3° BTDC
Ignition coil winding resistance (at 20°C):
  Primary . . . . 0.495 to 0.605 ohms
  Secondary . . . . 6660 to 8140 ohms

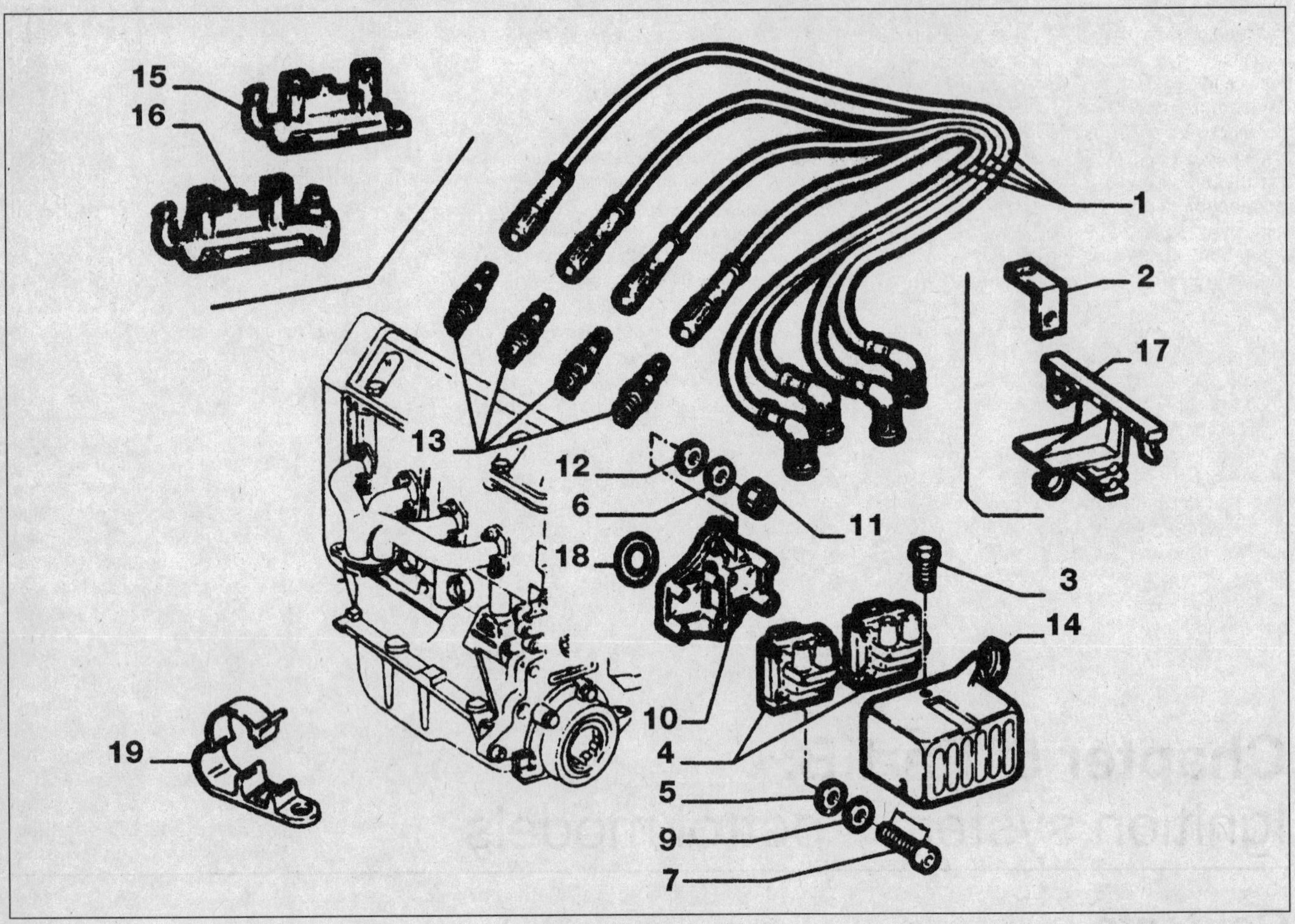

1.2a Ignition coils and HT leads

1 HT leads
2 Support
3 Cover mounting bolt
4 Ignition coils
5 Washer
6 Washer
7 Coil mounting bolt
9 Washer
10 Coil mounting bracket
11 Nut
12 Washer
13 Spark plugs
14 Coil cover
15 HT lead support
16 HT lead support
17 HT lead support
18 Seal
19 Bracket

1 General information

The ignition system is integrated with the fuel injection system to form a combined engine management system under the control of one ECU (see the relevant part of Chapter 4 for further information).

The ignition side of the system is of the static (distributorless) type, consisting only of two twin-output ignition coils located on the left-hand side of the cylinder head. Each ignition coil supplies two cylinders (one coil supplies cylinders 1 and 4, and the other cylinders 2 and 3) **(see illustrations)**. Under the control of the ECU, the ignition coils operate on the wasted spark principle, ie. each spark plug sparks twice for every cycle of the engine, once on the compression stroke and once on the exhaust stroke. The spark voltage is greatest in the cylinder which is under compression, the other cylinder having a very weak spark which has no effect on the exhaust gases. The ECU uses its inputs from the various sensors to calculate the required ignition advance setting and coil charging time.

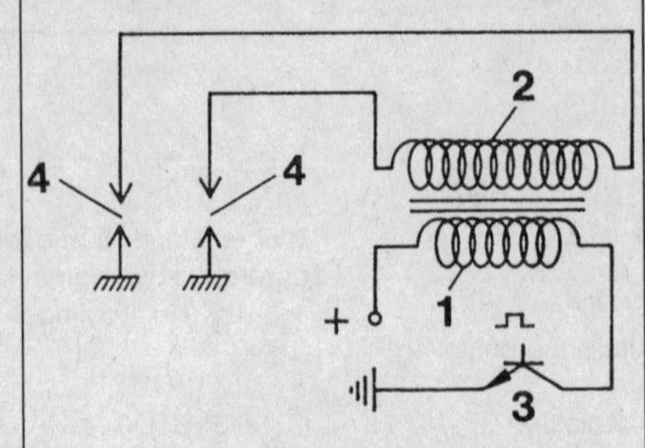

1.2b Ignition coil circuit

1 Primary windings
2 Secondary windings
3 Power module (inside ECU)
4 Spark plugs

2 Ignition system - testing

Warning: Voltages produced by an electronic ignition system are considerably higher than those produced by conventional ignition systems. Extreme care must be taken when working on the system with the ignition switched on. Persons with surgically-implanted cardiac pacemaker devices should keep well clear of the ignition circuits, components and test equipment.

1 If a fault appears in the engine management (fuel injection/ignition) system first ensure that the fault is not due to a poor electrical connection or poor maintenance; ie, check that the air cleaner filter element is clean, the spark plugs are in good condition and correctly gapped, that the engine breather hoses are clear and undamaged, referring to

Chapter 1A for further information. Also check that the accelerator cable is correctly adjusted as described in the relevant part of Chapter 4. If the engine is running very roughly, check the compression pressures and the valve clearances as described in the relevant parts of Chapters 1 and 2.

2 If these checks fail to reveal the cause of the problem, the vehicle should be taken to a suitably equipped Fiat dealer for testing. A wiring block connector is incorporated in the engine management circuit into which a special electronic diagnostic tester can be plugged. The tester will locate the fault quickly and simply alleviating the need to test all the system components individually which is a time consuming operation that carries a high risk of damaging the ECU.

3 The only ignition system checks which can be carried out by the home mechanic are those described in Chapter 1A, relating to the spark plugs, and the ignition coil test described in this Chapter. If necessary, the system wiring and wiring connectors can be checked as described in Chapter 12, Section 2, ensuring that the ECU wiring connector(s) have first been disconnected.

3 Ignition HT coil - removal, testing and refitting

Removal

1 On 8-valve engines, unscrew the bolt and remove the plastic cover from the left-hand end of the cylinder head **(see illustration)**. On 16-valve engines, remove the air cleaner, resonator and inlet air duct as described in Chapter 4B.

2 Identify the two HT leads for position then disconnect them from the coil HT terminals **(see illustration)**.

3 Disconnect the LT wiring plug.

4 Unscrew the mounting bolts and remove the relevant ignition coil from the end of the cylinder head.

Testing

5 Testing of the coil consists of using a multimeter set to its resistance function, to check the primary and secondary windings for continuity and resistance. Compare the results obtained to those given in the Specifications at the start of this Chapter. Note the resistance of the coil windings varies slightly according to the coil temperature; the results in the Specifications are approximate values for the coil at 20°C.

6 Check that there is no continuity between the HT lead terminals and the coil body/ mounting bracket.

7 Note that with the ignition switched on and the engine stationary, voltage will only be supplied to the ignition coils for approximately 2 seconds. However, when the engine is being cranked or running, voltage will be continually supplied.

8 If faulty, the coil should be renewed.

Refitting

9 Refitting is a reversal of the removal procedure ensuring that the wiring and HT leads are correctly reconnected **(see illustration)**.

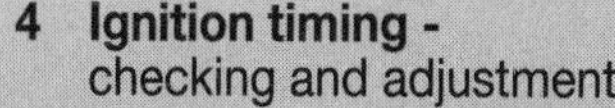

4 Ignition timing - checking and adjustment

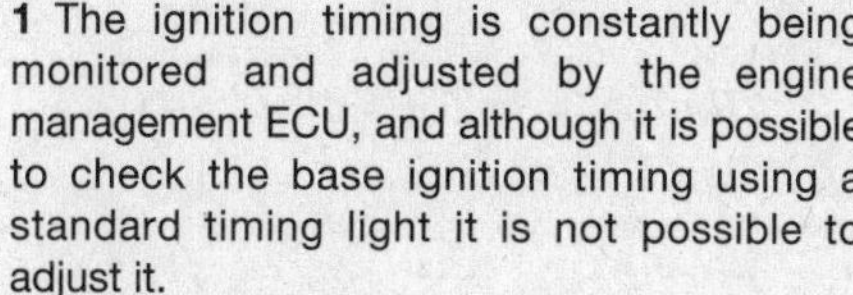

1 The ignition timing is constantly being monitored and adjusted by the engine management ECU, and although it is possible to check the base ignition timing using a standard timing light it is not possible to adjust it.

2 For those wishing to check the ignition timing a stroboscopic timing light will be required, and it will need to be the type which can determine the amount of advance from the TDC markings on the crankshaft pulley or flywheel. It is recommended that the timing mark is highlighted as follows.

3 Remove the plug from the top of the transmission then turn the engine slowly (raise the front right-hand wheel and engage 4th gear) until the timing mark scribed on the edge of the flywheel appears in the aperture. Highlight the line with quick-drying white paint - typist's correction fluid is ideal.

4 Start the engine and run it to normal operating temperature, then stop it.

5 Connect the timing light to No 1 cylinder spark plug lead (No 1 cylinder is at the timing belt end of the engine) as described in the timing light manufacturer's instructions.

6 Start the engine, allowing it to idle at the specified speed (Chapter 1A), and point the timing light at the transmission housing aperture. Adjust the timing light until the TDC marks are aligned with each other and read off the amount of advance.

7 If the ignition timing is incorrect, the car should be taken to a Fiat dealer who will be able to check the system quickly using special diagnostic equipment.

8 After making the check stop the engine, disconnect the timing light and refit the plug to the transmission.

3.1 Removing the ignition coil cover

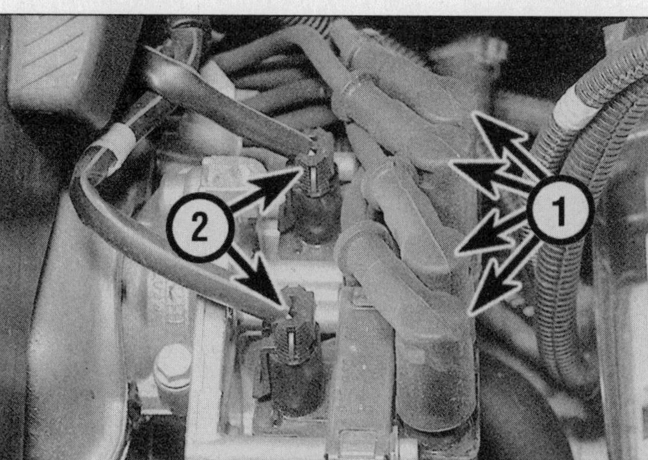

3.2 HT terminals (1) and LT wiring plugs (2) on the two ignition coils

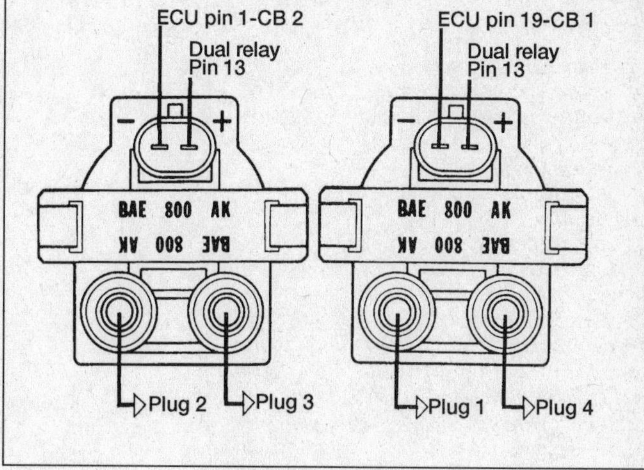

3.9 Ignition coil connections

5B

Chapter 5 Part C: Preheating system - diesel models

Contents

Degrees of difficulty

Easy, suitable for novice with little experience	Fairly easy, suitable for beginner with some experience	Fairly difficult, suitable for competent DIY mechanic	Difficult, suitable for experienced DIY mechanic	Very difficult, suitable for expert DIY or professional
		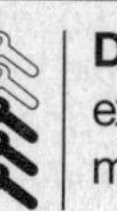		

Specifications

Preheating system

Glow plugs . . . . Bosch 0 250 201 039

Torque wrench setting

	Nm	lbf ft
Heater glow plugs	15	11

1 Preheating system - description and testing

Description

1 Each swirl chamber has a heater plug (commonly called a glow plug) screwed into it. The plugs are electrically-operated before and during start-up when the engine is cold.

2 Electrical feed to the glow plugs is controlled by a relay/timer unit. The coolant temperature determines the period of heating that takes place.

3 A warning light in the instrument panel tells the driver that preheating is taking place. When the light goes out, the engine is ready to be started. The voltage supply to the glow plugs continues for several seconds after the light goes out. If no attempt is made to start, the timer then cuts off the supply, in order to avoid draining the battery and overheating the glow plugs.

Testing

4 If the system malfunctions, testing is ultimately by substitution of known good units, but some preliminary checks may be made as follows.

5 Connect a voltmeter or 12-volt test lamp between the glow plug supply cable and earth (engine or vehicle metal). Make sure that the live connection is kept clear of the engine and bodywork.

6 Have an assistant switch on the ignition, and check that voltage is applied to the glow plugs. Note the time for which the warning light is lit, and the total time for which voltage is applied before the system cuts out. Switch off the ignition.

7 At an under-bonnet temperature of 20°C, typical times noted should be 5 or 6 seconds for warning light operation, followed by a further 10 seconds supply after the light goes out. Warning light time will increase with lower temperatures and decrease with higher temperatures.

8 If there is no supply at all, the relay or associated wiring is at fault.

9 To locate a defective glow plug, disconnect the main supply cable and the interconnecting strap from the top of the glow plugs. Be careful not to drop the nuts and washers.

10 Use a continuity tester, or a 12-volt test lamp connected to the battery positive terminal, to check for continuity between each glow plug terminal and earth. The resistance of a glow plug in good condition is very low (less than 1 ohm), so if the test lamp does not light or the continuity tester shows a high resistance, the glow plug is certainly defective.

11 If an ammeter is available, the current draw of each glow plug can be checked. After an initial surge of 15 to 20 amps, each plug should draw approximately 12 amps. Any plug which draws much more or less than this is probably defective.

12 As a final check, the glow plugs can be removed and inspected as described in the following Section.

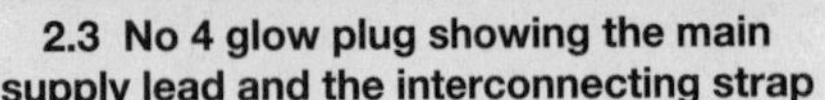

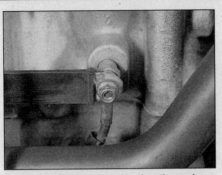

2.3 No 4 glow plug showing the main supply lead and the interconnecting strap

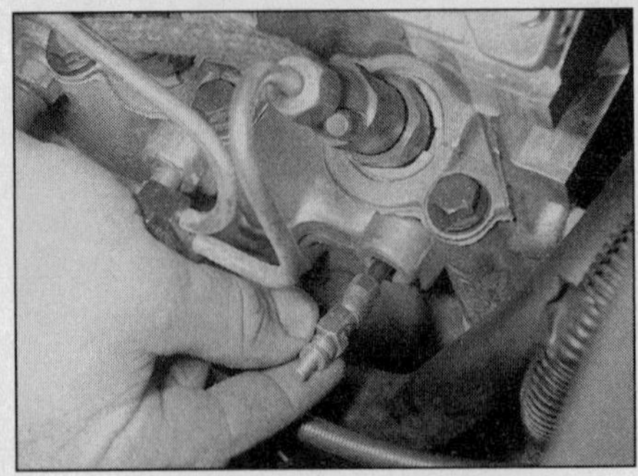

2.5 Removing a glow plug

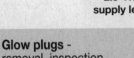

2 Glow plugs - removal, inspection and refitting

Removal

Caution: If the preheating system has just been energised, or if the engine has been running, the glow plugs will be very hot.

1 Disconnect the battery negative terminal (refer to *Disconnecting the battery* in the Reference Section of this manual).

2 Remove the air inlet ducting from the front of the engine with reference to Chapter 4C, Section 2.

3 Unscrew the nut from the relevant glow plug terminal(s), and recover the washer(s). Note that the main supply cable is connected to Number 4 cylinder glow plug and an interconnecting strap is fitted between the four plugs **(see illustration)**.

4 Where applicable, carefully move any obstructing pipes or wires to one side to enable access to the relevant glow plug(s).

5 Unscrew the glow plug(s) and remove from the cylinder head **(see illustration)**.

Inspection

6 Inspect each glow plug for physical damage. Burnt or eroded glow plug tips can be caused by a bad injector spray pattern. Have the injectors checked if this sort of damage is found.

7 If the glow plugs are in good physical condition, check them electrically using a 12 volt test lamp or continuity tester as described in the previous Section.

8 The glow plugs can be energised by applying 12 volts to them to verify that they heat up evenly and in the required time. Observe the following precautions.

a) Support the glow plug by clamping it carefully in a vice or self-locking pliers. Remember it will become red-hot.

b) Make sure that the power supply or test lead incorporates a fuse or overload trip to protect against damage from a short-circuit.

c) After testing, allow the glow plug to cool for several minutes before attempting to handle it.

9 A glow plug in good condition will start to glow red at the tip after drawing current for 5 seconds or so. Any plug which takes much longer to start glowing, or which starts glowing in the middle instead of at the tip, is defective.

Refitting

10 Refit by reversing the removal operations. Apply a smear of copper-based anti-seize compound to the plug threads and tighten the glow plugs to the specified torque. Do not overtighten, as this can damage the glow plug element.

3 Preheating system control unit - removal and refitting

Removal

1 Disconnect the battery negative terminal (refer to *Disconnecting the battery* in the Reference Section of this manual).

2 Unscrew the screws and remove the relay cover located at the left-hand end of the engine.

3 Disconnect the wiring then remove the control unit from the bracket.

Refitting

4 Refitting is a reversal of removal.

Chapter 6
Clutch

Contents

Degrees of difficulty

Easy, suitable for novice with little experience 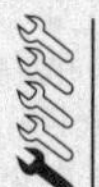	**Fairly easy,** suitable for beginner with some experience 	**Fairly difficult,** suitable for competent DIY mechanic	**Difficult,** suitable for experienced DIY mechanic 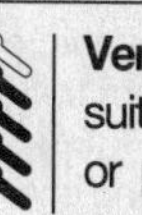	**Very difficult,** suitable for expert DIY or professional

Specifications

General

Type	Single dry plate with diaphragm spring, cable- or hydraulically-operated according to model
Clutch pedal travel (cable-operated mechanism)	140.0 ± 5.0 mm

Friction plate diameter

8-valve petrol engines	181.5 mm
16-valve petrol engines	190.0 mm
Diesel engines	200.0 mm

Torque wrench setting

	Nm	lbf ft
Pressure plate retaining bolts	16	12

1 General information

Vehicles with manual transmission are fitted with a pedal operated single dry plate clutch system. When the clutch pedal is depressed, effort is transmitted to the clutch release mechanism either mechanically by means of a cable, or hydraulically by means of a master cylinder and slave cylinder. The release mechanism transfers effort to the pressure plate diaphragm spring, which withdraws the pressure plate from the flywheel and releases the driven plate.

Where applicable, the hydraulic fluid employed in the clutch system is the same as that used in the braking system, hence fluid is supplied to the master cylinder from a tapping on the brake fluid reservoir. The clutch hydraulic system must be sealed before work is carried out on any of its components and then on completion, topped up and bled to remove any air bubbles.

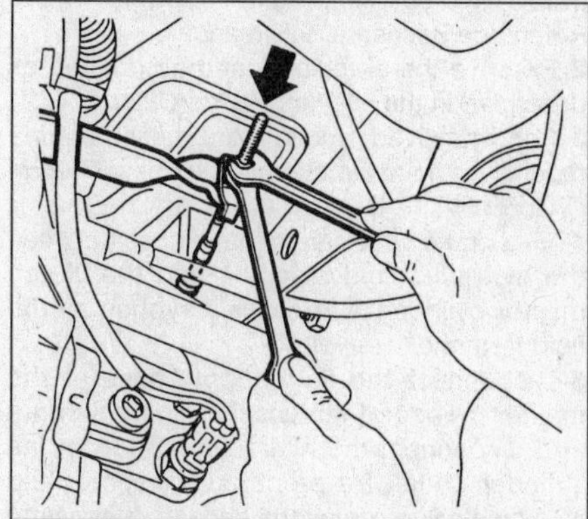

2.5 Clutch cable adjustment

2 Clutch - adjustment

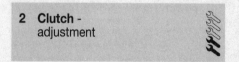

Note: *This procedure applies to models fitted with a cable-operated clutch release mechanism. No adjustment is possible on models with the hydraulically-operated system.*

1 The clutch adjustment is checked by measuring the clutch pedal travel. If a new cable has been fitted, settle it in position by depressing the clutch pedal at least thirty times.

2 Ensure that there are no obstructions beneath the clutch pedal then measure the distance from the centre of the clutch pedal pad to the base of the steering wheel with the pedal in the at-rest position. Depress the clutch pedal fully to the floor, and measure the distance from the centre of the clutch pedal pad to the base of the steering wheel.

3 Subtract the first measurement from the second to obtain the clutch pedal travel. If this is not with the range given in the Specifications at the start of this Chapter, adjust the clutch as follows.

4 The clutch cable is adjusted by means of the adjuster nut on the transmission end of the cable. Access to the nut is from under the vehicle. Apply the handbrake then jack up the front of the vehicle and support on axle stands (see *Jacking and vehicle support*).

5 Working under the left-hand side of the engine compartment, slacken the locknut from the end of the clutch cable. Adjust the position of the adjuster nut, then depress the clutch pedal ten times and re-measure the clutch pedal travel. Repeat this procedure until the clutch pedal travel is as specified **(see illustration).**

6 Once the adjuster nut is correctly positioned, and the pedal travel is correctly set, securely tighten the cable locknut then lower the vehicle to the ground.

6

3 Clutch cable - removal and refitting

Note: *This procedure applies to models fitted with a cable-operated clutch release mechanism.*

Removal

1 Remove the battery and tray as described in Chapter 5A. If necessary, also remove the inlet air ducting for improved access as described in the relevant part of Chapter 4.

2 Unscrew the adjustment locknut and adjuster nut from the end of the cable fitting, then release the inner and outer cables from the transmission housing. Note the position of the damper block.

3 Working inside the vehicle, unhook the inner cable from the top of the clutch pedal.

4 Returning to the engine compartment, unscrew the nuts securing the outer cable to the bulkhead, then withdraw the cable assembly from the engine compartment.

Refitting

5 Apply a smear of multi-purpose grease to the cable end fittings, then pass the cable through the bulkhead. Refit and tighten the nuts.

6 Inside the vehicle hook the inner cable onto the top of the clutch pedal.

7 In the engine compartment, attach the outer cable to the transmission housing and refit the damper block and nuts to the inner cable end.

8 Adjust the cable as described in Section 2.

9 Refit the air ducting and battery with reference to Chapters 4 and 5A.

4 Clutch hydraulic system - bleeding

Note: *This procedure applies to models fitted with the hydraulically-operated clutch release mechanism.*

Warning: Hydraulic fluid is poisonous; thoroughly wash off spills from bare skin without delay. Seek immediate medical advice if any fluid is swallowed or gets into the eyes. Certain types of hydraulic fluid are inflammable and may ignite when brought into contact with hot components; when servicing any hydraulic system, it is safest to assume that the fluid IS inflammable, and to take precautions against the risk of fire as though it were petrol that was being handled. Hydraulic fluid is an effective paint stripper and will also attack many plastics. If spillage occurs onto painted bodywork or fittings, it should be washed off immediately, using copious quantities of fresh water. It is also hygroscopic - it can absorb moisture from the air, which then renders it useless. Old fluid may have suffered contamination, and should never be re-used. When topping-up or renewing the fluid, always use the recommended grade, and ensure that it comes from a new sealed container.

General information

1 Whenever the clutch hydraulic lines are disconnected for service or repair, a certain amount of air will enter the system. The presence of air in any hydraulic system will introduce a degree of elasticity, and in the clutch system this will translate into poor pedal feel and reduced travel, leading to inefficient gear changes and even clutch system failure. For this reason, the hydraulic lines must be sealed using hose clamps before any work is carried out and then on completion, topped up and bled to remove any air bubbles.

2 To seal off the hydraulic supply to the clutch slave cylinder, fit a proprietary brake hose clamp to the flexible section of the hose located over the transmission and tighten it securely. It will be necessary to remove the battery and battery tray to access the hose.

3 The most effective way of bleeding the clutch hydraulic system is to use a pressure brake bleeding kit. These are readily available in motor accessories shops and are extremely effective; the following sub-section describes bleeding the clutch system using such a kit. The alternative method is to bleed the system by depressing the clutch pedal - refer to Chapter 9, Section 11, for details of this method.

Bleeding

4 Remove the protective cap from the bleed nipple on the slave cylinder. Access can be improved by removing the battery and tray with reference to Chapter 5A.

5 Fit a ring spanner over the bleed nipple head, but do not slacken it at this point. Connect a length of clear plastic hose over the nipple and insert the other end into a clean container. Pour hydraulic fluid into the container, such that the end of the hose is covered.

6 Following the manufacturer's instructions, pour hydraulic fluid into the bleeding kit vessel.

7 Unscrew the vehicle's fluid reservoir cap, then connect the bleeding kit fluid supply hose to the reservoir.

8 Connect the pressure hose to a supply of compressed air - a spare tyre is a convenient source.

Caution: Check that the pressure in the tyre does not exceed the maximum supply pressure quoted by the kit manufacturer, let some air escape to reduce the pressure, if necessary. Gently open the air valve and allow the air and fluid pressures to equalise. Check that there are no leaks before proceeding.

9 Using the spanner, slacken the bleed pipe nipple until fluid and air bubbles can be seen to flow through the tube, into the container. Maintain a steady flow until the emerging fluid is free of air bubbles; keep a watchful eye on the level of fluid in the bleeding kit vessel and the vehicle's fluid reservoir - if it is allowed to drop too low, air may be forced into the system, defeating the object of the exercise. To refill the vessel, turn off the compressed air supply, remove the lid and pour in an appropriate quantity of clean fluid from a new container - do not re-use the fluid collected in the receiving container. Repeat as necessary until the ejected fluid is bubble-free.

10 On completion, pump the clutch pedal several times to assess its feel and travel. If firm, constant pedal resistance is not felt throughout the pedal stroke, it is probable that air is still present in the system - repeat the bleeding procedure until the pedal feel is restored.

11 Depressurise the bleeding kit and remove it from the vehicle. At this point, the fluid reservoir may be over-full; the excess should be removed using a *clean* pipette to reduce the level to the MAX mark.

12 Tighten the bleed pipe nipple using the spanner and remove the receiving container. Refit the protective cap.

13 On completion, assess the feel of the clutch pedal; if it exhibits any sponginess or looseness, further bleeding may be required.

14 Where removed, refit the battery and tray.

15 Finally, road test the vehicle and check the operation of the clutch system whilst changing up and down through the gears, whilst pulling away from a standstill and from a hill start.

5 Clutch master cylinder - removal and refitting

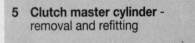

Note: *This procedure applies to models fitted with the hydraulically-operated clutch release mechanism.*

Note: *Refer to the warning at the beginning of Section 4 regarding the hazards of working with hydraulic fluid.*

Removal

1 Disconnect the battery negative terminal (refer to *Disconnecting the battery* in the Reference Section of this manual).

2 Remove the air cleaner and air ducting as described in the relevant Part of Chapter 4.

3 For improved access on petrol engine models, remove the alternator as described in Chapter 5A.

4 Fit a brake hose clamp to the hose between the hydraulic fluid reservoir and the clutch master cylinder. Alternatively syphon all the fluid from the reservoir.

5 Disconnect the fluid supply hose at the master cylinder, then unscrew the union nut and disconnect the hydraulic pipe from the cylinder outlet. Be prepared for some fluid loss by placing some rags beneath the master cylinder.

6 Working inside the vehicle, extract the split pin and remove the washer securing the master cylinder pushrod to the clutch pedal. Disconnect the pushrod from the pivot.

7 Have an assistant support the master cylinder in the engine compartment, then unscrew the mounting bolts. Withdraw the master cylinder from the engine compartment.

8 It is not possible to obtain an overhaul kit from Fiat however some motor factors may be able to supply one. Follow the instructions with the repair kit if obtained.

Refitting

9 Refit the clutch master cylinder by following the removal procedure in reverse, noting the following.

a) Apply a little high-melting point grease to the clutch pedal pivot.
b) Tighten the mounting bolts and union nut securely.
c) Fit a new split pin to the pushrod.
d) Where removed, refit the alternator as described in Chapter 5A.
e) On completion bleed the clutch hydraulic system as described in Section 4.

6 Clutch slave cylinder - removal and refitting

Note: *This procedure applies to models fitted with the hydraulically-operated clutch release mechanism.*

Note: *Refer to the warning at the beginning of Section 4 regarding the hazards of working with hydraulic fluid.*

Removal

1 Remove the battery and battery tray as described in Chapter 5A.

2 Fit a brake hose clamp to the hose leading to the clutch slave cylinder.

3 Unscrew the union nut and disconnect the hydraulic pipe from the slave cylinder. Be prepared for some fluid loss by placing rags beneath the cylinder.

4 Unscrew the mounting bolts and release the slave cylinder pushrod from the release arm on the transmission, then remove the unit from the engine compartment **(see illustration)**.

5 It is not possible to obtain an overhaul kit from Fiat however some motor factors may be able to supply one. Follow the instructions with the repair kit if obtained.

Refitting

6 Refit the clutch slave cylinder by following the removal procedure in reverse, noting the following.

a) Apply a little high-melting point grease to the tip of the slave cylinder pushrod.
b) Tighten the mounting bolts and union nut securely.
c) On completion bleed the clutch hydraulic system as described in Section 4.

7 Clutch assembly - removal, inspection and refitting

Warning: Dust created by clutch wear and deposited on the clutch components may contain asbestos, which is a health hazard. DO NOT blow it out with compressed air, or inhale any of it. DO NOT use petrol or petroleum-based solvents to clean off the dust. Brake system cleaner or methylated spirit should be used to flush the dust into a suitable receptacle. After the clutch components are wiped clean with rags, dispose of the contaminated rags and cleaner in a sealed, marked container.

Note: *Although some friction materials may no longer contain asbestos, it is safest to assume that they DO, and to take precautions accordingly.*

Removal

1 Unless the complete engine/transmission is to be removed from the car and separated for major overhaul (see Chapter 2D), the clutch can be reached by removing the transmission as described in Chapter 7A.

2 Before disturbing the clutch, use chalk or a marker pen to mark the relationship of the pressure plate assembly to the flywheel.

3 Working in a diagonal sequence, slacken the pressure plate bolts by half a turn at a time, until spring pressure is released and the bolts can be unscrewed by hand **(see illustration)**.

4 Prise the pressure plate assembly off its locating dowels, and collect the friction plate, noting which way round the friction plate is fitted **(see illustration)**.

Inspection

Note: *Due to the amount of work necessary to remove and refit clutch components, it is usually considered good practice to renew the clutch friction plate, pressure plate assembly and release bearing as a matched set, even if only one of these is actually worn enough to require renewal. It is also worth considering the renewal of the clutch components on a preventative basis if the engine and/or transmission have been removed for some other reason.*

6.4 Removing the clutch slave cylinder from the transmission

5 Separate the pressure plate and friction plate and place them on the bench.

6 When cleaning clutch components, read first the warning at the beginning of this Section; remove dust using a clean, dry cloth, and working in a well-ventilated atmosphere.

7 Check the friction plate facings for signs of wear, damage or oil contamination. If the friction material is cracked, burnt, scored or damaged, or if it is contaminated with oil or grease (shown by shiny black patches), the friction plate must be renewed.

8 If the friction material is still serviceable, check that the centre boss splines are unworn, that the torsion springs are in good condition and securely fastened, and that all the rivets are tight. If any wear or damage is found, the friction plate must be renewed.

9 If the friction material is fouled with oil, this must be due to an oil leak from the crankshaft rear (left-hand) oil seal, from the sump-to-cylinder block joint, or from the transmission input shaft. Renew the seal or repair the joint, as appropriate, before installing the new friction plate.

10 Check the pressure plate assembly for obvious signs of wear or damage; shake it to check for loose rivets or worn or damaged fulcrum rings, and check that the drive straps securing the pressure plate to the cover do not show signs (such as a deep yellow or blue discoloration) of overheating. If the diaphragm spring is worn or damaged, or if its pressure is in any way suspect, the pressure plate assembly should be renewed.

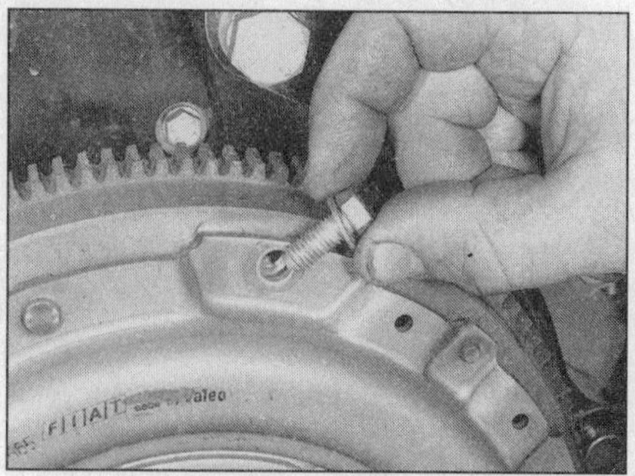

7.3 Removing the clutch pressure plate bolts

7.4 Removing the clutch pressure plate and friction plate

7.17 Using a clutch friction plate centralising tool

11 Examine the machined bearing surfaces of the pressure plate and of the flywheel; they should be clean, completely flat, and free from scratches or scoring. If either is discoloured from excessive heat, or shows signs of cracks, it should be renewed - although minor damage of this nature can sometimes be polished away using emery paper.

12 Check that the release bearing contact surface rotates smoothly and easily, with no sign of noise or roughness. Also check that the surface itself is smooth and unworn, with no signs of cracks, pitting or scoring. If there is any doubt about its condition, the bearing must be renewed.

Refitting

13 On reassembly, ensure that the bearing surfaces of the flywheel and pressure plate are completely clean, smooth, and free from oil or grease. Use solvent to remove any protective grease from new components.

14 Fit the friction plate so that its spring hub assembly faces away from the flywheel; there may also be a marking showing which way round the plate is to be refitted.

15 Refit the pressure plate assembly, aligning the marks made on dismantling (if the original pressure plate is re-used), and locating the pressure plate on its three locating dowels. Fit the pressure plate bolts, but tighten them only finger-tight, so that the friction plate can still be moved.

16 The friction plate must now be centralised, so that when the transmission is refitted, its input shaft will pass through the splines at the centre of the friction plate.

17 Centralisation can be achieved by passing a screwdriver or other long bar through the friction plate and into the hole in the crankshaft; the friction plate can then be moved around until it is centred on the crankshaft hole. Alternatively, a clutch-aligning tool can be used to eliminate the guesswork; these can be obtained from most accessory shops **(see illustration)**. A home-made aligning tool can be fabricated from a length of metal rod or wooden dowel which fits closely inside the crankshaft hole, and has insulating tape wound around it to match the diameter of the friction plate splined hole.

18 When the friction plate is centralised, tighten the pressure plate bolts evenly and in a diagonal sequence to the specified torque setting.

19 Apply a thin smear of molybdenum disulphide grease to the splines of the friction plate and the transmission input shaft, and also to the release bearing bore and release fork shaft.

20 Refit the transmission as described in Chapter 7A.

8 Clutch release mechanism - removal, inspection and refitting

Removal

1 Unless the complete engine/transmission is to be removed from the car and separated for major overhaul (see Chapter 2D), the clutch release mechanism can be reached by removing the transmission as described in Chapter 7A.

2 Unhook the release bearing from the fork and slide it off the guide tube **(see illustration)**.

3 Using circlip pliers extract the circlip from the top of the release fork shaft.

4 Note the position of the arm then slide it off the splines.

5 Using a small drift, tap out the upper release shaft bush from the transmission casing **(see illustration)**.

6 Lift the release shaft from the lower bush then remove it from inside the transmission casing.

7 Extract the lower bush from the casing.

Inspection

8 Check the release mechanism, renewing any worn or damaged parts. Carefully check all bearing surfaces and points of contact.

9 When checking the release bearing itself, note that it is often considered worthwhile to renew it as a matter of course. Check that the contact surface rotates smoothly and easily, with no sign of roughness, and that the surface itself is smooth and unworn, with no signs of cracks, pitting or scoring. If there is any doubt about its condition, the bearing must be renewed.

Refitting

10 Apply a smear of molybdenum disulphide grease to the shaft pivot bushes and the contact surfaces of the release fork.

11 Tap the lower bush into the casing and refit the release fork and shaft.

12 Slide the upper bush down the shaft and tap it into the casing making sure that the ridge engages with the cut-out, then slide the arm on the splines the correct way round.

13 Refit the circlip in the shaft groove.

14 Slide the release bearing onto the guide tube and engage it with the fork.

15 Refit the transmission as described in Chapter 7A.

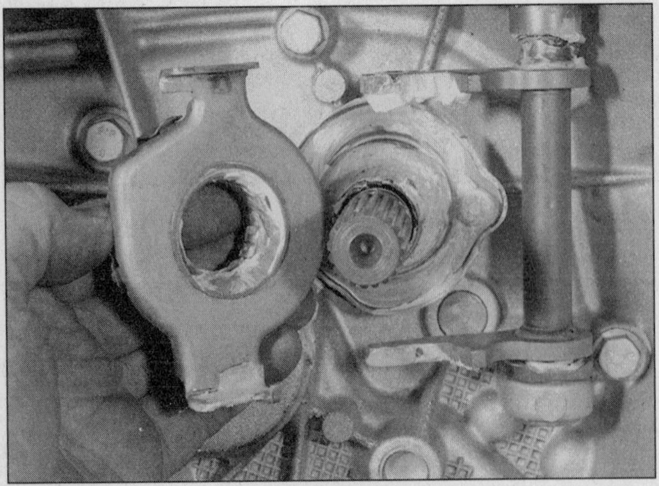
8.2 Removing the release bearing from the fork and guide tube

8.5 Clutch release shaft (1) and upper shaft bush (2)

Chapter 7 Part A: Manual transmission

Contents

Degrees of difficulty

Easy, suitable for novice with little experience 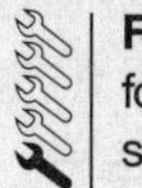	**Fairly easy,** suitable for beginner with some experience 	**Fairly difficult,** suitable for competent DIY mechanic 	**Difficult,** suitable for experienced DIY mechanic 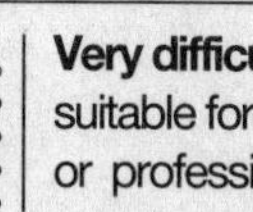	**Very difficult,** suitable for expert DIY or professional

Specifications

General

Type	Transverse mounted, front wheel drive layout with integral transaxle differential/final drive. 5 or 6 forward speeds, 1 reverse speed
Designation:	
1108 cc petrol engine	C.514.5.10 (5-speed) or C.514.6.10 (6-speed)
1242 cc petrol engine	C.514.5.10/13 (5-speed)
Non-turbo diesel engine	C.514.5.13 (5-speed)
Turbo diesel engine	C.510.5.17 (5-speed)

Torque wrench settings

Torque wrench settings	Nm	lbf ft
Gear lever support nut	6	4
Gear lever to mounting	49	36
Reverse gear inhibitor cable to transmission	30	22
Reversing light switch	40	30
Selector rod-to-gear lever nut	17	13
Speedometer drive	12	9
Transmission-to-engine bolt/nut	85	63

1 General information

The transmission is contained in a cast-aluminium alloy casing bolted to the engine's left-hand end, and consists of the gearbox and final drive differential.

Drive is transmitted from the crankshaft via the clutch to the input shaft, which has a splined extension to accept the clutch friction plate, and rotates in roller bearings at its right-hand end and ball bearings at its left-hand end (on 6-speed versions the left-hand extension rotates in a roller bearing). From the input shaft, drive is transmitted to the output shaft, which rotates in roller bearings at its right-hand end, and ball bearings at its left-hand end (on 6-speed versions the left-hand extension rotates in ball bearings). From the output shaft, the drive is transmitted to the differential crownwheel, which rotates with the differential case and gears in taper roller bearings, thus driving the sun gears and driveshafts. The rotation of the differential gears on their shaft allows the inner roadwheel to rotate at a slower speed than the outer roadwheel when the car is cornering.

The input and output shafts are arranged side by side, parallel to the crankshaft and driveshafts, so that their gear pinion teeth are in constant mesh. In the neutral position, the relevant input shaft and output shaft gear pinions rotate freely, so that drive cannot be transmitted to the output shaft and crownwheel.

Gear selection is via a floor-mounted lever and selector rod mechanism **(see illustration)**. The selector rod causes the appropriate selector fork to move its respective synchro-sleeve along the shaft, to lock the gear to the synchro-hub. Since the synchro-hubs are splined to the input and output shafts, this locks the gear to the shaft, so that drive can be transmitted. To ensure that gear-changing can be made quickly and quietly, a synchro-mesh system is fitted to all forward gears.

2 Gearchange lever and linkage - removal and refitting

Removal

1 Firmly apply the handbrake, then jack up the front of the car and support it securely on axle stands (see *Jacking and vehicle support*).

2 Remove the exhaust system with reference to Chapter 4D.

3 Unbolt the exhaust heatshield and remove it from under the vehicle.

4 Disconnect the gearchange cable and rod from the transmission and from the body. Also disconnect the reverse inhibitor cable.

5 Unscrew the single screw and remove the centre console from inside the vehicle.

6 Unscrew the front mounting securing the gearchange lower cover to the body.

7 Under the vehicle unscrew the lower cover mounting bolts, then lower the assembly and remove from under the vehicle.

8 The gearchange lever may be removed by disconnecting the cables and removing the pivot bolt. Note the location of the spacers and washers to ensure correct reassembly. If necessary the bushes may be renewed by unscrewing the mounting nuts.

9 Reassembly is a reversal of dismantling but apply a little multi-purpose grease to the bearing surfaces.

Refitting

10 Refitting is a reversal of removal. Tighten all nuts and bolts securely.

3 Manual transmission - removal and refitting

Petrol models

Removal

1 Select a solid, level surface to park the vehicle upon. Give yourself enough space to move around it easily. Apply the handbrake then jack up the front of the vehicle and support on axle stands (see *Jacking and vehicle support*). Remove both front wheels.

2 Disconnect the wiring connectors from the anti-theft alarm located next to the battery, then unbolt and remove the alarm.

3 Remove the battery and mounting tray as described in Chapter 5A.

4 Disconnect the wiring from the reversing light switch on the front of the transmission.

5 Unscrew the nut and disconnect the earth cable from its stud.

6 On models with a cable operated clutch,

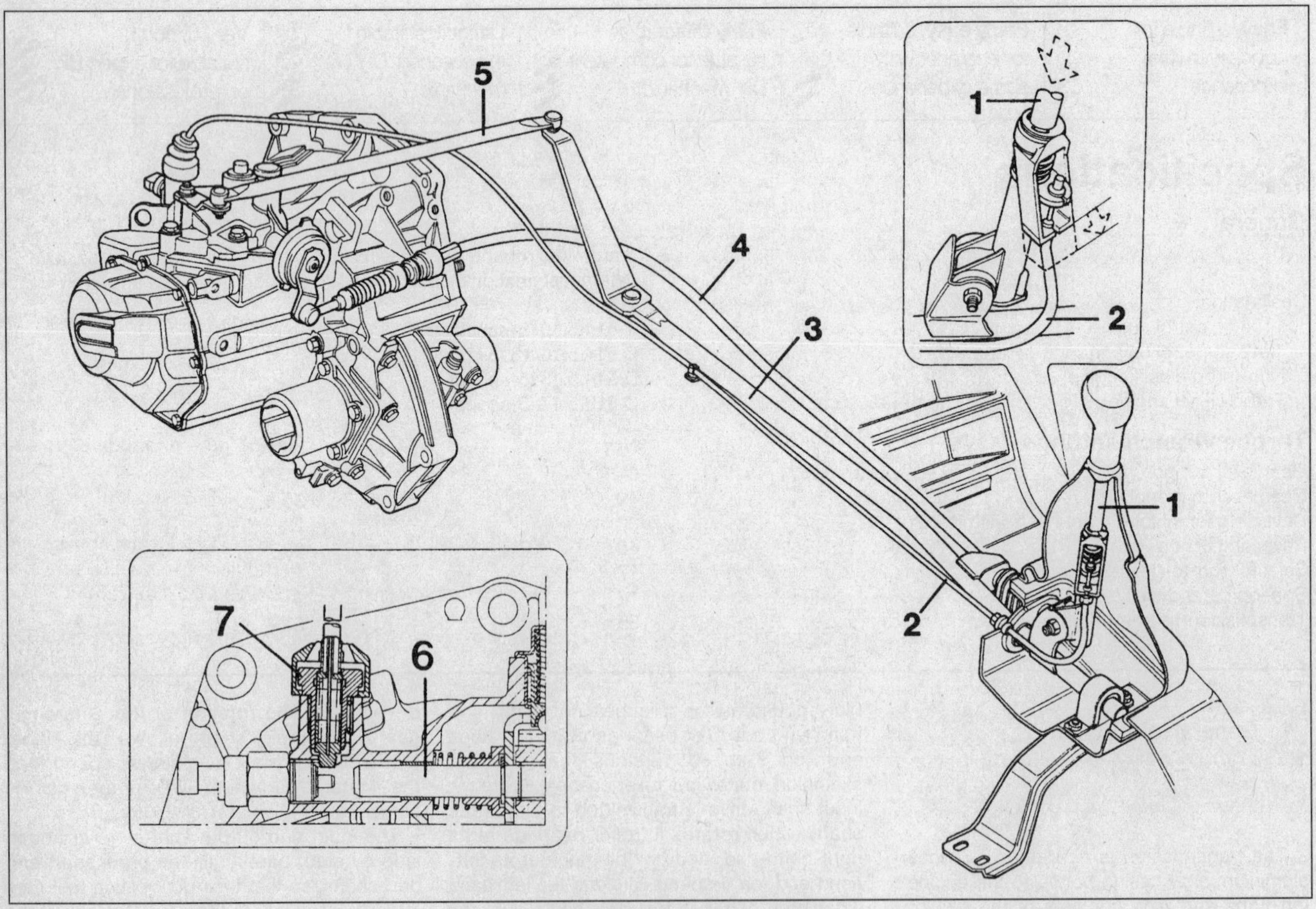

1.4 Gearchange lever and linkage

1 *Gear lever sliding part*
2 *Reverse gear inhibition cable*
3 *Gear selector control rod*
4 *Gear engagement control cable*
5 *Gear selector link rod*
6 *Gear selector control rod*
7 *Reverse gear inhibition device*

3.8 Unscrew the nut and disconnect the gear selector rod from the lever on the transmission

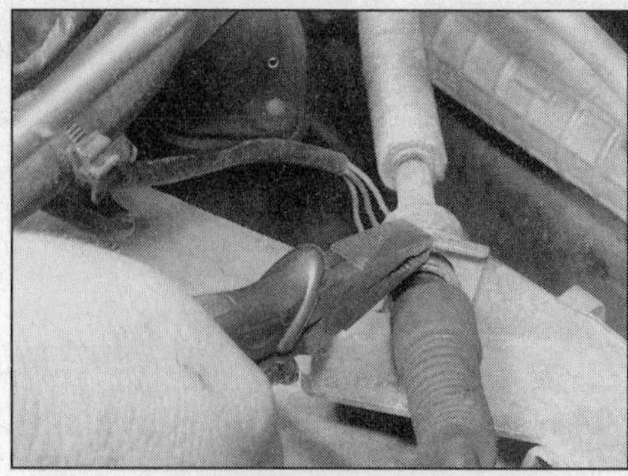
3.9a Remove the clip to release the gear engagement cable

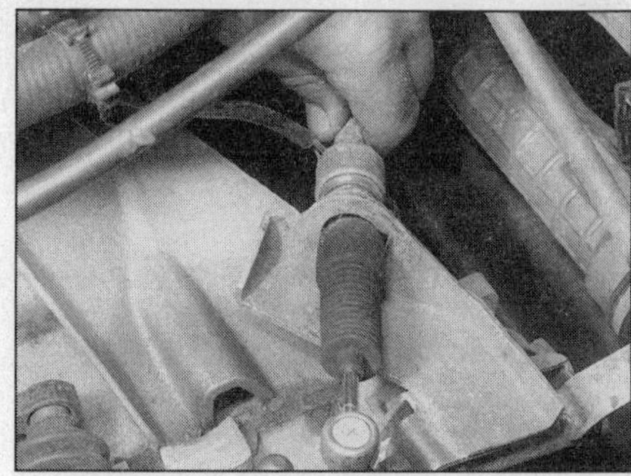
3.9b Removing the gear engagement cable from the mounting bracket

unscrew the locknut and adjusting nut from the end of the clutch cable and disconnect the cable from the transmission. Recover the damper block. On models with a hydraulically operated clutch, unscrew the mounting bolts, release the slave cylinder pushrod from the release arm on the transmission, then position the cylinder to one side.

7 Unscrew and remove the reverse gear inhibiting device from the transmission. Tie the cable to one side out of the way.

8 Unscrew the nut and disconnect the gear selector rod from the lever on the transmission **(see illustration)**.

9 Pull out the clip then disconnect the gear engagement cable from the control lever and release the cable from the mounting bracket **(see illustrations)**.

10 Unscrew and remove the two upper transmission-to-engine mounting bolts. Unscrew the single bolt securing the starter motor to the transmission.

11 Remove the air cleaner and air ducting with reference to Chapter 4A or 4B. This is necessary in order to fit the engine hoist.

12 On 5-speed transmissions, trace the wiring back from the electronic speedometer sensor and disconnect the connector located on the left-hand side of the engine **(see illustration)**.

13 On 6-speed transmissions, unscrew the knurled nut and disconnect the speedometer cable from the top of the final drive housing.

14 Support the weight of the engine using a hoist attached to the engine lifting eyes, or alternatively use a trolley jack and block of wood beneath the engine.

15 Unscrew the Lambda/oxygen sensor from the exhaust downpipe and position it in a safe place to prevent damage.

16 Unscrew the nuts securing the downpipe to the exhaust manifold, then lower it and support on an axle stand. Recover the gasket.

17 Unbolt the support bracket from the engine and transmission. Recover the spacer plate.

18 Unbolt and remove the transmission lower cover.

19 Unscrew the remaining starter motor mounting bolts and support the starter motor to one side.

20 Loosen and remove the clips securing the left- and right-hand driveshaft gaiters to the transmission output shafts.

21 Unscrew and remove the bolts securing the left-hand swivel hub assembly to the front suspension strut, then separate the components and support the swivel hub on an axle stand.

22 Move the swivel hub assembly outwards and disconnect the inner end of the driveshaft from the transmission output shaft. Support the shaft away from the transmission to prevent damage to the gaiters.

23 Working beneath the vehicle, unscrew the bolts securing the rear engine mounting to the underbody then unscrew the bolts securing the mounting to the transmission and withdraw the mounting assembly from under the vehicle.

24 Unscrew the bolts securing the left-hand engine/transmission mounting to the body then unscrew the bolts from the transmission and remove the mounting.

25 Support the weight of the transmission on a trolley jack then unscrew the remaining nut and bolt from the bellhousing and pull the transmission away from the engine. Lower it and remove from under the vehicle.

Warning: Support the transmission to ensure that it remains steady on the jack head. Keep the transmission level until the input shaft is fully withdrawn from the clutch friction plate.

Refitting

26 Refitting is a reversal of the removal procedure, but note the following points.

- *a) Apply a smear of high-melting-point grease to the clutch friction plate splines; take care to avoid contaminating the friction surfaces.*
- *b) Tighten all bolts to the specified torque.*
- *c) Fit new clips to secure the driveshaft gaiters to the transmission output shafts.*
- *d) Adjust the clutch cable (where applicable) as described in Chapter 6.*

Diesel models

Removal

27 Select a solid, level surface to park the vehicle upon. Give yourself enough space to move around it easily. Apply the handbrake then jack up the front of the vehicle and support on axle stands (see *Jacking and vehicle support*). Remove both front wheels.

28 Unbolt the relay support then remove the battery and mounting tray as described in Chapter 5A.

29 On models with a cable operated clutch, unscrew the locknut and adjusting nut from the end of the clutch cable and disconnect the cable from the transmission. Recover the damper block. On models with a hydraulically operated clutch, unscrew the mounting bolts, release the slave cylinder pushrod from the release arm on the transmission, then position the cylinder to one side.

30 Unscrew the nut and disconnect the gear selector rod from the lever on the transmission.

31 Disconnect the gear engagement cable from the control lever then slide out the clip and release the cable from the mounting bracket.

32 Unbolt the electronic rev counter sensor from the upper rear of the bellhousing and position it to one side **(see illustration)**.

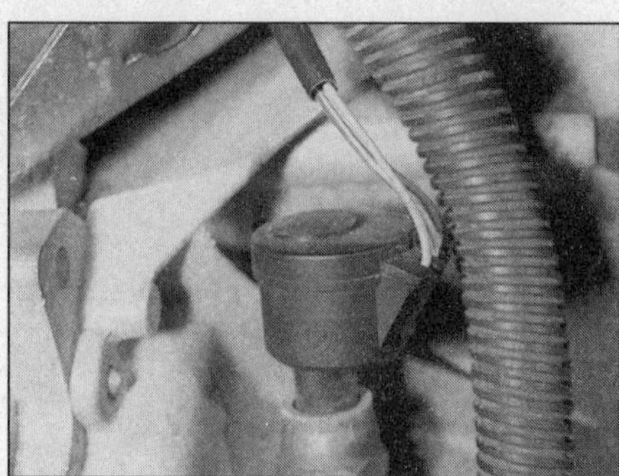
3.12 Electronic speedometer sensor fitted to 5-speed transmissions

3.32 Electronic rev counter sensor located in the upper rear of the bellhousing

33 Remove the air cleaner front section and air ducting with reference to Chapter 4C. Also disconnect the injection pump vacuum pipe from the clips on the left-hand end of the cylinder head. This work is necessary in order to fit the engine hoist.
34 Support the weight of the engine using a hoist attached to the engine lifting eyes, or alternatively use a trolley jack and block of wood beneath the engine.
35 Unscrew the nuts securing the downpipe to the exhaust manifold, then lower it and support on an axle stand. Recover the gasket.
36 Unscrew the starter motor mounting bolts and support the starter motor to one side.
37 Disconnect the wiring from the reversing light switch on the front of the transmission.
38 Unscrew the nut and disconnect the earth cable from its stud.
39 Trace the wiring back from the electronic speedometer sensor and disconnect the connector located on the left-hand side of the engine. If a mechanical speedometer is fitted unscrew the knurled collar and disconnect the cable from the transmission.
40 Unbolt and remove the transmission lower cover.
41 Using an Allen key unscrew the bolts securing the inner end of the left-hand driveshaft to the transmission flange. Remove the bolts and recover the spacer plates. Support the driveshaft on an axle stand.
42 Unscrew and remove the bolts securing the left-hand swivel hub assembly to the front suspension strut, then separate the components and support the swivel hub on an axle stand.
43 Move the swivel hub assembly outwards and support the driveshaft away from the transmission.
44 Using an Allen key unscrew the bolts securing the inner end of the right-hand driveshaft to the intermediate shaft flange. Remove the bolts and recover the spacer plates. Support the driveshaft on an axle stand.
45 Remove the intermediate driveshaft with reference to Chapter 8.
46 Working beneath the vehicle, unscrew the bolts securing the rear engine mounting to the underbody then unscrew the bolts securing the mounting to the transmission and withdraw the mounting assembly from under the vehicle.
47 Unscrew the bolts securing the left-hand engine/transmission mounting to the body then unscrew the bolts from the transmission and remove the mounting.
48 Support the weight of the transmission on a trolley jack then unscrew the remaining nut and bolts from the bellhousing and pull the transmission away from the engine.

⚠ ***Warning: Support the transmission to ensure that it remains steady on the jack head. Keep the transmission level until the input shaft is fully withdrawn from the clutch friction plate.***

Refitting

49 Refitting is a reversal of the removal procedure, but note the following points.
a) Apply a smear of high-melting-point grease to the clutch friction plate splines; take care to avoid contaminating the friction surfaces.
b) Tighten all bolts to the specified torque.
c) Fit new clips to secure the driveshaft gaiters to the transmission output shafts.
d) Adjust the clutch cable (where applicable) as described in Chapter 6.

4 Manual transmission overhaul - general information

Overhauling a manual transmission is a difficult and involved job for the DIY home mechanic. In addition to dismantling and reassembling many small parts, clearances must be precisely measured and, if necessary, changed by selecting shims and spacers. Internal transmission components are also often difficult to obtain, and in many instances, extremely expensive. Because of this, if the transmission develops a fault or becomes noisy, the best course of action is to have the unit overhauled by a specialist repairer, or to obtain an exchange reconditioned unit.

Nevertheless, it is not impossible for the more experienced mechanic to overhaul the transmission, provided the special tools are available, and the job is done in a deliberate step-by-step manner, so that nothing is overlooked.

The tools necessary for an overhaul include internal and external circlip pliers, bearing pullers, a slide hammer, a set of pin punches, a dial test indicator, and possibly a hydraulic press. In addition, a large, sturdy workbench and a vice will be required.

During dismantling of the transmission, make careful notes of how each component is fitted, to make reassembly easier and more accurate.

Before dismantling the transmission, it will help if you have some idea what area is malfunctioning. Certain problems can be closely related to specific areas in the transmission, which can make component examination and replacement easier. Refer to the *Fault Finding* Section at the end of this manual for more information.

5 Reversing light switch - testing, removal and refitting

Testing

1 The reversing light circuit is controlled by a plunger-type switch screwed into the front of the transmission casing. If a fault develops, first ensure that the circuit fuse has not blown.
2 To test the switch, disconnect the wiring connector, and use a multimeter (set to the resistance function) or a battery-and-bulb test circuit to check that there is continuity between the switch terminals only when reverse gear is selected. If this is not the case, and there are no obvious breaks or other damage to the wires, the switch is faulty, and must be renewed.

Removal

3 Access to the reversing light switch is best achieved from under the vehicle. Apply the handbrake then jack up the front of the vehicle and support on axle stands (see *Jacking and vehicle support*).
4 Disconnect the wiring connector, then unscrew it from the transmission casing.

Refitting

5 Refit the switch and tighten securely.
6 Reconnect the wiring then lower the vehicle to the ground.

Chapter 7 Part B: Automatic transmission

Contents

Degrees of difficulty

Easy, suitable for novice with little experience 	**Fairly easy,** suitable for beginner with some experience 	**Fairly difficult,** suitable for competent DIY mechanic 	**Difficult,** suitable for experienced DIY mechanic 	**Very difficult,** suitable for expert DIY or professional

Specifications

General

Type	ECVT (Electronic Continuously Variable Transmission)
Ratios (at transmission):	
Lowest	2.503
Highest	0.497
Final drive	4.647:1

Torque wrench settings

	Nm	lbf ft
Earth cable	14	10
Control unit	5	4
Electro-magnetic clutch to flywheel	34	25
Transmission-to-engine bolt/nut	85	63

1 General information

1 The automatic transmission fitted is designated ECVT (Electronic Continuously Variable Transmission). The main components of the transmission are an electro-magnetic clutch, a variable-ratio coupling, a final drive/differential unit, and the associated control mechanisms **(see illustrations overleaf)**.

2 The variable-ratio coupling consists of two pulleys and a flexible metal drivebelt. The effective diameter of the two pulleys can be varied to provide different transmission ratios between them.

3 During normal driving, the transmission automatically selects the ratio giving the best compromise between economy and speed. When the driver depresses the accelerator pedal to the floor, a kickdown effect is provided, and the transmission selects a lower ratio for improved acceleration.

4 The gear selector control resembles that fitted to conventional automatic transmissions. The control positions are as follows:

P (Parking)	*The transmission is mechanically locked by the engagement of a pawl with a toothed segment on the driven pulley.*
R (Reverse)	*Reverse gear is engaged.*
N (Neutral)	*The transmission is in neutral.*
D (Drive)	*Normal driving position. Transmission ratio is varied automatically to suit prevailing speed and load.*
L (Low)	*Prevents the transmission moving into high ratios. Provides maximum acceleration and maximum engine braking.*

5 The engine can only be started in positions P and N. A warning buzzer sounds if the selector is in any position other than P when the ignition is switched off or when the driver's door is opened.

6 The electro-magnetic clutch consists of a driving element bolted to the engine flywheel, and a driven element splined to the transmission input shaft. The degree of coupling between the two elements is determined by the intensity of a magnetic field generated by a current passing through windings in the driven element. The magnetic field acts on a layer of metallic powder between the driving and driven elements. When no magnetic field is present, the powder is loose and the two elements are effectively disconnected. As the magnetic field increases, the powder sticks together, and the coupling between the elements becomes increasingly rigid.

7 Selection of reverse, neutral and forward gears is by the movement of a sliding sleeve on a hub keyed to the drive pulley shaft. In forward gear, the sleeve engages with the gear on the end of the input shaft, which is then locked to the drive pulley shaft. When reverse is selected, the sleeve engages with reverse driven gear, which is in constant mesh with an idler gear driven by transfer gears from the input shaft gear. In neutral, the sleeve is in an intermediate position, and the two shafts are not connected.

8 The drive pulley and driven pulley both consist of fixed and moving halves. The movement of the drive pulley halves is controlled hydraulically, while the driven pulley halves move under the influence of a spring and the tension exerted by the drivebelt. As the drive pulley opens, the driven pulley closes, and vice-versa. In this way, the transmission ratio between the two pulleys can be varied. The ratios are continuously variable between preset limits; the difference between the lowest and highest ratios available is approximately 5:1.

9 Hydraulic pressure is generated by a gear-type pump inside the transmission. The pump driveshaft runs inside the input and drive pulley shafts, and is splined to the centre of the engine flywheel. This means that hydraulic pressure is only generated when the engine is running, which is why a car with this type of transmission cannot be push- or tow-started.

10 Application of hydraulic pressure to the pulley halves is via a control unit, which receives information on accelerator pedal position, transmission selector lever position, transmission ratio currently in use, and drive pulley speed. From this information, the control unit determines whether, and in which direction, to change the pulley ratios.

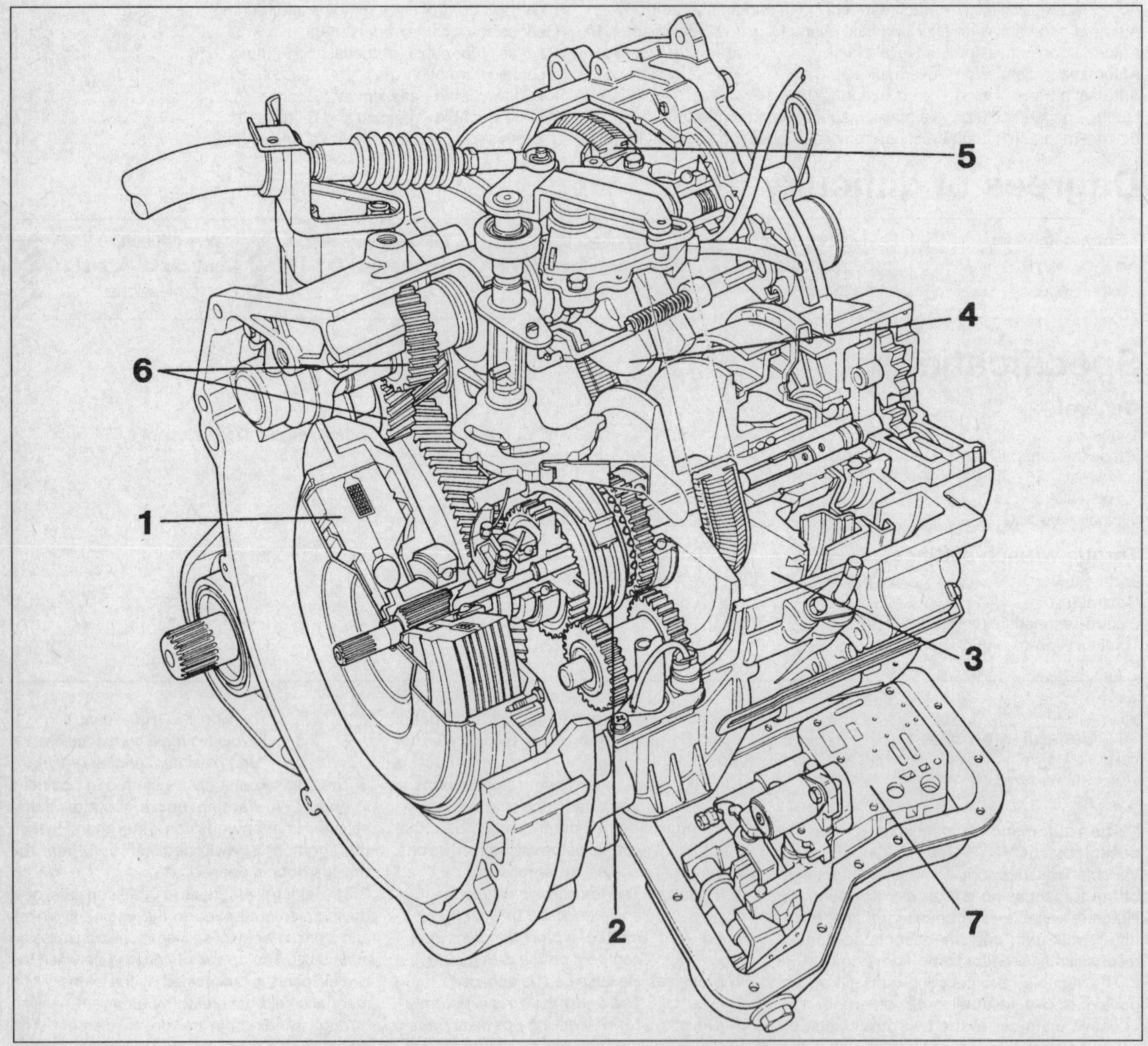

1.1a Cutaway view of the ECVT (electronic continuously variable transmission)

1 Electromagnetic clutch
2 Gear selector sleeve
3 Drive pulley
4 Driven pulley
5 Metal drivebelt
6 Final drive reduction gears
7 Hydraulic control unit

11 When reverse gear is selected, the control unit keeps the transmission in low ratio. If this were not the case, it would, in theory, be possible to drive as fast in reverse as in forward gear.

12 An electronic control unit supplies the current to energise the clutch. The control unit receives signals concerning engine speed, road speed, accelerator pedal position, and gear selector position. Sensors include the following.

a) Engine rpm sensor (from the injection/ignition control unit)
b) Accelerator pedal switch
c) Throttle valve position sensor
d) Selector lever position sensor
e) Vehicle speed sensor
f) Coolant temperature sensor
g) Air conditioning sensor
h) Brake switch
i) Torque signal

13 The final drive/differential unit is conventional. Drive from the driven pulley is transmitted to the differential by an intermediate reduction gear.

14 The ECVT incorporates a warning light which illuminates when a fault occurs.

Precautions

15 Observe the following precautions to avoid damage to the automatic transmission:

a) Do not attempt to start the engine by pushing or towing the car.
b) If the car has to be towed for recovery, the distance must not exceed 12 miles (20 km), and the speed must not exceed 19 mph (30 kph). If these conditions cannot be met, or if transmission damage is suspected, only tow the car with the front wheels clear of the ground.
c) Only engage P or R when the vehicle is stationary.

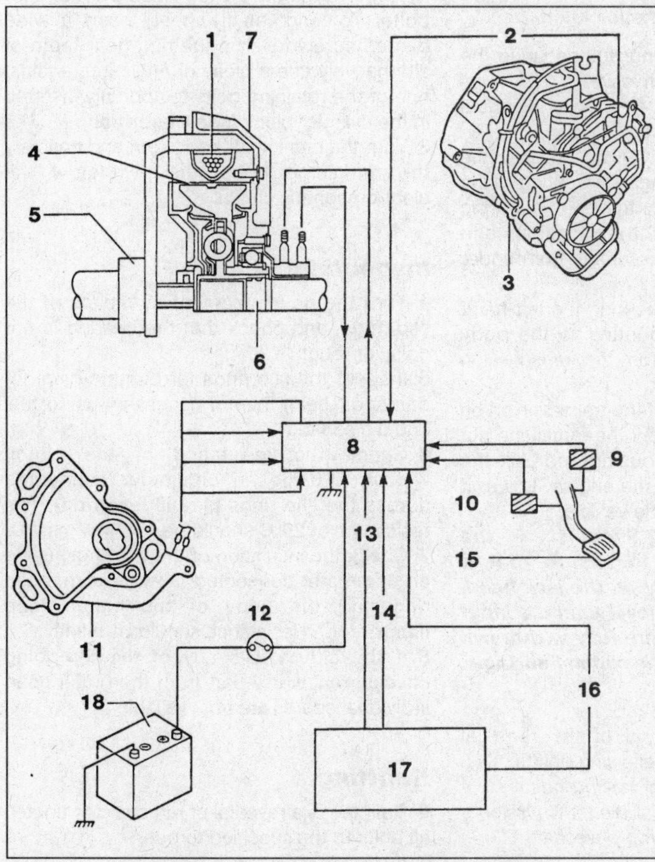

1.1b Electromagnetic clutch control system

1 Coil
2 Signal from vehicle speed sensor
3 Transmission
4 Electromagnetic powder
5 Drive shaft (driven by crankshaft)
6 Transmission input shaft
7 Electromagnetic clutch housing
8 ECVT control unit
9 Accelerator pedal micro switch
10 Throttle valve opening position potentiometer
11 Multifunction switch
12 Ignition switch
13 Air conditioning signal
14 Engine RPM signal
15 Accelerator pedal
16 Coolant temperature signal
17 Injection/ignition control unit
18 Battery

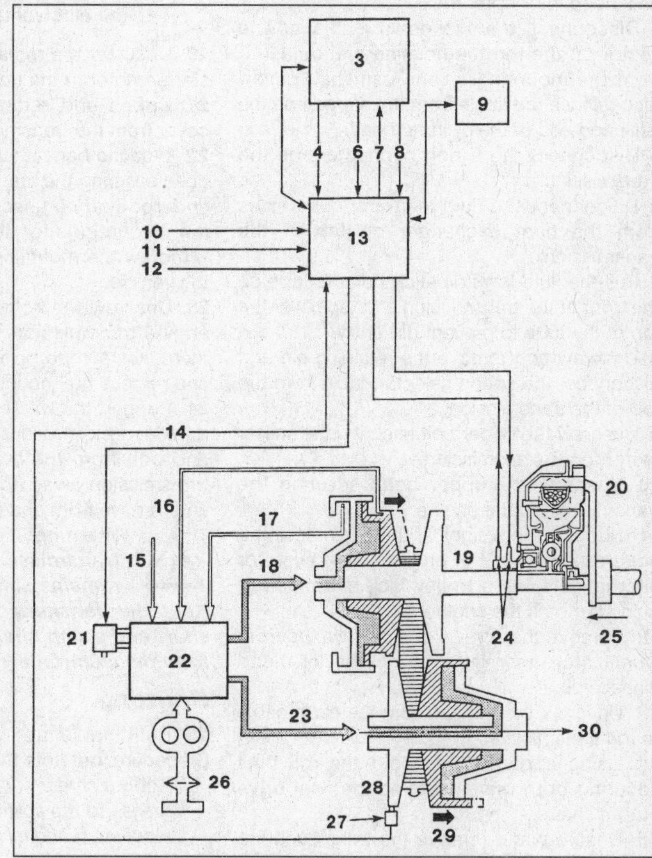

1.1c Hydraulic control system

3 Injection/ignition control unit
4 Air conditioner sensor signal
6 Coolant temperature signal
7 Clutch signal
8 Engine RPM signal
9 ECVT warning light
10 Selector lever position
11 Accelerator pedal switch/throttle valve potentiometer/torque signal
12 Brake switch
13 ECVT control unit
14 Signal from vehicle speed sensor
15 Accelerator pedal position switch
16 Pulley ratio
17 Input shaft RPM
18 Primary oil pressure
19 Primary pulley
20 Electromagnetic clutch
21 Pressure regulating solenoid valve
22 Oil pressure control valve
23 Secondary oil pressure
24 Slip ring
25 Drive from engine
26 Oil pump
27 Vehicle speed sensor
28 Secondary pulley
29 Belt and pulley
30 Drive to driveshafts

2 Automatic transmission - removal and refitting

Removal

1 Select a solid, level surface to park the vehicle upon. Give yourself enough space to move around it easily. Apply the handbrake then jack up the front of the vehicle and support on axle stands (see *Jacking and vehicle support*). Remove both front wheels.
2 Remove the battery and mounting tray as described in Chapter 5A.
3 Remove the air cleaner and air inlet duct as described in Chapter 4A.
4 Disconnect the kickdown cable at the sector on the throttle housing and detach it from the mounting on the camshaft cover. Also release the cable from the support on the left-hand end of the cylinder head.
5 Disconnect the wiring connectors on the transmission.
6 Disconnect the fluid inlet and outlet lines from the heat exchanger on top of the transmission.
7 Pull the fluid level dipstick from its tube on the front of the transmission and tape over the top of the tube to prevent dirt entry.
8 Unscrew and remove the retaining pin and disconnect the speed selector cable from the top of the transmission.
9 Unscrew the upper bolt securing the starter motor to the transmission.
10 Unscrew the upper bolts securing the transmission to the engine.
11 Support the weight of the engine using a hoist attached to the engine lifting eyes, or alternatively use a trolley jack and block of wood beneath the engine.
12 Remove the screws and remove the front wheel arch liner from under the left-hand wheel arch.
13 Unscrew the nut securing the earth cable to the transmission.
14 Using a punch drive out the roll pins securing both driveshafts to the final drive output shafts.
15 Unscrew and remove the bolts securing the left-hand swivel hub assembly to the front suspension strut, then separate the components and support the swivel hub on an axle stand.
16 Move the swivel hub assembly outwards and slide the inner end of the driveshaft from the splines on the transmission output shaft. Support the shaft away from the transmission to prevent damage to the gaiters.
17 Unscrew the Lambda/oxygen sensor from the exhaust downpipe and position it in a safe place to prevent damage.
18 Unscrew the nuts securing the downpipe to the exhaust manifold, then lower it and support on an axle stand. Recover the gasket.
19 Unscrew the knurled nut and disconnect the speedometer cable from the top of the final drive housing.

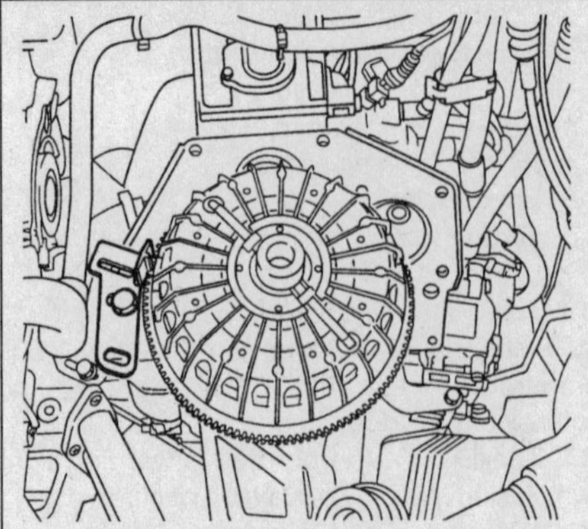

3.2 Locking the flywheel when removing the electromagnetic clutch

20 Unscrew the remaining bolt securing the starter motor to the transmission
21 Unbolt and remove the lower flywheel cover from the transmission.
22 Working beneath the vehicle, unscrew the bolts securing the rear engine mounting to the underbody then unscrew the bolts securing the mounting to the transmission and withdraw the mounting assembly from under the vehicle.
23 Unscrew the bolts securing the left-hand engine/transmission mounting to the body then unscrew the bolts from the transmission and remove the mounting.
24 Support the weight of the transmission on a trolley jack then unscrew the remaining nut and bolt from the bellhousing and pull the transmission away from the engine. Lower it and remove from under the vehicle.

Warning: Support the transmission to ensure that it remains steady on the jack head. Keep the transmission level until the input shaft and pump shaft are fully withdrawn from the electromagnetic clutch housing.

Refitting

25 Refitting is a reversal of the removal procedure, but note the following points.
a) Apply a smear of high-melting-point grease to the splines of the transmission input shaft and oil pump driveshaft.
b) Tighten all nuts and bolts to the specified torque, where given.
c) Renew both driveshaft roll pins.

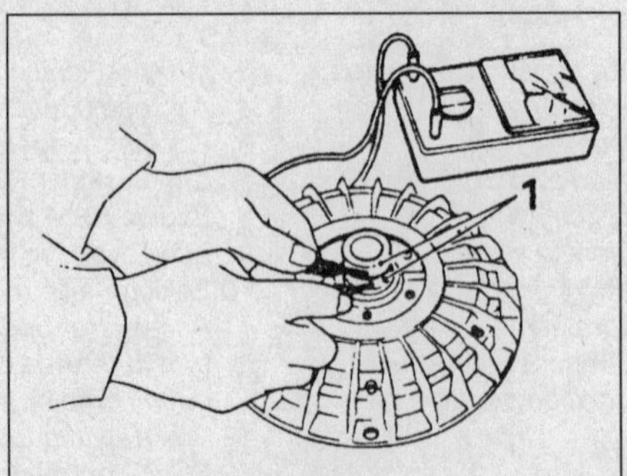

3.6 Checking the resistance of the clutch windings

1 Slip rings

3 Electro-magnetic clutch - removal, inspection and refitting

Removal

1 Remove the transmission as described in Section 2.
2 Turn the flywheel so that two of the four mounting bolts are accessible. Hold the flywheel stationary then unscrew the two bolts. To hold the flywheel, insert a wide bladed screwdriver in the ring gear teeth or alternatively use a piece of angle iron against one of the retaining bolts temporarily inserted in the cylinder block **(see illustration)**.
3 Turn the crankshaft half a turn and unscrew the remaining bolts, then withdraw the electromagnetic clutch.

Inspection

4 Turn the driven element by means of the slip rings, and check that the bearing is not noisy or rough.
5 Inspect the slip rings for burning or other damage. Clean them if necessary using fuel and a clean rag.
6 Check the resistance of the clutch windings, using an ohmmeter connected across the slip rings **(see illustration)**. The resistance at 20°C should be 2 to 4 ohms.
7 Check the insulation of the windings, using an ohmmeter connected between either slip ring and the body of the clutch **(see illustration)**. Resistance should be infinity.
8 If the clutch fails any of the foregoing checks, renew it. Apart from the brush gear, individual spares are not available.

Refitting

9 Refitting is a reversal of removal but tighten all bolts to the specified torque.

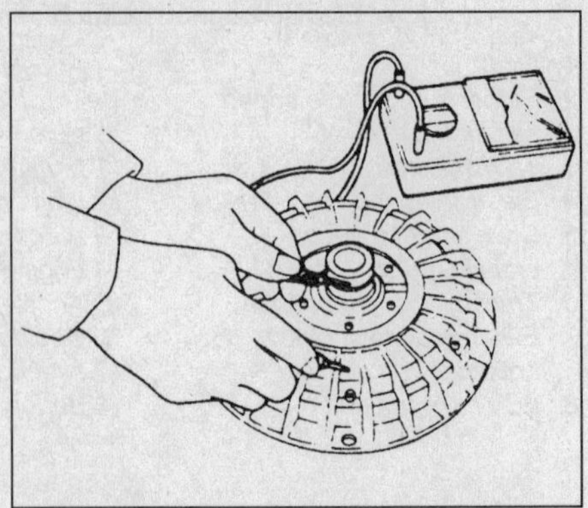

3.7 Checking the insulation of the clutch windings

4 Electro-magnetic clutch brushes - removal, inspection and refitting

Removal

1 Remove the battery and battery tray as described in Chapter 5A.

2 Disconnect the wiring connector for the brushes. The brush holder is located near the dipstick tube.

3 Unscrew the mounting screws and withdraw the brush holder from the transmission **(see illustration)**.

Inspection

4 Inspect the brushes. If they are worn down to the limit lines, or if they do not move smoothly in their holders, renew the brush carrier assembly **(see illustration)**. **Note:** *Be careful not to damage the brush supply leads when checking the brushes for free movement.* It is not possible to renew the brushes separately.

Refitting

5 Refitting is a reversal of removal.

5 Electronic control unit - removal and refitting

Removal

1 Disconnect the battery negative terminal (refer to *Disconnecting the battery* in the Reference Section of this manual).

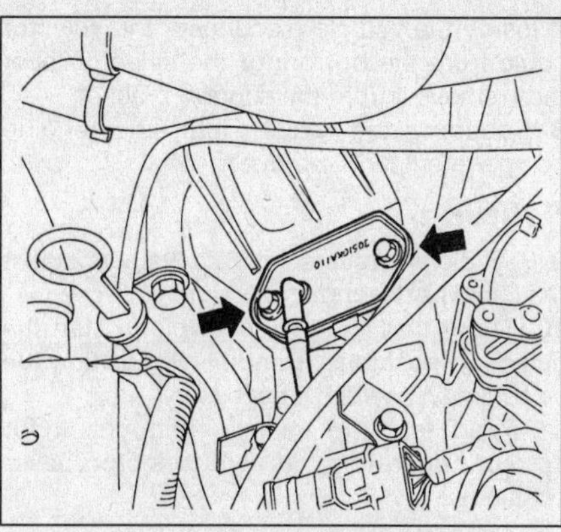

4.3 Brush holder mounting screws on top of the transmission

2 Unscrew the mounting screws and remove the centre console.

3 Unscrew the mounting bracket screws, lower the control unit then disconnect the two wiring connectors **(see illustration)**. Withdraw the unit from inside the vehicle.

Refitting

4 Refitting is a reversal of removal.

6 Kickdown cable - removal and refitting

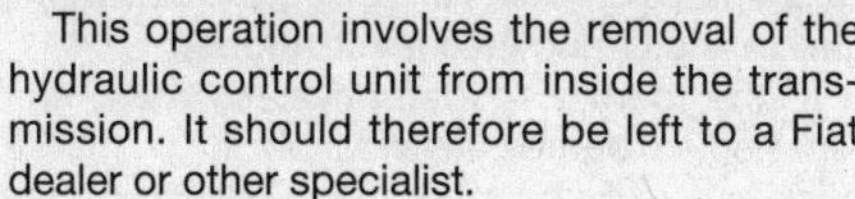

This operation involves the removal of the hydraulic control unit from inside the transmission. It should therefore be left to a Fiat dealer or other specialist.

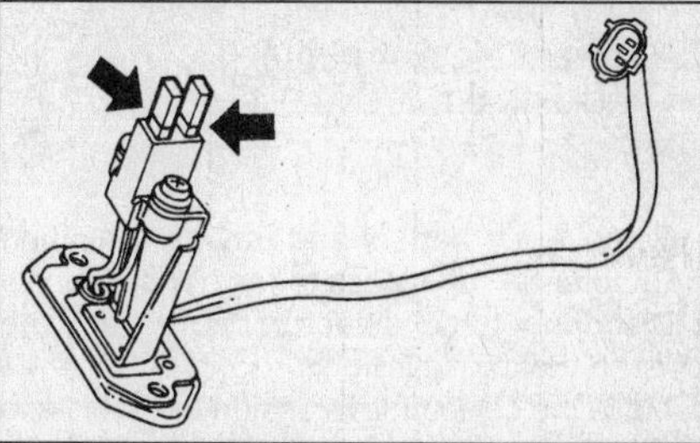

4.4 Wear limit lines on the brushes

7 Kickdown cable - adjustment

1 Remove the air cleaner and air inlet duct assembly as described in Chapter 4A. The throttle cable is located on top of the throttle housing sector and the kickdown cable is located on the bottom of the sector **(see illustration)**.

2 Turn the throttle housing sector fully clockwise so that the throttle is wide open, then position the kickdown outer cable so that its inner cable is slightly tensioned. Make the adjustment at the two adjustment nuts on the support bracket.

3 Check and if necessary adjust the accelerator cable as described in Chapter 4A.

4 Fully depress the accelerator pedal then check that there is approximately 0.5 to 1.0 mm free travel available on the kickdown cable. If necessary re-adjust the kickdown cable until it is set correctly.

5 Road test the vehicle and check for correct operation.

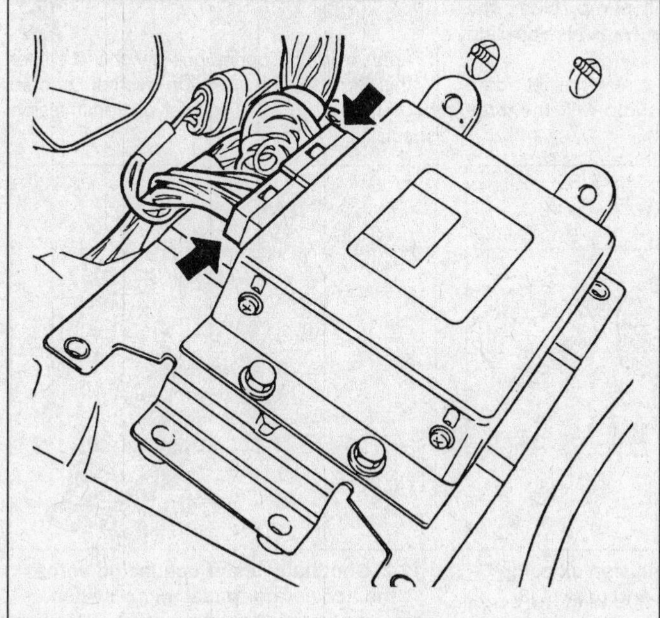

5.3 Wiring connectors on the electronic control unit

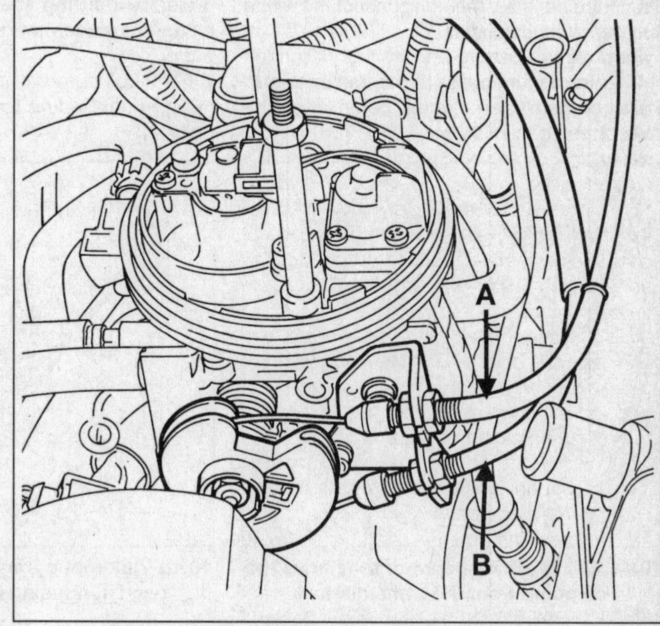

7.1 The throttle cable (A) is located on top of the throttle housing sector and the kickdown cable (B) on the bottom

8 Gear selector cable - adjustment

1 Remove the battery and tray as described in Chapter 5A for access to the transmission.
2 Disconnect the selector cable from the lever on the transmission.
3 Move the selector lever inside the vehicle to the N (Neutral) position, then move the lever on the transmission to its central (Neutral) position. Locate the cable end over the lever. If the cable end fitting does not line up exactly with the hole in the lever, loosen the adjustment nut and reposition the end fitting.
4 With the adjustment correct reconnect the cable to the lever, then move the selector lever to the P (Park) position. Check that the lever on the transmission has also moved to the P position.
5 Refit the battery and tray as described in Chapter 5A.
6 Road test the vehicle, and check for correct operation in all selector lever positions.

9 Gear selector cable - removal and refitting

Removal

1 Using an Allen key, unscrew the screw and remove the selector lever knob from the lever.
2 Remove the oddment tray and the ashtray.
3 Remove the screws and withdraw the centre console and selector mechanism cover.
4 Unscrew the mounting screws, slightly lift the centre console, then disconnect the wiring and remove the console.
5 Remove the battery and tray as described in Chapter 5A for access to the transmission.
6 Disconnect the selector cable from the lever on the transmission.
7 Inside the vehicle disconnect the selector cable from the bottom of the selector lever then remove it from the support bracket.
8 Withdraw the cable into the engine compartment, and remove it.

Refitting

9 Refitting is a reversal of removal, but adjust the cable as described in Section 8.
10 Check that it is only possible to start the engine in positions P and N. Reposition the selector lever switch if necessary.
11 Road test the vehicle, and check for correct operation in all selector lever positions.

10 Transmission oil pump - removal and refitting

Removal

1 Apply the handbrake, then jack up the front of the vehicle and support on axle stands (see *Jacking and vehicle support*). Remove the left-hand wheel.
2 Unscrew the screws and remove the wheel arch liner.
3 Working through the left-hand wheel arch, remove the three bolts which secure the oil pump.
4 Attach a slide hammer to the oil pump, using the two tapped holes provided. Withdraw the pump using the slide hammer. Be prepared for some oil spillage. Recover the gasket and O-ring **(see illustrations)**.
5 If the pump is defective, it must be renewed; no spares are available.

Refitting

6 Before refitting the oil pump, clean the mating surfaces of the transmission and pump.
7 Fit the oil pump, using a new gasket and a new O-ring. Secure the pump with the three bolts.
8 Refit the wheel arch liner, then refit the wheel and lower the vehicle to the ground.
9 Check the transmission fluid level as described earlier in this Section, and top-up if necessary.

11 Accelerator pedal micro-switch(es) - checking and adjustment

1 Correct adjustment of the micro-switch which senses the accelerator pedal position is essential for correct operation of the clutch. A quick check can be made by listening for the switch clicking as the accelerator is depressed. For an accurate check, proceed as follows.
2 Disconnect the microswitch wiring connector inside the vehicle. Connect a continuity tester across the terminals of the switch, located at the top of the pedal box **(see illustration)**.
3 Remove the air cleaner and air ducting as described in Chapter 4A.
4 With the accelerator pedal released, the switch must be closed (zero resistance). Slowly depress the pedal, and check that the switch opens when the throttle valve on the throttle housing is 30° open. This will occur when the pedal has travelled between 3 and 7 mm. Adjust the switch position if necessary.
5 If the switch is permanently open or permanently closed, and adjustment makes no difference, renew it.
6 Remake the original wiring connections on completion.

12 Automatic transmission - overhaul

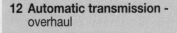

Apart from the operations described earlier in this Section, transmission overhaul should be entrusted to a Fiat dealer or transmission specialist.

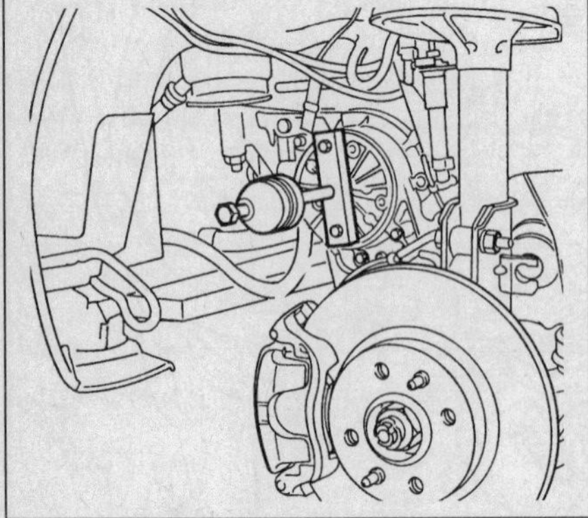

10.4a Using a slide hammer to remove the oil pump from the transmission

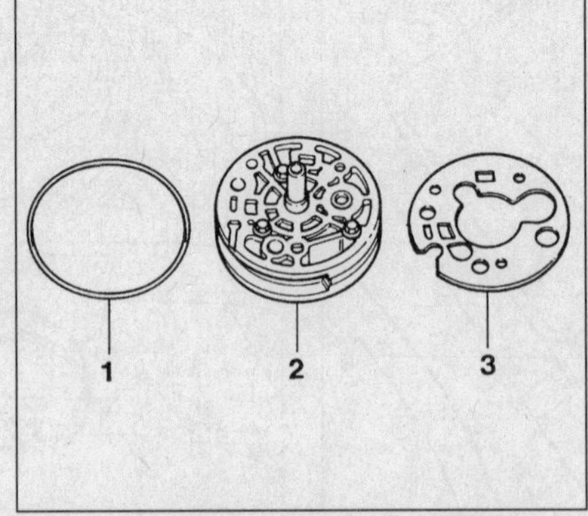

10.4b Automatic transmission oil pump O-ring (1), housing (2) and gasket (3)

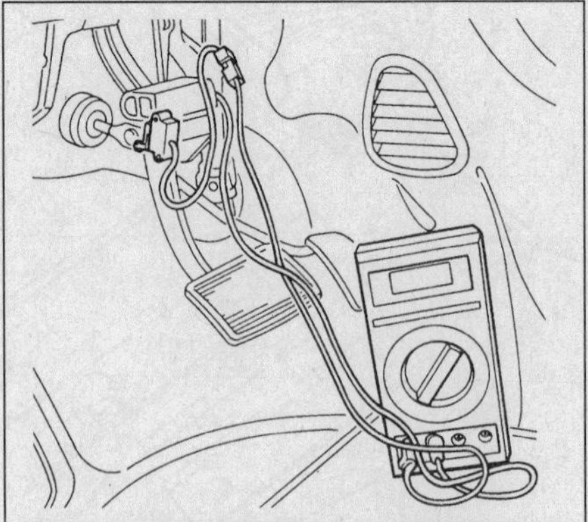

11.2 Continuity tester connected across the accelerator pedal micro-switch

Chapter 8
Driveshafts

Contents

Degrees of difficulty

Easy, suitable for novice with little experience 	**Fairly easy,** suitable for beginner with some experience 	**Fairly difficult,** suitable for competent DIY mechanic 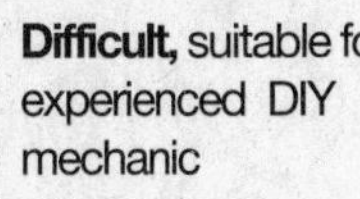	**Difficult,** suitable for experienced DIY mechanic 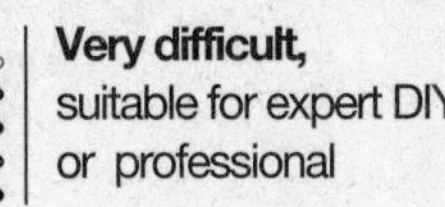	**Very difficult,** suitable for expert DIY or professional

Specifications

General

Type	Unequal-length, solid steel shafts, splined to inner and outer constant velocity joints. Intermediate shaft with support bearing on turbo diesel models with equal length driveshafts.

Lubrication

Lubricant type	Fiat specification grease, supplied with gaiter repair kit

Torque wrench settings

	Nm	lbf ft
Driveshaft nut*		
All models except turbo diesel (M22 plain)	240	177
Turbo diesel (M24 with staking and captive washer)	280	207
Roadwheel bolts	85	63
Suspension strut-to-hub carrier bolts	70	52
Track-rod balljoint-to-hub carrier	40	30

**Use a new nut.*

1 General information

Power is transmitted from the differential to the roadwheels by the driveshafts, via inboard and outboard constant velocity (CV) joints **(see illustrations)**.

An intermediate drive shaft, with its own support bearing is fitted between the gearbox output and right-hand drive shafts on turbo diesel models **(see illustration overleaf)**. This layout has the effect of equalising driveshaft angles at all suspension positions and reduces driveshaft flexing, which improves directional stability, particularly under acceleration.

The outer Rzeppa type CV joints allow smooth transmission of drive to the wheels at all steering and suspension angles. Drive is transmitted by means of a number of radially static steel balls that run in grooves between the two halves of the joint.

The type of inboard CV joint fitted is model dependant. Those fitted to all except the turbo diesel models are of the plunge-cup type; drive is transmitted across the joint by means of three rollers, mounted on the driveshaft in a tripod arrangement, that are radially static but are free to slide in the grooved plunge cup.

The inboard CV joints fitted to turbo diesel models are of the Rzeppa type, similar to those at the outboard end of the driveshaft. On the right-hand driveshaft, the joint is bolted directly to the end of the intermediate driveshaft flange. On the left-hand driveshaft, the joint is bolted to the transmission output shaft flange.

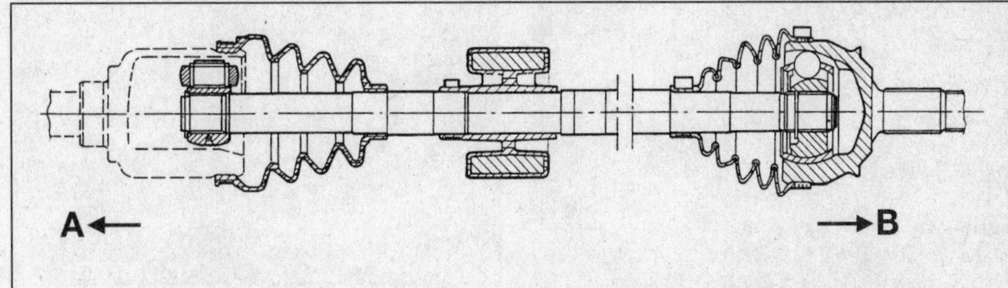

1.1a Cross section of driveshaft - petrol and non-turbo diesel models
A Transmission side *B Roadwheel side*

8

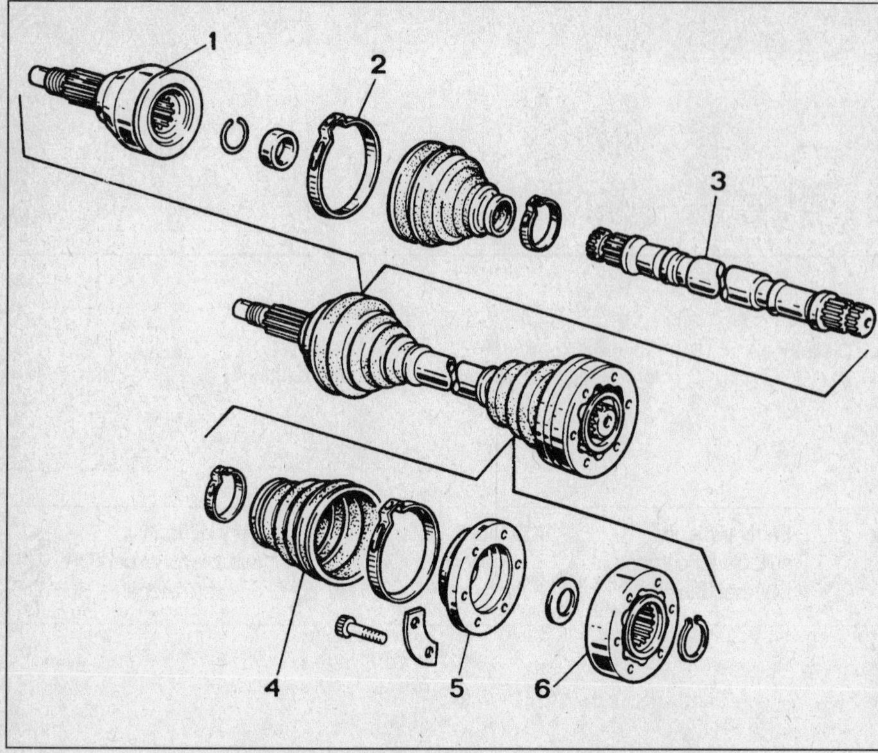

1.1b Exploded view of driveshaft - turbo diesel models

1 Outboard CV joint
2 Gaiter clip
3 Driveshaft
4 Gaiter
5 Flange
6 Inboard CV joint

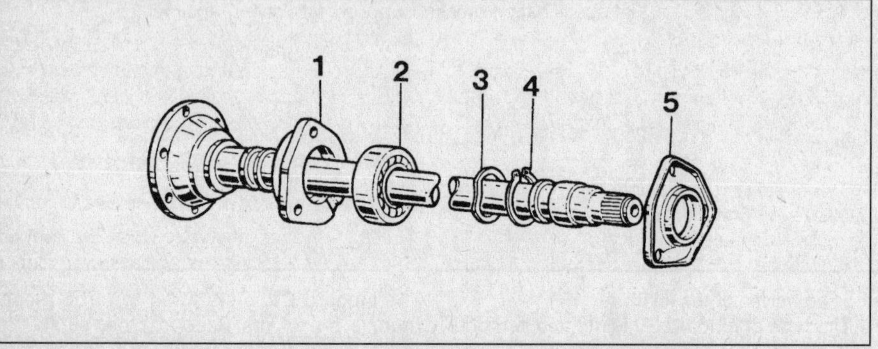

1.2 Intermediate driveshaft - turbo diesel models

1 Bearing flange
2 Bearing
3 Washer
4 Circlip
5 Retaining plate

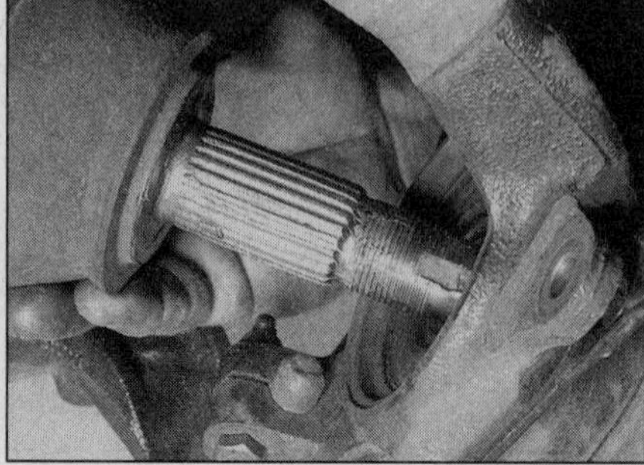

2.5 Extracting the driveshaft from the hub carrier

2.7 Remove the driveshaft gaiter clip (arrowed) from the CV joint at the transmission

The joints are protected by rubber gaiters and are packed with grease, to provide permanent lubrication. If wear is detected in the joint, it can be detached from the driveshaft and renewed. Normally, the CV joints do not require additional lubrication, unless they have been overhauled or the rubber gaiters have been damaged, allowing the grease to become contaminated. Refer to Chapter 1A or 1B for guidance in checking the condition of the driveshaft gaiters.

Both driveshafts are splined at their outer ends, to accept the wheel hubs, and are threaded so that the hubs can be fastened to the driveshafts by means of a large, staked nut.

2 Driveshafts - removal and refitting

Note: *A balljoint separator tool will be required for this operation. A new driveshaft nut and track-rod end nut should be used on refitting. In addition, new lower arm balljoint nuts should be used.*

Removal

1 Chock the rear wheels, apply the handbrake, then jack up the front of the vehicle and support on axle stands (see *Jacking and vehicle support*). Remove the appropriate roadwheel(s).

2 The front hub must be held stationary in order to loosen the driveshaft nut. Ideally, the hub should be held by a suitable tool bolted into place using two of the roadwheel nuts. Alternatively, have an assistant firmly apply the brake pedal to prevent the hub from rotating. Using a socket and extension bar, slacken and remove the driveshaft nut. Recover the washer (where fitted).

Warning: The nut is extremely tight. Discard the nut - a new one must be used on refitting.

3 Remove the locking clip and extract the brake caliper hydraulic hose (and where applicable, the brake pad wear indicator cable) from the bracket on the base of the suspension strut.

4 With reference to Chapter 10, Section 3, unbolt the base of the suspension strut from the top of the hub carrier.

5 Temporarily refit the driveshaft nut to the end of the driveshaft, to prevent damage to the driveshaft threads, then using a soft-faced mallet, carefully tap the driveshaft from the hub carrier **(see illustration)**. If the shaft is a tight fit, a suitable hub puller can be used to force the end of the shaft from the hub. Support the end of the driveshaft - do not allow the end of the driveshaft to hang down as this will strain the joint components and gaiters.

6 Proceed as follows, according to which driveshaft is to be removed.

All models except turbo diesels

7 Remove the driveshaft gaiter clip from the CV joint at the transmission **(see illustration)**,

2.9 **On turbo diesel models, unscrew the driveshaft Allen bolts (right-hand driveshaft shown)**

2.13 **Fitting a new driveshaft nut**

then pull the driveshaft away from the plunge cup. Position a container underneath the joint to catch any grease that may escape (driveshaft grease becomes liquid with use).

8 Remove the driveshaft from under the vehicle. Cover the open plunge cup on the vehicle to prevent the ingress of dirt; use a plastic bag secured with elastic bands.

Turbo diesel models

9 Unscrew the six Allen bolts securing the inboard end of the driveshaft to the intermediate shaft flange (right hand driveshaft) or gearbox output shaft flange (left hand driveshaft flange) **(see illustration)**. Recover the reinforcement plates (where fitted).

10 Remove the driveshaft from under the vehicle. Cover the exposed flange at the gearbox/intermediate shaft, to prevent the ingress of dirt; use a plastic bag secured with elastic bands.

11 Loosely refit one of the strut lower mounting bolts, to support the hub carrier whilst the driveshaft is out of the vehicle.

Refitting

12 After removing the temporarily-fitted bolt from the strut mounting, pivot the hub carrier away from the vehicle and push the splined end of the driveshaft into the hub.

13 Fit a new driveshaft nut, but do not fully tighten it at this point **(see illustration)**.

14 Support the driveshaft with one hand and push the hub carrier back towards the vehicle.

All models except turbo diesels

15 Re-engage the tripod at the inboard end of the driveshaft with the plunge cup at the gearbox. Slide the gaiter into position over the joint and briefly lift the lip of the gaiter to expel any air trapped inside. Ensure that the gaiter is seated squarely over the universal joint, then fit a new clip around the centre of the joint to secure it in place.

Turbo diesel models

16 Align the inboard end of the driveshaft joint with the intermediate shaft flange. Refit the six driveshaft bolts and tighten them securely.

All models

17 Refit the suspension strut-to-hub carrier bolts and tighten them to the correct torque - refer to Chapter 10 for details.

18 Refit the brake caliper hydraulic hose (and where applicable, the brake pad wear indicator cable) to the bracket on the base of the suspension strut.

19 Refit the roadwheel and bolts.

20 Lower the vehicle to the ground and tighten the driveshaft nut to the specified torque. Stake the rim of the nut into the machined recess in the end of the driveshaft, using a hammer and punch **(see illustrations)**.

21 Tighten the wheel bolts to the specified torque and refit the wheel trim/centre cap.

3 Driveshaft overhaul and rubber gaiter renewal

1 Remove the driveshaft from the vehicle as described in Section 2.

2 Unfasten the remainder of the rubber gaiter securing clips. Slide the gaiters towards the centre of the shaft, away from the joints. Wipe off the majority of the old grease with a rag.

Outboard CV joint - removal

All models except turbo diesels

3 Mark the relationship between the joint and the driveshaft using a scriber or a dab of paint. Using pair of circlip pliers, expand the circlip that holds the driveshaft in place and withdraw the shaft from the CV joint. Note that the circlip is captive in the joint, and need not be removed, unless it appears damaged or worn **(see illustration overleaf)**.

2.20a **Tighten the driveshaft nut to the specified torque (roadwheel removed for clarity)**

2.20b **Stake the rim of the nut into the recess in the driveshaft**

2.20c **Recess machined into end of the driveshaft**

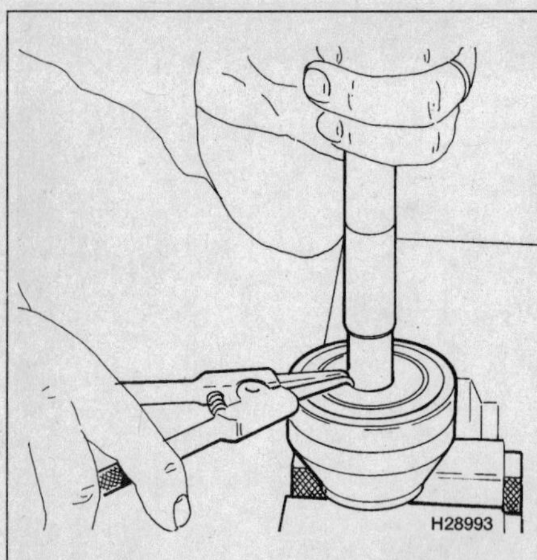

3.3 Using pair of circlip pliers, expand the circlip that holds the driveshaft in place

Turbo diesel models

4 Mark the relationship between the joint and the driveshaft using a scriber or a dab of paint. Attach a slide hammer to the driveshaft nut thread.

5 Draw the joint off the driveshaft using the slide hammer. Use just enough effort to overcome the tension of the internal circlip.

Inboard CV joint removal

All models except turbo diesels

6 At the inboard end of the driveshaft, use a hammer and centre punch to mark the relationship between the shaft and joint. Remove the circlip with a pair of circlip pliers, then using a three-legged puller if required, draw the tripod joint off the end of the driveshaft. Ensure that the legs of the puller bear upon the cast centre section of the joint, not the roller bearings **(see illustration)**.

Turbo diesel models

7 At the inboard end of the driveshaft, use a hammer and centre punch to mark the relationship between the shaft and joint. Remove the circlip with a pair of circlip pliers, then carefully slide the CV joint from the end of the shaft. Take great care to prevent the cage and ball bearings from falling out - secure the joint components together with wire or a nylon cable-tie.

8 Remove the washer then slide the flange from the end of the shaft.

Inspection

9 Slide both rubber gaiters off the driveshaft and discard them; it is recommended that new ones are fitted on reassembly as a matter of course. Recover the flexible washers (where fitted), making a note of their fitted positions, to aid correct refitting later.

10 Thoroughly clean the driveshaft splines, and CV joint components with paraffin or a suitable solvent, taking care not to destroy any alignment marks made during removal.

11 Examine the CV joint components for wear and damage; in particular, check the balls and corresponding grooves for pitting and corrosion. If evidence of wear is visible, then the joint must be renewed. Note that if the outboard CV joint is to be renewed on turbo diesel models, it must be matched to the driveshaft using the colour-coded paint markings.

12 Where applicable, examine the tripod joint components for wear. Check that the three rollers are free to rotate without resistance and are not worn, damaged or corroded. The rollers are supported by arrays of needle bearings; wear or damage will show up as play in the rollers and/or roughness in rotation. If wear is discovered, the tripod joint must be renewed.

13 Fit a new rubber gaiter (and where applicable, flexible washer) to the inboard end of the driveshaft and secure it in place on the shaft with a clip **(see illustration)**.

Inboard CV joint - refitting

All models except turbo diesels

14 Using the alignment marks made during removal, fit the tripod joint onto the splines of the driveshaft. Tap it into position using a soft faced mallet. To ensure that the tripod joint rollers and driveshaft splines are not damaged, use a socket with an internal diameter slightly larger than that of the driveshaft as a drift. Refit the circlip.

15 Slide the gaiter over the tripod joint and pack the gaiter with grease from the service kit.

Caution: Do not allow grease to come into contact with vehicles paintwork, as discolouring may result.

Turbo diesel models

16 Slide the flange and washer onto the end of the shaft, then fit the joint into position on the driveshaft splines, using the alignment marks made during removal. Fit the circlip.

17 Pack the gaiter with grease from the service kit, then slide the gaiter over the joint. Briefly lift the lip of the gaiter to expel all the air from the joint, then secure the gaiter over the joint with a new clip.

Caution: Do not allow grease to come into contact with the vehicle's paintwork, as discolouring may result.

Outboard CV joint - refitting

18 Fit a new rubber gaiter to the outboard end of the driveshaft and secure it place with a clip.

19 Pack the CV joint with grease from the service kit, pushing it into the ball grooves and expelling any air that may be trapped underneath.

20 Lubricate the splines of the drive shaft with a smear of grease, then whilst splaying the circlip open with a pair of circlip pliers, insert the driveshaft into CV joint, observing the alignment marks made during removal. **Note:** *On turbo diesel models, the circlip snaps into the CV joint groove as the driveshaft is inserted - no circlip pliers are required*. Ensure that the circlip snaps securely into place; pull on the shaft to check that it is held firmly in position.

21 Pack additional grease into the joint to displace any air pockets, then slide the rubber gaiter over the joint. Briefly lift the lip of the gaiter to expel all the air from the joint, then secure it in place with a clip.

22 Refit the driveshaft (see Section 2).

4 Intermediate driveshaft - removal and refitting

Note 1: *This procedure applies only to turbo diesel engined models.*

Note 2: *The intermediate shaft and bearing are not available as separate spares and can only be renewed as a complete assembly.*

Removal

1 Firmly apply the handbrake, then jack up the front of the car and support it securely on axle stands (see *Jacking and vehicle support*). Remove the appropriate roadwheel(s).

2 Unbolt the inboard end of the right-hand driveshaft from the intermediate shaft flange, as described in Section 2. Suspend the disconnected end of the driveshaft from a convenient point on the subframe, using wire or a cable-tie, to avoid straining the joint and gaiter.

3 Drain the oil from the transmission, with reference to Chapter 1B.

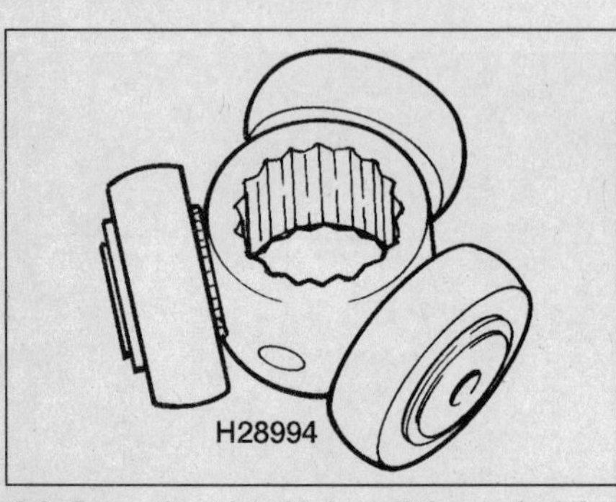

3.6 Draw the tripod joint off the end of the driveshaft

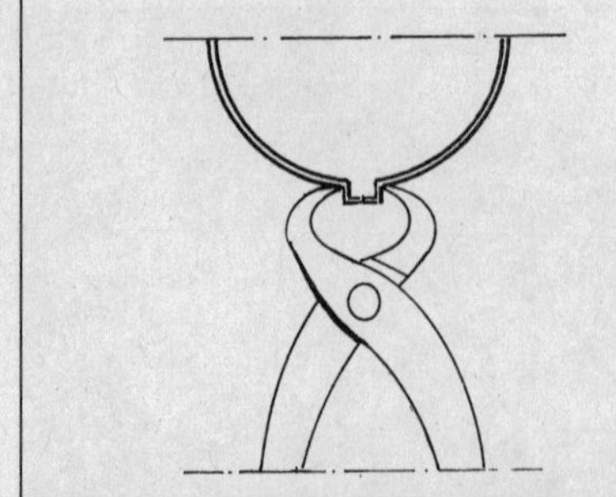

3.13 Fit a new rubber gaiter to the inboard end of the driveshaft and secure it in place with a clip

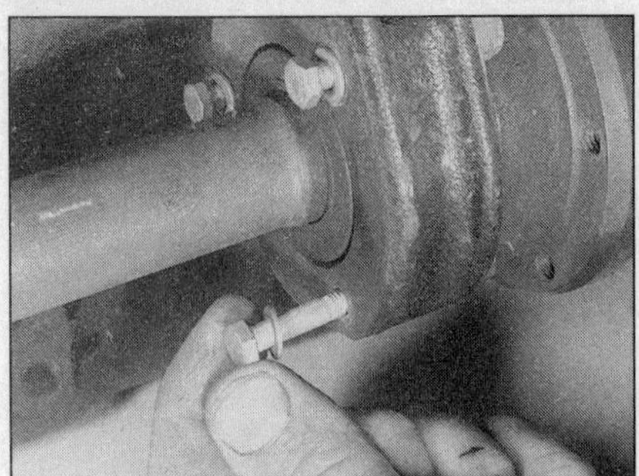
4.4 Unbolt the intermediate shaft from the support bracket

4.5a Withdraw the intermediate shaft from the transmission

4.5b Recover the dust seal

4 Unbolt the intermediate shaft from the support bracket **(see illustration)**.

5 Attach a slide hammer to the intermediate shaft flange and draw the splined end of the shaft out of the transmission. Take care to avoid damaging the oil seal. Recover the dust seal **(see illustrations)**.

Refitting

6 Before installing the driveshaft, examine the oil seal in the transmission for signs of damage or deterioration and, if necessary, renew it (it is advisable to renew the seal as a matter of course).

7 Thoroughly clean the intermediate shaft splines and the aperture in the transmission. Fit a new dust seal to the shaft, then apply a thin film of grease to the oil seal lips, and to the intermediate shaft splines and shoulders.

8 Push the shaft squarely into the transmission, taking care to avoid damaging the oil seal.

9 Line up the intermediate shaft bearing with the support bracket, then insert the bolts and tighten them securely.

10 Refit the right-hand driveshaft as described in Section 2, then refit the roadwheel and lower the vehicle to the ground. Tighten the roadwheel bolts to the specified torque.

11 On completion refill the transmission with the specified quantity and grade of oil, as described in Chapter 1B.

Chapter 9
Braking system

Contents

Degrees of difficulty

Easy, suitable for novice with little experience 

Fairly easy, suitable for beginner with some experience 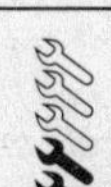

Fairly difficult, suitable for competent DIY mechanic 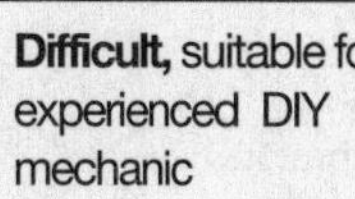

Difficult, suitable for experienced DIY mechanic

Very difficult, suitable for expert DIY or professional

Specifications

Front disc brakes

Type	Disc with single-piston sliding calipers
Disc diameter:	
Petrol models with single-point injection	240.0 mm
Petrol models with multi-point injection	257.0 mm
Non-turbo diesel models	240.0 mm
Turbo diesel models	257.0 mm
Disc thickness (new):	
Petrol models with single-point injection	10.80 to 11.10 mm
Petrol models with multi-point injection	11.80 to 12.10 mm
Non-turbo diesel models	10.80 to 11.10 mm
Turbo diesel models	11.80 to 12.10 mm
Minimum disc thickness (wear limit):	
Petrol models with single-point injection	9.20 mm
Petrol models with multi-point injection	10.20 mm
Non-turbo diesel models	9.20 mm
Turbo diesel models	10.20 mm
Maximum disc runout	0.15 mm
Brake pad friction material minimum thickness	1.5 mm

Rear drum brakes

Drum inner diameter (new)	180.0 to 180.25 mm
Maximum drum diameter (wear limit)	181.35 mm
Minimum brake shoe lining thickness	2.0 mm

Torque wrench settings

Torque wrench settings	Nm	lbf ft
Bleed screw	6	4
Brake disc locating studs	12	9
Brake drum locating studs	12	9
Brake pipe and hose unions	14	10
Front caliper mounting bracket-to-hub carrier bolts	53	39
Front caliper-to-caliper bracket guide pin bolts	12	9
Rear wheel cylinder mounting bolts	10	7
Roadwheel bolts	85	63

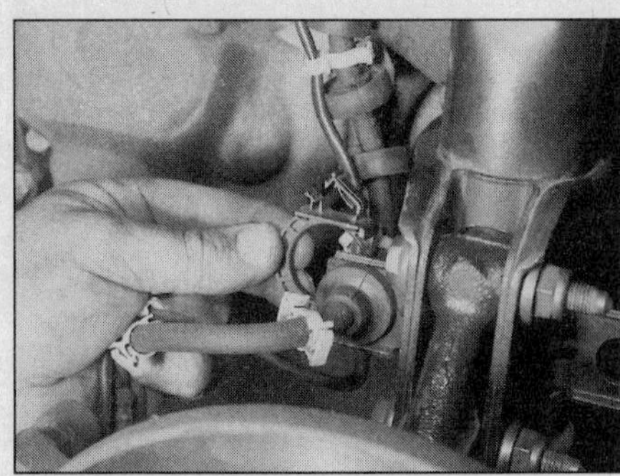

2.3a Release the locking clip . . .

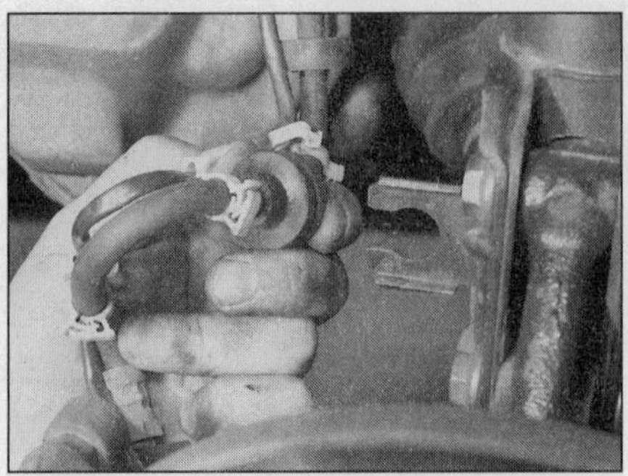

2.3b . . . and remove the pad wear indicator wiring and brake fluid line from the suspension strut

1 General information

The braking system is of the vacuum servo-assisted, dual-circuit hydraulic type. The arrangement of the hydraulic system is such that each circuit operates one front and one rear brake from a tandem master cylinder. Under normal circumstances, both circuits operate in unison. However, in the event of hydraulic failure in one circuit, full braking force will still be available at two diagonally-opposite wheels.

All models covered in this manual are fitted with front disc brakes and rear drum brakes.

The front disc brakes are actuated by single-piston sliding type calipers, which ensure that equal pressure is applied to each brake pad.

The rear drum brakes incorporate leading and trailing shoes, which are actuated by twin-piston wheel cylinders. A self-adjust mechanism is incorporated, to automatically compensate for brake shoe wear. As the brake shoe linings wear, the footbrake operation automatically operates the adjuster mechanism, which effectively lengthens the shoe strut and repositions the brake shoes, to remove the lining-to-drum clearance.

The mechanical handbrake linkage operates the brake shoes via a lever attached to the trailing brake shoe.

Load sensitive proportioning valves operate on the rear brake hydraulic circuits, to prevent the possibility of the rear wheels locking before the front wheels under heavy braking.

Note: *When servicing any part of the system, work carefully and methodically; also observe scrupulous cleanliness when overhauling any part of the hydraulic system. Always renew components (in axle sets, where applicable) if in doubt about their condition, and use only genuine Fiat replacement parts, or at least those of known good quality. Note the warnings given in Safety first and at relevant points in this Chapter concerning the dangers of asbestos dust and hydraulic fluid.*

Models with anti-lock braking system (ABS)

Available as an option on certain models, the anti-lock braking system prevents skidding which not only optimises stopping distances but allows full steering control to be maintained under maximum braking.

By electronically monitoring the speed of each roadwheel in relation to the other wheels, the system can detect when a wheel is about to lock-up, before control is actually lost. The brake fluid pressure applied to that wheel's brake caliper is then decreased and restored (or modulated) several times a second until control is regained.

The system components comprise an Electronic Control Unit (ECU), four wheel speed sensors, a hydraulic unit, brake lines and dashboard mounted warning lamps.

The hydraulic unit incorporates a tandem master cylinder, a valve block which modulates the pressure in the brake hydraulic circuits during ABS operation, an accumulator which provides a supply of highly pressurised brake fluid, a hydraulic pump to charge the accumulator and an integral electronic control unit (ECU).

The four wheel sensors are mounted on the wheel hubs. The ECU uses the signals produced by the sensors to calculate the rotational speed of each wheel.

The ECU has a self-diagnostic capability and will inhibit the operation of the ABS if a fault is detected, lighting the dashboard mounted warning lamp. The braking system will then revert to conventional, non-ABS operation. If the nature of the fault is not immediately obvious upon inspection, the vehicle must be taken to a Fiat dealer, who will have the diagnostic equipment required to interrogate the ABS ECU electronically and pin-point the problem.

2 Front brake pads - renewal

Warning: Renew BOTH sets of front brake pads at the same time - NEVER renew the pads on only one wheel, as uneven braking may result.

Warning: Note that the dust created by wear of the pads may contain asbestos, which is a health hazard. Never blow it out with compressed air, and don't inhale any of it. An approved filtering mask should be worn when working on the brakes. DO NOT use petrol or petroleum-based solvents to clean brake parts; use proprietary brake cleaner or methylated spirit only.

1 Firmly apply the handbrake, then jack up the front of the car and support it securely on axle stands (see *Jacking and vehicle support*). Remove the front roadwheels.

2 Working on one side of the vehicle, push the caliper piston into its bore by pulling the caliper outwards. If necessary, press the piston back into its bore using a large G-clamp or a piston retraction tool. Keep a careful eye on the level of brake fluid in the reservoir as you do this - ensure that the level does not rise above the MAX marking.

3 Where applicable, release the locking clip and remove the pad wear indicator wiring and brake fluid line from the bracket at the base of the suspension strut **(see illustrations)**.

Petrol models without ABS

4 Remove the locking clip and extract the lower guide pin from the caliper **(see illustrations)**

5 Pivot the caliper body upwards and support in position with a length of wire or a cable-tie. Avoid straining the hydraulic hose.

2.4a Remove the locking clip . . .

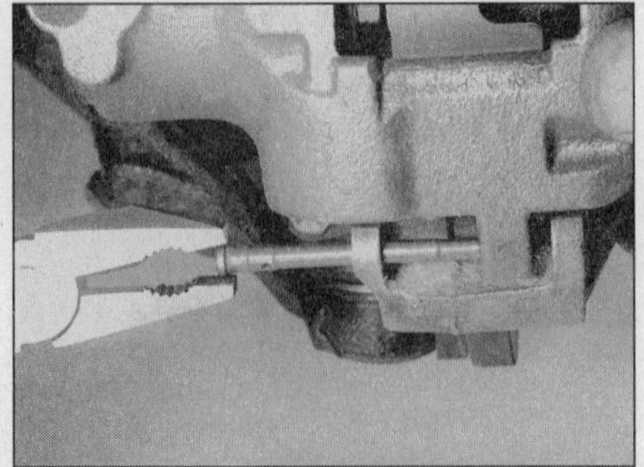

2.4b . . . and extract the lower guide pin from the caliper (petrol models without ABS)

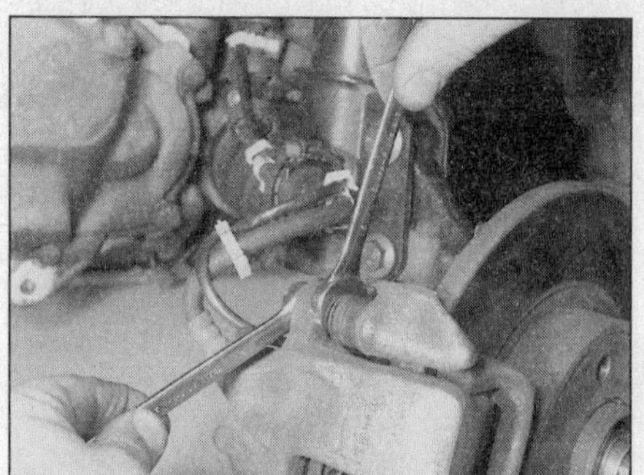

2.6a Unscrew the upper . . .

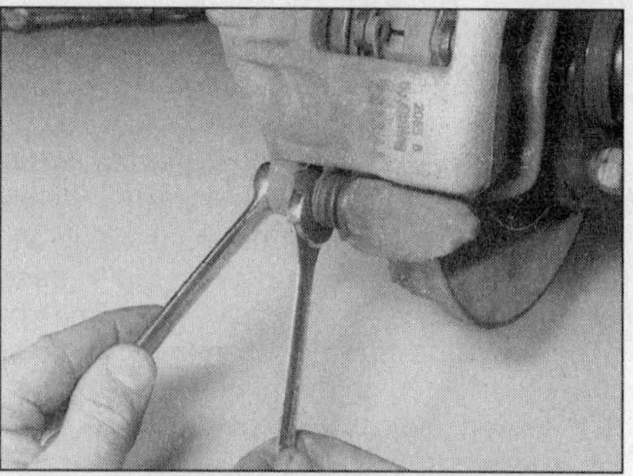

2.6b . . . and lower guide pin bolts (petrol models with ABS and diesel models)

2.7 Lift the caliper from the hub/disc assembly

Petrol models with ABS and diesel models

6 Unscrew the upper and lower caliper guide pin bolts, using a slim open-ended spanner to counterhold the head of the guide pin **(see illustrations)**. Discard the guide pin bolts - new items must be fitted on reassembly.

7 Lift the caliper from the hub/disc assembly **(see illustration)**. Suspend it from a suitable point on the suspension using a length of wire or a cable-tie, to avoid straining the hydraulic hose.

All models

Caution: Do not depress the brake pedal until the caliper is refitted, or the piston will be pushed out of its bore.

8 Withdraw the brake pads from the caliper bracket **(see illustrations)**.

9 Measure the thickness of each brake pad's friction material. If either pad is worn at any point to the specified minimum thickness or less, all four pads must be renewed. Also, the pads should be renewed if any are fouled with oil or grease; there is no satisfactory way of degreasing friction material, once contaminated. If any of the brake pads are worn unevenly, or are fouled with oil or grease, trace and rectify the cause before reassembly.

Warning: Do not be tempted to swap brake pads over to compensate for uneven wear.

10 If the brake pads are still serviceable, carefully clean them using a clean, fine wire brush or similar and brake cleaning fluid. Pay particular attention to the sides and back of the metal backing. Where applicable, clean out the grooves in the friction material, and pick out any large embedded particles of dirt or debris.

11 Clean the surfaces of the brake pad contact points in the caliper body and caliper mounting bracket.

12 Prior to fitting the pads, check that the guide pins can slide freely in the caliper body, and check that the rubber guide pin gaiters are undamaged. Brush the dust and dirt from the caliper and piston, but *do not* inhale it, as it may contain asbestos.

13 Inspect the dust seal and the area around the piston for signs of damage, corrosion or brake fluid leaks. If evident, refer to Section 3 and overhaul the caliper assembly.

14 If new brake pads are to be fitted, the caliper piston must be pushed back into the cylinder, to allow for the extra depth of the friction material. Either use a G-clamp or similar tool, or use suitable pieces of wood as levers. Provided that the master cylinder reservoir has not been overfilled with hydraulic fluid, there should be no spillage, but keep a careful watch on the fluid level while retracting the piston. If the fluid level rises above the MAX level line at any time, the surplus should be siphoned off.

Warning: Do not syphon the fluid by mouth, as it is poisonous; use a syringe or an old poultry baster.

15 Apply a little high temperature brake grease to the contact surfaces of the pad backing plates; take great care not to allow any grease onto the pad friction linings. Similarly, apply brake grease to the pad contact points on the caliper bracket - again take care not to apply excess grease, which may contaminate the pads.

16 Place the brake pads in position on the caliper bracket, with the friction material facing the surfaces of the brake disc. Feed the wear indicator cable through the caliper body aperture.

Petrol models without ABS

17 Pivot the caliper body down over the brake pads, then refit the guide pin and clip.

Petrol models with ABS and diesel models

18 Fit the caliper body in position on the caliper bracket, then fit the new guide pin bolts and tighten them to the specified torque.

All models

19 Check that the caliper body can slide freely on the guide pins. Ensure that the flexible hydraulic hose is not twisted or kinked in any way. Turn the steering from lock to lock and check that the hose does not chafe against the suspension or steering gear.

20 Where applicable, reconnect the pad wear indicator wiring and press it into the retaining clips on the suspension.

21 Repeat the above procedure on the remaining front caliper.

22 With both sets of front brake pads fitted, depress the brake pedal repeatedly until the pads are pressed into firm contact with the brake disc, and normal pedal pressure is restored. Any sponginess felt when depressing the pedal is most probably due to air trapped inside the hydraulic system - refer to Section 11 and bleed the braking system before progressing any further.

23 Refit the roadwheels, and lower the vehicle to the ground.

24 Check the hydraulic fluid level as described in *Weekly checks*.

25 Check the operation of the braking system thoroughly.

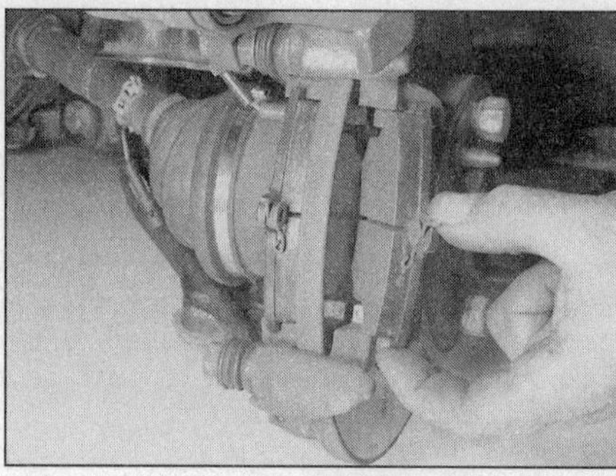

2.8a Withdraw the outboard . . .

2.8b . . . and inboard brake pads from the caliper bracket

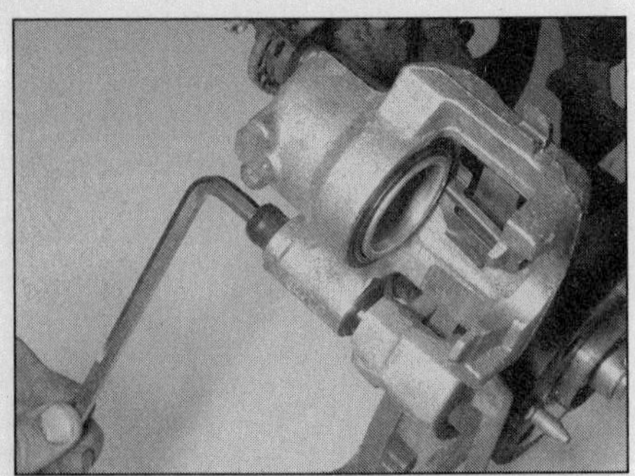

3.5 Unscrew the caliper upper guide pin bolt and remove the caliper body from the bracket

3 Front brake caliper - removal, overhaul and refitting

Warning: Before starting work, refer to the warnings at the beginning of Sections 2 and 11 concerning the dangers of handling asbestos dust and hydraulic fluid.

Removal

1 Chock the rear wheels, apply the handbrake, then jack up the front of the vehicle and support it on axle stands (see *Jacking and vehicle support*). Remove the appropriate front roadwheel.

2 Remove the brake pads as described in Section 2.

3 To minimise fluid loss during the following operations, remove the master cylinder reservoir cap, then tighten it down onto a piece of polythene, to obtain an airtight seal. Alternatively, use a brake hose clamp to seal off the flexible hose running to the caliper.

Warning: Do not use an ordinary G-clamp or mole grips for this purpose, as these can easily damage the hydraulic hose internally, possibly leading to failure.

4 Clean the area surrounding the brake hose union, then slacken it using a ring spanner. It won't be possible to separate the union completely without twisting the hose at this stage.

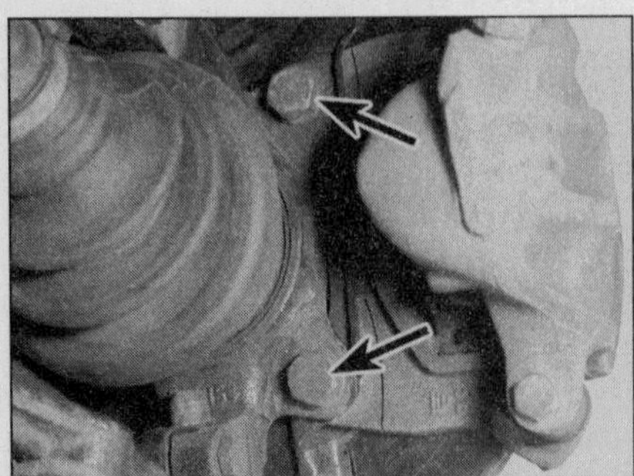

3.7 Unscrew the two securing bolts (arrowed) and remove the caliper mounting bracket from the hub carrier

5 On petrol models without ABS, unscrew the caliper upper guide pin bolt using a hex bit or Allen key and remove the caliper body from the bracket **(see illustration)**.

6 Hold the brake hose and rotate the caliper to unscrew the hose union from the caliper body. Cover the open ends of the union and the caliper fluid inlet, to prevent dirt ingress. Alternatively, the flexible brake hose may be separated from the rigid brake pipe, at the bracket mounted on the inner wheel arch.

7 If desired, the caliper mounting bracket can be removed from the hub carrier after unscrewing the two securing bolts **(see illustration)** but note that locking compound must be applied to the bolt threads on refitting.

Overhaul

Note: *Before commencing work, ensure that the appropriate caliper overhaul kit is obtained.*

8 With the caliper on the bench, wipe away all traces of dust and dirt, but *avoid inhaling the dust, as it is a health hazard.*

9 Place a small block of wood between the caliper body and the piston, to act as padding. Remove the piston by applying a jet of low pressure compressed air (such as that produced by a tyre foot pump) to the fluid inlet port.

Warning: Protect your hands and eyes when using compressed air in this manner - brake fluid may be ejected under pressure when the piston pops out of its bore.

10 Peel the dust seal from the piston, then use a soft, blunt instrument (ie **not** a screwdriver) to extract the piston seal from the caliper bore.

11 Thoroughly clean all components, using only methylated spirit or clean hydraulic fluid. Never use mineral-based solvents such as petrol or paraffin, which will attack the hydraulic system rubber components.

12 The caliper piston seal, the dust seal and the bleed nipple dust cap, are only available as part of a seal kit. Since the manufacturers recommend that the piston seal and dust seal are renewed whenever they are disturbed, all of these components should be discarded on disassembly and new ones fitted on reassembly as a matter of course.

13 Carefully examine all parts of the caliper assembly, looking for signs of wear or damage. In particular, the cylinder bore and piston must be free from any signs of scratches, corrosion or wear. If there is any doubt about the condition of any part of the caliper, the relevant part should be renewed. Note that the piston surface is plated, and **must not** be polished with emery or similar abrasives to remove corrosion or scratches. In addition, the pistons are matched to the caliper bores and can only be renewed as a part of a complete caliper assembly.

14 Check that the threads in the caliper body and the mounting bracket are in good condition. Check that both guide pins are undamaged, and (when cleaned) a reasonably tight sliding fit in the mounting bracket bores.

15 Use compressed air to blow clear the fluid passages.

Warning: Wear eye protection when using compressed air.

16 Before commencing reassembly, ensure that all components are spotlessly-clean and dry.

17 Soak the new piston seal in clean hydraulic fluid, and fit it to the groove in the cylinder bore, using your fingers only (no tools) to manipulate it into place.

18 Fit the new dust seal inner lip to the cylinder groove, smear clean hydraulic fluid over the piston and caliper cylinder bore, and twist the piston into the dust seal. Press the piston squarely into the cylinder, then slide the dust seal outer lip to the groove in the piston.

Refitting

19 Where applicable, refit the caliper mounting bracket to the hub carrier. Coat the threads of the mounting bolts with locking compound, then tighten them to the specified torque.

20 Hold the brake hose and rotate the caliper to screw the hose union back into the caliper body.

21 On petrol models without ABS, place the caliper in position on the bracket and tighten the caliper upper guide pin bolt to the specified torque.

22 Refit the brake pads as described in Section 2.

23 On all models, tighten the brake hose-to-caliper union securely.

24 Check that the caliper slides smoothly on its guide pins.

25 Where applicable, remove the polythene from the master cylinder reservoir cap, or remove the clamp from the fluid hose, as applicable.

26 Bleed the hydraulic fluid circuit as described in Section 11. Note that if no other part of the system has been disturbed, it should only be necessary to bleed the relevant front circuit.

27 Depress the brake pedal repeatedly to bring the pads into contact with the brake disc, and ensure that normal pedal pressure is restored.

28 Refit the roadwheel, and lower the vehicle to the ground.

4 Brake disc - inspection, removal and refitting

Inspection

1 Firmly apply the handbrake, then jack up the front of the car and support it securely on axle stands (see *Jacking and vehicle support*). Remove the front roadwheels.

2 Rotate the brake disc by hand and examine the whole of the surface area swept by the brake pads, on both sides of the disc. **Note:** *It will be necessary to remove the front brake pads to allow an adequate inspection of the disc's rear surface; refer to Section 2 for details.*

3 Typically, the disc surface will have a polished appearance and should be free from heavy scoring. Smooth rippling is produced by normal operation and does not indicate excessive wear. Deep scoring and cracks, however, are indications of more serious damage in need of correction.

4 If deep scoring is discovered, it may be possible to have the disc reground to restore the surface, depending on the extent of the damage. To determine whether this is a feasible course of action, it will be necessary to measure the thickness of the disc, as described later.

5 Check the whole surface of the disc for cracks, particularly around the roadwheel bolt holes. A cracked disc must be renewed.

6 A ridge of rust and brake dust at the inner and outer edges of the disc, beyond the pad contact area is normal - this can be scraped away quite easily.

7 Raised ridges caused by the brake pads eroding the disc material, however, are an indication of excessive wear. If close examination reveals such ridges, the thickness of the disc must be measured, to assess whether it is still fit for use.

8 To measure the thickness of the disc, take readings at several points on the surface using a micrometer, in the area swept by the brake pads **(see illustration)**. Include any points where the disc has been scored; align the jaws of the micrometer with the deepest area of scoring, to get a true indication of the extent of the wear. Compare these measurements with the limits listed in the Specifications. If the disc has worn below its minimum thickness, at any point, it must be renewed.

9 If the discs are suspected of causing brake judder, check the disc runout, using one of the following methods:

Runout measurement - DTI gauge method

10 Refit the four roadwheel bolts, together with one M14 plain washer per stud - this will ensure adequate disc to hub contact. Tighten the studs to 5 Nm (4 lbf ft).

11 Clamp the DTI gauge to a stand and attach the stand, preferably via a magnetic base, to the strut mounting bracket. Align the gauge so that its pointer rests upon the area of the disc swept by the brake pads, on an arc 2 mm from the outer edge of the disc **(see illustration)**.

12 Zero the gauge and slowly rotate the disc through one revolution, observing the pointer movement. Note the maximum deflection recorded and compare the figure with that listed in Specifications.

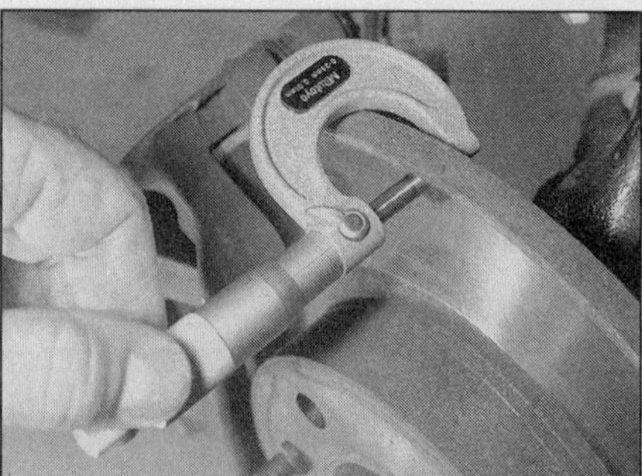

4.8 Measuring brake disc thickness with a micrometer

Runout measurement - feeler blade method

13 Use the feeler blades to measure the clearance between the disc and a convenient fixed point, such as the disc backplate. Rotate the disc and measure the variation in clearance at several points around the disc. Compare the maximum figure with that listed in Specifications.

14 If the disc runout is outside of its specified tolerance, first check that the hub is not worn (see *Steering and suspension* check in Chapter 1A or 1B). If the hub is in good condition, remove the disc (as described later in this Section), rotate it through 180° and refit it. This may improve the seating and eradicate the excessive runout.

15 If the runout is still unacceptable, then it may be possible to restore the disc by regrinding; consult your Fiat dealer or a machine shop for a professional opinion - it may prove more economical to purchase a new disc. If the disc cannot be reground, then it must be renewed.

Removal

16 Mark the relationship between the disc and the hub with chalk or a marker pen, to allow correct refitting.

17 To allow the disc to be removed, undo the two bolts securing the brake caliper mounting bracket to the hub carrier (see illustration 3.7). Withdraw the brake caliper and mounting bracket assembly, complete with brake pads, from the hub carrier, and hang it from a rigid point on the suspension, using wire or a cable-tie. Do not allow it to dangle freely as this will strain the brake hose.

18 Slacken and remove the disc locating stud(s). Support the disc as you do this and lift it off as it becomes free **(see illustrations)**.

19 Remove the polished glaze from the surface of the disc with sand/emery paper. Use small, circular motions to avoid producing a directional finish on the surface.

4.11 Brake disc runout measurement - DTI gauge method

Refitting

20 If a new disc is being fitted, remove the protective coating from the surface using an appropriate solvent.

21 Locate the disc on the hub so that the roadwheel bolt and locating stud holes are all correctly lined up; use the alignment marks made during removal. If the disc is being removed in an attempt to improve seating and hence runout, turn the disc through 180° and then refit it.

22 Refit the locating stud and retaining screw, tightening them securely.

23 Re-check the disc runout, using one of the methods described earlier in this Section.

24 Refit the brake caliper and mounting bracket assembly to the hub carrier. Coat the threads of the mounting bolts with locking compound, then tighten them to the specified torque.

25 Depress the brake pedal several times to bring the brake pads into contact with the disc.

26 Refit the roadwheel and lower the vehicle to the ground. Tighten the roadwheel bolts to the specified torque.

27 Check the hydraulic fluid level as described in *Weekly checks.*

4.18a Slacken and remove the disc locating studs . . .

4.18b . . . and lift off the disc as it becomes free

5.4a Detaching the lower return spring

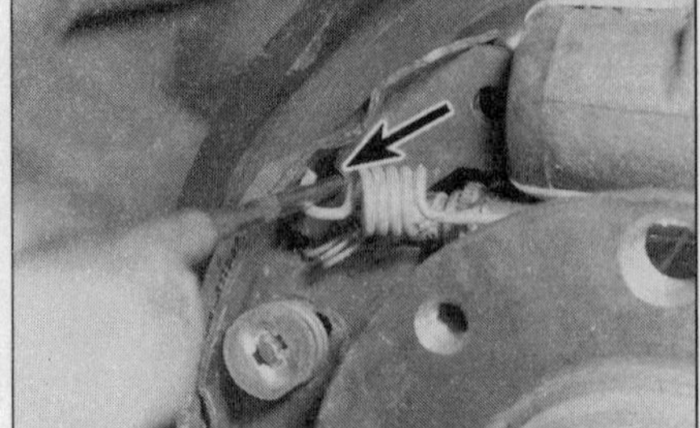

5.4b Detaching the upper return spring from the leading . . .

5.4c . . . and trailing brake shoes

5 Rear brake shoes - renewal

Warning: Renew BOTH sets of rear brake shoes at the same time - NEVER renew the shoes on only one wheel, as uneven braking may result.

Warning: Before starting work, refer to the warning given at the beginning of Section 2, concerning the dangers of asbestos dust.

1 Remove the rear brake drums, as described in Section 6.

2 Working on one side of the vehicle, brush the dirt and dust from the brake backplate and drum. Avoid inhaling the dust, as it may contain asbestos, which is a health hazard.

3 Note the position of each shoe, and the location of the return and steady springs. Also make a note of the adjuster component locations, to aid refitting later. It is advisable, at this stage to wrap a stout rubber band or a cable-tie over the wheel cylinder, to prevent the pistons from being accidentally ejected.

4 Detach the upper and lower return springs from both brake shoes **(see illustrations)**.

5 Unhook the self-adjuster mechanism return spring from the leading brake shoe **(see illustration)**. Remove the hold-down cup and spring from the leading shoe. The spring cups are a bayonet-style fit - use a large pair of pliers to depress and then turn the cup through 90°, while holding the pin from behind the backplate. Remove the pin.

6 Carefully pull the leading brake shoe away from the backplate and remove it **(see illustration)**.

7 Using a suitable pair of pliers, unhook the self-adjuster mechanism from the trailing shoe and remove it **(see illustrations)**.

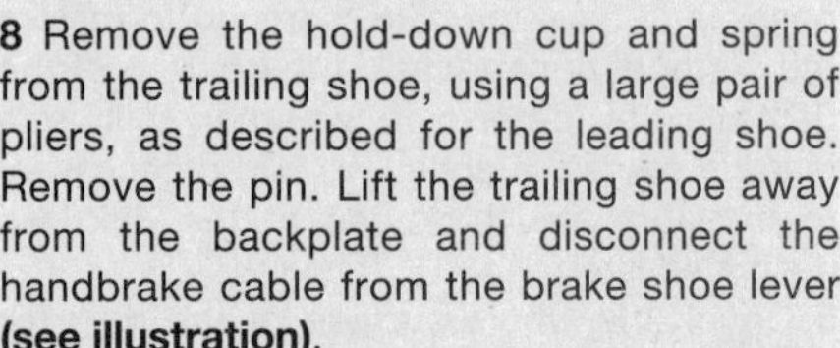

8 Remove the hold-down cup and spring from the trailing shoe, using a large pair of pliers, as described for the leading shoe. Remove the pin. Lift the trailing shoe away from the backplate and disconnect the handbrake cable from the brake shoe lever **(see illustration)**.

9 Thoroughly clean the surface of the backplate using brake component cleaner to remove all traces of dust and old lubricant. Examine all components for signs of corrosion.

10 Apply brake grease sparingly to the shoe contact surfaces of the brake backplate **(see illustration)**.

11 Connect the handbrake cable to the lever on the trailing brake shoe, locate the trailing shoe on the backplate and secure in position with the pin, hold down spring and cup. Using pliers, turn the cup through 90° and then release it, to lock it in position.

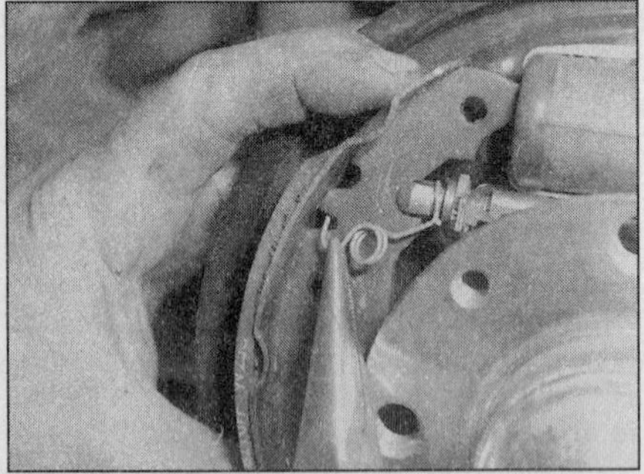

5.5 Unhook the self-adjuster mechanism return spring from the leading brake shoe

5.6 Carefully pull the leading brake shoe away from the backplate and remove it

5.7a Unhook the self-adjuster mechanism from the trailing shoe . . .

5.7b . . . and remove it

5.8a Remove the hold-down cup and spring from the trailing shoe

5.8b Lift the trailing shoe away from the backplate . . .

5.8c . . . and disconnect the handbrake cable from the brake shoe lever

5.10 Apply brake grease sparingly to the shoe contact surfaces (arrowed) of the brake backplate

5.12 Fit the self-adjuster mechanism into the recess (arrowed) in the trailing brake shoe

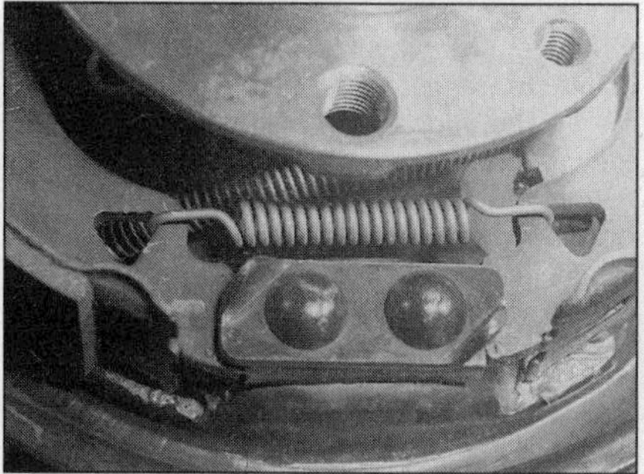

5.14a Lower return spring fitted in place

5.14b Correct location of upper return spring in leading shoe . . .

5.14c . . . and trailing shoe

12 Fit the self-adjuster mechanism into the recess in the trailing brake shoe and anchor the retaining spring in the slot provided in the shoe **(see illustration)**.

13 Fit the leading shoe in position on the backplate and secure it with the hold down pin, spring and cup as described for the trailing shoe. Engage the end of the self-adjuster mechanism with the recess in the leading brake shoe. Hook the retaining spring into the slot provided.

14 Fit the upper and lower shoe return springs, engaging them with the slots in the shoes as shown **(see illustrations)**. Remove the elastic band from the wheel cylinder.

15 Turn the serrated wheel at the end of the self-adjuster mechanism, to retract the brake shoes - this will give additional clearance to allow the drum to pass over the shoes during refitting.

16 Repeat the procedure on the remaining side of the vehicle.

17 Refit the brake drums as described in Section 6. Check and if necessary adjust the operation of the handbrake, as described in Section 9.

18 Apply the brake pedal and handbrake lever several times to settle the self-adjusting mechanism. With both rear roadwheels refitted and the rear of the vehicle still raised, turn the wheels by hand to check that the brake shoes are not binding.

19 Lower the vehicle to the ground and thoroughly check the operation of the braking system.

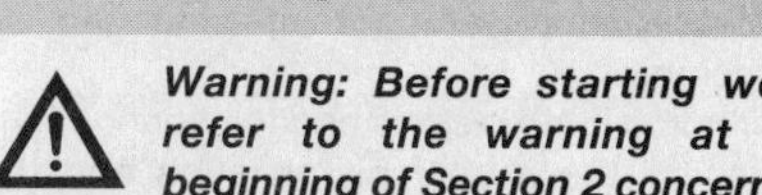

6 Rear brake drums - removal, inspection and refitting

Warning: Before starting work, refer to the warning at the beginning of Section 2 concerning the dangers of asbestos dust.

Removal

1 Chock the front wheels, then jack up the rear of the vehicle and support it on axle stands (see *Jacking and vehicle support*). Remove the appropriate rear roadwheel. Fully release the handbrake.

2 If the original drum is to be refitted, mark the relationship between the drum and the hub. Slacken and remove the two locating studs and pull the drum from the hub **(see illustration)**.

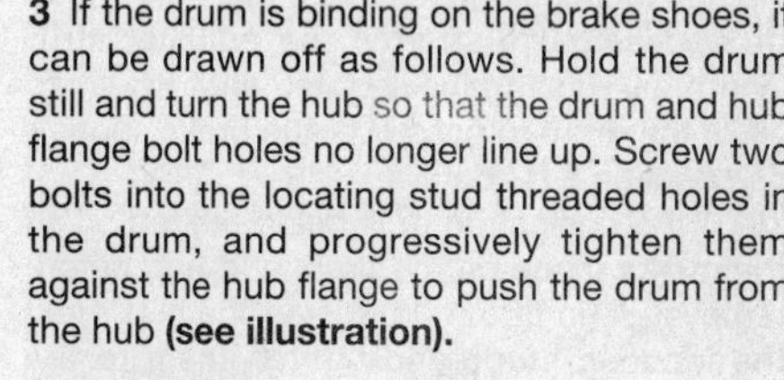

3 If the drum is binding on the brake shoes, it can be drawn off as follows. Hold the drum still and turn the hub so that the drum and hub flange bolt holes no longer line up. Screw two bolts into the locating stud threaded holes in the drum, and progressively tighten them against the hub flange to push the drum from the hub **(see illustration)**.

Inspection

Note: *If either drum requires renewal, BOTH should be renewed at the same time, to ensure even and consistent braking. New brake shoes should also be fitted.*

4 Working carefully, remove all traces of brake dust from the drum, but *avoid inhaling the dust, as it is a health hazard.*

5 Clean the outside of the drum, and check it for obvious signs of wear or damage, such as cracks around the roadwheel stud holes; renew the drum if necessary.

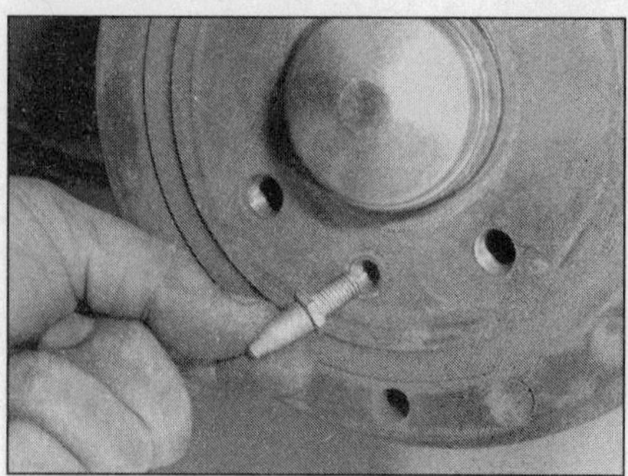

6.2 Slacken and remove the two drum locating studs

6.3 Using two bolts to draw the drum off the brake shoes

6 Carefully examine the inside of the drum. Light scoring of the friction surface is normal, but if heavy scoring is found, the drum must be renewed.

7 It is usual to find a lip on the drum's inboard edge which consists of a mixture of rust and brake dust; this should be carefully scraped away, to leave a smooth surface which can be polished with fine (120 to 150-grade) emery paper. If, however, the lip is due to the friction surface being recessed by excessive wear, then the drum must be renewed.

8 If the drum is thought to be excessively worn, or oval, its internal diameter must be measured at several points using an internal micrometer. Take measurements in pairs, the second at right-angles to the first, and compare the two, to check for signs of ovality. Provided that it does not enlarge the drum to beyond the specified maximum diameter, it may be possible to have the drum refinished by skimming or grinding; if this is not possible, the drums on both sides must be renewed. Note that if the drum is to be skimmed, BOTH drums must be refinished, to maintain a consistent internal diameter on both sides.

Refitting

9 If a new brake drum is to be installed, use a suitable solvent to remove any preservative coating that may have been applied to its internal friction surfaces. Note that it may also be necessary to shorten the adjuster strut length, by rotating the serrated strut wheel, to allow the drum to pass over the brake shoes - see Section 5 for details.

10 If the original drum is being refitted, align the marks made on the drum and hub before removal, then fit the drum over the hub. Refit the locating studs and tighten them to the specified torque.

11 Depress the footbrake repeatedly to expand the brake shoes against the drum, and ensure that normal pedal pressure is restored.

12 Check and if necessary adjust the handbrake cable as described in Section 9.

13 Refit the roadwheels, and lower the vehicle to the ground.

7 Rear wheel cylinder - removal, overhaul and refitting

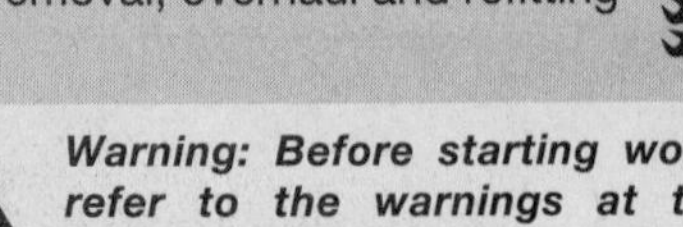

Warning: Before starting work, refer to the warnings at the beginning of Sections 2 and 11 concerning the dangers of handling asbestos dust and hydraulic fluid.

Removal

1 Remove the brake drum (see Section 6).

2 Remove the brake shoes (see Section 5).

3 To minimise fluid loss during the following operations, remove the master cylinder reservoir cap, then tighten it down onto a piece of polythene, to obtain an airtight seal.

7.4 Unscrew the union nut and disconnect the hydraulic pipe from the rear of the wheel cylinder

4 Clean the brake backplate around the wheel cylinder mounting bolts and the hydraulic pipe union, then unscrew the union nut and disconnect the hydraulic pipe **(see illustration)**. Cover the open ends of the pipe and the master cylinder to prevent dirt ingress.

5 Remove the securing bolts, then withdraw the wheel cylinder from the backplate **(see illustration)**.

Overhaul

Note: *Before commencing work, ensure that the appropriate wheel cylinder overhaul kit is obtained.*

6 Clean the assembly thoroughly, using only methylated spirit or clean brake fluid.

7 Peel off both rubber dust covers, then use paint or similar to mark one of the pistons so that the pistons are not interchanged on reassembly.

8 Withdraw both pistons and the spring.

9 Discard the rubber piston cups and the dust covers. These components should be renewed as a matter of course, and are available as part of an overhaul kit, which also includes the bleed nipple dust cap.

10 Check the condition of the cylinder bore and the pistons - the surfaces must be perfect and free from scratches, scoring and corrosion. It is advisable to renew the complete wheel cylinder if there is any doubt as to the condition of the cylinder bore or pistons.

11 Ensure that all components are clean and dry. The pistons, spring and cups should be fitted wet, using hydraulic fluid as a lubricant - soak them in clean fluid before installation.

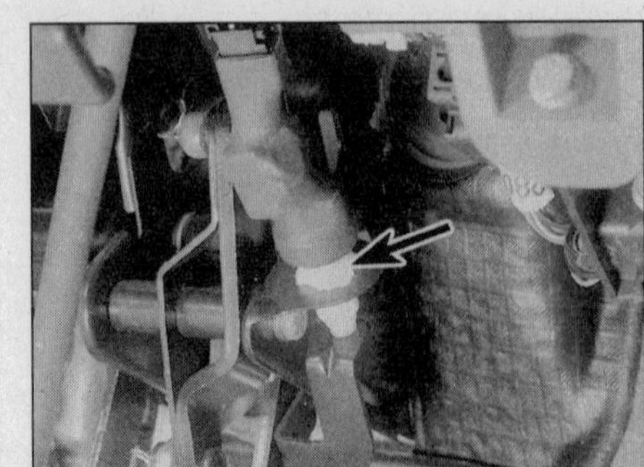

8.4 Location of brake light switch - LHD model shown

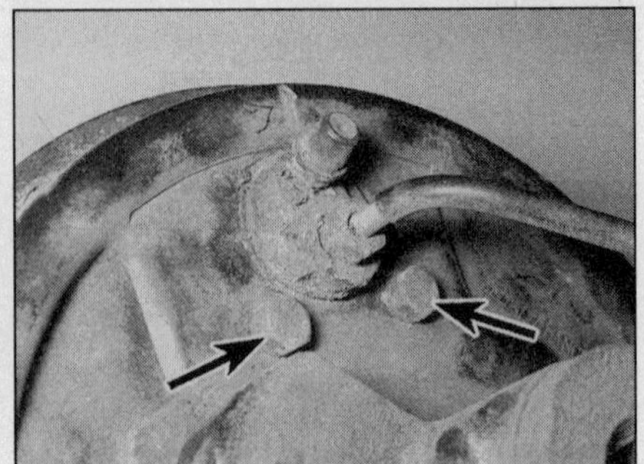

7.5 Remove the securing bolts then withdraw the wheel cylinder from the backplate

12 Fit the cups to the pistons, ensuring that they are the correct way round. Use only your fingers (no tools) to manipulate the cups into position.

13 Fit the first piston to the cylinder, taking care not to distort the cup. If the original pistons are being re-used, the marks made on dismantling should be used to ensure that the pistons are refitted to their original bores.

14 Refit the spring and the second piston.

15 Apply a smear of rubber grease to the exposed end of each piston and to the dust cover sealing lips, then fit the dust covers to each end of the wheel cylinder.

Refitting

16 Refitting is a reversal of removal, bearing in mind the following points:

a) Tighten the mounting bolts to the specified torque.

b) Refit the brake shoes as described in Section 5, and refit the brake drum as described in Section 6.

c) Before refitting the roadwheel and lowering the vehicle to the ground, remove the polythene from the fluid reservoir, and bleed the hydraulic system as described in Section 11. Note that if no other part of the system has been disturbed, it should only be necessary to bleed the relevant rear circuit.

8 Stop-light switch - adjustment, removal and refitting

Adjustment

1 The switch plunger operates on a ratchet.

2 If adjustment is required, pull the plunger fully out - the switch then self-adjusts as the brake pedal is applied and released.

Removal

3 Ensure that the ignition is switched to OFF.

4 For improved access, remove the driver's side lower facia panel, as described in Chapter 11 **(see illustration)**.

5 Disconnect the wiring plug from the switch.

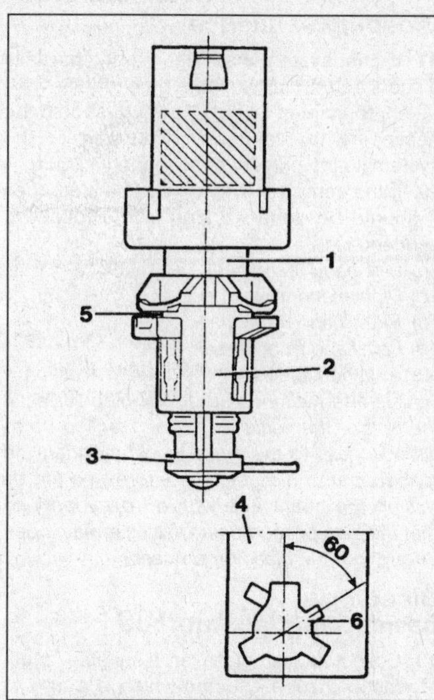

8.8 Brake light switch assembly

1 *Hexagonal section*
2 *Bush*
3 *Spacer*
4 *Mounting bracket*
5 *Locating lug*

6 Twist the switch anti-clockwise through about half a turn, and withdraw the switch from the pedal bracket. Note the position of the spacer and fitting bush.

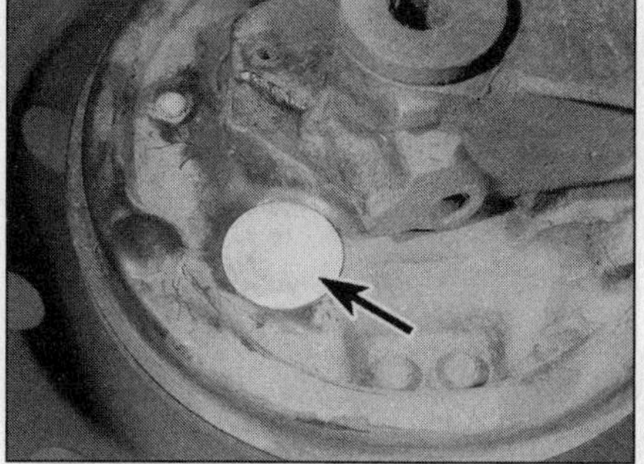

10.3a Prise the bung (arrowed) from the access hatch in the rear of the relevant brake backplate

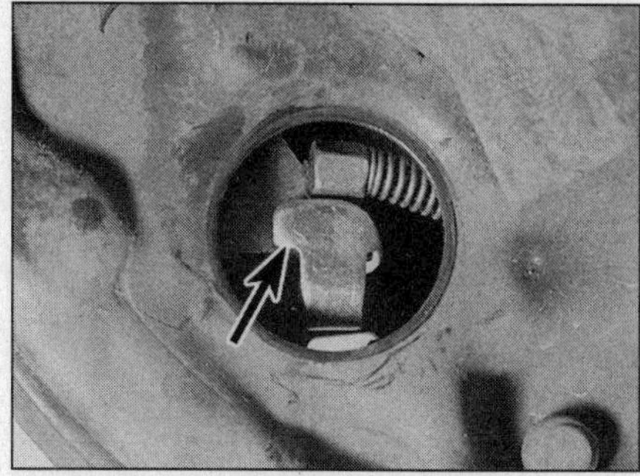

10.3b Unhook the cable end from the brake shoe lever (arrowed)

Refitting

7 Depress the brake pedal and hold it in this position.

8 Fit the bush and spacer over the end of the switch, then insert the switch into its mounting bracket. Rotate the switch body clockwise through 60° until the locating lug is felt to engage in its recess **(see illustration)**.

9 Release the brake pedal and allow it to rest against the switch spacer tab - this adjusts the position of the switch body inside the bush.

10 Now depress the brake pedal again - this has the effect of breaking off the spacer tab and fixes the position of the switch inside the bush.

11 Restore the wiring at the connector, then refit the facia lower trim panel.

12 Switch on the ignition and test the operation of the brake lights.

9 Handbrake - checking and adjustment

Checking

1 Apply the handbrake by pulling it through three to four clicks of the ratchet mechanism and check that this locks the rear wheels, holding the vehicle stationary on an incline. In this position, there should be sufficient reserve travel in the handbrake lever to allow for brake shoe wear and cable stretching. If not, the handbrake mechanism is need of adjustment.

Adjustment

2 Remove the securing screws and lift off the handbrake lever trim cover - refer to Chapter 11, Section 19, for details.

3 Pull the handbrake lever through three clicks of the ratchet mechanism and leave it in this position.

4 The adjustment mechanism is underneath the handbrake lever. Hold the locknut with a ring spanner, then rotate the adjustment screw through one turn anticlockwise, so that the adjustment mechanism tensions the handbrake cable draw bar **(see illustration)**.

5 Release the handbrake lever, then re-apply it and check the operation of the handbrake as described in paragraph 1. Repeat the adjustment procedure as necessary.

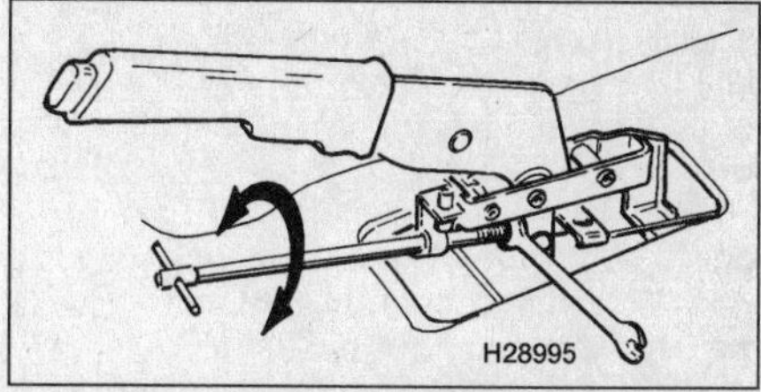

9.4 Method of adjusting the operation of the handbrake

6 Chock the front wheels then jack up the rear of the car and support it on axle stands (see *Jacking and Vehicle Support*). Release the handbrake lever and check that the rear wheels are free to rotate without binding. Re-adjust the cable if the brakes appear to be binding.

7 On completion, tighten the cable locknut and refit the handbrake lever trim cover. Lower the car to the ground.

10 Handbrake cables - removal and refitting

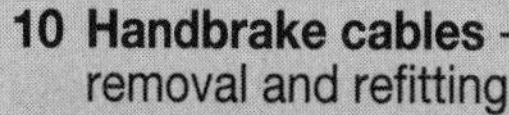

Removal

1 There are two rear handbrake cables, one on each side of the vehicle. To renew either rear cable, proceed as follows.

2 Chock the front wheels, then jack up the rear of the vehicle and support securely on axle stands (see *Jacking and vehicle support*). Release the handbrake fully.

3 Working under the rear of the car, prise the bung from the access hatch in the rear of the relevant brake backplate. Using pointed-nose pliers, compress the cable spring and release the cable end from the brake shoe lever **(see illustrations)**.

4 Extract the handbrake outer cable from the brake backplate, then withdraw the end of the cable from the brake assembly.

5 Unscrew the nuts and bolts securing the handbrake cable bracket to the suspension lower arm. Release the cable from the clips on the floorpan heatshield **(see illustrations)**.

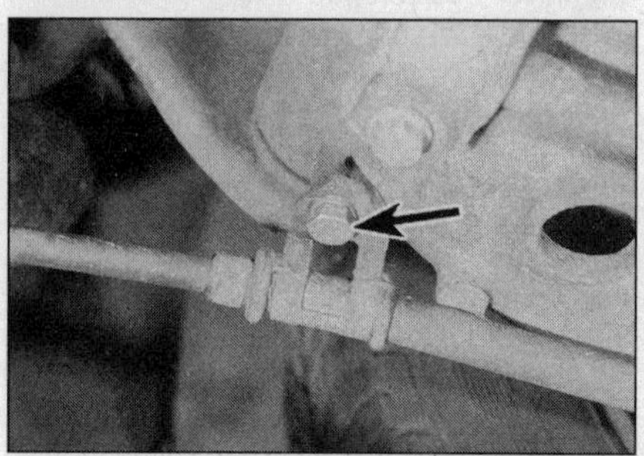

10.5a Unscrew the bolts (arrowed) securing the handbrake cable bracket to the suspension lower arm

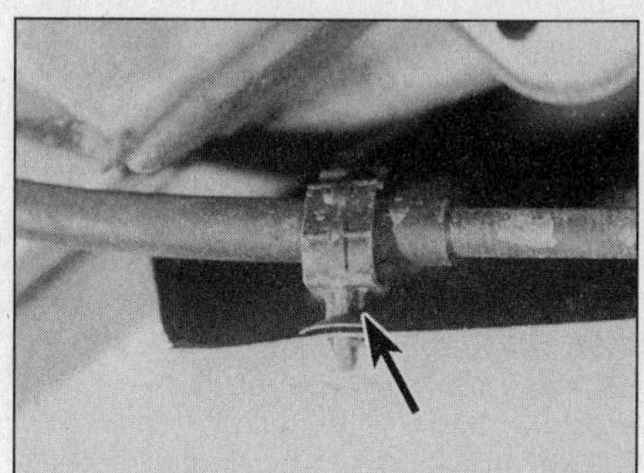

10.5b Release the cable from the clips (arrowed) on the floorpan heatshield

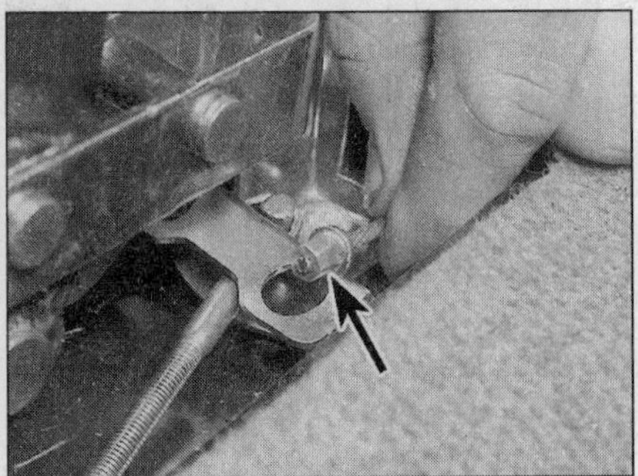

10.6 Disconnect the relevant handbrake inner cable (arrowed) from the draw bar

6 Working inside the vehicle, remove the screws and lift off the handbrake lever trim panel (refer to Section 9 for more detail). At the base of the handbrake lever, fully slacken off the handbrake adjusting screw and locknut, to remove all tension from the cable draw bar, then disconnect the relevant handbrake inner cable from the cable draw bar **(see illustration)**

7 Release the cable grommet from the floor-pan, then withdraw the cable from the vehicle.

Refitting

8 Refitting is a reversal of removal, bearing in mind the following points:

a) *Ensure that the cables are securely fastened in the clips on the floorpan heatshield and lower suspension arm.*

b) *On completion, check the handbrake adjustment, as described in Section 9.*

11 Hydraulic system - bleeding

Warning: Hydraulic fluid is poisonous; wash off immediately and thoroughly in the case of skin contact, and seek immediate medical advice if any fluid is swallowed, or gets into the eyes. Certain types of hydraulic fluid are inflammable, and may ignite when allowed into contact with hot components. When servicing any hydraulic system, it is safest to assume that the fluid IS inflammable, and to take precautions against the risk of fire as though it is petrol that is being handled. Hydraulic fluid is also an effective paint stripper, and will attack plastics; if any is spilt, it should be washed off immediately, using copious quantities of fresh water. Finally, it is hygroscopic (it absorbs moisture from the air) - old fluid may be contaminated and unfit for further use. When topping-up or renewing the fluid, always use the recommended type, and ensure that it comes from a freshly-opened sealed container.

11.17 Bleeding a rear brake line

General

1 The correct operation of any hydraulic system is only possible after removing all air from the components and circuit; and this is achieved by bleeding the system.

2 During the bleeding procedure, add only clean, unused hydraulic fluid of the recommended type; never re-use fluid that has already been bled from the system. Ensure that sufficient fluid is available before starting work.

3 If there is any possibility of incorrect fluid being already in the system, the brake components and circuit must be flushed completely with uncontaminated, correct fluid, and new seals should be fitted throughout the system.

4 If hydraulic fluid has been lost from the system, or air has entered because of a leak, ensure that the fault is cured before proceeding further.

5 Park the vehicle on level ground, switch off the engine and select first or reverse gear (or P), then chock the wheels and release the handbrake.

6 Check that all pipes and hoses are secure, unions tight and bleed screws closed. Remove the dust caps (where applicable), and clean any dirt from around the bleed screws.

7 Unscrew the master cylinder reservoir cap, and top the master cylinder reservoir up to the MAX level line; refit the cap loosely. Remember to maintain the fluid level at least above the MIN level line throughout the procedure, otherwise there is a risk of further air entering the system.

8 There are a number of one-man, do-it-yourself brake bleeding kits currently available from motor accessory shops. It is recommended that one of these kits is used whenever possible, as they greatly simplify the bleeding operation, and also reduce the risk of expelled air and fluid being drawn back into the system. If such a kit is not available, the basic (two-man) method must be used, which is described in detail below.

9 If a kit is to be used, prepare the vehicle as described previously, and follow the kit manufacturer's instructions, as the procedure may vary slightly according to the type being used; generally, they are as outlined below in the relevant sub-section.

10 Whichever method is used, the same sequence must be followed (paragraphs 11 and 12) to ensure the removal of all air from the system.

Bleeding sequence

11 If the system has been only partially disconnected, and suitable precautions were taken to minimise fluid loss, it should be necessary to bleed only that part of the system (ie the primary or secondary circuit).

12 If the complete system is to be bled, then it should be done working in the following sequence:

a) *Left-hand rear wheel.*

b) *Right-hand front wheel.*

c) *Right-hand rear wheel.*

d) *Left-hand front wheel.*

Note: *When bleeding the rear brakes on a vehicle fitted with load proportioning valves: if the rear of the vehicle has been jacked up to allow access to the brake wheel cylinder, the rear suspension must be compressed (eg by raising the beam axle with a trolley jack) so that the load proportioning valves remain open throughout the bleeding process.*

Bleeding - basic (two-man) method

13 Collect a clean glass jar, a suitable length of plastic or rubber tubing which is a tight fit over the bleed screw, and a ring spanner to fit the screw. The help of an assistant will also be required.

14 Remove the dust cap from the first screw in the sequence if not already done. Fit a suitable spanner and tube to the screw, place the other end of the tube in the jar, and pour in sufficient fluid to cover the end of the tube.

15 Ensure that the master cylinder reservoir fluid level is maintained at least above the MIN level line throughout the procedure.

16 Have the assistant fully depress the brake pedal several times to build up pressure, then maintain it on the final downstroke.

17 While pedal pressure is maintained, unscrew the bleed screw (approximately one turn) and allow the compressed fluid and air to flow into the jar. The assistant should maintain pedal pressure, following the pedal down to the floor if necessary, and should not release the pedal until instructed to do so. When the flow stops, tighten the bleed screw again, have the assistant release the pedal slowly, and recheck the reservoir fluid level **(see illustration)**.

18 Repeat the steps given in paragraphs 16 and 17 until the fluid emerging from the bleed screw is free from air bubbles. If the master cylinder has been drained and refilled, and air is being bled from the first screw in the sequence, allow approximately five seconds between cycles for the master cylinder passages to refill.

19 When no more air bubbles appear, tighten the bleed screw securely, remove the tube and spanner, and refit the dust cap (where applicable). Do not overtighten the bleed screw.

20 Repeat the procedure on the remaining screws in the sequence, until all air is removed from the system, and the brake pedal feels firm again.

Bleeding - using a one-way valve kit

21 As their name implies, these kits consist of a length of tubing with a one-way valve fitted, to prevent expelled air and fluid being drawn back into the system; some kits include a translucent container, which can be positioned so that the air bubbles can be more easily seen flowing from the end of the tube.

22 The kit is connected to the bleed screw, which is then opened. The user returns to the driver's seat, depresses the brake pedal with a smooth, steady stroke, and slowly releases it; this is repeated until the expelled fluid is clear of air bubbles.

23 Note that these kits simplify work so much that it is easy to forget the master cylinder reservoir fluid level; ensure that this is maintained at least above the MIN level line at all times.

Bleeding - using a pressure-bleeding kit

24 These kits are usually operated by the reservoir of pressurised air contained in the spare tyre. However, note that it will probably be necessary to reduce the pressure to a lower level than normal; refer to the instructions supplied with the kit.

25 By connecting a pressurised, fluid-filled container to the master cylinder reservoir, bleeding can be carried out simply by opening each screw in turn (in the specified sequence), and allowing the fluid to flow out until no more air bubbles can be seen in the expelled fluid.

26 This method has the advantage that the large reservoir of fluid provides an additional safeguard against air being drawn into the system during bleeding.

27 Pressure-bleeding is particularly effective when bleeding 'difficult' systems, or when bleeding the complete system at the time of routine fluid renewal.

All methods

28 When bleeding is complete, and firm pedal feel is restored, wash off any spilt fluid, tighten the bleed screws securely, and refit their dust caps (where applicable).

29 Check the hydraulic fluid level in the master cylinder reservoir, and top-up if necessary.

30 Discard any hydraulic fluid that has been bled from the system; it will not be fit for re-use.

31 Check the feel of the brake pedal. If it feels at all spongy, air must still be present in the system, and further bleeding is required. Failure to bleed satisfactorily after a reasonable repetition of the bleeding procedure may be due to worn master cylinder seals.

12 Master cylinder - removal and refitting

Warning: Before starting work, refer to the warning at the beginning of Section 11 concerning the dangers of hydraulic fluid.

Removal

1 Remove the master cylinder fluid reservoir cap, and syphon the hydraulic fluid from the reservoir. **Note:** *Do not syphon the fluid by mouth, as it is poisonous; use a syringe or an old poultry baster.* Alternatively, open any convenient bleed screw in the system, and gently pump the brake pedal to expel the fluid through a tube connected to the screw (see Section 11). Disconnect the wiring connector from the brake fluid level sender unit.

2 Carefully prise the fluid reservoir from the seals and release it from the top of the master cylinder.

3 Wipe clean the area around the brake pipe unions on the side of the master cylinder, and place absorbent rags beneath the pipe unions to catch any surplus fluid. Make a note of the correct fitted positions of the unions, then unscrew the union nuts and carefully withdraw the pipes. Plug or tape over the pipe ends and master cylinder orifices, to minimise the loss of brake fluid, and to prevent the entry of dirt into the system. Wash off any spilt fluid immediately with cold water.

HAYNES HiNT ***Cut the finger tips from an old rubber glove and secure them over the open ends of the brake pipes with elastic bands - this will help to minimise fluid loss and prevent the ingress of contaminants.***

4 Slacken and remove the nuts securing the master cylinder to the vacuum servo unit, then withdraw the unit from the engine compartment.

5 Where applicable, recover the seals from the rear of the master cylinder, and discard them; new items must be used on refitting.

6 With the master cylinder removed, check that the distance between the end of the vacuum servo unit pushrod and the master cylinder mating surface is as shown in the diagram. If necessary, the distance may be adjusted by turning the nut at the end of the servo unit pushrod **(see illustration)**.

Refitting

7 Fit new rubber seals and then press the fluid reservoir into the ports at the top of the master cylinder

8 Remove all traces of dirt from the master cylinder and servo unit mating surfaces, and where applicable, fit a new seal between the master cylinder body and the servo.

9 Fit the master cylinder to the servo unit, ensuring that the servo unit pushrod enters the master cylinder bore centrally. Refit the

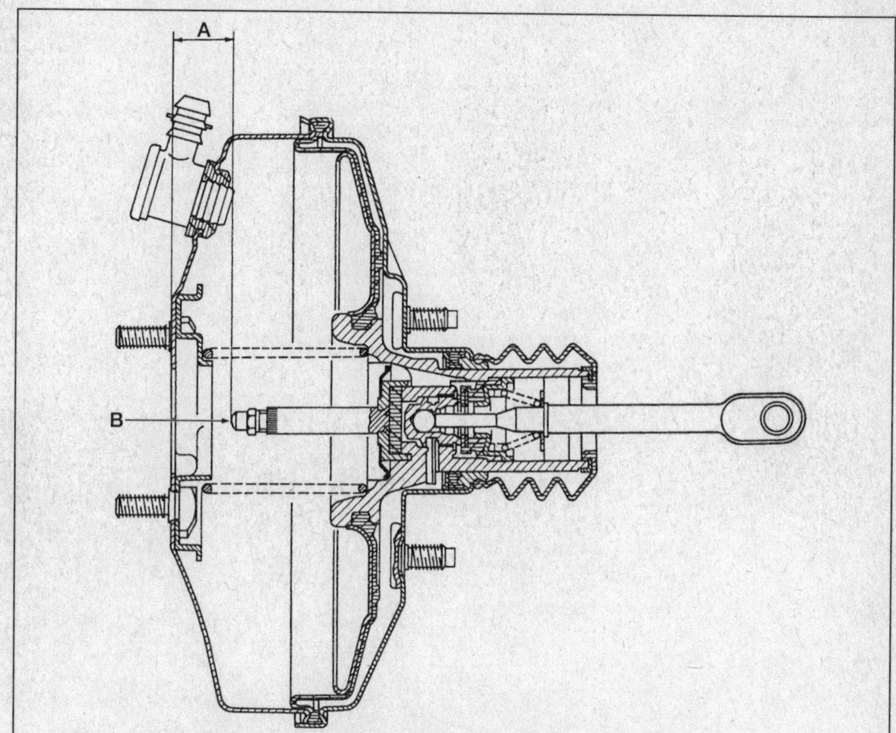

12.6 Cross-sectional view of vacuum servo unit

A 22.45 to 22.65 mm *B Adjustment nut*

9

master cylinder mounting nuts, and tighten them securely.

10 Wipe clean the brake pipe unions, then refit them to the correct master cylinder ports, as noted before removal, and tighten the union nuts securely.

11 Refill the master cylinder reservoir with new fluid, and bleed the complete hydraulic system as described in Section 11.

12 Check the operation of the braking system thoroughly.

13 Hydraulic pipes and hoses - renewal

Warning: Before starting work, refer to the warning at the beginning of Section 11 concerning the dangers of hydraulic fluid.

1 If any pipe or hose is to be renewed, minimise fluid loss by first removing the master cylinder reservoir cap, then tighten the cap down onto a piece of polythene to obtain an airtight seal. Alternatively, flexible hoses can be sealed, if required, using a proprietary brake hose clamp; metal brake pipe unions can be plugged (if care is taken not to allow dirt into the system) or capped immediately they are disconnected. Place a wad of rag under any union that is to be disconnected, to catch any spilt fluid.

2 If a flexible hose is to be disconnected, unscrew the brake pipe union nut before removing the spring clip which secures the hose to its mounting bracket.

3 To unscrew the union nuts, it is preferable to obtain a brake pipe spanner of the correct size; these are available from most large motor accessory shops. Failing this, a close-fitting open-ended spanner will be required, though if the nuts are tight or corroded, their flats may be rounded-off if the spanner slips. In such a case, a self-locking wrench is often the only way to unscrew a stubborn union, but it follows that the pipe and the damaged nuts must be renewed on reassembly. Always clean a union and surrounding area before disconnecting it. If disconnecting a component with more than one union, make a careful note of the connections before disturbing any of them.

4 If a brake pipe is to be renewed, it can be obtained, cut to length and with the union nuts and end flares in place, from Fiat dealers. All that is then necessary is to bend it to shape, following the line of the original, before fitting it to the vehicle. Alternatively, most motor accessory shops can make up brake pipes from kits, but this requires very careful measurement of the original, to ensure that the replacement is of the correct length. The safest answer is usually to take the original to the shop as a pattern.

5 On refitting, do not overtighten the union nuts. It is not necessary to exercise brute force to obtain a sound joint.

6 Ensure that the pipes and hoses are correctly routed, with no kinks, and that they are secured in the clips or brackets provided. After fitting, remove the polythene from the reservoir, and bleed the hydraulic system as described in Section 11. Wash off any spilt fluid, and check carefully for fluid leaks.

Chapter 10
Suspension and steering

Contents

Degrees of difficulty

Easy, suitable for novice with little experience 	**Fairly easy,** suitable for beginner with some experience 	**Fairly difficult,** suitable for competent DIY mechanic	**Difficult,** suitable for experienced DIY mechanic	**Very difficult,** suitable for expert DIY or professional

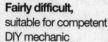

Specifications

Front suspension

Type . . . Independent, incorporating transverse lower wishbones and coil spring-over-telescopic damper strut units. Anti-roll bar fitted to all models.

Rear suspension

Type . . . Independent, incorporating trailing arms with telescopic dampers and coil springs.

Steering

Type	Rack-and-pinion, manual or power assisted, depending on model
Turns lock-to-lock:	
Manual	4.4 approx.
Power assisted	2.9 approx.
Toe setting (front)	0° (parallel) ± 1°

Roadwheels and tyres

See *Weekly checks*

Torque wrench settings

	Nm	lbf ft
Front suspension		
Anti-roll bar bush bracket bolts	30	22
Driveshaft nut:*		
All models except turbo diesel (M22 plain)	240	177
Turbo diesel (M24 with staking and captive washer)	280	207
Lower arm balljoint to hub carrier	30	22
Lower arm front bush securing bolt	95	70
Lower arm rear bush securing bolt	70	52
Suspension strut damper nut	60	44
Suspension strut to hub carrier	70	52
Suspension strut to inner wing	50	37

10

Torque wrench settings (continued)

	Nm	lbf ft
Rear suspension		
Damper lower securing bolt	95	70
Damper upper securing bolt	60	44
Handbrake cable support bracket-to-trailing arm screws	15	11
Hub nut	280	207
Trailing arm securing bolt	150	111
Steering		
Ignition switch/steering column lock securing bolts	4	3
Steering column mounting bolts	55	41
Steering gear mounting bolts	70	52
Steering wheel nut*	50	37
Subframe-to-body bolts	110	81
Track-rod end to hub carrier	40	30
Universal joint clamp bolts	20	15
Roadwheels		
Roadwheel bolts	85	63

* *Use a new nut*

1 General information

Front suspension

The front suspension is independent, comprising transverse lower wishbones, coil spring-over-damper strut units and an anti-roll bar. The hub carriers are bolted to the base of the strut units and are linked to the lower arms by means of balljoints. The entire front suspension assembly is mounted on a subframe, which is in turn bolted to the vehicle body.

Rear suspension

The rear suspension incorporates a torsion beam axle, trailing arms, coil springs and separate telescopic dampers. In addition, a rear anti-roll bar is fitted to certain models. The components form a discrete sub-assembly which can be unbolted from the underside of the vehicle separately or as a complete unit.

Steering

The two-piece steering shaft runs in a tubular column assembly, which is bolted to a bracket mounted on the vehicles bulkhead. The shaft is articulated at its lower end by means of a universal joint, which is clamped to the steering shaft and the steering gear pinion by means of clamp bolts.

The steering gear is mounted on the engine compartment bulkhead, and is connected to the steering arms projecting rearwards from the hub carriers. The track-rods are fitted with balljoints at their inner and outer ends, to allow for suspension movement, and are threaded to facilitate adjustment.

Hydraulically-assisted power steering is fitted to some models. The hydraulic system is powered by a belt-driven servo pump, which is driven from the crankshaft pulley.

Certain models are fitted with an airbag system. Sensors built into the vehicle body are triggered in the event of a front end collision and prompt an Electronic Control Unit (ECU) to activate the airbag, mounted in the centre of the steering wheel and the facia. This reduces the risk of the front seat occupants striking the steering wheel, windscreen or facia during an accident.

Warning: For safety reasons, owners are strongly advised to entrust to an authorised Fiat dealer any work which involves disturbing the airbag system components. The airbag inflation devices contain explosive material and legislation exists to control their handling and storage. In addition, specialised test equipment is needed to check that the airbag system is fully operational following reassembly.

2 Front hub bearings - renewal

Note: *A balljoint separator tool, and a press or suitable alternative tools (see text) will be required for this operation. The bearing will be destroyed during the removal procedure.*

Removal

1 Chock the rear wheels, apply the handbrake, then jack up the front of the vehicle and support on axle stands (see *Jacking and vehicle support*). Remove the appropriate roadwheel.

2 Remove the brake disc and caliper, with reference to Chapter 9. Note that the caliper body can remain bolted to its bracket: there is no need to disconnect the brake fluid hose from the caliper.

3 With reference to Chapter 8, slacken and remove the driveshaft hub nut.

4 On models with ABS, unbolt the ABS wheel sensor, and remove the screw securing the ABS sensor wiring to the hub carrier. Suspend the sensor away from the working area, to avoid the possibility of damage.

5 With reference to Section 17, separate the track-rod end from the hub carrier, using a suitable balljoint splitter.

6 Remove the two nuts from the bolts securing the hub carrier to the base of the suspension strut (refer to Section 3). Withdraw the bolts and separate the top of hub carrier from the strut.

7 Disconnect the outboard end of the driveshaft from the hub, as described during the driveshaft removal and refitting procedure in Chapter 8. **Note:** *There is no need to disconnect the inboard end of the driveshaft from the transmission.*

Caution: Do not allow the end of the driveshaft to hang down under its own weight, as this places strain on the CV joints; support the end of the shaft using wire or string.

8 Slacken and remove the nut and clamp bolt, then push the lower arm down and separate the balljoint from the base of the hub carrier **(see illustrations).**

9 At this stage, it is recommended that the hub carrier be taken to a engineering workshop, as the hub and bearing should ideally be removed from the hub carrier using a hydraulic press.

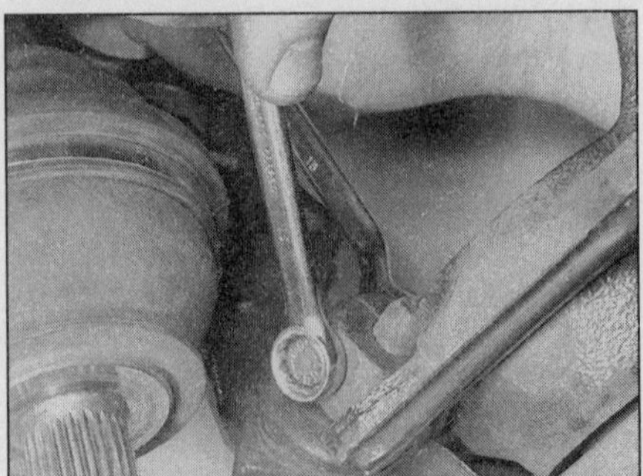

2.8a . . . Slacken and remove the nut . . .

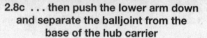

2.8b . . . and clamp bolt . . .

2.8c . . . then push the lower arm down and separate the balljoint from the base of the hub carrier

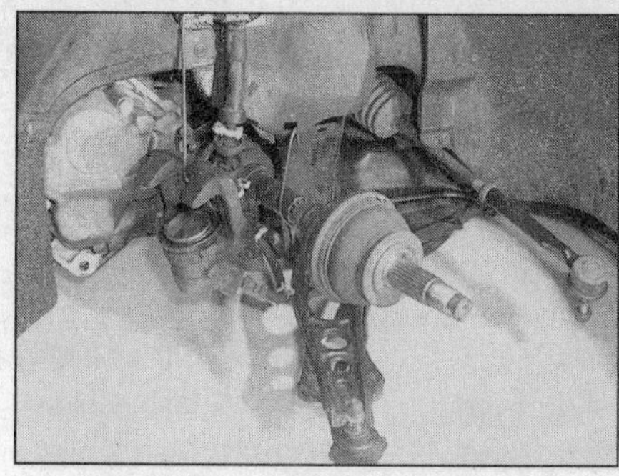

2.8d View of front suspension components with hub carrier removed

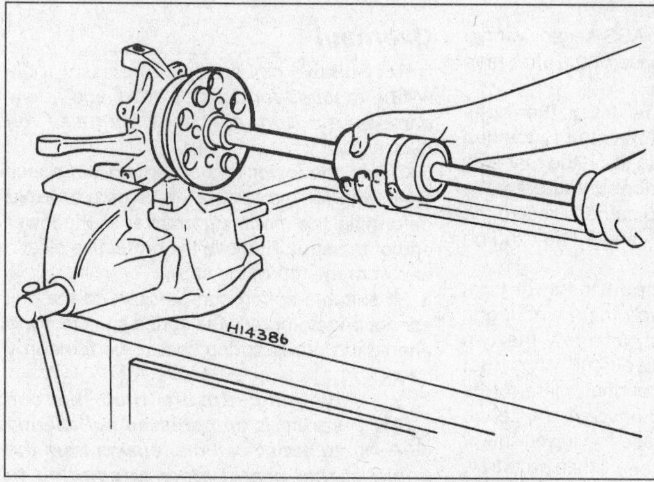

2.10 Using a slide hammer to extract the hub

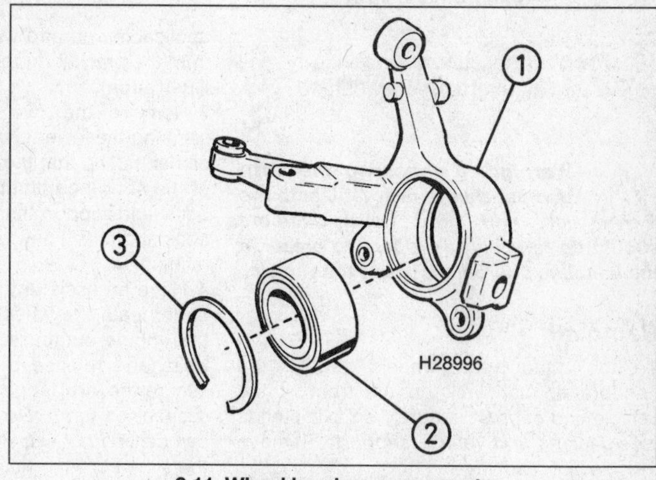

2.11 Wheel bearing components

1 Hub carrier *2 Wheel bearing* *3 Circlip*

Owners wishing to attempt the work themselves should proceed as follows.

10 Mount the hub carrier firmly in a bench vice. Attach a slide hammer to the hub flange and extract the hub, together with the inner bearing race, if it has remained attached to the hub. Unbolt and remove the heat shield **(see illustration).**

11 Mount the hub carrier horizontally in the vice, then remove the bearing retaining circlip. Using a suitable length of tubing as a drift, drive the bearing outer race from the carrier **(see illustration).** Note that a flange on the outboard side of the carrier means that the bearing can only be driven out in one direction.

12 Support the inner bearing race, if it has remained attached to the hub, then press or drive the hub from the race. Alternatively, pull the bearing race from the hub using a suitable two or three-legged puller.

13 Before installing the new bearing, thoroughly clean the bearing location in the hub carrier.

14 Fit the new bearing from the inboard side the hub; press or drive the bearing into position, applying pressure only to the bearing outer race. **Do not** lubricate the mating surface of the bearing in an attempt to ease installation.

15 Fit the bearing retaining circlip to its groove in the hub carrier, then refit the heat shield and tighten the retaining screw securely.

16 Support the outer face of the hub carrier across the jaws of a bench vice.

17 Carefully press or draw the hub into the bearing, noting that the bearing inner race must be supported during this operation, to prevent it from being separated from the outer race. This can be achieved using a suitable socket, threaded rod, washers and a length of bar **(see illustration).**

18 On completion, check that the hub rotates freely in the hub carrier without resistance or roughness.

2.17 Typical method of drawing the hub into the wheel bearing using improvised tools

Refitting

19 Reconnect the outboard end of the driveshaft to the hub as described in Chapter 8. Ensure that the driveshaft nut is tightened to the correct torque and adequately staked. Ideally, for safety reasons due to the very high torque of the driveshaft nut, carry out final tightening and staking of the nut after refitting the roadwheel and lowering the car to the ground.

20 Reconnect the hub carrier to the lower arm balljoint, then fit a new clamp bolt nut. Tighten the nut to the specified torque.

21 Engage the hub carrier with the suspension strut, then refit the securing bolts and nuts, tightening them to the specified torque.

22 Reconnect the steering track-rod balljoint to the hub carrier steering arm. Use a new nut and tighten it to the specified torque.

23 Refer to Chapter 9 and refit the brake disc and caliper.

24 Where applicable, fit the ABS wheel sensor into its mounting hole and tighten the securing screw.

25 Refit the roadwheel, and lower the vehicle to the ground.

26 Have the front wheel alignment checked by a Fiat dealer or a tyre specialist at the earliest opportunity.

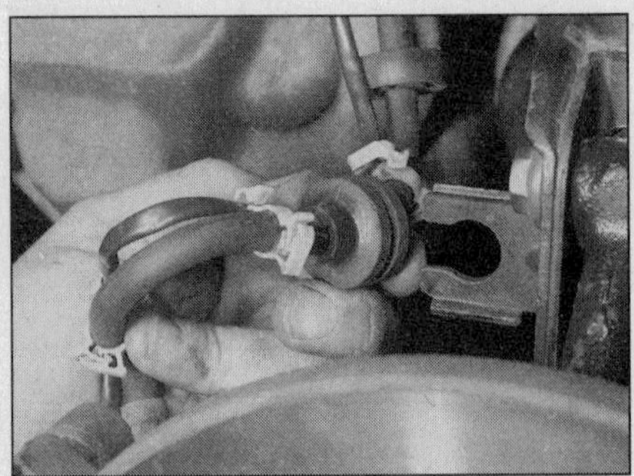
3.2 Release the brake fluid line (and where applicable, the pad wear/ABS sensor wiring) from the strut

3.3a Remove the two bolts (arrowed) . . .

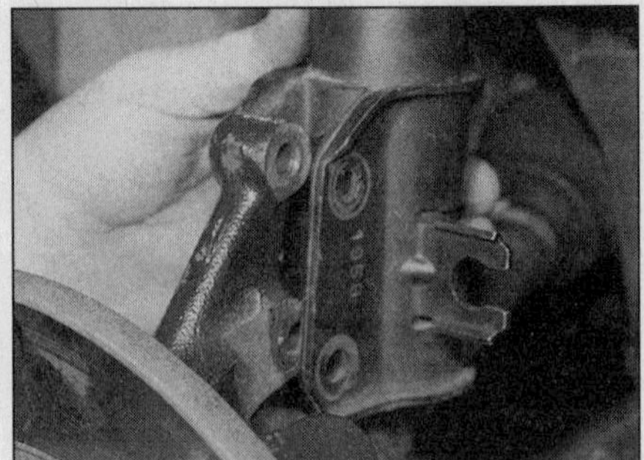
3.3b . . . and detach the lower end of the strut from the hub carrier

3 Front suspension strut - removal, overhaul and refitting

Warning: If renewing the strut damper during overhaul, both the left and right hand dampers should be renewed as a pair, to preserve the handling characteristics of the vehicle.

Removal

1 Chock the rear wheels, apply the handbrake, then jack up the front of the vehicle and support securely on axle stands (see *Jacking and vehicle support*). Remove the relevant roadwheel.

2 Release the brake fluid line (and where applicable, the pad wear/ABS sensor wiring) from the bracket on the base of the strut **(see illustration).**

3 Remove the two nuts from the bolts securing the lower end of the strut to the hub carrier, noting that the nuts fit on the rear side of the strut **(see illustrations).** Withdraw the bolts, and support the hub carrier. Discard the bolts and nuts - new ones should be used on refitting.

4 Have an assistant support the strut from underneath the wheel arch then, working in the engine compartment, unscrew the two bolts and release the two stud clips that secure the strut upper mounting plate to the suspension turret. *Do not unscrew the centre damper rod nut yet.* Release the lower end of the strut from the hub carrier, then withdraw the assembly from under the wheel arch.

Overhaul

Note: *Suitable coil spring compressor tools will be required for this operation, and a new damper rod top nut must be used on reassembly.*

5 Clamp the lower end of the strut in a vice fitted with jaw protectors - take care to avoid deforming the mounting bracket at the lower end of the strut. Remove the protective plastic cap from the top of the strut.

6 Fit suitable spring compressors to the coil spring, and compress the spring sufficiently to enable the upper spring seat to be turned by hand.

Warning: Ensure that the coil spring is compressed sufficiently to remove all the tension from the upper spring seat, before attempting to remove the damper rod nut.

7 Fully unscrew and remove the damper rod top nut. Counterhold the damper rod, using a suitable Allen key or hex bit, as the nut is unscrewed - do not allow the rod to rotate inside the damper **(see illustration).** Discard the nut - a new one must be used on reassembly.

8 Withdraw the washer, bush, upper mounting plate and upper spring seat - make a careful note of the order of assembly **(see illustrations).**

9 Withdraw the spring, complete with the compressors, then withdraw the dust cover, bump rubber and the lower spring seat rubber (where fitted) **(see illustrations).**

3.7 Fully unscrew and remove the damper rod top nut

3.8a Withdraw the washer . . .

3.8b . . . bush . . .

3.8c . . . upper mounting plate . . .

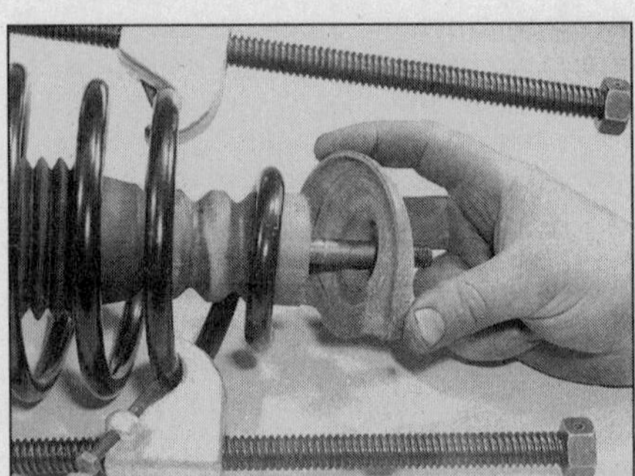
3.8d . . . and upper spring seat

3.9a Withdraw the coil spring, complete with the compressors . . .

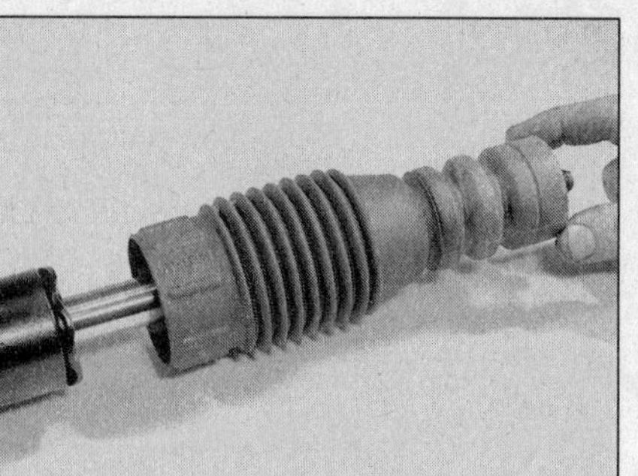

3.9b . . . then withdraw the dust cover and bump rubber

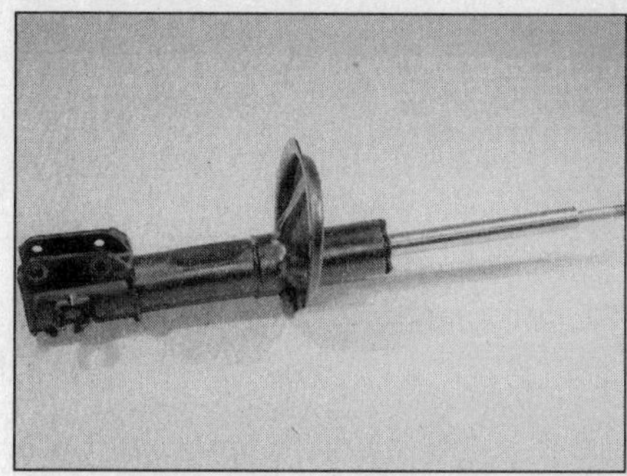

3.9c Fully dismantled strut

10 With the strut assembly now dismantled, examine all the components for wear, damage or deformation. Check the rubber components for deterioration. Renew any of the components as necessary.

11 Examine the damper for signs of fluid leakage. Check the damper rod for signs of pitting along its entire length, and check the strut body for signs of damage. While holding it in an upright position, test the operation of the strut by moving the damper rod through a full stroke, and then through short strokes of 50 to 100 mm. In both cases, the resistance felt should be smooth and continuous. If the resistance is jerky, or uneven, or if there is any visible sign of wear or damage to the strut, renewal is necessary. Note that the damper cannot be renewed independently, and if leakage, damage or corrosion is evident, the complete strut/damper assembly must be renewed (in which case, the spring, upper mounting components, bushes, and associated components can be transferred to the new strut).

12 If any doubt exists about the condition of the coil spring, carefully remove the spring compressors, and check the spring for distortion and signs of cracking. Renew the spring if it is damaged or distorted, or if there is any doubt about its condition.

Warning: Coil springs are classified by their height when under load - this is indicated by a coloured paint marking on the side of the coil windings (either green or yellow). All coil springs fitted to the vehicle must be of the same classification to ensure the correct ride height.

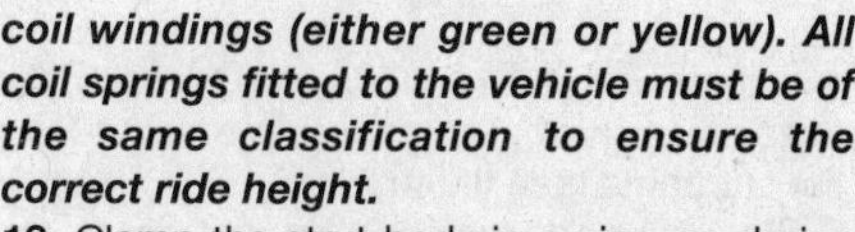

13 Clamp the strut body in a vice, as during dismantling, then refit the lower spring seat rubber (where fitted), dust cover and bump rubber.

14 Ensure that the coil spring is compressed sufficiently to enable the upper mounting components to be fitted, then fit the spring over the damper rod, ensuring that the lower end of the spring is correctly located in the recess on the lower spring seat **(see illustration)**.

15 Refit the upper spring seat and upper mounting plate ensuring that the top end of the spring is correctly located on the upper spring seat. Note that when the strut is reassembled, the orientation marking on the upper rubber mounting must be positioned in relation to the metal section of the upper mounting plate as shown, to maintain the correct front wheel castor setting **(see illustration)**.

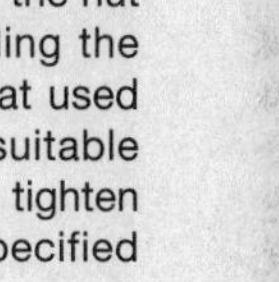

16 Fit the new damper rod top nut together with its washer and bush, then tighten the nut to the specified torque, counterholding the damper rod in a manner similar to that used during dismantling. Note that a suitable crows-foot adapter will be required to tighten the damper rod top nut to the specified torque.

17 Remove the spring compressors. Where applicable, refit the protective plastic cap over the damper rod top nut.

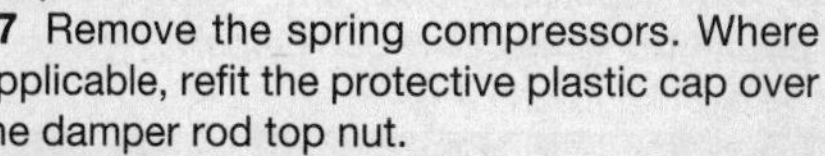

Refitting

18 Manoeuvre the strut assembly into position under the wheel arch, passing the locating stud clip through the holes in the body turret. Note that when the strut is refitted, the orientation marking on the upper mounting plate rubber mounting must be positioned in relation to the vehicle as shown, to maintain the correct front wheel castor setting - refer to illustration 3.15. Fit the upper mounting bolts, and tighten them to the specified torque **(see illustration)**.

19 Engage the lower end of the strut with the

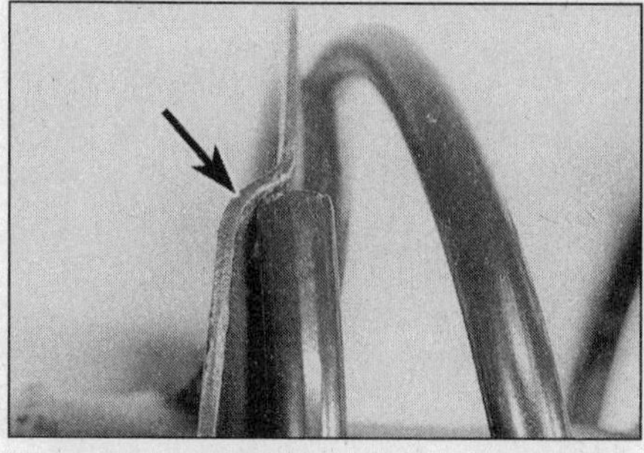

3.14 Ensure that the lower end of the spring is correctly located in the recess (arrowed) on the lower spring seat

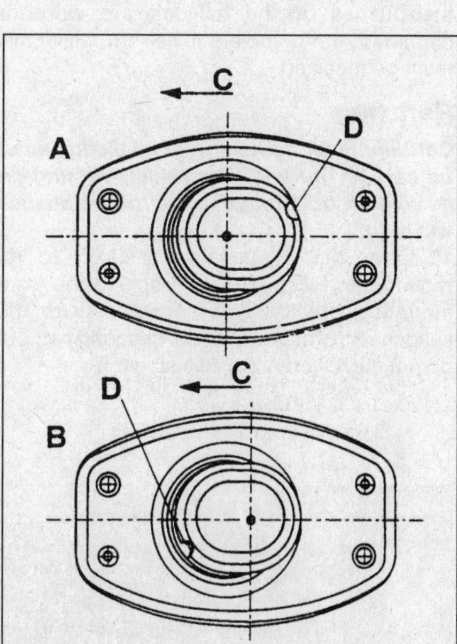

3.15 Correct positioning of the suspension strut upper mounting components

A Left hand mounting for vehicles with manual steering
B Left hand mounting for vehicles with power-assisted steering
C To front of vehicle
D Orientation marking

3.18 Fit the strut upper mounting bolts, and tighten them to the specified torque

hub carrier, then fit the securing bolts and nuts, noting that the nuts fit on the rear side of the strut, and tighten to the specified torque **(see illustrations).**

20 Refit the brake fluid line to the bracket on the base of the strut.

21 Where applicable, press the ABS wheel sensor wiring into its retaining bracket.

22 Refit the roadwheel, and lower the vehicle to the ground.

3.19a Fit the securing bolts, noting that the nuts fit on the rear side of the strut . . .

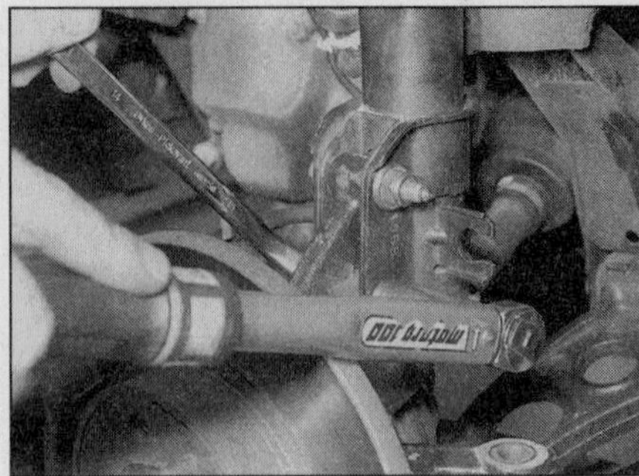
3.19b . . . and tighten them to the specified torque

4 Front suspension lower arm - removal and refitting

Removal

1 Chock the rear wheels, apply the handbrake, then jack up the front of the vehicle and support securely on axle stands (see *Jacking and vehicle support*). Remove the relevant roadwheel.

2 Unscrew the bolts securing the anti-roll bar mountings to the suspension lower arms on either side of the vehicle. Similarly, unscrew the bolts securing the anti-roll bar mountings to the suspension sub-frame **(see illustrations).** Allow the ends of the anti-roll bar to pivot away from the suspension lower arms.

3 With reference to Section 2, unscrew the nut, withdraw the clamp bolt and lever the end of the suspension lower arm down to release it from the base of the hub carrier.

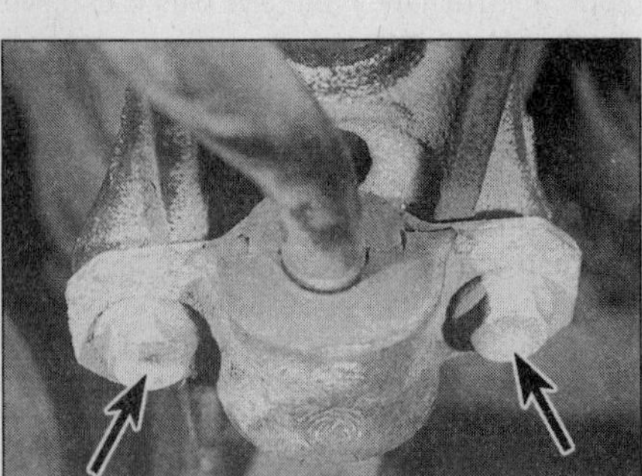
4.2a Unscrew the bolts (arrowed) securing the anti-roll bar mountings to the suspension lower arms . . .

4 Unscrew the two bolts and detach the suspension arm rear mounting bracket from the subframe **(see illustration).**

5 Slacken and remove the nut from the through-bolt at the lower arm front mounting **(see illustration).** Withdraw the bolt.

6 Withdraw the suspension lower arm from under the vehicle.

7 With the lower arm removed, examine the lower arm itself, and the mounting bushes, for wear, cracks or damage.

8 Check the balljoint for wear, excessive play, or stiffness. Also check the balljoint dust boot for cracks or damage.

9 The mounting bushes and balljoint assembly are integral with the lower arm, and cannot be renewed independently. If either the bushes or the balljoint are worn or damaged, the complete lower arm assembly must be renewed.

Refitting

Caution: Final tightening of all fixings must be carried out with the vehicle resting on its wheels, or damage to the rubber bushes will result.

10 Offer the suspension arm up to its mountings. Fit the through-bolt to the front mounting bracket and engage it with the suspension arm bush. Fit the securing nut, but do not fully tighten it at this stage.

11 Bolt the rear mounting bracket to the subframe, but do not fully tighten the bolts at this stage.

12 Engage the lower arm balljoint with the hub carrier, then refit the balljoint clamp bolt and nut. Do not fully tighten the nut at this stage.

13 Raise the anti-roll bar into position, then bolt the mounting brackets to the subframe. The anti-roll bar must be pre-loaded before its outer mounting brackets can be bolted to the suspension arms. Do this by raising the ends of the anti-roll bar with a trolley jack and holding them in this position whilst the bracket mounting bolts are inserted and hand tightened. Do not fully tighten the bolts at this stage. Line up the holes at the ends of the anti-roll bar with those on the suspension lower arm.

14 Refit the roadwheel, and lower the vehicle to the ground.

15 Make sure that the vehicle is parked on level ground, then release the handbrake. Roll the vehicle backwards and forwards, and bounce the front of the vehicle to settle the suspension components.

16 Chock the wheels, then tighten all the anti-roll bar and suspension arm mounting nuts and bolts to the specified torque.

17 On completion the front wheel alignment should be checked by a Fiat dealer.

4.2b . . . and the suspension sub-frame (arrowed)

4.4 Unscrew the two bolts (arrowed) and detach the suspension arm rear mounting bracket from the subframe

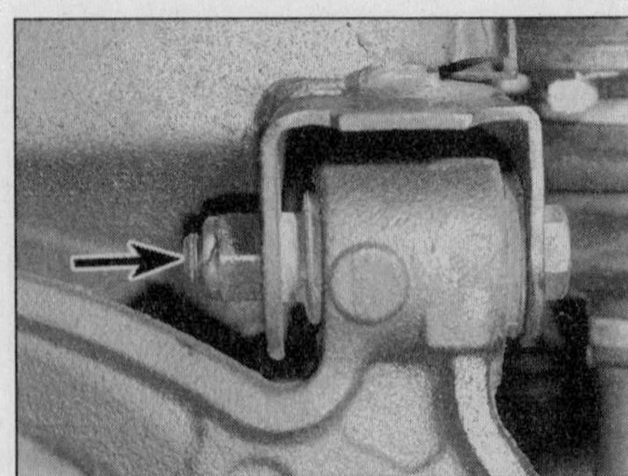
4.5 Slacken and remove the nut (arrowed) from the through-bolt at the lower arm front mounting

5 Front suspension lower arm balljoint - renewal

The balljoint is integral with the suspension lower arm **(see illustration).** If the balljoint is worn or damaged, the complete lower arm must be renewed as described in Section 4.

5.1 Front suspension lower arm balljoint

6 Front suspension anti-roll bar - removal and refitting

Removal

1 Chock the rear wheels, apply the handbrake, then jack up the front of the vehicle and support securely on axle stands (see *Jacking and vehicle support*). If required, remove the relevant roadwheels.

2 Refer to the Chapter 4D and unbolt the front section of the exhaust pipe.

3 Unscrew the bolts securing the anti-roll bar mountings to the suspension lower arms on either side of the vehicle. Similarly, unscrew the bolts securing the anti-roll bar mountings to the suspension sub-frame (refer to the illustrations in Section 4).

4 Lower the anti-roll bar away from the underside of the vehicle.

5 Inspect the rubber bushes for cracks or deterioration. If renewal is necessary, slide the old bushes from the bar, and fit the new items, using soapy water as a lubricant. Do not apply grease or oil as this will attack the rubber.

6 Check the anti-roll bar for signs of damage, wear or serious corrosion.

Refitting

7 Refitting is a reversal of removal, bearing in mind the following points:

a) *Line up the holes at the ends of the anti-roll bar with those on the suspension lower arm.*

b) *Tighten all fixings to the specified torque, but do not do this until the vehicle is resting on its roadwheels, and the suspension has been settled, or damage to the bushes may result.*

7 Rear hub bearings - renewal

Note: *The bearing will be destroyed during the removal operation, and a new rear hub/bearing assembly must be used on refitting - the old hub cannot be re-used. A new rear hub nut must be used on refitting.*

1 The rear hub bearings are integral with the hubs themselves, and cannot be renewed separately. If the bearings require renewal, the complete hub assembly must be renewed as follows.

2 Chock the front wheels, then jack up the rear of the vehicle and support securely on axle stands (see *Jacking and vehicle support*). Remove the appropriate rear roadwheel.

3 Remove the brake drum as described in Chapter 9. **Do not** depress the brake pedal whilst the brake drum is removed.

4 Prise the dust cap from the hub, using a mallet and punch.

5 Slacken and remove the hub nut and recover the washer/spacers **(see illustration).** ***Caution: The nut is tightened to a very high torque. Use a long extension bar to remove the nut and ensure that you have access to torque wrench capable of tightening the new nut to the specified torque setting, before removing the existing nut.***

6 Withdraw the hub and bearing assembly from the stub axle, and recover the inner washer. Discard the hub nut - a new one must be used on refitting.

7 Thoroughly clean the stub axle, then slide the inner washer and new hub assembly into position.

8 Fit the outer washer, then thread a new hub nut onto the end of the stub axle by hand - do not fully tighten the nut at this stage.

9 Refit the brake drum (Chapter 9).

10 Tighten the hub nut to the specified torque, then check that the hub spins smoothly and freely. Carefully tap the dust cap into position over the nut.

11 Refit the roadwheel, then lower the vehicle to the ground and tighten the roadwheel bolts to the specified torque.

8 Rear suspension components - removal, overhaul and refitting

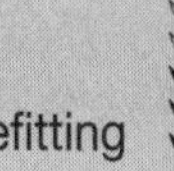

1 Chock the front wheels, then jack up the rear of the vehicle and support on axle stands (see *Jacking and vehicle support*). Remove the relevant rear roadwheel.

Damper

Removal

2 Using a trolley jack positioned under the trailing arm, raise the trailing arm to take the strain from the damper.

3 Slacken and withdraw the damper lower retaining bolt **(see illustration).**

4 Lower the jack and allow the damper to separate from the trailing arm. Take care to avoid displacing the coil spring.

5 Slacken and withdraw the damper upper retaining bolt **(see illustration).**

6 Lower the damper away from the suspension subframe.

Refitting

7 Refitting is a reversal of removal. Tighten the damper upper and lower retaining bolts to the specified torque, but delay this operation until the full weight vehicle is resting on the roadwheels - this prevents the damper bushes from being strained.

Coil spring

Removal

8 With reference to the previous sub-Section,

7.5 Slacken and remove the rear hub nut

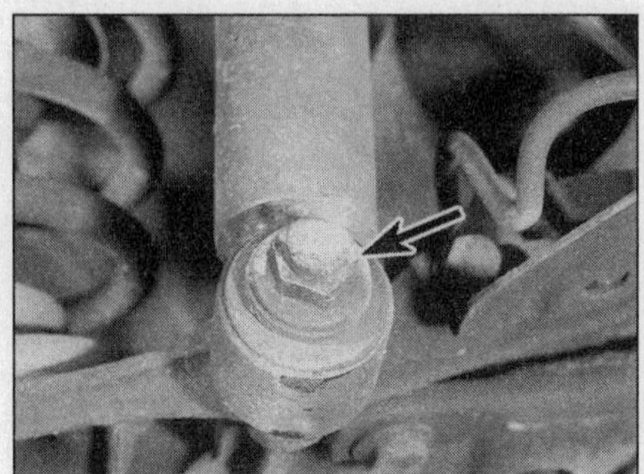

8.3 Slacken and withdraw the damper lower retaining bolt (arrowed)

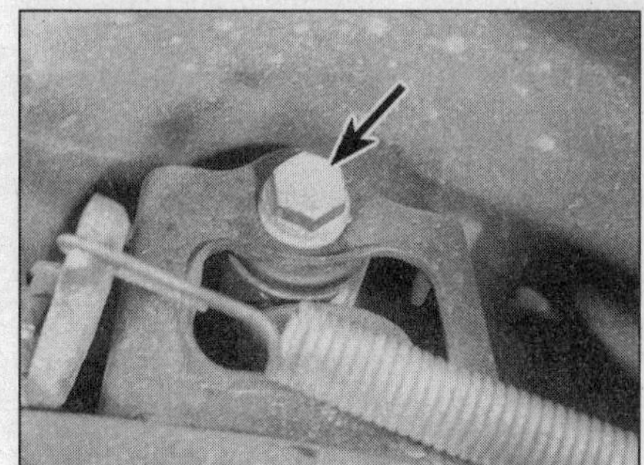

8.5 Slacken and withdraw the damper upper retaining bolt (arrowed)

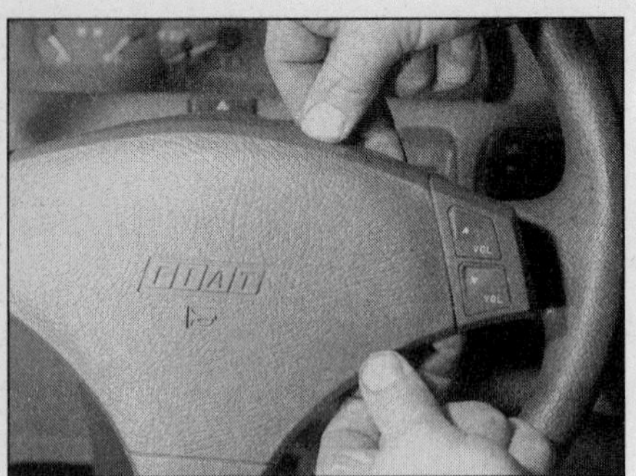
9.1 Prise the horn centre pad from the steering wheel hub

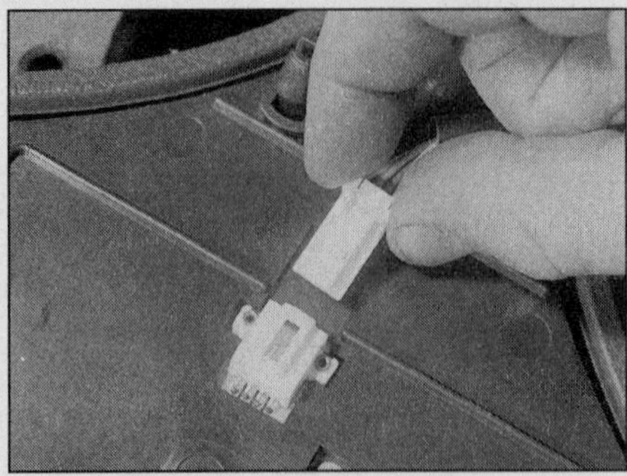
9.2 Unplug the wiring from the centre pad at the connector(s)

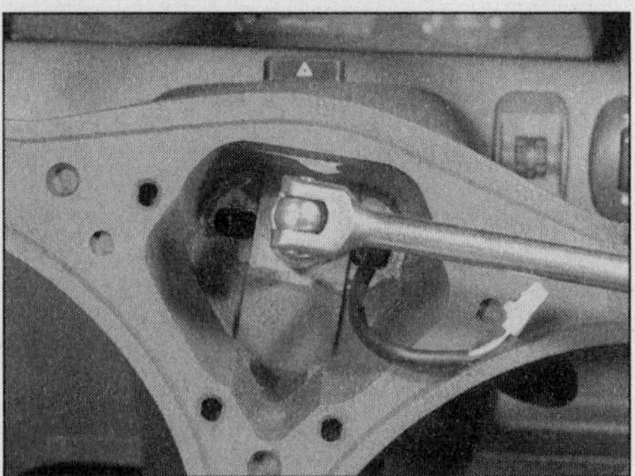
9.5 Slacken and remove the steering wheel securing nut

unbolt the lower end of the damper from the trailing arm.

9 Lower the trailing arm gradually using a trolley jack, until the coil spring is released from its lower seat on the trailing arm and its upper seat on the subframe. Make a note of the orientation of the coil spring, to aid correct refitting later.

Refitting

10 Refitting is a reversal of removal. Tighten the damper lower retaining bolt to the specified torque.

Trailing arm

Note: *The rear stub axles are integral with the trailing arm assemblies and cannot be renewed separately.*

Removal

11 With reference to Chapter 9, carry out the following:

a) *Remove the brake drum, shoes and adjuster assembly.*
b) *Unbolt the brake hose union from the rear of the wheel cylinder.*
c) *Unbolt the brake pipe mounting bracket from the trailing arm.*

12 Refer to Section 7 and remove the rear hub and bearing assembly.

13 With reference to the relevant sub-Section, unbolt the lower end of the damper from the trailing arm.

14 Raise the trailing arm using a trolley jack so that the coil spring is compressed, then slacken and withdraw the trailing arm front mounting bolt.

15 With reference to the previous sub-Section, gradually lower the trailing arm using a trolley jack and remove the coil spring.

16 Allow the trailing arm to hang down, then pull the leading edge of the arm down from its mounting bracket.

Refitting

17 Refitting is a reversal of removal. Tighten all suspension fixings to the specified torque settings, but delay this operation until the full weight vehicle is resting on the roadwheels - this prevents the damper and trailing arm bushes from being strained.

18 On completion, bleed the brake hydraulic system and adjust the operation of the handbrake, with reference to Chapter 9.

9 Steering wheel - removal and refitting

Note: *This procedure does not apply to vehicles fitted with an airbag*

Warning: For safety reasons, owners are strongly advised to entrust to an authorised Fiat dealer any work which involves disturbing the airbag system components. The airbag inflation devices contain explosive material and legislation exists to control their handling and storage. In addition, specialised test equipment is needed to check that the airbag system is fully operational following reassembly.

Removal

1 Ensure that the ignition is switched off, then prise the horn centre pad from the steering wheel hub. Use the blade of a screwdriver, padded with PVC tape to protect the steering wheel **(see illustration)**

2 Unplug the horn and (where applicable) radio/cassette control switch wiring from the centre pad at the connector(s) **(see illustration)**.

3 Turn the steering wheel to its centre position, so that the roadwheels are pointing straight ahead.

4 Make alignment marks between the steering wheel and the end of the steering column shaft, to aid correct refitting later.

5 Relieve the staking and then slacken and remove the steering wheel securing nut **(see illustration)**. Discard the nut as a new item must used on refitting.

6 Lift the steering wheel off the column splines. If it is tight, tap it near the centre, using the palm of your hand, or twist it from side to side, whilst pulling upwards to release it from the shaft splines. If the wheel is particularly tight, a suitable puller should be used.

Refitting

7 Before commencing refitting, lightly coat the surfaces of the direction indicator cancelling mechanism with grease.

8 Refitting is a reversal of removal, bearing in mind the following points:

a) *Use a new steering wheel securing nut and tighten it to the specified torque. Ensure that its outer collar is adequately staked to the column shaft using a hammer and punch* ***(see illustrations).***
b) *Ensure that the direction indicator switch is in the central (cancelled/off) position, otherwise the switch may be damaged as the wheel is refitted.*
c) *Align the marks made on the wheel and the steering column shaft during removal.*

9 Note that if necessary, the position of the steering wheel on the column shaft can be altered in order to centralise the wheel (ensure that the front roadwheels are pointing in the straight-ahead position), by moving the wheel the required number of splines on the shaft. Fine adjustment can be carried out by adjusting the length of both track-rods simultaneously, but this operation is best entrusted to a Fiat dealer or tyre specialist.

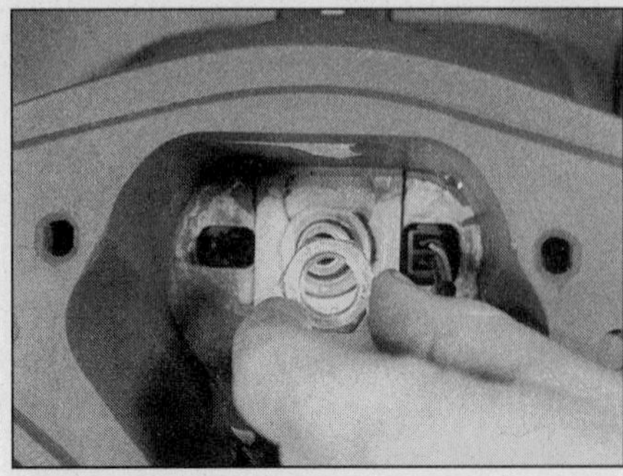
9.8a Fit a new steering wheel securing nut . . .

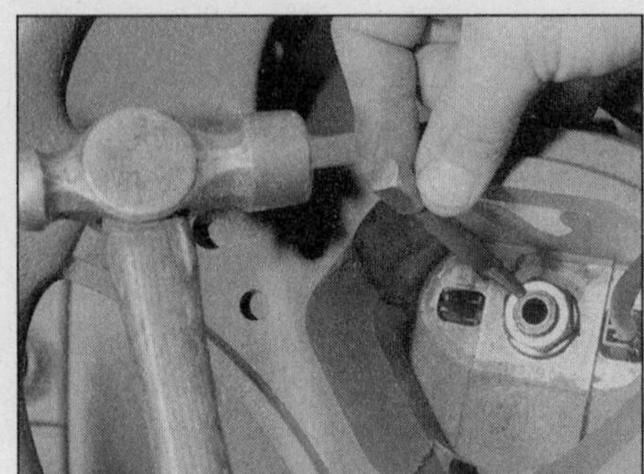
9.8b . . . and stake it to the steering column shaft using a hammer and punch

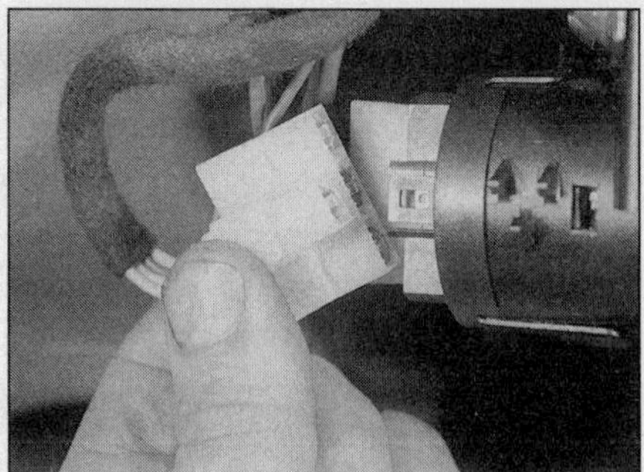

10.3 Unplug the multi-way wiring connector from the rear of the lock assembly

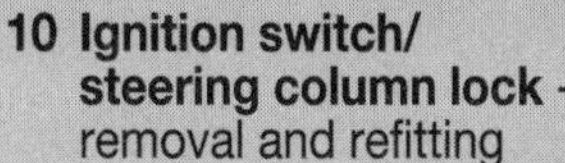

10 Ignition switch/ steering column lock - removal and refitting

Caution: The ignition switch/steering column lock has an integral anti-theft mechanism. Any attempt to rotate the lock shaft using tools (ie without using the correct key) results in the steering column being locked and irreparable damage to the lock mechanism. This renders the vehicle unusable until the lock assembly is renewed.

Removal

1 Disconnect the battery negative terminal (refer to *Disconnecting the battery* in the Reference Section of this manual).

2 Remove the lower section of the steering column shroud.

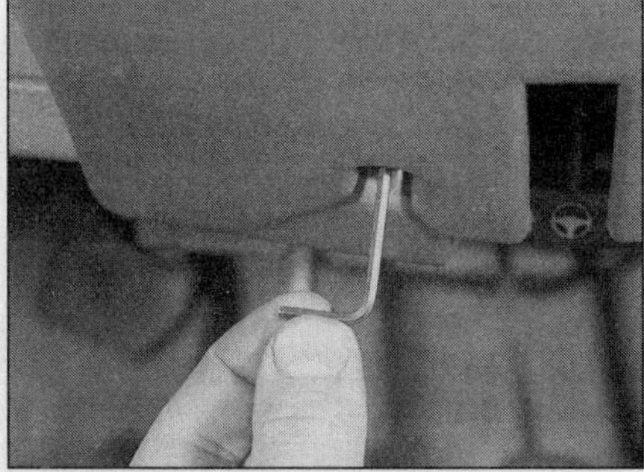

11.3a Unscrew the fixings using an Allen key . . .

11.3b . . . and remove the upper and lower halves of the plastic shroud from the steering column

10.4 On vehicles fitted with a Fiat immobiliser, unclip the receiver ring from the lock cylinder

3 Unplug the multi-way wiring connector from the rear of the lock assembly **(see illustration)**.

4 On vehicles fitted with a Fiat immobiliser, unclip the receiver ring from the lock cylinder **(see illustration)**. Insert the key into the ignition switch and turn it to the ON position.

5 Working underneath the steering column, insert a small flat bladed screwdriver into the access slot in the base of the lock assembly bracket. Depress the release button and withdraw the lock assembly from its bracket, complete with the key **(see illustrations)**.

Refitting

6 To refit the lock, first insert the key and turn it to the ON position. Depress the release button slide the assembly into the retaining bracket until the release button clicks into the access slot.

7 Turn the key back to the OFF position, then reconnect the wiring connector.

8 Refit the steering column lower shroud.

9 Reconnect the negative cable to the battery terminal.

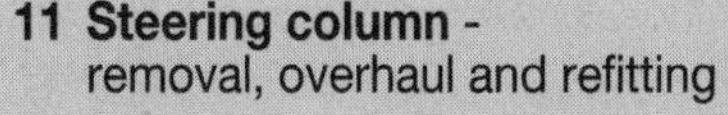

11 Steering column - removal, overhaul and refitting

Removal

1 Disconnect the battery negative terminal (refer to *Disconnecting the battery* in the Reference Section of this manual).

2 Remove the steering wheel (Section 9).

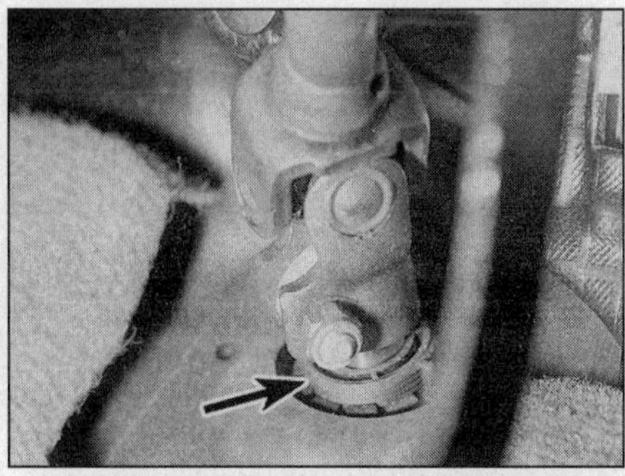

11.6 Slacken the nut (arrowed) and clamp bolt on the lower half of the universal joint

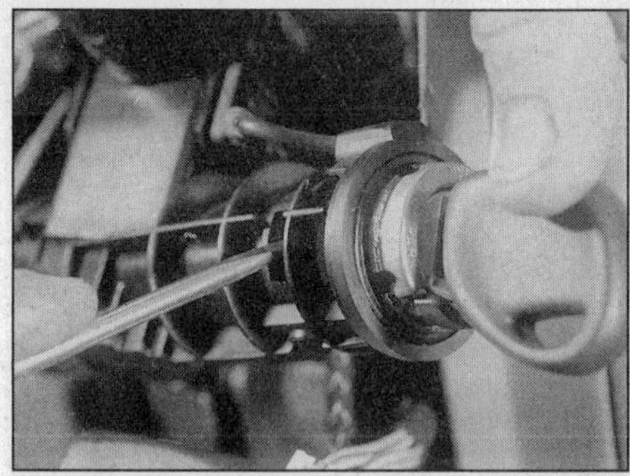

10.5a Insert a small, flat-bladed screwdriver into the access slot in the base of the lock assembly bracket

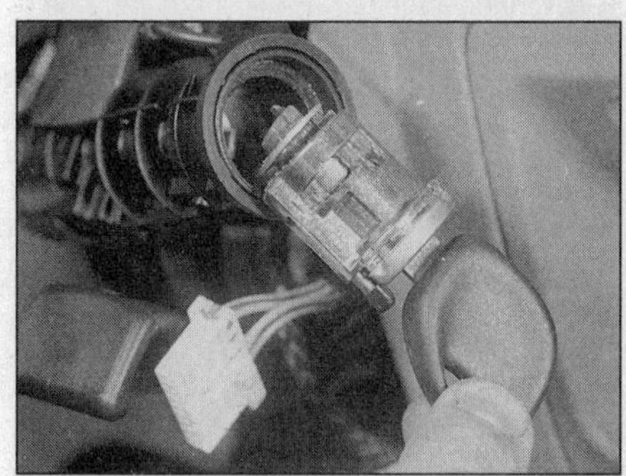

10.5b Depress the release button and withdraw the lock cylinder

3 Unscrew the fixings using an Allen key and remove the upper and lower halves of the plastic shroud from the steering column **(see illustrations)**

4 Working as described in Chapter 12, Section 14, remove the column stalk switch assembly.

5 Unplug the wiring from the rear of the ignition switch/column lock at the multi-way connector - refer to Section 10 for details.

6 Working in the drivers footwell, peel back the carpet trim to gain access to the base of the steering column. Slacken the nut and clamp bolt on the lower half of the universal joint **(see illustration).**

7 Remove the nuts from the four upper steering column mounting bolts and lower the assembly away from the bulkhead bracket **(see illustration).**

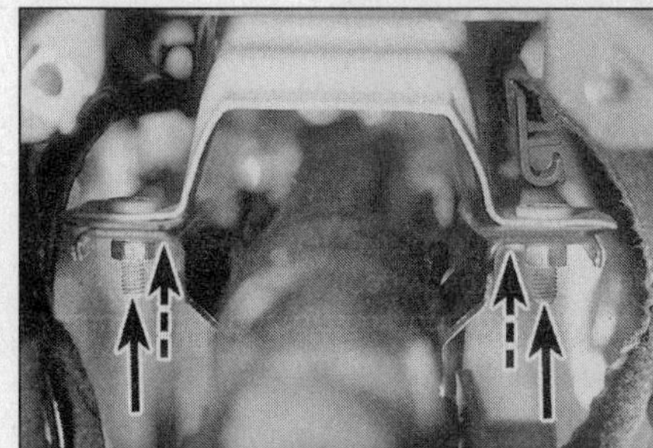

11.7 Remove the nuts from the four upper steering column mounting bolts (two arrowed, two concealed)

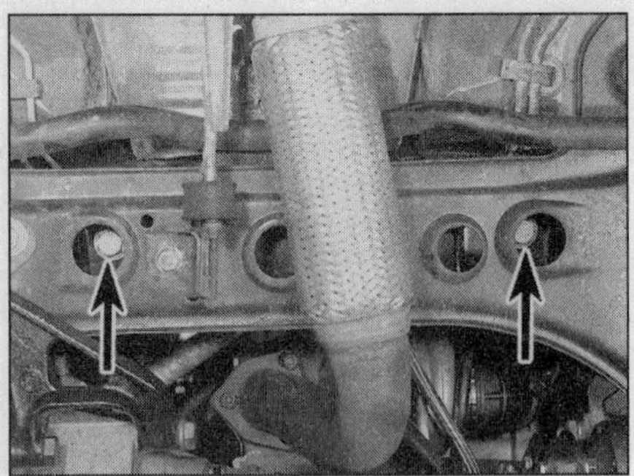

12.8 Slacken and remove the two steering gear-to-subframe bolts (arrowed)

8 Disconnect the universal joint at the base of the steering column from the steering gear pinion. Note the position of the safety clip - this must be refitted in the same position on reassembly.
9 Remove the steering column from the vehicle.

Overhaul

10 The height adjustment mechanism can be removed by removing the nut from the end of the pivot shaft and withdrawing it.
11 The upper and lower bushes are held in position by staking at the ends of the column tube. Relieve the staking using a mallet and punch to extract the bushes.
12 Check for excessive radial and axial play in the universal joints at both ends of the lower steering column. The lower section of the steering column may be renewed separately if required, by slackening the clamp bolt and detaching it from the upper section.
13 If the vehicle has been involved in an accident, check for deformation in all of the steering column components, particularly the mounting bracket and centre tube. Renew as required.

Refitting

14 Refitting the steering column is by following the removal procedure in reverse. Tighten all fixings to the specified torque setting.

12 Manual steering gear assembly - removal, overhaul and refitting

Removal

1 Firmly apply the handbrake, then jack up the front of the car and support it securely on axle stands (see *Jacking and vehicle support*). Remove the front roadwheels.
2 Disconnect the battery negative terminal (refer to *Disconnecting the battery* in the Reference Section of this manual).
3 With reference to Section 11, slacken the clamp bolt at the base of steering column lower universal joint, to separate it from the steering gear pinion.

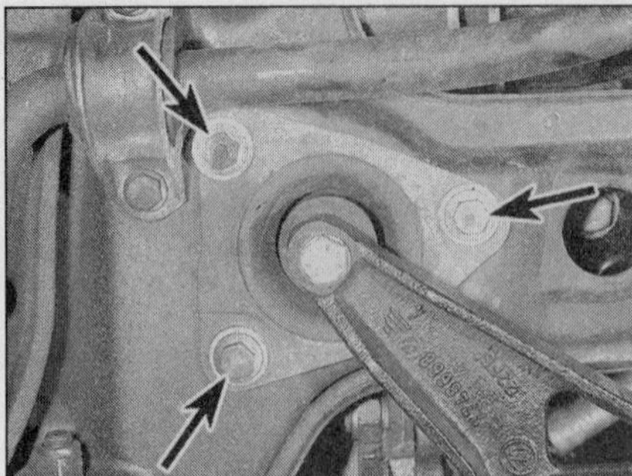

12.9 Unbolt the rear engine mounting-to-subframe bolts (arrowed)

4 Remove the safety clip from the steering gear pinion, noting its fitted position to aid correct refitting later. Lift off the sound insulating pad.
5 Refer to Section 17 and detach the track-rod end balljoints from the hub carriers, using a balljoint splitter.
6 Working underneath the vehicle, remove the clips and detach the gear selection cable and the reverse gear inhibitor cable from the steering gear.
7 Detach the gear selector rod from the top of the steering gear.
8 Slacken and remove the two steering gear-to-subframe bolts **(see illustration)**.
9 Support the underside of the transmission using a trolley jack, then unbolt the rear engine mounting-to-subframe bolts **(see illustration)**.
10 With reference to Chapter 4D, unbolt the front section of the exhaust pipe from the catalytic converter.
11 Unclip the plastic steering gear pinion cup from the bulkhead.
12 Withdraw the steering gear through the wheel arch.

Refitting

13 Refitting is a reversal of removal, noting the following:
a) *Tighten all fixings to the specified torque settings.*
b) *On completion, have the front wheel alignment checked at the earliest opportunity by a Fiat dealer or a tyre specialist.*

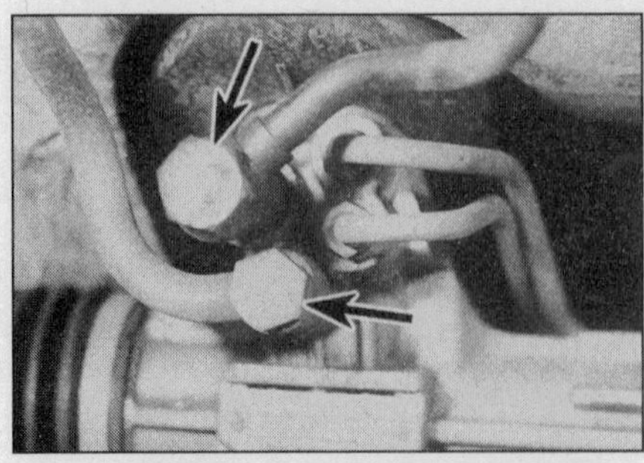

13.10 Disconnect the fluid delivery and return pipes (arrowed) from the power steering gear

13 Power steering gear assembly - removal and refitting

Removal

1 Chock the rear wheels, apply the handbrake, then jack up the front of the vehicle and support securely on axle stands (see *Jacking and vehicle support*). Remove both front roadwheels to improve access.
2 Disconnect the battery negative terminal (refer to *Disconnecting the battery* in the Reference Section of this manual).
3 With reference to Section 11, slacken the clamp bolt at the base of steering column lower universal joint, to separate it from the steering gear pinion.
4 Remove the safety clip from the steering gear pinion, noting its fitted position to aid correct refitting later. Lift off the sound insulating pad.
5 Refer to Section 17 and detach the track-rod end balljoints from the hub carriers, using a balljoint splitter.
6 Working underneath the vehicle, remove the clips and detach the power steering fluid pipe from the steering gear casing.
7 With reference to Chapter 4D, unbolt the front section of the exhaust pipe from the manifold and catalytic converter/intermediate silencer (as applicable).
8 Refer to Chapter 7A and disconnect the gear selector rod from the relay rod. Disconnect the relay rod from the mounting on the top of the steering gear casing.
9 Drain as much fluid as possible from the power steering reservoir, using a pipette or an old poultry baster.
10 Slacken the unions and disconnect the fluid delivery and return pipes from the power steering gear. Be prepared for an amount of fluid loss - position a container underneath the unions and pad the surrounding area with absorbent rags **(see illustration)**.
11 Slacken and remove the two steering gear-to-subframe bolts **(see illustrations)**.
12 Support the engine and transmission assembly using either blocks of wood positioned under the transmission casing, or a lifting beam positioned across the engine bay

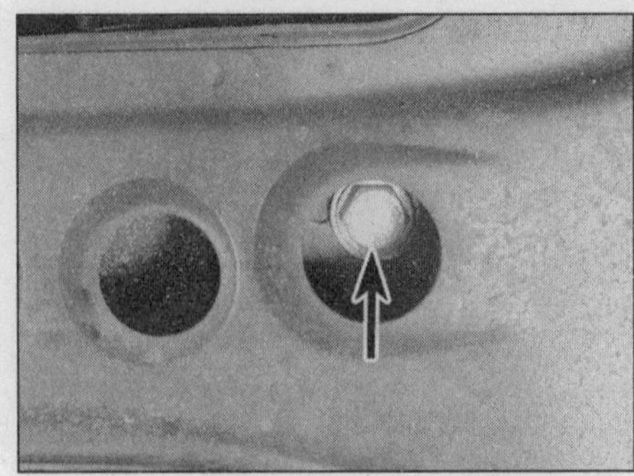

13.11a Slacken and remove the right-hand . . .

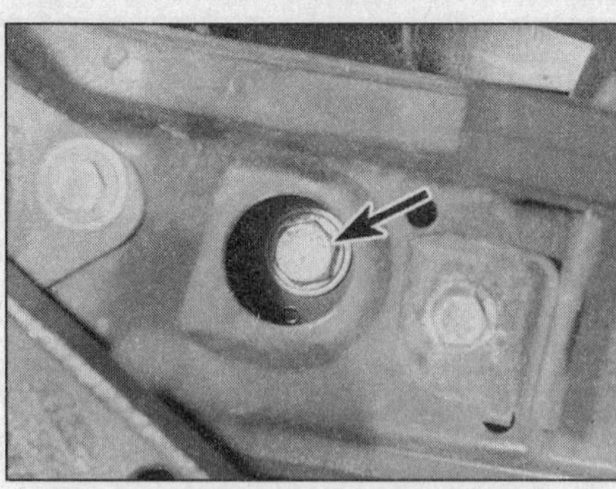

13.11b . . . and left-hand steering gear-to-subframe bolts

hooked onto the engine lifting eyelet on the cylinder head. Working underneath the vehicle, unbolt and remove the transmission-to-subframe rear mounting bracket.

13 Position a trolley jack under the right hand side of the subframe crossmember. Raise the jack to take the weight of the crossmember and the attached components.

14 With reference to Section 4, slacken and remove the two bolts that secure the suspension lower arm rear bush to the subframe. Slacken and withdraw the subframe-to-bodywork bolt, located adjacent to the rear of the suspension lower arm. Thread two flange head bolts of the same thread size, but approximately 25 mm longer into the vacated holes, then carefully lower the trolley jack and allow the subframe to rest on the heads of the temporary bolts **(see illustration)**.

15 Repeat the operations in paragraphs 13 and 14 at the left-hand side of the vehicle. On completion, the subframe should be resting at a height approximately 25 mm lower than normal.

16 The additional clearance will now permit the steering gear pinion to be lowered away from the bulkhead. When the end of the pinion has cleared the aperture, manoeuvre the entire steering gear assembly through the wheelarch.

Refitting

17 Refitting is a reversal of removal, noting the following points:

a) Remove the temporary bolts and refit the original length fixings.

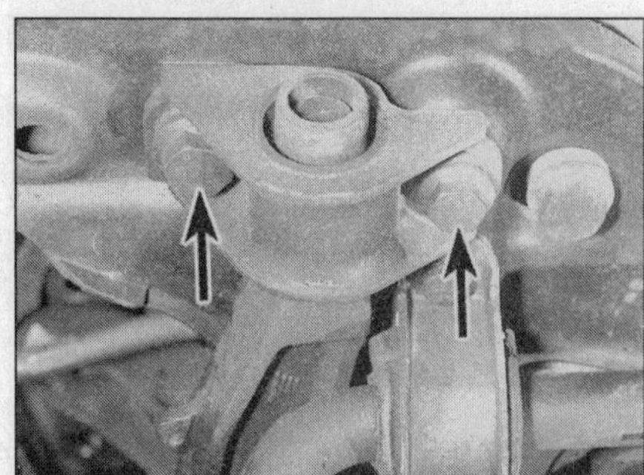

13.14 Slacken and remove the subframe-to-bodywork bolts (arrowed)

b) Tighten all fixings to the specified torque settings.

c) Refill the hydraulic system with the specified grade and quantity of power steering fluid (see Lubricants and fluids in Weekly checks), then thoroughly bleed the system as described in Section 15.

d) On completion, have the front wheel alignment checked at the earliest opportunity by a Fiat dealer or a tyre specialist.

14 Steering gear rubber gaiters - renewal

Note: *New gaiter retaining clips should be used on refitting.*

1 Remove the relevant track-rod end as described in Section 17.

2 If not already done, unscrew the track-rod end locknut from the end of the track-rod.

3 Mark the correct fitted position of the gaiter on the track-rod, then release the gaiter securing clips. Slide the gaiter from the steering gear, and off the end of the track-rod.

4 Thoroughly clean the track-rod and the steering gear housing, using fine abrasive paper to polish off any corrosion, burrs or sharp edges, which might damage the new gaiter sealing lips on installation. Scrape off all the grease from the old gaiter, and apply it to the track-rod inner balljoint. (This assumes that grease has not been lost or contaminated as a result of damage to the old gaiter. Use fresh grease if in doubt.)

5 Carefully slide the new gaiter onto the track-rod, and locate it on the steering gear housing. Align the outer edge of the gaiter with the mark made on the track-rod prior to removal, then secure it in position with new retaining clips.

6 Screw the track-rod end locknut onto the end of the track-rod.

7 Refit the track-rod end as described in Section 17.

15 Power steering hydraulic system - bleeding

General

1 The following symptoms indicate that there is air present in the power steering hydraulic system:

a) Generation of air bubbles in fluid reservoir.

b) Clicking noises from power steering pump.

c) Excessive buzzing or groaning from power steering pump.

2 Note that when the vehicle is stationary, or while moving the steering wheel slowly, a hissing noise may be produced in the steering gear or the fluid pump. This noise is inherent in the system, and does not indicate any cause for concern.

Bleeding

3 Chock the rear wheels, apply the handbrake, then jack up the front of the vehicle and support securely on axle stands (see *Jacking and vehicle support*).

4 Check the fluid level in the power steering fluid reservoir (bear in mind that the vehicle will be tilted, so the level cannot be read accurately), and if necessary top-up to just above the relevant level mark.

5 Have an assistant turn the steering quickly from lock to lock, and observe the fluid level. If the fluid level drops, add more fluid, and repeat the operation until the fluid level no longer drops. Failure to achieve this within a reasonable period may indicate a leak in the system.

6 Start the engine and repeat the procedure described in the previous paragraph.

7 Once the fluid level has stabilised, and all air has been bled from the system, lower the vehicle to the ground.

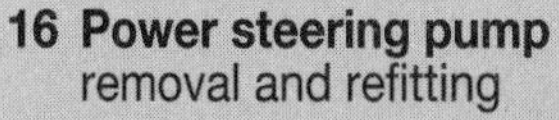

16 Power steering pump - removal and refitting

Removal

1 Drain as much fluid as possible from the power steering reservoir, using a pipette or an old poultry baster.

2 Remove the clip and disconnect the rubber fluid supply hose from the port on the top of the power steering pump. Be prepared for an amount of fluid loss - position a container underneath the port and pad the surrounding area with absorbent rags.

3 Slacken the union and disconnect the fluid delivery hose from the side of the power steering pump. Again, be prepared for an amount of fluid loss.

4 Unscrew the clamp bolt and through-bolt at either end of the drivebelt guard, then detach the guard from the power steering pump **(see illustrations)**.

5 Partially unscrew the two power steering pump mounting bolts then rotate the pump towards the engine slightly, to release the tension from the belt. Carefully ease the drivebelt from the pump pulley.

16.4a Unscrew the clamp bolt . . .

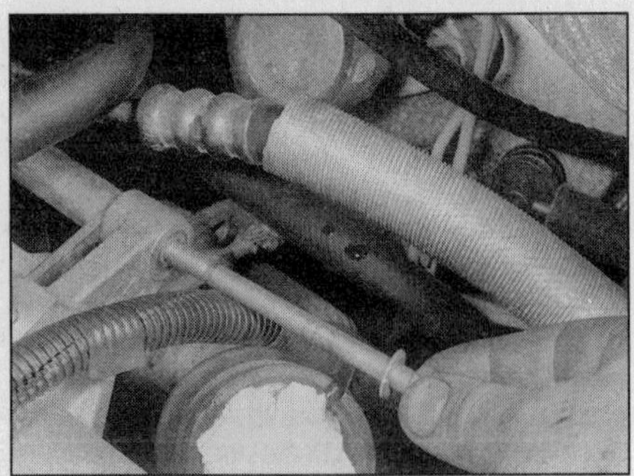
16.4b . . . and through-bolt . . .

16.4c . . . then detach the guard from the power steering pump

16.6a Power steering pump front . . .

6 Remove the two pump mounting bolts **(see illustrations)** that were slackened earlier, then remove the pump from the engine.

Refitting

7 Refitting is a reversal, noting the following points:

a) *On completion, check and if necessary adjust the drivebelt tension as described in Chapter 1A or 1B.*
b) *Refill the hydraulic system with the specified grade and quantity of power steering fluid (see lubricants and fluids in Weekly checks), then thoroughly bleed the system as described in Section 15.*
c) *Tighten all fixings to the specified torque setting.*

17 Track-rod end - removal and refitting

Removal

Note: *A balljoint separator tool will be required for this operation. A new track-rod end nut split pin should be used on refitting.*

1 Chock the rear wheels, apply the handbrake, then jack up the front of the vehicle and support on axle stands (see *Jacking and vehicle support*). Remove the relevant front roadwheel.

2 Partially unscrew the nut securing the track-rod end to the steering arm. Using a balljoint separator tool, separate the track-rod end from the steering arm **(see illustrations)**.

3 Counterhold the track-rod end using the flats provided, then loosen the track-rod end locknut **(see illustration)**.

4 Unscrew the track-rod end from the track-rod, counting the exact number of turns required to do so. Alternatively, mark the relationship between the track-rod end and the track-rod using a dab of paint.

Refitting

5 Carefully clean the track-rod end and the track-rod threads.

6 Renew the track-rod end if the rubber dust cover is cracked, split or perished, or if the movement of the balljoint is either sloppy or too stiff. Also check for other signs of damage such as worn threads.

7 Screw the track-rod end onto the track-rod by the number of turns noted before removal. Tighten the locknut temporarily.

8 Ensure that the balljoint taper is clean, then engage the taper with the steering arm on the hub carrier.

9 Refit the balljoint nut, and tighten to the specified torque.

10 Refit the roadwheel, and lower the vehicle to the ground.

11 Have the front wheel alignment checked by a Fiat dealer or tyre specialist at the earliest opportunity. **Note:** *If the vehicle has to be driven to have the wheel alignment checked, the track-rod end locknut should be tightened before driving the vehicle.*

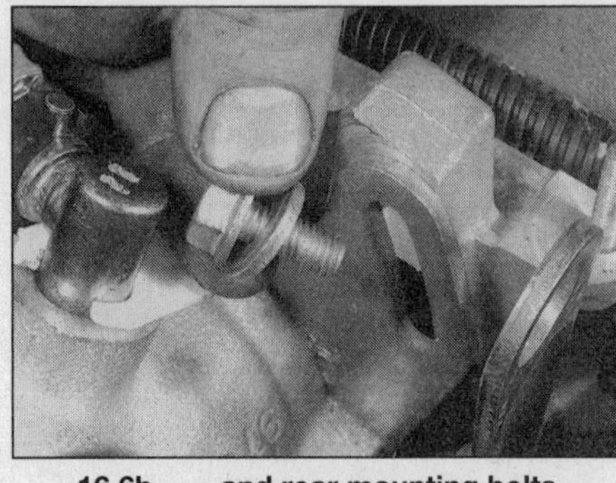
16.6b . . . and rear mounting bolts

18 Wheel alignment and steering angles - general information

General information

1 A car's steering and suspension geometry is defined in four basic settings - with the exception of toe setting, all angles are expressed in degrees; the relevant settings are camber, castor, steering axis inclination, and toe-setting. With the exception of toe-setting, none of these settings are adjustable.

Front wheel toe setting

Checking

2 Due to the special measuring equipment necessary to check the wheel alignment, and

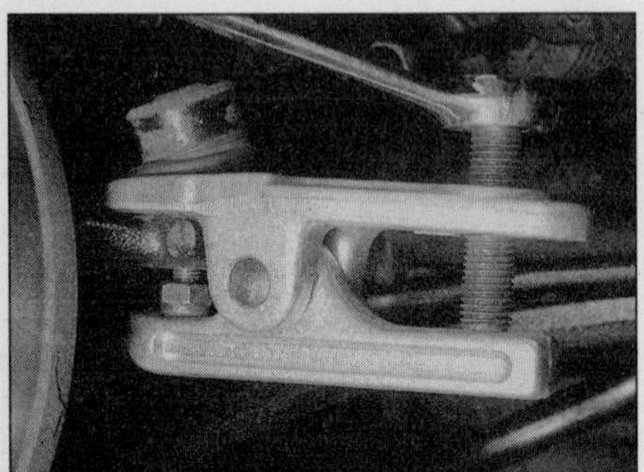
17.2a Balljoint separator tool in use on the track-rod end

17.2b Separate the track-rod end from the steering arm

17.3 Counterhold the track-rod end, then loosen the locknut (arrowed)

the skill required to use it properly, the checking and adjustment of these settings is best left to a Fiat dealer or similar expert. Most tyre-fitting shops now possess sophisticated checking equipment.

3 For accurate checking, the vehicle must be at the kerb weight specified in *Dimensions and weights.*

4 Before starting work, check first that the tyre sizes and types are as specified (see *Tyre pressures* in *Weekly checks*), then check tyre pressures and tread wear. Also check roadwheel run-out, the condition of the hub bearings, the steering wheel free play and the condition of the front suspension components (*Steering and suspension check* in Chapter 1A or 1B). Correct any faults found.

5 Park the vehicle on level ground, with the front roadwheels in the straight-ahead position. Rock the rear and front ends to settle the suspension. Release the handbrake and roll the vehicle backwards approximately 1 metre, then forwards again, to relieve any stresses in the steering and suspension components.

6 Two methods are available to the home mechanic for checking the front wheel toe setting. One method is to use a gauge to measure the distance between the front and rear inside edges of the roadwheels. The other method is to use a scuff plate, in which each front wheel is rolled across a movable plate which records any deviation, or scuff, of the tyre from the straight-ahead position as it moves across the plate. Such gauges are available in relatively-inexpensive form from accessory outlets. It is up to the owner to decide whether the expense is justified, in view of the small amount of use such equipment would normally receive.

7 Prepare the vehicle as described in paragraphs 3 to 5 above.

8 If the measurement procedure is being used, carefully measure the distance between the front edges of the roadwheel rims and the rear edges of the rims. Subtract the front measurement from the rear measurement, and check that the result is within the specified range. If not, adjust the toe setting as described in paragraph 10.

9 If scuff plates are to be used, roll the vehicle backwards, check that the roadwheels are in the straight-ahead position, then roll it across the scuff plates so that each front roadwheel passes squarely over the centre of its respective plate. Note the angle recorded by the scuff plates. To ensure accuracy, repeat the check three times, and take the average of the three readings. If the roadwheels are running parallel, there will of course be no angle recorded; if a deviation value is shown on the scuff plates, compare the reading obtained for each wheel with that supplied by the scuff plate manufacturers. If the value recorded is outside the specified tolerance, the toe setting is incorrect, and must be adjusted as follows.

Adjustment

10 Apply the handbrake, then jack up the front of the vehicle and support it securely on axle stands (see *Jacking and vehicle support*). Turn the steering wheel onto full-left lock, and record the number of exposed threads on the right-hand track-rod. Now turn the steering onto full-right lock, and record the number of threads on the left-hand side. If there are the same number of threads visible on both sides, then subsequent adjustment should be made equally on both sides. If there are more threads visible on one side than the other, it will be necessary to compensate for this during adjustment. **Note:** *It is important to ensure that, after adjustment, the same number of threads are visible on the end of each track-rod.*

11 First clean the track-rod threads; if they are corroded, apply penetrating fluid before starting adjustment. Release the steering gear rubber gaiter outboard clips, then peel back the gaiters and apply a smear of grease, so that both gaiters are free and will not be twisted or strained as their respective track-rods are rotated.

12 Use a straight-edge and a scriber or similar to mark the relationship of each track-rod to the track-rod end. Working on each track-rod end in turn, unscrew its locking nut.

13 Alter the length of the track-rods, bearing in mind the note in paragraph 10, by screwing them into or out of the track-rod ends. Rotate the track-rod using an open-ended spanner fitted to the flats provided. If necessary, counterhold the track-rod end using a second spanner. Shortening the track-rods (screwing them into their track-rod ends) will reduce toe-in and increase toe-out.

14 When the setting is correct, hold the track-rods and securely tighten the locking nuts. Check that the balljoints are seated correctly in their sockets, and count the exposed threads on the ends of the track-rods. If the number of threads exposed is not the same on both sides, then the adjustment has not been made equally, and problems will be encountered with tyre scrubbing in turns; also, the steering wheel spokes will no longer be horizontal when the wheels are in the straight-ahead position.

15 When the track-rod lengths are the same, lower the vehicle to the ground and re-check the toe setting; readjust if necessary. When the setting is correct, tighten the locking nuts. Ensure that the steering gear rubber gaiters are seated correctly and are not twisted or strained, then secure them in position with new retaining clips.

Chapter 11
Bodywork and fittings

Contents

Degrees of difficulty

Easy, suitable for novice with little experience 

Fairly easy, suitable for beginner with some experience 

Fairly difficult, suitable for competent DIY mechanic

Difficult, suitable for experienced DIY mechanic

Very difficult, suitable for expert DIY or professional

Specifications

Torque wrench settings	Nm	lbf ft
Bonnet-to-hinge bolts	8	6
Door hinge-to-body bolts	35	26

1 General information

The bodyshell is composed of pressed-steel sections which are welded together, although some use of structural adhesives is made. In addition, the front wings are bolted on.

The bonnet, door and some other panels vulnerable to corrosion are fabricated from zinc-coated metal. A coating of anti-chip primer, applied prior to paint spraying provides further protection.

Extensive use is made of plastic materials, mainly in the interior, but also in exterior components. The outer sections of the front and rear bumpers are injection-moulded from a synthetic material which is very strong, and yet light. Plastic components such as wheel arch liners are fitted to the underside of the vehicle, to improve the body's resistance to corrosion.

2 Maintenance - bodywork and underframe

The general condition of a vehicle's bodywork is the one thing that significantly affects its value. Maintenance is easy, but needs to be regular. Neglect, particularly after minor damage, can lead quickly to further deterioration and costly repair bills. It is important also to keep watch on those parts of the vehicle not immediately visible, for instance the underside, inside all the wheel arches, and the lower part of the engine compartment.

The basic maintenance routine for the bodywork is washing - preferably with a lot of water, from a hose. This will remove all the loose solids which may have stuck to the vehicle. It is important to flush these off in such a way as to prevent grit from scratching the finish. The wheel arches and underframe need washing in the same way, to remove any accumulated mud, which will retain moisture and tend to encourage rust. Paradoxically enough, the best time to clean the underframe and wheel arches is in wet weather, when the mud is thoroughly wet and soft. In very wet weather, the underframe is usually cleaned of large accumulations automatically, and this is a good time for inspection.

Periodically, except on vehicles with a wax-based underbody protective coating, it is a good idea to have the whole of the underframe of the vehicle steam-cleaned, engine compartment included, so that a thorough inspection can be carried out to see what minor repairs and renovations are necessary. Steam-cleaning is available at many garages, and is necessary for the removal of the accumulation of oily grime, which sometimes is allowed to become thick in certain areas. If steam-cleaning facilities are not available, there are some excellent grease solvents available which can be brush-applied; the dirt can then be simply hosed off. Note that these methods should not be used on vehicles with wax-based underbody protective coating, or the coating will be removed. Such vehicles should be inspected annually, preferably just prior to Winter, when the underbody should be washed down, and any damage to the wax coating repaired. Ideally, a completely fresh coat should be applied. It would also be worth considering the use of such wax-based protection for injection into door panels, sills, box sections, etc, as an additional safeguard against rust damage, where such protection is not provided by the vehicle manufacturer.

After washing paintwork, wipe off with a chamois leather to give an unspotted clear finish. A coat of clear protective wax polish will give added protection against chemical pollutants in the air. If the paintwork sheen has dulled or oxidised, use a cleaner/polisher combination to restore the brilliance of the shine. This requires a little effort, but such dulling is usually caused because regular washing has been neglected. Care needs to be taken with metallic paintwork, as special non-abrasive cleaner/polisher is required to avoid damage to the finish. Always check that the door and ventilator opening drain holes and pipes are completely clear, so that water can be drained out. Brightwork should be treated in the same way as paintwork. Windscreens and windows can be kept clear of the smeary film which often appears, by the use of proprietary glass cleaner. Never use any form of wax or other body or chromium polish on glass.

3 Maintenance - upholstery and carpets

Mats and carpets should be brushed or vacuum-cleaned regularly, to keep them free of grit. If they are badly stained, remove them from the vehicle for scrubbing or sponging, and make quite sure they are dry before refitting. Seats and interior trim panels can be kept clean by wiping with a damp cloth. If they do become stained (which can be more apparent on light-coloured upholstery), use a little liquid detergent and a soft nail brush to scour the grime out of the grain of the material. Do not forget to keep the headlining clean in the same way as the upholstery. When using liquid cleaners inside the vehicle, do not over-wet the surfaces being cleaned. Excessive damp could get into the seams and padded interior, causing stains, offensive odours or even rot.

If the inside of the vehicle gets wet accidentally, it is worthwhile taking some trouble to dry it out properly, particularly where carpets are involved. Do not leave oil or electric heaters inside the vehicle for this purpose.

4 Minor body damage - repair

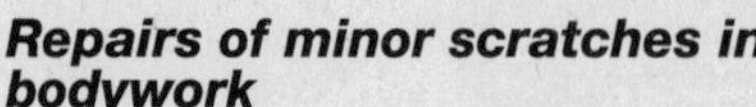

Repairs of minor scratches in bodywork

If the scratch is very superficial, and does not penetrate to the metal of the bodywork, repair is very simple. Lightly rub the area of the scratch with a paintwork renovator, or a very fine cutting paste, to remove loose paint from the scratch, and to clear the surrounding bodywork of wax polish. Rinse the area with clean water.

Apply touch-up paint to the scratch using a fine paint brush; continue to apply fine layers of paint until the surface of the paint in the scratch is level with the surrounding paintwork. Allow the new paint at least two weeks to harden, then blend it into the surrounding paintwork by rubbing the scratch area with a paintwork renovator or a very fine cutting paste. Finally, apply wax polish.

Where the scratch has penetrated right through to the metal of the bodywork, causing the metal to rust, a different repair technique is required. Remove any loose rust from the bottom of the scratch with a penknife, then apply rust-inhibiting paint to prevent the formation of rust in the future. Using a rubber or nylon applicator, fill the scratch with bodystopper paste. If required, this paste can be mixed with cellulose thinners to provide a very thin paste which is ideal for filling narrow scratches. Before the stopper-paste in the scratch hardens, wrap a piece of smooth cotton rag around the top of a finger. Dip the finger in cellulose thinners, and quickly sweep it across the surface of the stopper-paste in the scratch; this will ensure that the surface of the stopper-paste is slightly hollowed. The scratch can now be painted over as described earlier in this Section.

Repairs of dents in bodywork

When deep denting of the vehicle's bodywork has taken place, the first task is to pull the dent out, until the affected bodywork almost attains its original shape. There is little point in trying to restore the original shape completely, as the metal in the damaged area will have stretched on impact, and cannot be reshaped fully to its original contour. It is better to bring the level of the dent up to a point which is about 3 mm below the level of the surrounding bodywork. In cases where the dent is very shallow anyway, it is not worth trying to pull it out at all. If the underside of the dent is accessible, it can be hammered out gently from behind, using a mallet with a wooden or plastic head. Whilst doing this, hold a suitable block of wood firmly against the outside of the panel, to absorb the impact from the hammer blows and thus prevent a large area of the bodywork from being 'belled-out'.

Should the dent be in a section of the bodywork which has a double skin, or some other factor making it inaccessible from behind, a different technique is called for. Drill several small holes through the metal inside the area - particularly in the deeper section. Then screw long self-tapping screws into the holes, just sufficiently for them to gain a good purchase in the metal. Now the dent can be pulled out by pulling on the protruding heads of the screws with a pair of pliers.

The next stage of the repair is the removal of the paint from the damaged area, and from an inch or so of the surrounding 'sound' bodywork. This is accomplished most easily by using a wire brush or abrasive pad on a power drill, although it can be done just as effectively by hand, using sheets of abrasive paper. To complete the preparation for filling, score the surface of the bare metal with a screwdriver or the tang of a file, or alternatively, drill small holes in the affected area. This will provide a really good 'key' for the filler paste.

To complete the repair, see the Section on filling and respraying.

Repairs of rust holes or gashes in bodywork

Remove all paint from the affected area, and from an inch or so of the surrounding 'sound' bodywork, using an abrasive pad or a wire brush on a power drill. If these are not available, a few sheets of abrasive paper will do the job most effectively. With the paint removed, you will be able to judge the severity of the corrosion, and therefore decide whether to renew the whole panel (if this is possible) or to repair the affected area. New body panels are not as expensive as most people think, and it is often quicker and more satisfactory to fit a new panel than to attempt to repair large areas of corrosion.

Remove all fittings from the affected area, except those which will act as a guide to the original shape of the damaged bodywork (eg headlight shells etc). Then, using tin snips or a hacksaw blade, remove all loose metal and any other metal badly affected by corrosion. Hammer the edges of the hole inwards, in order to create a slight depression for the filler paste.

Wire-brush the affected area to remove the powdery rust from the surface of the remaining metal. Paint the affected area with rust-inhibiting paint, if the back of the rusted area is accessible, treat this also.

Before filling can take place, it will be necessary to block the hole in some way. This can be achieved by the use of aluminium or plastic mesh, or aluminium tape.

Aluminium or plastic mesh, or glass-fibre matting, is probably the best material to use for a large hole. Cut a piece to the approximate size and shape of the hole to be filled, then position it in the hole so that its edges are below the level of the surrounding bodywork. It can be retained in position by several blobs of filler paste around its periphery.

Aluminium tape should be used for small or very narrow holes. Pull a piece off the roll, trim it to the approximate size and shape required, then pull off the backing paper (if used) and stick the tape over the hole; it can be overlapped if the thickness of one piece is insufficient. Burnish down the edges of the tape with the handle of a screwdriver or similar, to ensure that the tape is securely attached to the metal underneath.

Bodywork repairs - filling and respraying

Before using this Section, see the Sections on dent, deep scratch, rust holes and gash repairs.

Many types of bodyfiller are available, but generally speaking, those proprietary kits which contain a tin of filler paste and a tube of resin hardener are best for this type of repair. A wide, flexible plastic or nylon applicator will be found invaluable for imparting a smooth and well-contoured finish to the surface of the filler.

Mix up a little filler on a clean piece of card or board - measure the hardener carefully (follow the maker's instructions on the pack), otherwise the filler will set too rapidly or too slowly. Using the applicator, apply the filler paste to the prepared area; draw the applicator across the surface of the filler to achieve the correct contour and to level the surface. As soon as a contour that approximates to the correct one is achieved, stop working the paste - if you carry on too long, the paste will become sticky and begin to 'pick-up' on the applicator. Continue to add thin layers of filler paste at 20-minute intervals, until the level of the filler is just proud of the surrounding bodywork.

Once the filler has hardened, the excess can be removed using a metal plane or file. From then on, progressively-finer grades of abrasive paper should be used, starting with a 40-grade production paper, and finishing with a 400-grade wet-and-dry paper. Always wrap the abrasive paper around a flat rubber, cork, or wooden block - otherwise the surface of the filler will not be completely flat. During the smoothing of the filler surface, the wet-and-dry paper should be periodically rinsed in water. This will ensure that a very smooth finish is imparted to the filler at the final stage.

At this stage, the dent should be surrounded by a ring of bare metal, which in turn should be encircled by the finely 'feathered' edge of the good paintwork. Rinse the repair area with clean water, until all of the dust produced by the rubbing-down operation has gone.

Spray the whole area with a light coat of primer - this will show up any imperfections in the surface of the filler. Repair these imperfections with fresh filler paste or bodystopper, and once more smooth the surface with abrasive paper. Repeat this spray-and-repair procedure until you are satisfied that the surface of the filler, and the feathered edge of the paintwork, are perfect. Clean the repair area with clean water, and allow to dry fully.

If bodystopper is used, it can be mixed with cellulose thinners to form a really thin paste which is ideal for filling small holes.

The repair area is now ready for final spraying. Paint spraying must be carried out in a warm, dry, windless and dust-free atmosphere. This condition can be created artificially if you have access to a large indoor working area, but if you are forced to work in the open, you will have to pick your day very carefully. If you are working indoors, dousing the floor in the work area with water will help to settle the dust which would otherwise be in the atmosphere. If the repair area is confined to one body panel, mask off the surrounding panels; this will help to minimise the effects of a slight mis-match in paint colours. Bodywork fittings (eg chrome strips, door handles etc) will also need to be masked off. Use genuine masking tape, and several thicknesses of newspaper, for the masking operations.

Before commencing to spray, agitate the aerosol can thoroughly, then spray a test area (an old tin, or similar) until the technique is mastered. Cover the repair area with a thick coat of primer; the thickness should be built up using several thin layers of paint, rather than one thick one. Using 400-grade wet-and-dry paper, rub down the surface of the primer until it is really smooth. While doing this, the work area should be thoroughly doused with water, and the wet-and-dry paper periodically rinsed in water. Allow to dry before spraying on more paint.

Spray on the top coat, again building up the thickness by using several thin layers of paint. Start spraying at one edge of the repair area, and then, using a side-to-side motion, work until the whole repair area and about 2 inches of the surrounding original paintwork is covered. Remove all masking material 10 to 15 minutes after spraying on the final coat of paint.

Allow the new paint at least two weeks to harden, then, using a paintwork renovator, or a very fine cutting paste, blend the edges of the paint into the existing paintwork. Finally, apply wax polish.

Plastic components

With the use of more and more plastic body components by the vehicle manufacturers (eg bumpers. spoilers, and in some cases major body panels), rectification of more serious damage to such items has become a matter of either entrusting repair work to a specialist in this field, or renewing complete components. Repair of such damage by the DIY owner is not really feasible, owing to the cost of the equipment and materials required for effecting such repairs. The basic technique involves making a groove along the line of the crack in the plastic, using a rotary burr in a power drill. The damaged part is then welded back together, using a hot-air gun to heat up and fuse a plastic filler rod into the groove. Any excess plastic is then removed, and the area rubbed down to a smooth finish. It is important that a filler rod of the correct plastic is used, as body components can be made of a variety of different types (eg polycarbonate, ABS, polypropylene).

Damage of a less serious nature (abrasions, minor cracks etc) can be repaired by the DIY owner using a two-part epoxy filler repair material. Once mixed in equal proportions, this is used in similar fashion to the bodywork filler used on metal panels. The filler is usually cured in twenty to thirty minutes, ready for sanding and painting.

If the owner is renewing a complete component himself, or if he has repaired it with epoxy filler, he will be left with the problem of finding a suitable paint for finishing which is compatible with the type of plastic used. At one time, the use of a universal paint was not possible, owing to the complex range of plastics encountered in body component applications. Standard paints, generally speaking, will not bond to plastic or rubber satisfactorily. However, it is now possible to obtain a plastic body parts finishing kit which consists of a pre-primer treatment, a primer and coloured top coat. Full instructions are normally supplied with a kit, but basically, the method of use is to first apply the pre-primer to the component concerned, and allow it to dry for up to 30 minutes. Then the primer is applied, and left to dry for about an hour before finally applying the special-coloured top coat. The result is a correctly-coloured component, where the paint will flex with the plastic or rubber, a property that standard paint does not normally possess.

5 Major body damage - repair

Where serious damage has occurred, or large areas need renewal due to neglect, it means that complete new panels will need welding-in, and this is best left to professionals. If the damage is due to impact, it will also be necessary to check completely the alignment of the bodyshell, and this can only be carried out accurately by a Fiat dealer using special jigs. If the alignment of the bodyshell is not corrected, the car's handling may be seriously affected. In addition, excessive stress may be imposed on the steering, suspension, tyres or transmission, causing abnormal wear or even complete failure.

6.3a Remove the screws . . .

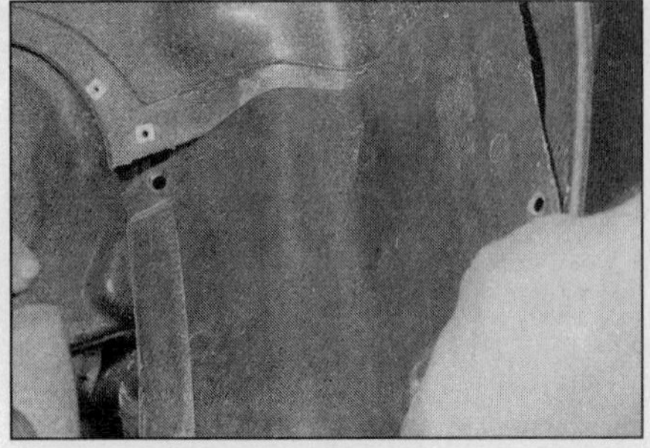

6.3b . . . and lower the front section of the plastic wheel arch liners away from the bodywork

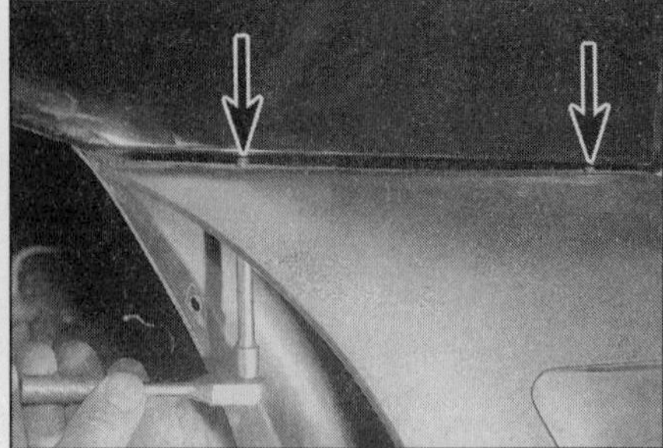

6.4 Remove the retaining screws (arrowed) from the trailing edges of the bumper moulding

6 Front bumper - removal and refitting

Removal

1 Access to the front bumper mountings may be improved by raising the front of the vehicle and resting it securely on axle stands (see *Jacking and vehicle support*).

2 Remove the direction indicator units from both front wings, as described in Chapter 12, Section 6.

3 Remove the screws and lower both plastic wheel arch liners away from the bodywork **(see illustrations)**.

4 Reach inside the wheel arch and remove the retaining screws from the trailing edges of the bumper moulding **(see illustration)**.

5 Slacken and withdraw the four screws from the lower edge of the bumper **(see illustration)**.

6.5 Slacken and withdraw the four screws from the lower edge of the bumper

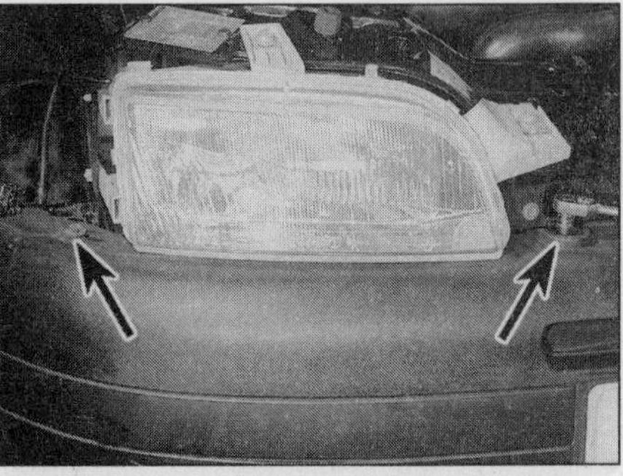

6.6 Remove the retaining bolts (arrowed) from either side of the headlight units

6 Support the bumper moulding, then remove the four retaining bolts from the upper edge of the bumper (located either side of the headlight units) **(see illustration)**.

7 Where applicable, unplug the wiring from the rear of the foglamp units.

8 Unclip any electrical cabling secured to the rear side of the bumper and then carefully draw the bumper away from the front of the vehicle.

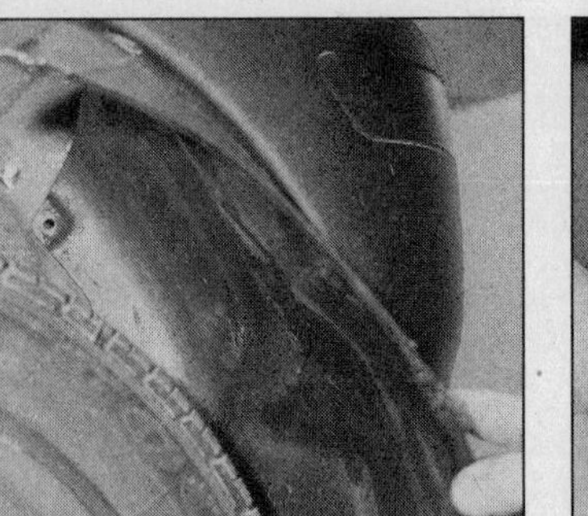

7.2 Lower the rear wheel arch plastic liners away from the bodywork

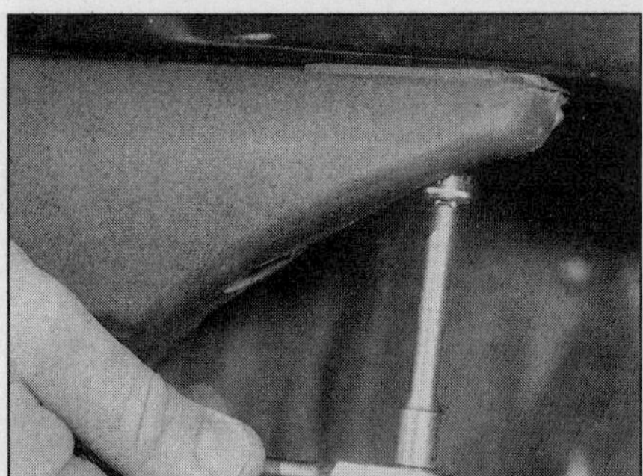

7.3 Remove the retaining screws from the leading edges of the bumper moulding

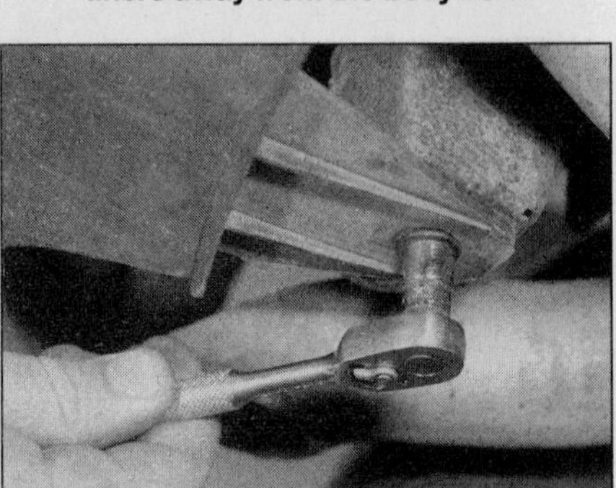

7.4 Slacken and withdraw the four screws from the lower edge of the bumper

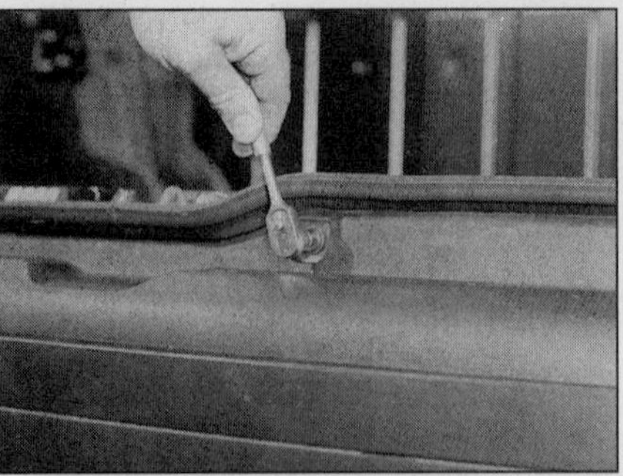

7.5 Remove the four retaining bolts from the upper edge of the bumper

Refitting

9 The bumper is refitted by following the removal procedure in reverse.

7 Rear bumper - removal and refitting

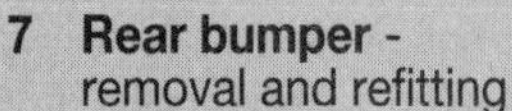

Removal

1 Access to the rear bumper mountings may be improved by raising the rear of the vehicle and resting it securely on axle stands (see *Jacking and vehicle support*).

2 After removing the retaining screws and nuts, lower both rear wheel arch plastic liners away from the bodywork **(see illustration)**.

3 Reach inside the rear wheel arches and remove the retaining screws from the leading edges of the bumper moulding **(see illustration)**.

4 Slacken and withdraw the four screws from the lower edge of the bumper **(see illustration)**.

5 Support the bumper moulding, then remove the four retaining bolts from the upper edge of the bumper **(see illustration)**.

6 Unclip any electrical cabling that may be secured to the inside of the bumper, then carefully draw the bumper off its guide brackets and away from the rear of the vehicle.

8.2 Release the fixings and lower the trim panel away from the tailgate

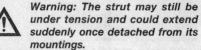

Refitting

7 The bumper is refitted by following the removal procedure in reverse.

8 Tailgate - removal and refitting

Removal

1 Disconnect the battery negative terminal (refer to *Disconnecting the battery* in the Reference Section of this manual).

2 Release the press stud fixings and extract the screws, then lower the trim panel away from the tailgate **(see illustration)**.

3 Working inside the tailgate, disconnect all wiring harness connectors and unbolt the earth leads. Check for any other wiring connectors which must be disconnected to facilitate tailgate removal. **Note:** *Carefully label each wiring harness connector to aid correct refitting.*

4 Tie a length of cord to the wiring harness, then bind the loose ends of the cabling together using PVC tape. Prise the wiring harness grommets from the upper edge of the tailgate, then feed the wiring through the aperture in the tailgate. Untie the cord from the harness, but leave it in place in the tailgate, to aid refitting later.

5 Where applicable, remove the fluid hose from the tailgate washer nozzle, as described in Chapter 12, Section 16, then tie a length of

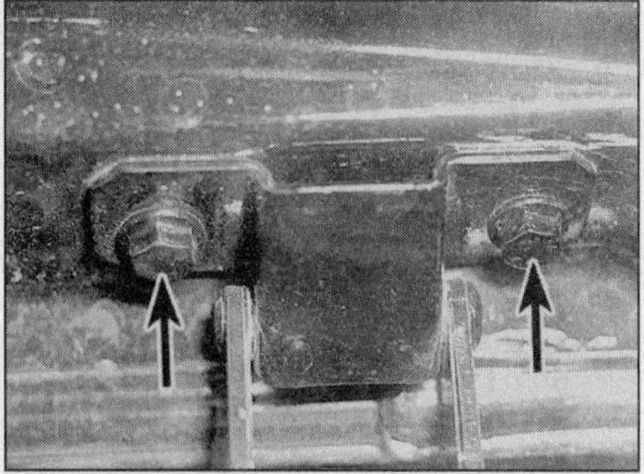

8.8 Slacken and unscrew the bolts (arrowed) securing the hinges to the tailgate

cord to the hose and draw it out of the tailgate, using the same procedure carried out on the wiring harness.

6 Have an assistant support the tailgate in the open position.

7 Detach the upper ends of the support struts from the tailgate as described in Section 9.

8 Slacken and unscrew the bolts securing the hinges to the tailgate **(see illustration)**, then lift the tailgate from the vehicle.

Refitting

9 Refitting is a reversal of removal, bearing in mind the following points.

a) *Tie the cord to the wiring harness and use it to pull the harness through the aperture and into the tailgate. Where applicable, repeat the procedure on the washer fluid hose.*

b) *Do not fully tighten the hinge bolts until the tailgate adjustment has been checked, as described in the following paragraphs.*

Adjustment

10 Close the tailgate **carefully**, in case the alignment is incorrect, which may cause scratching on the tailgate or the body as the tailgate is closed, and check for alignment with the adjacent panels. If necessary, slacken the bolts that secure the hinges to the bodywork and re-align the tailgate to suit. Once the tailgate is correctly aligned, tighten the hinge bolts securely.

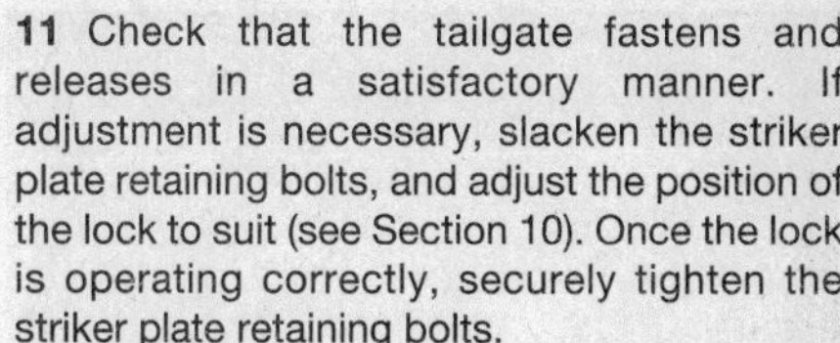

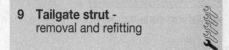

11 Check that the tailgate fastens and releases in a satisfactory manner. If adjustment is necessary, slacken the striker plate retaining bolts, and adjust the position of the lock to suit (see Section 10). Once the lock is operating correctly, securely tighten the striker plate retaining bolts.

12 If necessary, adjust the protrusion of the rubber buffers at the lower edge of the tailgate, by screwing them in or out as appropriate.

9 Tailgate strut - removal and refitting

Removal

1 Open the tailgate and support it using suitable wooden props.

2 At the upper end of each strut, lever off the balljoint spring clip. Compress the strut slightly by hand and then prise strut balljoint from the stud on the tailgate **(see illustrations)**.

Warning: The strut may still be under tension and could extend suddenly once detached from its mountings.

3 At the lower end of the strut, unbolt the joint from the bodywork.

Refitting

4 Refitting is a reversal of removal.

10 Tailgate lock components - removal and refitting

Lock and cylinder assembly

Removal

1 With the tailgate held in the fully open position, slacken and unscrew the bolts securing the lock assembly to the lower edge of the tailgate **(see illustration)**.

2 Carefully withdraw the lock assembly, together with the lock cylinder **(see illustration)**.

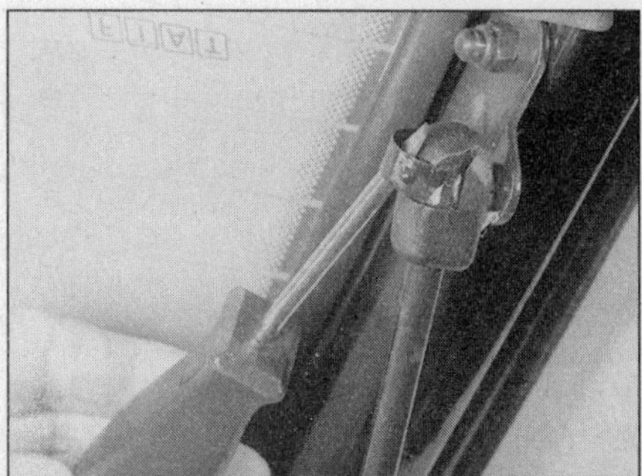

9.2a Lever off the balljoint spring clip . . .

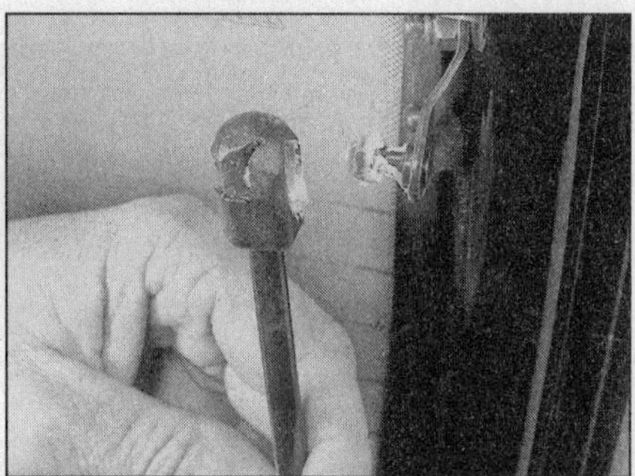

9.2b . . . and then prise strut balljoint from the stud on the tailgate

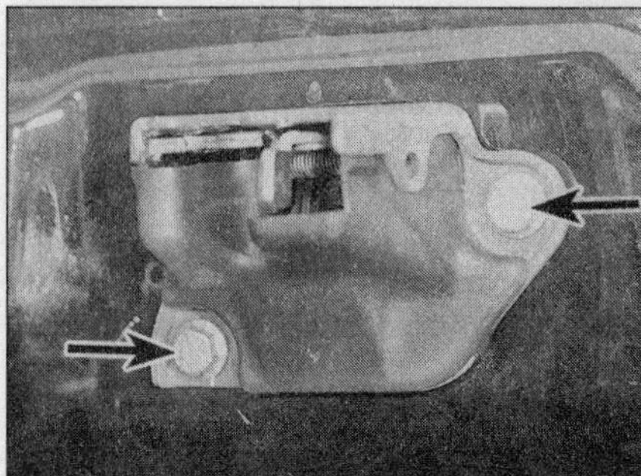

10.1 Unscrew the bolts (arrowed) securing the lock assembly to the lower edge of the tailgate

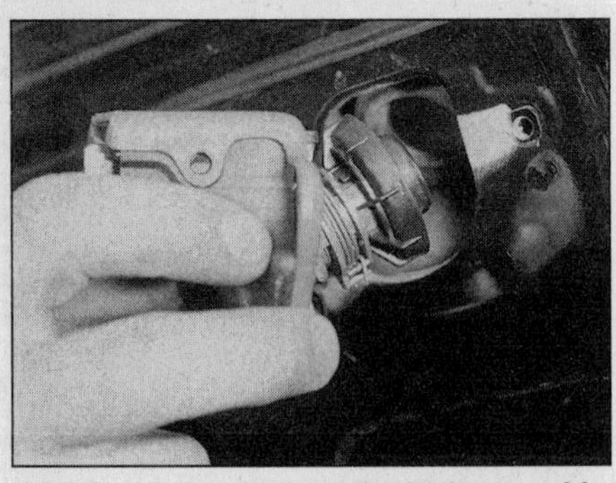
10.2 Carefully withdraw the lock assembly

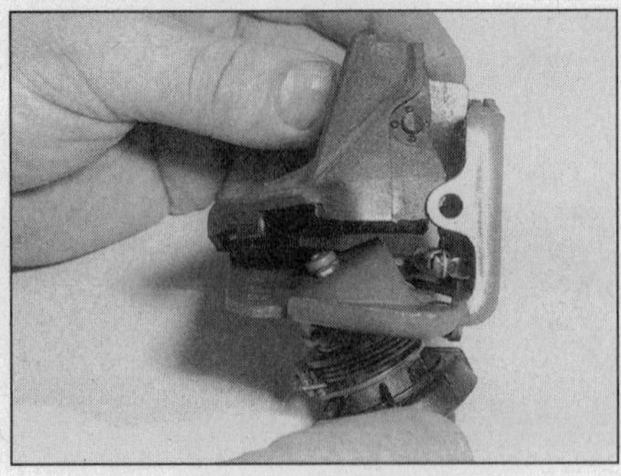
10.3a Unclip the plastic shield . . .

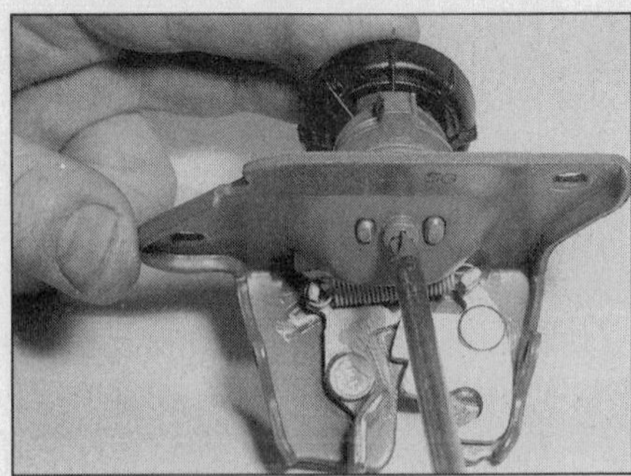
10.3b . . . remove the screw . . .

10.3c . . . and lift off the lock cylinder

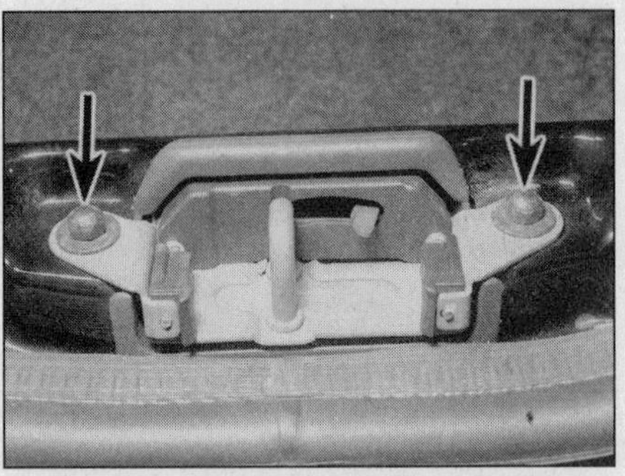
10.6 Slacken and unscrew the bolts (arrowed) securing the striker plate to the bodywork

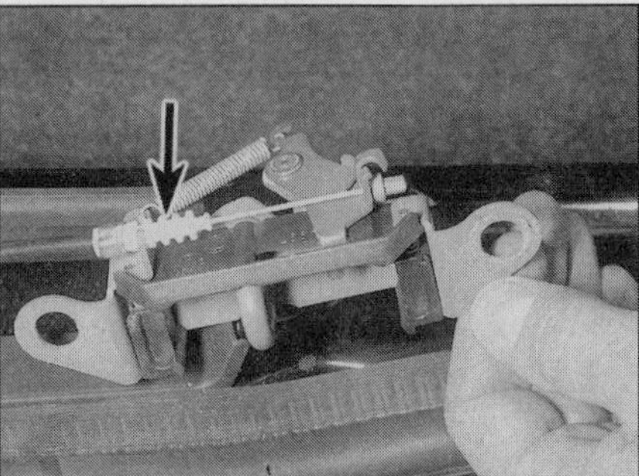
10.8 Adjust the release cable by altering the position of the cable outer sheath within its bracket (arrowed)

3 The lock cylinder may be separated from the assembly by first unclipping the plastic shield and then removing the securing screw **(see illustrations).**

Refitting

4 Refitting is the reversal of removal.

Striker plate

Removal

5 With the tailgate held in the fully open position, mark the position of the striker plate in relation to the bodywork using a pencil or marker pen, to aid accurate refitting.

6 Slacken and unscrew the bolts securing the striker plate to the bodywork **(see illustration).**

7 Remove the striker plate from its aperture, to expose the remote release cable.

8 The release cable may be adjusted by altering the position of the cable outer sheath within its retaining bracket **(see illustration)**

Refitting

9 Refitting is a reversal of removal. Use the markings made during removal to give the correct alignment.

10 Check that the tailgate fastens and releases in a satisfactory manner. If adjustment is necessary, slacken the striker plate retaining bolts, and adjust the position of the plate to suit. Once the lock is operating correctly, securely tighten the striker plate retaining bolts.

11 Bonnet - removal and refitting

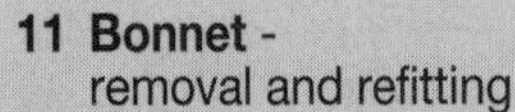

Removal

1 Open the bonnet and prop it up with a stout pole.

2 Disconnect the washer jet hoses at the three way joint **(see illustration).**

3 Mark the relationship between the hinges and the edge of the bonnet using a soft pencil or marker pen. Slacken and unscrew the bolts; have an assistant support the bonnet as the last bolts are removed **(see illustration).**

4 With the help of an assistant, lift off the bonnet and set it down on its edge, using a dust sheet to protect the paintwork.

Refitting

5 Refit the bonnet by reversing the removal process, using the markings made during removal to achieve the correct alignment. Note that the bolt mounting holes are slotted to allow adjustment if required. On completion, tighten the bolts to the specified torque.

6 Check that the bonnet fastens and releases in a satisfactory manner. If necessary, adjust the bonnet lock components, as described in Section 12.

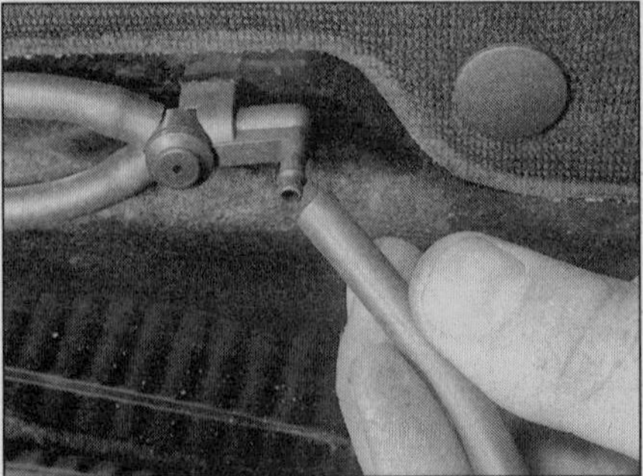
11.2 Disconnect the washer jet hoses at the three way joint

11.3 Slacken and unscrew the bonnet hinge bolts

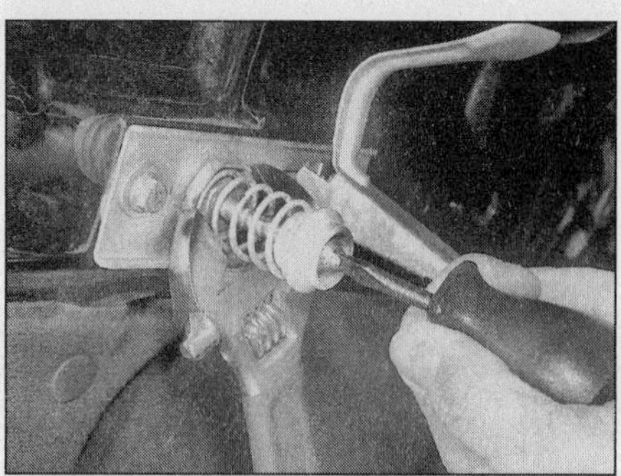
12.4 Adjusting the extension of the bonnet pin

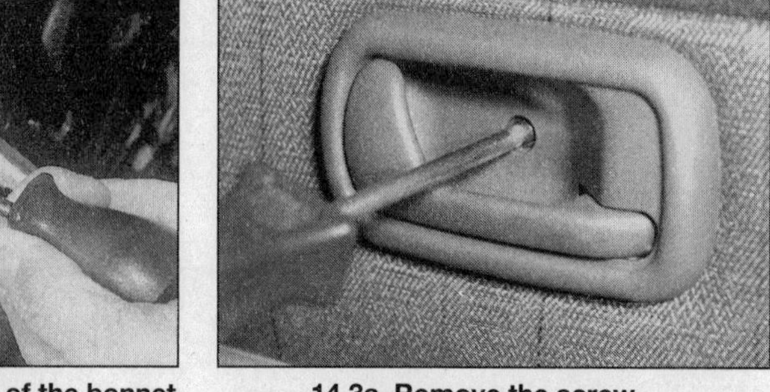
14.3a Remove the screw . . .

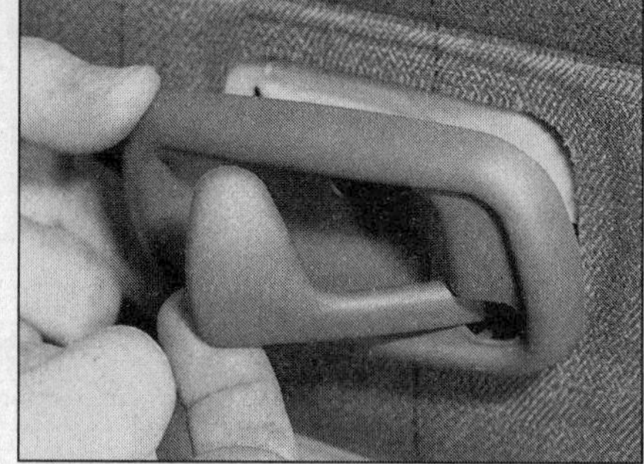
14.3b . . . then prise out the door grab handle moulding

12 Bonnet lock components - removal and refitting

Latch and release lever assembly

Removal

1 Secure the bonnet in the fully open position using the stay. Mark the relationship between the latch and the surface of the bonnet using a soft pencil or marker pen.

2 Slacken and unscrew the bolts, then lower the latch assembly away from the bonnet.

Refitting

3 Refitting is a reversal of removal. Use the alignment markings made during removal to aid accurate refitting. Note that the mounting holes are slotted to allow adjustment if required. On completion, tighten the bolts securely.

4 The extension of the bonnet pin may be adjusted in necessary, by slackening the locknut and turning the pin with a flat-bladed screwdriver **(see illustration)**.

Striker plate

Removal

5 Mark the relationship between the striker plate and the bodywork using a soft pencil or marker pen. The striker plate can then be removed by slackening and withdrawing the three securing bolts and unhooking the release cable from the operating lever.

Refitting

6 Refitting is a reversal of removal. Use the alignment markings made during removal to aid accurate refitting. Note that the mounting holes are slotted to allow adjustment if required. On completion, tighten the bolts securely.

Buffers

7 If necessary, adjust the protrusion of the rubber buffers on the front crossmember, (located above each headlamp unit) by screwing them in or out as appropriate. When the rubber buffers are correctly adjusted, there should be just enough free movement to allow the bonnet to be closed and locked easily, without using excessive force, but not enough to allow the bonnet to rattle when secured in the locked position.

13 Bonnet release cable - removal and refitting

Removal

1 Secure the bonnet in the fully open position. With reference to Section 12, detach the bonnet release cable from the striker plate operating lever.

2 Unscrew the cable clip from above the right hand headlamp unit.

3 Working around the engine bay, extract the release cable from its securing clips.

4 In the drivers footwell, extract the fixings and lower the sound insulation panel (where fitted) away from the underside of the steering column/facia.

5 Push the bonnet release handle towards the bulkhead slightly, then free the release cable end fitting from its recess in the handle. Lift the cable inner up, pass the end fitting through the larger hole and withdraw it from the handle. Extract the release cable outer from the mounting bracket by carefully pulling down on the plastic collar.

6 Release the cable from the remaining clips under the facia, then carefully pull the entire cable through the bulkhead grommet into the engine bay.

Refitting

7 Refit the cable by reversing the removal process. On completion, close the bonnet to check that it locks securely, then check the operation of the release mechanism. If adjustment is required, this can be achieved by repositioning the slotted plastic collar fitted to the cable outer sheath, in the mounting lug on the underside of the striker plate.

14 Door inner trim panel - removal and refitting

Removal

Note: *This section describes the removal of the front door trim panel; the procedure for removing the rear door trim panel is essentially the same.*

1 Disconnect the battery negative terminal (refer to *Disconnecting the battery* in the Reference Section of this manual).

2 With reference to Section 17, remove the trim panel from the rear of the door mirror fixings.

3 Lift off the caps and remove the screw, then prise out the door grab handle moulding **(see illustrations)**

4 Prise the electric window/mirror adjustment switch from the armrest and unplug the wiring connector(s). Label them to aid correct refitting later **(see illustrations)**.

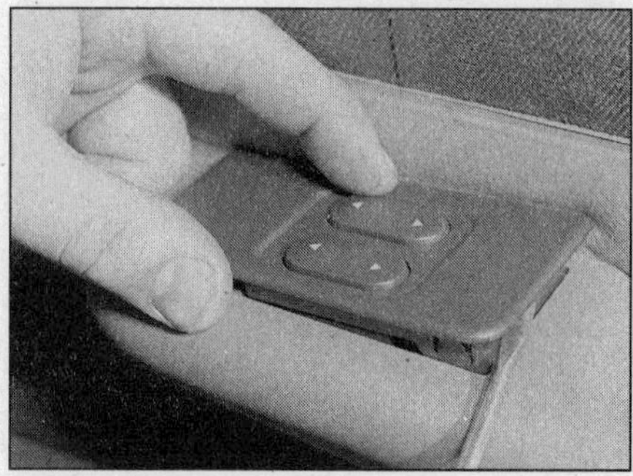
14.4a Prise the electric window/mirror adjustment switch from the armrest . . .

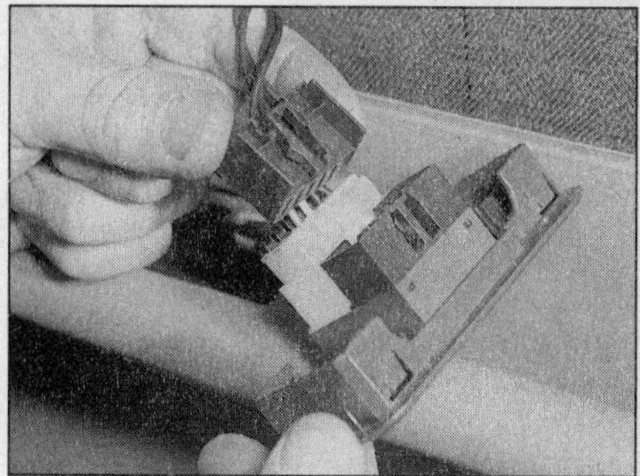
14.4b . . . and unplug the wiring connector

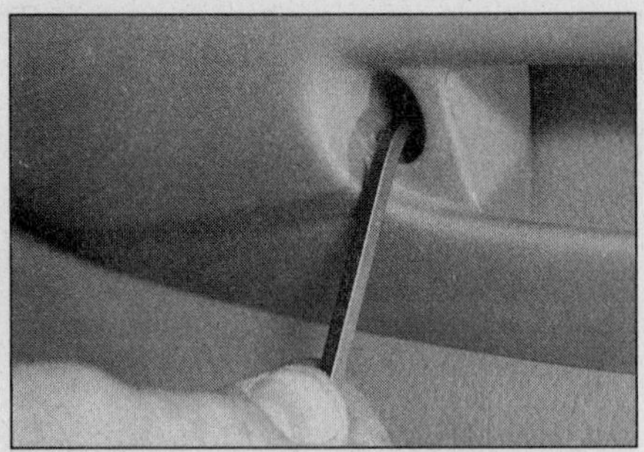

14.5a Unscrew the door panel securing screws, located on the edge of the armrest moulding . . .

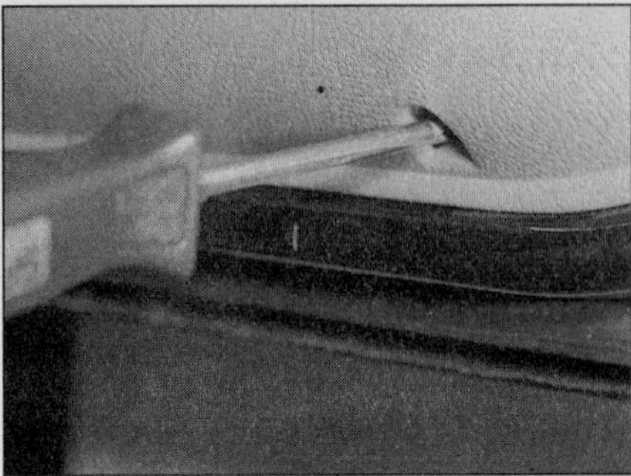

14.5b . . . and around the outside edge of the door trim panel

5 Unscrew the door panel securing screws, located on the edge of the armrest moulding and around the outside edge of the door trim panel - note that some are concealed beneath plastic caps **(see illustrations)**.

6 Using a suitable forked tool inserted between the door and the trim panel, release the press-stud clips located around the edge of the panel, then lift the trim panel upwards. Recover the locking knob trim collars **(see illustrations)**.

7 Pull the panel from the door, noting that the lower window aperture weatherstrip is integral with the trim panel and must be released from the door as the panel is withdrawn.

8 If work is to be carried out on the door internal components, it will be necessary to remove the plastic sealing sheet from the inside of the door. Start at one corner of the sheet and carefully peel it away, using a sharp blade to split the sealant bead **(see llustration)**.

9 Store the detached sealing sheet such that it cannot become contaminated with dust; this will allow it to be re-used later.

Refitting

10 Refitting is a reversal of removal, bearing in mind the following points:

a) *Ensure that the sealing sheet is correctly refitted, press it on firmly to ensure that it is adequately sealed around its edges. It should be possible to use the original sealant, but if necessary, new sealant can be obtained from a Fiat dealer.*
b) *Before refitting the trim panel, feed the electric window switch wiring through the aperture in the front of the panel.*
c) *Make sure that the weatherstrip engages securely with the edge of the door as the panel is refitted.*

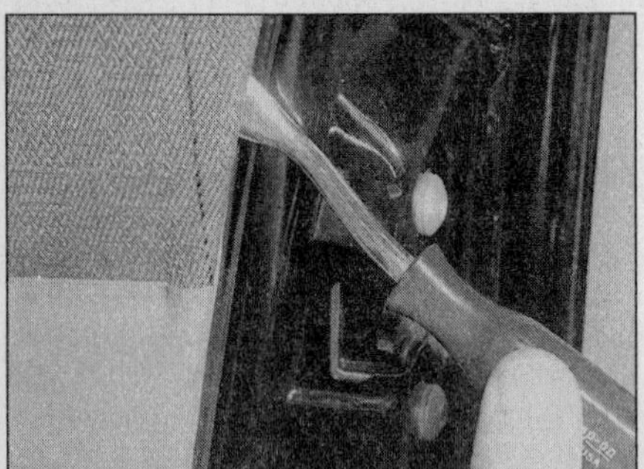

14.6a Release the press-stud clips located around the edge of the panel . . .

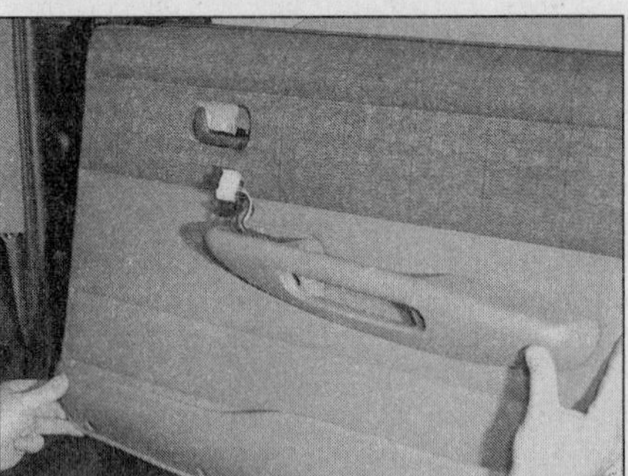

14.6b . . . then lift the trim panel upwards . . .

15 Door - removal and refitting

Note: *This procedure is applicable both to the front and rear doors.*

Removal

Note: *A new door check strap roll-pin will be required on refitting.*

1 Disconnect the battery negative terminal (refer to *Disconnecting the battery* in the Reference Section of this manual).

2 Unplug the multiway electrical connector from the inner edge of the door.

3 Have an assistant support the door, then unscrew the door hinges centre bolts, and lift the door from the vehicle.

Refitting

4 Refitting is a reversal of removal. On completion, tighten the hinge centre bolts securely.

Adjustment

5 Close the door **carefully**, in case the alignment is incorrect, which may cause scratching on the door or the body as the door is closed, and check the fit of the door with the surrounding panels.

6 If adjustment is required, loosen the hinge-to-body securing bolts (the bolt holes are elongated to allow for adjustment) and move the hinges as required to achieve satisfactory alignment. Tighten the securing bolts securely on completion.

7 Check the operation of the door lock. If necessary, slacken the securing bolts, and adjust the position of the lock striker on the body pillar to achieve satisfactory alignment. Tighten the bolts securely on completion.

16 Door handle and lock components - removal and refitting

1 Ensure that the door window glass is in the fully closed position, then disconnect the battery negative terminal (refer to *Disconnecting the battery* in the Reference Section of this

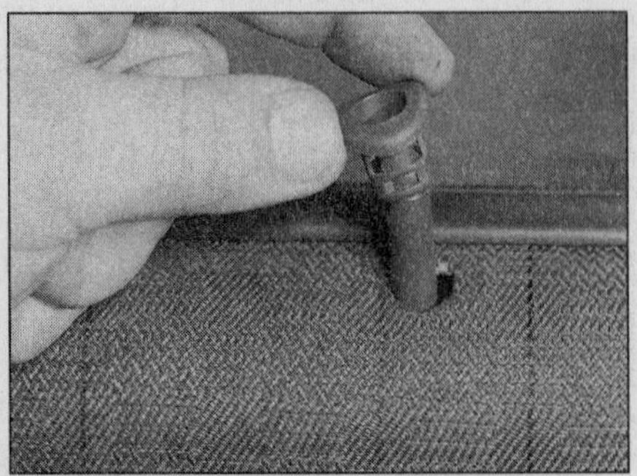

14.6c . . . and recover the locking knob trim collars from above . . .

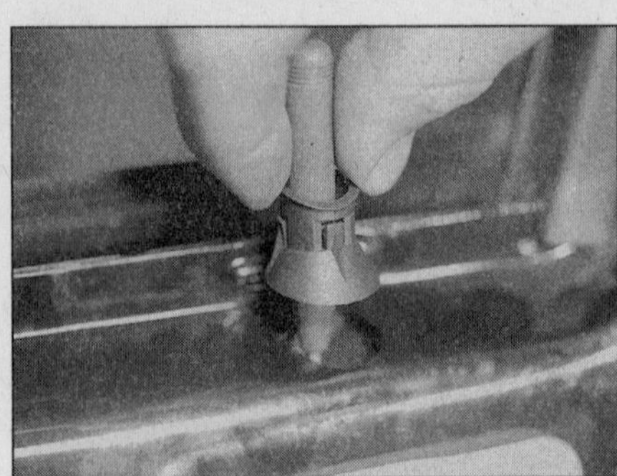

14.6d . . . and below the panel

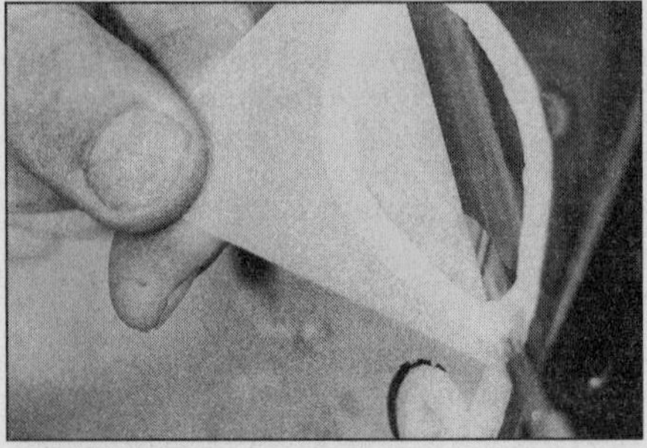

14.8 Carefully peel the sealing sheet away, using a sharp blade to split the sealant bead

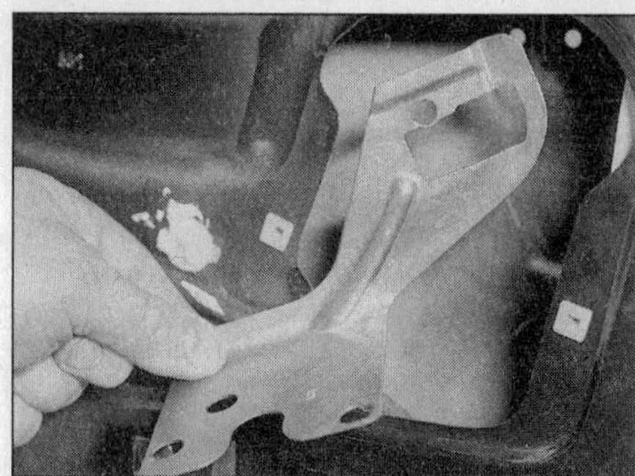

16.3 Unbolt and remove the anti-theft bracket from the rear of the door handle

16.4 Detach the link rod (arrowed) from the door lock mechanism

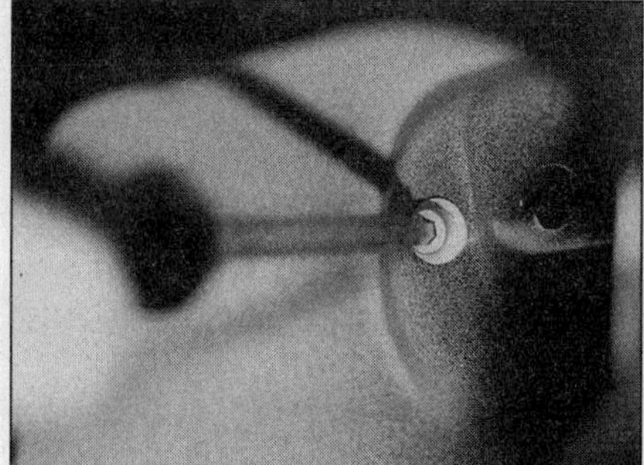

16.5a Slacken and remove the handle retaining screws . . .

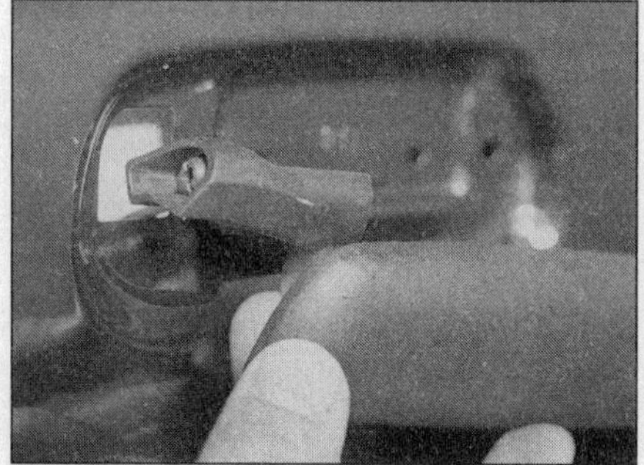

16.5b . . . and lift the handle assembly from the door

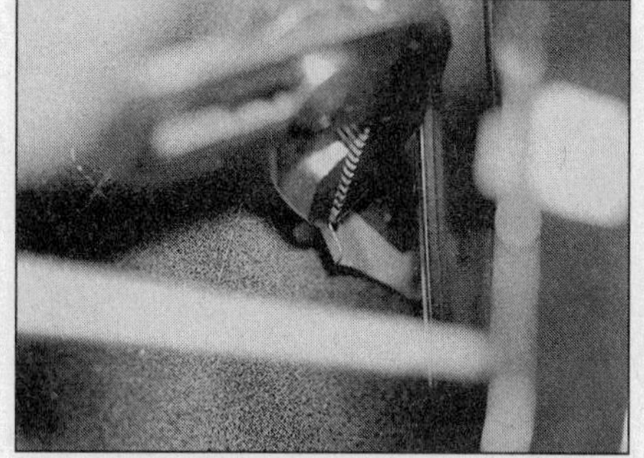

16.7a Release the retaining clip from the rear of the cylinder using a pair of pliers

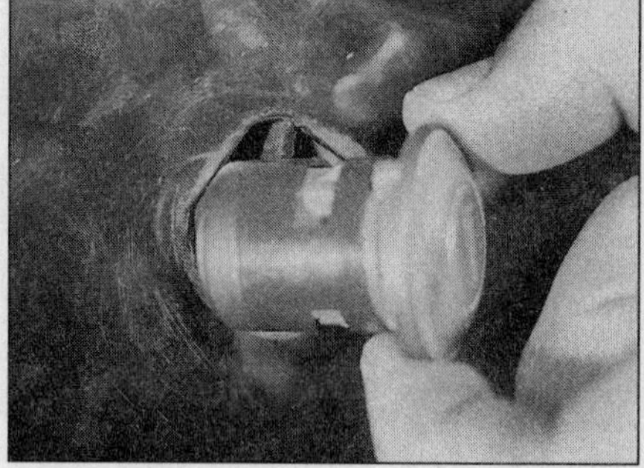

16.7b Extract the lock cylinder from the door

manual). Refer to Section 14 and remove the door inner trim panel and sealing sheet.

Door handle

Removal

2 Where applicable on 3-door models, refer to Section 18 and remove the bolts that secure the window glass guide rail to the door, then remove the guide rail.

3 Working inside the door space, unbolt and remove the anti-theft bracket from the rear of the door handle **(see illustration)**.

4 Detach the link rod from the door lock mechanism **(see illustration)**.

5 Slacken and remove the handle retaining screws and lift the handle assembly from the door **(see illustrations)**.

Refitting

6 Refit the door handle by following the removal procedure in reverse. Ensure that the link rod engages correctly with the lock mechanism operating lever.

Lock cylinder

7 Working inside the door space, release the metal retaining clip from the rear of the cylinder using a pair of pliers **(see illustrations)**. Extract the lock cylinder from the door.

Refitting

8 Refitting is a reversal of removal. Ensure that the lugs on the rear of the cylinder engage correctly with the lock mechanism.

Lock mechanism

Removal

9 Working inside the door space, unplug the wiring for the central locking motor and switches, at the multiway connector **(see illustration)**.

10 At the trailing edge of the door, remove the three screws that secure the lock mechanism to the door **(see illustration)**.

11 Disconnect the locking knob link rod from the lever on the top of the lock mechanism. **Note:** *On models fitted with a plastic anti-theft lock shield, the locking knob link rod remains connected to the lock mechanism and is then removed with the mechanism as a complete assembly.*

12 With reference to the relevant sub-section, detach the exterior door handle link rod from the lock mechanism operating lever.

13 Unclip the link rod for the interior door handle from its guide, then manoeuvre the lock mechanism out of the door **(see illustration)**.

Refitting

14 Refitting is a reversal of removal. On completion, tighten the lock mechanism retaining screws securely.

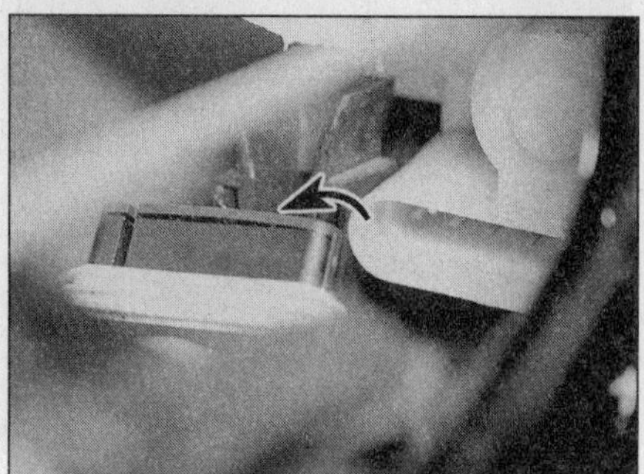

16.9 Unplug the wiring at the multiway connector

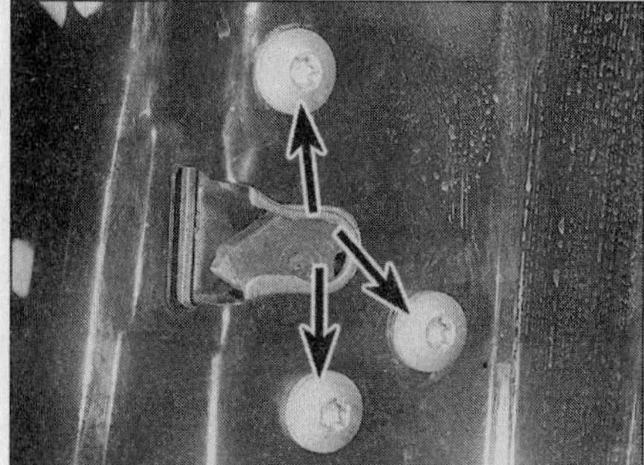

16.10 Remove the three screws that secure the lock mechanism to the door

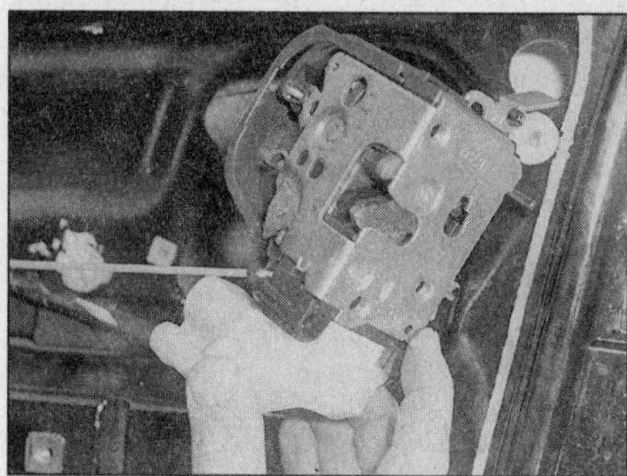

16.13 Manoeuvre the lock mechanism out of the door

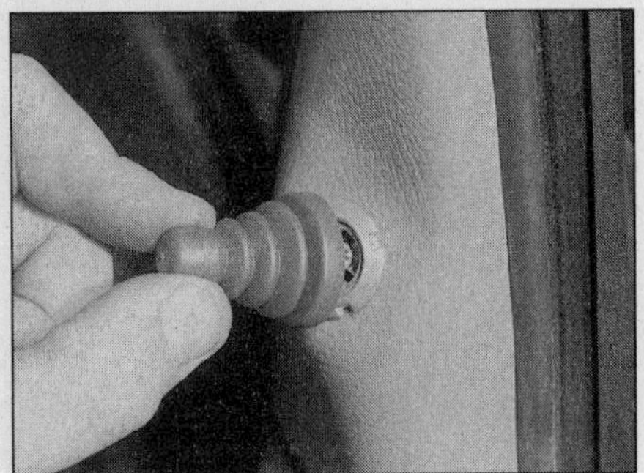

17.3a Prise the rubber cover off the adjustment lever . . .

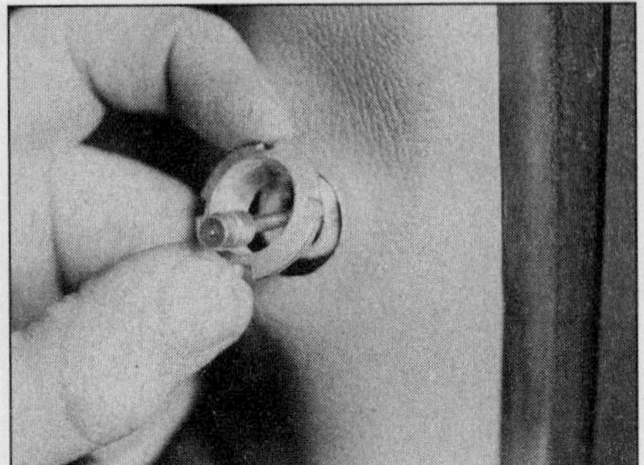

17.3b . . . then unscrew and remove the locking collar

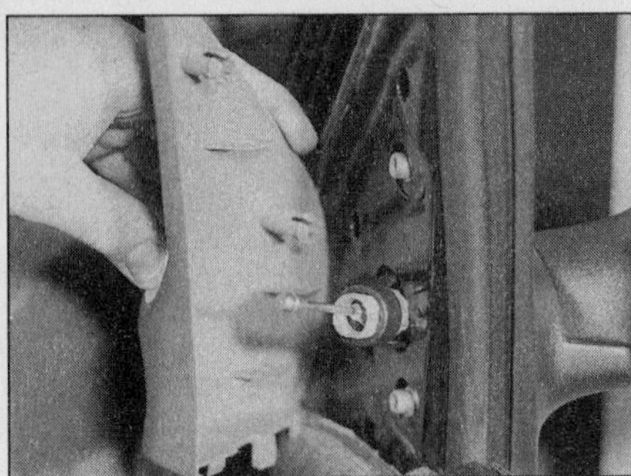

17.4 Remove the plastic trim panel, to expose the mirror securing screws

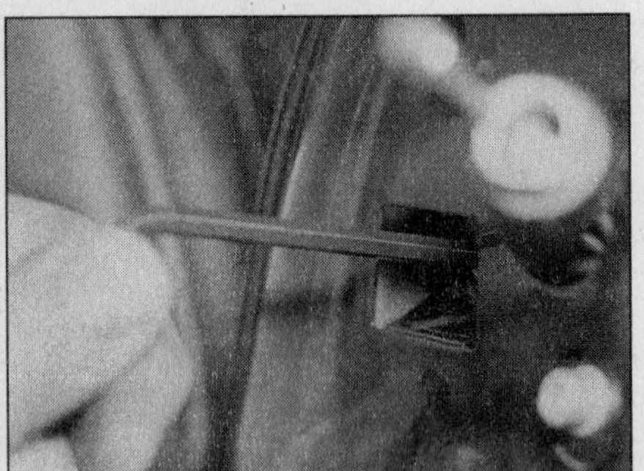

17.5a Remove the securing screws . . .

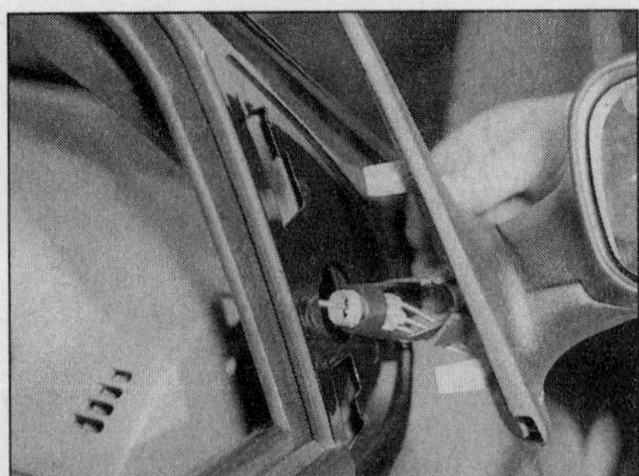

17.5b . . . and withdraw the mirror assembly from the door

17 Exterior mirror components - removal and refitting

Mirror assembly

Removal - models with electrically-adjustable mirrors

1 Disconnect the battery negative terminal (refer to *Disconnecting the battery* in the Reference Section of this manual).

2 Refer to Section 14 and remove the door inner trim panel. Reach inside the door space and unplug the electrical supply to the mirror at the multiway connector. Unclip the mirror wiring from the door, noting its routing.

Removal - models with manually-adjustable mirrors

3 Prise the rubber cover off the adjustment lever, then unscrew and remove the locking collar **(see illustrations)**.

All models

4 Remove the plastic trim panel, to expose the mirror securing screws **(see illustration).**

5 Remove the securing screws, and withdraw the mirror assembly from the door **(see illustrations)**.

Refitting

6 Refitting is a reversal of removal. Tighten the mirror securing screws securely. On models with electric mirrors, ensure that the electrical wiring is correctly routed so that it cannot foul the electric window mechanism.

Mirror glass

Removal

7 On models with electric mirrors, disconnect the battery negative terminal (refer to *Disconnecting the battery* in the Reference Section of this manual).

8 Insert a suitable thin plastic or wooden tool between the mirror glass and the mirror body, and carefully lever the glass forward to release the securing clips.

Warning: Protect your hands and eyes from glass splinters.

9 Where applicable, disconnect the heater element wiring from the rear of the glass, and withdraw the glass from the mirror assembly.

Refitting

10 Where applicable, reconnect the wires to the rear of the mirror glass, then push the glass into position to engage the securing clips.

To aid refitting, lightly grease the securing clips on the rear of the mirror glass.

18 Electric window components - removal and refitting

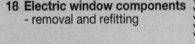

Door window glass

Removal

1 Operate the window regulator mechanism, such that the glass is positioned halfway down the aperture. On models with electric windows, disconnect the battery negative terminal (refer to *Disconnecting the battery* in the Reference Section of this manual).

2 Remove the door inner trim panel and the plastic sealing sheet, as described in Section 14.

3 On three door models, remove the screws at the trailing edge of the door and lift out the window glass rear guide channel. Similarly, remove the screws at the front edge of the door and remove the window glass front guide channel.

4 Support the glass, then unclip the plastic fastener that secures the window glass to the regulator mechanism. Disengage the regulator mechanism from the hole at the base of the window glass **(see illustrations)**.

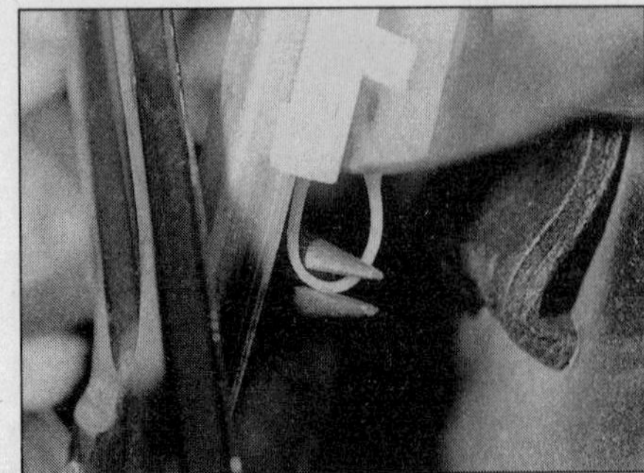

18.4a Unclip the plastic fastener that secures the window glass to the regulator mechanism

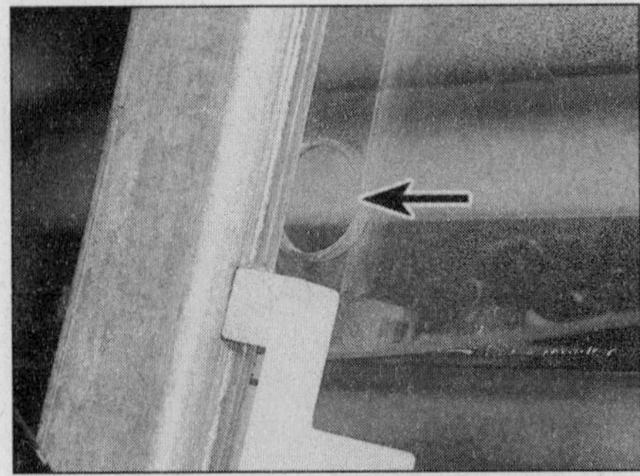

18.4b Disengage the regulator mechanism from the hole (arrowed) at the base of the window glass

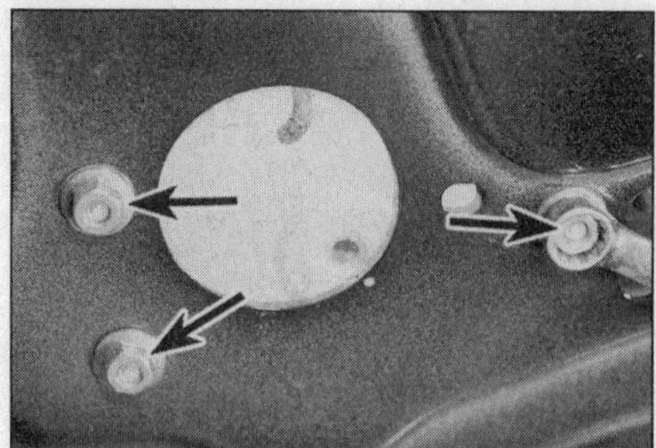
18.10 Unscrew the bolts (arrowed) securing the motor assembly/winder mechanism to the door

5 Lift the glass out through the window aperture in the top of the door, manipulating the glass past the weatherstrips as it is withdrawn. On 3-door models, it will be necessary to partially remove the weatherstrip from the upper edge of the window aperture, to allow the glass to be withdrawn.

Refitting

6 Refitting is a reversal of removal, bearing in mind the following points:

a) Ensure that all weather strips are securely seated on the edges of the window aperture.
b) Check the operation of the window regulator mechanism before refitting the door inner trim panel.
c) Refit the door inner trim panel with reference to Section 14.

Door window regulator

Removal

7 Separate the window glass from the regulator mechanism, as described earlier.
8 Fully raise the window glass, and secure the glass in position using suitable tape, or by wedging the glass in position using rags between the glass and the edge of the door - ensure that the glass cannot drop into the door. Alternatively, lift the glass panel out through the window aperture.
9 Where applicable, separate the two halves of the regulator motor wiring connector.
10 Unscrew the bolts securing the motor assembly/winder mechanism to the door **(see illustration)**.
11 Unscrew the two upper and the two lower regulator mechanism securing bolts, then manipulate the complete regulator assembly out through the aperture in the door **(see illustrations)**.
12 The winder/motor assembly, together with its associated control cables remains connected to the regulator mechanism **(see illustration)**. **Note:** *Carefully mark the relationship between the guide rails and the door to ensure correct adjustment on refitting.*

Refitting

13 Refitting is a reversal of removal, bearing in mind the following points:

a) Ensure that all weather strips are securely seated on the edges of the window aperture

18.11a Unscrew the upper . . .

18.11c . . . then manipulate the complete regulator assembly out through the aperture in the door

b) Check the operation of the window mechanism before refitting the door inner trim panel.
c) Refit the door inner trim panel with reference to Section 14.

19 Facia - removal and refitting

Removal

1 Disconnect the battery negative terminal (refer to *Disconnecting the battery* in the Reference Section of this manual).
2 Refer to Chapter 12 and carry out the following:

a) Remove the instrument panel from the facia.

19.5a Prise open the plastic covers . . .

18.11b . . . and the lower regulator mechanism securing bolts . . .

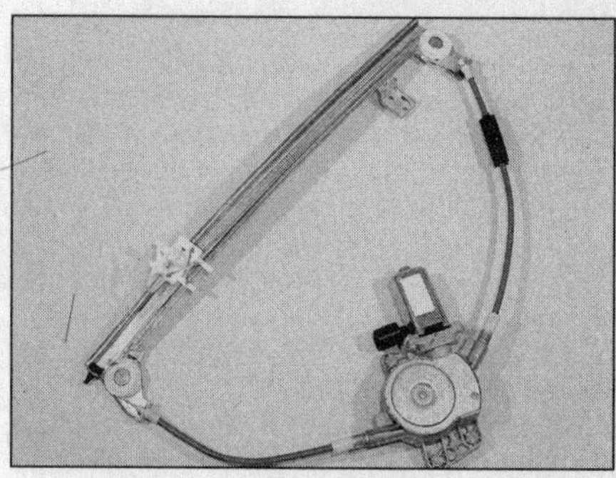
18.12 The electric window regulator assembly

b) Remove the radio/cassette unit from the facia

3 Unscrew the fixings for the storage bin above the radio aperture, then remove the bin from the facia.
4 Remove the steering wheel (see Chapter 10) and the steering column shroud.
5 Prise open the plastic covers, remove the fixings and lift off the handbrake lever console **(see illustrations)**.
6 Work around the outside of the centre console and unscrew the fixings. Unclip the gear lever gaiter, lift the centre console over the gear lever, then label and unplug the wiring connector beneath and remove the console from the vehicle.
7 Remove the heater control panel from the facia, with reference to Chapter 3.
8 Unscrew the fixings from the upper and lower edges of the combined ventilation/

19.5b . . . remove the fixings . . .

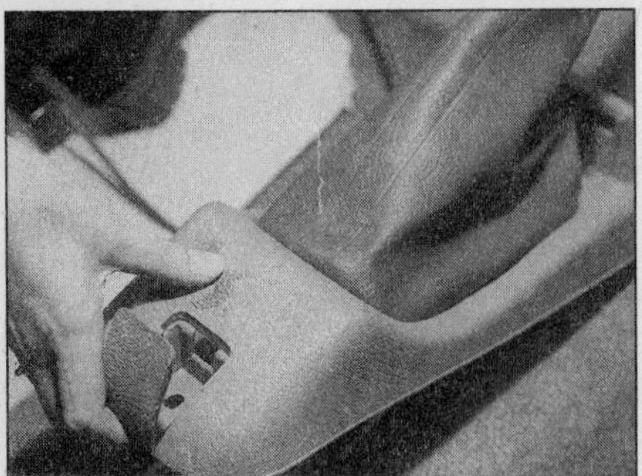

19.5c . . . and lift off the handbrake lever console

19.8 Remove the combined ventilation/switch panel from the facia

switch panel, then remove the panel from the facia **(see illustration)**. Label the wiring connector to aid refitting, then unplug it.

9 Work along the lower edge of the facia and remove all the securing screws; there are three on the drivers side and three on the passenger side - one is concealed inside the glove compartment, behind a plastic cap.

10 With reference to Chapter 12, remove the cover and open the main fuse box. Where applicable, unscrew the fixings that secure the electronic control unit to its mounting bracket. Remove the facia mounting bolts located adjacent to the mounting bracket **(see illustration)**.

11 Refer to Chapter 10 and unbolt the steering column from its support bracket, allowing the column to rest in the footwell. There is no need to slacken the clamp bolt at the base of the steering column to separate it from the steering gear.

12 With reference to Chapter 12, remove front right and left speaker grilles. Remove the two facia upper mounting screws that are now exposed. Similarly, prise open the plastic cover from centre of upper edge of the facia and remove the mounting screw behind.

13 Carefully pull whole facia moulding forward away from the bulkhead slightly. Label all wiring connectors to aid correct refitting later, then unplug them. Check that nothing remains connected between the facia and bulkhead then draw the facia moulding away and remove it from the vehicle.

20.8 Remove the bolt (arrowed) and detach the backrest from the mounting bracket

Refitting

14 Refit the facia by following the removal procedure in reverse, noting the following points:

a) Reinstate all electrical connections according to the labels made during removal and ensure that cables are secured in their clips, using the original routing.

b) Ensure that all ventilation ducting locates correctly over the rear of the grilles before tightening the facia retaining screws.

c) On completion, reconnect the battery negative cable and check the operation of all controls, gauges and instruments disturbed during the removal process, including the ventilation/heating system.

20 Seats - removal and refitting

Front seats

Removal

Warning: On models with seat belt pre-tensioners, entrust the work of seat removal to a Fiat dealer. DO NOT attempt to remove the seat on vehicles so equipped.

1 The front seats frames are secured to the floorpan by four bolts. Where applicable, prise out the caps from the plastic trim panel to expose the bolt heads.

2 Slide the seat towards the rear of the car to gain access to the two bolts at the front, then slacken and withdraw them.

3 Slide the seat fully forwards and remove the two rearmost bolts.

4 Lift the seat out of the cabin area.

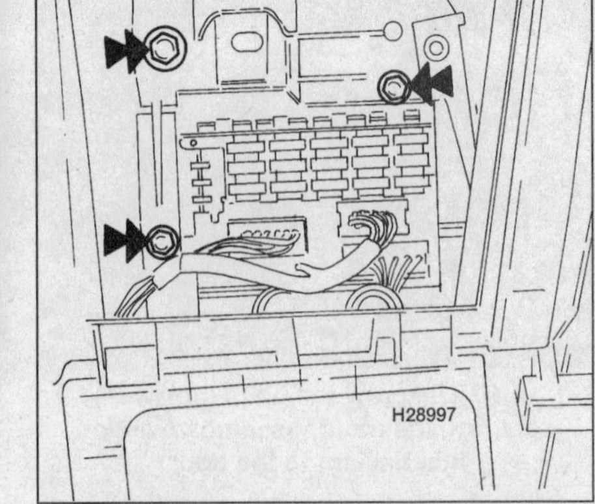

19.10 Remove the facia mounting bolts (arrowed) located adjacent to the control unit mounting bracket

Refitting

5 Refit the seat by reversing the removal procedure.

Rear seat back rests

Removal

6 Using the hand straps, raise the seat cushion and tilt it fully forward.

7 The rear seat back rests are mounted on hinged brackets which are bolted to the floorpan. To remove both back rests together, first remove the screws and detach the load space carpet panel.

8 Unbolt the back rest panel from the mounting brackets **(see illustration)**.

Refitting

9 Refit the back rests by reversing the removal procedure.

Rear seat cushion

Removal

10 Using the hand straps, raise the seat cushion and tilt it fully forward.

11 Remove the screws that secure the hinged brackets to the floorpan, then lift out the cushion **(see illustration)**.

Refitting

12 Refit the seat cushion by reversing the removal procedure.

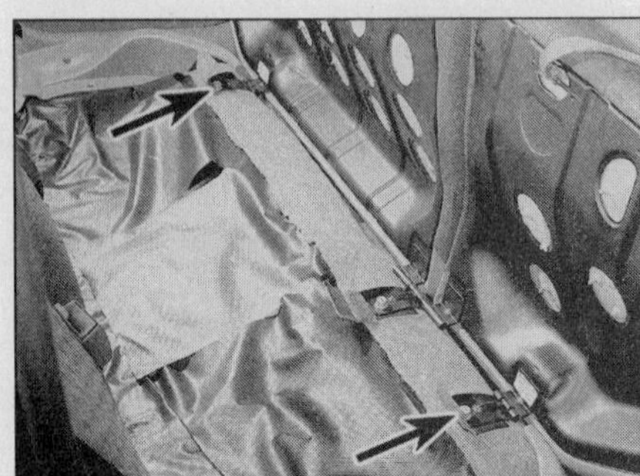

20.11 Remove the screws (arrowed) that secure the hinged brackets to the floorpan

Chapter 12
Body electrical systems

Contents

Degrees of difficulty

Easy, suitable for novice with little experience 	**Fairly easy,** suitable for beginner with some experience 	**Fairly difficult,** suitable for competent DIY mechanic 	**Difficult,** suitable for experienced DIY mechanic	**Very difficult,** suitable for expert DIY or professional

Specifications

Bulb ratings

	Watts
Headlights	60/55
Front long range driving light	55
Front foglight	55
Front direction indicator light	21
Front sidelight	5
Front direction indicator repeater light	5
Stop light	21
Tail light	5
Rear direction indicator light	21
Reversing light	21
Rear foglight	21
Rear number plate light	5
Courtesy light	10
Map reading light	5

1 General information and precautions

Warning: *Before carrying out any work on the electrical system, read through the precautions given in Safety first! at the beginning of this manual, and in Chapter 5.*

The electrical system is of 12-volt negative earth type. Power for the lights and all electrical accessories is supplied by a lead/acid type battery, which is charged by the alternator.

This Chapter covers repair and service procedures for the various electrical components not associated with the engine. Information on the battery, alternator and starter motor can be found in Chapter 5.

It should be noted that, prior to working on any component in the electrical system, the battery negative terminal should first be disconnected, to prevent the possibility of electrical short-circuits and/or fires.

Caution: Before proceeding, refer to Disconnecting the battery in the Reference Section of this manual for further information.

2 Electrical fault finding - general information

Note: *Refer to the precautions given in Safety first! and in Section 1 of this Chapter before starting work. The following tests relate to testing of the main electrical circuits, and should not be used to test delicate electronic circuits (such as anti-lock braking systems), particularly where an electronic control module is used.*

General

1 A typical electrical circuit consists of an electrical component, any switches, relays, motors, fuses, fusible links or circuit breakers related to that component, and the wiring and connectors which link the component to both the battery and the chassis. To help to pinpoint a problem in an electrical circuit, wiring diagrams are included at the end of this manual.

2 Before attempting to diagnose an electrical fault, first study the appropriate wiring diagram, to obtain a more complete understanding of the components included in the particular circuit concerned. The possible sources of a fault can be narrowed down by noting whether other components related to the circuit are operating properly. If several components or circuits fail at one time, the problem is likely to be related to a shared fuse or earth connection.

3 Electrical problems usually stem from simple causes, such as loose or corroded connections, a faulty earth connection, a blown fuse, a melted fusible link, or a faulty relay (refer to Section 3 for details of testing relays). Visually inspect the condition of all fuses, wires and connections in a problem circuit before testing the components. Use the wiring diagrams to determine which terminal connections will need to be checked, in order to pinpoint the trouble-spot.

4 The basic tools required for electrical fault-finding include a circuit tester or voltmeter (a 12-volt bulb with a set of test leads can also be used for certain tests); a self-powered test light (sometimes known as a continuity tester); an ohmmeter (to measure resistance); a battery and set of test leads; and a jumper wire, preferably with a circuit breaker or fuse incorporated, which can be used to bypass suspect wires or electrical components. Before attempting to locate a problem with test instruments, use the wiring diagram to determine where to make the connections.

5 To find the source of an intermittent wiring fault (usually due to a poor or dirty connection, or damaged wiring insulation), a wiggle test can be performed on the wiring. This involves wiggling the wiring by hand, to see if the fault occurs as the wiring is moved. It should be possible to narrow down the source of the fault to a particular section of wiring. This method of testing can be used in conjunction with any of the tests described in the following sub-Sections.

6 Apart from problems due to poor connections, two basic types of fault can occur in an electrical circuit - open-circuit, or short-circuit.

7 Open-circuit faults are caused by a break somewhere in the circuit, which prevents current from flowing. An open-circuit fault will prevent a component from working, but will not cause the relevant circuit fuse to blow.

8 Short-circuit faults are caused by a short somewhere in the circuit, which allows the current flowing in the circuit to escape along an alternative route, usually to earth. Short-circuit faults are normally caused by a breakdown in wiring insulation, which allows a feed wire to touch either another wire, or an earthed component such as the bodyshell. A short-circuit fault will normally cause the relevant circuit fuse to blow.

Finding an open-circuit

9 To check for an open-circuit, connect one lead of a circuit tester or voltmeter to either the negative battery terminal or a known good earth.

10 Connect the other lead to a connector in the circuit being tested, preferably nearest to the battery or fuse.

11 Switch on the circuit, bearing in mind that some circuits are live only when the ignition switch is moved to a particular position.

12 If voltage is present (indicated either by the tester bulb lighting or a voltmeter reading, as applicable), this means that the section of the circuit between the relevant connector and the battery is problem-free.

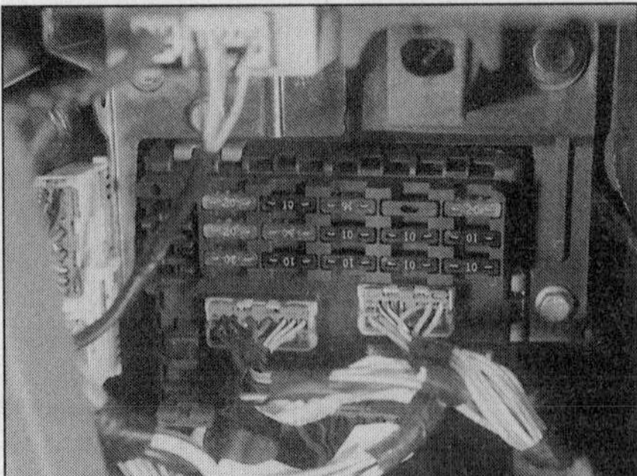

3.2 Main fusebox, located on the driver's side of the facia

13 Continue to check the remainder of the circuit in the same fashion.

14 When a point is reached at which no voltage is present, the problem must lie between that point and the previous test point with voltage. Most problems can be traced to a broken, corroded or loose connection.

Finding a short-circuit

15 To check for a short-circuit, first disconnect the load(s) from the circuit (loads are the components which draw current from a circuit, such as bulbs, motors, heating elements, etc).

16 Remove the relevant fuse from the circuit, and connect a circuit tester or voltmeter to the fuse connections.

17 Switch on the circuit, bearing in mind that some circuits are live only when the ignition switch is moved to a particular position.

18 If voltage is present (indicated either by the tester bulb lighting or a voltmeter reading, as applicable), this means that there is a short-circuit.

19 If no voltage is present, but the fuse still blows with the load(s) connected, this indicates an internal fault in the load(s).

Finding an earth fault

20 The battery negative terminal is connected to 'earth' - the metal of the engine/transmission and the car body - and most systems are wired so that they only receive a positive feed, the current returning via the metal of the car body. This means that the component mounting and the body form part of that circuit. Loose or corroded mountings can therefore cause a range of electrical faults, ranging from total failure of a circuit, to a puzzling partial fault. In particular, lights may shine dimly (especially when another circuit sharing the same earth point is in operation), motors (eg wiper motors or the radiator cooling fan motor) may run slowly, and the operation of one circuit may have an apparently-unrelated effect on another. Note that on many vehicles, earth straps are used between certain components, such as the engine/transmission and the body, usually where there is no metal-to-metal contact between components, due to flexible rubber mountings, etc.

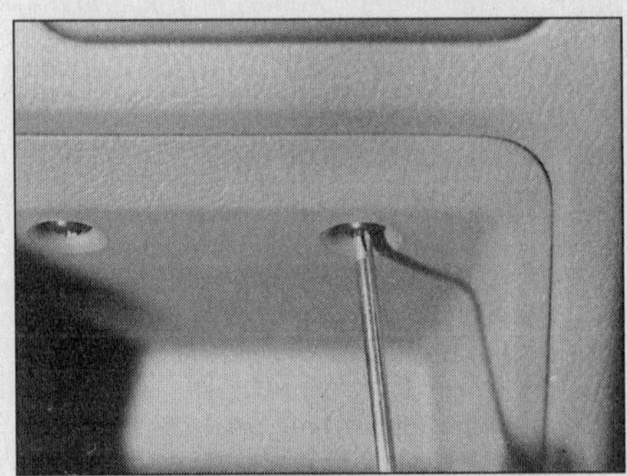

3.3 To gain access to the fuses, remove the screw and pull the stowage bin away from the facia

21 To check whether a component is properly earthed, disconnect the battery, and connect one lead of an ohmmeter to a known good earth point. Connect the other lead to the wire or earth connection being tested. The resistance reading should be zero; if not, check the connection as follows.

22 If an earth connection is thought to be faulty, dismantle the connection, and clean back to bare metal both the bodyshell and the wire terminal or the component earth connection mating surface. Be careful to remove all traces of dirt and corrosion, then use a knife to trim away any paint, so that a clean metal-to-metal joint is made. On reassembly, tighten the joint fasteners securely; if a wire terminal is being refitted, use serrated washers between the terminal and the bodyshell, to ensure a clean and secure connection. When the connection is remade, prevent the onset of corrosion in the future by applying a coat of petroleum jelly or silicone-based grease, or by spraying on (at regular intervals) a proprietary ignition sealer, or a water-dispersant lubricant.

3 Fuses and relays - general information

Fuses

1 Fuses are designed to break a circuit when a predetermined current is reached, in order to protect the components and wiring which could be damaged by excessive current flow. Any excessive current flow will be due to a fault in the circuit, usually a short-circuit (see Section 2).

2 The main fuses are located in the fusebox on the driver's side of the facia **(see illustration)**.

3 To gain access to the fuses, remove the screw and pull the stowage bin moulding away from the facia **(see illustration)**.

4 Additional fuses and circuit-breakers are located in the engine compartment, and in an

3.4 The auxiliary fusebox, located inside the glovebox behind a drop-down panel

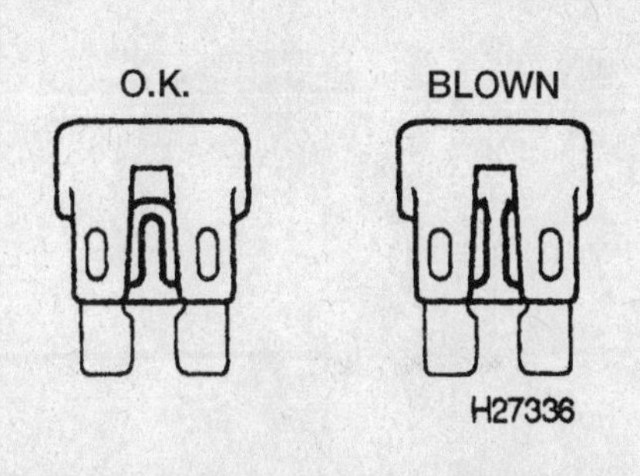

3.5 A blown fuse can be recognised from its melted or broken wire

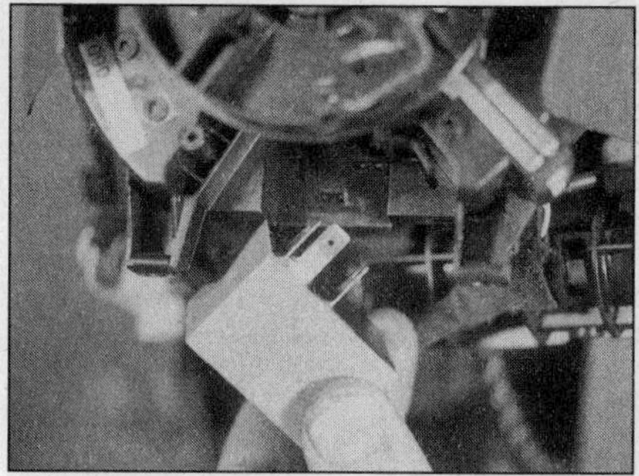

3.14 Removing the direction indicator/hazard warning flasher unit

auxiliary fusebox, which is located inside the glovebox behind a drop-down panel **(see illustration)**.

5 A blown fuse can be recognised from its melted or broken wire **(see illustration)**.

6 To remove a fuse, first ensure that the relevant circuit is switched off.

7 Using the plastic tool clipped to the main fusebox lid, pull the fuse from its location.

8 Spare fuses are provided in the main fusebox.

9 Before renewing a blown fuse, trace and rectify the cause, and always use a fuse of the correct rating (fuse ratings are specified on the inside of the fusebox cover flap). Never substitute a fuse of a higher rating, or make temporary repairs using wire or metal foil; more serious damage, or even fire, could result.

10 Note that the fuses are colour-coded as follows. Refer to the wiring diagrams for details of the fuse ratings used and the circuits protected.

Colour	Rating
Orange	5A
Red	10A
Blue	15A
Yellow	20A
Clear or White	25A
Green	30A

11 The radio/cassette player fuse is located in the rear of the unit, and can be accessed after removing the radio/cassette player - refer to Section 12 for greater detail.

Relays

12 A relay is an electrically-operated switch, which is used for the following reasons:

a) *A relay can switch a heavy current remotely from the circuit in which the current is flowing, therefore allowing the use of lighter-gauge wiring and switch contacts.*
b) *A relay can receive more than one control input, unlike a mechanical switch.*
c) *A relay can have a timer function - for example, the intermittent wiper relay.*

13 The main and optional equipment relays are located in the main and auxiliary fuseboxes (see *Fuses*). A number of additional relays may be fitted, depending on model and specification. These are generally mounted adjacent to the component being controlled; e.g. the radiator cooling fan relay(s) are mounted on a bracket next the cooling fan itself.

14 The direction indicator/hazard warning flasher unit is mounted on the underside of the steering column stalk switch unit. It can be accessed by removing the steering column lower shroud panel **(see illustration)**.

15 If a circuit or system controlled by a relay develops a fault, and the relay is suspect, operate the system. If the relay is functioning, it should be possible to hear it click as it is energised. If this is the case, the fault lies with the components or wiring of the system. If the relay is not being energised, then either the relay is not receiving a main supply or a switching voltage, or the relay itself is faulty. Testing is by the substitution of a known good unit, but be careful - while some relays are identical in appearance and in operation, others look similar but perform different functions.

16 To remove a relay, first ensure that the relevant circuit is switched off. The relay can then simply be pulled out from the socket, and pushed back into position.

4 Bulbs (exterior lights) - renewal

General

1 Whenever a bulb is renewed, note the following points:

a) *Ensure that the relevant electrical circuit is isolated before removing a bulb. If in doubt, disconnect the battery negative lead before starting work.*
b) *Remember that, if the circuit has just been in use, the bulb may be extremely hot.*
c) *Always check the bulb contacts and holder, ensuring that there is clean metal-to-metal contact between the bulb and its live contact(s) and earth. Clean off any corrosion or dirt before fitting a new bulb.*
d) *Wherever bayonet-type bulbs are fitted, ensure that the live contact(s) bear firmly against the bulb contact.*
e) *Always ensure that the new bulb is of the correct rating (see Specifications), and that it is completely clean before fitting it; this applies particularly to headlight/foglight bulbs (see following paragraphs).*
f) *Pay attention to the orientation when fitting multi-filament bulbs (e.g. combined tail/brake light bulbs) - incorrect fitting will cause the filaments to illuminate in the wrong sequence.*

Headlight

2 Open the bonnet. Ensure that the headlights are turned off at the stalk switch.

Models with single reflector

3 Pull the wiring plug from the rear of the bulb **(see illustration)**.

4 Pull the rubber boot from the rear of the headlight unit **(see illustration)**.

4.3 Pull the wiring plug from the rear of the bulb

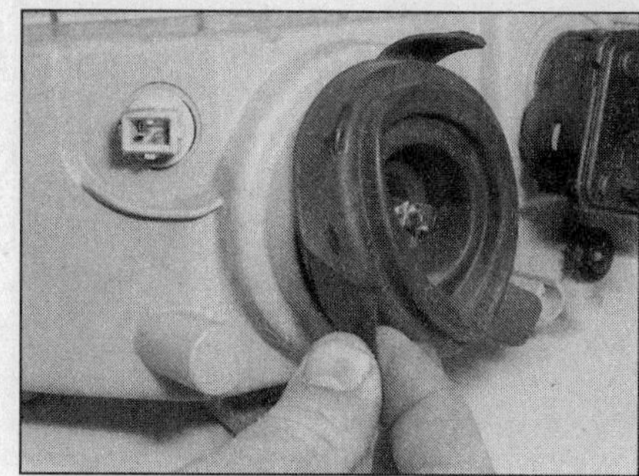

4.4 Pull the rubber boot from the rear of the headlight unit

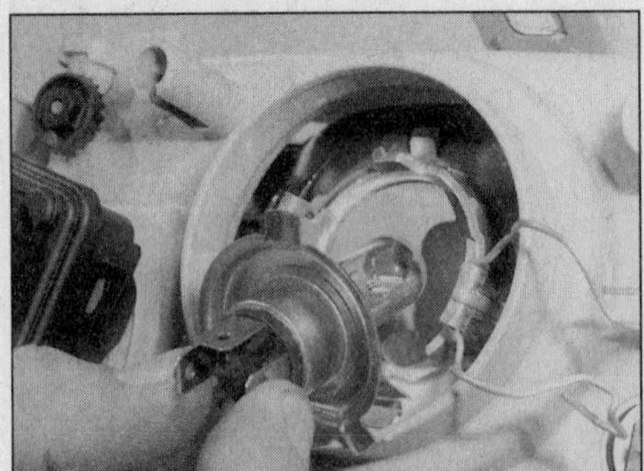

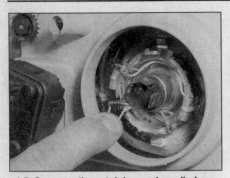

4.5 Squeeze the retaining spring-clip lugs, and release the clip from the rear of the bulb

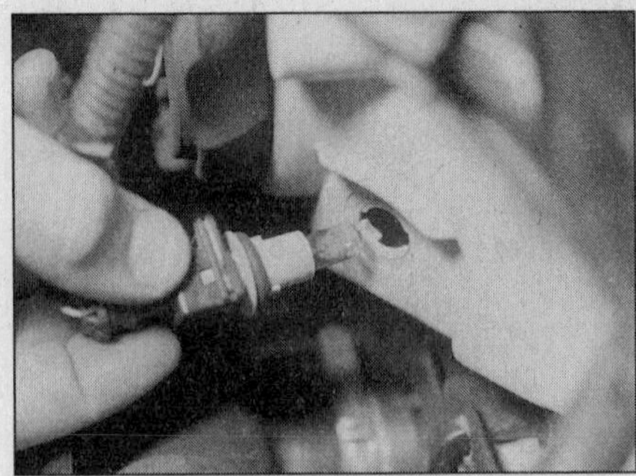

4.6 Withdraw the bulb

4.14 Twist the bulbholder to release it from the rear of the light unit

5 Squeeze the retaining spring-clip lugs, and release the clip from the rear of the bulb **(see illustration)**

6 Withdraw the bulb **(see illustration)**.

Models with twin reflectors

7 Unclip the cover from the rear of the headlight unit. Note that the light unit houses three bulbholders; one for the combined main/dipped beam bulb, one for the long range main beam bulb and one for the sidelight bulb.

8 Pull the wiring plug from the rear of the bulb.

9 Squeeze the retaining spring-clip lugs, and release the clip from the rear of the bulb.

10 Withdraw the bulb.

All models

11 When handling the new bulb, use a tissue or clean cloth, to avoid touching the glass with the fingers; moisture and grease from the skin can cause blackening and rapid failure of this type of bulb. If the glass is accidentally touched, wipe it clean using methylated spirit. Avoid knocking or shaking the bulb as this may weaken the filament.

12 Install the new bulb, using a reversal of the removal procedure, ensuring that its locating tabs are correctly located in the light unit cut-outs. Secure the bulb in position with the retaining clip.

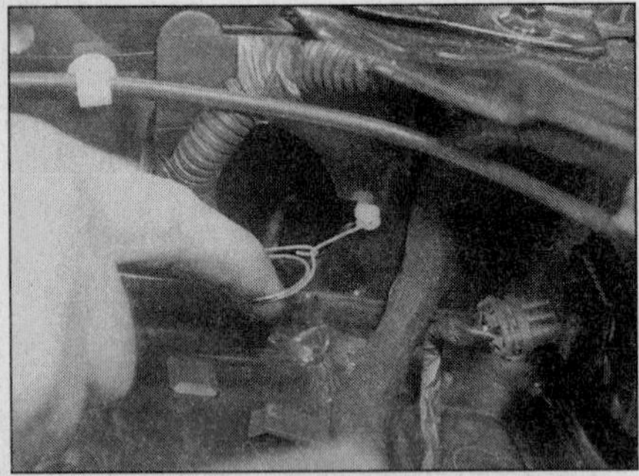

4.21 Unhook the light unit spring clip from the recess in the inner wing

Sidelight

Models with single reflector

13 Open the bonnet. Ensure that the sidelights are turned off at the stalk switch.

14 Twist the bulbholder to release it from the rear of the light unit **(see illustration)**

15 The bulb is a push fit in the bulbholder.

16 Fit the new bulb using a reversal of the removal procedure.

Models with twin reflectors

17 Unclip the cover from the rear of the headlight unit. Note that the light unit houses three bulbholders; one for the combined main/dipped beam bulb, one for the long range main beam bulb and one for the sidelight bulb.

18 Twist the bulbholder to release it from the rear of the light unit.

19 The bulb is a push fit in the bulbholder.

20 Fit the new bulb using a reversal of the removal procedure.

Front direction indicator

21 Open the bonnet. Unhook the light unit spring clip from the recess in the inner wing, directly behind the indicator light unit **(see illustration)**.

22 Pull the light unit forwards from its housing.

23 Twist the bulbholder anti-clockwise and withdraw it from the light unit **(see illustration)**.

24 The bulb is a bayonet fit in the bulbholder.

25 Fit the new bulb, then refit the light assembly using a reversal of the removal procedure. Ensure that the pegs on the side of the light unit engage with the lugs in the side of the headlight unit and the body panel **(see illustration)**. Hook the retaining spring clip securely into the recess in the inner wing.

Front direction indicator side repeater

26 Slide the light unit towards the front of the vehicle slightly, then insert a plastic implement behind the rear edge of the unit and lever it out of the wing aperture **(see illustration)**.

27 Withdraw the light unit, then twist the bulbholder anti-clockwise to release it from the light unit **(see illustration)**.

28 The bulb is a push fit in the bulbholder.

29 Fit the new bulb using a reversal of the removal procedure.

4.23 Twist the bulbholder anti-clockwise and withdraw it from the light unit

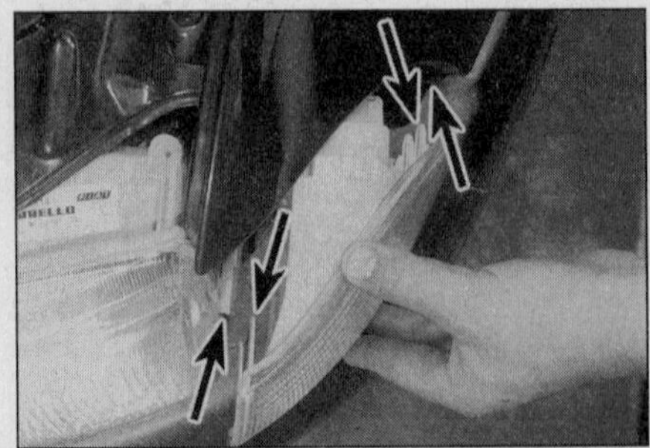

4.25 Ensure that the pegs (arrowed) on the side of the light unit engage with the lugs in the side of the headlight unit and the body panel

4.26 Slide the light unit towards the front of the vehicle slightly, then insert a plastic implement behind the rear edge

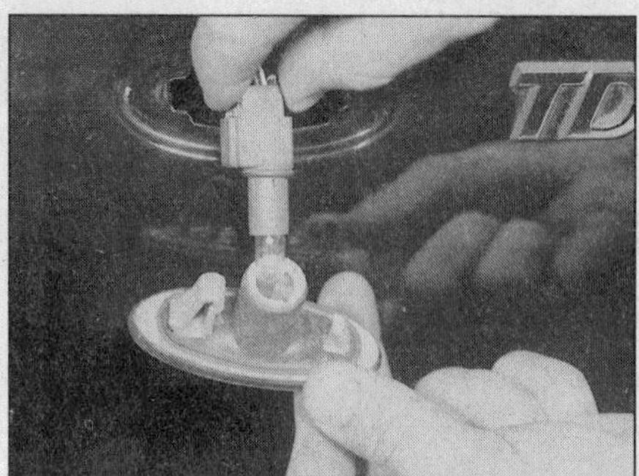

4.27 Withdraw the light unit, then twist the bulbholder anti-clockwise to release it from the light unit

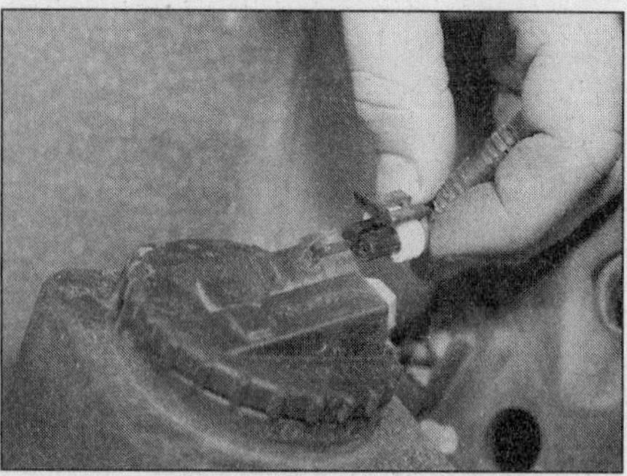
4.32 Disconnect the wiring from the rear of the foglight unit at the connector

4.33 Unscrew the rear cover from the foglight unit by turning it anticlockwise

Front foglight

30 Access to the rear of the foglight units can be gained by via removable hatches in plastic inner wheel arch liners.

31 Turn the steering wheel to angle the roadwheel away from the rear of the relevant foglight.

32 Reach through the wheel arch liner and disconnect the wiring from the rear of the foglight unit at the connector **(see illustration).**

33 Unscrew the rear cover from the foglight unit by turning it anticlockwise **(see illustration).**

34 Unplug the flying lead from the push-fit connector inside of the rear cover. Release the spring clip, and withdraw the bulb from the rear of the light unit **(see illustrations).**

35 Fit the new bulb using a reversal of the removal procedure, ensuring that the recess in the bulb flange engages with the lug in the bulbholder.

Rear light cluster bulbs

36 Open the tailgate. Working from within the loadspace, prise the plastic caps from the rear pillar trim panel **(see illustration).**

37 Using the special socket provided with the vehicle's toolkit, unscrew the rear light cluster securing bolts **(see illustrations).**

38 Pull the light cluster away from the bodywork. Unplug the electrical wiring at the connector **(see illustrations).**

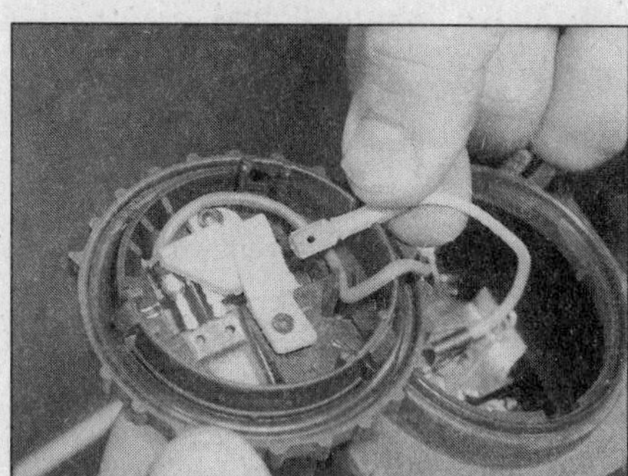
4.34a Unplug the flying lead from the push-fit connector inside of the rear cover

4.34b Release the spring clip, and withdraw the bulb from the rear of the light unit

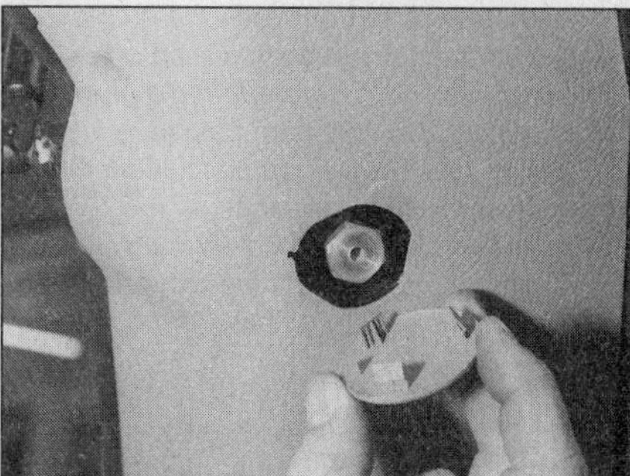
4.36 Prise the plastic caps from the rear pillar trim panel

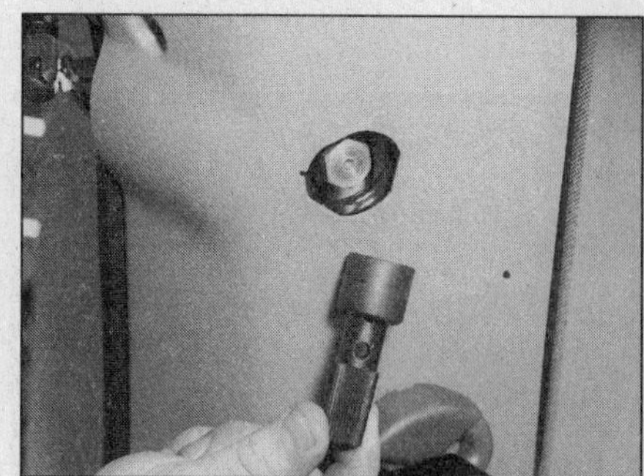
4.37a Using the special socket provided with the vehicles tool kit . . .

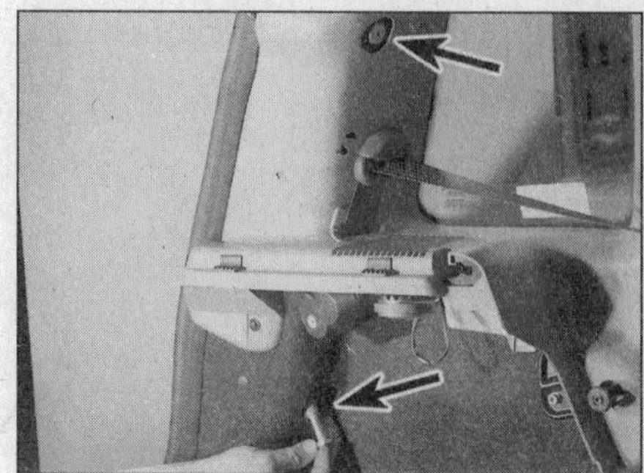
4.37b . . . unscrew the rear light cluster securing bolts (arrowed)

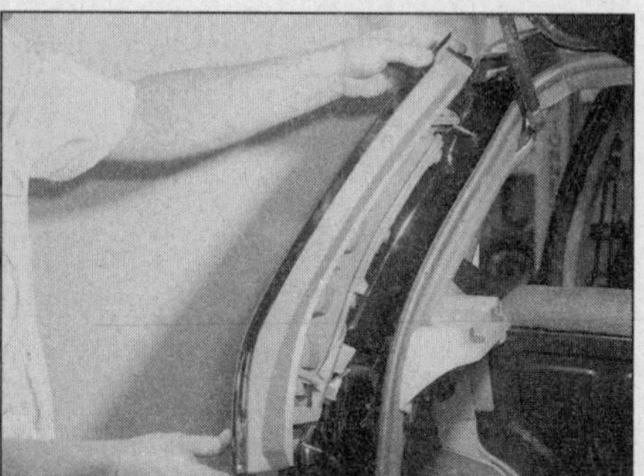
4.38a Pull the light cluster away from the bodywork . . .

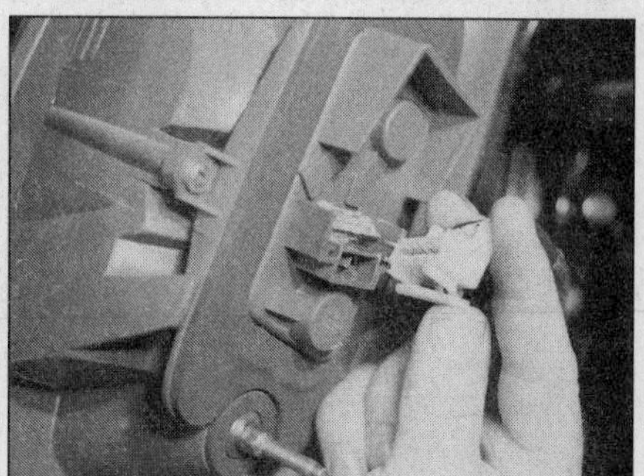
4.38b . . . unplug the electrical wiring at the connector

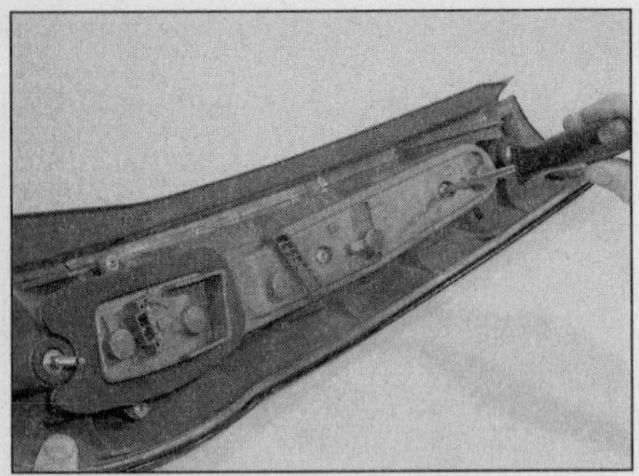

4.39a Remove the screws . . .

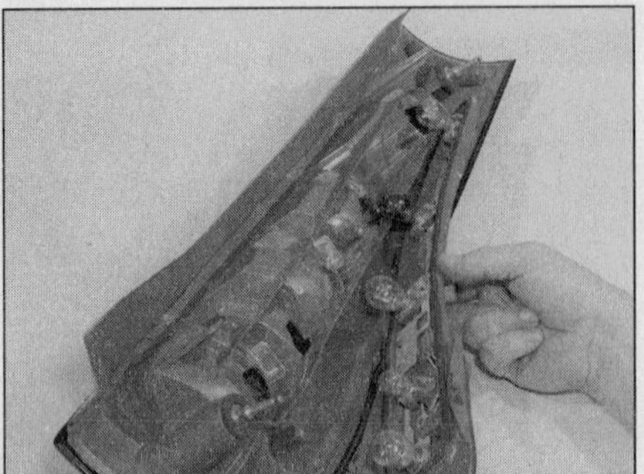

4.39b . . . and separate the bulbholder from the lens unit

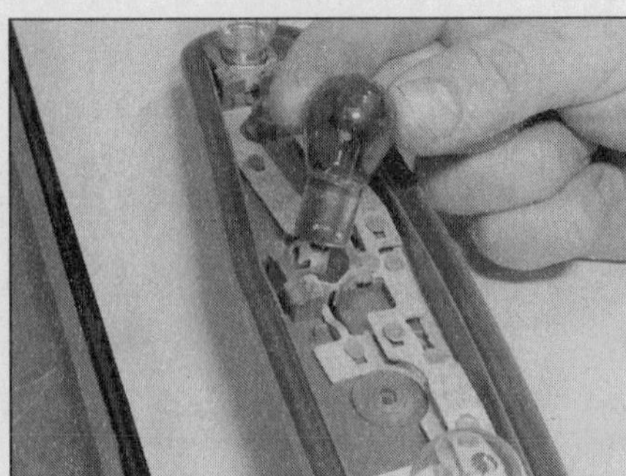

4.40 The bulbs are a bayonet fit in the bulbholder

39 Remove the screws and separate the bulbholder from the lens unit **(see illustrations).**

40 The bulbs are a bayonet fit in the bulbholder **(see illustration).**

41 Fit the new bulb using a reversal of the removal procedure. Note that the stop/tail light bulb has offset locking pins, to ensure correct orientation.

Rear number plate light

42 Remove the securing screws, and lower the light unit lens from the tailgate handle **(see illustration).**

43 The bulb is a push fit in the light unit.

44 Fit the new bulb using a reversal of the removal procedure.

5.3a On models with a manually operated sunroof, remove the sunroof crank handle

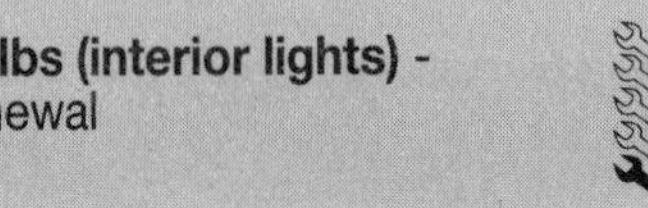

5 Bulbs (interior lights) - renewal

General

1 Whenever a bulb is renewed, note the following points:

a) Ensure that the relevant electrical circuit is isolated before removing a bulb. If in doubt, disconnect the battery negative terminal (refer to Disconnecting the battery in the Reference Section of this manual) before starting work.

b) Remember that, if the light has just been in use, the bulb may be extremely hot.

c) Always check the bulb contacts and holder, ensuring that there is clean metal-to-metal contact between the bulb and its live contact(s) and earth. Clean off any corrosion or dirt before fitting a new bulb.

d) Wherever bayonet-type bulbs are fitted, ensure that the live contact(s) bear firmly against the bulb contact.

e) Always ensure that the new bulb is of the correct rating (see Specifications), and that it is completely clean before fitting it.

Courtesy light

2 On Punto S models (except those with a manually operated sunroof and/or theft alarm) access to the courtesy light bulb can gained by unclipping the lens from the roof lining. The bulb can then be prised from its spring loaded contacts.

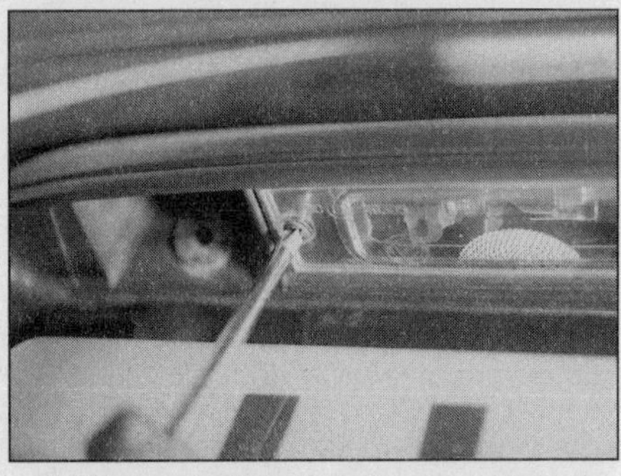

4.42 Remove the securing screws, and lower the light unit lens from the tailgate handle

3 On all other variants, carefully prise out the plastic caps and remove the screws that secure the overhead console to the roof. **Note:** *On models fitted with a manually operated sunroof, it will be necessary to remove the screw and detach the sunroof crank handle from its shaft, before the overhead console can be removed **(see illustrations).***

4 Unplug the wiring from the console at the connector **(see illustration).**

5 Unclip the plastic cover from the rear of the overhead console **(see illustration).**

6 Carefully prise the bulb from the spring contacts **(see illustration).**

7 Fit the new bulb using a reversal of the removal procedure.

Luggage compartment light

8 The light unit is located under the left hand parcel shelf support panel.

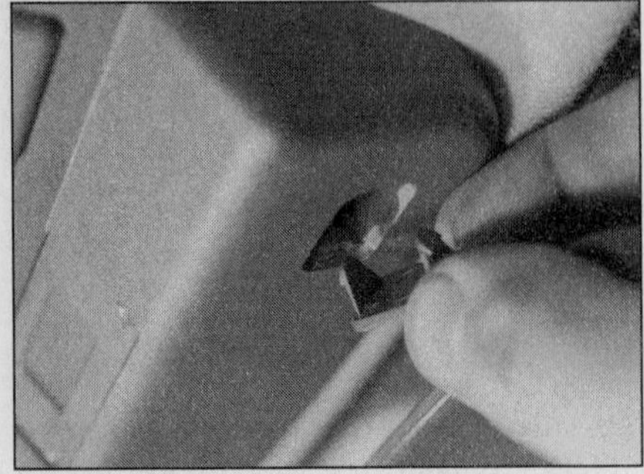

5.3b Carefully prise out the plastic caps . . .

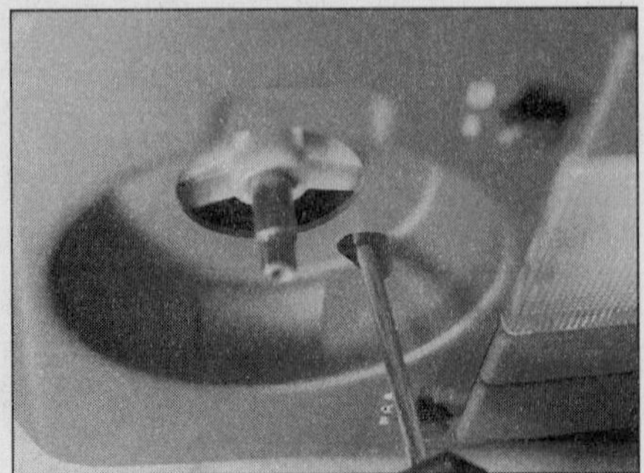

5.3c . . . and remove the screws that secure the overhead console to the roof

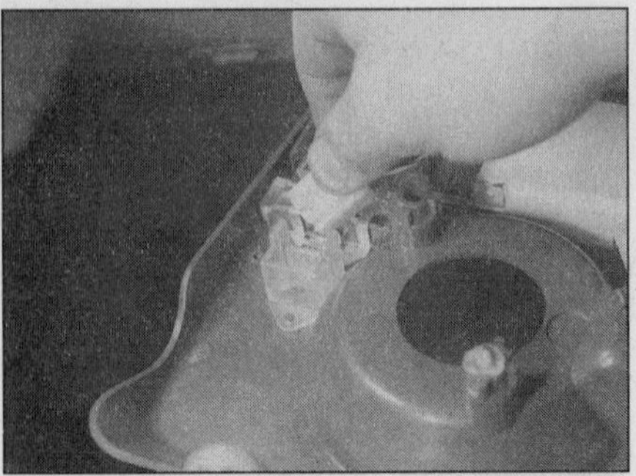

5.4 Unplug the wiring from the console at the connector

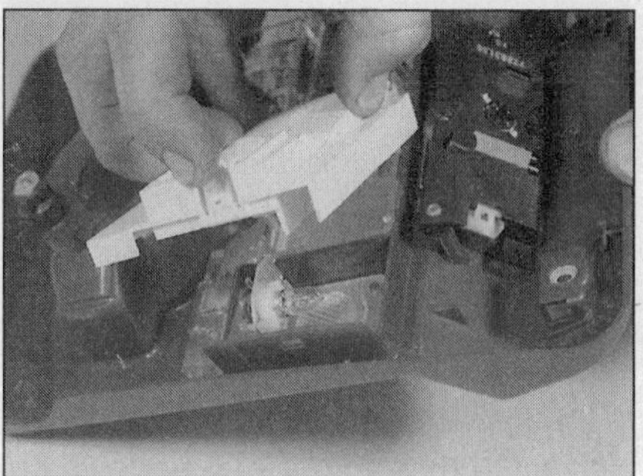

5.5 Unclip the plastic cover from the rear of the overhead console

9 Unclip the lens from the support panel **(see illustration)**.

10 The bulb can be prised from its spring-loaded contacts **(see illustration)**.

11 Fit the new bulb using a reversal of the removal procedure.

Instrument panel gauge illumination

12 Remove the instrument panel as described in Section 7.

13 The bulbs are a bayonet fit in the rear of the instrument panel **(see illustration)**. The colour of the bulb casing denotes its wattage - ensure that a replacement bulb of the correct rating is used.

Switch illumination

14 The bulbs that illuminate the facia-mounted switches are integral with the switch body and cannot be renewed separately.

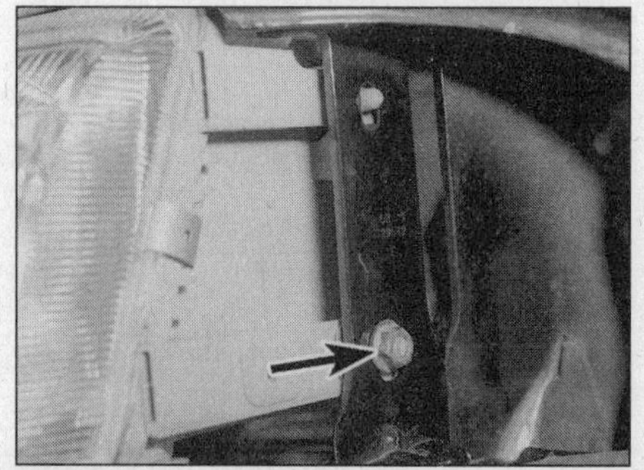

6.3a Unscrew the headlight side securing bolt (arrowed) . . .

5.6 Overhead console bulb location

A Map reading bulb
B Courtesy bulb
C Clock illumination bulb

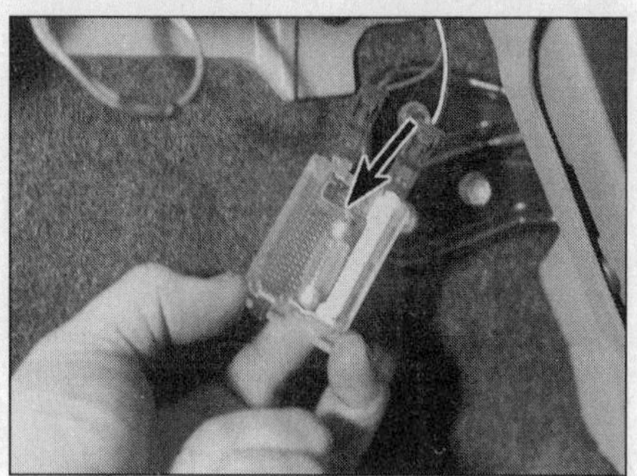

5.10 The bulb can be prised from its spring-loaded contacts (arrowed)

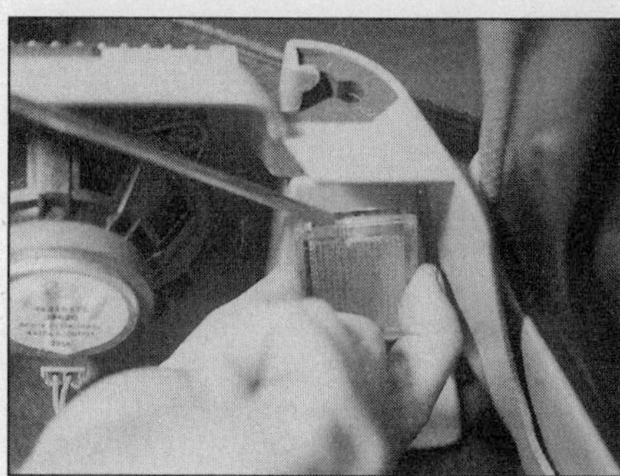

5.9 Unclip the lens from the support panel

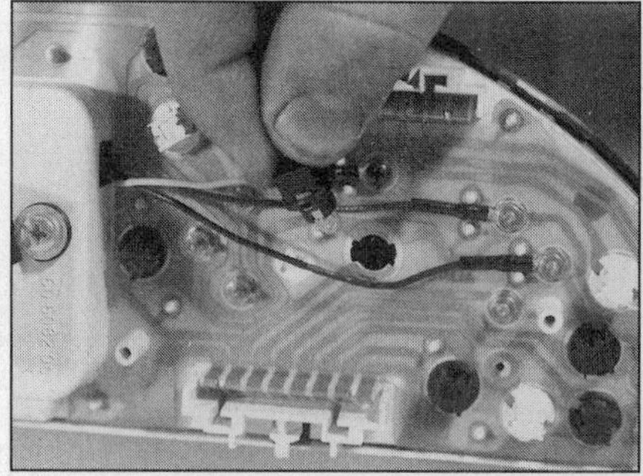

5.13 The bulbs are a bayonet fit in the rear of the instrument panel

6 Exterior light units - removal and refitting

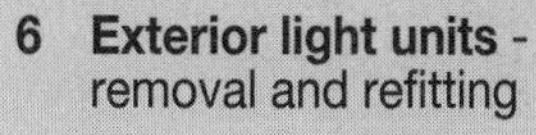

Caution: Ensure that the relevant electrical circuit is isolated before removing a light unit. If in doubt, disconnect the battery negative terminal (refer to Disconnecting the battery in the Reference Section of this manual).

Headlight

Removal

1 Remove the adjacent direction indicator light unit as described in Section 4.

2 Disconnect all wiring from the rear of the light unit at the connectors.

3 Unscrew the headlight side and upper securing bolts **(see illustrations)**.

4 Withdraw the headlight unit from the vehicle **(see illustration)**.

Refitting

5 Refitting is a reversal of removal. On completion, it is advisable to have the headlight beam alignment checked with reference to Section 8.

Front direction indicator light

6 The procedure is described as part of the bulb renewal procedure in Section 4. Note that the wiring harness can be disconnected from the light unit without removing the bulb holder **(see illustration)**.

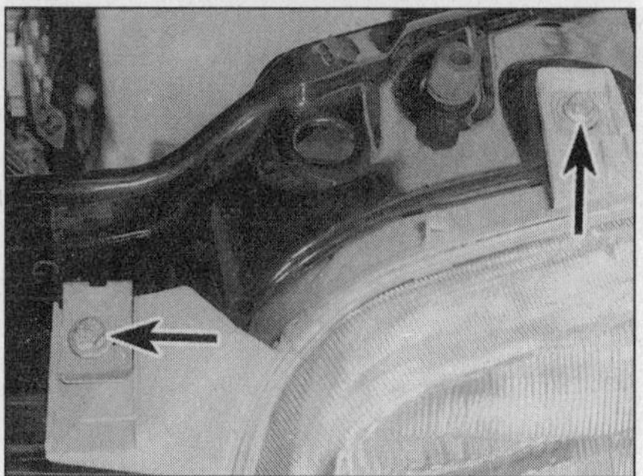

6.3b . . . and upper securing bolts (arrowed)

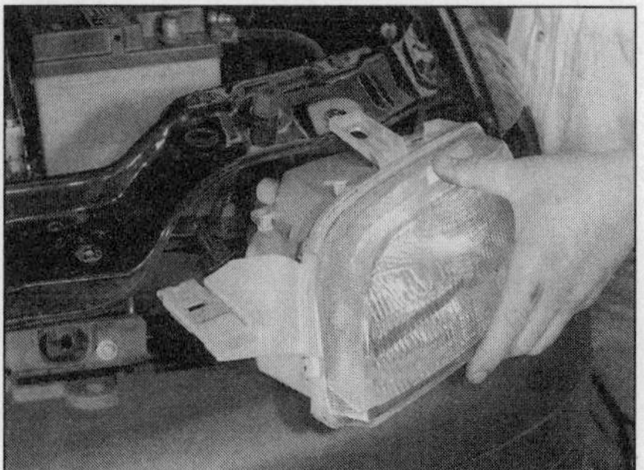

6.4 Withdraw the headlight unit from the vehicle

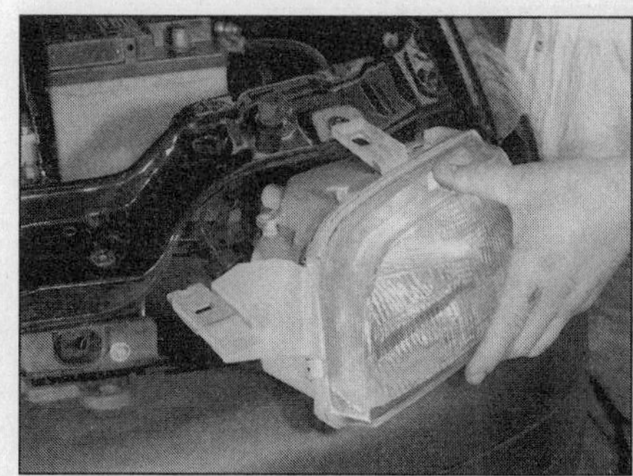

6.6 Disconnecting the direction indicator light unit wiring from the bulb holder

6.10 Front foglamp beam adjustment screw (arrowed)

7.3a Carefully pull the panel away from the facia

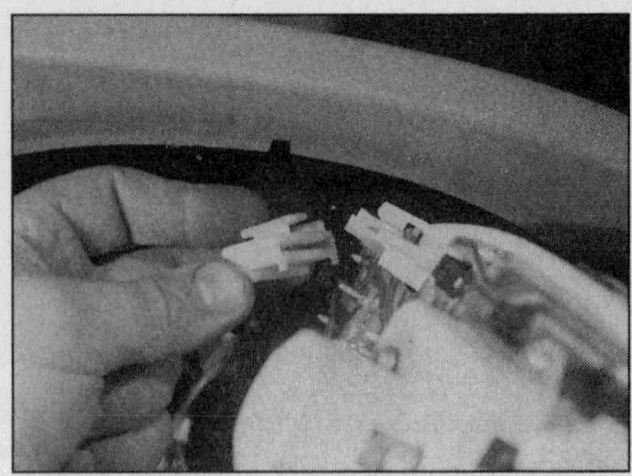

7.3b Label and then unplug the wiring connectors

Front direction indicator side repeater light

7 The procedure is described as part of the bulb renewal procedure in Section 4.

Front foglight

8 Remove the hatch from the wheel arch liner and unplug the wiring from the rear of the foglamp unit.

9 The front foglamps are secured to the valence by three screws - one directly above the light unit, accessed from the front and two accessed from below the valence. Once these are removed, the foglamp can be removed via the hatch in the wheel arch liner.

10 Refitting is a reversal of removal. On completion, it is advisable to check the foglight beam alignment. If necessary, the beam may be altered using the adjustment screw **(see illustration)**.

Rear light cluster

11 The procedure is described as part of the bulb renewal procedure in Section 4.

7 Instrument panel - removal and refitting

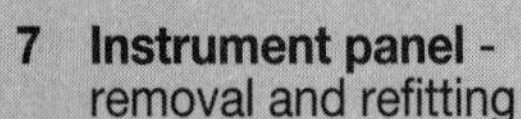

Removal

1 Disconnect the battery negative terminal (refer to *Disconnecting the battery* in the Reference Section of this manual).

2 Remove the securing screws from the instrument panel surround.

3 Carefully pull the panel away from the facia. Label each bundle of electrical cables carefully to aid refitting later and then unplug them at the connectors **(see illustrations)**. Where a mechanical speedometer drive is fitted, disconnect the drive cable from the rear of the instrument panel.

4 The individual gauges are illuminated by filament bulbs. These are a bayonet fit in the rear of the instrument panel and can be removed individually by rotating them through a quarter turn and withdrawing them - refer to Section 5 for details.

Refitting

5 Refit the instrument panel by following the removal procedure in reverse.

8 Headlight beam alignment - general information

Accurate adjustment of the headlight beam is only possible using optical beam-setting equipment, and this work should therefore be carried out by a Fiat dealer or suitably-equipped workshop. Incorrectly adjusted headlamps can dazzle other drivers and cause accidents.

Certain models are equipped with a headlight aim adjustment switch, located on the facia, which allows the aim of the headlights to be adjusted to compensate for the varying loads carried in the vehicle. The switch should be positioned according to the load being carried in the vehicle - refer to the vehicle's handbook for details.

9 Horn - removal and refitting

Removal

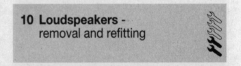

1 The horn is mounted on the lower edge of the front left hand wing, behind the front bumper moulding. To gain access, remove the screws and detach the hatch from the wheel arch liner.

2 Reach through the aperture in the wheel arch liner and unplug the wiring from the horn at the connector **(see illustration)**.

3 Unscrew the securing bolt **(see illustration)** and remove the horn sounder.

Refitting

4 Refit the horn by following the removal procedure in reverse.

10 Loudspeakers - removal and refitting

1 Ensure that the radio/cassette unit is switched off.

Facia mounted front speakers

2 Remove the screw and lift off the facia grille **(see illustration)**.

9.2 Unplug the wiring from the horn at the connector (arrowed)

9.3 Unscrew the securing bolt (arrowed) and remove the horn sounder

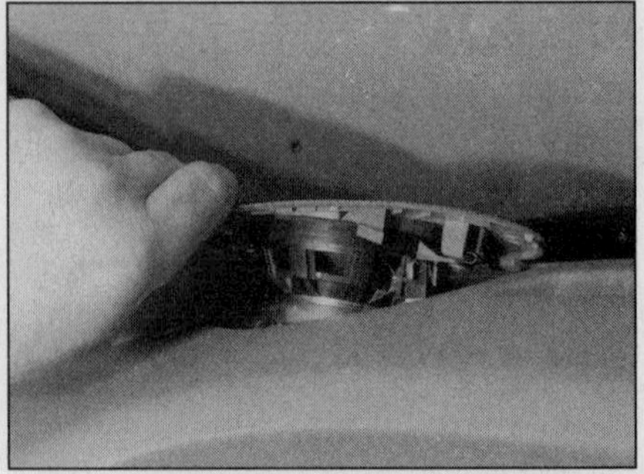

10.2 Remove the screw and lift off the facia grille

3 Undo the mounting screws and lift out the speaker **(see illustration)**. Unplug the wiring at the connector.

4 Refitting is a reversal of removal.

Rear parcel shelf speakers

5 Working underneath the relevant parcel shelf support bracket, remove the securing screws and lower the loudspeaker from the support bracket. Unplug the wiring at the connector **(see illustration).**

6 Refitting is a reversal of removal.

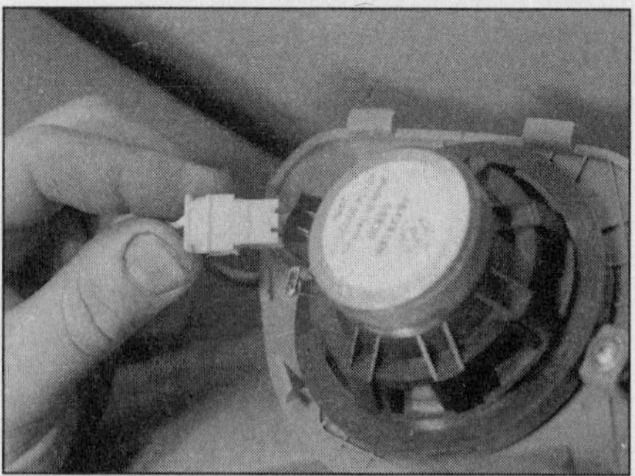

10.3 Lift out the speaker and unplug the wiring at the connector

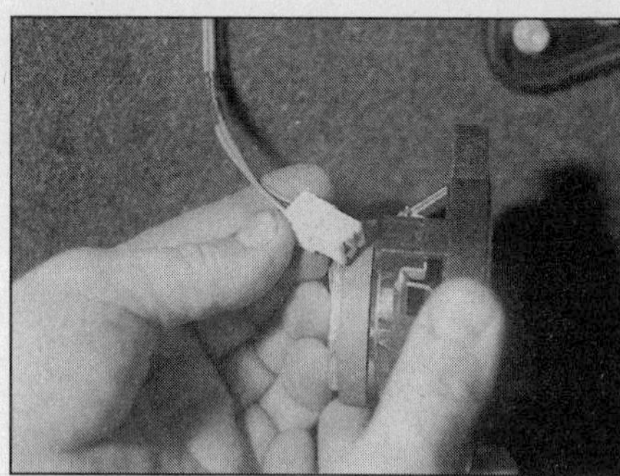

10.5 Lower the loudspeaker from the support bracket and unplug the wiring at the connector

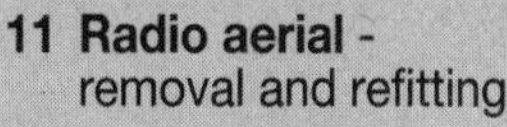

11 Radio aerial - removal and refitting

Removal

1 Carefully prise off the plastic cap, then remove the securing screws and withdraw the aerial from the roof.

2 Draw the aerial co-axial cable through the roof aperture and disconnect it. If there is insufficient slack in the aerial cable, remove the courtesy light unit/overhead panel from the inside of the vehicle (as described earlier in this Chapter) to gain access to the cable connector.

Refitting

3 Refitting is a reversal of removal, but ensure that seal between the aerial housing and the roof panel is in good condition.

12.2 Removing the radio/cassette unit using the special extraction tools

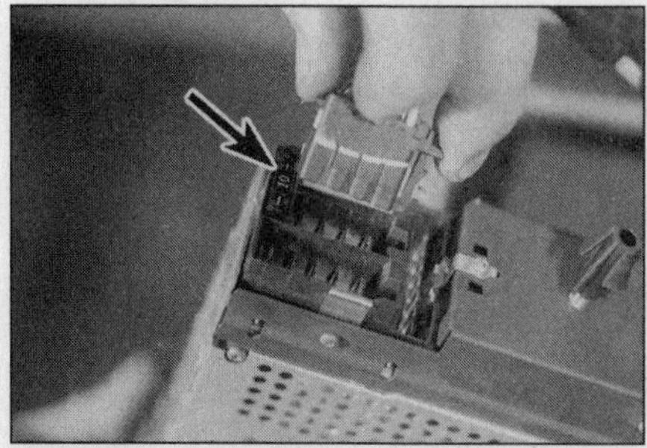

12.3 Disconnect the wiring plugs from the rear of the unit. Note the bayonet fuse (arrowed) which is a push fit in the rear of the unit

12 Radio/cassette player - removal and refitting

Removal

Note: *Once the battery has been disconnected, the radio/cassette unit cannot be re-activated until the appropriate security code has been entered. Do not remove the unit unless the appropriate code is known.*

1 Disconnect the battery negative terminal (refer to *Disconnecting the battery* in the Reference Section of this manual).

2 Insert the special extraction tools supplied with the vehicle into the holes on either side of the radio/cassette unit. Press them home until the internal clips can be felt to release **(see illustration)**.

3 Pull the unit forwards from the facia, then disconnect the wiring plugs and the aerial lead from the rear of the unit. Note the bayonet fuse, which is a push fit in the rear of the unit. **(see illustration)**.

Refitting

4 Refitting is a reversal of removal, ensuring that the wiring is routed freely behind the unit.

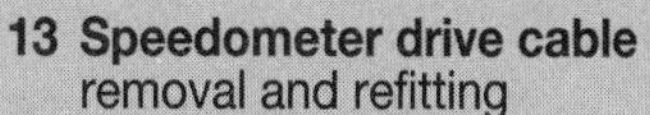

13 Speedometer drive cable - removal and refitting

Note: *Later vehicles are fitted with an electronic transducer in place of the mechanical speedometer drive. This is mounted on the transmission casing; refer to Chapter 7A*, Section 3, *for details.*

Removal

1 Remove the instrument panel as described in Section 7.

2 Working in the engine compartment, unscrew the sleeve securing the cable end to gearbox, then pull the cable from gearbox.

3 Where applicable, release the cable from the brackets in the engine compartment bulkhead, then pull the cable through into the engine compartment. If necessary, pull the cable grommet from the bulkhead.

Refitting

4 Refitting is a reversal of removal, bearing in mind the following points:

a) Ensure that the bulkhead grommet is securely seated.

b) Refit the instrument panel with reference to Section 7.

c) Note that certain models have alignment marks on the cable outer for use when refitting. The marks should be aligned with the bulkhead bracket when the cable is correctly refitted and routed.

14 Switches - removal and refitting

Steering column stalk switches

Note: *On vehicles equipped with steering wheel-mounted radio controls, the column stalk switch unit also incorporates the rotary contacts for the steering wheel switches.*

Removal

1 Disconnect the battery negative cable and position it away from the terminal. Turn the steering wheel so that the roadwheels are pointing in the straight-ahead position.

2 Refer to Chapter 10 and remove the steering wheel from the column.

3 Remove the screws and lift off the upper and lower steering column shrouds.

4 Using an Allen key, slacken the clamp ring at the rear of the switch unit **(see illustration)**.

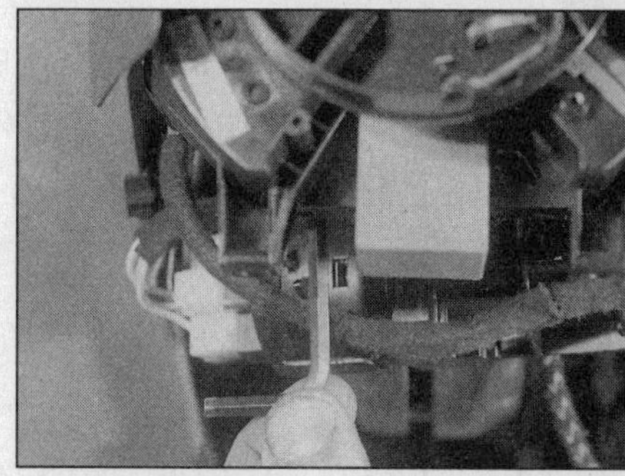

14.4 Using an Allen key, slacken the clamp ring at the rear of the switch unit

14.5 Remove the switch unit the steering column and unplug the wiring connectors

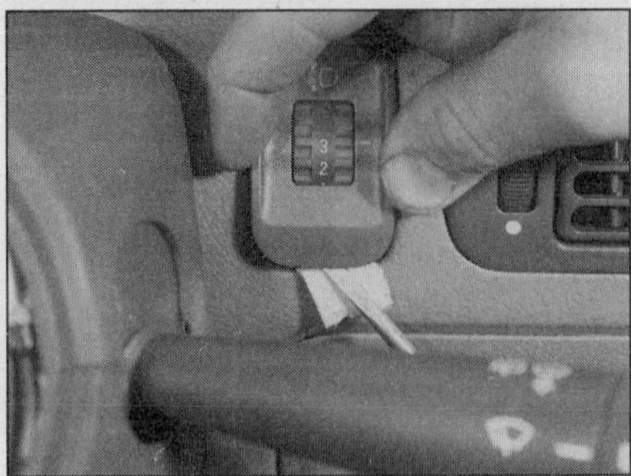
14.9 Carefully lever the switch body out of the facia, using a flat bladed instrument

14.10 Unplug the wiring from the rear of the switch body at the connector

14.14 Remove the screws and lift the switch bank from the rear of the facia panel

5 Pull the switch unit along the steering column slightly, then label and unplug the wiring connectors from the rear of the unit **(see illustration)**.

6 Remove the switch unit from the steering column.

Refitting

7 Refitting is reversal of removal - ensure that the steering column/roadwheels are still in the straight-ahead position. On completion, ensure that the direction indicator cancelling mechanism functions correctly.

Headlamp beam adjustment switch

8 Disconnect the battery negative cable and position it away from the terminal.

9 Carefully lever the switch body out of the facia, using a flat bladed instrument. Pad the facia with a small piece of card to prevent the instrument blade from damaging it **(see illustration)**.

10 Unplug the wiring from the rear of the switch body at the connector **(see illustration)**.

11 Refitting is a reversal of removal.

Stop-light switch

12 Refer to the information in Chapter 9

Centre console switches

13 With reference to Chapter 11, Section 19, remove the combined air ventilation/switch panel from the facia.

14 Remove the screws and lift the switch bank from the rear of the panel **(see illustration)**.

15 Refitting is a reversal of removal.

Courtesy light/door ajar warning switches

16 Disconnect the battery negative terminal (refer to *Disconnecting the battery* in the Reference Section of this manual).

17 Open the door to expose the switch in the door B-pillar.

18 Remove the securing screw, then remove the rubber gaiter (where applicable) and withdraw the switch from the door pillar. Disconnect the wiring connector as it becomes accessible.

Tape the wiring to the door pillar, or tie a length of string to the wiring, to retrieve it if it falls back into the door pillar.

19 Refitting is a reversal of removal, but ensure that the rubber gaiter is securely seated over the switch.

Electric window switches

20 Refer to the information given in Chapter 11, Section 14.

15 Tailgate wiper motor - removal and refitting

Removal

1 Disconnect the battery negative terminal (refer to *Disconnecting the battery* in the Reference Section of this manual).

2 Remove the tailgate inner trim panel with reference to Chapter 11, Section 8.

3 Remove the wiper arm with reference to Section 18.

4 Working inside the tailgate, unplug the tailgate wiper motor wiring at the connector and disconnect the washer hose at the union **(see illustrations)**.

5 Unscrew the bolts securing the motor mounting bracket to the tailgate **(see illustration)**.

6 Withdraw the motor assembly through the aperture in the tailgate **(see illustration)**.

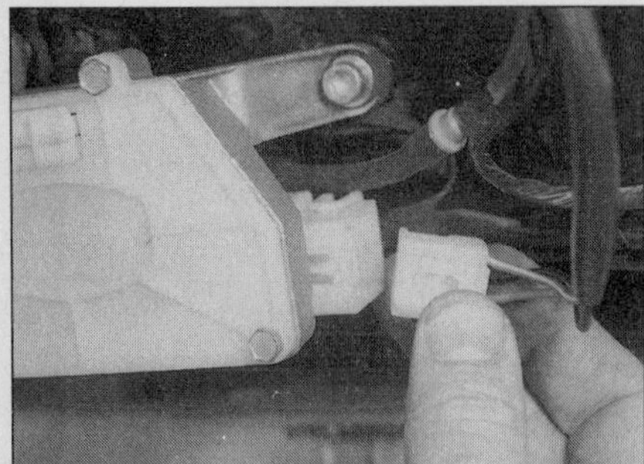
15.4a Working inside the tailgate, unplug the tailgate wiper motor wiring at the connector . . .

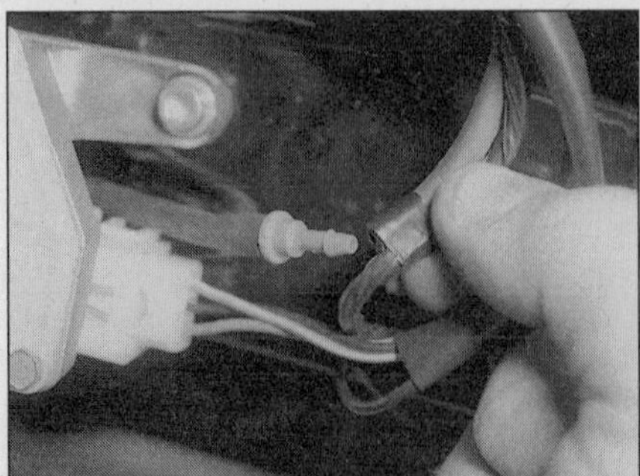
15.4b . . . and disconnect the washer hose at the union

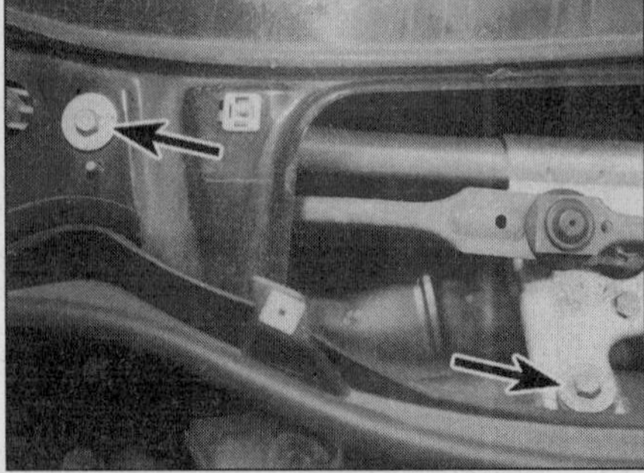
15.5 Unscrew the bolts securing the motor mounting bracket to the tailgate

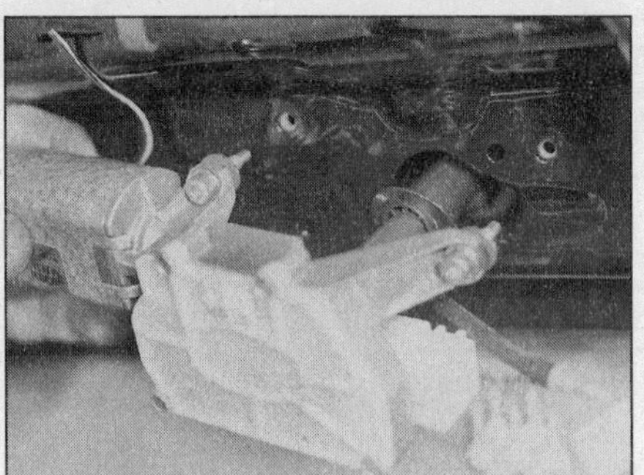
15.6 Withdraw the motor assembly through the aperture in the tailgate

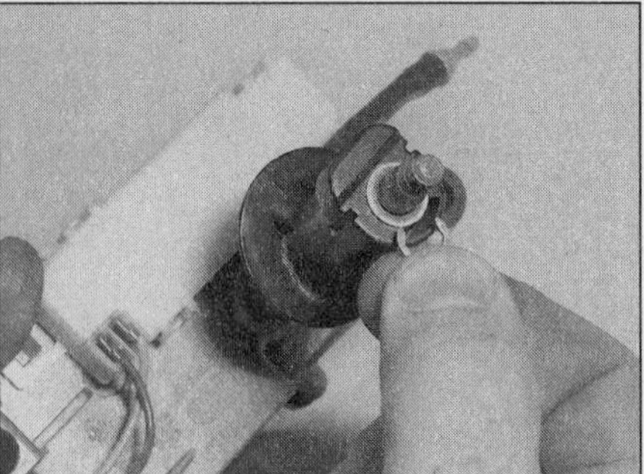
16.20a Remove the circlip . . .

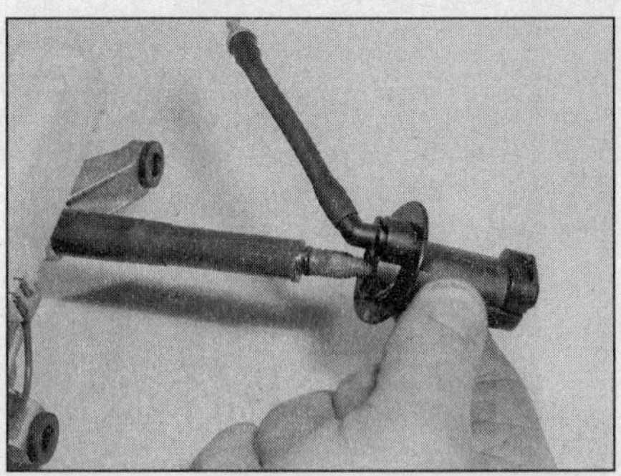
16.20b . . . and then slide the nozzle housing from the end of the wiper shaft

Refitting

7 Refitting is a reversal of removal. Refit the wiper arm with reference to Section 18.

16 Windscreen/tailgate washer system components - removal and refitting

Washer fluid reservoir

Removal

1 Ensure that the vehicle is parked on a level surface. Apply the handbrake and chock the rear wheels. Slacken the left hand front roadwheel bolts.

2 Raise the front of the vehicle, rest it securely on axle stands (see *Jacking and vehicle support*) and remove the left hand front roadwheel.

3 Disconnect the battery negative terminal (refer to *Disconnecting the battery* in the Reference Section of this manual).

4 Working from the engine bay, remove washer fluid reservoir upper securing screws.

5 Remove the securing screws and lift off the front and rear sections of the wheel arch liner.

6 Remove fluid reservoir lower securing screws.

7 Disconnect the wiring plugs from the washer pumps, and from the fluid level sensor, where applicable. Label each connector to aid correct refitting later.

8 Disconnect the fluid hoses from the washer pumps - if the reservoir still contains fluid, be prepared for spillage.

9 Where applicable, release the wiring harness from its clips, and move the harness to one side to allow sufficient clearance to remove the reservoir.

10 Lower the reservoir from under the wheel arch.

Refitting

11 Refitting is a reversal of removal.

Washer fluid reservoir and washer pump(s)

Removal

12 Remove the washer fluid reservoir, as described in the previous sub-Section.

13 Disconnect the wiring plug and the fluid hose from the relevant washer pump.

14 Release the spring clip, then pull the washer pump from the reservoir. Where applicable, recover the grommet.

Refitting

15 Refitting is a reversal of removal.

Windscreen washer nozzle

Removal

16 Open the bonnet.

17 Working under the bonnet, release the securing tabs using a suitable screwdriver, then push the nozzle from the bonnet. Disconnect the fluid hose, and withdraw the nozzle.

Refitting

18 Refitting is a reversal of removal.

Tailgate washer nozzle

Removal

19 The tailgate washer nozzle is integral with the wiper motor shaft; remove the wiper motor as described in Section 15.

20 Remove the circlip and then slide the nozzle housing from the end of the wiper shaft **(see illustrations)**.

Refitting

21 Refitting is a reversal of removal, but ensure that the fluid hose is securely reconnected.

17 Windscreen wiper motor - removal and refitting

Removal

1 Disconnect the battery negative terminal (refer to *Disconnecting the battery* in the Reference Section of this manual).

2 Refer to Section 18 and remove both wiper arms.

3 Remove the securing screws and plastic clips, and withdraw the cowl panel **(see illustrations)**.

4 Disconnect the motor wiring plug.

5 Slacken and withdraw the motor and linkage securing bolts, then withdraw the assembly from the bulkhead **(see illustrations)**.

17.3a Remove the securing screws and plastic clips . . .

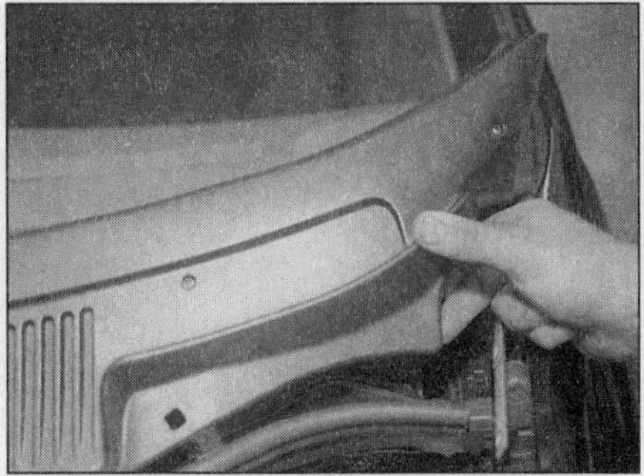
17.3b . . . and withdraw the cowl panel

17.5a Wiper motor and linkage left-hand . . .

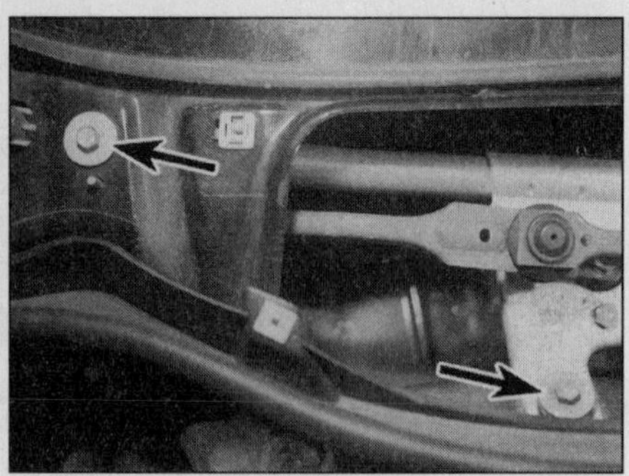

17.5b . . . and right-hand securing bolts (arrowed)

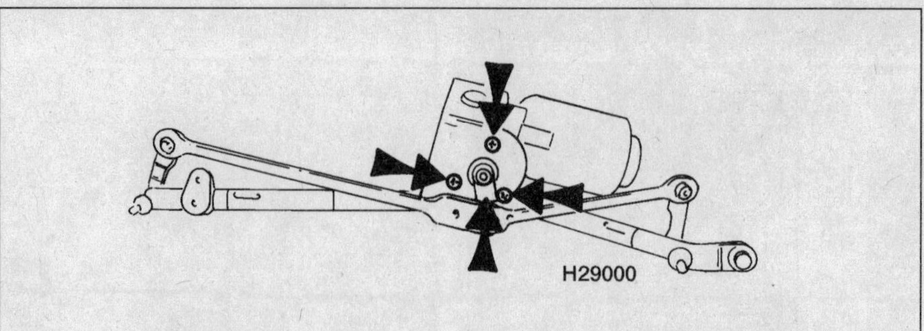

17.6 If desired, the motor may be detached from the linkage by removing the securing screws (arrowed)

6 If desired, the motor may be detached from the linkage by removing the securing screws **(see illustration)**.

Refitting

7 Refitting is a reversal of removal, but ensure that the motor drive is in the 'parked' position before reconnecting the crank arm.

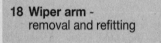

18 Wiper arm - removal and refitting

Removal

1 Operate the wiper motor, then switch it off so that the wiper arm returns to the at-rest/parked position.

2 If a windscreen or tailgate wiper is being removed, stick a length of masking tape on the glass below the edge of the wiper blade, to use as an alignment aid on refitting.

3 Where applicable, lift up the wiper arm spindle nut cover, then slacken and remove the spindle nut **(see illustrations)**.

4 Lift the blade off the glass, and pull the wiper arm off its spindle. If necessary, the arm can be carefully levered off the spindle using a suitable flat-bladed screwdriver. If both windscreen wiper arms are removed, note their locations, as different arms are fitted to the driver's and passenger's sides.

Refitting

5 Ensure that the wiper arm and spindle splines are clean and dry.

6 When refitting a windscreen or tailgate wiper arm, refit the arm to the spindle, aligning the wiper blade with the tape fitted before removal. If both windscreen wiper arms have been removed, ensure that the arms are refitted to their correct positions as noted before removal.

7 Refit the spindle nut, tighten it securely, and where applicable, clip the nut cover back into position.

18.3a Lift up the wiper arm spindle nut cover . . .

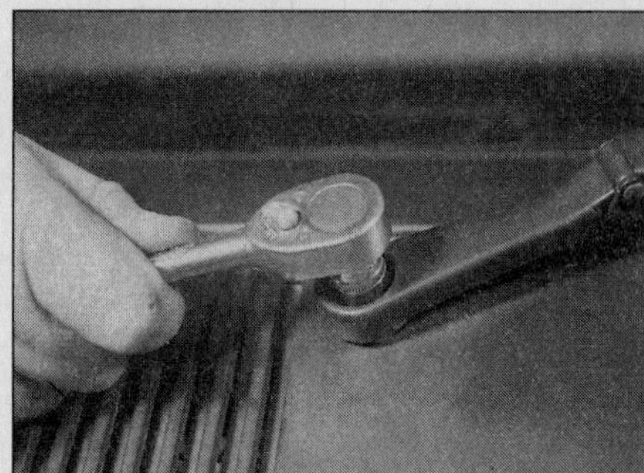

18.3b . . . then slacken and remove the spindle nut

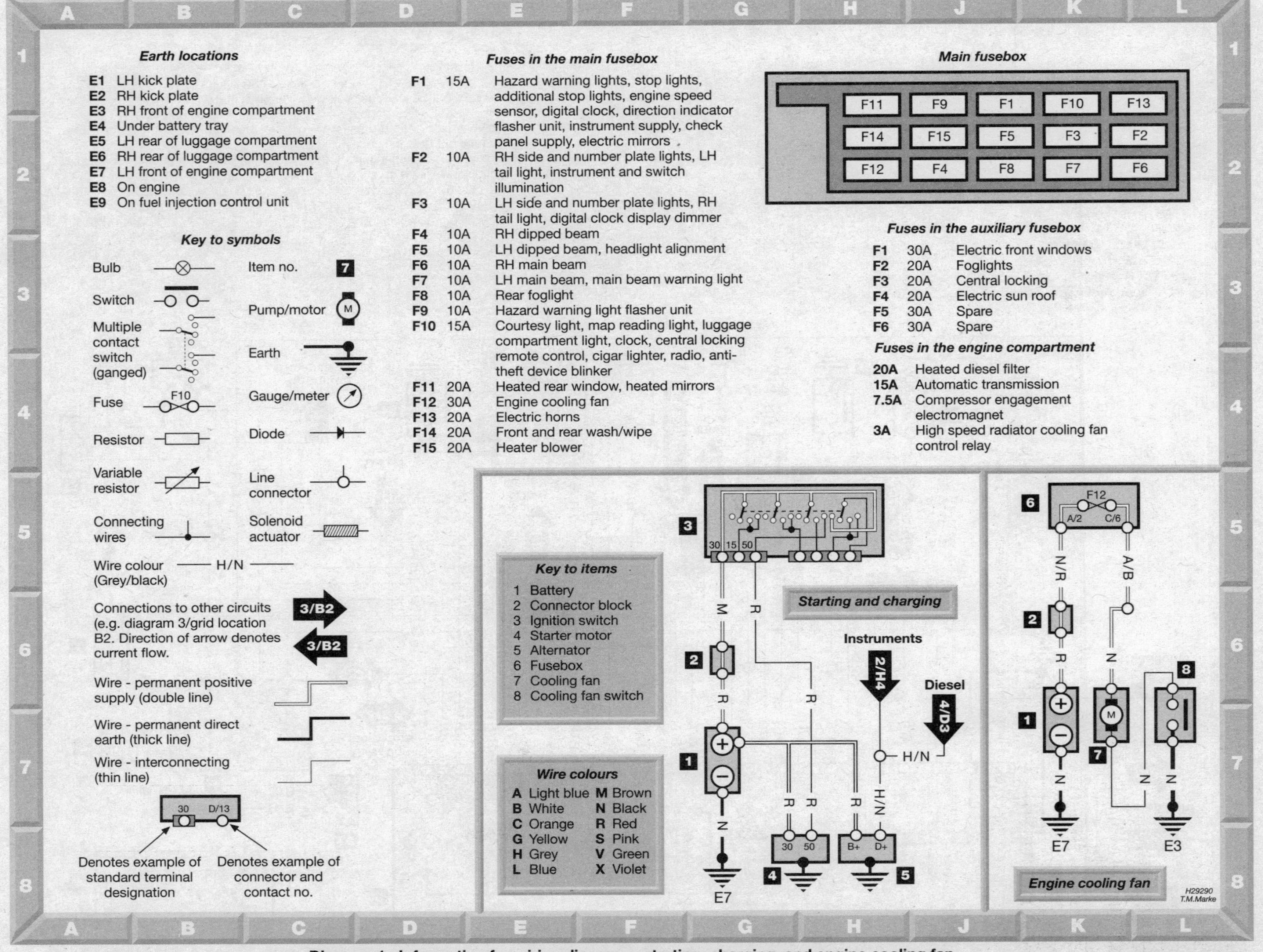

Earth locations

E1	LH kick plate
E2	RH kick plate
E3	RH front of engine compartment
E4	Under battery tray
E5	LH rear of luggage compartment
E6	RH rear of luggage compartment
E7	LH front of engine compartment
E8	On engine
E9	On fuel injection control unit

Fuses in the main fusebox

F1	15A	Hazard warning lights, stop lights, additional stop lights, engine speed sensor, digital clock, direction indicator flasher unit, instrument supply, check panel supply, electric mirrors
F2	10A	RH side and number plate lights, LH tail light, instrument and switch illumination
F3	10A	LH side and number plate lights, RH tail light, digital clock display dimmer
F4	10A	RH dipped beam
F5	10A	LH dipped beam, headlight alignment
F6	10A	RH main beam
F7	10A	LH main beam, main beam warning light
F8	10A	Rear foglight
F9	10A	Hazard warning light flasher unit
F10	15A	Courtesy light, map reading light, luggage compartment light, clock, central locking remote control, cigar lighter, radio, anti-theft device blinker
F11	20A	Heated rear window, heated mirrors
F12	30A	Engine cooling fan
F13	20A	Electric horns
F14	20A	Front and rear wash/wipe
F15	20A	Heater blower

Fuses in the auxiliary fusebox

F1	30A	Electric front windows
F2	20A	Foglights
F3	20A	Central locking
F4	20A	Electric sun roof
F5	30A	Spare
F6	30A	Spare

Fuses in the engine compartment

20A	Heated diesel filter
15A	Automatic transmission
7.5A	Compressor engagement electromagnet
3A	High speed radiator cooling fan control relay

Key to items

1 Battery
2 Connector block
3 Ignition switch
4 Starter motor
5 Alternator
6 Fusebox
7 Cooling fan
8 Cooling fan switch

Wire colours

A	Light blue	**M**	Brown
B	White	**N**	Black
C	Orange	**R**	Red
G	Yellow	**S**	Pink
H	Grey	**V**	Green
L	Blue	**X**	Violet

Diagram 1 : Information for wiring diagrams, starting, charging, and engine cooling fan

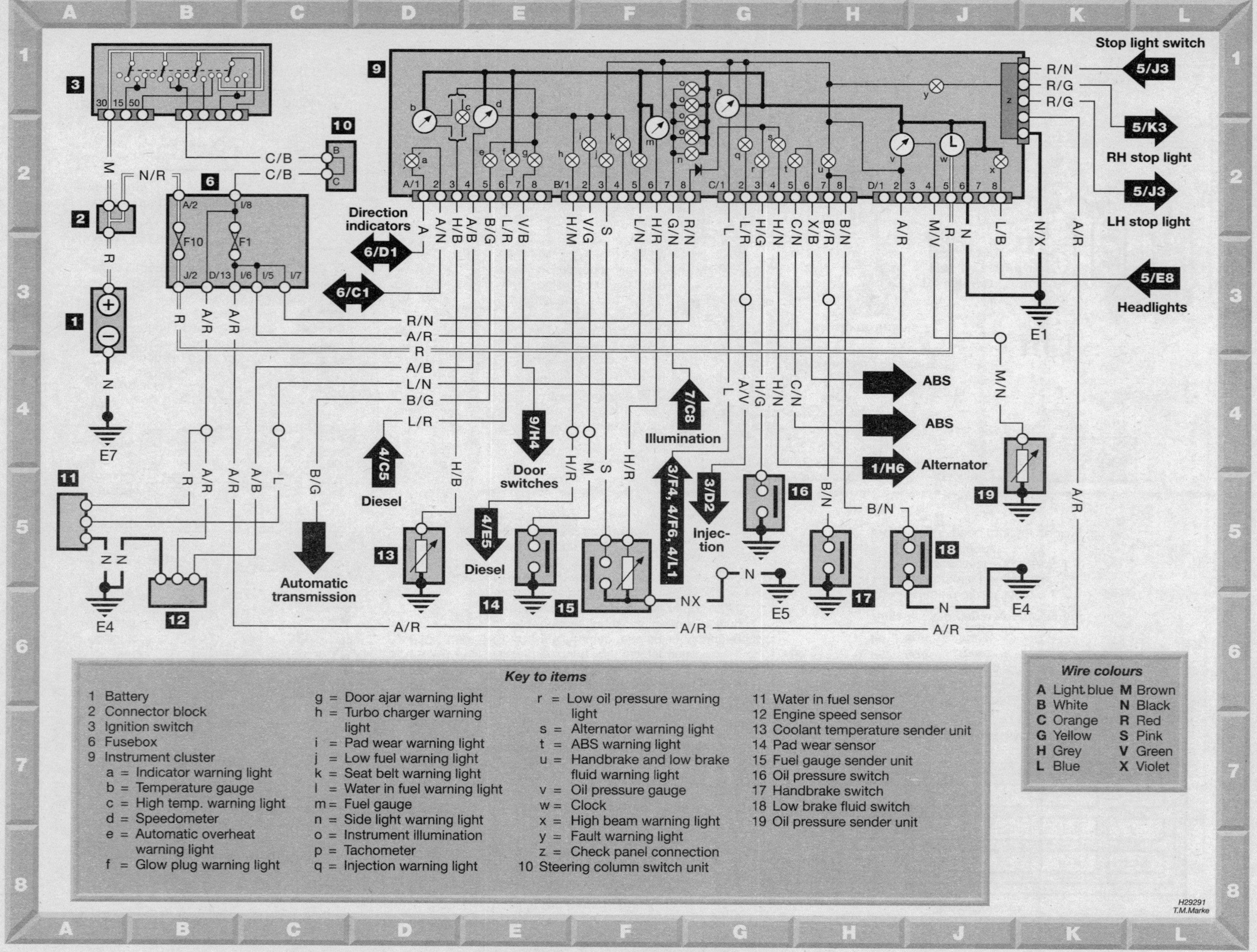

Stop light switch
5/J3
5/K3
RH stop light
5/J3
LH stop light
5/E8
Headlights
Direction indicators
6/D1
6/C1
4/C5
Diesel
Automatic transmission
9/H4
Door switches
4/E5
Diesel
7/C8
Illumination
3/F4, 4/F6, 4/L1
3/D2
Injection
ABS
ABS
1/H6
Alternator
Key to items
1 Battery
2 Connector block
3 Ignition switch
6 Fusebox
9 Instrument cluster
a = Indicator warning light
b = Temperature gauge
c = High temp. warning light
d = Speedometer
e = Automatic overheat warning light
f = Glow plug warning light
g = Door ajar warning light
h = Turbo charger warning light
i = Pad wear warning light
j = Low fuel warning light
k = Seat belt warning light
l = Water in fuel warning light
m = Fuel gauge
n = Side light warning light
o = Instrument illumination
p = Tachometer
q = Injection warning light
r = Low oil pressure warning light
s = Alternator warning light
t = ABS warning light
u = Handbrake and low brake fluid warning light
v = Oil pressure gauge
w = Clock
x = High beam warning light
y = Fault warning light
z = Check panel connection
10 Steering column switch unit
11 Water in fuel sensor
12 Engine speed sensor
13 Coolant temperature sender unit
14 Pad wear sensor
15 Fuel gauge sender unit
16 Oil pressure switch
17 Handbrake switch
18 Low brake fluid switch
19 Oil pressure sender unit
Wire colours
A Light blue
B White
C Orange
G Yellow
H Grey
L Blue
M Brown
N Black
R Red
S Pink
V Green
X Violet
H29291
T.M.Marke

Diagram 2 : Warning lights and gauges

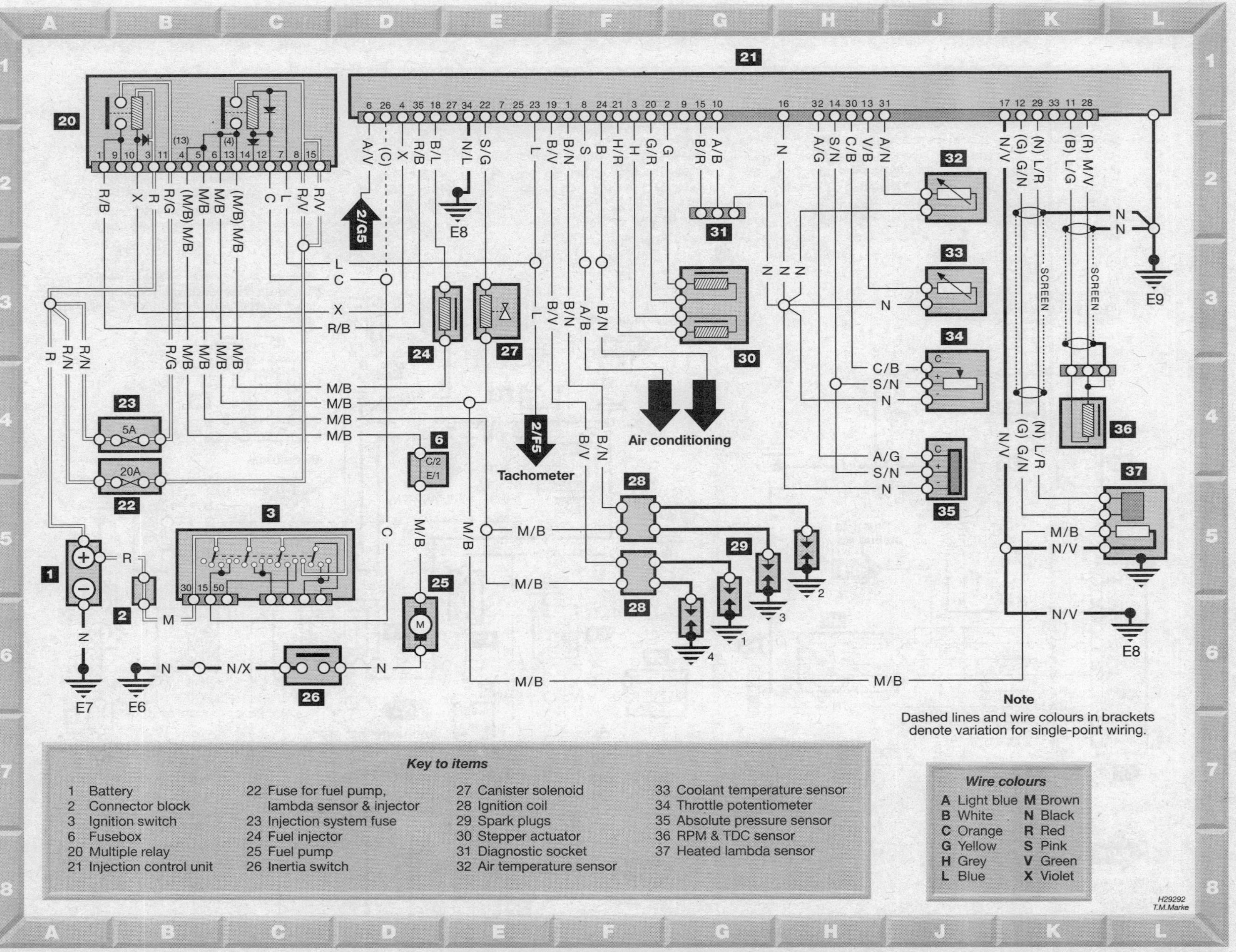

Key to items
1 Battery
2 Connector block
3 Ignition switch
6 Fusebox
20 Multiple relay
21 Injection control unit
22 Fuse for fuel pump, lambda sensor & injector
23 Injection system fuse
24 Fuel injector
25 Fuel pump
26 Inertia switch
27 Canister solenoid
28 Ignition coil
29 Spark plugs
30 Stepper actuator
31 Diagnostic socket
32 Air temperature sensor
33 Coolant temperature sensor
34 Throttle potentiometer
35 Absolute pressure sensor
36 RPM & TDC sensor
37 Heated lambda sensor
Wire colours
A Light blue
B White
C Orange
G Yellow
H Grey
L Blue
M Brown
N Black
R Red
S Pink
V Green
X Violet
Note
Dashed lines and wire colours in brackets denote variation for single-point wiring.
Air conditioning
Tachometer
2/F5
2/G5
SCREEN
H29292
T.M.Marke

Diagram 3 : Petrol - fuel injection and ignition

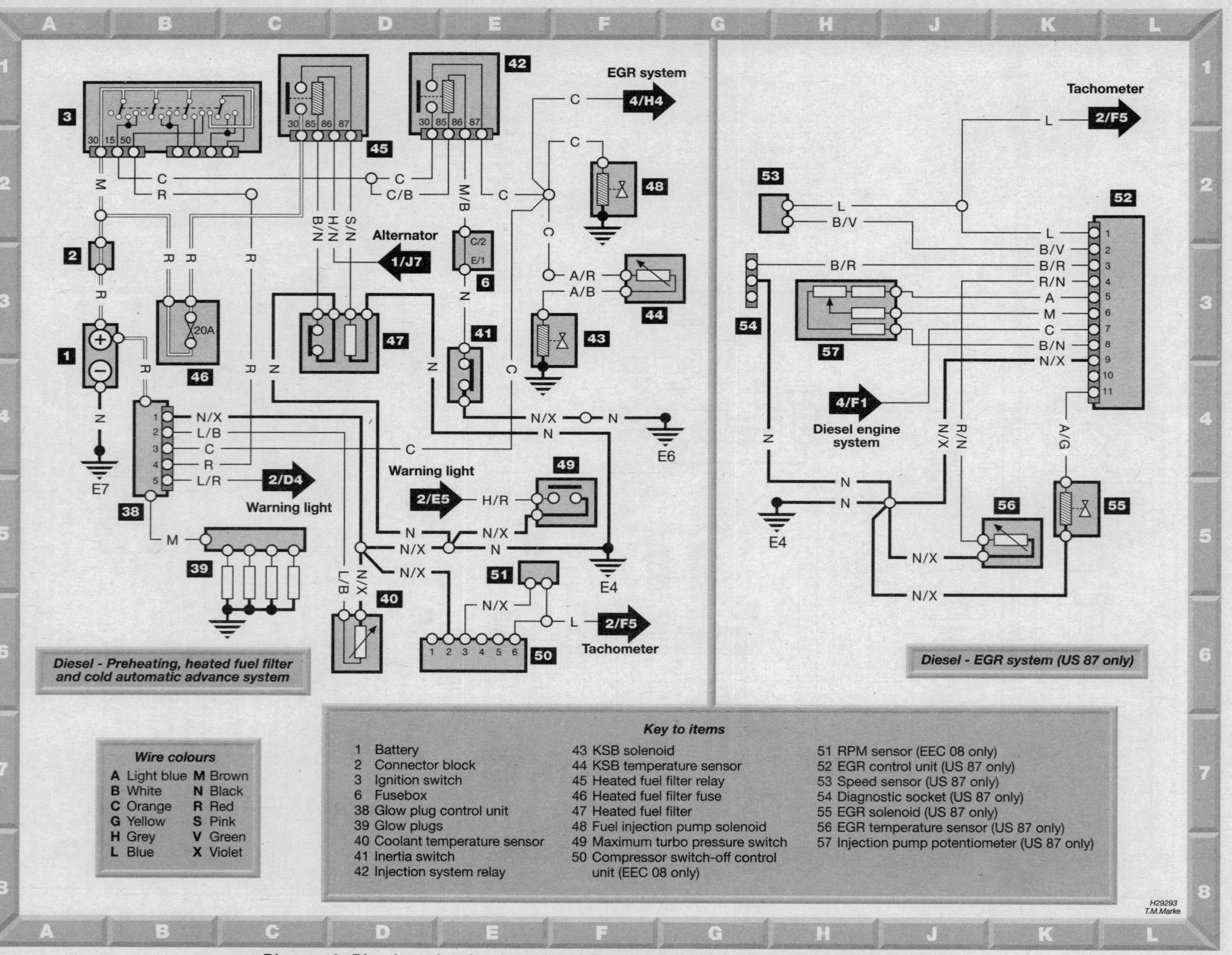

Diesel - Preheating, heated fuel filter and cold automatic advance system
Diesel - EGR system (US 87 only)
EGR system
Tachometer
Alternator
Warning light
Diesel engine system
H29293
T.M.Marke
Wire colours
A Light blue
B White
C Orange
G Yellow
H Grey
L Blue
M Brown
N Black
R Red
S Pink
V Green
X Violet
Key to items
1 Battery
2 Connector block
3 Ignition switch
6 Fusebox
38 Glow plug control unit
39 Glow plugs
40 Coolant temperature sensor
41 Inertia switch
42 Injection system relay
43 KSB solenoid
44 KSB temperature sensor
45 Heated fuel filter relay
46 Heated fuel filter fuse
47 Heated fuel filter
48 Fuel injection pump solenoid
49 Maximum turbo pressure switch
50 Compressor switch-off control unit (EEC 08 only)
51 RPM sensor (EEC 08 only)
52 EGR control unit (US 87 only)
53 Speed sensor (US 87 only)
54 Diagnostic socket (US 87 only)
55 EGR solenoid (US 87 only)
56 EGR temperature sensor (US 87 only)
57 Injection pump potentiometer (US 87 only)

Diagram 4 : Diesel - preheating, heated fuel filter, cold automatic advance and EGR systems

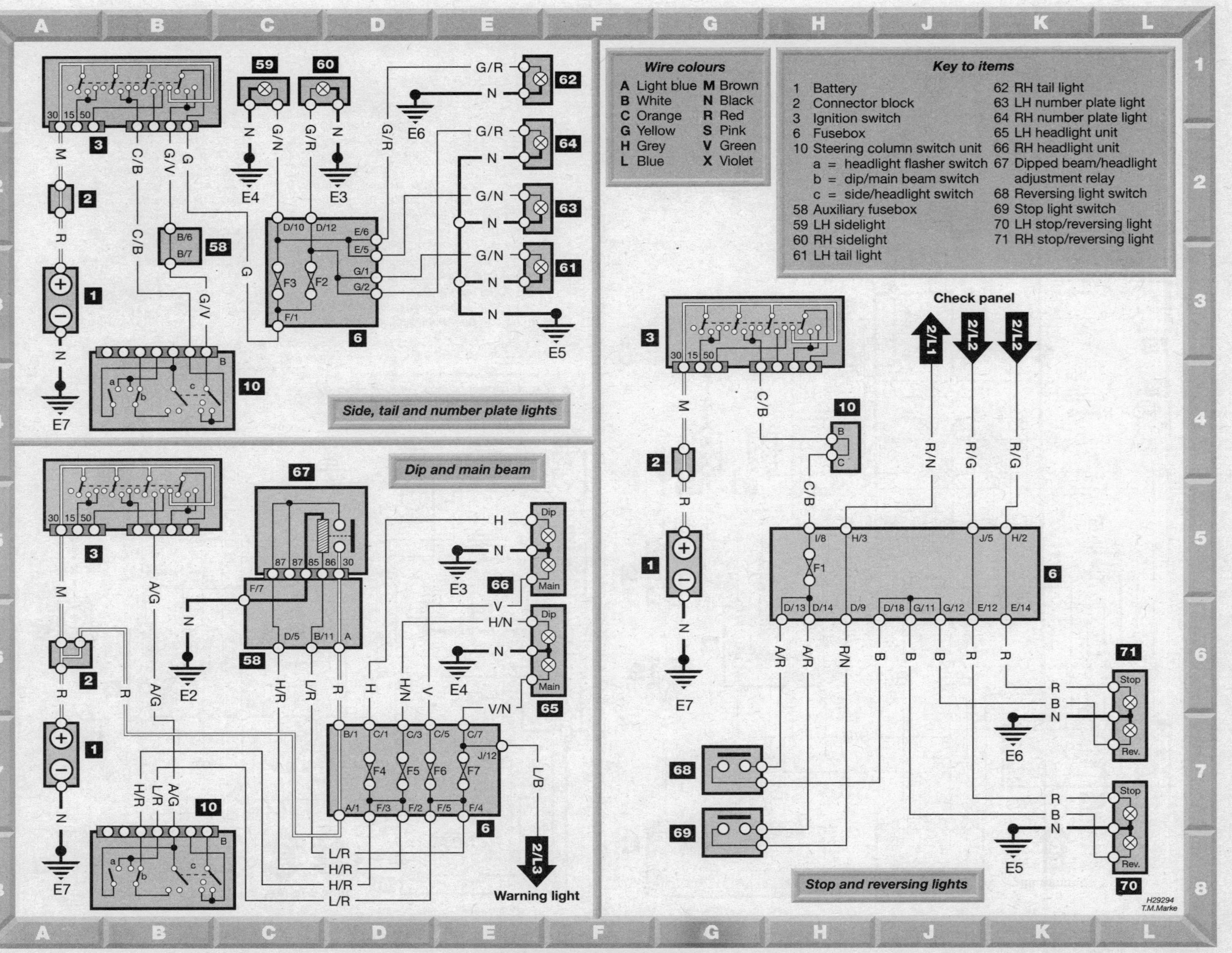

Diagram 5 : Exterior lighting

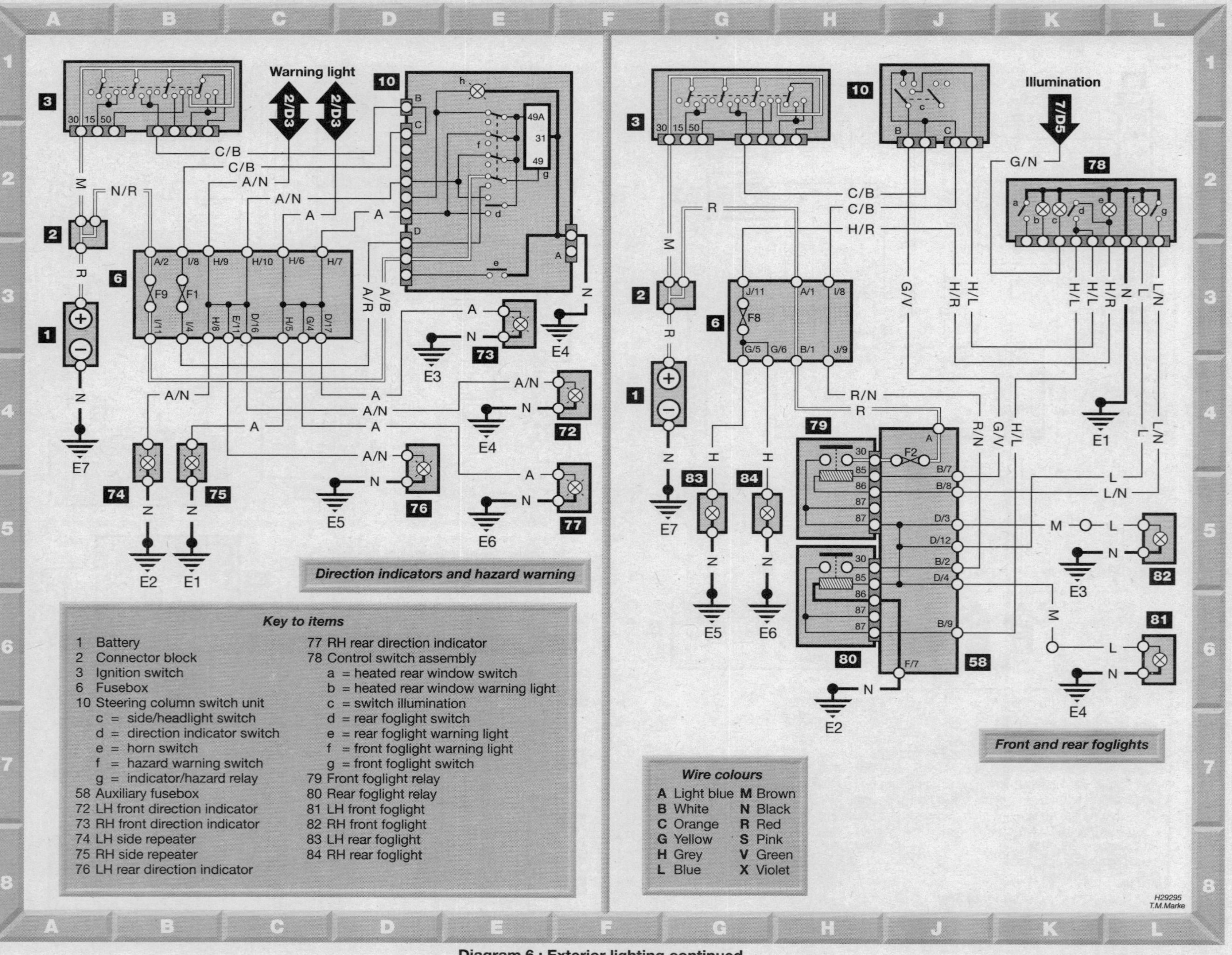

Warning light
2/D3
2/D3
Illumination
7/D5
Direction indicators and hazard warning
Front and rear foglights
Key to items
1 Battery
2 Connector block
3 Ignition switch
6 Fusebox
10 Steering column switch unit
c = side/headlight switch
d = direction indicator switch
e = horn switch
f = hazard warning switch
g = indicator/hazard relay
58 Auxiliary fusebox
72 LH front direction indicator
73 RH front direction indicator
74 LH side repeater
75 RH side repeater
76 LH rear direction indicator
77 RH rear direction indicator
78 Control switch assembly
a = heated rear window switch
b = heated rear window warning light
c = switch illumination
d = rear foglight switch
e = rear foglight warning light
f = front foglight warning light
g = front foglight switch
79 Front foglight relay
80 Rear foglight relay
81 LH front foglight
82 RH front foglight
83 LH rear foglight
84 RH rear foglight
Wire colours
A Light blue
B White
C Orange
G Yellow
H Grey
L Blue
M Brown
N Black
R Red
S Pink
V Green
X Violet
H29295
T.M.Marke

Diagram 6 : Exterior lighting continued

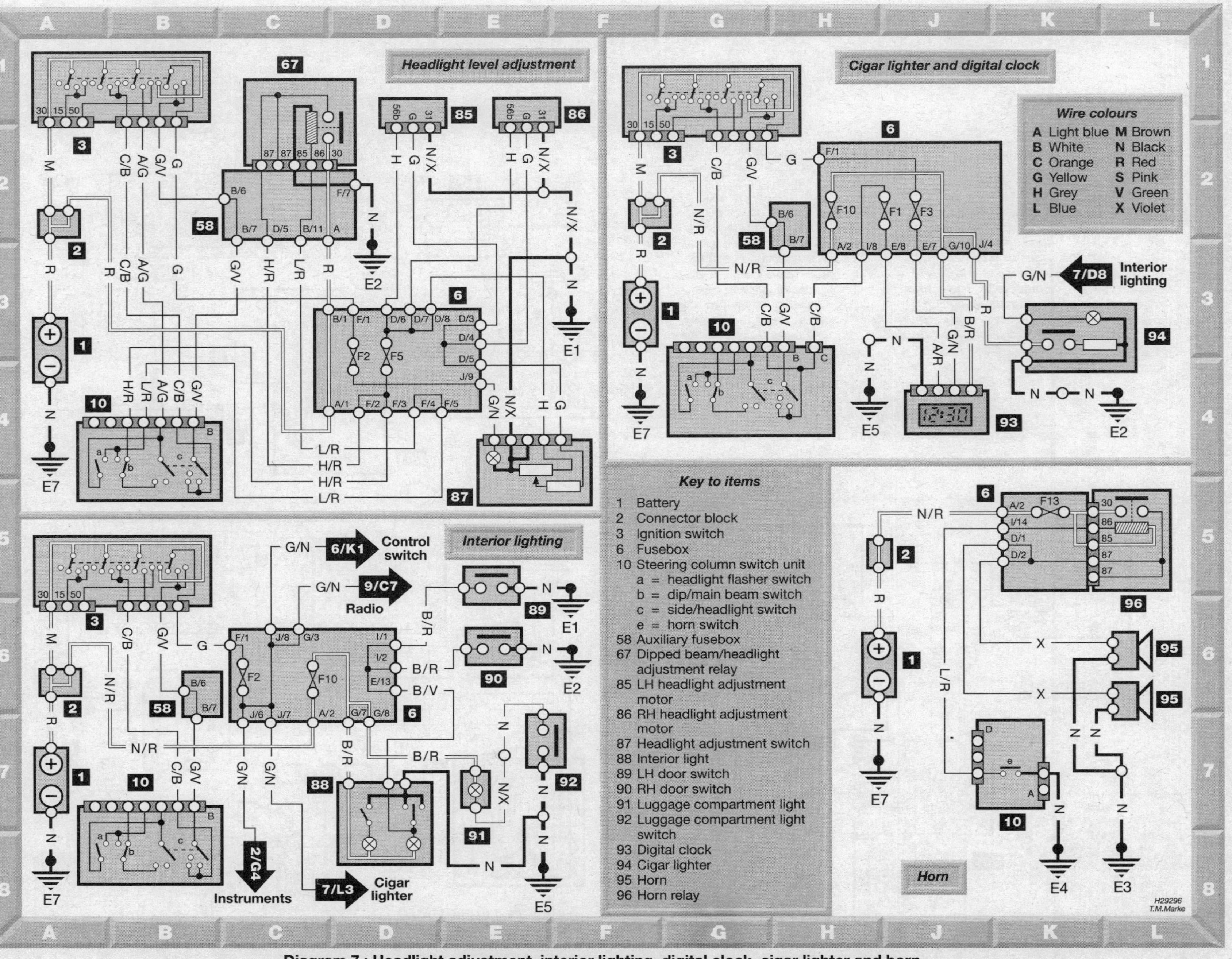
Headlight level adjustment
Cigar lighter and digital clock
Interior lighting
Horn
Wire colours
A Light blue
B White
C Orange
G Yellow
H Grey
L Blue
M Brown
N Black
R Red
S Pink
V Green
X Violet
Key to items
1 Battery
2 Connector block
3 Ignition switch
6 Fusebox
10 Steering column switch unit
a = headlight flasher switch
b = dip/main beam switch
c = side/headlight switch
e = horn switch
58 Auxiliary fusebox
67 Dipped beam/headlight adjustment relay
85 LH headlight adjustment motor
86 RH headlight adjustment motor
87 Headlight adjustment switch
88 Interior light
89 LH door switch
90 RH door switch
91 Luggage compartment light
92 Luggage compartment light switch
93 Digital clock
94 Cigar lighter
95 Horn
96 Horn relay
6/K1 Control switch
9/C7 Radio
2/G4 Instruments
7/L3 Cigar lighter
7/D8 Interior lighting
H29296
T.M.Marke

Diagram 7 : Headlight adjustment, interior lighting, digital clock, cigar lighter and horn

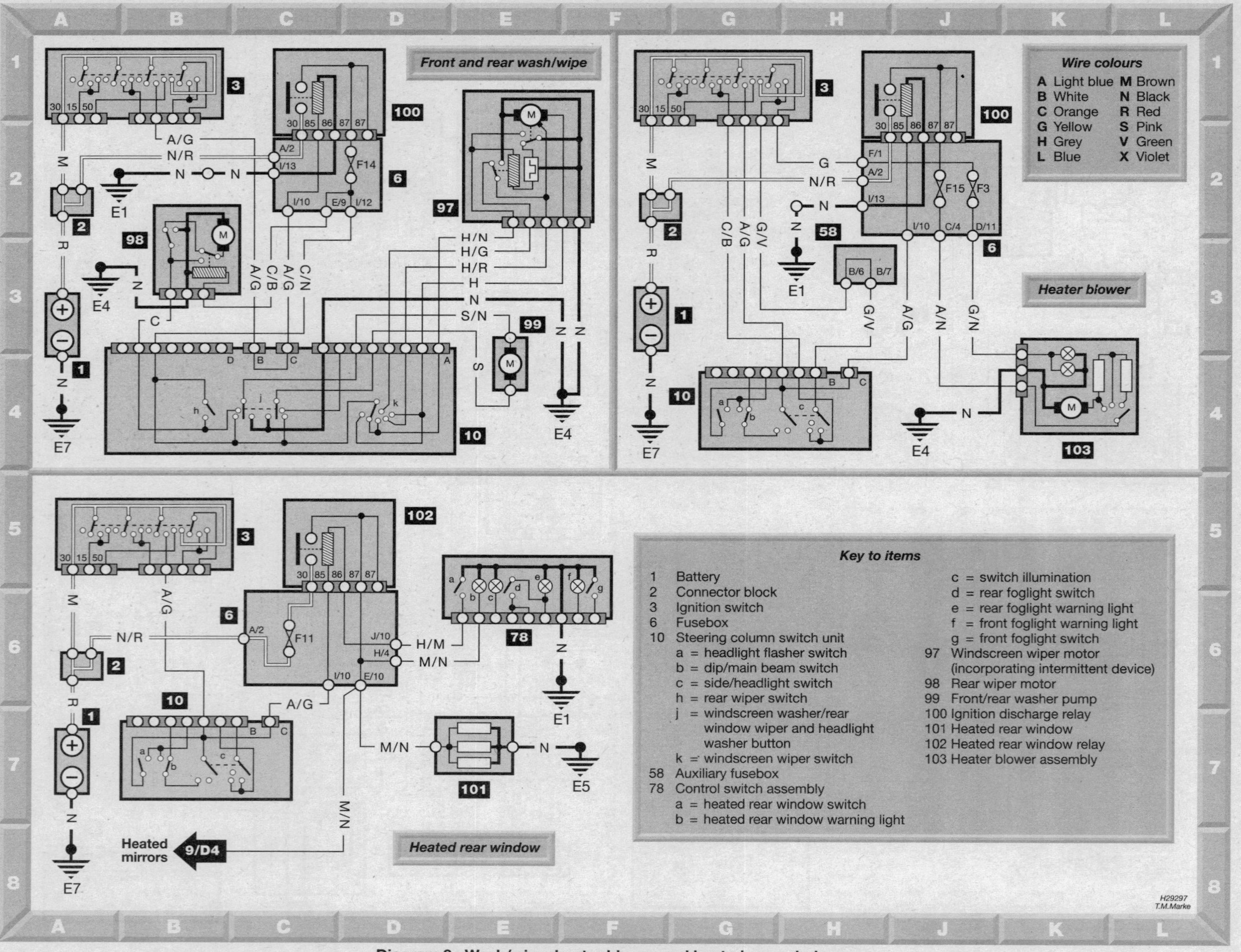

Front and rear wash/wipe
Heater blower
Wire colours
A Light blue M Brown
B White N Black
C Orange R Red
G Yellow S Pink
H Grey V Green
L Blue X Violet
Heated rear window
Heated mirrors
9/D4
Key to items
1 Battery
2 Connector block
3 Ignition switch
6 Fusebox
10 Steering column switch unit
a = headlight flasher switch
b = dip/main beam switch
c = side/headlight switch
h = rear wiper switch
j = windscreen washer/rear window wiper and headlight washer button
k = windscreen wiper switch
58 Auxiliary fusebox
78 Control switch assembly
a = heated rear window switch
b = heated rear window warning light
c = switch illumination
d = rear foglight switch
e = rear foglight warning light
f = front foglight warning light
g = front foglight switch
97 Windscreen wiper motor (incorporating intermittent device)
98 Rear wiper motor
99 Front/rear washer pump
100 Ignition discharge relay
101 Heated rear window
102 Heated rear window relay
103 Heater blower assembly
H29297
T.M.Marke

Diagram 8 : Wash/wipe, heater blower and heated rear window

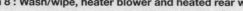

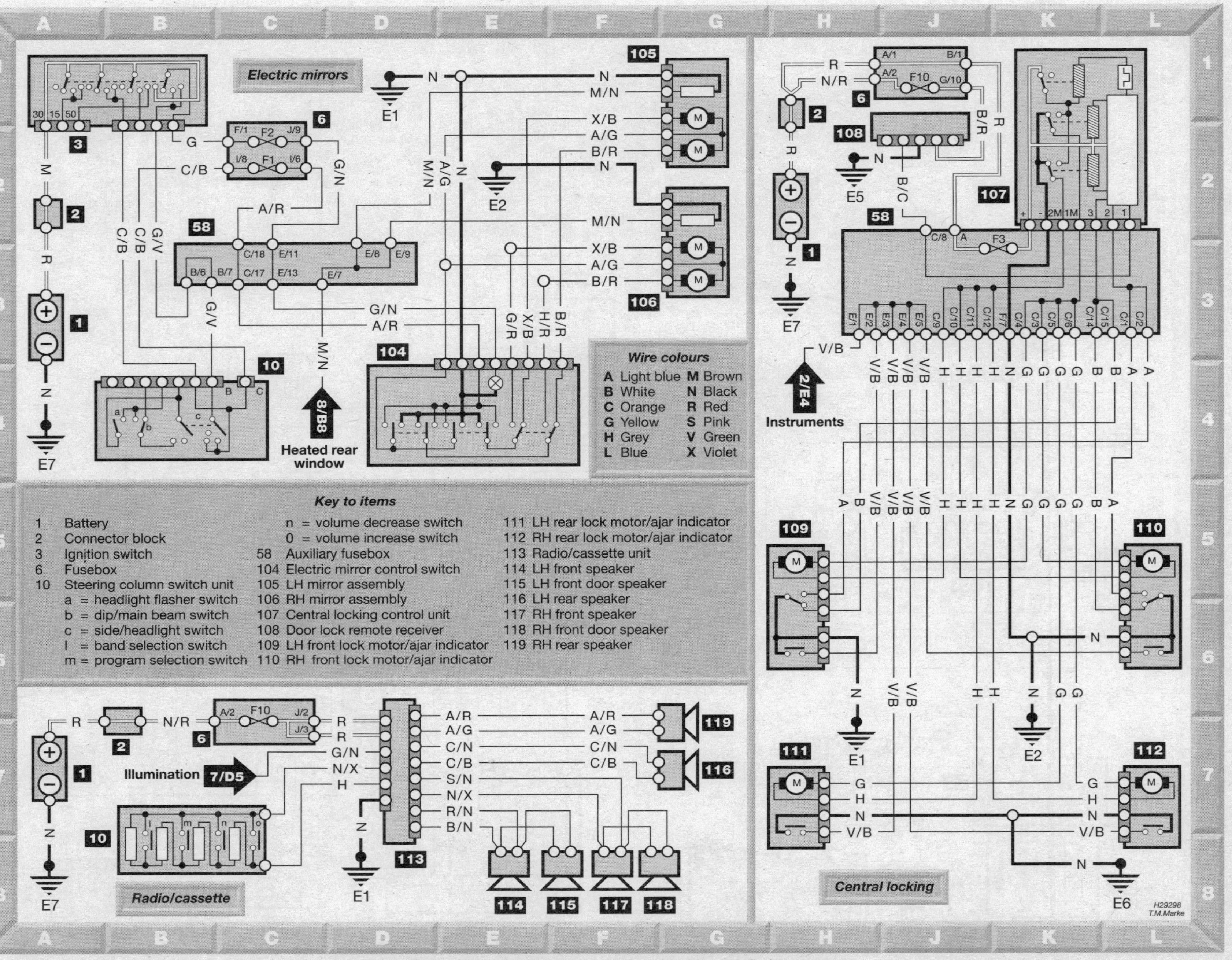

Electric mirrors
Heated rear window
8/B8
Radio/cassette
Illumination
7/D5
Central locking
Instruments
2/E4
Wire colours
A Light blue
B White
C Orange
G Yellow
H Grey
L Blue
M Brown
N Black
R Red
S Pink
V Green
X Violet
Key to items
1 Battery
2 Connector block
3 Ignition switch
6 Fusebox
10 Steering column switch unit
a = headlight flasher switch
b = dip/main beam switch
c = side/headlight switch
l = band selection switch
m = program selection switch
n = volume decrease switch
0 = volume increase switch
58 Auxiliary fusebox
104 Electric mirror control switch
105 LH mirror assembly
106 RH mirror assembly
107 Central locking control unit
108 Door lock remote receiver
109 LH front lock motor/ajar indicator
110 RH front lock motor/ajar indicator
111 LH rear lock motor/ajar indicator
112 RH rear lock motor/ajar indicator
113 Radio/cassette unit
114 LH front speaker
115 LH front door speaker
116 LH rear speaker
117 RH front speaker
118 RH front door speaker
119 RH rear speaker
H29298
T.M.Marke

Diagram 9 : Electric mirrors, central locking and radio/cassette

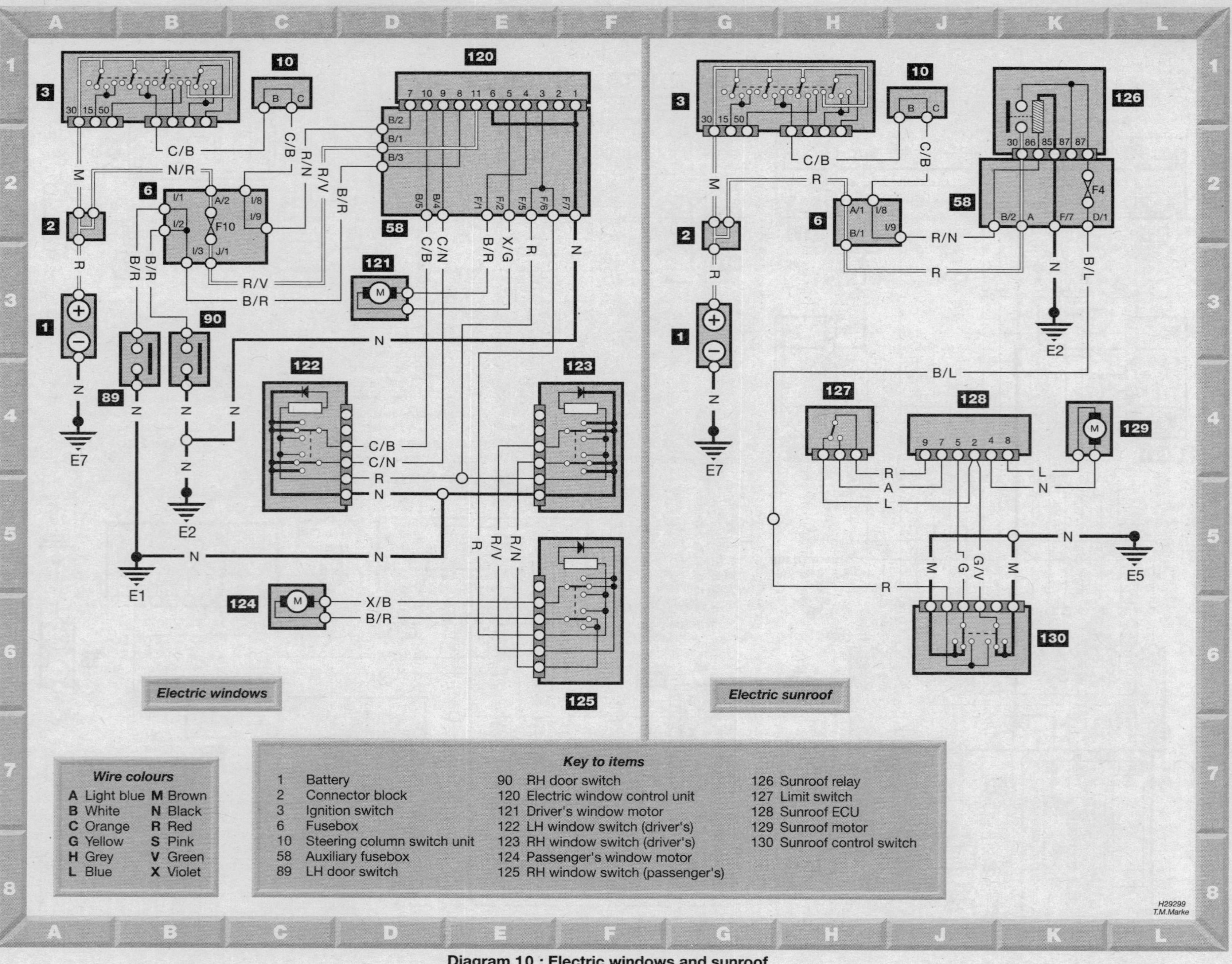
Electric windows
Electric sunroof
E7
E2
E1
E5
Wire colours
A Light blue
B White
C Orange
G Yellow
H Grey
L Blue
M Brown
N Black
R Red
S Pink
V Green
X Violet
Key to items
1 Battery
2 Connector block
3 Ignition switch
6 Fusebox
10 Steering column switch unit
58 Auxiliary fusebox
89 LH door switch
90 RH door switch
120 Electric window control unit
121 Driver's window motor
122 LH window switch (driver's)
123 RH window switch (driver's)
124 Passenger's window motor
125 RH window switch (passenger's)
126 Sunroof relay
127 Limit switch
128 Sunroof ECU
129 Sunroof motor
130 Sunroof control switch
H29299
T.M.Marke

Diagram 10 : Electric windows and sunroof

Dimensions and weights

Note: *All figures are approximate, and may vary according to model. Refer to manufacturer's data for exact figures.*

Dimensions

Overall length	3770 mm
Overall width	1625 mm
Overall height (unladen)	1460 mm
Wheelbase	2450 mm

Weights

Kerb weight*:	
Petrol models	840 to 1000 kg
Diesel models	1010 to 1060 kg
Maximum gross vehicle weight*:	
Petrol models	1310 to 1405 kg
Diesel models	1495 to 1510 kg
Maximum roof rack load	75 kg
Maximum towing weight*:	
Braked trailer	900 to 1100 kg
Unbraked trailer	400 kg
Maximum trailer nose weight (braked trailer)	70 kg

**Depending on model and specification.*

Conversion factors

Length (distance)

Inches (in)	x 25.4	= Millimetres (mm)	x 0.0394	= Inches (in)
Feet (ft)	x 0.305	= Metres (m)	x 3.281	= Feet (ft)
Miles	x 1.609	= Kilometres (km)	x 0.621	= Miles

Volume (capacity)

Cubic inches (cu in; in^3)	x 16.387	= Cubic centimetres (cc; cm^3)	x 0.061	= Cubic inches (cu in; in^3)
Imperial pints (Imp pt)	x 0.568	= Litres (l)	x 1.76	= Imperial pints (Imp pt)
Imperial quarts (Imp qt)	x 1.137	= Litres (l)	x 0.88	= Imperial quarts (Imp qt)
Imperial quarts (Imp qt)	x 1.201	= US quarts (US qt)	x 0.833	= Imperial quarts (Imp qt)
US quarts (US qt)	x 0.946	= Litres (l)	x 1.057	= US quarts (US qt)
Imperial gallons (Imp gal)	x 4.546	= Litres (l)	x 0.22	= Imperial gallons (Imp gal)
Imperial gallons (Imp gal)	x 1.201	= US gallons (US gal)	x 0.833	= Imperial gallons (Imp gal)
US gallons (US gal)	x 3.785	= Litres (l)	x 0.264	= US gallons (US gal)

Mass (weight)

Ounces (oz)	x 28.35	= Grams (g)	x 0.035	= Ounces (oz)
Pounds (lb)	x 0.454	= Kilograms (kg)	x 2.205	= Pounds (lb)

Force

Ounces-force (ozf; oz)	x 0.278	= Newtons (N)	x 3.6	= Ounces-force (ozf; oz)
Pounds-force (lbf; lb)	x 4.448	= Newtons (N)	x 0.225	= Pounds-force (lbf; lb)
Newtons (N)	x 0.1	= Kilograms-force (kgf; kg)	x 9.81	= Newtons (N)

Pressure

Pounds-force per square inch (psi; lbf/in^2; lb/in^2)	x 0.070	= Kilograms-force per square centimetre (kgf/cm^2; kg/cm^2)	x 14.223	= Pounds-force per square inch (psi; lbf/in^2; lb/in^2)
Pounds-force per square inch (psi; lbf/in^2; lb/in^2)	x 0.068	= Atmospheres (atm)	x 14.696	= Pounds-force per square inch (psi; lbf/in^2; lb/in^2)
Pounds-force per square inch (psi; lbf/in^2; lb/in^2)	x 0.069	= Bars	x 14.5	= Pounds-force per square inch (psi; lbf/in^2; lb/in^2)
Pounds-force per square inch (psi; lbf/in^2; lb/in^2)	x 6.895	= Kilopascals (kPa)	x 0.145	= Pounds-force per square inch (psi; lbf/in^2; lb/in^2)
Kilopascals (kPa)	x 0.01	= Kilograms-force per square centimetre (kgf/cm^2; kg/cm^2)	x 98.1	= Kilopascals (kPa)
Millibar (mbar)	x 100	= Pascals (Pa)	x 0.01	= Millibar (mbar)
Millibar (mbar)	x 0.0145	= Pounds-force per square inch (psi; lbf/in^2; lb/in^2)	x 68.947	= Millibar (mbar)
Millibar (mbar)	x 0.75	= Millimetres of mercury (mmHg)	x 1.333	= Millibar (mbar)
Millibar (mbar)	x 0.401	= Inches of water (inH_2O)	x 2.491	= Millibar (mbar)
Millimetres of mercury (mmHg)	x 0.535	= Inches of water (inH_2O)	x 1.868	= Millimetres of mercury (mmHg)
Inches of water (inH_2O)	x 0.036	= Pounds-force per square inch (psi; lbf/in^2; lb/in^2)	x 27.68	= Inches of water (inH_2O)

Torque (moment of force)

Pounds-force inches (lbf in; lb in)	x 1.152	= Kilograms-force centimetre (kgf cm; kg cm)	x 0.868	= Pounds-force inches (lbf in; lb in)
Pounds-force inches (lbf in; lb in)	x 0.113	= Newton metres (Nm)	x 8.85	= Pounds-force inches (lbf in; lb in)
Pounds-force inches (lbf in; lb in)	x 0.083	= Pounds-force feet (lbf ft; lb ft)	x 12	= Pounds-force inches (lbf in; lb in)
Pounds-force feet (lbf ft; lb ft)	x 0.138	= Kilograms-force metres (kgf m; kg m)	x 7.233	= Pounds-force feet (lbf ft; lb ft)
Pounds-force feet (lbf ft; lb ft)	x 1.356	= Newton metres (Nm)	x 0.738	= Pounds-force feet (lbf ft; lb ft)
Newton metres (Nm)	x 0.102	= Kilograms-force metres (kgf m; kg m)	x 9.804	= Newton metres (Nm)

Power

Horsepower (hp)	x 745.7	= Watts (W)	x 0.0013	= Horsepower (hp)

Velocity (speed)

Miles per hour (miles/hr; mph)	x 1.609	= Kilometres per hour (km/hr; kph)	x 0.621	= Miles per hour (miles/hr; mph)

Fuel consumption*

Miles per gallon, Imperial (mpg)	x 0.354	= Kilometres per litre (km/l)	x 2.825	= Miles per gallon, Imperial (mpg)
Miles per gallon, US (mpg)	x 0.425	= Kilometres per litre (km/l)	x 2.352	= Miles per gallon, US (mpg)

Temperature

Degrees Fahrenheit = (°C x 1.8) + 32

Degrees Celsius (Degrees Centigrade; °C) = (°F - 32) x 0.56

** It is common practice to convert from miles per gallon (mpg) to litres/100 kilometres (l/100km), where mpg x l/100 km = 282*

Spare parts are available from many sources, including maker's appointed garages, accessory shops, and motor factors. To be sure of obtaining the correct parts, it may sometimes be necessary to quote the vehicle identification number. If possible, it can also be useful to take the old parts along for positive identification. Items such as starter motors and alternators may be available under a service exchange scheme - any parts returned should always be clean.

Our advice regarding spare part sources is as follows.

Officially-appointed garages

This is the best source of parts which are peculiar to your car, and are not otherwise generally available (eg, badges, interior trim, certain body panels, etc). It is also the only place at which you should buy parts if the vehicle is still under warranty.

Accessory shops

These are very good places to buy materials and components needed for the maintenance of your car (oil, air and fuel filters, spark plugs, light bulbs, drivebelts, oils and greases, brake pads, touch-up paint, etc). Parts like this sold by a reputable shop are of the same standard as those used by the car manufacturer.

Motor factors

Good factors will stock all the more important components which wear out comparatively quickly and can sometimes supply individual components needed for the overhaul of a larger assembly. They may also handle work such as cylinder block reboring, crankshaft regrinding and balancing, etc.

Tyre and exhaust specialists

These outlets may be independent or members of a local or national chain. They frequently offer competitive prices when compared with a main dealer or local garage, but it will pay to obtain several quotes before making a decision. Also ask what 'extras' may be added to the quote - for instance, fitting a new valve and balancing the wheel are both often charged on top of the price of a new tyre.

Other sources

Beware of parts or materials obtained from market stalls, car boot sales or similar outlets. Such items are not invariably sub-standard, but there is little chance of compensation if they do prove unsatisfactory. In the case of safety-critical components such as brake pads, there is the risk not only of financial loss, but also of an accident causing injury or death.

Second-hand components or assemblies obtained from a car breaker can be a good buy in some circumstances, but this sort of purchase is best made by the experienced DIY mechanic.

Vehicle identification

Modifications are a continuing and unpublicised process in vehicle manufacture, quite apart from major model changes. Spare parts manuals and lists are compiled upon a numerical basis, the individual vehicle identification numbers being essential to correct identification of the component concerned.

When ordering spare parts, always give as much information as possible. Quote the car model, year of manufacture and registration, chassis and engine numbers as appropriate.

The *Vehicle Identification Number (VIN)* plate is riveted to the front of the engine compartment, behind and above the right hand headlamp unit. The vehicle identification number is also stamped into the floorpan, beneath the carpet between the drivers door and seat **(see illustration)**.

The engine number is stamped on the left hand face of the cylinder block.

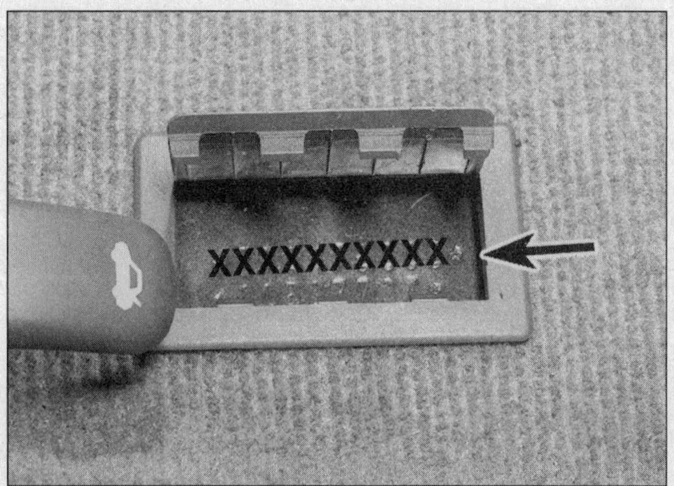

The vehicle identification number (arrowed) is stamped into the floorpan, beneath the carpet between the driver's door and seat.

Whenever servicing, repair or overhaul work is carried out on the car or its components, observe the following procedures and instructions. This will assist in carrying out the operation efficiently and to a professional standard of workmanship.

Joint mating faces and gaskets

When separating components at their mating faces, never insert screwdrivers or similar implements into the joint between the faces in order to prise them apart. This can cause severe damage which results in oil leaks, coolant leaks, etc upon reassembly. Separation is usually achieved by tapping along the joint with a soft-faced hammer in order to break the seal. However, note that this method may not be suitable where dowels are used for component location.

Where a gasket is used between the mating faces of two components, a new one must be fitted on reassembly; fit it dry unless otherwise stated in the repair procedure. Make sure that the mating faces are clean and dry, with all traces of old gasket removed. When cleaning a joint face, use a tool which is unlikely to score or damage the face, and remove any burrs or nicks with an oilstone or fine file.

Make sure that tapped holes are cleaned with a pipe cleaner, and keep them free of jointing compound, if this is being used, unless specifically instructed otherwise.

Ensure that all orifices, channels or pipes are clear, and blow through them, preferably using compressed air.

Oil seals

Oil seals can be removed by levering them out with a wide flat-bladed screwdriver or similar implement. Alternatively, a number of self-tapping screws may be screwed into the seal, and these used as a purchase for pliers or some similar device in order to pull the seal free.

Whenever an oil seal is removed from its working location, either individually or as part of an assembly, it should be renewed.

The very fine sealing lip of the seal is easily damaged, and will not seal if the surface it contacts is not completely clean and free from scratches, nicks or grooves. If the original sealing surface of the component cannot be restored, and the manufacturer has not made provision for slight relocation of the seal relative to the sealing surface, the component should be renewed.

Protect the lips of the seal from any surface which may damage them in the course of fitting. Use tape or a conical sleeve where possible. Lubricate the seal lips with oil before fitting and, on dual-lipped seals, fill the space between the lips with grease.

Unless otherwise stated, oil seals must be fitted with their sealing lips toward the lubricant to be sealed.

Use a tubular drift or block of wood of the appropriate size to install the seal and, if the seal housing is shouldered, drive the seal down to the shoulder. If the seal housing is unshouldered, the seal should be fitted with its face flush with the housing top face (unless otherwise instructed).

Screw threads and fastenings

Seized nuts, bolts and screws are quite a common occurrence where corrosion has set in, and the use of penetrating oil or releasing fluid will often overcome this problem if the offending item is soaked for a while before attempting to release it. The use of an impact driver may also provide a means of releasing such stubborn fastening devices, when used in conjunction with the appropriate screwdriver bit or socket. If none of these methods works, it may be necessary to resort to the careful application of heat, or the use of a hacksaw or nut splitter device.

Studs are usually removed by locking two nuts together on the threaded part, and then using a spanner on the lower nut to unscrew the stud. Studs or bolts which have broken off below the surface of the component in which they are mounted can sometimes be removed using a stud extractor. Always ensure that a blind tapped hole is completely free from oil, grease, water or other fluid before installing the bolt or stud. Failure to do this could cause the housing to crack due to the hydraulic action of the bolt or stud as it is screwed in.

When tightening a castellated nut to accept a split pin, tighten the nut to the specified torque, where applicable, and then tighten further to the next split pin hole. Never slacken the nut to align the split pin hole, unless stated in the repair procedure.

When checking or retightening a nut or bolt to a specified torque setting, slacken the nut or bolt by a quarter of a turn, and then retighten to the specified setting. However, this should not be attempted where angular tightening has been used.

For some screw fastenings, notably cylinder head bolts or nuts, torque wrench settings are no longer specified for the latter stages of tightening, "angle-tightening" being called up instead. Typically, a fairly low torque wrench setting will be applied to the bolts/nuts in the correct sequence, followed by one or more stages of tightening through specified angles.

Locknuts, locktabs and washers

Any fastening which will rotate against a component or housing during tightening should always have a washer between it and the relevant component or housing.

Spring or split washers should always be renewed when they are used to lock a critical component such as a big-end bearing retaining bolt or nut. Locktabs which are folded over to retain a nut or bolt should always be renewed.

Self-locking nuts can be re-used in non-critical areas, providing resistance can be felt when the locking portion passes over the bolt or stud thread. However, it should be noted that self-locking stiffnuts tend to lose their effectiveness after long periods of use, and should then be renewed as a matter of course.

Split pins must always be replaced with new ones of the correct size for the hole.

When thread-locking compound is found on the threads of a fastener which is to be re-used, it should be cleaned off with a wire brush and solvent, and fresh compound applied on reassembly.

Special tools

Some repair procedures in this manual entail the use of special tools such as a press, two or three-legged pullers, spring compressors, etc. Wherever possible, suitable readily-available alternatives to the manufacturer's special tools are described, and are shown in use. In some instances, where no alternative is possible, it has been necessary to resort to the use of a manufacturer's tool, and this has been done for reasons of safety as well as the efficient completion of the repair operation. Unless you are highly-skilled and have a thorough understanding of the procedures described, never attempt to bypass the use of any special tool when the procedure described specifies its use. Not only is there a very great risk of personal injury, but expensive damage could be caused to the components involved.

Environmental considerations

When disposing of used engine oil, brake fluid, antifreeze, etc, give due consideration to any detrimental environmental effects. Do not, for instance, pour any of the above liquids down drains into the general sewage system, or onto the ground to soak away. Many local council refuse tips provide a facility for waste oil disposal, as do some garages. If none of these facilities are available, consult your local Environmental Health Department, or the National Rivers Authority, for further advice.

With the universal tightening-up of legislation regarding the emission of environmentally-harmful substances from motor vehicles, most vehicles have tamperproof devices fitted to the main adjustment points of the fuel system. These devices are primarily designed to prevent unqualified persons from adjusting the fuel/air mixture, with the chance of a consequent increase in toxic emissions. If such devices are found during servicing or overhaul, they should, wherever possible, be renewed or refitted in accordance with the manufacturer's requirements or current legislation.

OIL CARE
FOLLOW THE CODE
OIL BANK LINE
0800 66 33 66
www.oilbankline.org.uk

Note: It is antisocial and illegal to dump oil down the drain. To find the location of your local oil recycling bank, call this number free.

The jack supplied with the vehicle tool kit should only be used for changing the roadwheels in an emergency- see *Wheel changing* at the front of this manual. When carrying out any other kind of work, raise the vehicle using a hydraulic (or trolley) jack, and always supplement the jack with axle stands positioned under the vehicle jacking points.

When using a hydraulic jack to raise the front of the vehicle, position the jack head under the transmission differential housing **(see illustration). Do not** jack the vehicle under the sill, sump, or any of the steering or suspension components. With the vehicle raised, an axle stand should be positioned beneath the reinforced vehicle jack location point on the sill. Position a block of wood with a groove cut in it on the jack head to prevent the vehicle weight resting on the sill edge; align the sill edge with the groove in the wood so that the vehicle weight is spread evenly over the surface of the block.

To raise the rear of the vehicle, position the jack head centrally under the member to which the lower edge of the rear bumper is fixed - use an interposed block of wood to protect the bodywork and spread the load evenly **(see illustration). Do not** attempt to raise the vehicle with the jack positioned underneath the beam axle or suspension components. With the vehicle raised, an axle stand should be positioned beneath the reinforced vehicle jacking location points on the sill. Position a grooved block of wood on the jack as described in the previous paragraph.

Warning: Never work under, around, or near a raised vehicle, unless it is adequately supported in at least two places.

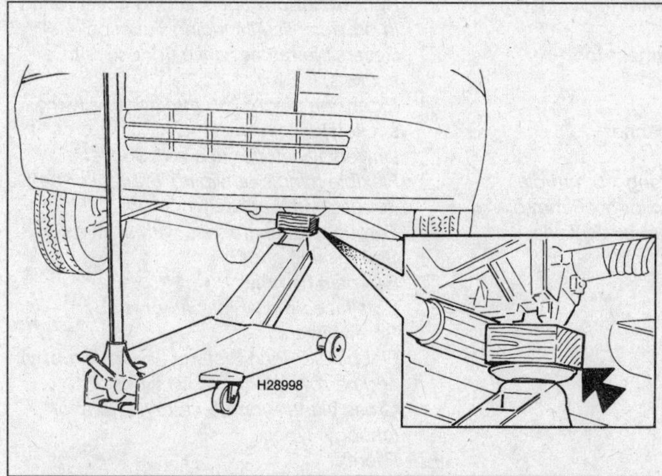

When using a hydraulic jack to raise the front of the vehicle, position the jack head under the transmission differential housing

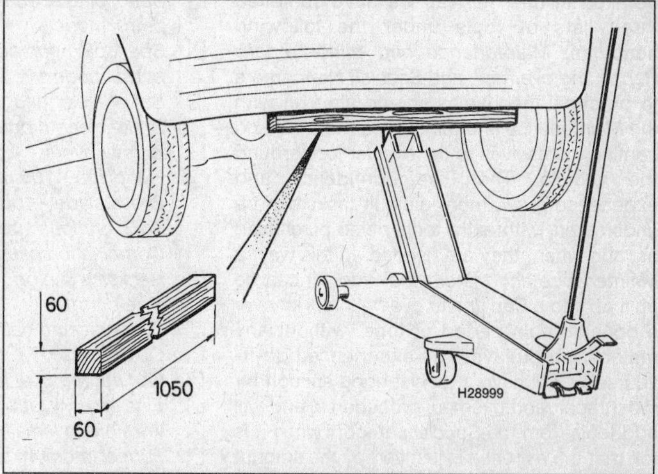

To raise the rear of the vehicle, position the jack head centrally under the member to which the lower edge of the rear bumper is fixed - use an interposed block of wood to protect the bodywork and spread the load evenly

Disconnecting the battery

Several systems fitted to the vehicle require battery power to be available at all times, either to ensure their continued operation (such as the clock) or to maintain control unit memories which would be wiped if the battery were to be disconnected. Whenever the battery is to be disconnected therefore, first note the following, to ensure that there are no unforeseen consequences of this action:

a) First, on any vehicle with central locking, it is a wise precaution to remove the key from the ignition, and to keep it with you, so that it does not get locked in if the central locking should engage accidentally when the battery is reconnected.

b) If a security-coded audio unit is fitted, and the unit andlor the battery is disconnected, the unit will not function again on reconnecfion until the correct security code is entered. Details of this procedure, which varies according to the unit fitted, are given in the vehicle owner's handbook. Ensure you have the correct code before you disconnect the battery. If you do not have the code or details of the correct procedure, but can supply proof of ownership and a legitimate reason for wanting this information, a Fiat dealer may be able to help.

c) On petrol engine models, the engine management system electronic control unit is of the 'self-learning' type, meaning that as it operates, it also monitors and stores the settings which give optimum engine performance under all operating conditions. When the battery is disconnected, these settings are lost and the ECU reverts to the base settings programmed into its memory at the factory. On restarting, this may lead to the engine running/idling roughly until the ECU has re-learned the optimum settings. This process is best accomplished by taking the vehicle on a road test (for approximately 15 minutes), covering all engine speeds and loads, concentrating mainly in the 2,500 to 3,500 rpm region.

Devices known as 'memory-savers' (or 'code-savers') can be used to avoid some of the above problems. Precise details vary according to the device used. Typically, it is plugged into the cigarette lighter, and is connected by its own wires to a spare battery; the vehicle's own battery is then disconnected from the electrical system, leaving the memory-saver to pass sufficient current to maintain audio unit security codes and any other memory values, and also to run permanently-live circuits such as the clock.

Warning: Some of these devices allow a considerable amount of current to pass, which can mean that many of the vehicle's systems are still operational when the main battery is disconnected. If a memory saver is used, ensure that the circuit concerned is actually 'dead' before carrying out any work on it!

Introduction

A selection of good tools is a fundamental requirement for anyone contemplating the maintenance and repair of a motor vehicle. For the owner who does not possess any, their purchase will prove a considerable expense, offsetting some of the savings made by doing-it-yourself. However, provided that the tools purchased meet the relevant national safety standards and are of good quality, they will last for many years and prove an extremely worthwhile investment.

To help the average owner to decide which tools are needed to carry out the various tasks detailed in this manual, we have compiled three lists of tools under the following headings: *Maintenance and minor repair*, *Repair and overhaul*, and *Special*. Newcomers to practical mechanics should start off with the *Maintenance and minor repair* tool kit, and confine themselves to the simpler jobs around the vehicle. Then, as confidence and experience grow, more difficult tasks can be undertaken, with extra tools being purchased as, and when, they are needed. In this way, a *Maintenance and minor repair* tool kit can be built up into a *Repair and overhaul* tool kit over a considerable period of time, without any major cash outlays. The experienced do-it-yourselfer will have a tool kit good enough for most repair and overhaul procedures, and will add tools from the *Special* category when it is felt that the expense is justified by the amount of use to which these tools will be put.

Maintenance and minor repair tool kit

The tools given in this list should be considered as a minimum requirement if routine maintenance, servicing and minor repair operations are to be undertaken. We recommend the purchase of combination spanners (ring one end, open-ended the other); although more expensive than open-ended ones, they do give the advantages of both types of spanner.

- ☐ *Combination spanners:*
  Metric - 8 to 19 mm inclusive
- ☐ *Adjustable spanner - 35 mm jaw (approx.)*
- ☐ *Spark plug spanner (with rubber insert) - petrol models*
- ☐ *Spark plug gap adjustment tool - petrol models*
- ☐ *Set of feeler gauges*
- ☐ *Brake bleed nipple spanner*
- ☐ *Screwdrivers:*
  Flat blade - 100 mm long x 6 mm dia
  Cross blade - 100 mm long x 6 mm dia
  Torx - various sizes (not all vehicles)
- ☐ *Combination pliers*
- ☐ *Hacksaw (junior)*
- ☐ *Tyre pump*
- ☐ *Tyre pressure gauge*
- ☐ *Oil can*
- ☐ *Oil filter removal tool*
- ☐ *Fine emery cloth*
- ☐ *Wire brush (small)*
- ☐ *Funnel (medium size)*
- ☐ *Sump drain plug key (not all vehicles)*

Repair and overhaul tool kit

These tools are virtually essential for anyone undertaking any major repairs to a motor vehicle, and are additional to those given in the *Maintenance and minor repair* list. Included in this list is a comprehensive set of sockets. Although these are expensive, they will be found invaluable as they are so versatile - particularly if various drives are included in the set. We recommend the half-inch square-drive type, as this can be used with most proprietary torque wrenches.

The tools in this list will sometimes need to be supplemented by tools from the *Special* list:

- ☐ *Sockets (or box spanners) to cover range in previous list (including Torx sockets)*
- ☐ *Reversible ratchet drive (for use with sockets)*
- ☐ *Extension piece, 250 mm (for use with sockets)*
- ☐ *Universal joint (for use with sockets)*
- ☐ *Flexible handle or sliding T "breaker bar" (for use with sockets)*
- ☐ *Torque wrench (for use with sockets)*
- ☐ *Self-locking grips*
- ☐ *Ball pein hammer*
- ☐ *Soft-faced mallet (plastic or rubber)*
- ☐ *Screwdrivers:*
  Flat blade - long & sturdy, short (chubby), and narrow (electrician's) types
  Cross blade – long & sturdy, and short (chubby) types
- ☐ *Pliers:*
  Long-nosed
  Side cutters (electrician's)
  Circlip (internal and external)
- ☐ *Cold chisel - 25 mm*
- ☐ *Scriber*
- ☐ *Scraper*
- ☐ *Centre-punch*
- ☐ *Pin punch*
- ☐ *Hacksaw*
- ☐ *Brake hose clamp*
- ☐ *Brake/clutch bleeding kit*
- ☐ *Selection of twist drills*
- ☐ *Steel rule/straight-edge*
- ☐ *Allen keys (inc. splined/Torx type)*
- ☐ *Selection of files*
- ☐ *Wire brush*
- ☐ *Axle stands*
- ☐ *Jack (strong trolley or hydraulic type)*
- ☐ *Light with extension lead*
- ☐ *Universal electrical multi-meter*

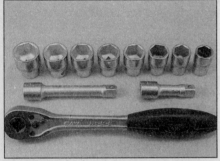

Sockets and reversible ratchet drive

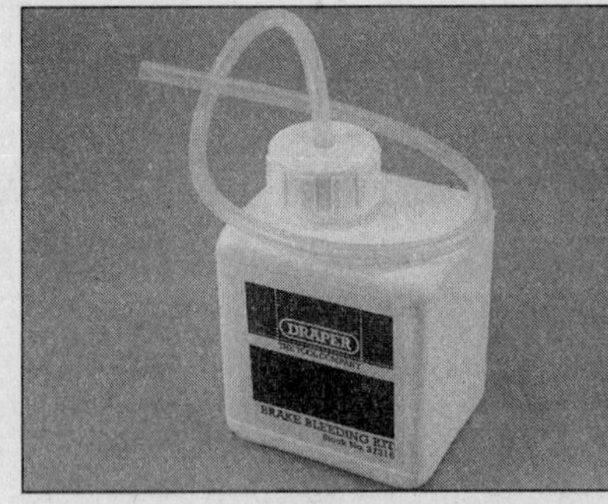

Brake bleeding kit

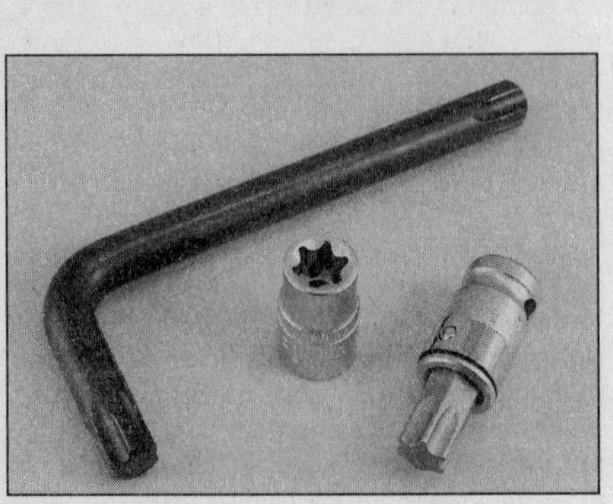
Torx key, socket and bit

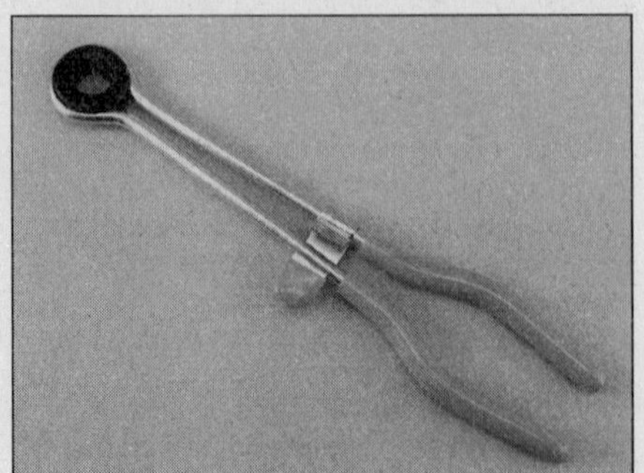
Hose clamp

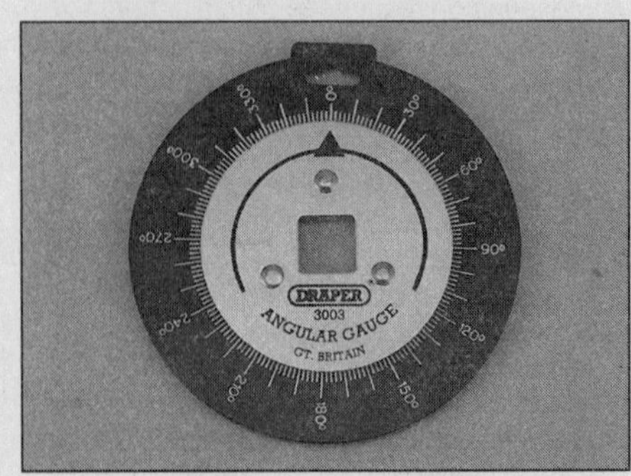

Angular-tightening gauge

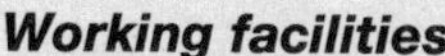

Special tools

The tools in this list are those which are not used regularly, are expensive to buy, or which need to be used in accordance with their manufacturers' instructions. Unless relatively difficult mechanical jobs are undertaken frequently, it will not be economic to buy many of these tools. Where this is the case, you could consider clubbing together with friends (or joining a motorists' club) to make a joint purchase, or borrowing the tools against a deposit from a local garage or tool hire specialist. It is worth noting that many of the larger DIY superstores now carry a large range of special tools for hire at modest rates.

The following list contains only those tools and instruments freely available to the public, and not those special tools produced by the vehicle manufacturer specifically for its dealer network. You will find occasional references to these manufacturers' special tools in the text of this manual. Generally, an alternative method of doing the job without the vehicle manufacturers' special tool is given. However, sometimes there is no alternative to using them. Where this is the case and the relevant tool cannot be bought or borrowed, you will have to entrust the work to a dealer.

- ☐ *Angular-tightening gauge*
- ☐ *Valve spring compressor*
- ☐ *Valve grinding tool*
- ☐ *Piston ring compressor*
- ☐ *Piston ring removal/installation tool*
- ☐ *Cylinder bore hone*
- ☐ *Balljoint separator*
- ☐ *Coil spring compressors (where applicable)*
- ☐ *Two/three-legged hub and bearing puller*
- ☐ *Impact screwdriver*
- ☐ *Micrometer and/or vernier calipers*
- ☐ *Dial gauge*
- ☐ *Stroboscopic timing light*
- ☐ *Dwell angle meter/tachometer*
- ☐ *Fault code reader*
- ☐ *Cylinder compression gauge*
- ☐ *Hand-operated vacuum pump and gauge*
- ☐ *Clutch plate alignment set*
- ☐ *Brake shoe steady spring cup removal tool*
- ☐ *Bush and bearing removal/installation set*
- ☐ *Stud extractors*
- ☐ *Tap and die set*
- ☐ *Lifting tackle*
- ☐ *Trolley jack*

Buying tools

Reputable motor accessory shops and superstores often offer excellent quality tools at discount prices, so it pays to shop around.

Remember, you don't have to buy the most expensive items on the shelf, but it is always advisable to steer clear of the very cheap tools. Beware of 'bargains' offered on market stalls or at car boot sales. There are plenty of good tools around at reasonable prices, but always aim to purchase items which meet the relevant national safety standards. If in doubt, ask the proprietor or manager of the shop for advice before making a purchase.

Care and maintenance of tools

Having purchased a reasonable tool kit, it is necessary to keep the tools in a clean and serviceable condition. After use, always wipe off any dirt, grease and metal particles using a clean, dry cloth, before putting the tools away. Never leave them lying around after they have been used. A simple tool rack on the garage or workshop wall for items such as screwdrivers and pliers is a good idea. Store all normal spanners and sockets in a metal box. Any measuring instruments, gauges, meters, etc, must be carefully stored where they cannot be damaged or become rusty.

Take a little care when tools are used. Hammer heads inevitably become marked, and screwdrivers lose the keen edge on their blades from time to time. A little timely attention with emery cloth or a file will soon restore items like this to a good finish.

Working facilities

Not to be forgotten when discussing tools is the workshop itself. If anything more than routine maintenance is to be carried out, a suitable working area becomes essential.

It is appreciated that many an owner-mechanic is forced by circumstances to remove an engine or similar item without the benefit of a garage or workshop. Having done this, any repairs should always be done under the cover of a roof.

Wherever possible, any dismantling should be done on a clean, flat workbench or table at a suitable working height.

Any workbench needs a vice; one with a jaw opening of 100 mm is suitable for most jobs. As mentioned previously, some clean dry storage space is also required for tools, as well as for any lubricants, cleaning fluids, touch-up paints etc, which become necessary.

Another item which may be required, and which has a much more general usage, is an electric drill with a chuck capacity of at least 8 mm. This, together with a good range of twist drills, is virtually essential for fitting accessories.

Last, but not least, always keep a supply of old newspapers and clean, lint-free rags available, and try to keep any working area as clean as possible.

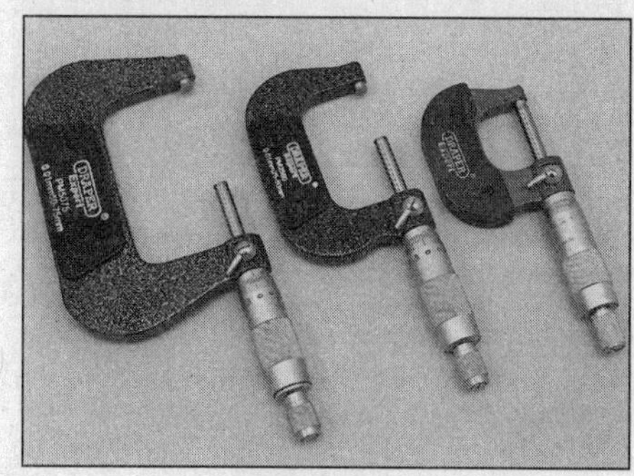

Micrometers

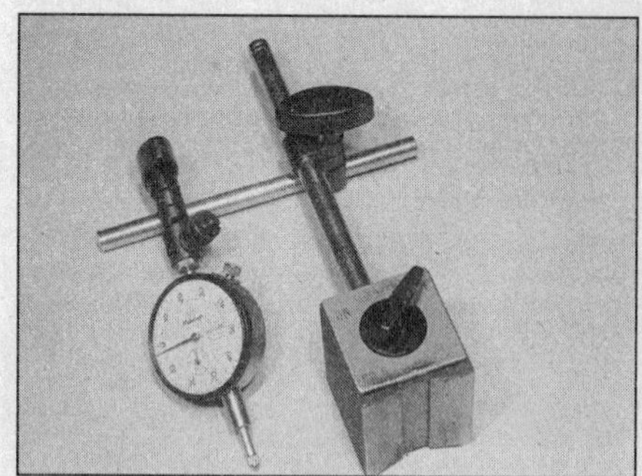

Dial test indicator ("dial gauge")

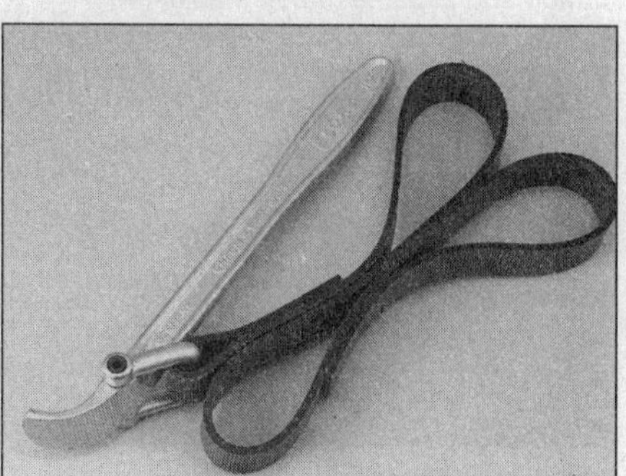

Strap wrench

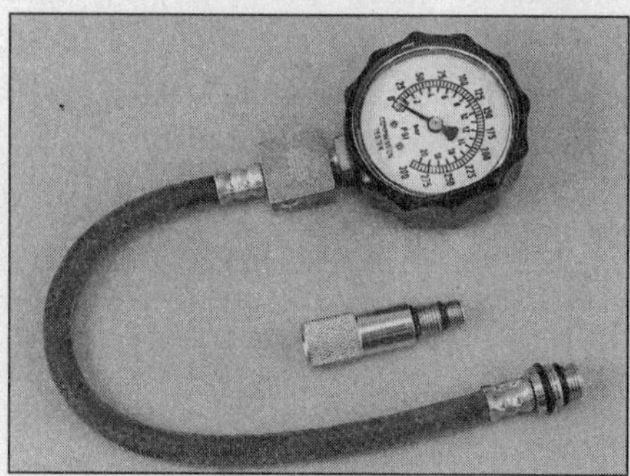

Compression tester

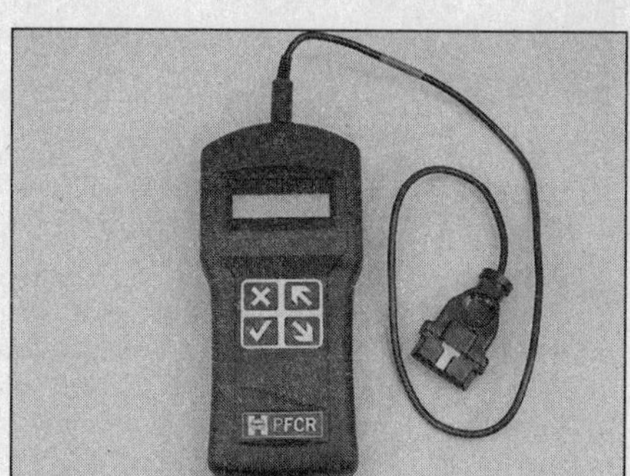

Fault code reader

This is a guide to getting your vehicle through the MOT test. Obviously it will not be possible to examine the vehicle to the same standard as the professional MOT tester. However, working through the following checks will enable you to identify any problem areas before submitting the vehicle for the test.

Where a testable component is in borderline condition, the tester has discretion in deciding whether to pass or fail it. The basis of such discretion is whether the tester would be happy for a close relative or friend to use the vehicle with the component in that condition. If the vehicle presented is clean and evidently well cared for, the tester may be more inclined to pass a borderline component than if the vehicle is scruffy and apparently neglected.

It has only been possible to summarise the test requirements here, based on the regulations in force at the time of printing. Test standards are becoming increasingly stringent, although there are some exemptions for older vehicles.

An assistant will be needed to help carry out some of these checks.

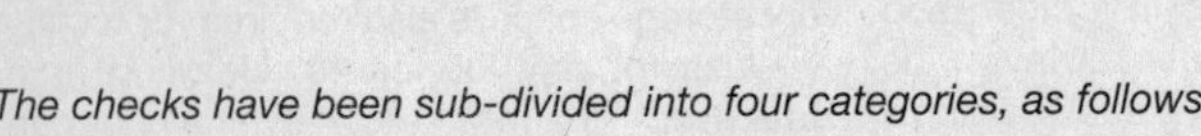

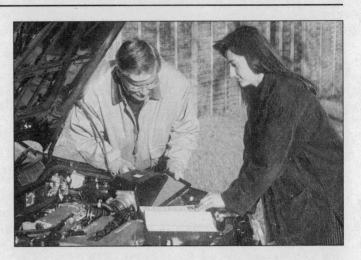

The checks have been sub-divided into four categories, as follows:

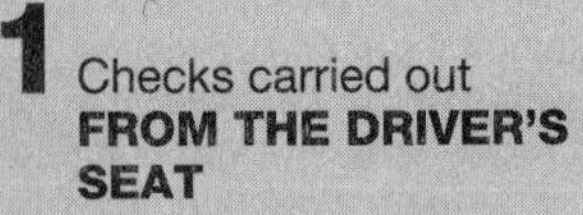

1 Checks carried out **FROM THE DRIVER'S SEAT**

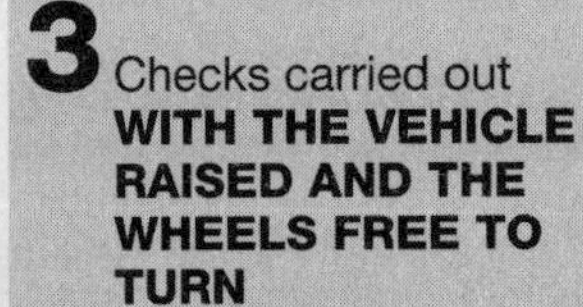

2 Checks carried out **WITH THE VEHICLE ON THE GROUND**

3 Checks carried out **WITH THE VEHICLE RAISED AND THE WHEELS FREE TO TURN**

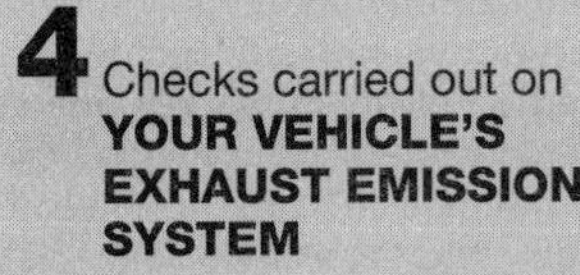

4 Checks carried out on **YOUR VEHICLE'S EXHAUST EMISSION SYSTEM**

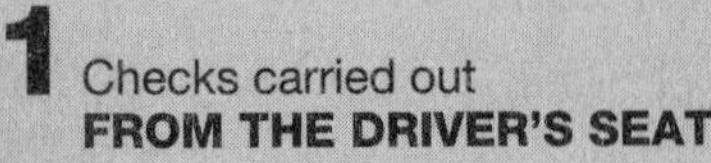

1 Checks carried out FROM THE DRIVER'S SEAT

Handbrake

☐ Test the operation of the handbrake. Excessive travel (too many clicks) indicates incorrect brake or cable adjustment.

☐ Check that the handbrake cannot be released by tapping the lever sideways. Check the security of the lever mountings.

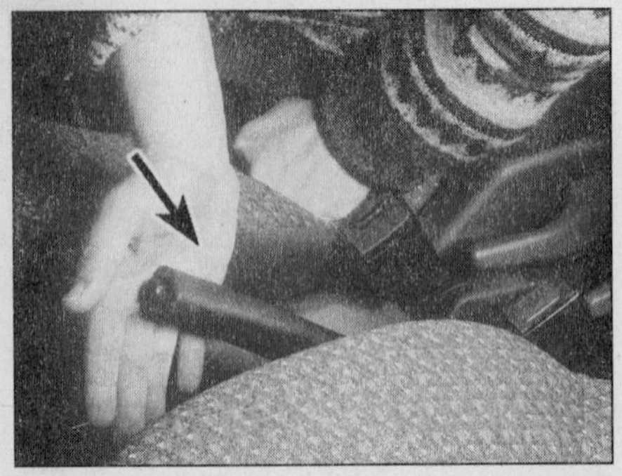

Footbrake

☐ Depress the brake pedal and check that it does not creep down to the floor, indicating a master cylinder fault. Release the pedal, wait a few seconds, then depress it again. If the pedal travels nearly to the floor before firm resistance is felt, brake adjustment or repair is necessary. If the pedal feels spongy, there is air in the hydraulic system which must be removed by bleeding.

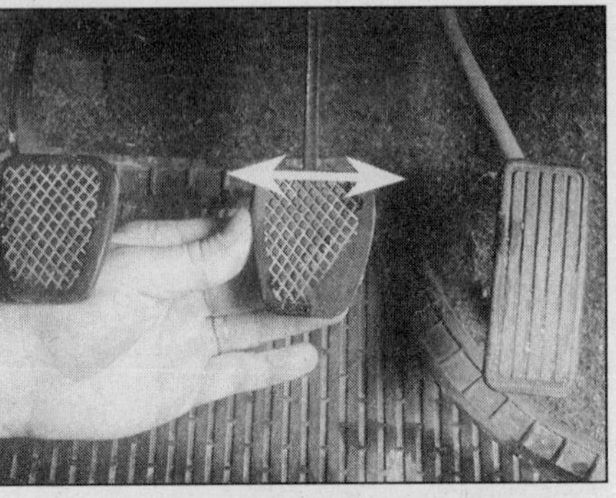

☐ Check that the brake pedal is secure and in good condition. Check also for signs of fluid leaks on the pedal, floor or carpets, which would indicate failed seals in the brake master cylinder.

☐ Check the servo unit (when applicable) by operating the brake pedal several times, then keeping the pedal depressed and starting the engine. As the engine starts, the pedal will move down slightly. If not, the vacuum hose or the servo itself may be faulty.

Steering wheel and column

☐ Examine the steering wheel for fractures or looseness of the hub, spokes or rim.

☐ Move the steering wheel from side to side and then up and down. Check that the steering wheel is not loose on the column, indicating wear or a loose retaining nut. Continue moving the steering wheel as before, but also turn it slightly from left to right.

☐ Check that the steering wheel is not loose on the column, and that there is no abnormal

movement of the steering wheel, indicating wear in the column support bearings or couplings.

Windscreen, mirrors and sunvisor

☐ The windscreen must be free of cracks or other significant damage within the driver's field of view. (Small stone chips are acceptable.) Rear view mirrors must be secure, intact, and capable of being adjusted.

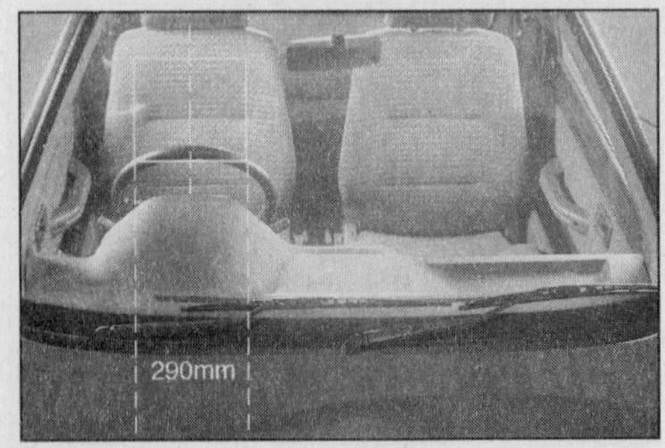

☐ The driver's sunvisor must be capable of being stored in the "up" position.

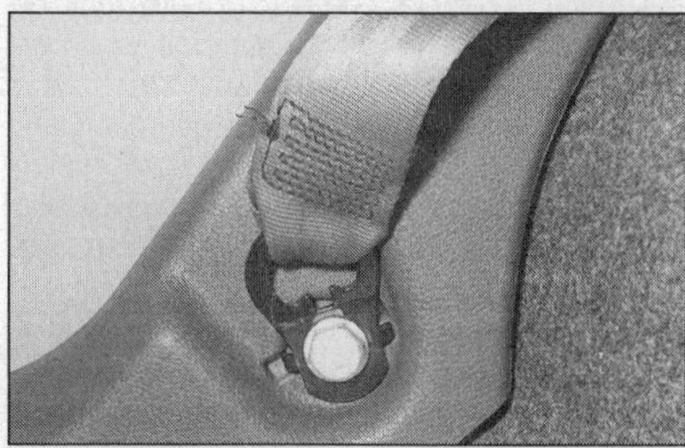

Seat belts and seats

Note: *The following checks are applicable to all seat belts, front and rear.*

☐ Examine the webbing of all the belts (including rear belts if fitted) for cuts, serious fraying or deterioration. Fasten and unfasten each belt to check the buckles. If applicable, check the retracting mechanism. Check the security of all seat belt mountings accessible from inside the vehicle.

☐ Seat belts with pre-tensioners, once activated, have a "flag" or similar showing on the seat belt stalk. This, in itself, is not a reason for test failure.

☐ The front seats themselves must be securely attached and the backrests must lock in the upright position.

Doors

☐ Both front doors must be able to be opened and closed from outside and inside, and must latch securely when closed.

2 Checks carried out WITH THE VEHICLE ON THE GROUND

Vehicle identification

☐ Number plates must be in good condition, secure and legible, with letters and numbers correctly spaced – spacing at (A) should be at least twice that at (B).

☐ The VIN plate and/or homologation plate must be legible.

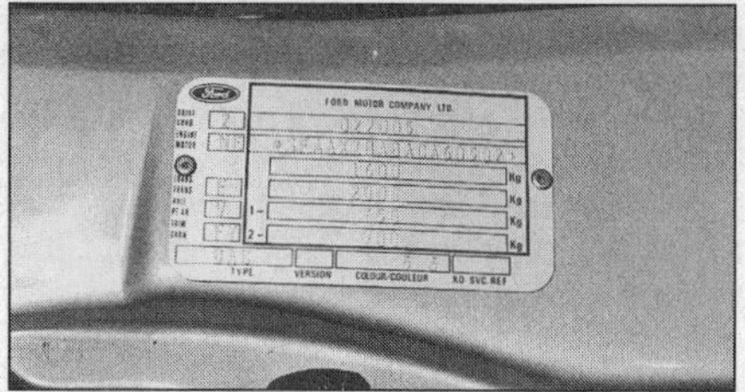

Electrical equipment

☐ Switch on the ignition and check the operation of the horn.

☐ Check the windscreen washers and wipers, examining the wiper blades; renew damaged or perished blades. Also check the operation of the stop-lights.

☐ Check the operation of the sidelights and number plate lights. The lenses and reflectors must be secure, clean and undamaged.

☐ Check the operation and alignment of the headlights. The headlight reflectors must not be tarnished and the lenses must be undamaged.

☐ Switch on the ignition and check the operation of the direction indicators (including the instrument panel tell-tale) and the hazard warning lights. Operation of the sidelights and stop-lights must not affect the indicators - if it does, the cause is usually a bad earth at the rear light cluster.

☐ Check the operation of the rear foglight(s), including the warning light on the instrument panel or in the switch.

☐ The ABS warning light must illuminate in accordance with the manufacturers' design. For most vehicles, the ABS warning light should illuminate when the ignition is switched on, and (if the system is operating properly) extinguish after a few seconds. Refer to the owner's handbook.

Footbrake

☐ Examine the master cylinder, brake pipes and servo unit for leaks, loose mountings, corrosion or other damage.

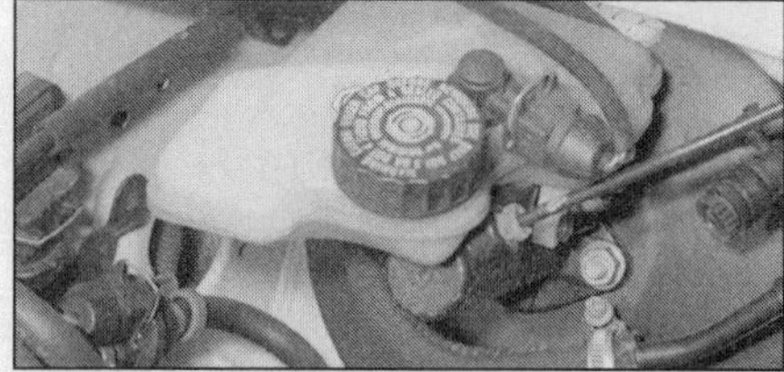

☐ The fluid reservoir must be secure and the fluid level must be between the upper (**A**) and lower (**B**) markings.

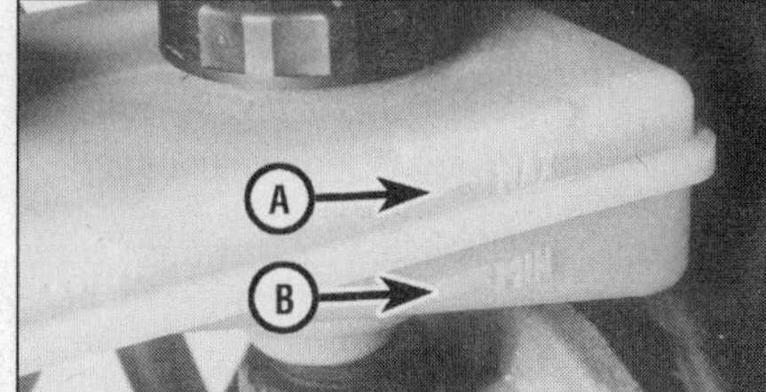

☐ Inspect both front brake flexible hoses for cracks or deterioration of the rubber. Turn the steering from lock to lock, and ensure that the hoses do not contact the wheel, tyre, or any part of the steering or suspension mechanism. With the brake pedal firmly depressed, check the hoses for bulges or leaks under pressure.

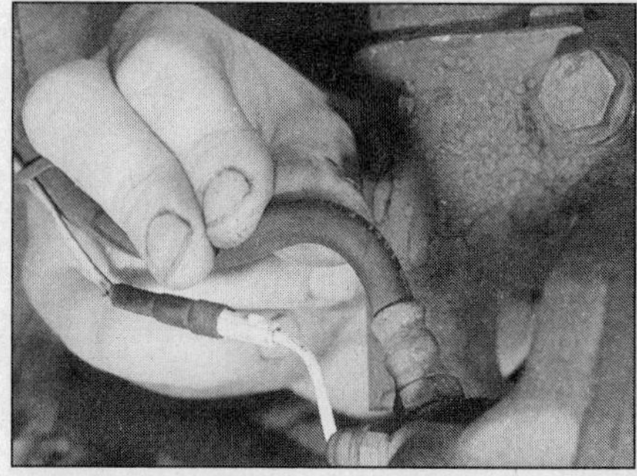

Steering and suspension

☐ Have your assistant turn the steering wheel from side to side slightly, up to the point where the steering gear just begins to transmit this movement to the roadwheels. Check for excessive free play between the steering wheel and the steering gear, indicating wear or insecurity of the steering column joints, the column-to-steering gear coupling, or the steering gear itself.

☐ Have your assistant turn the steering wheel more vigorously in each direction, so that the roadwheels just begin to turn. As this is done, examine all the steering joints, linkages, fittings and attachments. Renew any component that shows signs of wear or damage. On vehicles with power steering, check the security and condition of the steering pump, drivebelt and hoses.

☐ Check that the vehicle is standing level, and at approximately the correct ride height.

Shock absorbers

☐ Depress each corner of the vehicle in turn, then release it. The vehicle should rise and then settle in its normal position. If the vehicle continues to rise and fall, the shock absorber is defective. A shock absorber which has seized will also cause the vehicle to fail.

Exhaustive system

☐ Start the engine. With your assistant holding a rag over the tailpipe, check the entire system for leaks. Repair or renew leaking sections.

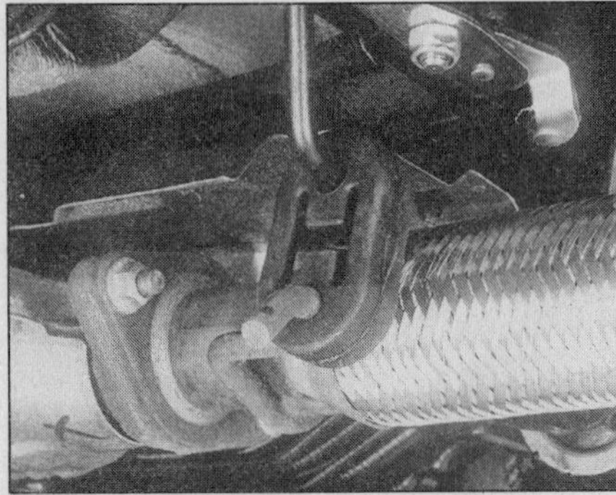

3 Checks carried out WITH THE VEHICLE RAISED AND THE WHEELS FREE TO TURN

Jack up the front and rear of the vehicle, and securely support it on axle stands. Position the stands clear of the suspension assemblies. Ensure that the wheels are clear of the ground and that the steering can be turned from lock to lock.

Steering mechanism

☐ Have your assistant turn the steering from lock to lock. Check that the steering turns smoothly, and that no part of the steering mechanism, including a wheel or tyre, fouls any brake hose or pipe or any part of the body structure.

☐ Examine the steering rack rubber gaiters for damage or insecurity of the retaining clips. If power steering is fitted, check for signs of damage or leakage of the fluid hoses, pipes or connections. Also check for excessive stiffness or binding of the steering, a missing split pin or locking device, or severe corrosion of the body structure within 30 cm of any steering component attachment point.

Front and rear suspension and wheel bearings

☐ Starting at the front right-hand side, grasp the roadwheel at the 3 o'clock and 9 o'clock positions and rock gently but firmly. Check for free play or insecurity at the wheel bearings, suspension balljoints, or suspension mountings, pivots and attachments.

☐ Now grasp the wheel at the 12 o'clock and 6 o'clock positions and repeat the previous inspection. Spin the wheel, and check for roughness or tightness of the front wheel bearing.

☐ If excess free play is suspected at a component pivot point, this can be confirmed by using a large screwdriver or similar tool and levering between the mounting and the component attachment. This will confirm whether the wear is in the pivot bush, its retaining bolt, or in the mounting itself (the bolt holes can often become elongated).

☐ Carry out all the above checks at the other front wheel, and then at both rear wheels.

Springs and shock absorbers

☐ Examine the suspension struts (when applicable) for serious fluid leakage, corrosion, or damage to the casing. Also check the security of the mounting points.

☐ If coil springs are fitted, check that the spring ends locate in their seats, and that the spring is not corroded, cracked or broken.

☐ If leaf springs are fitted, check that all leaves are intact, that the axle is securely attached to each spring, and that there is no deterioration of the spring eye mountings, bushes, and shackles.

☐ The same general checks apply to vehicles fitted with other suspension types, such as torsion bars, hydraulic displacer units, etc. Ensure that all mountings and attachments are secure, that there are no signs of excessive wear, corrosion or damage, and (on hydraulic types) that there are no fluid leaks or damaged pipes.

☐ Inspect the shock absorbers for signs of serious fluid leakage. Check for wear of the mounting bushes or attachments, or damage to the body of the unit.

Driveshafts (fwd vehicles only)

☐ Rotate each front wheel in turn and inspect the constant velocity joint gaiters for splits or damage. Also check that each driveshaft is straight and undamaged.

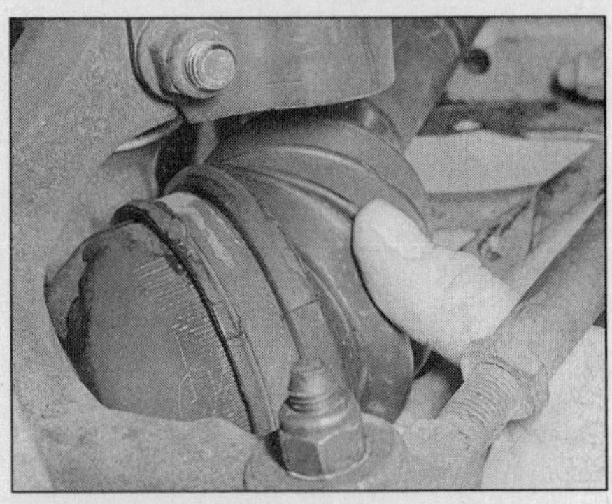

Braking system

☐ If possible without dismantling, check brake pad wear and disc condition. Ensure that the friction lining material has not worn excessively, (A) and that the discs are not fractured, pitted, scored or badly worn (B).

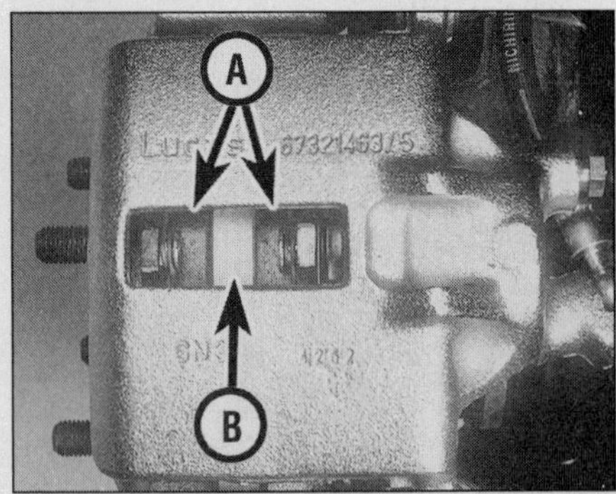

☐ Examine all the rigid brake pipes underneath the vehicle, and the flexible hose(s) at the rear. Look for corrosion, chafing or insecurity of the pipes, and for signs of bulging under pressure, chafing, splits or deterioration of the flexible hoses.

☐ Look for signs of fluid leaks at the brake calipers or on the brake backplates. Repair or renew leaking components.

☐ Slowly spin each wheel, while your assistant depresses and releases the footbrake. Ensure that each brake is operating and does not bind when the pedal is released.

☐ Examine the handbrake mechanism, checking for frayed or broken cables, excessive corrosion, or wear or insecurity of the linkage. Check that the mechanism works on each relevant wheel, and releases fully, without binding.

☐ It is not possible to test brake efficiency without special equipment, but a road test can be carried out later to check that the vehicle pulls up in a straight line.

Fuel and exhaust systems

☐ Inspect the fuel tank (including the filler cap), fuel pipes, hoses and unions. All components must be secure and free from leaks.

☐ Examine the exhaust system over its entire length, checking for any damaged, broken or missing mountings, security of the retaining clamps and rust or corrosion.

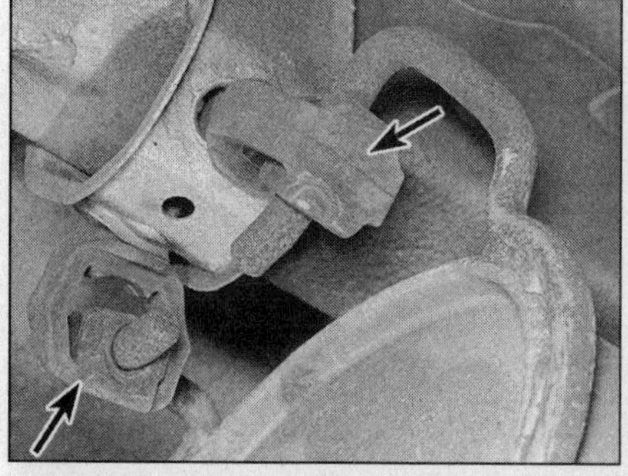

Wheels and tyres

☐ Examine the sidewalls and tread area of each tyre in turn. Check for cuts, tears, lumps, bulges, separation of the tread, and exposure of the ply or cord due to wear or damage. Check that the tyre bead is correctly seated on the wheel rim, that the valve is sound and properly seated, and that the wheel is not distorted or damaged.

☐ Check that the tyres are of the correct size for the vehicle, that they are of the same size and type on each axle, and that the pressures are correct.

☐ Check the tyre tread depth. The legal minimum at the time of writing is 1.6 mm over at least three-quarters of the tread width. Abnormal tread wear may indicate incorrect front wheel alignment.

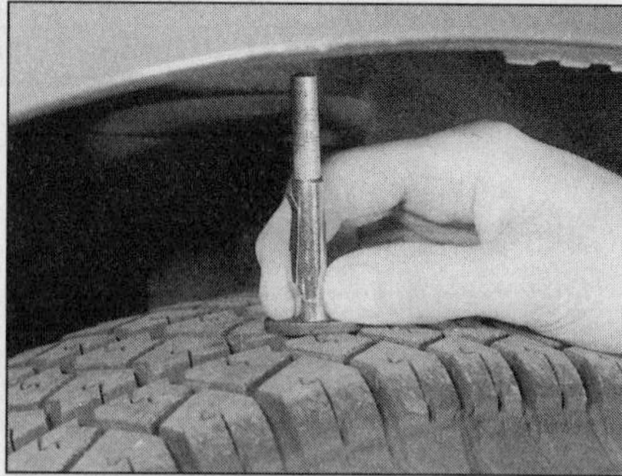

Body corrosion

☐ Check the condition of the entire vehicle structure for signs of corrosion in load-bearing areas. (These include chassis box sections, side sills, cross-members, pillars, and all suspension, steering, braking system and seat belt mountings and anchorages.) Any corrosion which has seriously reduced the thickness of a load-bearing area is likely to cause the vehicle to fail. In this case professional repairs are likely to be needed.

☐ Damage or corrosion which causes sharp or otherwise dangerous edges to be exposed will also cause the vehicle to fail.

4 Checks carried out on YOUR VEHICLE'S EXHAUST EMISSION SYSTEM

Petrol models

☐ Have the engine at normal operating temperature, and make sure that it is in good tune (ignition system in good order, air filter element clean, etc).

☐ Before any measurements are carried out, raise the engine speed to around 2500 rpm, and hold it at this speed for 20 seconds. Allow the engine speed to return to idle, and watch for smoke emissions from the exhaust tailpipe. If the idle speed is obviously much too high, or if dense blue or clearly-visible black smoke comes from the tailpipe for more than 5 seconds, the vehicle will fail. As a rule of thumb, blue smoke signifies oil being burnt (engine wear) while black smoke signifies unburnt fuel (dirty air cleaner element, or other carburettor or fuel system fault).

☐ An exhaust gas analyser capable of measuring carbon monoxide (CO) and hydrocarbons (HC) is now needed. If such an instrument cannot be hired or borrowed, a local garage may agree to perform the check for a small fee.

CO emissions (mixture)

☐ At the time of writing, for vehicles first used between 1st August 1975 and 31st July 1986 (P to C registration), the CO level must not exceed 4.5% by volume. For vehicles first used between 1st August 1986 and 31st July 1992 (D to J registration), the CO level must not exceed 3.5% by volume. Vehicles first used after 1st August 1992 (K registration) must conform to the manufacturer's specification. The MOT tester has access to a DOT database or emissions handbook, which lists the CO and HC limits for each make and model of vehicle. The CO level is measured with the engine at idle speed, and at "fast idle". The following limits are given as a general guide:

At idle speed -
CO level no more than 0.5%
At "fast idle" (2500 to 3000 rpm) -
CO level no more than 0.3%
(Minimum oil temperature 60°C)

☐ If the CO level cannot be reduced far enough to pass the test (and the fuel and ignition systems are otherwise in good condition) then the carburettor is badly worn, or there is some problem in the fuel injection system or catalytic converter (as applicable).

HC emissions

☐ With the CO within limits, HC emissions for vehicles first used between 1st August 1975 and 31st July 1992 (P to J registration) must not exceed 1200 ppm. Vehicles first used after 1st August 1992 (K registration) must conform to the manufacturer's specification. The MOT tester has access to a DOT database or emissions handbook, which lists the CO and HC limits for each make and model of vehicle. The HC level is measured with the engine at "fast idle". The following is given as a general guide:

At "fast idle" (2500 to 3000 rpm) -
HC level no more than 200 ppm
(Minimum oil temperature 60°C)

☐ Excessive HC emissions are caused by incomplete combustion, the causes of which can include oil being burnt, mechanical wear and ignition/fuel system malfunction.

Diesel models

☐ The only emission test applicable to Diesel engines is the measuring of exhaust smoke density. The test involves accelerating the engine several times to its maximum unloaded speed.

Note: *It is of the utmost importance that the engine timing belt is in good condition before the test is carried out.*

☐ The limits for Diesel engine exhaust smoke, introduced in September 1995 are:

Vehicles first used before 1st August 1979:
Exempt from metered smoke testing, but must not emit "dense blue or clearly visible black smoke for a period of more than 5 seconds at idle" or "dense blue or clearly visible black smoke during acceleration which would obscure the view of other road users".

Non-turbocharged vehicles first used after 1st August 1979: 2.5m^{-1}

Turbocharged vehicles first used after 1st August 1979: 3.0m^{-1}

☐ Excessive smoke can be caused by a dirty air cleaner element. Otherwise, professional advice may be needed to find the cause.

Engine

- ☐ Engine fails to rotate when attempting to start
- ☐ Engine rotates, but will not start
- ☐ Engine difficult to start when cold
- ☐ Engine difficult to start when hot
- ☐ Starter motor noisy or excessively-rough in engagement
- ☐ Engine starts, but stops immediately
- ☐ Engine idles erratically
- ☐ Engine misfires at idle speed
- ☐ Engine misfires throughout the driving speed range
- ☐ Engine hesitates on acceleration
- ☐ Engine stalls
- ☐ Engine lacks power
- ☐ Engine backfires
- ☐ Oil pressure warning light illuminated with engine running
- ☐ Engine runs-on after switching off
- ☐ Engine noises

Cooling system

- ☐ Overheating
- ☐ Overcooling
- ☐ External coolant leakage
- ☐ Internal coolant leakage
- ☐ Corrosion

Fuel and exhaust systems

- ☐ Excessive fuel consumption
- ☐ Fuel leakage and/or fuel odour
- ☐ Excessive noise or fumes from exhaust system

Clutch

- ☐ Pedal travels to floor - no pressure or very little resistance
- ☐ Clutch fails to disengage (unable to select gears)
- ☐ Clutch slips (engine speed increases, with no increase in vehicle speed)
- ☐ Judder as clutch is engaged
- ☐ Noise when depressing or releasing clutch pedal

Manual transmission

- ☐ Noisy in neutral with engine running
- ☐ Noisy in one particular gear
- ☐ Difficulty engaging gears
- ☐ Jumps out of gear
- ☐ Vibration
- ☐ Lubricant leaks

Automatic transmission

- ☐ Fluid leakage
- ☐ Transmission fluid brown, or has burned smell
- ☐ General gear selection problems
- ☐ Transmission will not downshift (kickdown) with accelerator fully depressed
- ☐ Engine will not start in any gear, or starts in gears other than Park or Neutral
- ☐ Transmission slips, shifts roughly, is noisy, or has no drive in forward or reverse gears

Driveshafts

- ☐ Clicking or knocking noise on turns (at slow speed on full-lock)
- ☐ Vibration when accelerating or decelerating

Braking system

- ☐ Vehicle pulls to one side under braking
- ☐ Noise (grinding or high-pitched squeal) when brakes applied
- ☐ Excessive brake pedal travel
- ☐ Brake pedal feels spongy when depressed
- ☐ Excessive brake pedal effort required to stop vehicle
- ☐ Judder felt through brake pedal or steering wheel when braking
- ☐ Brakes binding
- ☐ Rear wheels locking under normal braking

Suspension and steering systems

- ☐ Vehicle pulls to one side
- ☐ Wheel wobble and vibration
- ☐ Excessive pitching and/or rolling around corners, or during braking
- ☐ Wandering or general instability
- ☐ Excessively-stiff steering
- ☐ Excessive play in steering
- ☐ Lack of power assistance
- ☐ Tyre wear excessive

Electrical system

- ☐ Battery will not hold a charge for more than a few days
- ☐ Ignition/no-charge warning light remains illuminated with engine running
- ☐ Ignition/no-charge warning light fails to come on
- ☐ Lights inoperative
- ☐ Instrument readings inaccurate or erratic
- ☐ Horn inoperative, or unsatisfactory in operation
- ☐ Windscreen/tailgate wipers inoperative, or unsatisfactory in operation
- ☐ Windscreen/tailgate washers inoperative, or unsatisfactory in operation
- ☐ Electric windows inoperative, or unsatisfactory in operation

Introduction

The vehicle owner who does his or her own maintenance according to the recommended service schedules should not have to use this section of the manual very often. Modern component reliability is such that, provided those items subject to wear or deterioration are inspected or renewed at the specified intervals, sudden failure is comparatively rare. Faults do not usually just happen as a result of sudden failure, but develop over a period of time. Major mechanical failures in particular are usually preceded by characteristic symptoms over hundreds or even thousands of miles. Those components which do occasionally fail without warning are often small and easily carried in the vehicle.

With any fault-finding, the first step is to decide where to begin investigations. Sometimes this is obvious, but on other occasions, a little detective work will be necessary. The owner who makes half a dozen haphazard adjustments or replacements may be successful in curing a fault (or its symptoms), but will be none the wiser if the fault recurs, and ultimately may have spent more time and money than was necessary. A calm and logical approach will be found to be more satisfactory in the long run. Always take into account any warning signs or abnormalities that may have been noticed in the period preceding the fault - power loss, high or low gauge readings, unusual smells, etc - and remember that failure of components such as fuses or spark plugs may only be pointers to some underlying fault.

The pages which follow provide an easy-reference guide to the more common problems which may occur during the operation of the vehicle. These problems and their possible causes are grouped under headings denoting various components or systems, such as Engine, Cooling system, etc. The Chapter and/or Section which deals with the problem is also shown in brackets. Whatever the fault, certain basic principles apply. These are as follows:

Verify the fault. This is simply a matter of being sure that you know what the symptoms are before starting work. This is particularly important if you are investigating a fault for someone else, who may not have described it very accurately.

Don't overlook the obvious. For example, if the vehicle won't start, is there petrol in the tank? (Don't take anyone else's word on this particular point, and don't trust the fuel gauge either!) If an electrical fault is indicated, look for loose or broken wires before digging out the test gear.

Cure the disease, not the symptom. Substituting a flat battery with a fully-charged one will get you off the hard shoulder, but if the underlying cause is not attended to, the new battery will go the same way. Similarly, changing oil-fouled spark plugs (petrol models) for a new set will get you moving again, but remember that the reason for the fouling (if it wasn't simply an incorrect grade of plug) will have to be established and corrected.

Don't take anything for granted. Particularly, don't forget that a new component may itself be defective (especially if it's been rattling around in the boot for months), and don't leave components out of a fault diagnosis sequence just because they are new or recently-fitted. When you do finally diagnose a difficult fault, you'll probably realise that all the evidence was there from the start.

Engine

Engine fails to rotate when attempting to start

- ☐ Battery terminal connections loose or corroded (*Weekly Checks*).
- ☐ Battery discharged or faulty (Chapter 5A).
- ☐ Broken, loose or disconnected wiring in the starting circuit (Chapter 5A).
- ☐ Defective starter solenoid or switch (Chapter 5A).
- ☐ Defective starter motor (Chapter 5A).
- ☐ Starter pinion or flywheel ring gear teeth loose or broken (Chapters 2A, 2B, 2C and 5A).
- ☐ Engine earth strap broken or disconnected (Chapter 5A).

Engine rotates, but will not start

- ☐ Fuel tank empty.
- ☐ Battery discharged (engine rotates slowly) (Chapter 5A).
- ☐ Battery terminal connections loose or corroded (*Weekly checks*).
- ☐ Ignition components damp or damaged - petrol models (Chapters 1A and 5B).
- ☐ Broken, loose or disconnected wiring in the ignition circuit - petrol models (Chapters 1 and 5B).
- ☐ Worn, faulty or incorrectly-gapped spark plugs - petrol models (Chapter 1A).
- ☐ Preheating system faulty - diesel models (Chapter 5C).
- ☐ Fuel injection system fault - petrol models (Chapter 4A or 4B).
- ☐ Stop solenoid faulty - diesel models (Chapter 4C).
- ☐ Air in fuel system - diesel models (Chapter 4C).
- ☐ Major mechanical failure (eg camshaft drive) (Chapter 2A, 2B or 2C).

Engine difficult to start when cold

- ☐ Battery discharged (Chapter 5A).
- ☐ Battery terminal connections loose or corroded (*Weekly checks*).
- ☐ Worn, faulty or incorrectly-gapped spark plugs - petrol models (Chapter 1A).
- ☐ Preheating system faulty - diesel models (Chapter 5C).
- ☐ Fuel injection system fault - petrol models (Chapter 4A or 4B).
- ☐ Other ignition system fault - petrol models (Chapters 1A and 5B).
- ☐ Fast idle valve incorrectly adjusted - diesel models (Chapter 4C).
- ☐ Low cylinder compressions (Chapter 2A, 2B or 2C).

Engine difficult to start when hot

- ☐ Air filter element dirty or clogged (Chapter 1A or 1B).
- ☐ Fuel injection system fault - petrol models (Chapter 4A or 4B).
- ☐ Low cylinder compressions (Chapter 2A, 2B or 2C).

Starter motor noisy or excessively-rough in engagement

- ☐ Starter pinion or flywheel ring gear teeth loose or broken (Chapters 2A, 2B, 2C and 5A).
- ☐ Starter motor mounting bolts loose or missing (Chapter 5A).
- ☐ Starter motor internal components worn or damaged (Chapter 5A).

Engine starts, but stops immediately

- ☐ Loose or faulty electrical connections in the ignition circuit - petrol models (Chapters 1A and 5B).
- ☐ Vacuum leak at the throttle body or inlet manifold - petrol models (Chapter 4A or 4B).
- ☐ Blocked injector/fuel injection system fault - petrol models (Chapter 4A or 4B).

Engine idles erratically

- ☐ Air filter element clogged (Chapter 1A or 1B).
- ☐ Vacuum leak at the throttle body, inlet manifold or associated hoses - petrol models (Chapter 4A or 4B).
- ☐ Worn, faulty or incorrectly-gapped spark plugs - petrol models (Chapter 1A).
- ☐ Uneven or low cylinder compressions (Chapter 2A, 2B or 2C).
- ☐ Camshaft lobes worn (Chapter 2A, 2B , 2Cor 2D).
- ☐ Timing belt incorrectly tensioned (Chapter 2A, 2B or 2C).
- ☐ Blocked injector/fuel injection system fault - petrol models (Chapter 4A or 4B).
- ☐ Faulty injector(s) - diesel models (Chapter 4C).

Engine misfires at idle speed

- ☐ Worn, faulty or incorrectly-gapped spark plugs - petrol models (Chapter 1A).
- ☐ Faulty spark plug HT leads - petrol models (Chapter 1A).
- ☐ Vacuum leak at the throttle body, inlet manifold or associated hoses - petrol models (Chapter 4A or 4B).
- ☐ Blocked injector/fuel injection system fault - petrol models (Chapter 4A or 4B).
- ☐ Faulty injector(s) - diesel models (Chapter 4C).
- ☐ Uneven or low cylinder compressions (Chapter 2A, 2B or 2C).
- ☐ Disconnected, leaking, or perished crankcase ventilation hoses (Chapter 4D).

Engine misfires throughout the driving speed range

- ☐ Fuel filter choked (Chapter 1A or 1B).
- ☐ Fuel pump faulty, or delivery pressure low - petrol models (Chapter 4A or 4B).
- ☐ Fuel tank vent blocked, or fuel pipes restricted (Chapter 4A, 4B or 4C).
- ☐ Vacuum leak at the throttle body, inlet manifold or associated hoses - petrol models (Chapter 4A or 4B).
- ☐ Worn, faulty or incorrectly-gapped spark plugs - petrol models (Chapter 1A).
- ☐ Faulty spark plug HT leads - petrol models (Chapter 1A).
- ☐ Faulty injector(s) - diesel models (Chapter 4C).
- ☐ Faulty ignition coil - petrol models (Chapter 5B).
- ☐ Uneven or low cylinder compressions (Chapter 2A, 2B or 2C).
- ☐ Blocked injector/fuel injection system fault - petrol models (Chapter 4A or 4B).

Engine (continued)

Engine hesitates on acceleration

- ☐ Worn, faulty or incorrectly-gapped spark plugs - petrol models (Chapter 1A).
- ☐ Vacuum leak at the throttle body, inlet manifold or associated hoses - petrol models (Chapter 4A or 4B).
- ☐ Blocked injector/fuel injection system fault - petrol models (Chapter 4A or 4B).
- ☐ Faulty injector(s) - diesel models (Chapter 4C).

Engine stalls

- ☐ Vacuum leak at the throttle body, inlet manifold or associated hoses - petrol models (Chapter 4A or 4B).
- ☐ Fuel filter choked (Chapter 1A or 1B).
- ☐ Fuel pump faulty, or delivery pressure low - petrol models (Chapter 4A or 4B).
- ☐ Fuel tank vent blocked, or fuel pipes restricted (Chapter 4A, 4B or 4C).
- ☐ Blocked injector/fuel injection system fault - petrol models (Chapter 4A or 4B).
- ☐ Faulty injector(s) - diesel models (Chapter 4C).

Engine lacks power

- ☐ Timing belt incorrectly fitted or tensioned (Chapter 2A, 2B or 2C).
- ☐ Fuel filter choked (Chapter 1A or 1B).
- ☐ Fuel pump faulty, or delivery pressure low - petrol models (Chapter 4A or 4B).
- ☐ Uneven or low cylinder compressions (Chapter 2A, 2B or 2C).
- ☐ Worn, faulty or incorrectly-gapped spark plugs - petrol models (Chapter 1A).
- ☐ Vacuum leak at the throttle body, inlet manifold or associated hoses - petrol models (Chapter 4A or 4B).
- ☐ Blocked injector/fuel injection system fault - petrol models (Chapter 4A or 4B).
- ☐ Faulty injector(s) - diesel models (Chapter 4C).
- ☐ Injection pump timing incorrect - diesel models (Chapter 4C).
- ☐ Brakes binding (Chapter 9).
- ☐ Clutch slipping (Chapter 6).

Engine backfires

- ☐ Timing belt incorrectly fitted or tensioned (Chapter 2A, 2B or 2C).
- ☐ Vacuum leak at the throttle body, inlet manifold or associated hoses - petrol models (Chapter 4A or 4B).
- ☐ Blocked injector/fuel injection system fault - petrol models (Chapter 4A or 4B).

Oil pressure warning light illuminated with engine running

- ☐ Low oil level, or incorrect oil grade (*Weekly checks*).
- ☐ Faulty oil pressure sensor (Chapter 5A).
- ☐ Worn engine bearings and/or oil pump (Chapter 2D).
- ☐ High engine operating temperature (Chapter 3).
- ☐ Oil pressure relief valve defective (Chapter 2A, 2B or 2C).
- ☐ Oil pick-up strainer clogged (Chapter 2A, 2B or 2C).

Engine runs-on after switching off

- ☐ Excessive carbon build-up in engine (Chapter 2D).
- ☐ High engine operating temperature (Chapter 3).
- ☐ Fuel injection system fault - petrol models (Chapter 4A or 4B).
- ☐ Faulty stop solenoid - diesel models (Chapter 4C).

Engine noises

Pre-ignition (pinking) or knocking during acceleration or under load

- ☐ Ignition timing incorrect/ignition system fault - petrol models (Chapters 1A and 5B).
- ☐ Incorrect grade of spark plug - petrol models (Chapter 1A).
- ☐ Incorrect grade of fuel (Chapter 1A).
- ☐ Vacuum leak at the throttle body, inlet manifold or associated hoses - petrol models (Chapter 4A or 4B).
- ☐ Excessive carbon build-up in engine (Chapter 2D).
- ☐ Blocked injector/fuel injection system fault - petrol models (Chapter 4A or 4B).

Whistling or wheezing noises

- ☐ Leaking inlet manifold or throttle body gasket - petrol models (Chapter 4A or 4B).
- ☐ Leaking exhaust manifold gasket or pipe-to-manifold joint (Chapter 4A, 4B or 4C).
- ☐ Leaking vacuum hose (Chapters 4A, 4B, 4C, 5B and 9).
- ☐ Blowing cylinder head gasket (Chapter 2A, 2B or 2C).

Tapping or rattling noises

- ☐ Worn valve gear or camshaft (Chapter 2A, 2B, 2C or 2D).
- ☐ Ancillary component fault (coolant pump, alternator, etc) (Chapters 3, 5A, etc).

Knocking or thumping noises

- ☐ Worn big-end bearings (regular heavy knocking, perhaps less under load) (Chapter 2D).
- ☐ Worn main bearings (rumbling and knocking, perhaps worsening under load) (Chapter 2D).
- ☐ Piston slap (most noticeable when cold) (Chapter 2D).
- ☐ Ancillary component fault (coolant pump, alternator, etc) (Chapters 3, 5A, etc).

Cooling system

Overheating

- ☐ Insufficient coolant in system (*Weekly checks*).
- ☐ Thermostat faulty (Chapter 3).
- ☐ Radiator core blocked, or grille restricted (Chapter 3).
- ☐ Electric cooling fan or thermoswitch faulty (Chapter 3).
- ☐ Pressure cap faulty (Chapter 3).
- ☐ Ignition timing incorrect/ignition system fault - petrol models (Chapters 1A and 5B).
- ☐ Inaccurate temperature gauge sender unit (Chapter 3).
- ☐ Airlock in cooling system.

Overcooling

- ☐ Thermostat faulty (Chapter 3).
- ☐ Inaccurate temperature gauge sender unit (Chapter 3).

External coolant leakage

- ☐ Deteriorated or damaged hoses or hose clips (Chapter 1A or 1B).
- ☐ Radiator core or heater matrix leaking (Chapter 3).
- ☐ Pressure cap faulty (Chapter 3).
- ☐ Water pump seal leaking (Chapter 3).
- ☐ Boiling due to overheating (Chapter 3).
- ☐ Core plug leaking (Chapter 2D).

Cooling system (continued)

Internal coolant leakage

- ☐ Leaking cylinder head gasket (Chapter 2A, 2B or 2C).
- ☐ Cracked cylinder head or cylinder bore (Chapter 2A, 2B, 2C or 2D).

Corrosion

- ☐ Infrequent draining and flushing (Chapter 1A or 1B).
- ☐ Incorrect coolant mixture or inappropriate coolant type (Chapter 1A or 1B).

Fuel and exhaust systems

Excessive fuel consumption

- ☐ Air filter element dirty or clogged (Chapter 1A or 1B).
- ☐ Fuel injection system fault - petrol models (Chapter 4A or 4B).
- ☐ Faulty injector(s) - diesel models (Chapter 4C).
- ☐ Ignition timing incorrect/ignition system fault - petrol models (Chapters 1A and 5B).
- ☐ Tyres under-inflated (*Weekly checks*).

Fuel leakage and/or fuel odour

- ☐ Damaged or corroded fuel tank, pipes or connections (Chapter 4A, 4B or 4C).

Excessive noise or fumes from exhaust system

- ☐ Leaking exhaust system or manifold joints (Chapters 1A, 1B and 4D).
- ☐ Leaking, corroded or damaged silencers or pipe (Chapters 1A, 1B and 4D).
- ☐ Broken mountings causing body or suspension contact (Chapter 1A or 1B).

Clutch

Pedal travels to floor - no pressure or very little resistance

- ☐ Broken clutch cable - cable-operated clutch (Chapter 6).
- ☐ Incorrect clutch cable adjustment/automatic adjuster faulty - cable-operated clutch (Chapter 6).
- ☐ Hydraulic fluid level low/air in the hydraulic system - hydraulically-operated clutch (Chapter 6).
- ☐ Broken clutch release bearing or fork (Chapter 6).
- ☐ Broken diaphragm spring in clutch pressure plate (Chapter 6).

Clutch fails to disengage (unable to select gears).

- ☐ Incorrect clutch cable adjustment/automatic adjuster faulty - cable-operated clutch (Chapter 6).
- ☐ Incorrect clutch cable adjustment/automatic adjuster faulty - cable-operated clutch (Chapter 6).
- ☐ Hydraulic fluid level too high - hydraulically-operated clutch (Chapter 6).
- ☐ Clutch disc sticking on gearbox input shaft splines (Chapter 6).
- ☐ Clutch disc sticking to flywheel or pressure plate (Chapter 6).
- ☐ Faulty pressure plate assembly (Chapter 6).
- ☐ Clutch release mechanism worn or incorrectly assembled (Chapter 6).

Clutch slips (engine speed increases, with no increase in vehicle speed).

- ☐ Incorrect clutch cable adjustment/automatic adjuster faulty - cable-operated clutch (Chapter 6).
- ☐ Hydraulic fluid level too high - hydraulically-operated clutch (Chapter 6).
- ☐ Clutch disc linings excessively worn (Chapter 6).
- ☐ Clutch disc linings contaminated with oil or grease (Chapter 6).
- ☐ Faulty pressure plate or weak diaphragm spring (Chapter 6).

Judder as clutch is engaged

- ☐ Clutch disc linings contaminated with oil or grease (Chapter 6).
- ☐ Clutch disc linings excessively worn (Chapter 6).
- ☐ Clutch cable sticking or frayed - cable-operated clutch (Chapter 6).
- ☐ Faulty or distorted pressure plate or diaphragm spring (Chapter 6).
- ☐ Worn or loose engine or gearbox mountings (Chapter 2A, 2B or 2C).
- ☐ Clutch disc hub or gearbox input shaft splines worn (Chapter 6).

Noise when depressing or releasing clutch pedal

- ☐ Worn clutch release bearing (Chapter 6).
- ☐ Worn or dry clutch pedal bushes (Chapter 6).
- ☐ Faulty pressure plate assembly (Chapter 6).
- ☐ Pressure plate diaphragm spring broken (Chapter 6).
- ☐ Broken clutch disc cushioning springs (Chapter 6).

Manual transmission

Noisy in neutral with engine running

- ☐ Input shaft bearings worn (noise apparent with clutch pedal released, but not when depressed) (Chapter 7A).*
- ☐ Clutch release bearing worn (noise apparent with clutch pedal depressed, possibly less when released) (Chapter 6).

Noisy in one particular gear

- ☐ Worn, damaged or chipped gear teeth (Chapter 7A).*

Difficulty engaging gears

- ☐ Clutch fault (Chapter 6).
- ☐ Worn or damaged gearchange linkage/cable (Chapter 7A).
- ☐ Incorrectly-adjusted gearchange linkage/cable (Chapter 7A).
- ☐ Worn synchroniser units (Chapter 7A).*

Jumps out of gear

- ☐ Worn or damaged gearchange linkage/cable (Chapter 7A).
- ☐ Incorrectly-adjusted gearchange linkage/cable (Chapter 7A).
- ☐ Worn synchroniser units (Chapter 7A).*
- ☐ Worn selector forks (Chapter 7A).*

Vibration

- ☐ Lack of oil (Chapter 1A or 1B).
- ☐ Worn bearings (Chapter 7A).*

Lubricant leaks

- ☐ Leaking differential output oil seal (Chapter 7A).
- ☐ Leaking housing joint (Chapter 7A).*
- ☐ Leaking input shaft oil seal (Chapter 7A).*

**Although the corrective action necessary to remedy the symptoms described is beyond the scope of the home mechanic, the above information should be helpful in isolating the cause of the condition, so that the owner can communicate clearly with a professional mechanic.*

Automatic transmission

Note: *Due to the complexity of the automatic transmission, it is difficult for the home mechanic to properly diagnose and service this unit. For problems other than the following, the vehicle should be taken to a dealer service department or automatic transmission specialist. Do not be too hasty in removing the transmission if a fault is suspected, as most of the testing is carried out with the unit still fitted.*

Fluid leakage

- ☐ Automatic transmission fluid is usually dark in colour. Fluid leaks should not be confused with engine oil, which can easily be blown onto the transmission by airflow.
- ☐ To determine the source of a leak, first remove all built-up dirt and grime from the transmission housing and surrounding areas using a degreasing agent, or by steam-cleaning. Drive the vehicle at low speed, so airflow will not blow the leak far from its source. Raise and support the vehicle, and determine where the leak is coming from. The following are common areas of leakage:

a) Oil pan (Chapter 1A and 7B).
b) Dipstick tube (Chapter 1A and 7B).
c) Transmission-to-fluid cooler pipes/unions (Chapter 7B).

Transmission fluid brown, or has burned smell

- ☐ Transmission fluid level low, or fluid in need of renewal (Chapter 1A).

General gear selection problems

- ☐ Chapter 7B deals with checking and adjusting the selector cable on automatic transmissions. The following are common problems which may be caused by a poorly-adjusted cable:

a) Engine starting in gears other than Park or Neutral.
b) Indicator panel indicating a gear other than the one actually being used.
c) Vehicle moves when in Park or Neutral.

- ☐ Refer to Chapter 7B for the selector cable adjustment procedure.

Transmission will not downshift (kickdown) with accelerator pedal fully depressed

- ☐ Low transmission fluid level (*Weekly checks*).
- ☐ Incorrect selector cable adjustment (Chapter 7B).

Engine will not start in any gear, or starts in gears other than Park or Neutral

- ☐ Incorrect selector cable adjustment (Chapter 7B).

Transmission slips, is noisy, or has no drive in forward or reverse gears

- ☐ There are many probable causes for the above problems, but the home mechanic should be concerned with only one possibility - fluid level. Before taking the vehicle to a dealer or transmission specialist, check the fluid level and condition of the fluid as described in *Weekly checks* and Chapter 1A. Correct the fluid level as necessary, or change the fluid and filter if needed. If the problem persists, professional help will be necessary.

Driveshafts

Clicking or knocking noise on turns (at slow speed on full-lock).

- ☐ Lack of constant velocity joint lubricant, possibly due to damaged gaiter (Chapter 8).
- ☐ Worn outer constant velocity joint (Chapter 8).

Vibration when accelerating or decelerating

- ☐ Worn inner constant velocity joint (Chapter 8).
- ☐ Bent or distorted driveshaft (Chapter 8).

Braking system

Note: *Before assuming that a brake problem exists, make sure that the tyres are in good condition and correctly inflated, that the front wheel alignment is correct, and that the vehicle is not loaded with weight in an unequal manner. Apart from checking the condition of all pipe and hose connections, any faults occurring on the anti-lock braking system should be referred to a Fiat dealer for diagnosis.*

Vehicle pulls to one side under braking

- ☐ Worn, defective, damaged or contaminated brake pads/shoes on one side (Chapters 1A, 1B and 9).
- ☐ Seized or partially-seized front brake caliper/wheel cylinder piston (Chapters 1A, 1B and 9).
- ☐ A mixture of brake pad/shoe lining materials fitted between sides (Chapters 1A, 1B and 9).
- ☐ Brake caliper or backplate mounting bolts loose (Chapter 9).
- ☐ Worn or damaged steering or suspension components (Chapters 1A, 1B and 10).

Noise (grinding or high-pitched squeal) when brakes applied

- ☐ Brake pad or shoe friction lining material worn down to metal backing (Chapters 1A, 1B and 9).
- ☐ Excessive corrosion of brake disc or drum. (May be apparent after the vehicle has been standing for some time (Chapters 1A, 1B and 9).
- ☐ Foreign object (stone chipping, etc) trapped between brake disc and shield (Chapters 1A, 1B and 9).

Excessive brake pedal travel

- ☐ Inoperative rear brake self-adjust mechanism - drum brakes (Chapter 9).
- ☐ Faulty master cylinder (Chapter 9).
- ☐ Air in hydraulic system (Chapter 9).

Brake pedal feels spongy when depressed

- ☐ Air in hydraulic system (Chapter 9).
- ☐ Deteriorated flexible rubber brake hoses (Chapters 1A, 1B and 9).
- ☐ Master cylinder mounting nuts loose (Chapter 9).
- ☐ Faulty master cylinder (Chapter 9).

Excessive brake pedal effort required to stop vehicle

- ☐ Faulty vacuum servo unit (Chapter 9).
- ☐ Faulty vacuum pump - diesel models (Chapter 9).
- ☐ Disconnected, damaged or insecure brake servo vacuum hose (Chapter 9).
- ☐ Primary or secondary hydraulic circuit failure (Chapter 9).
- ☐ Seized brake caliper or wheel cylinder piston(s) (Chapter 9).
- ☐ Brake pads or brake shoes incorrectly fitted (Chapter 9).
- ☐ Incorrect grade of brake pads or brake shoes fitted (Chapter 9).
- ☐ Brake pads or brake shoe linings contaminated (Chapter 9).

Braking system (continued)

Judder felt through brake pedal or steering wheel when braking

- ☐ Excessive run-out or distortion of discs/drums (Chapter 9).
- ☐ Brake pad or brake shoe linings worn (Chapters 1A, 1B and 9).
- ☐ Brake caliper or brake backplate mounting bolts loose (Chapter 9).
- ☐ Wear in suspension or steering components or mountings (Chapters 1A, 1B and 10).

Brakes binding

- ☐ Seized brake caliper or wheel cylinder piston(s) (Chapter 9).
- ☐ Incorrectly-adjusted handbrake mechanism (Chapter 9).
- ☐ Faulty master cylinder (Chapter 9).

Rear wheels locking under normal braking

- ☐ Rear brake shoe linings contaminated (Chapters 1A, 1B and 9).
- ☐ Faulty brake pressure regulator (Chapter 9).

Suspension and steering

Note: *Before diagnosing suspension or steering faults, be sure that the trouble is not due to incorrect tyre pressures, mixtures of tyre types, or binding brakes.*

Vehicle pulls to one side

- ☐ Defective tyre (*Weekly checks*).
- ☐ Excessive wear in suspension or steering components (Chapters 1A, 1B and 10).
- ☐ Incorrect front wheel alignment (Chapter 10).
- ☐ Accident damage to steering or suspension components (Chapter 1A or 1B).

Wheel wobble and vibration

- ☐ Front roadwheels out of balance (vibration felt mainly through the steering wheel) (Chapters 1A, 1B and 10).
- ☐ Rear roadwheels out of balance (vibration felt throughout the vehicle) (Chapters 1A, 1B and 10).
- ☐ Roadwheels damaged or distorted (Chapters 1A, 1B and 10).
- ☐ Faulty or damaged tyre (*Weekly checks*).
- ☐ Worn steering or suspension joints, bushes or components (Chapters 1A, 1B and 10).
- ☐ Wheel bolts loose (Chapters 1A, 1B and 10).

Excessive pitching and/or rolling around corners, or during braking

- ☐ Defective shock absorbers (Chapter 10).
- ☐ Broken or weak spring and/or suspension component (Chapter 10).
- ☐ Worn or damaged anti-roll bar or mountings (Chapter 10).

Wandering or general instability

- ☐ Incorrect front wheel alignment (Chapter 10).
- ☐ Worn steering or suspension joints, bushes or components (Chapters 1A, 1B and 10).
- ☐ Roadwheels out of balance (Chapters 1A, 1B and 10).
- ☐ Faulty or damaged tyre (*Weekly checks*).
- ☐ Wheel bolts loose (Chapters 1A, 1B and 10).
- ☐ Defective shock absorbers (Chapter 10).

Excessively-stiff steering

- ☐ Lack of steering gear lubricant (Chapter 10).
- ☐ Seized track rod end balljoint or suspension balljoint (Chapters 1A, 1B and 10).
- ☐ Broken or incorrectly-adjusted auxiliary drivebelt - power steering (Chapter 1A or 1B).
- ☐ Incorrect front wheel alignment (Chapter 10).
- ☐ Steering rack or column bent or damaged (Chapter 10).

Excessive play in steering

- ☐ Worn steering column intermediate shaft universal joint (Chapter 10).
- ☐ Worn steering track rod end balljoints (Chapters 1A, 1B and 10).
- ☐ Worn rack-and-pinion steering gear (Chapter 10).
- ☐ Worn steering or suspension joints, bushes or components (Chapters 1A, 1B and 10).

Lack of power assistance

- ☐ Broken or incorrectly-adjusted auxiliary drivebelt (Chapter 1A or 1B).
- ☐ Incorrect power steering fluid level (*Weekly checks*).
- ☐ Restriction in power steering fluid hoses (Chapter 1A or 1B).
- ☐ Faulty power steering pump (Chapter 10).
- ☐ Faulty rack-and-pinion steering gear (Chapter 10).

Tyre wear excessive

Tyres worn on inside or outside edges

- ☐ Tyres under-inflated (wear on both edges) (*Weekly checks*).
- ☐ Incorrect camber or castor angles (wear on one edge only) (Chapter 10).
- ☐ Worn steering or suspension joints, bushes or components (Chapters 1A, 1B and 10).
- ☐ Excessively-hard cornering.
- ☐ Accident damage.

Tyre treads exhibit feathered edges

- ☐ Incorrect toe setting (Chapter 10).

Tyres worn in centre of tread

- ☐ Tyres over-inflated (*Weekly checks*).

Tyres worn on inside and outside edges

- ☐ Tyres under-inflated (*Weekly checks*).

Tyres worn unevenly

- ☐ Tyres/wheels out of balance (Chapter 1A or 1B).
- ☐ Excessive wheel or tyre run-out (Chapter 1A or 1B).
- ☐ Worn shock absorbers (Chapters 1A, 1B and 10).
- ☐ Faulty tyre (*Weekly checks*).

Electrical system

Note: *For problems associated with the starting system, refer to the faults listed under Engine earlier in this Section.*

Battery will not hold a charge for more than a few days

- ☐ Battery defective internally (Chapter 5A).
- ☐ Battery terminal connections loose or corroded (*Weekly checks*).
- ☐ Auxiliary drivebelt worn or incorrectly adjusted (Chapter 1A or 1B).
- ☐ Alternator not charging at correct output (Chapter 5A).
- ☐ Alternator or voltage regulator faulty (Chapter 5A).
- ☐ Short-circuit causing continual battery drain (Chapters 5A and 12).

Ignition/no-charge warning light remains illuminated with engine running

- ☐ Auxiliary drivebelt broken, worn, or incorrectly adjusted (Chapter 1A or 1B).
- ☐ Alternator brushes worn, sticking, or dirty (Chapter 5A).
- ☐ Alternator brush springs weak or broken (Chapter 5A).
- ☐ Internal fault in alternator or voltage regulator (Chapter 5A).
- ☐ Broken, disconnected, or loose wiring in charging circuit (Chapter 5A).

Ignition/no-charge warning light fails to come on

- ☐ Warning light bulb blown (Chapter 12).
- ☐ Broken, disconnected, or loose wiring in warning light circuit (Chapter 12).
- ☐ Alternator faulty (Chapter 5A).

Lights inoperative

- ☐ Bulb blown (Chapter 12).
- ☐ Corrosion of bulb or bulbholder contacts (Chapter 12).
- ☐ Blown fuse (Chapter 12).
- ☐ Faulty relay (Chapter 12).
- ☐ Broken, loose, or disconnected wiring (Chapter 12).
- ☐ Faulty switch (Chapter 12).

Instrument readings inaccurate or erratic

Instrument readings increase with engine speed

- ☐ Faulty voltage regulator (Chapter 12).

Fuel or temperature gauges give no reading

- ☐ Faulty gauge sender unit (Chapters 3 and 4A, 4B or 4C).
- ☐ Wiring open-circuit (Chapter 12).
- ☐ Faulty gauge (Chapter 12).

Fuel or temperature gauges give continuous maximum reading

- ☐ Faulty gauge sender unit (Chapters 3 and 4A, 4B or 4C).
- ☐ Wiring short-circuit (Chapter 12).
- ☐ Faulty gauge (Chapter 12).

Horn inoperative, or unsatisfactory in operation

Horn operates all the time

- ☐ Horn push either earthed or stuck down (Chapter 12).
- ☐ Horn cable-to-horn push earthed (Chapter 12).

Horn fails to operate

- ☐ Blown fuse (Chapter 12).
- ☐ Cable or cable connections loose, broken or disconnected (Chapter 12).
- ☐ Faulty horn (Chapter 12).

Horn emits intermittent or unsatisfactory sound

- ☐ Cable connections loose (Chapter 12).
- ☐ Horn mountings loose (Chapter 12).
- ☐ Faulty horn (Chapter 12).

Windscreen/tailgate wipers inoperative, or unsatisfactory in operation

Wipers fail to operate, or operate very slowly

- ☐ Wiper blades stuck to screen, or linkage seized or binding (Chapters 1A, 1B and 12).
- ☐ Blown fuse (Chapter 12).
- ☐ Cable or cable connections loose, broken or disconnected (Chapter 12).
- ☐ Faulty relay (Chapter 12).
- ☐ Faulty wiper motor (Chapter 12).

Wiper blades sweep over too large or too small an area of the glass

- ☐ Wiper arms incorrectly positioned on spindles (Chapter 1A or 1B).
- ☐ Excessive wear of wiper linkage (Chapter 12).
- ☐ Wiper motor or linkage mountings loose or insecure (Chapter 12).

Wiper blades fail to clean the glass effectively

- ☐ Wiper blade rubbers worn or perished (*Weekly checks*).
- ☐ Wiper arm tension springs broken, or arm pivots seized (Chapter 12).
- ☐ Insufficient windscreen washer additive to adequately remove road film (*Weekly checks*).

Windscreen/tailgate washers inoperative, or unsatisfactory in operation

One or more washer jets inoperative

- ☐ Blocked washer jet (Chapter 1A or 1B).
- ☐ Disconnected, kinked or restricted fluid hose (Chapter 12).
- ☐ Insufficient fluid in washer reservoir (*Weekly checks*).

Washer pump fails to operate

- ☐ Broken or disconnected wiring or connections (Chapter 12).
- ☐ Blown fuse (Chapter 12).
- ☐ Faulty washer switch (Chapter 12).
- ☐ Faulty washer pump (Chapter 12).

Washer pump runs for some time before fluid is emitted from jets

- ☐ Faulty one-way valve in fluid supply hose (Chapter 12).

Electric windows inoperative, or unsatisfactory in operation

Window glass will only move in one direction

- ☐ Faulty switch (Chapter 12).

Window glass slow to move

- ☐ Regulator seized or damaged, or in need of lubrication (Chapter 11).
- ☐ Door internal components or trim fouling regulator (Chapter 11).
- ☐ Faulty motor (Chapter 11).

Window glass fails to move

- ☐ Blown fuse (Chapter 12).
- ☐ Faulty relay (Chapter 12).
- ☐ Broken or disconnected wiring or connections (Chapter 12).
- ☐ Faulty motor (Chapter 11).

A

ABS (Anti-lock brake system) A system, usually electronically controlled, that senses incipient wheel lockup during braking and relieves hydraulic pressure at wheels that are about to skid.
Air bag An inflatable bag hidden in the steering wheel (driver's side) or the dash or glovebox (passenger side). In a head-on collision, the bags inflate, preventing the driver and front passenger from being thrown forward into the steering wheel or windscreen.
Air cleaner A metal or plastic housing, containing a filter element, which removes dust and dirt from the air being drawn into the engine.
Air filter element The actual filter in an air cleaner system, usually manufactured from pleated paper and requiring renewal at regular intervals.

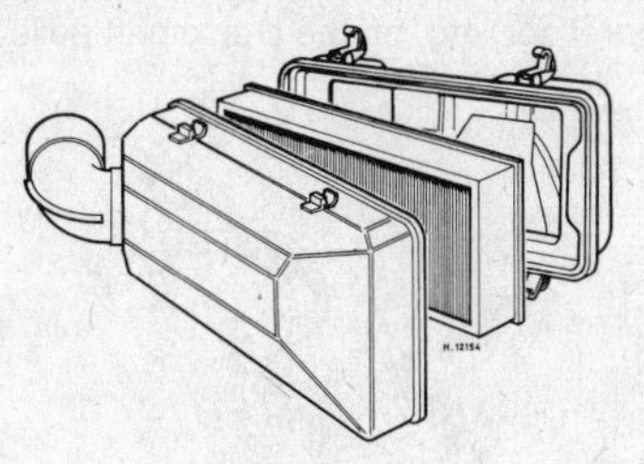

Air filter

Allen key A hexagonal wrench which fits into a recessed hexagonal hole.
Alligator clip A long-nosed spring-loaded metal clip with meshing teeth. Used to make temporary electrical connections.
Alternator A component in the electrical system which converts mechanical energy from a drivebelt into electrical energy to charge the battery and to operate the starting system, ignition system and electrical accessories.

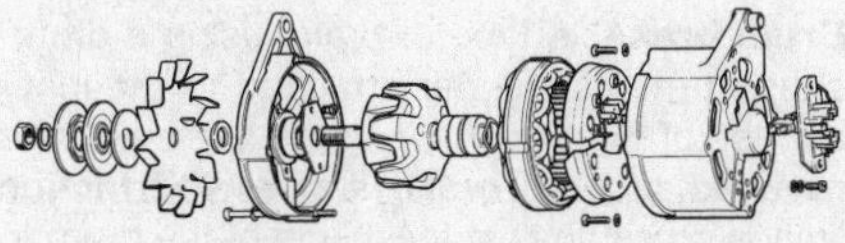

Alternator (exploded view)

Ampere (amp) A unit of measurement for the flow of electric current. One amp is the amount of current produced by one volt acting through a resistance of one ohm.
Anaerobic sealer A substance used to prevent bolts and screws from loosening. Anaerobic means that it does not require oxygen for activation. The Loctite brand is widely used.
Antifreeze A substance (usually ethylene glycol) mixed with water, and added to a vehicle's cooling system, to prevent freezing of the coolant in winter. Antifreeze also contains chemicals to inhibit corrosion and the formation of rust and other deposits that would tend to clog the radiator and coolant passages and reduce cooling efficiency.
Anti-seize compound A coating that reduces the risk of seizing on fasteners that are subjected to high temperatures, such as exhaust manifold bolts and nuts.

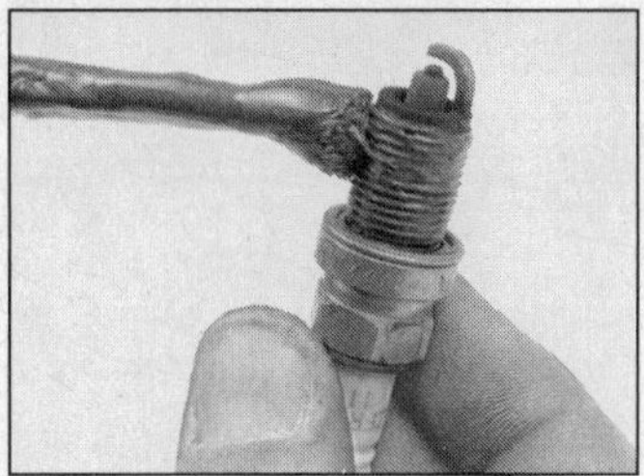

Anti-seize compound

Asbestos A natural fibrous mineral with great heat resistance, commonly used in the composition of brake friction materials. Asbestos is a health hazard and the dust created by brake systems should never be inhaled or ingested.
Axle A shaft on which a wheel revolves, or which revolves with a wheel. Also, a solid beam that connects the two wheels at one end of the vehicle. An axle which also transmits power to the wheels is known as a live axle.

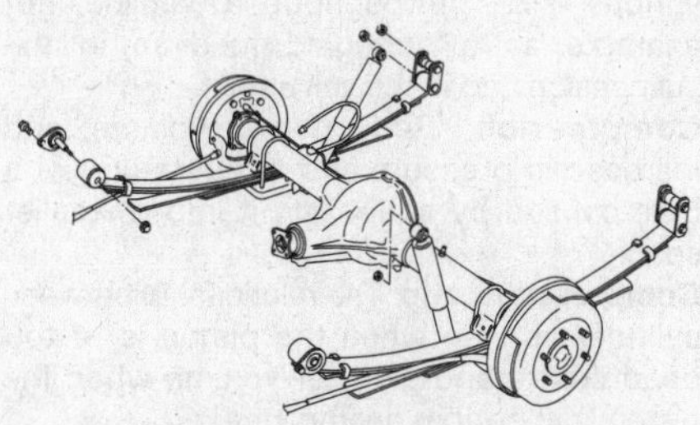

Axle assembly

Axleshaft A single rotating shaft, on either side of the differential, which delivers power from the final drive assembly to the drive wheels. Also called a driveshaft or a halfshaft.

B

Ball bearing An anti-friction bearing consisting of a hardened inner and outer race with hardened steel balls between two races.

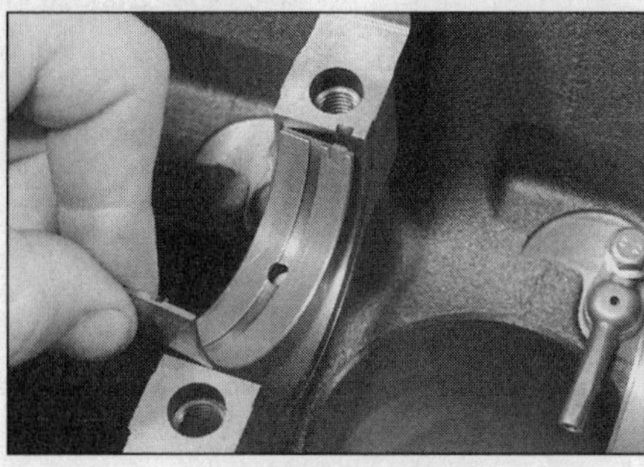

Bearing

Bearing The curved surface on a shaft or in a bore, or the part assembled into either, that permits relative motion between them with minimum wear and friction.
Big-end bearing The bearing in the end of the connecting rod that's attached to the crankshaft.
Bleed nipple A valve on a brake wheel cylinder, caliper or other hydraulic component that is opened to purge the hydraulic system of air. Also called a bleed screw.

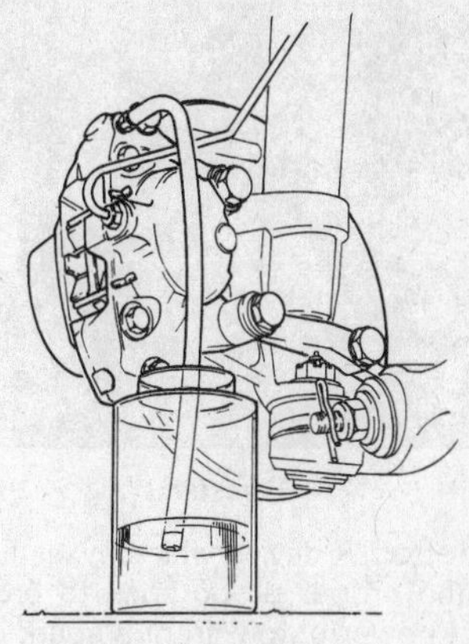

Brake bleeding

Brake bleeding Procedure for removing air from lines of a hydraulic brake system.
Brake disc The component of a disc brake that rotates with the wheels.
Brake drum The component of a drum brake that rotates with the wheels.
Brake linings The friction material which contacts the brake disc or drum to retard the vehicle's speed. The linings are bonded or riveted to the brake pads or shoes.
Brake pads The replaceable friction pads that pinch the brake disc when the brakes are applied. Brake pads consist of a friction material bonded or riveted to a rigid backing plate.
Brake shoe The crescent-shaped carrier to which the brake linings are mounted and which forces the lining against the rotating drum during braking.
Braking systems For more information on braking systems, consult the *Haynes Automotive Brake Manual*.
Breaker bar A long socket wrench handle providing greater leverage.
Bulkhead The insulated partition between the engine and the passenger compartment.

C

Caliper The non-rotating part of a disc-brake assembly that straddles the disc and carries the brake pads. The caliper also contains the hydraulic components that cause the pads to pinch the disc when the brakes are applied. A caliper is also a measuring tool that can be set to measure inside or outside dimensions of an object.

Camshaft A rotating shaft on which a series of cam lobes operate the valve mechanisms. The camshaft may be driven by gears, by sprockets and chain or by sprockets and a belt.

Canister A container in an evaporative emission control system; contains activated charcoal granules to trap vapours from the fuel system.

Canister

Carburettor A device which mixes fuel with air in the proper proportions to provide a desired power output from a spark ignition internal combustion engine.

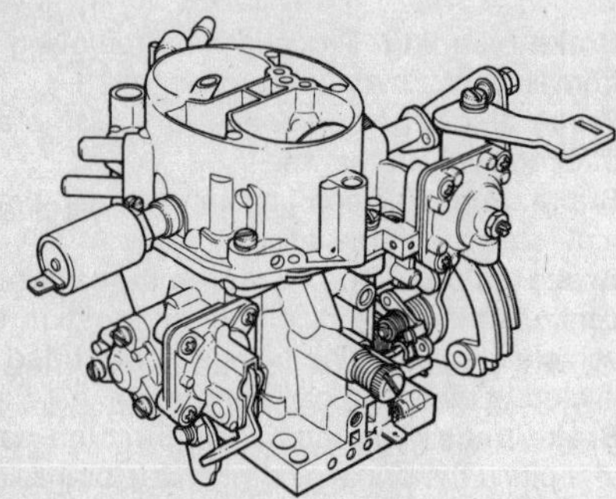

Carburettor

Castellated Resembling the parapets along the top of a castle wall. For example, a castellated balljoint stud nut.

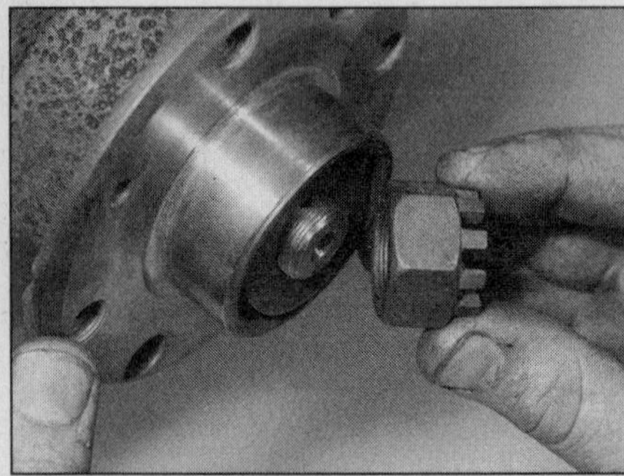

Castellated nut

Castor In wheel alignment, the backward or forward tilt of the steering axis. Castor is positive when the steering axis is inclined rearward at the top.

Catalytic converter A silencer-like device in the exhaust system which converts certain pollutants in the exhaust gases into less harmful substances.

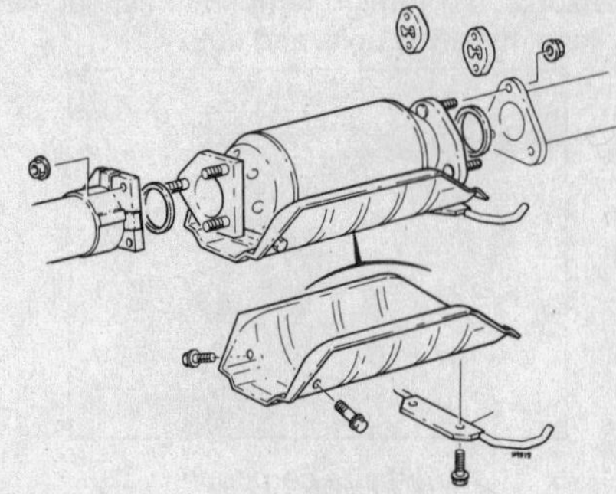

Catalytic converter

Circlip A ring-shaped clip used to prevent endwise movement of cylindrical parts and shafts. An internal circlip is installed in a groove in a housing; an external circlip fits into a groove on the outside of a cylindrical piece such as a shaft.

Clearance The amount of space between two parts. For example, between a piston and a cylinder, between a bearing and a journal, etc.

Coil spring A spiral of elastic steel found in various sizes throughout a vehicle, for example as a springing medium in the suspension and in the valve train.

Compression Reduction in volume, and increase in pressure and temperature, of a gas, caused by squeezing it into a smaller space.

Compression ratio The relationship between cylinder volume when the piston is at top dead centre and cylinder volume when the piston is at bottom dead centre.

Constant velocity (CV) joint A type of universal joint that cancels out vibrations caused by driving power being transmitted through an angle.

Core plug A disc or cup-shaped metal device inserted in a hole in a casting through which core was removed when the casting was formed. Also known as a freeze plug or expansion plug.

Crankcase The lower part of the engine block in which the crankshaft rotates.

Crankshaft The main rotating member, or shaft, running the length of the crankcase, with offset "throws" to which the connecting rods are attached.

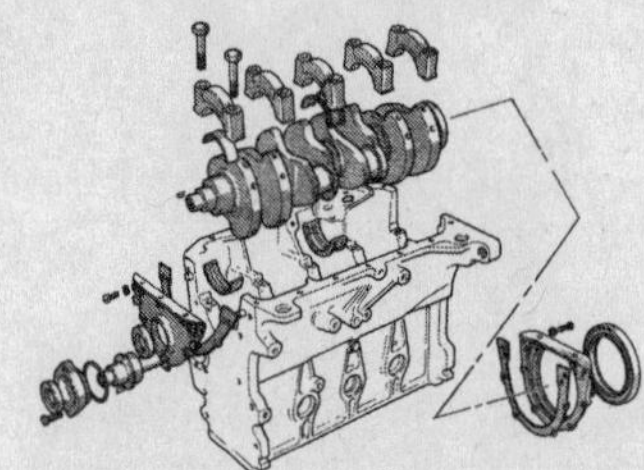

Crankshaft assembly

Crocodile clip See Alligator clip

D

Diagnostic code Code numbers obtained by accessing the diagnostic mode of an engine management computer. This code can be used to determine the area in the system where a malfunction may be located.

Disc brake A brake design incorporating a rotating disc onto which brake pads are squeezed. The resulting friction converts the energy of a moving vehicle into heat.

Double-overhead cam (DOHC) An engine that uses two overhead camshafts, usually one for the intake valves and one for the exhaust valves.

Drivebelt(s) The belt(s) used to drive accessories such as the alternator, water pump, power steering pump, air conditioning compressor, etc. off the crankshaft pulley.

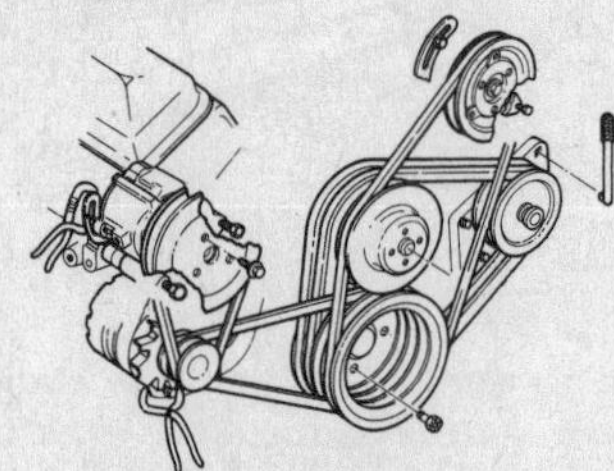

Accessory drivebelts

Driveshaft Any shaft used to transmit motion. Commonly used when referring to the axleshafts on a front wheel drive vehicle.

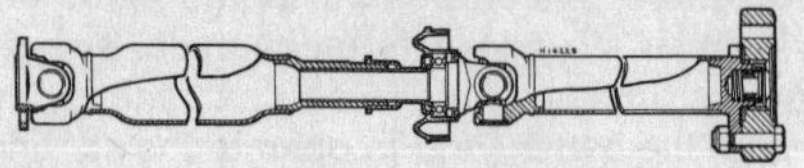

Driveshaft

Drum brake A type of brake using a drum-shaped metal cylinder attached to the inner surface of the wheel. When the brake pedal is pressed, curved brake shoes with friction linings press against the inside of the drum to slow or stop the vehicle.

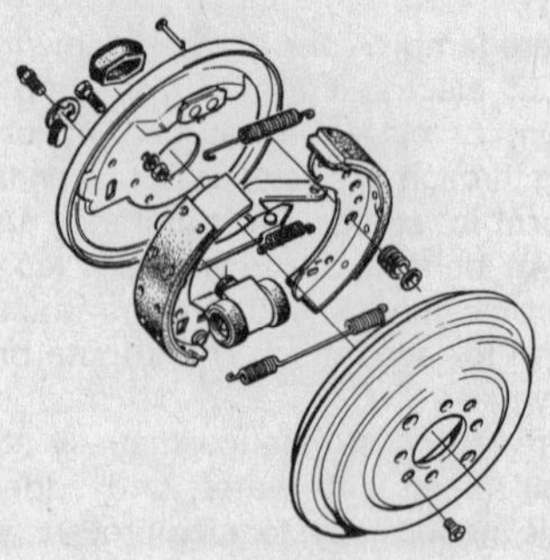

Drum brake assembly

E

EGR valve A valve used to introduce exhaust gases into the intake air stream.

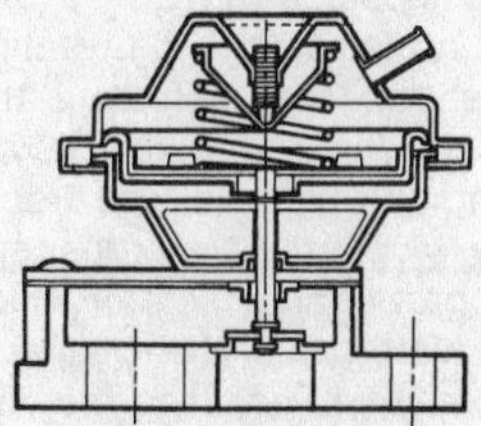

EGR valve

Electronic control unit (ECU) A computer which controls (for instance) ignition and fuel injection systems, or an anti-lock braking system. For more information refer to the *Haynes Automotive Electrical and Electronic Systems Manual.*

Electronic Fuel Injection (EFI) A computer controlled fuel system that distributes fuel through an injector located in each intake port of the engine.

Emergency brake A braking system, independent of the main hydraulic system, that can be used to slow or stop the vehicle if the primary brakes fail, or to hold the vehicle stationary even though the brake pedal isn't depressed. It usually consists of a hand lever that actuates either front or rear brakes mechanically through a series of cables and linkages. Also known as a handbrake or parking brake.

Endfloat The amount of lengthwise movement between two parts. As applied to a crankshaft, the distance that the crankshaft can move forward and back in the cylinder block.

Engine management system (EMS) A computer controlled system which manages the fuel injection and the ignition systems in an integrated fashion.

Exhaust manifold A part with several passages through which exhaust gases leave the engine combustion chambers and enter the exhaust pipe.

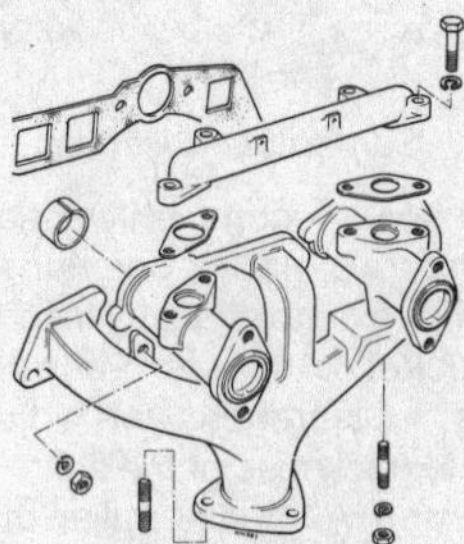

Exhaust manifold

F

Fan clutch A viscous (fluid) drive coupling device which permits variable engine fan speeds in relation to engine speeds.

Feeler blade A thin strip or blade of hardened steel, ground to an exact thickness, used to check or measure clearances between parts.

Feeler blade

Firing order The order in which the engine cylinders fire, or deliver their power strokes, beginning with the number one cylinder.

Flywheel A heavy spinning wheel in which energy is absorbed and stored by means of momentum. On cars, the flywheel is attached to the crankshaft to smooth out firing impulses.

Free play The amount of travel before any action takes place. The "looseness" in a linkage, or an assembly of parts, between the initial application of force and actual movement. For example, the distance the brake pedal moves before the pistons in the master cylinder are actuated.

Fuse An electrical device which protects a circuit against accidental overload. The typical fuse contains a soft piece of metal which is calibrated to melt at a predetermined current flow (expressed as amps) and break the circuit.

Fusible link A circuit protection device consisting of a conductor surrounded by heat-resistant insulation. The conductor is smaller than the wire it protects, so it acts as the weakest link in the circuit. Unlike a blown fuse, a failed fusible link must frequently be cut from the wire for replacement.

G

Gap The distance the spark must travel in jumping from the centre electrode to the side electrode in a spark plug. Also refers to the spacing between the points in a contact breaker assembly in a conventional points-type ignition, or to the distance between the reluctor or rotor and the pickup coil in an electronic ignition.

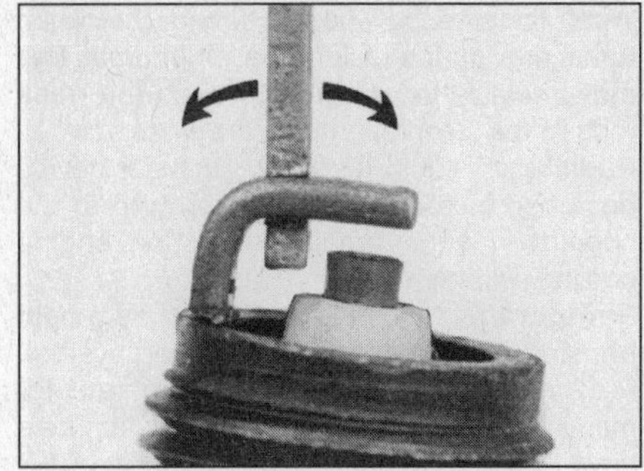

Adjusting spark plug gap

Gasket Any thin, soft material - usually cork, cardboard, asbestos or soft metal - installed between two metal surfaces to ensure a good seal. For instance, the cylinder head gasket seals the joint between the block and the cylinder head.

Gasket

Gauge An instrument panel display used to monitor engine conditions. A gauge with a movable pointer on a dial or a fixed scale is an analogue gauge. A gauge with a numerical readout is called a digital gauge.

H

Halfshaft A rotating shaft that transmits power from the final drive unit to a drive wheel, usually when referring to a live rear axle.

Harmonic balancer A device designed to reduce torsion or twisting vibration in the crankshaft. May be incorporated in the crankshaft pulley. Also known as a vibration damper.

Hone An abrasive tool for correcting small irregularities or differences in diameter in an engine cylinder, brake cylinder, etc.

Hydraulic tappet A tappet that utilises hydraulic pressure from the engine's lubrication system to maintain zero clearance (constant contact with both camshaft and valve stem). Automatically adjusts to variation in valve stem length. Hydraulic tappets also reduce valve noise.

I

Ignition timing The moment at which the spark plug fires, usually expressed in the number of crankshaft degrees before the piston reaches the top of its stroke.

Inlet manifold A tube or housing with passages through which flows the air-fuel mixture (carburettor vehicles and vehicles with throttle body injection) or air only (port fuel-injected vehicles) to the port openings in the cylinder head.

J

Jump start Starting the engine of a vehicle with a discharged or weak battery by attaching jump leads from the weak battery to a charged or helper battery.

L

Load Sensing Proportioning Valve (LSPV) A brake hydraulic system control valve that works like a proportioning valve, but also takes into consideration the amount of weight carried by the rear axle.

Locknut A nut used to lock an adjustment nut, or other threaded component, in place. For example, a locknut is employed to keep the adjusting nut on the rocker arm in position.

Lockwasher A form of washer designed to prevent an attaching nut from working loose.

M

MacPherson strut A type of front suspension system devised by Earle MacPherson at Ford of England. In its original form, a simple lateral link with the anti-roll bar creates the lower control arm. A long strut - an integral coil spring and shock absorber - is mounted between the body and the steering knuckle. Many modern so-called MacPherson strut systems use a conventional lower A-arm and don't rely on the anti-roll bar for location.

Multimeter An electrical test instrument with the capability to measure voltage, current and resistance.

N

NOx Oxides of Nitrogen. A common toxic pollutant emitted by petrol and diesel engines at higher temperatures.

O

Ohm The unit of electrical resistance. One volt applied to a resistance of one ohm will produce a current of one amp.

Ohmmeter An instrument for measuring electrical resistance.

O-ring A type of sealing ring made of a special rubber-like material; in use, the O-ring is compressed into a groove to provide the sealing action.

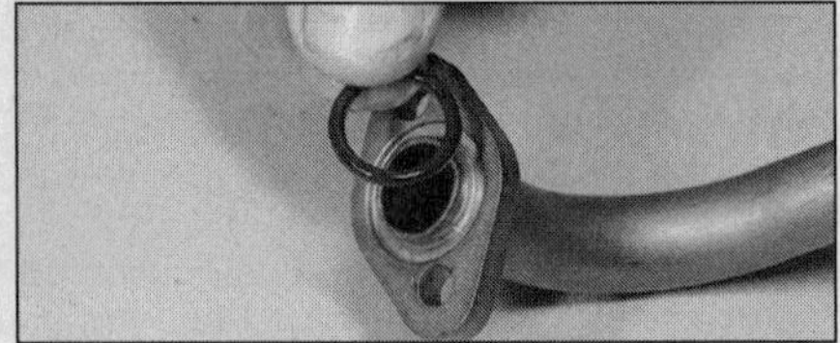

O-ring

Overhead cam (ohc) engine An engine with the camshaft(s) located on top of the cylinder head(s).

Overhead valve (ohv) engine An engine with the valves located in the cylinder head, but with the camshaft located in the engine block.

Oxygen sensor A device installed in the engine exhaust manifold, which senses the oxygen content in the exhaust and converts this information into an electric current. Also called a Lambda sensor.

P

Phillips screw A type of screw head having a cross instead of a slot for a corresponding type of screwdriver.

Plastigage A thin strip of plastic thread, available in different sizes, used for measuring clearances. For example, a strip of Plastigage is laid across a bearing journal. The parts are assembled and dismantled; the width of the crushed strip indicates the clearance between journal and bearing.

Plastigage

Propeller shaft The long hollow tube with universal joints at both ends that carries power from the transmission to the differential on front-engined rear wheel drive vehicles.

Proportioning valve A hydraulic control valve which limits the amount of pressure to the rear brakes during panic stops to prevent wheel lock-up.

R

Rack-and-pinion steering A steering system with a pinion gear on the end of the steering shaft that mates with a rack (think of a geared wheel opened up and laid flat). When the steering wheel is turned, the pinion turns, moving the rack to the left or right. This movement is transmitted through the track rods to the steering arms at the wheels.

Radiator A liquid-to-air heat transfer device designed to reduce the temperature of the coolant in an internal combustion engine cooling system.

Refrigerant Any substance used as a heat transfer agent in an air-conditioning system. R-12 has been the principle refrigerant for many years; recently, however, manufacturers have begun using R-134a, a non-CFC substance that is considered less harmful to the ozone in the upper atmosphere.

Rocker arm A lever arm that rocks on a shaft or pivots on a stud. In an overhead valve engine, the rocker arm converts the upward movement of the pushrod into a downward movement to open a valve.

Rotor In a distributor, the rotating device inside the cap that connects the centre electrode and the outer terminals as it turns, distributing the high voltage from the coil secondary winding to the proper spark plug. Also, that part of an alternator which rotates inside the stator. Also, the rotating assembly of a turbocharger, including the compressor wheel, shaft and turbine wheel.

Runout The amount of wobble (in-and-out movement) of a gear or wheel as it's rotated. The amount a shaft rotates "out-of-true." The out-of-round condition of a rotating part.

S

Sealant A liquid or paste used to prevent leakage at a joint. Sometimes used in conjunction with a gasket.

Sealed beam lamp An older headlight design which integrates the reflector, lens and filaments into a hermetically-sealed one-piece unit. When a filament burns out or the lens cracks, the entire unit is simply replaced.

Serpentine drivebelt A single, long, wide accessory drivebelt that's used on some newer vehicles to drive all the accessories, instead of a series of smaller, shorter belts. Serpentine drivebelts are usually tensioned by an automatic tensioner.

Serpentine drivebelt

Shim Thin spacer, commonly used to adjust the clearance or relative positions between two parts. For example, shims inserted into or under bucket tappets control valve clearances. Clearance is adjusted by changing the thickness of the shim.

Slide hammer A special puller that screws into or hooks onto a component such as a shaft or bearing; a heavy sliding handle on the shaft bottoms against the end of the shaft to knock the component free.

Sprocket A tooth or projection on the periphery of a wheel, shaped to engage with a chain or drivebelt. Commonly used to refer to the sprocket wheel itself.

Starter inhibitor switch On vehicles with an automatic transmission, a switch that prevents starting if the vehicle is not in Neutral or Park.
Strut See MacPherson strut.

T

Tappet A cylindrical component which transmits motion from the cam to the valve stem, either directly or via a pushrod and rocker arm. Also called a cam follower.
Thermostat A heat-controlled valve that regulates the flow of coolant between the cylinder block and the radiator, so maintaining optimum engine operating temperature. A thermostat is also used in some air cleaners in which the temperature is regulated.
Thrust bearing The bearing in the clutch assembly that is moved in to the release levers by clutch pedal action to disengage the clutch. Also referred to as a release bearing.
Timing belt A toothed belt which drives the camshaft. Serious engine damage may result if it breaks in service.
Timing chain A chain which drives the camshaft.
Toe-in The amount the front wheels are closer together at the front than at the rear. On rear wheel drive vehicles, a slight amount of toe-in is usually specified to keep the front wheels running parallel on the road by offsetting other forces that tend to spread the wheels apart.
Toe-out The amount the front wheels are closer together at the rear than at the front. On front wheel drive vehicles, a slight amount of toe-out is usually specified.
Tools For full information on choosing and using tools, refer to the *Haynes Automotive Tools Manual.*
Tracer A stripe of a second colour applied to a wire insulator to distinguish that wire from another one with the same colour insulator.
Tune-up A process of accurate and careful adjustments and parts replacement to obtain the best possible engine performance.
Turbocharger A centrifugal device, driven by exhaust gases, that pressurises the intake air. Normally used to increase the power output from a given engine displacement, but can also be used primarily to reduce exhaust emissions (as on VW's "Umwelt" Diesel engine).

U

Universal joint or U-joint A double-pivoted connection for transmitting power from a driving to a driven shaft through an angle. A U-joint consists of two Y-shaped yokes and a cross-shaped member called the spider.

V

Valve A device through which the flow of liquid, gas, vacuum, or loose material in bulk may be started, stopped, or regulated by a movable part that opens, shuts, or partially obstructs one or more ports or passageways. A valve is also the movable part of such a device.
Valve clearance The clearance between the valve tip (the end of the valve stem) and the rocker arm or tappet. The valve clearance is measured when the valve is closed.
Vernier caliper A precision measuring instrument that measures inside and outside dimensions. Not quite as accurate as a micrometer, but more convenient.
Viscosity The thickness of a liquid or its resistance to flow.
Volt A unit for expressing electrical "pressure" in a circuit. One volt that will produce a current of one ampere through a resistance of one ohm.

W

Welding Various processes used to join metal items by heating the areas to be joined to a molten state and fusing them together. For more information refer to the *Haynes Automotive Welding Manual.*
Wiring diagram A drawing portraying the components and wires in a vehicle's electrical system, using standardised symbols. For more information refer to the *Haynes Automotive Electrical and Electronic Systems Manual.*

Note: *References throughout this index are in the form "Chapter number" • "Page number"*

M

O

P

R

S

T

U

V

W

Haynes Manuals – The Complete List

Title	Book No.
ALFA ROMEO Alfasud/Sprint (74 - 88) up to F *	**0292**
Alfa Romeo Alfetta (73 - 87) up to E *	**0531**
AUDI 80, 90 & Coupe Petrol (79 - Nov 88) up to F	**0605**
Audi 80, 90 & Coupe Petrol (Oct 86 - 90) D to H	**1491**
Audi 100 & 200 Petrol (Oct 82 - 90) up to H	**0907**
Audi 100 & A6 Petrol & Diesel (May 91 - May 97) H to P	**3504**
Audi A3 (96 - May 03) P to 03	**4253**
Audi A4 Petrol & Diesel (95 - Feb 00) M to V	**3575**
AUSTIN A35 & A40 (56 - 67) up to F *	**0118**
Austin/MG/Rover Maestro 1.3 & 1.6 Petrol (83 - 95) up to M	**0922**
Austin/MG Metro (80 - May 90) up to G	**0718**
Austin/Rover Montego 1.3 & 1.6 Petrol (84 - 94) A to L	**1066**
Austin/MG/Rover Montego 2.0 Petrol (84 - 95) A to M	**1067**
Mini (59 - 69) up to H *	**0527**
Mini (69 - 01) up to X	**0646**
Austin/Rover 2.0 litre Diesel Engine (86-93) C to L	**1857**
AUSTIN HEALEY 100/6 & 3000 (56 - 68) up to G *	**0049**
BEDFORD CF Petrol (69 - 87) up to E	**0163**
Bedford/Vauxhall Rascal & Suzuki Supercarry (86 - Oct 94) C to M	**3015**
BMW 316, 320 & 320i (4-cyl) (75 - Feb 83) up to Y *	**0276**
BMW 320, 320i, 323i & 325i (6-cyl) (Oct 77 - Sept 87) up to E	**0815**
BMW 3- & 5-Series Petrol (81 - 91) up to J	**1948**
BMW 3-Series Petrol (Apr 91 - 96) H to N	**3210**
BMW 3-Series Petrol (Sept 98 - 03) S-reg. on	**4067**
BMW 520i & 525e (Oct 81 - June 88) up to E	**1560**
BMW 525, 528 & 528i (73 - Sept 81) up to X *	**0632**
BMW 5-Series Petrol (April 96 - Aug 03) N to 03	**4151**
BMW 1500, 1502, 1600, 1602, 2000 & 2002 (59 - 77) up to S *	**0240**
CHRYSLER PT Cruiser Petrol (00 - 03) W-reg. onwards	**4058**
CITROËN 2CV, Ami & Dyane (67 - 90) up to H	**0196**
Citroën AX Petrol & Diesel (87 - 97) D to P	**3014**
Citroën BX Petrol (83 - 94) A to L	**0908**
Citroën C15 Van Petrol & Diesel (89 - Oct 98) F to S	**3509**
Citroën C3 (02 - 05) 51 to 05	**4197**
Citroën CX Petrol (75 - 88) up to F	**0528**
Citroën Saxo Petrol & Diesel (96 - 01) N to X	**3506**
Citroën Visa Petrol (79 - 88) up to F	**0620**
Citroën Xantia Petrol & Diesel (93 - 01) K to Y	**3082**
Citroën XM Petrol & Diesel (89 - 00) G to X	**3451**
Citroën Xsara Petrol & Diesel (97 - Sept 00) R to W	**3751**
Citroën Xsara Picasso Petrol & Diesel (00 - 02) W-reg. onwards	**3944**
Citroën ZX Diesel (91 - 98) J to S	**1922**
Citroën ZX Petrol (91 - 98) H to S	**1881**
Citroën 1.7 & 1.9 litre Diesel Engine (84 - 96) A to N	**1379**
FIAT 126 (73 - 87) up to E *	**0305**
Fiat 500 (57 - 73) up to M *	**0090**
Fiat Bravo & Brava Petrol (95 - 00) N to W	**3572**
Fiat Cinquecento (93 - 98) K to R	**3501**
Fiat Panda (81 - 95) up to M	**0793**
Fiat Punto Petrol & Diesel (94 - Oct 99) L to V	**3251**
Fiat Punto Petrol (Oct 99 - July 03) V-reg onwards	**4066**
Fiat Regata Petrol (84 - 88) A to F	**1167**
Fiat Tipo Petrol (88 - 91) E to J	**1625**
Fiat Uno Petrol (83 - 95) up to M	**0923**
Fiat X1/9 (74 - 89) up to G *	**0273**
FORD Anglia (59 - 68) up to G *	**0001**
Ford Capri II (& III) 1.6 & 2.0 (74 - 87) up to E *	**0283**
Ford Capri II (& III) 2.8 & 3.0 V6 (74 - 87) up to E	**1309**
Ford Cortina Mk III 1300 & 1600 (70 - 76) up to P *	**0070**
Ford Escort Mk I 1100 & 1300 (68 - 74) up to N *	**0171**
Ford Escort Mk I Mexico, RS 1600 & RS 2000 (70 - 74) up to N *	**0139**
Ford Escort Mk II Mexico, RS 1800 & RS 2000 (75 - 80) up to W *	**0735**
Ford Escort (75 - Aug 80) up to V *	**0280**
Ford Escort Petrol (Sept 80 - Sept 90) up to H	**0686**
Ford Escort & Orion Petrol (Sept 90 - 00) H to X	**1737**
Ford Escort & Orion Diesel (Sept 90 - 00) H to X	**4081**
Ford Fiesta (76 - Aug 83) up to Y	**0334**
Ford Fiesta Petrol (Aug 83 - Feb 89) A to F	**1030**
Ford Fiesta Petrol (Feb 89 - Oct 95) F to N	**1595**
Ford Fiesta Petrol & Diesel (Oct 95 - Mar 02) N to 02	**3397**
Ford Fiesta Petrol & Diesel (Apr 02 - 05) 02 to 54	**4170**
Ford Focus Petrol & Diesel (98 - 01) S to Y	**3759**
Ford Focus Petrol & Diesel (Oct 01 - 04) 51 to 54 reg.	**4167**
Ford Galaxy Petrol & Diesel (95 - Aug 00) M to W	**3984**
Ford Granada Petrol (Sept 77 - Feb 85) up to B *	**0481**
Ford Granada & Scorpio Petrol (Mar 85 - 94) B to M	**1245**
Ford Ka (96 - 02) P-reg. onwards	**3570**
Ford Mondeo Petrol (93 - Sept 00) K to X	**1923**
Ford Mondeo Petrol & Diesel (Oct 00 - Jul 03) X to 03	**3990**
Ford Mondeo Diesel (93 - 96) L to N	**3465**
Ford Orion Petrol (83 - Sept 90) up to H	**1009**
Ford Sierra 4-cyl Petrol (82 - 93) up to K	**0903**
Ford Sierra V6 Petrol (82 - 91) up to J	**0904**
Ford Transit Petrol (Mk 2) (78 - Jan 86) up to C	**0719**
Ford Transit Petrol (Mk 3) (Feb 86 - 89) C to G	**1468**
Ford Transit Diesel (Feb 86 - 99) C to T	**3019**
Ford 1.6 & 1.8 litre Diesel Engine (84 - 96) A to N	**1172**
Ford 2.1, 2.3 & 2.5 litre Diesel Engine (77 - 90) up to H	**1606**
FREIGHT ROVER Sherpa Petrol (74 - 87) up to E	**0463**
HILLMAN Avenger (70 - 82) up to Y	**0037**
Hillman Imp (63 - 76) up to R *	**0022**
HONDA Civic (Feb 84 - Oct 87) A to E	**1226**
Honda Civic (Nov 91 - 96) J to N	**3199**
Honda Civic Petrol (Mar 95 - 00) M to X	**4050**
HYUNDAI Pony (85 - 94) C to M	**3398**
JAGUAR E Type (61 - 72) up to L *	**0140**
Jaguar MkI & II, 240 & 340 (55 - 69) up to H *	**0098**
Jaguar XJ6, XJ & Sovereign; Daimler Sovereign (68 - Oct 86) up to D	**0242**
Jaguar XJ6 & Sovereign (Oct 86 - Sept 94) D to M	**3261**
Jaguar XJ12, XJS & Sovereign; Daimler Double Six (72 - 88) up to F	**0478**
JEEP Cherokee Petrol (93 - 96) K to N	**1943**
LADA 1200, 1300, 1500 & 1600 (74 - 91) up to J	**0413**
Lada Samara (87 - 91) D to J	**1610**
LAND ROVER 90, 110 & Defender Diesel (83 - 95) up to N	**3017**
Land Rover Discovery Petrol & Diesel (89 - 98) G to S	**3016**
Land Rover Freelander Petrol & Diesel (97 - 02) R-reg. onwards	**3929**
Land Rover Series IIA & III Diesel (58 - 85) up to C	**0529**
Land Rover Series II, IIA & III 4-cyl Petrol (58 - 85) up to C	**0314**
MAZDA 323 (Mar 81 - Oct 89) up to G	**1608**
Mazda 323 (Oct 89 - 98) G to R	**3455**
Mazda 626 (May 83 - Sept 87) up to E	**0929**
Mazda B1600, B1800 & B2000 Pick-up Petrol (72 - 88) up to F	**0267**
Mazda RX-7 (79 - 85) up to C *	**0460**
MERCEDES-BENZ 190, 190E & 190D Petrol & Diesel (83 - 93) A to L	**3450**
Mercedes-Benz 200D, 240D, 240TD, 300D & 300TD 123 Series Diesel (Oct 76 - 85) up to C	**1114**
Mercedes-Benz 250 & 280 (68 - 72) up to L *	**0346**
Mercedes-Benz 250 & 280 123 Series Petrol (Oct 76 - 84) up to B *	**0677**
Mercedes-Benz 124 Series Petrol & Diesel (85 - Aug 93) C to K	**3253**
Mercedes-Benz C-Class Petrol & Diesel (93 - Aug 00) L to W	**3511**
MGA (55 - 62) *	**0475**
MGB (62 - 80) up to W	**0111**
MG Midget & Austin-Healey Sprite (58 - 80) up to W *	**0265**
MITSUBISHI Shogun & L200 Pick-Ups Petrol (83 - 94) up to M	**1944**
MORRIS Ital 1.3 (80 - 84) up to B	**0705**
Morris Minor 1000 (56 - 71) up to K	**0024**
NISSAN Almera Petrol (95 - Feb 00) N to V	**4053**
Nissan Bluebird (May 84 - Mar 86) A to C	**1223**
Nissan Bluebird Petrol (Mar 86 - 90) C to H	**1473**
Nissan Cherry (Sept 82 - 86) up to D	**1031**
Nissan Micra (83 - Jan 93) up to K	**0931**
Nissan Micra (93 - 99) K to T	**3254**
Nissan Primera Petrol (90 - Aug 99) H to T	**1851**
Nissan Stanza (82 - 86) up to D	**0824**
Nissan Sunny Petrol (May 82 - Oct 86) up to D	**0895**
Nissan Sunny Petrol (Oct 86 - Mar 91) D to H	**1378**
Nissan Sunny Petrol (Apr 91 - 95) H to N	**3219**
OPEL Ascona & Manta (B Series) (Sept 75 - 88) up to F *	**0316**
Opel Ascona Petrol (81 - 88)	**3215**
Opel Astra Petrol (Oct 91 - Feb 98)	**3156**
Opel Corsa Petrol (83 - Mar 93)	**3160**
Opel Corsa Petrol (Mar 93 - 97)	**3159**
Opel Kadett Petrol (Nov 79 - Oct 84) up to B	**0634**
Opel Kadett Petrol (Oct 84 - Oct 91)	**3196**
Opel Omega & Senator Petrol (Nov 86 - 94)	**3157**
Opel Rekord Petrol (Feb 78 - Oct 86) up to D	**0543**
Opel Vectra Petrol (Oct 88 - Oct 95)	**3158**
PEUGEOT 106 Petrol & Diesel (91 - 02) J-reg. onwards	**1882**
Peugeot 205 Petrol (83 - 97) A to P	**0932**
Peugeot 206 Petrol & Diesel (98 - 01) S to X	**3757**
Peugeot 306 Petrol & Diesel (93 - 99) K to T	**3073**
Peugeot 307 Petrol & Diesel (01 - 04) Y-reg. onwards	**4147**
Peugeot 309 Petrol (86 - 93) C to K	**1266**

* Classic reprint

Title	Book No.
Peugeot 405 Petrol (88 - 97) E to P	**1559**
Peugeot 405 Diesel (88 - 97) E to P	**3198**
Peugeot 406 Petrol & Diesel (96 - Mar 99) N to T	**3394**
Peugeot 406 Petrol & Diesel (Mar 99-02) T-reg. on	**3982**
Peugeot 505 Petrol (79 - 89) up to G	**0762**
Peugeot 1.7/1.8 & 1.9 litre Diesel Engine (82 - 96) up to N	**0950**
Peugeot 2.0, 2.1, 2.3 & 2.5 litre Diesel Engines (74 - 90) up to H	**1607**
PORSCHE 911 (65 - 85) up to C	**0264**
Porsche 924 & 924 Turbo (76 - 85) up to C	**0397**
PROTON (89 - 97) F to P	**3255**
RANGE ROVER V8 Petrol (70 - Oct 92) up to K	**0606**
RELIANT Robin & Kitten (73 - 83) up to A *	**0436**
RENAULT 4 (61 - 86) up to D *	**0072**
Renault 5 Petrol (Feb 85 - 96) B to N	**1219**
Renault 9 & 11 Petrol (82 - 89) up to F	**0822**
Renault 18 Petrol (79 - 86) up to D	**0598**
Renault 19 Petrol (89 - 96) F to N	**1646**
Renault 19 Diesel (89 - 96) F to N	**1946**
Renault 21 Petrol (86 - 94) C to M	**1397**
Renault 25 Petrol & Diesel (84 - 92) B to K	**1228**
Renault Clio Petrol (91 - May 98) H to R	**1853**
Renault Clio Diesel (91 - June 96) H to N	**3031**
Renault Clio Petrol & Diesel (May 98 - May 01) R to Y	**3906**
Renault Clio Petrol & Diesel (June 01 - 04) Y-reg. onwards	**4168**
Renault Espace Petrol & Diesel (85 - 96) C to N	**3197**
Renault Laguna Petrol & Diesel (94 - 00) L to W	**3252**
Renault Mégane & Scénic Petrol & Diesel (96 - 98) N to R	**3395**
Renault Mégane & Scénic Petrol & Diesel (Apr 99 - 02) T-reg. onwards	**3916**
ROVER 213 & 216 (84 - 89) A to G	**1116**
Rover 214 & 414 Petrol (89 - 96) G to N	**1689**
Rover 216 & 416 Petrol (89 - 96) G to N	**1830**
Rover 211, 214, 216, 218 & 220 Petrol & Diesel (Dec 95 - 99) N to V	**3399**
Rover 25 & MG ZR Petrol & Diesel (Oct 99 - 04) V-reg. onwards	**4145**
Rover 414, 416 & 420 Petrol & Diesel (May 95 - 98) M to R	**3453**
Rover 618, 620 & 623 Petrol (93 - 97) K to P	**3257**
Rover 820, 825 & 827 Petrol (86 - 95) D to N	**1380**
Rover 3500 (76 - 87) up to E *	**0365**
Rover Metro, 111 & 114 Petrol (May 90 - 98) G to S	**1711**
SAAB 95 & 96 (66 - 76) up to R *	**0198**
Saab 90, 99 & 900 (79 - Oct 93) up to L	**0765**
Saab 900 (Oct 93 - 98) L to R	**3512**
Saab 9000 (4-cyl) (85 - 98) C to S	**1686**
Saab 9-5 4-cyl Petrol (97 - 04) R-reg onwards	**4156**
SEAT Ibiza & Cordoba Petrol & Diesel (Oct 93 - Oct 99) L to V	**3571**
Seat Ibiza & Malaga Petrol (85 - 92) B to K	**1609**
SKODA Estelle (77 - 89) up to G	**0604**
Skoda Favorit (89 - 96) F to N	**1801**
Skoda Felicia Petrol & Diesel (95 - 01) M to X	**3505**
SUBARU 1600 & 1800 (Nov 79 - 90) up to H *	**0995**
SUNBEAM Alpine, Rapier & H120 (67 - 74) to N *	**0051**
SUZUKI SJ Series, Samurai & Vitara (4-cyl) Petrol (82 - 97) up to P	**1942**
TALBOT Alpine, Solara, Minx & Rapier (75 - 86) up to D	**0337**

Title	Book No.
Talbot Horizon Petrol (78 - 86) up to D	**0473**
Talbot Samba (82 - 86) up to D	**0823**
TOYOTA Carina E Petrol (May 92 - 97) J to P	**3256**
Toyota Corolla (80 - 85) up to C	**0683**
Toyota Corolla (Sept 83 - Sept 87) A to E	**1024**
Toyota Corolla (Sept 87 - Aug 92) E to K	**1683**
Toyota Corolla Petrol (Aug 92 - 97) K to P	**3259**
Toyota Hi-Ace & Hi-Lux Petrol (69 - Oct 83) to A	**0304**
TRIUMPH GT6 & Vitesse (62 - 74) up to N *	**0112**
Triumph Herald (59 - 71) up to K *	**0010**
Triumph Spitfire (62 - 81) up to X	**0113**
Triumph Stag (70 - 78) up to T *	**0441**
Triumph TR2, TR3, TR3A, TR4 & TR4A (52 - 67) up to F *	**0028**
Triumph TR5 & 6 (67 - 75) up to P *	**0031**
Triumph TR7 (75 - 82) up to Y *	**0322**
VAUXHALL Astra Petrol (80 - Oct 84) up to B	**0635**
Vauxhall Astra & Belmont Petrol (Oct 84 - Oct 91) B to J	**1136**
Vauxhall Astra Petrol (Oct 91 - Feb 98) J to R	**1832**
Vauxhall/Opel Astra & Zafira Petrol (Feb 98 - Apr 04) R-reg onwards	**3758**
Vauxhall/Opel Astra & Zafira Diesel (Feb 98 - Apr 04) R-reg onwards	**3797**
Vauxhall/Opel Calibra (90 - 98) G to S	**3502**
Vauxhall Carlton Petrol (Oct 78 - Oct 86) up to D	**0480**
Vauxhall Carlton & Senator Petrol (Nov 86 - 94) D to L	**1469**
Vauxhall Cavalier Petrol (81 - Oct 88) up to F	**0812**
Vauxhall Cavalier Petrol (Oct 88 - 95) F to N	**1570**
Vauxhall Chevette (75 - 84) up to B	**0285**
Vauxhall/Opel Corsa Diesel (Mar 93 - Oct 00) K to X	**4087**
Vauxhall Corsa Petrol (Mar 93 - 97) K to R	**1985**
Vauxhall/Opel Corsa Petrol (Apr 97 - Oct 00) P to X	**3921**
Vauxhall/Opel Corsa Petrol & Diesel (Oct 00 - Sept 03) X-reg onwards	**4079**
Vauxhall/Opel Frontera Petrol & Diesel (91 - Sept 98) J to S	**3454**
Vauxhall Nova Petrol (83 - 93) up to K	**0909**
Vauxhall/Opel Omega Petrol (94 - 99) L to T	**3510**
Vauxhall/Opel Vectra Petrol & Diesel (95 - Feb 99) N to S	**3396**
Vauxhall/Opel Vectra Petrol & Diesel (Mar 99 - May 02) T-reg. onwards	**3930**
Vauxhall/Opel 1.5, 1.6 & 1.7 litre Diesel Engine (82 - 96) up to N	**1222**
VOLKSWAGEN 411 & 412 (68 - 75) up to P *	**0091**
Volkswagen Beetle 1200 (54 - 77) up to S	**0036**
Volkswagen Beetle 1300 & 1500 (65 - 75) up to P	**0039**
Volkswagen Beetle 1302 & 1302S (70 - 72) up to L *	**0110**
Volkswagen Beetle 1303, 1303S & GT (72 - 75) up to P	**0159**
Volkswagen Beetle Petrol & Diesel (Apr 99 - 01) T-reg. onwards	**3798**
Volkswagen Golf & Bora Petrol & Diesel (April 98 - 00) R to X	**3727**
Volkswagen Golf & Jetta Mk 1 Petrol 1.1 & 1.3 (74 - 84) up to A	**0716**
Volkswagen Golf, Jetta & Scirocco Mk 1 Petrol 1.5, 1.6 & 1.8 (74 - 84) up to A	**0726**
Volkswagen Golf & Jetta Mk 1 Diesel (78 - 84) up to A	**0451**

Title	Book No.
Volkswagen Golf & Jetta Mk 2 Petrol (Mar 84 - Feb 92) A to J	**1081**
Volkswagen Golf & Vento Petrol & Diesel (Feb 92 - Mar 98) J to R	**3097**
Volkswagen Golf & Bora 4-cyl Petrol & Diesel (01 - 03) X to 53	**4169**
Volkswagen LT Petrol Vans & Light Trucks (76 - 87) up to E	**0637**
Volkswagen Passat & Santana Petrol (Sept 81 - May 88) up to E	**0814**
Volkswagen Passat 4-cyl Petrol & Diesel (May 88 - 96) E to P	**3498**
Volkswagen Passat 4-cyl Petrol & Diesel (Dec 96 - Nov 00) P to X	**3917**
Volkswagen Polo & Derby (76 - Jan 82) up to X	**0335**
Volkswagen Polo (82 - Oct 90) up to H	**0813**
Volkswagen Polo Petrol (Nov 90 - Aug 94) H to L	**3245**
Volkswagen Polo Hatchback Petrol & Diesel (94 - 99) M to S	**3500**
Volkswagen Polo Hatchback Petrol (00 - Jan 02) V to 51	**4150**
Volkswagen Scirocco (82 - 90) up to H *	**1224**
Volkswagen Transporter 1600 (68 - 79) up to V	**0082**
Volkswagen Transporter 1700, 1800 & 2000 (72 - 79) up to V *	**0226**
Volkswagen Transporter (air-cooled) Petrol (79 - 82) up to Y *	**0638**
Volkswagen Transporter (water-cooled) Petrol (82 - 90) up to H	**3452**
Volkswagen Type 3 (63 - 73) up to M *	**0084**
VOLVO 120 & 130 Series (& P1800) (61 - 73) up to M *	**0203**
Volvo 142, 144 & 145 (66 - 74) up to N *	**0129**
Volvo 240 Series Petrol (74 - 93) up to K	**0270**
Volvo 262, 264 & 260/265 (75 - 85) up to C *	**0400**
Volvo 340, 343, 345 & 360 (76 - 91) up to J	**0715**
Volvo 440, 460 & 480 Petrol (87 - 97) D to P	**1691**
Volvo 740 & 760 Petrol (82 - 91) up to J	**1258**
Volvo 850 Petrol (92 - 96) J to P	**3260**
Volvo 940 Petrol (90 - 96) H to N	**3249**
Volvo S40 & V40 Petrol (96 - Mar 04) N-reg. onwards	**3569**
Volvo S70, V70 & C70 Petrol (96 - 99) P to V	**3573**

AUTOMOTIVE TECHBOOKS

Automotive Air Conditioning Systems	**3740**
Automotive Electrical and Electronic Systems	**3049**
Automotive Gearbox Overhaul Manual	**3473**
Automotive Service Summaries Manual	**3475**
Automotive Timing Belts Manual - Austin/Rover	**3549**
Automotive Timing Belts Manual - Ford	**3474**
Automotive Timing Belts Manual - Peugeot/Citroën	**3568**
Automotive Timing Belts Manual - Vauxhall/Opel	**3577**

DIY MANUAL SERIES

Haynes Manual on Bodywork	**4198**
Haynes Manual on Brakes	**4178**
Haynes Manual on Carburettors	**4177**
Haynes Manual on Diesel Engines	**4174**
Haynes Manual on Engine Management	**4199**
Haynes Manual on Fault Codes	**4175**
Haynes Manual on Practical Electrical Systems	**4267**
Haynes Manual on Small Engines	**4250**
Haynes Manual on Welding	**4176**

* Classic reprint

All the products featured on this page are available through most motor accessory shops, cycle shops and book stores. Our policy of continuous updating and development means that titles are being constantly added to the range. For up-to-date information on our complete list of titles, please telephone: (UK) **+44 1963 442030** • (USA) **+1 805 498 6703** • (France) **+33 1 47 17 66 29** • (Sweden) **+46 18 124016** • (Australia) **+61 3 9763 8100**

Preserving Our Motoring Heritage

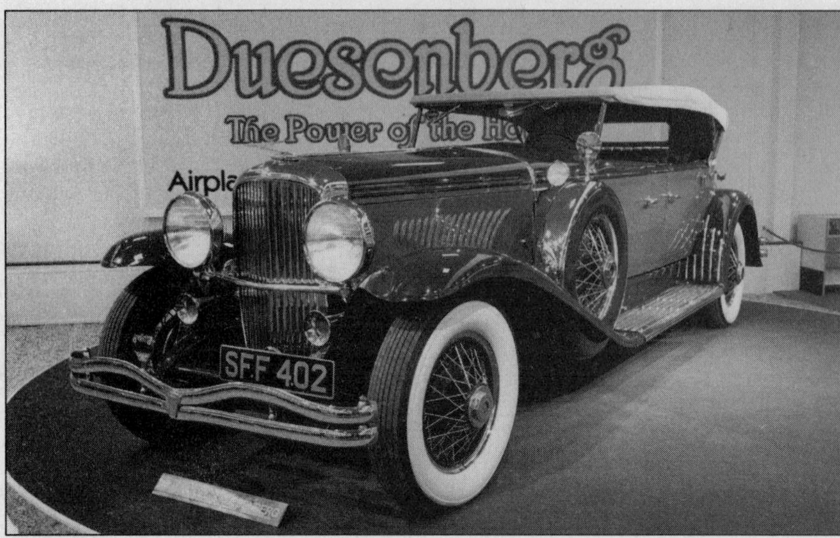

The Model J Duesenberg Derham Tourster. Only eight of these magnificent cars were ever built – this is the only example to be found outside the United States of America

Almost every car you've ever loved, loathed or desired is gathered under one roof at the Haynes Motor Museum. Over 300 immaculately presented cars and motorbikes represent every aspect of our motoring heritage, from elegant reminders of bygone days, such as the superb Model J Duesenberg to curiosities like the bug-eyed BMW Isetta. There are also many old friends and flames. Perhaps you remember the 1959 Ford Popular that you did your courting in? The magnificent 'Red Collection' is a spectacle of classic sports cars including AC, Alfa Romeo, Austin Healey, Ferrari, Lamborghini, Maserati, MG, Riley, Porsche and Triumph.

A Perfect Day Out

Each and every vehicle at the Haynes Motor Museum has played its part in the history and culture of Motoring. Today, they make a wonderful spectacle and a great day out for all the family. Bring the kids, bring Mum and Dad, but above all bring your camera to capture those golden memories for ever. You will also find an impressive array of motoring memorabilia, a comfortable 70 seat video cinema and one of the most extensive transport book shops in Britain. The Pit Stop Cafe serves everything from a cup of tea to wholesome, home-made meals or, if you prefer, you can enjoy the large picnic area nestled in the beautiful rural surroundings of Somerset.

John Haynes O.B.E., Founder and Chairman of the museum at the wheel of a Haynes Light 12.

Graham Hill's Lola Cosworth Formula 1 car next to a 1934 Riley Sports.

The Museum is situated on the A359 Yeovil to Frome road at Sparkford, just off the A303 in Somerset. It is about 40 miles south of Bristol, and 25 minutes drive from the M5 intersection at Taunton.

Open 9.30am - 5.30pm (10.00am - 4.00pm Winter) 7 days a week, *except Christmas Day, Boxing Day and New Years Day*

Special rates available for schools, coach parties and outings Charitable Trust No. 292048